T0328895

Data Science and Machine Learning for Non-Programmers

As data continues to grow exponentially, knowledge of data science and machine learning has become more crucial than ever. Machine learning has grown exponentially; however, the abundance of resources can be overwhelming, making it challenging for new learners. This book aims to address this disparity and cater to learners from various non-technical fields, enabling them to utilize machine learning effectively.

Adopting a hands-on approach, readers are guided through practical implementations using real datasets and SAS Enterprise Miner, a user-friendly data mining software that requires no programming. Throughout the chapters, two large datasets are used consistently, allowing readers to practice all stages of the data mining process within a cohesive project framework. This book also provides specific guidelines and examples on presenting data mining results and reports, enhancing effective communication with stakeholders.

Designed as a guiding companion for both beginners and experienced practitioners, this book targets a wide audience, including students, lecturers, researchers, and industry professionals from various backgrounds.

Dothang Truong, PhD, is a Professor of Graduate Studies at Embry Riddle Aeronautical University, Daytona Beach, Florida. He has extensive teaching and research experience in machine learning, data analytics, air transportation management, and supply chain management. In 2022, Dr. Truong received the Frank Sorenson Award for outstanding achievement of excellence in aviation research and scholarship.

Chapman & Hall/CRC Data Mining and Knowledge Discovery Series

Series Editor: Vipin Kumar

Data Science and Machine Learning for Non-Programmers: Using SAS Enterprise Miner
Dothang Truong

Healthcare Data Analytics
Chandan K. Reddy and Charu C. Aggarwal

Accelerating Discovery: Mining Unstructured Information for Hypothesis Generation
Scott Spangler

Event Mining: Algorithms and Applications
Tao Li

Text Mining and Visualization: Case Studies Using Open-Source Tools
Markus Hofmann and Andrew Chisholm

Graph-Based Social Media Analysis
Ioannis Pitas

Data Mining: A Tutorial-Based Primer, Second Edition
Richard J. Roiger

Data Mining with R: Learning with Case Studies, Second Edition
Luís Torgo

Social Networks with Rich Edge Semantics
Quan Zheng and David Skillicorn

Large-Scale Machine Learning in the Earth Sciences
Ashok N. Srivastava, Ramakrishna Nemani, and Karsten Steinhaeuser

Data Science and Analytics with Python
Jesús Rogel-Salazar

Feature Engineering for Machine Learning and Data Analytics
Guozhu Dong and Huan Liu

Exploratory Data Analysis Using R
Ronald K. Pearson

Human Capital Systems, Analytics, and Data Mining
Robert C. Hughes

For more information about this series please visit: https://www.routledge.com/
Chapman--HallCRC-Data-Mining-and-Knowledge-Discovery-Series/book-series/
CHDAMINODIS

Data Science and Machine Learning for Non-Programmers
Using SAS Enterprise Miner

Dothang Truong

CRC Press
Taylor & Francis Group
Boca Raton London New York

CRC Press is an imprint of the
Taylor & Francis Group, an **informa** business

A CHAPMAN & HALL BOOK

First edition published 2024
by CRC Press
2385 NW Executive Center Drive, Suite 320, Boca Raton FL 33431

and by CRC Press
4 Park Square, Milton Park, Abingdon, Oxon, OX14 4RN

CRC Press is an imprint of Taylor & Francis Group, LLC

© 2024 Dothang Truong

ISBN: 978-0-367-75538-6 (hbk)
ISBN: 978-0-367-75196-8 (pbk)
ISBN: 978-1-003-16287-2 (ebk)

DOI: 10.1201/9781003162872

Typeset in Palatino LT Std
by KnowledgeWorks Global Ltd.

Dedication

To my beloved parents, Mr. Tin and Mrs. Thinh, whose unwavering love and support have shaped me into the person I am today.

To my cherished wife, Thanh Van, the love of my life. You are the cornerstone of my life, my constant companion, and my greatest source of strength.

To my sweet daughter, Nga My, and brave son, Phi Long, you are my inspiration and the reason I strive to be the best version of myself.

And to my dear brother, Do Lan, your friendship and camaraderie have been a guiding light throughout my journey.

This book is dedicated to all of you, the pillars of my existence and the driving force behind my pursuit of knowledge and creativity. With heartfelt gratitude and love, this endeavor is for each one of you.

Contents

Preface..ix

Part I   Introduction to Data Mining

1. Introduction to Data Mining and Data Science 3

2. Data Mining Processes, Methods, and Software 30

3. Data Sampling and Partitioning 63

4. Data Visualization and Exploration 97

5. Data Modification..133

Part II   Data Mining Methods

6. Model Evaluation... 169

7. Regression Methods...204

8. Decision Trees 250

9. Neural Networks 300

10. Ensemble Modeling 338

11. Presenting Results and Writing Data Mining Reports 359

12. Principal Component Analysis..403

13. Cluster Analysis...424

Part III   Advanced Data Mining Methods

14. Random Forest..455

15. Gradient Boosting 479

16. Bayesian Networks...505

Term Definitions..541

References 555

Appendices: Data Descriptions 561

Index..565

Preface

In recent years, the field of machine learning has seen an unprecedented surge in popularity and innovation, which has revolutionized industries and transformed the way we interact with technology. In this rapidly evolving field, the pursuit of knowledge hidden within vast datasets has led to groundbreaking discoveries, insightful patterns, and novel applications across diverse domains. It is an exciting time as we find ourselves immersed in the realm of true Artificial Intelligence (AI). I still vividly recall my amazement when I had a chance to test out Tesla's full self-driving technology last year. The car effortlessly drove itself from a hotel to the airport, leaving a lasting impression of the limitless potential of AI. More recently, as I was finishing the final chapter of this book, ChatGPT was introduced. Honestly, I was a little bit skeptical at first, given some other applications that claimed to be true AI before, and then disappointed. Regardless, I decided to test it out anyway, and I was thoroughly surprised. What a game changer! The capability of this generative AI goes beyond anyone's imagination. A few months later, when my book was completed, ChatGPT had already evolved so much. I use it frequently for different tasks, and it gets better every day. With each passing day, ChatGPT continues to evolve, further affirming its capacity to learn and adapt independently. I firmly believe that this technology is a breakthrough that takes us closer to true AI.

Declaration of generative AI in the writing process

During the preparation of this work, the author used ChatGPT in order to search and gather information relevant to some parts of the book content. After using this tool/service, the author reviewed, edited, corrected, and rewrote the content, and verified the sources as needed and takes full responsibility for the content of the book.

Why This Book?

For the past 12 years, I have taught courses on data mining and machine learning. My students have thoroughly enjoyed the challenges of the course, and their encouragement, along with that of my colleagues, compelled me to write this book. I carefully considered the endeavor, understanding the difficulty of presenting this advanced topic in a manner accessible to all audiences. Nonetheless, having accumulated ample course notes and online lectures, I felt it was time to take on this endeavor.

As data continues to grow exponentially, learning data mining techniques becomes more crucial than ever. The field of machine learning has experienced explosive growth, with new techniques, algorithms, and applications emerging rapidly. However, the abundance of resources can be overwhelming, making it challenging for learners to identify a structured path for their education, particularly those without strong programming skills or a background in mathematics and computer science. My students are among these learners. They are successful professionals in their fields, and they want to learn to use data mining and machine learning to improve the effectiveness of their businesses and operations. This book aims to address this disparity. Many learners come from various fields, such as business management, marketing, finance, aviation, social sciences, and the humanities, and may feel left out amidst the overwhelming emphasis on training data scientists who excel in programming, coding, and algorithm development. Similarly, researchers and instructors in these non-technical fields face challenges when teaching or conducting research in the emerging field of data mining without programming skills and a solid foundation in computer science. I have observed that many textbooks and articles in this field are highly technical, laden with mathematical foundations and coding requirements, leading learners to believe that this is the only path to learning data mining and machine learning. However, this is far from the truth. As software technologies evolve, many applications allow users to build machine learning models and perform data mining without writing a single line of code. These applications feature user-friendly interfaces that enable non-programmers to harness the power of data mining. What we need is a different approach to explaining the concepts, principles, and processes of data mining, which is a book that effectively communicates essential information to the target audience.

With this book, my goal is to provide a comprehensive yet approachable resource that equips readers with fundamental concepts and practical skills to tackle real-world machine learning challenges. This book aims to be your guiding companion in this exciting journey, catering to both beginners who are just stepping into the world of machine learning and seasoned practitioners seeking to deepen their understanding and broaden their skills.

Who Should Read This Book?

This book is designed to be accessible to a wide range of readers, including students, instructors, researchers, and industry professionals. Regardless of your background – whether in business, finance, marketing, aviation, social science, computer science, statistics, engineering, or any other field – my goal is to present complex concepts in an intuitive manner, avoiding excessive jargon and heavy mathematical formulas. Throughout the text, I provide insightful examples that resonate with a diverse range of experiences.

What This Book Covers

The book begins with Part I, introducing the core concepts of data science, data mining, and machine learning. My aim is to present these principles without overwhelming readers with complex math, empowering them to comprehend the underlying mechanisms of various algorithms and models. This foundational knowledge will enable readers to make informed choices when selecting the right tool for specific problems. In Part II, I focus on the most popular machine learning algorithms, including regression methods, decision trees, neural networks, ensemble modeling, principal component analysis, and cluster analysis. Once readers feel confident with these methods, Part III introduces more advanced techniques, such as random forest, gradient boosting, and Bayesian networks, enabling them to build more complicated machine learning models. These principles and methods are beneficial for learners from all backgrounds. If you come from a non-technical background (business, finance, marketing, aviation, and social science), you will enjoy the simple explanations of the machine learning methods and the tips I provide. If you come from a technical background (computer science, statistics, and engineering), these chapters offer insights into fundamental concepts and principles of machine learning without delving into intricate mathematical theorems and formulas.

Once a solid foundation is established, readers have the opportunity to practice the methods through practical examples. The book adopts a hands-on approach, guiding readers through practical implementations using real datasets and SAS Enterprise Miner. SAS is one of the pioneer software companies in data science and machine learning. It is essentially still a capable programming language that has been adopted by many governmental and industrial organizations. SAS offers a user-friendly version called SAS Enterprise Miner. This software allows non-programmers to perform data mining without having to learn a programming language while maintaining the rigor of the data mining process. I provide step-by-step guidelines, accompanied by screenshots, to ensure readers can follow the process effortlessly. And the good news is that the educational version of SAS Enterprise Miner is completely free while having the full features of the professional version. Furthermore, while this book emphasizes SAS Enterprise Miner, it is worth noting that other popular data science software, such as SPSS Modeler and Rapid Miner, will be covered in subsequent books.

How to Use This Book

This book is designed to offer flexibility in your learning journey. Each chapter builds upon the knowledge gained in the previous ones, but readers can also navigate to specific topics or algorithms of interest, using it as a reference guide. Throughout the text, I provide specific configurations, software guidelines, and examples that help you solidify your understanding and gain practical experience. Unlike many data science books that employ numerous small datasets in examples, I have chosen to use only two large datasets – one for classification and one for association – across all chapters. In essence, the examples in the chapters are interconnected, representing different steps of the same project. This approach allows readers to practice all steps in the data mining process within the context of a cohesive project. Furthermore, even the chapter exercises are built upon the same two datasets throughout, offering readers a seamless application of learned principles. All exercises contribute to a larger project, ensuring a comprehensive learning experience.

One chapter that stands out in this book is Chapter 11. In this chapter, I provide specific guidelines and examples on how to present data mining results and write a data mining report. Data mining methods often lack standardization, making it challenging for users to produce effective reports that communicate the project's purpose, data characteristics, and analysis results to stakeholders. This chapter offers thorough guidance on all components of the report, supported by concrete examples.

Final Thoughts

Machine learning holds the potential to unlock endless possibilities, revolutionizing industries and addressing some of the world's most pressing challenges. I hope this book sparks your curiosity and passion for data mining and machine learning, inspiring you to explore, innovate, and create a meaningful impact in the world of data. As you embark on this exciting journey, remember that learning is a continuous process. Embrace challenges, celebrate your successes, and, most importantly, have fun exploring the fascinating world of machine learning.

Let's embark on this journey together and unlock the power of machine learning!
Happy mining!

Part I

Introduction to Data Mining

1

Introduction to Data Mining and Data Science

LEARNING OUTCOMES

Upon completion of this chapter, you will be able to

1. Define data mining.
2. Provide examples of data mining applications in real-life business practices.
3. Differentiate between reactive, proactive, and predictive strategies.
4. Explain the differences and overlaps between data science and data mining.
5. Describe the primary characteristics of data mining, how it differs from traditional statistical methods, and the potential advantages and disadvantages.
6. Discuss the evolution of Artificial Intelligence, data mining, machine learning, and deep learning.
7. Define big data and describe the primary characteristics of big data.
8. Explain the big data analytics process.
9. Identify ethical considerations in data mining.
10. Describe the Institutional Review Board requirements.
11. Implement the data de-identification process.

Introduction

This chapter covers some basic and important concepts in data mining and data science. Data mining is not a new term, but it is emerging and evolving. While many people talk about data science and mining, I wonder how many of them can understand and explain clearly what those terms mean and their purposes. There are many buzzwords in our world, and they are often misused or misquoted. In this chapter, I will cover many different concepts and classifications regarding data mining, data science,

machine learning (ML), big data, and predictive research. This fundamental understanding will allow you to go deeper into data mining methods and how to use them in the

DOI: 10.1201/9781003162872-2

next few chapters. If you still get confused after reading this chapter, don't worry. We will return to those fundamental concepts with specific examples of data and analysis results.

Are you ready for this exciting journey into the data analytics world? Let's begin.

What Is Data Mining?

We are living in a world of shared information, social networks, wireless connectivity, and digital communications. In this world, data are streamed and collected continuously in real time. Data exist in many forms, including numbers, texts, images, and videos. Big tech companies like Apple, Amazon, Facebook, and Twitter continue to collect and archive users' data on their servers. Manufacturing companies collect data on their products, operations, supply chains, inventories, logistics, and retailers. Service providers, such as hotels, resorts, casinos, banks, and airlines, gather data on their markets and customers. Our normal lives are also captured constantly via security cameras installed almost everywhere. We also choose to share our own data by sharing information, thoughts, pictures, and videos on social networks. If we go to the Internet and Google, we can find everything that we need. It is not an understatement that we are overwhelmed with the amount of data that we have access to, not to mention the proprietary data that are not accessible to the public. Remember, not seeing the data does not mean they don't exist. They are on the CLOUD.

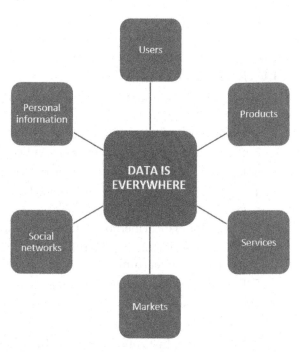

Has Anyone Seen the TV Show "Person of Interest"?

With that vast amount of data stored in cloud-based servers, the question is how can we make use of data to improve our lives, businesses, or customer experience? Let me start with one of my favorite TV shows, Person of Interest. It is a CBS sci-fi thriller show that aired from 2011 until 2016. The main character is Harold Finch, a math and computer genius. He received very large government funding to develop an advanced ML algorithm and build an Artificial Intelligence (AI) called "the Machine." The main goal of this AI is to process and analyze all data being fed into it from various sources, including personal information, social networks, traffic data, business information, security information, government information, banking transactions, etc. Basically, the Machine receives all kinds of data that the government can provide, including numbers, texts, videos, images, and voices. The data are fed to the system in real time. So you can imagine the volume of data the Machine receives every second. Storing such a vast amount of data demands both a substantial bandwidth and an exceptionally powerful server. Additionally, the energy required to keep the server operational is significant. Furthermore, computers with very high computing power are needed to quickly process and analyze that huge amount of data to produce practical outputs.

Mr. Finch developed a very robust and novel ML algorithm for the Machine, which took him several years to make it work. It was a tedious process with a lot of statistics, data analytics, computer programming, model training, and validation. But he finally succeeded. (Of course, we are never shown the actual algorithm on the show.) Using the algorithm, the Machine is capable of discovering unknown patterns from the data to do one thing and one thing only, which is to predict a specific individual, a person of interest, that will be involved in crime- or national security-related incidents. The prediction is not the name or address but the individual's social security number since it is a unique number assigned to each citizen. However, the Machine does not know whether this individual is a good guy or a bad guy; it only predicts that this person will be involved in an incident. It also does not know the reason or what causes the incident. In order to prevent the incident from happening, Mr. Finch hired an ex-CIA operative, John Reese, who has a set of special skills in hand-on-hand combat, weaponry, tactics, and covert operations. Mr. Reese's job is to find and follow that person of interest and intervene to stop the bad thing from happening. Each episode shows a prediction made by the Machine, and the team has to rush to follow the person of interest to determine if they are the victim or perpetrator, so they can either save this person or stop them from doing the bad thing.

While the synopsis may sound complicated, how the Machine works is fairly straightforward. I have demonstrated the working mechanism of the system in Figure 1.1. The input of the system is all data collected from various data sources in different forms, such as numbers, texts, voices, and images. The data are collected, stored, and fed to the cloud in real time. Imagine the amount of data the system has to process every second. The model uses ML algorithms to mine all of that data. It is a highly intelligent model that can learn, adapt, and improve itself, hence the name Artificial Intelligence. Of course, there are a lot of complicated algorithms used in this model. The interesting thing is that the more data we collect and feed to the system, the more the model can learn and improve itself with new data. In other words, the Machine learns from data (now you can see where the term "Machine Learning" comes from). Finally, the output of this system is the prediction of the target variable, more specifically, the person of interest represented by the social security number. It is a unique number assigned to one person, so there are no duplications.

The key takeaway from this series is that the Machine does not try to explain how the incident will happen, because it has not yet happened, nor explain contributing factors based on any theory. It only analyzes the big data given to it and predicts what will happen in the

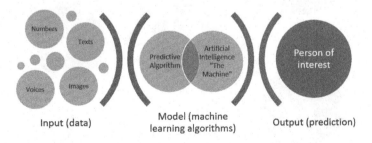

FIGURE 1.1
How does the Machine in Person of Interest work?

near future. It does not know whether the person of interest is a victim or a perpetrator. Nonetheless, its prediction is never wrong; something terrible will happen involving that individual. Sounds fictional, right? Remember, it is a sci-fi show. Realistically, we should always account for the margin of error in prediction. In essence, it does not try to explain the incident but rather predicts it. Once Mr. Reese intervenes and stops the incident, then we will know what causes or may cause the incident, but it is what we learn at the end of each episode. It is a great TV show, and if you are a fan of sci-fi thrillers, I strongly recommend watching it.

Definitions of Data Mining

SAS Institute defines data mining as "the process of finding anomalies, patterns, and correlations within large data sets to predict outcomes." Additionally, Nisbet et al. (2012) define data mining as the use of "machine learning algorithms to find faint patterns of relationship between data elements in large, noisy, and messy data sets, which can lead to actions to increase benefit in some form (diagnosis, profit, detection, etc.)."

In this book, I define *data mining* as *a method of using ML algorithms to detect unknown patents involving relationships among variables within large datasets to predict outcomes of interest, which can lead to informed business decisions*. Figure 1.2 illustrates the concept of data mining.

Thus, what the Machine in the TV show Person of Interest does is nothing more than data mining. The futuristic part is that this AI can do it so well with the huge amount of data, it has to process to make the prediction very quickly, so necessary mitigations can be implemented on time. In reality, that task requires significant resources to get it to work, and we have to account for the margin of error in prediction. There is no such thing as a perfect prediction in the real world.

> **DEFINITION**
>
> **Data mining:**
> Data mining is a method of using machine learning algorithms to detect unknown patents involving relationships among variables within large datasets to predict outcomes of interest, which can lead to informed business decisions.

In real life, small businesses, corporations, and governmental organizations can use data mining to analyze large datasets and detect unknown relationships between variables to make a prediction of outcomes, including performance, risk, revenue, customer satisfaction, etc. The predictive model and the relationships among variables can be used to provide the leaders with useful information about their operations and the importance

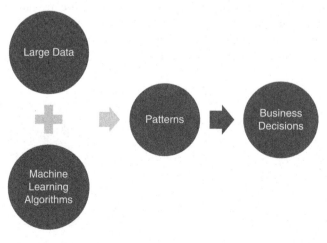

FIGURE 1.2
Data mining concept.

of business variables, based on which they can develop necessary business strategies and make informed decisions to enhance operational efficiency or mitigate the risks. It may sound too scientific and may be hard to understand. Let me show you some examples of how data mining can be used in real-life scenarios.

Practical Examples of Data Mining in Practice

There are numerous applications of data mining in the business world that we experience every day. Organizations and corporations have been using data mining to make sense of the data they collect and make informed decisions to enhance their operations or businesses. I provide below some typical examples of data mining applications in various domains.

Media Streaming

Many streaming services, such as Netflix, Amazon Prime, and Hulu, collect daily data from users on their preferences for movies and TV shows and watching habits. The companies use ML algorithms to uncover patterns from the data, which show the relationship between the user's preference and their demographic information. Then, the streaming application can predict what types of TV shows or movies a user may  want to watch at a certain time and make suggestions of other similar shows or movies to that specific user. For example, I am a fan of action movies, and I watched numerous Tom Cruise's and Will Smith's movies. The next time I logged in to my Netflix, I would see several suggestions of other action movies played by the same actors. On the home page, I also see several TV shows and movies in the same genre. Cool, right? In addition, Netflix can use the information from the patterns and predictions to decide what kind of shows or movies they should invest in making to increase their user subscriptions. Some examples of popular Netflix TV shows and movies include Stranger Things, Game of Cards, The Crown, The Iris Man, and Red Notice.

Social Networks

Top social media companies, such as Facebook or Twitter, have been collecting users' demographic information, their search for products or services, and their posts, photos, and communications with others on social media. Algorithms are developed to predict user behavior and the relationship with their demographic information. Then the application suggests relevant sites or built-in applications for a specific user to use, shows ads relevant to the user's preferences,  and suggests potential friends or posts that the user may want to check out. For example, I searched for some new posts or news on Lexus vehicles on Facebook, and the next day, I started seeing more ads on Lexus vehicles for sale. I also see suggested friends based on my friend database, and many times I found my long-lost friends through this useful feature. The companies also use the data mining outputs to decide how to make adjustments or change the applications to meet users' demands and attract more users.

Online Shopping

Nowadays, online shopping gradually out-performs the brick-and-mortar business model (in-person shopping). Amazon is a dominant company in e-commerce and has achieved great success. Most traditional retailers have transitioned to e-commerce models to improve their profitability. Online retailers, such as Amazon, Bestbuy, and Walmart, have used ML algorithms to predict customers' shopping behaviors. Their online shopping applications can suggest substituting products or new products

to the customers based on their demographic, past order history, or search history. The other day, I searched on Amazon for a smart outlet. The next day, my Amazon app suggested numerous smart outlets from different sellers with various types for me to choose. Very convenient! The companies can also predict the rising demand for certain products at a specific time in the future and have those items ready to fulfill the orders. They also use the information to enhance their supply chain efficiency to reduce inventory costs while reducing shipping time and maintaining service satisfaction.

Airline Industry

The airline industry is one of the largest and most competitive industries in the United States. Airline executives have been using data mining to improve passenger satisfaction and enhance their operational effectiveness. The airlines collect passenger demographic information and travel behaviors to uncover relationships between them, based on which future travel demand can be predicted, and passengers receive promotional and special offers from the airlines based on their travel histories. For example, I have been flying domestically and internationally with American Airlines. The airline

application records my travel histories and sends me recommendations for reasonable ticket prices to the same location or similar ones from time to time. They also send me various offers for frequent flyers, such as bonus reward points for specific trips or free 60,000 miles for the American Airlines credit card. Airlines can also identify the relationship among factors such as onboard services, Wi-Fi, cleanliness, leg room, food, flight delay, flight cancellation, and the passengers' decision to continue to fly with the airline. Thus, they can develop strategies to improve their operations and services to retain and increase loyal passengers.

Banking and Financing

Banks and mortgage companies have been using data mining extensively to predict customers' decisions in banking and their creditability in financing. Most of us have checking accounts with banks, and from time to time, we decide to switch to another bank for various reasons. Banks use data mining to predict the probability and time that a customer may close a bank account based on their demographics and banking history. Using this outcome, the  bank manager can offer the customer attractive offers to keep them with the bank. They also offer customers attractive credit card deals or new financing services. The benefits of predictive modeling are endless for banks. Additionally, in financing services, it is imperative to know if the borrowers are capable of paying their principal and interest for the loans they receive. Thus, mortgage companies use data mining to predict customer creditability based on demographics and credit histories. Then, they can decide whether to lend money to that customer, the loan amount, and the term. Data mining plays an important role in minimizing the lender's risks.

Healthcare

Data mining plays a vital role in healthcare since it helps doctors and providers improve the quality of their healthcare services. Doctors' offices and hospitals record all patients' personal information, demographics, health histories, and past and current treatments. Predictive models can be used to support patient treatments in multiple ways. First, when a new patient comes in with some  symptoms, the doctor enters the information into the system, and the system automatically maps the patient's issues and even provides a preliminary diagnosis. It can predict the level of severity and probability that the patient will get worse. It can also suggest effective treatments and prescriptions that work for similar cases. Furthermore, the system can predict whether it is an isolated case or a part of the pattern, based on which the doctors and hospitals can take proper actions to intervene and mitigate the risks.

Transportation

We all know that with the extensive highway system in the United States and many developed countries, traffic jams are a big issue that results in traffic delays, increased emissions, and lost time. A lot of traffic data are being collected in real time, and they can be used to predict the probability of traffic jams at a specific location, time, and delay time. The authorities can use this output to mitigate the traffic

situation and develop a strategic plan to optimize the transportation system, build new roads, or leverage new modes of transportation to reduce the traffic density in metropolitan areas. Furthermore, accidents happen very often and could result in serious injuries or even fatalities. We see accidents between cars on highways. We also observe way too many accidents occurring to bicyclists and pedestrians in big cities. A predictive model can be developed to predict the probability of an accident along with time and location. Thus, the authorities can allocate the resources efficiently so the emergency medical technicians (EMTs) can be ready to be at the scene promptly to help the victims. Remember, every second counts.

Those are just some examples of how data mining is being used and can be used in practice to enable businesses and organizations to enhance their operations, improve profitability, increase customer satisfaction, and enhance safety. There are a lot more applications that we can see in other areas, including education, training, manufacturing, engineering, aerospace, social science, biology, etc. Through examples in this book, we will get into specific cases in some areas. Then, depending on the industry or sector that you are working in, you can decide how data mining can be applied. The good news is that we will follow the same process and use the same algorithms to analyze the data. The difference is how we use the outputs to make informed business decisions.

Reactive, Proactive, and Predictive Strategies

In order to use data mining effectively in businesses, it is essential to understand the primary purpose of data mining in predictive projects. I want to show you how the Federal Aviation Administration (FAA) differentiates between reactive, proactive, and predictive strategies. While
it is meant for aviation safety strategies, I find this classification represents different types of research projects and where predictive research fits in very well. The FAA's primary responsibility is to ensure safety in air transportation. In aviation safety, the FAA categorizes three types of safety strategies, which are fundamentally different: reactive, proactive, and predictive (Figure 1.3). Aviation organizations can follow those strategies to enhance their operational safety.

The first type is the **Reactive strategy**, which focuses on examining events that have already happened and identifying the root causes of a specific incident or accident. Based on the identified root causes, the organizations can form appropriate strategies to mitigate

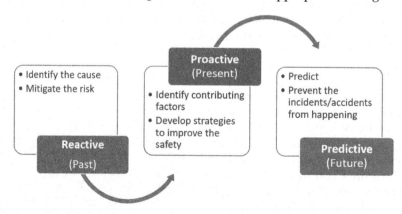

FIGURE 1.3
Reactive, Proactive, and Predictive safety strategies. (Source: Federal Aviation Administration.)

the risk. This strategy requires experts to investigate the incident very thoroughly, examine the black box, interview involved parties, and examine the scene of the incident. Depending on the scope and severity of the incident/accident, the investigation may take a long time to complete. For example, an airline accident may take months or even years to complete the investigation and confirm the causes. Nonetheless, the results are very useful for improvement in safety training and policies.

The second type is the **Proactive strategy**, which looks into the present. In other words, organizations examine contributing factors to an incident/accident from various aspects of hazardous conditions and organizational processes and see how they are related to the incident or accident. This action does not examine the causality but rather the correlations between contributing factors and the incident/accident. Common methods include statistical analysis, scientific theories, aeronautical scientific models, and engineering mechanisms. Using the correlation between variables, organizations can form necessary strategies and action plans to make impacts on those contributing factors, which will lead to safer operations. In addition, they can develop applications that detect incidents based on various parameters. Using sensors and collected data, an incident can be detected in real time, allowing authorities to make decisions to mitigate or reduce the risks. Since those incidents happen at the present time, it may not be possible to prevent them from happening, but proper actions can be taken to minimize the injuries or damages.

The third type is **Predictive strategy**, which looks into the future. In other words, organizations analyze a large amount of data to predict new potential safety problems in the future. By mining big data, they can develop a predictive model that predicts an incident or accident before it happens. While the first two strategies focus on explaining why and how an incident happened, the predictive strategy focuses on predicting the incident before it happens to prevent it. Since it has yet to happen, we are not able to explain how it will happen, but we can predict it. Explaining how it happens will come later. What important is that we can predict what, where, and when the incident will happen along with the probability. It is done by mining large data and discovering unknown patterns. Note that it is the first time we can actually prevent the incident from happening rather than just mitigate the risk. We will need a lot of data to make it happen. This is the type of event we see in the Person of Interest TV show. And data mining is the method used for predictive modeling.

All three strategies benefit businesses and organizations. In this book, we focus on the predictive strategy. In business operations, we can use predictive modeling to develop and validate a predictive model that accurately predicts a pre-defined outcome (target variable). We can also identify important predictors contributing to the prediction. Then, based on the potential or forecast future values of these predictors, we can predict the outcome in the future. We can also run various what-if-scenario to see how the outcome changes as we modify the values of specific predictors. These scenarios would allow the decision maker to decide the best strategies or decisions to solve the business problem with minimal uncertainty.

Data Mining and Data Science

In recent years, the term *data science* has become very popular in the analytics world and other fields. Many job openings are created to hire data scientists, and many people put *data scientist* or *data science expert* in their resumes. However, it is one of the buzzwords that people keep using and

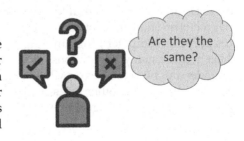

talking about but may not be able to clearly explain what it is. The main reason is that there is no consistent definition of the term *data science*. Before *data science*, we have seen intriguing terms such as *data mining, data analytics, business analytics,* and *big data*. Note that in those terms, including *data science*, the key part is not *data* but the other part of the term. We all know that we need data, but what to do with the data is the important part. In this section, I will explain the differences between *data science* and *data mining* and how they are related. Please note that you may find many comparisons on the Internet, but they are not consistent, and in some cases, there are discrepancies in those comparisons, which causes more confusion than helps us understand the difference. I noticed some comparisons mixed up concepts of data mining and data science. So we want to be careful and should rely on more reliable sources.

Data science is not a new term. Actually, an official definition of *data science* was introduced back in 1998 by Hayashi (1998). According to the author, data science is a "concept to unify statistics, data analysis and their related methods" in order to "understand and analyze actual phenomena" with data. In 2013, Dr. Vasant Dhar provided a definition of *data science* at a higher level in the Communications of ACM. He defined data science as "the study of the generalizable extraction of knowledge from data" (Dhar, 2013). It uses theories and techniques from various fields, including mathematics, statistics, computer science, and domain knowledge (Cao, 2017). *Data scientist* is a professional who "creates programming codes and combines them with statistical knowledge to create insights from data" (Davenport & Patil, 2012).

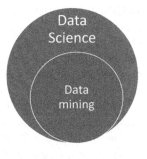

Thus, we can say that *data mining* and *data science* serve the same purposes of enabling us to explore and uncover patterns from large data to provide organizations and individuals with newly discovered information so they can make informed decisions. These terms overlap or

Data mining is an essential component of Data science

can even be considered the same in some cases since both involve ML, big data, and analytics. A common understanding is that data mining is a method or interdisciplinary subfield, while data science is a discipline. From that perspective, we can consider data science broader than data mining, but data mining is an essential component of data science. Let's put it this way. Data mining covers methods of using ML to uncover patterns from large data to predict outcomes. Statistics, mathematics, and other rule-based methods are the core of data mining. On the other hand, data science is a larger and multidisciplinary field, focusing on capturing and extracting knowledge from data and communicating the outcomes. Data science consists of data mining as an essential part of analyzing data and other components such as data collection and management, data treatment, data visualization, computer programming, and AI application development.

Data scientists are expected to do a task or a combination of tasks involving analytics, data collection and treatment, data mining, ML, and programming. Thus, their job could be just data mining or more multidisciplinary. If their primary responsibility is data mining, they focus on analyzing data and using various ML methods to build predictive models. For this purpose, computer programming skills are an advantage but not necessarily required skills because many applications allow us to do data mining without writing codes (as a reminder, this book focuses on ML for non-programmers). However, suppose the job responsibilities also include other tasks such as big data collection and management, developing complex deep learning algorithms, and deploying the predictive model in an implementable application. In that case, programming skills are very necessary. This explains why you will see discrepancies in job qualifications and skill requirements for data scientist jobs.

What I can say here is that we will continue to see different definitions of these terms. Both data mining and data science continue to evolve, and we will see more aspects of them in the near future. I incorporate my comparison in Figure 1.4 to help you see that difference. Since this book is for non-programmers, we will focus mainly on the data mining part of data science; i.e., we cover the process and methods of using ML to uncover hidden patterns from large data. Nonetheless, I cover useful parts regarding data visualization and treatment that may be useful for you to learn. Accordingly, in essence, it is not wrong to say that

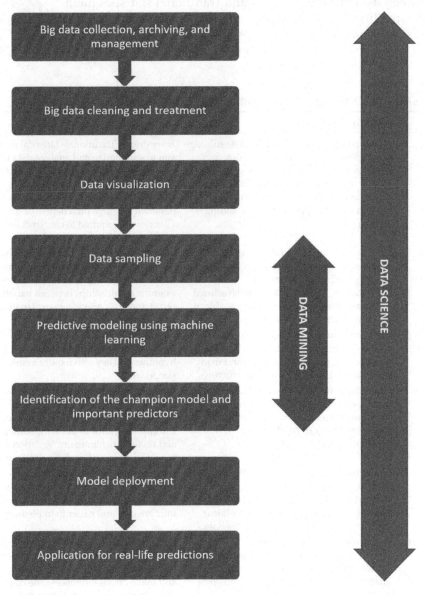

FIGURE 1.4
Data science and data mining.

this book is about data science because it is. And I will use the term *data scientists* to refer to the specialists using ML methods to analyze data. But we will not cover data scientists who are also responsible for collecting, archiving, and managing data, as well as those responsible for deploying the predictive algorithm and making actual computer applications.

Characteristics of Data Mining

One of the common confusions in data mining research is the differences between data mining methods and traditional statistics methods. Understanding those differences allows us to understand better characteristics of data mining methods and know when to use them instead of traditional statistical methods. Table 1.1 summarizes the

TABLE 1.1

Differences between Data Mining and Traditional Statistical Methods

Items	Data Mining Methods	Traditional Statistical Methods
Objectives	*Data-driven*: The primary goal of data mining is to discover patterns, relationships, and insights in large datasets that may not be readily apparent. It focuses on extracting useful information from data, often with the aim of making predictions or finding hidden patterns.	*Theory-driven*: Traditional statistical methods aim to summarize and analyze data to make inferences about a population. They focus on understanding relationships between variables, testing hypotheses, and estimating parameters with a high degree of confidence. Theories are required to construct hypotheses in those models.
Exploratory vs. explanatory	*Exploratory*: Data mining techniques emphasize exploring large and complex datasets to identify patterns and relationships. They can handle unstructured and semi-structured data and are capable of handling high-dimensional datasets.	*Explanatory*: Traditional statistical methods typically start with a pre-defined hypothesis or research question and use statistical tests to examine relationships between variables. As a result, they can provide an explanation for those relationships.
Data requirements	Data mining methods require large data for model training and validation. The datasets usually have many rows of data and many variables in different forms and structures.	Traditional statistical methods do not need many variables since they focus on proposed hypotheses. They also require a small sample size to work.
Assumptions	Data mining methods typically make fewer assumptions about the underlying data distribution and relationships between variables. They can handle noisy, incomplete, and inconsistent data.	Traditional statistical methods often assume specific data distributions (e.g., normality) and require adherence to certain statistical assumptions, such as linearity, homogeneity, and non-multicollinearity. Violation of these assumptions can affect the validity of results.
Model complexity	Data mining techniques can handle complex models, including decision trees, neural networks, and ensemble methods. They are capable of capturing complex, non-linear relationships and interactions in the data.	Traditional statistical methods often use simpler models, such as linear regression, ANOVA, or logistic regression. These models are typically interpretable and easier to implement.
Interpretation	Data mining techniques prioritize discovering patterns and relationships, but the interpretability of the models can be a challenge. The focus is often on predictive accuracy rather than the explicit understanding of underlying mechanisms.	Traditional statistical methods emphasize interpretability, allowing researchers to understand the relationship between variables and make causal inferences. The emphasis is often on parameter estimation and hypothesis testing.

primary characteristics of data mining and how they are different from other traditional statistical methods.

First, data mining is a data-driven method. We use data mining to discover unknown or new patterns from large data. In other words, we use ML algorithms to extract information or uncover unknown patterns solely from the data. In essence, we want to know what data tells us. It differs from traditional statistical research, which tends to be theory-driven. They construct relationships and hypotheses from existing theories. In these studies, data are collected to test the proposed hypotheses and confirm with evidence whether they are supported or not. The studies focus mainly on the variables of interest, supported by the literature. Traditional statistical methods are commonly used in these studies, such as t-test, ANOVA, and MANOVA for comparison and multiple linear regression, logistic regression, and structural equation modeling for testing correlations. On the contrary, in data mining, we do not have hypotheses or use any theories as the foundation since we want to find out new patterns from the data rather than from the theories or literature. Hence, the quality of the data plays a very important role since noisy and incomplete data may provide meaningless results or even false outcomes. Therefore, in order to make data mining useful, we need large datasets with a large number of variables and records. We will get to the characteristics of big data later.

Second, data mining research is exploratory; i.e., we use data mining to explore new variables and relationships from data. We do not try to speculate in advance on what relationships are significant and which variables are important. Essentially, we want the data to tell us these outcomes. On the other hand, traditional statistical research is explanatory and tends to focus on confirming hypothesized relationships. Hence, those studies are limited to pre-identified variables of interest and their relationships based on the literature. One question that usually arises in data mining research is, "Do you discover any new variables, relationships, or patterns?" In other words, the findings of data mining research may surprise us, which makes them meaningful in predictive research.

Of course, in order to discover new variables and relationships, we cannot limit ourselves to small datasets with limited variables. Therefore, the third characteristic of data mining is large data. Large data means the dataset with a large number of variables and records in different forms and structures. Since we do not know what we may find, we need large data. As in the Person of Interest TV show, the AI needs to have access to a huge amount of data, many of which are rather sensitive, to be able to make an accurate prediction. This is different from theory-driven, explanatory research, which usually uses a smaller dataset with limited variables. As you know, when we perform statistical analysis techniques such as ANOVA and multiple regression, or even structural equation modeling, we usually use some formula to find the minimum sample size needed to detect the relationships at a particular significance level and expected test power. In most cases, we should be fine with a sample size between 100 and 300. And our models tend to have 3–10 variables. On the other hand, in data mining research, we need to analyze data with hundreds of variables and million rows of data. Since data mining is data-driven, the noise and missing values may have a negative effect on the quality of the outcomes. Having larger data would help address those issues.

Due to the size of the data, data mining methods are not subject to strict statistical assumptions, and they can handle noisy and unstructured data. They usually do not require specific underlying data distributions. Many ML algorithms can perform well with missing values and outliers since they are rule-based rather than statistics-based. Of course, we still need to ensure the quality of the data to obtain meaningful outcomes. The phrase "garbage in, garbage out" still applies here. On the other hand, theory-driven studies tend to use statistical techniques with a smaller sample size, which requires meeting strict statistical assumptions, such as normality, non-multicollinearity, linearity, and homogeneity. These requirements tend to create obstacles in the data analysis process and limit the inclusion of variables in the model.

Given the large data and variety of ML algorithms, data mining allows us to build complex predictive models with non-linear relationships or interactions between variables. Since we do not know what data may tell us, it is impossible to assume any type of relationships we are dealing with (linear or non-linear) or how many variables are in the final model. Advanced ML methods, such as decision trees, neural networks, or ensemble modeling can model the complexity of the data. On the other hand, traditional statistical methods often use simpler models, such as t-test, ANOVA, linear regression, or logistic regression. They rely on proposed hypotheses and may not be able to capture complex, non-linear models.

Last but not least, the interpretability. Since data mining can detect complex, non-linear models with interactions of variables, the model is often considered a *black box*, meaning uninterpretable. The reason is that the relationships of variables are too complex to follow. Note that the model is not literally uninterpretable. The data mining outcomes do allow us to examine those relationships using either trees or mathematical formulas. However, it requires a deeper understanding of the scientific background of the method. Note that the focus of data mining is not really to explain the underlying mechanism but rather to achieve an accurate prediction. On the other hand, traditional statistical methods focus on explaining the relationship between variables and making causal inferences. The emphasis of those studies is often on parameter estimation and hypothesis testing. That is why it is easier to interpret the results of traditional statistical models.

That comparison shows us the strengths of data mining, but it is not without weaknesses. The most obvious weakness is the tendency to overfit the model to data, given the size of the data. Overfitting basically means we train our predictive model with a lot of data and achieve a predictive model with very high accuracy. However, the model fits the training sample so well that it is not generalizable to other samples; i.e., when we run this model with another dataset we achieve a very low accuracy. Thus, the model is overfitted to the training sample and has no use in real life since it lacks generalizability. Usually, we can evaluate the overfitting by partitioning the data randomly into training and validation samples. The training sample is used to train the model, and the validation sample is used to validate the model. If the model fit metrics are similar between both samples, we have a reliable model without overfitting issues. We will get deeper into overfitting in Chapter 6.

In addition, some ML algorithms may require a lot of computer power to finish the analysis. More specifically, neural network algorithms usually require a very high number of iterations to search for the optimal solution. This search process tends to require a lot of computation, which demands high computing power and running time. An effective search algorithm and high-power computer are needed to deal with the situation. More importantly, in data mining, the most time-consuming part is data preparation and treatment. Usually, 80% of the time in data mining projects is dedicated to data cleaning and preparation.

Note that those are general disadvantages of data mining. When we cover each ML method, we will get into its specific advantages and disadvantages. The rule of thumb is that *there is no such thing as a perfect ML method, but there is the best method for a specific dataset.* While some methods are more complicated

There is no such thing as a perfect machine learning method. But there is the best method for a specific set of data.

or advanced than others, all methods have pros and cons. Which method works best will depend on the data. Otherwise, if there was a perfect method that worked well for all types of data, we could just always use that one for all projects. But the reality is that we don't know which method would work best for our data until we train the model with the data. Hence, the common strategy is to use multiple methods and develop multiple predictive models. By comparing those models, we can identify the best predictive model, also called the champion model. We will get into the details of this step in Chapter 6.

Evolution of Artificial Intelligence, Machine Learning, and Deep Learning

There are several buzzwords related to data mining and predictive modeling that we hear or read every day. They are *Artificial Intelligence, Machine Learning,* and *Deep Learning.* Accordingly, I want to explain briefly the differences among them since they are overlapping, and people tend to get confused about those terms. I will not get into the detail since each of them is a field of study and a degree by itself. I will also explain the evolution of those fields of study over time (Figure 1.5).

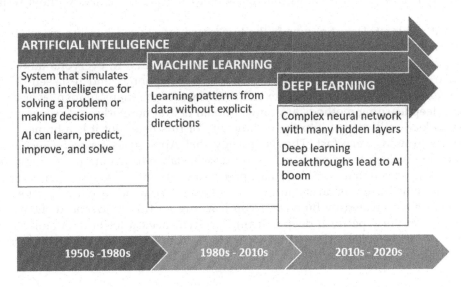

FIGURE 1.5
Evolution of Artificial Intelligence, machine learning, and deep learning.

First, *Artificial Intelligence* or AI. While AI is a growing trend in research, it is not a new term. The term AI was created back in the 1950s to refer to software that uses complex logic to automate any operations. AI has evolved significantly over time with the advances of computer science and robotics. But AI is not just about building robots. A more current definition of AI is "a system that simulates human intelligence for solving problems or making decisions." AI can learn, predict, improve, and solve. Basically, AI could be an application or solution that automatically operates and acts with minimal human interference. Siri, Alexa, and Google Assistant are some examples of AI virtual assistants that make our life easier with smartphones, smart homes, and smart cars. Tesla's self-driving application is an AI that drives the advance of autonomous vehicles. Chat GPT is an AI chatbot that can do a lot of intelligent work based on users' demands. Those applications are just the beginning of the AI era. We will soon see more amazing AI tools in all industries. Of course, when the machine gets smarter, there will be concerns regarding ethics and social impacts. However, it is a topic for a different book.

Machine Learning is a vital part of AI, and it started in the 1980s. ML is an algorithm that learns patterns from data without explicit directions. The data mining that we have been talking about uses ML algorithms. These algorithms are developed based on the foundation of mathematics, statistics, and computer science. In the next chapters, I will describe specific ML algorithms that we can use in our research. In the old times, in order to use ML, heavy coding was a must since there was a lot of math involved, and only some software, such as MATLAB, could handle the algorithms. Fortunately, in the last few years, more and more user-friendly applications have been created. So ML is no longer just the venue for mathematicians or computer scientists. ML can also be used for applied research rather than just basic research. While data scientists still use programming languages, such as Python or R, for ML work, non-programmers have more options to leverage this method for their research or businesses. Software applications, such as SAS Enterprise Miner, Rapid Miner, and SPSS Modeler, are point-and-click data mining tools that allow us to analyze large data without writing codes.

Last but not least, *Deep Learning* is the buzzword we started hearing more often in the past few years, even though it was introduced in the 2010s. No one mentioned it then because only a few people understood this concept. Now, everyone talks about Deepfake, voice recognition, facial recognition on smartphones, and Tesla self-driving. In essence, deep learning is a complex neural network with many hidden layers. Some popular deep learning methods are convolutional neural networks and recurrent neural networks. I will not get into the technicality of this field, but it is a branch of ML that starts growing very fast. The technology that Apple uses for facial recognition and cameras is deep learning. It is also used in Tesla's self-driving technology. Deep learning is also used in natural language processing, art and music creation, and many others. You may have seen arts and music created by AI, which are hard for us to tell that they are not created by humans. Deep learning is still an advanced subject, and in order to properly perform deep learning, we will need a lot of data and complex algorithms. Hence, it is harder to find software that can handle deep learning without programming and coding.

MACHINE LEARNING: CAN MACHINES ACTUALLY LEARN?

The term *machine learning* is being used very often nowadays in many books, papers, and online articles. But someone may wonder if machines can actually learn, and what *machine learning* actually means. It is one of the buzzwords people keep using without fully understanding the meaning of it. I will avoid providing a scientific definition of machine learning and will explain it in a simpler way. I illustrate it in Figure 1.6.

Basically, in order to develop a predictive model from data, we need to have a large dataset and a target variable. Then we need to choose one or more algorithms to use. Those algorithms are either math-based, statistics-based, or rule-based. For each algorithm, a model is built by expressing relationships among variables with specific sets of formulas and rules. The data scientist makes these configurations based on exploring the data and the foundation of the machine learning method. The next step is to fit that model to the actual dataset and evaluate the model fit. If the model fits the data, we have a good fit model. This process is called *training the model with data*. In other words, we could say the model is learning from data; hence, the term *machine learning*.

If the model fit is poor, there is a significant difference between the model and the data (we call it *residual*). In this case, the data scientist needs to reconfigure the algorithm or use a different one and retrain the model. The process repeats until we receive a good model fit. In other words, machine must continue to learn until it learns well, even though we are the one training it. Of course, if we overtrain the model, it will be overfitted, i.e., it would work only with that dataset and may not work with other datasets. Accordingly, we need to be more careful not to overtrain the model.

> We train the model with data, and the algorithm gets better through training. So we can say machine does learn through the training we provide it.

Over time, when we use the predictive model for actual predictions, we need to make adjustments to make sure it still works. By training the model with new data, we can continue to improve its performance. An advanced programming can be developed to automate this training process, which allows the model to continue to learn from new data. Basically, when we achieve this step, machine can learn by itself without needing us to train it. Thus, we will have a true AI.

I hope those explanations help you understand the meaning of the term "machine learning."

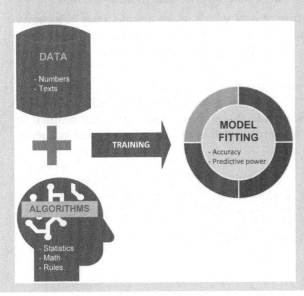

FIGURE 1.6
Machine learning: Can machines actually learn?

Big Data

I want to provide a quick introduction to big data. First, what is *big data*? A common-sense answer would be "a lot of data," which is not wrong. The AI in the Person of Interest TV show has to collect and process a huge amount of data in different types and formats coming in from many different sources in real time. And, of course, it would require a super supercomputer to store and process that amount of data promptly. The prediction would not be meaningful and useful if it took days to make one prediction. SAS Institute defines big data as "large volume of data – both structured and unstructured – that inundates a business on a day-to-day basis. But it's not the amount of data that's important. It's what organizations do with the data that matters. Big data can be analyzed for insights that lead to better decisions and strategic business moves".

> **DEFINITION**
>
> "Big data is a term that describes the large volume of data – both structured and unstructured – that inundates a business on a day-to-day basis. But it's not the amount of data that's important. It's what organizations do with the data that matters. Big data can be analyzed for insights that lead to better decisions and strategic business moves." (SAS)

Thus, big data is not only the amount of data but also what we do with the data. Essentially, big data can be characterized by five dimensions: volume, velocity, variety, variability, and veracity (Figure 1.7).

VOLUME pertains to the quantity of data, encompassing various sources such as business transactions, smart devices, industrial equipment, videos, social media, and more. Historically, managing such data would have posed challenges, but advancements in cloud computing and the availability of cost-effective storage solutions like data lakes and Hadoop have alleviated this burden.

VELOCITY relates to the speed at which data is generated and transmitted. With the proliferation of the Internet of Things (IoTs), data streams into servers at an unprecedented rate, necessitating timely processing. RFID tags, sensors, and smart meters are driving the demand for handling these torrents of data in near-real time.

VARIETY refers to the diverse nature of data which spans a wide array of formats. This encompasses structured, numeric data typically found in traditional databases, as well as unstructured data such as text documents, email, video, audio, and financial transactions.

VARIABILITY pertains to the diversity and fluctuations in data flows. In addition to the increasing speed and variety of data, data flows exhibit unpredictability due to frequent changes and significant variations. Businesses must stay attuned to trends in social media and effectively manage daily, seasonal, and event-triggered surges in data loads.

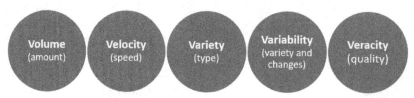

FIGURE 1.7
Big data dimensions.

VERACITY denotes data quality. Given the multitude of data sources, linking, matching, cleansing, and transforming data across systems can be challenging. Businesses must establish connections and discern relationships, hierarchies, and multiple data linkages; otherwise, their data may quickly become unmanageable.

Now we understand more about the complexity of big data. It is no longer just a very large dataset. It is a business framework for success. So how do we implement big data analytics? We will need to follow the five steps presented in Figure 1.8. For each step, I list important questions we need to find answers to.

1. **Set a big data strategy.**
   - What is our goal?
   - What do we want to achieve with big data?
2. **Identify big data sources.**
   - What data are available?
   - Where do we get the data?
   - Do we have permission to access and use the data?
   - What data can we use for business purposes, and what restrictions do we have to follow?
3. **Access, manage, and store the data.**
   - How do we collect that huge amount of data from different sources?
   - Where do we store them?
   - Do we have enough infrastructure and computing power to categorize and store the data?
   - What equipment and protocol are needed to ensure the security of the data?
   - How do we access the data as needed without delay, lagging, or disruption?
4. **Analyze big data.**
   - What are our purposes?
   - What dataset do we analyze?
   - What variables do we use? How do we prepare and clean the data?
   - What analytic methods should we use?
   - How do we interpret the results?
5. **Make data-driven decisions.**
   - Given the analysis results from the previous step, what are possible solutions?
   - What are the outcomes of various scenarios?
   - What is the best solution to solve the business problem?

FIGURE 1.8
Big data implementation process.

In this book, we focus more on predictive modeling and won't cover big data. However, it is important to understand the concept and importance of big data and big data analytics. After all, we live in a world of data and digitization. I take you back to the Person of Interest TV show that I introduced at the beginning. The Machine possesses big data which streams to it in real time. It processes all data to make predictions. These predictions help to save people's lives and, sometimes, save the world. It is certainly not an easy task. In conclusion, we live in a world with too much data that overwhelms us. Some may say too much data have created chaos in our society. But we cannot change that fact. We have to move forward and make the best of it. I think if we can find patterns and orders in chaos, we will be able to succeed.

Ethical Consideration

When we work with data, especially a lot of data, naturally, we have to ask a question about ethics. Data tends to include personal, private, and sensitive information. While that information can help us develop good predictive algorithms, if it is leaked out, it can harm those individuals. Accordingly, before we can conduct data mining research, we must evaluate and address any ethical concerns to ensure no harm to human subjects.

Ethical Principles and Data Collection

Ethical consideration is an important topic in data mining because we must ensure we comply with any requirements and restrictions regarding data access to protect human subjects and avoid violating privacy. Essentially, ethical consideration refers to the principles, guidelines, and moral values that govern the responsible and respectful use of data throughout the entire data mining process. According to the Belmont report (1979), there are three basic ethical principles that all researchers or investigators must follow. These principles include (1) respect for persons, (2) beneficence, and (3) justice. First, respect for persons means individuals should be treated as autonomous agents, and persons with diminished autonomy are entitled to protection. Second, beneficent actions ensure that the research does not harm persons and maximizes possible benefits and minimizes possible harms. Finally, justice is to ensure "fairness in distribution" to all participants. All researchers and investigators must comply with these ethical principles in their research projects.

Acquiring data is a challenging task, as not many organizations are willing to share their own data with the public. Some websites on data mining share the so-called example datasets, mainly for practice purposes. Those datasets could be fictional or have been de-identified, modified, or even reduced. Accordingly, they are not usable for research purposes since we are not certain about the validity of the data or do not have information on the variables, timeframe, or context that are needed to make a project meaningful.

There are limited organizations that put de-identified data on the Internet for public use. Examples include NASA, FAA, NTSB, BTS, U.S. Census Bureau, Department of Education, etc. Of course, those datasets have been scrubbed carefully and thoroughly to make sure no personal information or identification is revealed. Although these databases are valid and can be used for research purposes, they are very limited, which may not provide us with the data we actually need for our project. An advantage of these publicly accessed data sources is that no permission or conditions are required to use the data. Since the data have been cleaned and de-identified, we are allowed to publish our results on the Internet or in peer-reviewed journals. Since there is no information about the human subjects or participants in the data, there should be no ethical concerns.

Private organizations usually have very current and relevant data that they frequently collect for business purposes. Examples include airlines, manufacturers, retailers, e-commerce companies, hotels, hospitals, social network providers, media providers, banks, and real estate companies. However, they consider the data proprietary and do not want to publish it on the Internet for public use. They usually have an in-house data analytics team to analyze data to get insights to help them make business decisions. Nonetheless, sometimes they may agree to share the data for research purposes with some restricted conditions, mostly through research grants or contracts. In this case, researchers usually need permission from the organization to access the data on the condition that the researcher accepts all terms established by the organization. The consent should be in writing and formal. The document is called Non-Disclosure Agreement (NDA), and all parties should agree and sign it before the data can be shared with the researcher. Researchers should make sure that permission is given before attempting to access and collect the data. They also need to review the terms and conditions carefully and thoroughly before accepting them. In some cases, the permission includes the expiration date for data access, the purpose of the project, the expectation for the final report submission, and whether the findings can be published in a peer-reviewed journal. Usually, the permission to publish comes with restrictions that the data must be thoroughly de-identified, and the identification of the data provider is not revealed in the report in any form.

In some cases, government agencies or private parties agree to provide non-public data for research purposes but require the researcher to hold the publication of the results for a certain amount of time. For example, a funding organization provides the researcher with the necessary data. However, the data may contain some information that is time sensitive; i.e., the information should be kept from the public at this time but should be publicly available in two years. Hence, the organization may require the researcher to hold the publication of the results

> Ethics is very important. We cannot proceed with our research until we prove that there are no harm to individuals.

for two years. After that expiration date, the researcher is free to publish the results, provided that it is approved by the data provider. This requirement is usually included in the contract or non-disclosure agreement signed by the organization and the researcher.

When we work with datasets provided by those organizations, we need to follow the three above basic ethical principles. We should begin with performing a systematic assessment of risks and benefits to the organization and individuals involved in the data. By understanding potential risks and harms for the organizations and individuals, we can decide proper action plan to avoid any harm to them. Revealing sensitive and private information can harm not only individuals but also organizations. In addition, misinformation or misinterpretation of the results also poses the same level of harm. Once we complete the risk and benefit analysis, we develop an action plan to make sure no harm will be done to individuals as well as organizations.

Institutional Research Board (IRB) and the Review Process

An Institutional Research Board (IRB), alternatively known as an Independent Ethics Committee (IEC), Ethical Review Board (ERB), or Research Ethics Board (REB), constitutes a committee tasked with the application of research ethics. Its role primarily involves scrutinizing proposed research methods to ascertain their ethical validity. These boards are officially authorized to either grant approval or withhold it, oversee, and evaluate research that involves human subjects. Frequently, they engage in a thorough risk-benefit analysis to determine the ethical suitability of conducting the research. The primary objective of the IRB is to ensure the implementation of necessary measures for safeguarding the rights and well-being of individuals participating as subjects in a research study. When a researcher conducts a study involving human subjects, they need to submit an application and get approved by two different IRBs, one at their own institution and another one at the data provider's organization. For example, suppose I conduct a study that may involve individuals at an airline. In that case, I will need to submit the application to two different IRBs, one at the university where I am working and another board at the airline (airlines may use a different name than IRB). Both IRBs will review my application, and upon approval by both of them, I can proceed with my research.

Each organization has different rules, processes, and requirements for IRB application. The typical process includes the following steps.

- The researcher completes an application for IRB review. The application usually asks for the research purposes, methodology, possibility of using human subjects, data collection process, experimental design, questionnaire, potential harms to human subjects, and what efforts will be made to avoid those harms.

- The IRB coordinator reviews the application and decides whether the application needs to be reviewed by an IRB committee. If not, the researcher will be informed of the exempt decision and can proceed with the research. If yes, an IRB committee will be formed, including experts in the field.

- The IRB committee reviews the application, discusses it, and votes. They may decide to ask the researcher for more information or clarification.

- The IRB committee's decision is communicated to the researcher. The decision includes several options: exempt, approved, approved with conditions, or declined (resubmission is required). Based on the decision, the researcher can either proceed with the research or must make changes and resubmit.

Figure 1.9 presents a diagram that explains the common IRB decision process that allows the researcher to determine whether IRB application and review are needed.

How to De-Identify Data?

Data de-identification is the process of removing or altering identifying information from a dataset to protect the privacy and anonymity of individuals. Data de-identification is typically unnecessary for publicly available data since the data provider already de-identifies the data before posting it online. Nonetheless, it is essential to review the terms and conditions posted by the data provider regarding how to use the data. In many cases, the researcher has to agree to terms and conditions before being granted access to the data.

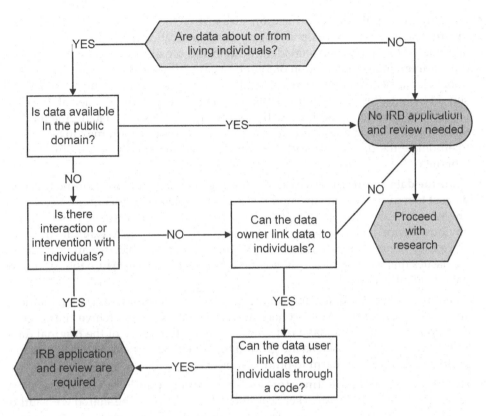

FIGURE 1.9
IRB decision process. (Adapted from the National Institute of Health, 2019.)

If we have access to secondary data with sensitive and private information, it is important to de-identify the data before analyzing them. We should first check with the data provider for any particular information that they want to take out and any conditions they have in terms of how the data is being used. For example, some organizations may not allow us to publish the findings or require us to hold the publication for a certain amount of time before sending it to a journal. Some other organizations may require us to submit the final report with detailed findings for their review, while others may want to hold the right to the reports for different reasons. All these conditions should be discussed and agreed upon in advance. In addition, any relevant privacy rules must be reviewed and discussed. When we have a complete list of information that must be removed from the data, we can proceed to de-identification.

The de-identification process usually includes the following steps.

- **Identify risks for re-identification**: In this step, we need to evaluate any harm to individuals or organizations if the data is re-identified. The severity of the impacts must be reviewed and recorded for risk assessment purposes. In addition, we also must assess the possibility that someone may be able to re-identify the data based on the information of de-identified data. What it means is that sometimes the de-identified data may still contain some information that allows others to guess the hidden information, which is a serious issue.

- **Develop and apply de-identification measures**: Once we know the risks of re-identification, we can develop and apply de-identification measures. The common approach is to remove personal identification and sensitive information or replace it with anonymous information or temporary ID. While it sounds simple, we need to develop a clear and detailed protocol to avoid missing anything. The protocol should include the variables that should be removed or changed, the values being used for replacement, and the location of those variables and data in the dataset. Since we are dealing with large datasets, some macros or programs can be written to automate the de-identification process to save time and avoid missing important data.

- **Examine data again**: Once we de-identify the data, it is vital to examine this new dataset to make sure the data is properly and completely de-identified. We are the one who de-identified the data, which may lead to bias or missing of something obvious. Hence, it is recommended to use external reviewers to examine the data. Since they review the data the first time, they are totally objective and can detect any issues that we may have missed. It is a necessary step to ensure the validity of data de-identification.

- **Document the method**: It is important to document the de-identification methods and process carefully. We also need to document how we archive the original data and de-identify the data and how we ensure the safety of the original data. The document can be used as the ground to prove that we have followed a proper protocol to reduce any harm to human subjects.

- **Keep the codes and guidelines for re-identification by authorized parties**: These codes and guidelines must be kept confidential and can only be shared with authorized parties because they will allow them to re-identify the data.

How Is the Book Structured?

In order to help you follow the chapters in this book easily, I present the general structure of each chapter in Table 1.2. Each chapter consists of many sections, details, and examples. Some information may be complicated or advanced for the audience, especially if you are new to data mining concepts. By understanding the general structure of those chapters, you should be able to follow the introduction, details, guidelines, software references, and examples. I use this structure for most chapters, especially those focusing on ML methods.

Writing Tone and Style

In my research papers, I typically adopt a scholarly writing style, which is academic-focused, objective, and evidence-based. Each statement is meticulously supported by references through proper citations. Moreover, passive voice is frequently used to maintain a formal and authoritative tone.

However, for the purpose of this book, I have adopted a different writing strategy that primarily employs active voice to connect with readers and facilitate their understanding of the concepts and processes. In the initial seven chapters, I adopt a casual writing tone

TABLE 1.2

General Structure of the Chapters

Sections	Description
Learning outcomes	Set of outcomes you are expected to learn and implement after completing the chapter.
Keywords	Primary terms used in the chapter.
Introduction	A brief introduction of the ML method and any important thing you need to pay attention to when reading the chapter.
Definitions of the method	Clear definitions of the method and related important terms.
Principle	The principle of the method is explained in detail to allow you to gain a fundamental understanding of the method and how it works.
Practical applications	Examples of how the method is applied in various domains.
Basic concepts	Basic concepts in the method and descriptions. Those terms are used often in the chapter. You can refer to those concepts as you go through the chapter if you need a reminder of what they mean.
Process	The steps you need to follow to perform the method.
Advantages and disadvantages	Advantages and disadvantages of the method in comparison with other ML methods.
Detailed components	Detailed components of the method. I use figures, formulas, functions, and rules to explain them. These details help you understand how the method works and how to configure the model. The length of this section depends on the details I provide in the chapter. The chapters covering important methods, including regression, decision trees, and neural networks, consist of more details. The chapters covering advanced methods, including random forest, gradient boosting, and Bayesian networks, are shorter because I want to avoid complicated mathematical foundations in those methods. Instead, I focus on the analysis process, key takeaways, and common configurations.
Configurations provided by SAS Enterprise Miner	Specific configurations are provided by the software. Note that not all configurations described above are provided by SAS Enterprise Miner. This section allows you to decide what properties you can change in the predictive modeling using the software.
SAS Enterprise Miner guidelines and references	Specific guidelines and references provided by SAS Enterprise Miner. These details are extracted directly from SAS references and resources. However, I try to keep the most relevant parts and make some clarification to avoid confusion. The full guidelines can be accessed via the provided links.
Examples of predictive modeling	Specific examples of how to use the method with an actual dataset. The examples provide detailed steps with screenshots for property settings, how to use the software, explanations of decisions you can make, how to get the outcomes, which outcomes are important, and how to understand and interpret the results. This section is the most important section in each chapter, as it allows you to follow the steps and practice with the software and the data.
	In order to make it easy for you to follow through multiple steps of the data mining process, I use mainly two datasets throughout the book: the *airline recommendation* dataset and the *Boston housing* dataset. Thus, you can see the whole picture and process of analyzing one big dataset using data mining.
Chapter summary	Summary of the method with key concepts and takeaways.
Chapter discussion questions	Important discussion questions covering all information and required content for the method. By answering those questions, you can test your understanding of the method in this chapter.
Exercises	Useful exercises that allow you to practice your understanding and skills in predictive modeling. Make sure to practice with the examples before doing these exercises. Following the steps in the examples should allow you to complete those exercises successfully.

to infuse the topics with a sense of fun and engagement. By incorporating more real-life examples, I aim to explain the principles and concepts of ML in an accessible manner. Recognizing that ML can appear daunting, especially with its scientific terminologies and mathematical foundations, I assume that most readers do not possess a strong background in mathematics or computer science, and many may be non-programmers. Therefore, I strive to commence this complex subject with relatable statements, practical examples, and my personal experiences, all geared toward fostering interest and curiosity in the subject. Additionally, I have incorporated figures, tables, definition boxes, tips, and warnings to help readers follow the concepts and steps seamlessly.

As readers become more accustomed to terminologies, concepts, and processes, the writing tone and style will gradually shift toward a more scholarly approach starting from Chapter 8 onwards. The intention behind this transition is to foster the readers' comfort in reading and writing quality reports. By the book's conclusion, the readers should feel proficient in reading and writing various report types, including business reports, technical reports, and academic reports. It is essential to note that, as this book is not a research project or research reference book, I do not provide citations in the chapter content, as you regularly see in published articles, to avoid distraction while reading. However, a comprehensive list of references that served as the foundation for this book is available at the end, enabling readers to explore additional sources if desired.

Finally, in writing this book, I draw upon my extensive expertise and experience in teaching data mining in my classes and using ML in my research. As a result, some guidelines and rules of thumb are based on my perspectives and practical experience with these methods. It is important to recognize that the world of ML is dynamic, and information and guidelines may not always align across different books and sources. This variation arises from the fact that different authors possess their unique perspectives and experiences in using ML techniques. In several aspects of ML, particularly in model performance evaluation, there are no standardized cut-off values or thresholds. In the book, I provide various rules of thumb based on my experience with the methods, which have also been employed in my published articles, indicating acceptance within the academic community. Moreover, I endeavor to maintain consistency in terminologies, concepts, and steps throughout the book, facilitating a smoother understanding of the content for readers.

Summary

Data science and data mining are emergent fields of study, and they allow us to analyze big data and use the analysis results to make informed business decisions. This chapter introduces some key concepts in data science and data mining, the evolution of AI and ML, how data mining is used in different industries to improve safety and enhance operation efficiency, big data characteristics, and ethical considerations. These are important concepts we need to understand clearly before diving into the details of the data mining process and ML methods. Unlike traditional statistical studies, which tend to be theory-driven and use a small sample size, data mining projects are exploratory, data-driven, and use large data. Essentially, we aim to discover unknown patterns from data. In other words, we have collected a large amount of data for our business, and we need to find out what useful insights the data can tell us about our business operations. The patterns we uncover from the data allow us to make informed decisions to improve our business operations.

This chapter also covers the ethical considerations in data mining. Data mining involves the extraction of patterns, knowledge, and insights from large datasets, and while it provides valuable information, it also raises significant ethical concerns. Ethical considerations in data mining refer to the principles, guidelines, and moral values that govern the responsible and respectful use of data throughout the entire data mining process. Adhering to these ethical principles and guidelines ensures that data mining is conducted responsibly and with respect for individuals' rights and well-being. It helps build trust between data scientists and the public and promotes the positive impact of data-driven insights while minimizing potential harm.

CHAPTER DISCUSSION QUESTIONS

1. Define data mining and data science. What are the differences between them?
2. What are the primary differences between data mining methods and traditional statistic methods?
3. Describe the characteristics of data mining. What are the major challenges when using data mining?
4. Give a specific example of how data mining can be applied in various domains in real life.
5. Search on the Internet to find information on a business or organization using data mining and machine learning to enhance their operations. Describe the purpose of their data mining projects, database, analytical methods, and findings.
6. Explain the concept of machine learning. Can machines learn? Why do we call it machine learning?
7. What is big data? What are the five dimensions of big data?
8. Describe the process of implementing big data analytics.
9. Describe the ethical principle in using secondary data. Why is ethical consideration important in data mining projects?
10. What are the main responsibilities of the Institutional Review Board (IRB)? Describe the IRB decision process.
11. Why do we need to de-identify data? Describe the data de-identification steps.

2

Data Mining Processes, Methods, and Software

LEARNING OUTCOMES

Upon completion of this chapter, you will be able to

1. Define the data mining process.
2. Describe the SEMMA process, its steps, and when it should be used.
3. Describe the CRISP-DM process, its steps, and when it should be used.
4. Define the target variable and predictors.
5. Evaluate the scales of variables.
6. Compare the association model and classification model.
7. Differentiate between supervised learning and unsupervised learning.
8. Classify machine learning methods based on the target variable and study purposes.
9. List the primary characteristics of those machine learning methods.
10. Select the appropriate machine-learning method for a data mining project.
11. Compare different data mining software applications.

Introduction

In this chapter, we will go deeper into the data mining process, various machine learning methods, how to select the appropriate method for our study purpose, and the software options for non-programmers. I will introduce multiple data mining terminologies. Don't be alarmed if you get confused or do not get them immediately. While they may sound strange to you at first, you will see them repeatedly in almost every chapter. After a couple of chapters, you will become a master of those terminologies. The primary challenge is that those terminologies are not used consistently in other books, materials, or online resources. Hence, it is common to get confused when we read those materials. In order to avoid that situation, in this chapter,

DOI: 10.1201/9781003162872-3

I provide the terms and definitions that I will use consistently throughout the book. Anytime you need to look up the terms, you can always return to this chapter or check the definitions. In each chapter, I will also provide key basic concepts for that method along with descriptions.

Keep in mind that these are the terms I use, and other authors may use different terms. Data mining is emerging, and there are discrepancies in terminologies if you read from different sources. Nonetheless, I am confident my terms are used properly and consistently, which will help you understand the methods, analysis process, and results covered in the next chapters. I try to use those terms consistently throughout the chapters to avoid confusion. Imagine if I keep using different terms to refer to the same concept. That is what we experience when we google data mining methods. I also provide references for equivalent terms, so you can still follow other authors' studies without any difficulties.

I also compare various software options and focus on the ones appropriate for non-programmers. Unlike what you may see online, there are more and more data mining software applications that do not require coding, and non-programmers like us can take advantage of these applications and use them for our data mining projects. Data mining and machine learning is no longer the field for computer engineering majors. Nonetheless, those applications are not perfect, and they all have pros and cons. I will explain why I selected SAS Enterprise Miner for this book but also briefly discuss other options. I am sure when we finish this book, you will be master of data mining skills with this software.

Data Mining Processes

In Chapter 1, we defined data mining and discussed some primary characteristics of data mining. It is an exploratory, data-driven method to detect unknown patterns from large data and provide insights about our business, allowing us to make informed business decisions. In order to properly perform data mining, we need to follow a process that guides us through specific steps to explore and analyze the data properly. Since large data tend to be noisy, there is a chance that the outcome of our analysis may be affected by the noise and be less accurate, which could lead to wrong decisions. In the business world, misprediction of the variable of interest could have substantial consequences. Imagine if an airline sends the promotion package to the wrong passenger and ends up losing another passenger. Or a bank executive decides to open a new branch in an incorrect location and ends up losing a lot of money. Or even worse, in healthcare, when the prediction is a false negative, leading to a patient's treatment delay. The consequences of those incorrect business decisions could be catastrophic to the business and customers. We all know that any prediction has a margin of error. Our goal is to keep that margin of error within our acceptable range. How low it should be acceptable will depend on the organization and the executives. Depending on the organization's strategies, it could be 1%, 5%, or even 10%. In the service industry with high demand fluctuation, the executives may accept a 10% error. On the other hand, prediction errors in healthcare or aviation safety may significantly affect the outcomes, and they may only accept a 1% error.

So, how to avoid, or at least, minimize, that problem? The best practice is to follow a valid data mining process while analyzing the data. A good process guides us through important steps to ensure the analysis is correctly conducted, avoiding data mining mistakes. Note that on the Internet or in other books, you may find different steps for the data mining process. Many of them are based on the authors' opinions and experiences. Some of them are useful, especially for some specific types of projects. However, in some cases, we wonder whether such a process has been validated and can be generalized to other types of projects. Using an invalid process may result in questionable outcomes. As stated in Chapter 1, data mining is an exploratory, data-driven method. This means the outcome of the study is dependent on the quality of the data and the analysis process. Hence, it is imperative to do the analysis correctly to produce quality outcomes. Following incorrect steps could lead to invalid results, which, in turn, will lead to wrong business decisions. For example, if we trained the model without cleaning the data first, the noise in the data might lead to rather messy outcomes, which are either not interpretable or meaningful. Basically, the prediction outcomes may be all over the place or contradictory, and decision-makers cannot use them to make any decisions. In another case, we overtrained the model with a lot of data and received a predictive model with high accuracy. However, we did not validate the model with a validation sample. Consequently, our model turned out to be not generalizable to other datasets due to the overfitting issue. In other words, when we applied that model with new datasets, the prediction came out with a high margin of error, making the model invalid and unusable in the real world. Accordingly, decision-makers may be misinformed and make wrong decisions based on incorrect predictions. Having said that, it is important to follow a valid data mining process to ensure the quality of the prediction outcomes.

In this book, I would like to introduce the data mining processes that are validated, widely accepted, and used in both academia and industry. They are Sample-Explore-Modify-Model-Assess (SEMMA) and Cross-Industry Standard Process for Data Mining (CRISP-DM).

> A valid data mining process plays a vital role in producing an effective and usable predictive model.

SEMMA Process

The first process is SEMMA, which stands for Sample-Explore-Modify-Model-Assess. This process is proposed by SAS Institute, but it has been used in many industries and, especially by academic researchers. SEMMA is actually integrated into SAS Enterprise Miner software to guide users in conducting data mining. SEMMA is the sequence of data mining steps that should be followed to analyze large data to uncover new patterns (Figure 2.1).

The following explains each step in the SEMMA process.

> **SAMPLE:** In the Sample step, we start with data sampling, which is to select a portion of the whole dataset (sample) for analysis purposes. The sample should be large enough to contain sufficient information to retrieve yet small enough to be used efficiently. If the original dataset is too large, we can decide to sample a part

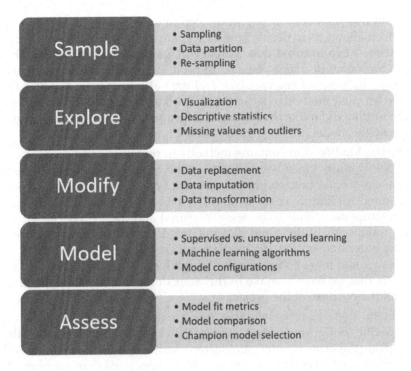

FIGURE 2.1
SEMMA process.

of it. For example, we have a dataset with 10 million data points, and using the whole dataset may increase the computing time. For data mining purposes, 10% of it would provide us with one million records and should be sufficient. So we want to sample 10% of the data for analysis. However, if we do not sample it correctly, our sample may be skewed from the original data, and we will have sampling biases. In other words, our sample is not representative of the full dataset, and the data mining results may be invalid. Accordingly, we need to choose the right sampling method to minimize sampling biases and have a quality dataset for data mining. In addition, this phase also deals with data partitioning, in which the data is split into sub-samples. The training sample is used to train the model, and the validation sample is used to validate the model. In some cases, we can also use a test sample to test the final model. Finally, if we have an imbalanced dataset, our model may suffer from overfitting. In this case, re-sampling may be needed to ensure the balance of the dataset. Details of different sampling methods will be covered later in Chapter 3.

EXPLORE: In the Explore step, we need to explore and understand the data by dis-covering anticipated and unanticipated relationships between the variables and also abnormalities with the help of data visualization. By using data visualization, we can produce multiple charts in different formats for different variables. Thus, we can gain a deep understanding of the variables, scales, and values. Features such as descriptive statistics, missing value detection, and variable selection can be used in this step. It is an important step to understand the variables and the data, which allows us to decide how to prepare and modify the data before analyzing them. Keep in mind that "garbage in, garbage out" still applies here. We want to have quality data to be able to produce quality output. Furthermore, a deep understanding of the variables and data also allows us to select the right machine learning method, choose the right configurations for the models, interpret the results, and make the necessary adjustments to the model configurations to improve the model fit.

MODIFY: The Modify step contains methods to transform and prepare variables for model training. Once we understand the quality and completeness of the data, we can decide how to improve the data quality and reduce noise. While data mining can handle noisy data, clean data is very useful in building valid models. Large data tends to be less structured and messy. We can also handle missing values and outliers and perform any data transformation as needed. By reducing noise and outliers in the data and handling missing values, we will have cleaner and more complete data for analysis. Note that there will be judgment calls that we have to make in this step, depending on the type of data we have and the purpose of the project.

MODEL: In the Model step, we select the appropriate machine learning methods and apply specific configurations to the prepared variables to train models that possibly provide the desired outcome. Machine learning algorithms are used in this step to build multiple predictive models, either supervised or unsupervised learning. Depending on the purpose of the project, the target variable, and the data, we can build multiple models using different methods or use a few methods but configure them differently to produce more models. It is an iterative process, and we will have to configure and reconfigure the models several times until we achieve satisfactory models. The deeper our understanding of the variables, scales, data, and machine learning, the more likely we can build good models. We will get into detailed configurations for each machine learning method later in the book.

ASSESS: The last step is Assess, in which we evaluate model performance and compare models using appropriate metrics. Model fit metrics are decided based on the study purpose and the type of data mining model. Based on the model comparison, we select the champion model, which is the best model. We also examine the usefulness and usability of the model and identify important predictors. The champion model is recommended to decision-makers along with important predictors so they can make informed decisions on how to use the tool to improve business operations.

The SEMMA process explains well the steps we need to follow to import, explore, and analyze data to produce quality outcomes. If we build our project diagram following those steps, we can keep track of the steps we have taken, the results of each step, and the final outcomes. Thus, if there is an error or misprediction in the modeling process, we can trace back to our steps, identify where and why the error occurred, and make the necessary corrections. Figure 2.2 presents an example of a project diagram in SAS Enterprise Miner following SEMMA steps. The process can be applied to any data mining project and has been widely accepted and used in both

> SEMMA is most appropriate for data mining project. We use SEMMA in this book.

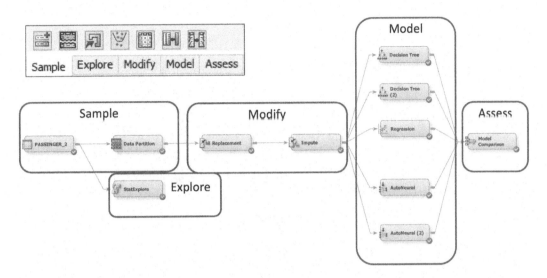

FIGURE 2.2
SEMMA steps in SAS Enterprise Miner.

industry and academia. Keep in mind that the SEMMA process does not include model deployment. It stops at recommending the champion model and important predictors to decision-makers. How they use the tool and information in practical applications will be the scope of another project.

CRISP-DM Process

Another data mining process is CRISP-DM, which stands for Cross-Industry Standard Process for Data Mining. This process is founded based on the European Strategic Program on Research in Information Technology initiative (ESPRIT). It is more popular in the industry than in academia. IBM is the one that has adopted and is using this process in the software SPSS Modeler.

CRISP-DM breaks the process of data mining into six major steps: Business Understanding, Data Understanding, Data Preparation, Modeling, Evaluation, and Deployment (Figure 2.3). I won't go into the details of those steps because some of its steps are very similar to SEMMA steps. Specifically, Data Understanding is similar to Explore, Data Preparation is similar to Modify, Modeling is similar to Model, and Evaluation is similar to Assess. However, two steps in CRISP-DM that are different from SEMMA are Business Understanding and Deployment. I describe briefly CRISP-DM steps as follows.

> **BUSINESS UNDERSTANDING**: The Business Understanding step focuses on the business problem that drives data mining. We aim to understand the project objectives and requirements from a business perspective, based on which we can describe it as a data mining problem and develop a preliminary plan.

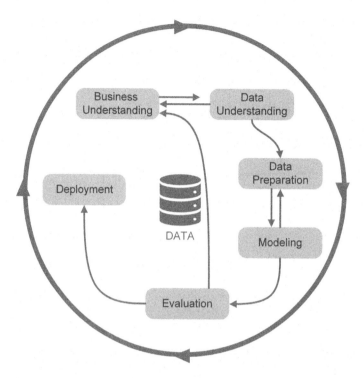

FIGURE 2.3
CRISP-DM process.

DATA UNDERSTANDING: In the Data Understanding step, we collect and get familiarized with the data. We need to explore the data, all variables, and scales, and identify any problems with the data, such as missing values and outliers.

DATA PREPARATION: The Data Preparation step covers specific activities to clean the data and make any data transformation as needed. Missing values and outliers need to be handled carefully to remove noise from the data and, at the same time, not to lose important information.

MODELING: In the Modeling step, we develop predictive models using appropriate machine learning algorithms and make specific configurations for those models. It is an iterative process.

EVALUATION: In the Evaluation step, we evaluate, compare, and choose the model with high prediction accuracy but also generalizable. In this step, we need to validate the models carefully to make sure the models are reliable and valid. The end result is the champion model.

DEPLOYMENT: In the final step, Deployment, we deploy the predictive algorithm of the champion model as codes and create a practical application in an operating system. The application uses real-life data and the validated algorithm to make actual predictions. Organizations and businesses can commercialize this application.

Note that the sequence of the steps is not linear. Actually, the process requires moving back and forth between specific steps. The process diagram employs arrows to signify the primary and recurring interconnections between phases. The outer circle within the diagram serves as a representation of the iterative aspect inherent to data mining. The data mining process continues even after the deployment of a solution. Insights gained throughout this process have the potential to instigate fresh business inquiries, and future data mining endeavors stand to gain from the insights accumulated in prior iterations.

As we can see, CRISP-DM is very practical-oriented, which is why practitioners widely use it in the industry for real-life business problems. From an academic research standpoint, SEMMA is more suitable since it focuses more on the process of performing data mining. Having said that, what process works best will depend on the purpose of your data mining project. In this book, we will use the SEMMA process for our data mining examples and projects since we do not cover deploying the predictive algorithms in real-life applications. It is important to note that SAS Enterprise Miner has all the needed features for deploying the champion model into real life operating system, but programming skills are required for that task.

> CRISP-DM is practical-oriented and more appropriate for industrial and commercial applications

USELEI Process

In some special cases, our business problem may require us to make causal inferences among variables from large data. It is a common problem in risk analysis projects since we want to know if the change in one variable may lead to a change in another variable. In this case, the expected outcome is the probability of the target variable based on the change in one predictor. In order to discover such as causal network, a specific method, Bayesian Networks, should be used, and at the end, the causal inference must be made, assuming we have prior domain knowledge and causal assumptions. I developed a new process for this type of project since there isn't one in the literature. I named it the Understanding-Sampling-Exploring-Learning-Evaluating-Inferring (USELEI) process (Figure 2.4). This process is particularly useful for the so-called causal data mining. I will get into the details of this process and the Bayesian Network method in Chapter 16.

FIGURE 2.4
The USELEI process.

How to Categorize Data Mining Methods?

For someone who is new to data mining, the common question is, "which method should I use to analyze my data?" This is the question that instructors tend to receive when teaching statistics courses. In this case, students usually expect a clear and concrete answer so they can use that exact method to complete their class assignments or projects. I face the same question in my data mining course, in which my students usually expect 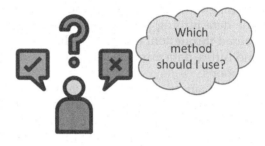 me to tell them exactly what method to use and which variables to include in the analysis. However, things are not that simple with data mining since data mining projects are exploratory rather than confirmatory. We aim to discover unknown patterns from data. Remember? We want to know what data will tell us about the relationships between variables.

The choice is not straightforward and clear as black and white. We need to consider many factors, and even then, trials and errors are required. But no one says data mining is easy. That is why the data scientist job is very attractive because it requires a specific set of skills. I remembered that Netflix used to host a data mining competition in which all teams were given the same dataset and a target variable. The team that selected the right method and configured the right algorithm to produce the best prediction would win the competition. So, you see, the difficulties in data mining allow us to tell a great data scientist from a mediocre one.

As described in Chapter 1, data mining is an exploratory, data-driven method. The purpose of a data mining project is not to explain what happened or what is happening but rather to uncover unknown, hidden patterns from the data to predict what will happen in the near future. Hence, the simple answer to the above question is, "it depends on your data and the purpose of your project." Of course, no one will be satisfied with this answer because it is too vague. However, the fact is that we do not know what method may work best until we explore and understand the data. And even then, given the large volume and noise in the data, it is very hard to speculate which method would produce the best predictive model. But it is the reality of this type of project when we, as data scientists, are expected to explore and discover new patterns from the data, not to confirm what we already know or think we know.

Data mining is a very broad area that consists of numerous methods, which may cause confusion to data scientists. Hence, it is important that we determine how to select the appropriate method for the purpose of our project. In many cases, we select multiple methods for our analysis, train multiple models using those methods, and select the best one. As mentioned in the previous section, this best model is called *the champion model*. The reason we need to use multiple methods is due to the exploratory nature of data mining. Since we cannot speculate which method can produce the best model, developing models using only one method with one set of configurations will likely lead to an inferior model that fails to make a good prediction for our business operations. And we may not even know that it is inferior because we do not have anything to compare it with. As with other business activities, in order to find the best one, we have to have a baseline and other options for comparison.

There are several ways to categorize data mining methods, by data type or by the purpose of analysis. Data types typically include quantitative and qualitative. Quantitative data are numbers using interval, ratio, or ordinal scales. Qualitative data are text, voices, images, and videos. We also have mixed data, which consists of both quantitative and qualitative data. Naturally, the majority of data mining methods are quantitative since there are many methods of analyzing data quantitatively. On the other hand, qualitative methods are much scarce due to the nature of qualitative data. Text mining is a typical method that we use to analyze textual data. Even when we use text mining, we eventually apply some quantitative methods to make sense of the results. Advanced methods that are used to analyze voice, images, and videos are generally quantitative-based, such as convolutional neural networks, natural language processing, or voice recognition. As you can see, even when we have data and know what type of data we have, it is still hard to determine which method works best.

In this book, I categorize data mining methods primarily based on the purpose of the analysis. Thus, when you know your variables and their scales and have a clear purpose for data analysis, you should be able to determine appropriate methods that you can use to develop your predictive models. However, note that each method has its own advantages and disadvantages, and since data mining is a data-driven approach, there is never a

There is no such thing as a perfect data mining method. But there is the best method for a specific set of data.

certainty in which method works best. In other words, we cannot speculate which algorithm will work best for the given data before running the data analysis. Basically, we explore multiple options and determine the best method based on the analysis results, which is the primary goal of data mining. My recommendation is to select several methods and configure various models to see which model produces the best prediction. Or even if we choose to use only one method, we should develop several models with different configurations and compare them to choose the best one. Again, that model is called the *champion model*. Please keep in mind that the term *best model* here is relative; i.e., it is not the true best one because we have to test all possible models to find the true best one. The best model refers to the one with the highest prediction accuracy and predictive power among the available models we have. Hence, it is a relative best.

Common Terms Used in This Book

Before we get into the details of the method categorization, it is important to understand different terms that are being used in data mining books and papers. Some of them are used interchangeably, while, on the other hand, one term could be used for two different meanings. For example, it is not uncommon to see some authors use *regression* to refer to a model with a continuous target variable, while others use *prediction* for the same model.

Let's standardize these terms

From my perspective, either of them could cause confusion. First, *prediction* is a more general term referring to a predicting act, so it is unclear why it only applies to continuous target variables. Furthermore, *regression* seems to be specific to the regression analysis methods, so it does not make much sense to use this term to refer to methods such as decision trees or neural networks. In addition, we have the *logistic regression* method that handles binary or categorical target variables but is not considered a regression model, which could cause further confusion. To make the topic further confusing, we have the term *predictive modeling*, which is a common reference to a data mining process in general. Hence, we need to differentiate between predictive models with different types of target variables.

I also noted that the terms used for variables also vary. Some authors use terms like in traditional statistical analysis, i.e., *dependent variable* for the output, and *independent variable* for the input. Other authors use *predictor* for the input and *target variable* for the output. While the former is technically correct, it is often used in traditional statistical research. The latter seems to be a more popular way in data mining research since it does capture the prediction intention. In data mining materials, I also often notice authors use *features* to refer to *variables*. That is why you will see terms such as *feature selection* and *feature importance* instead of *variable selection* and *variable importance* in some places.

It is hard to say which terms work better than others since they are all, technically, correct. The challenge is that authors tend to choose using the terms they like, and in some cases they don't use them consistently, which causes a great deal of confusion for readers. The importance is to be consistent so the readers understand what we are talking about. For that purpose, in this book, I standardize the terms and use them consistently, as defined in Table 2.1. Thus, when I use terms such as *association model, classification model,* or *predictors,* you will know exactly what I am talking about without confusion.

Datasets Used in This Book

In order to demonstrate how to develop both the association model and classification model, I will use two primary datasets in this book.

- Association model: Boston housing dataset; target variable: *medium housing price* (interval).
- Classification model: Airline recommendation dataset; target variable: *recommendation of the airline* (binary: Yes – recommend; No – not recommend).

In order to help you follow the steps in the SEMMA process, I use those two datasets throughout all chapters to demonstrate how to complete each step. It allows you to connect those steps together and see the whole picture of a data mining project. We will go into the details of these datasets in the next few chapters. I am confident this approach works better than using a different dataset for each chapter.

TABLE 2.1

Standardized Terms Used in This Book and Equivalent Terms

Terms	Description
Prediction	A general term for a predicting act
Target variable	The output being predicted *Equivalent terms*: dependent variable, output, target
Predictors	Inputs being used in predicting the output *Equivalent terms*: independent variables, input variables, features
Predictive model	A model predicting either a continuous or categorical target variable *Equivalent terms*: prediction model, data mining model, machine learning model
Predictive modeling	A process of using machine learning algorithms to develop a model that predicts future or unseen events or outcomes based on data. *Equivalent terms*: data mining process, machine learning process
Machine learning	Machine learning is data analytic methods that detect unknown patterns from large data to predict the outcomes of interest.
Association model	A predictive model with an interval target variable *Equivalent terms*: regression model
Classification model	A predictive model with a binary or nominal target variable
Supervised learning	A machine learning approach for structured data, in which a model is trained from labeled data to make predictions of a pre-defined target variable.
Class	A class refers to a distinct category or label that represents a specific group or type of data instances in a dataset, which is often the target. *Equivalent terms*: category, label, level
Unsupervised learning	A machine learning approach for unstructured data, in which a model is trained from unlabeled data without a specific target variable.
Training sample	A sample of data used to train the model
Validation sample	A sample of data used to validate the model
Test sample	A sample of data used to perform the final test of the model
Model fit	A measure of how well the model fist the data *Equivalent terms*: model performance, goodness of fit
Model fit metrics	Criteria used to evaluate model fit *Equivalent terms*: evaluation metrics, goodness-of-fit indices, evaluation criteria
Overfitting	A situation in which the model is overtrained to the training sample and not generalized to other datasets
Model reliability	The model's ability to produce consistent results with different runs using different data sets (internal consistency)
Model validity	The model's ability to consistently produce an accurate prediction of the target variable (accuracy of the model)
Predictive power	The model's ability to accurately capture and represent the underlying patterns, relationships, or trends present in the data and generalize the results to other datasets
Prediction accuracy	A measure of how well the model performs in terms of accurately predicting the target variable
Champion model	The model with the best model fit among compared models.
Variable importance	Relative importance of each predictor in determining the prediction of the target variable *Equivalent terms*: feature importance
Variable scale	A characteristic that describes the nature and properties of a variable; it indicates the type of values that a variable can take and the operations that can be performed on it *Equivalent terms:* level of measurement, scale of measurement, measurement scale, measurement of variable

Variable Measurement Scales

Another topic that needs consistency is measurement scales for variables. The scale of variable measurement is one of the key factors that determine the methods that we use to analyze the data. Basically, it is the way we define and categorize variables or numbers in our dataset. It is also called *variable scale, measurement scale, scales of measurement,* or *measurements of variables.* Understanding the differences between scales is the key to determining the right analytical method. In this book, I call it *variable scale.*

OMG, what are these things?

In statistics, we usually have two types of scales: continuous (metric) and categorical (non-metric). For those types, we have four specific scales: interval and ratio (continuous), and ordinal and nominal (categorical). Those four scales are described in Table 2.2, along with some examples.

However, SAS Enterprise Miner has a slightly different scale setup, with four scales: interval, ordinal, binary, and nominal. To avoid confusion, I include SAS scales in the same table so you know which ones we should use when using the software.

> **DEFINITION**
>
> Variable scale is a characteristic that describes the nature and properties of a variable; it indicates the type of values that a variable can take and the operations that can be performed on it.

TABLE 2.2

Variable Measurement Scales

Types	Traditional Scales	Characteristics	Examples	SAS Enterprise Miner Scales (Used in This Book)
Continuous (metric)	Interval	Numeric; rank order; no true zero values; difference between values is the same	F degree (0 degree is not true zero)	Interval
	Ratio	Numeric; rank order; having true zero values; difference between values is the same	Age, distance, population, accident rate	Interval
Categorical (non-metric)	Ordinal	Non-numeric classes; rank order; difference between responses is inconsistent	Usage: never; sometimes; often Agreement: disagree, somewhat disagree, somewhat agree, agree	Ordinal
	Nominal	Non-numeric classes; no rank order; difference between responses is meaningless	Region: north, south, east, west Travel purpose: business, pleasure	Nominal
		Nominal scale with only two levels	Decision: yes, no Answer: true, false	Binary

Interval and Ratio

Interval and ratio are both continuous scales that are represented by numerical numbers, can be ranked by order, and have consistent gaps (intervals) between levels across the measurements (to avoid confusion with the interval scale, I use *gaps* instead). The only difference between those two is that the ratio has the true zero value, while the interval does not. For example, Fahrenheit degrees are interval because 0 F degree does not mean any degree. It is a specific value representing a very cold temperature. On the other hand, ratio variables, such as age, distance, or scores, do have true zero values since they mean 0 year, 0 distance, and 0 point. As you can see, we have more ratio variables than interval variables since interval variables may appear more in scientific fields rather than in real-life or business activities. However, you may notice that on the Internet and in many materials, the term interval is used much more often than *ratio*. One possible explanation is that authors tend to use *interval* for the continuous scale. Perhaps for that reason, SAS Enterprise Miner does not differentiate between these two. It has only one scale, *interval*, that can be used for both cases. It should not affect the analysis results since these two scales are used exactly the same way in the analysis. Only when we interpret the results we need to understand the difference. Accordingly, in this book, I will use the term *interval* for both of these scales to simplify the content and be consistent with SAS Enterprise Miner.

Ordinal

On the other hand, we have non-metric scales, ordinal and nominal. They are represented by non-numeric classes. The ordinal scale has a ranking order, but the gaps between levels can be inconsistent. Examples may include the level of usage (never, sometimes, often) or agreement (disagree, somewhat disagree, somewhat agree, and agree). These are classes showing the participants' responses to questions about their choices or perceptions. They are non-numerical but can be ranked by order.

Nominal

Finally, the nominal scale is represented by non-metric classes but without any rank order, and the difference between levels is meaningless. For example, the Region variable has four levels: north, south, east, and west. But these levels have no association with each other and cannot be ranked. These levels mainly represent different classes of variables of interest in a qualitative way. SAS Enterprise Miner has a Nominal scale, but it adds a special case, Binary scale. The binary scale is essentially nominal with one difference; it has only two levels. For example, Decision can be either Yes or No, or Answer can be True or False. This scale is often used in predicting risks or decisions, which explains why SAS Enterprise Miner dedicates a separate scale to it.

Likert Scale

A very popular scale is the Likert scale, either with 5 points or 7 points, which is used widely to measure people's perceptions, behaviors, or attitudes. The Likert scale has only two forms, 5-point scale or 7-point scale, and always has a middle point (Figure 2.5). Examples include Satisfaction (very dissatisfied, dissatisfied, neutral, satisfied, very satisfied) or Quality

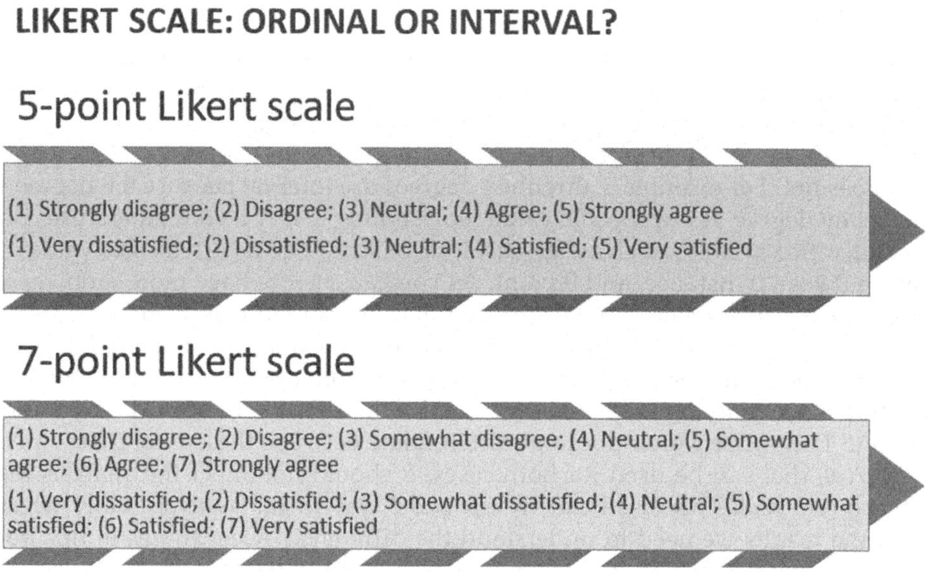

LIKERT SCALE: ORDINAL OR INTERVAL?

5-point Likert scale

(1) Strongly disagree; (2) Disagree; (3) Neutral; (4) Agree; (5) Strongly agree

(1) Very dissatisfied; (2) Dissatisfied; (3) Neutral; (4) Satisfied; (5) Very satisfied

7-point Likert scale

(1) Strongly disagree; (2) Disagree; (3) Somewhat disagree; (4) Neutral; (5) Somewhat agree; (6) Agree; (7) Strongly agree

(1) Very dissatisfied; (2) Dissatisfied; (3) Somewhat dissatisfied; (4) Neutral; (5) Somewhat satisfied; (6) Satisfied; (7) Very satisfied

FIGURE 2.5
Likert scale.

(very poor, poor, fair, good, excellent). The difference between levels is usually very consistent and considered equal. As you can see, it is used very widely in business management and social studies.

An important question is how do we categorize Likert scale variables? Interval or ordinal. Based on the way the responses are coded, it looks like an ordinal scale. However, in many studies, researchers decide to treat Likert scale variables as interval variables. The main reason is that by doing so they can use parametric statistical techniques that require metric variables. There are some non-parametric techniques, but they are very limited and usually lack robustness. For example, when researchers have multiple hypotheses indicating complicated relationships among variables, they need to use multiple regression or structural equation modeling (SEM) methods to test these hypotheses. However, these are parametric methods and require metric variables. Unfortunately, there are no substitute non-parametric methods. Hence, in this case, researchers use interval scales for Likert scale variables, which allows them to use these parametric methods.

The decision to use Likert scale variables as interval tends to receive criticism sometimes because Likert scale is not a true interval scale. Nonetheless, researchers in the fields of marketing, management, and social behavior have been treating Likert scale as interval in their studies. Although there are some limitations due to the number of levels (5 or 7) and the challenge of meeting test assumptions, this approach allows researchers to achieve meaningful and practical analysis results. The key point is that we need to make sure the gaps between levels are equal throughout the measurement (it is a key difference between continuous scales and categorical scales). For example, when we design a survey questionnaire, we need to make sure the gap between Very dissatisfied and

Somewhat dissatisfied should be the same as the gap between Somewhat satisfied and Very satisfied, and so on.

There is another reason that researchers prefer treating Likert scale variables as interval. It is easier to interpret the results. Since Likert scale data are coded as 1–5 or 1–7, the statistical outputs, such as correlation coefficients, model fit, and explained variance, are easier to interpret and understand in the form of metric values. If we use an ordinal scale for these variables, then the result interpretation should be done in the same way as nominal variables, which is much harder to do because the responses are non-metric instead of metric. You will see some specific examples in Chapter 7

In data mining, we should use Interval for Likert scale variables <u>unless</u> we intentionally treat them as Ordinal and have a plan for analysis and results interpretation. We need to show evidence that the gaps between levels are equal.

when we learn about logistic regression. In fact, ordinal regression works almost the same way as logistic regression or multinomial regression.

Having said that, depending on the purpose of our study, we can decide how to treat Likert scale, either as ordinal or interval. My rule of thumb is unless we have specific reasons to use Likert scale variables as ordinal and have a plan for data analysis and results interpretation, we should treat them as interval. In this case, we need to show evidence that the gaps between levels are equal, and we still need to test the assumptions required for the parametric method we choose.

Classification of Machine Learning Methods

Let's move to machine learning algorithms, the core of data mining, data science, and even artificial intelligence. SAS defines machine learning as "a method of data analysis that automates analytical model building. It is a branch of artificial intelligence based on the idea that systems can learn from data, identify patterns, and make decisions

DEFINITION

Machine learning is data analytic methods that detect unknown patterns from large data to predict the outcomes of interest.

with minimal human intervention." This definition brings machine learning closer to Artificial Intelligence. Though machine learning algorithms have existed for a considerable duration, the capability to autonomously employ intricate mathematical computations on extensive datasets, repeatedly and with increasing speed, represents a recent advancement. Examples include Tesla self-driving and autopilot applications, online recommendations by Amazon, Facebook, or Netflix, fraud detection by banks, AI assistants, such as Siri, Alexa, or Google Assistant, and Generative AI, such as ChatGPT and Google Bard.

In this book, we define machine learning methods as "data analytic methods that detect unknown patterns from large data to predict the outcomes of interest." This definition fits the data mining definition we have in Chapter 1 and the methods we cover in this book. The methods we cover will allow us to train the model and build predictive algorithms with the accuracy and predictive power needed for making actual predictions.

Supervised vs. Unsupervised learning

Machine learning algorithms can be categorized as *supervised learning* and *unsupervised learning*. Supervised learning works best with structured data. It requires a target variable, and models are developed to predict the target variable based on numerous predictors. On the other hand, unsupervised learning works well with less structured data. It does not have a specific target variable and treats all variables as input variables. Models are developed mainly to detect the intrinsic structure of variables. The rule of thumb to decide whether you need supervised or unsupervised learning is to see if you have a target variable and whether the purpose of your research is to predict it.

DEFINITION

Supervised learning: A machine learning approach for structured data, in which a model is trained from labeled data to make predictions of a pre-defined target variable.

Unsupervised learning: A machine learning approach for unstructured data, in which a model is trained from unlabeled data without a specificc target variable.

Naturally, there are more supervised learning methods compared to unsupervised learning methods. Some examples of supervised learning methods include regression and logistic regression, decision trees, random forests, gradient boosting, memory-based reasoning, support vector machine, neural network, and Bayesian network. What method is the appropriate choice for your research depends on the study's purpose and the target variable's scale. Methods such as regression and logistic regression are based on the same foundation as in traditional statistical methods, but in data

Look for a target variable in the dataset. If you have a target variable and intent to predict it, then use supervised learning. Otherwise, use unsupervised learning.

mining, they are used to analyze much larger data and are subject to less strict assumptions such as normal distributions. It is also worth noting that random forest and gradient boosting are essentially the ensemble of decision trees, in which a lot more trees are constructed to find a better predictive model. We will get to those machine learning methods and their characteristics later. It is a common practice to use several methods to construct multiple predictive models and compare them to identify the champion model.

Examples of unsupervised learning algorithms may include cluster analysis, principal components, or multi-dimensional scaling. These methods are used to group individual cases by similarity or detect underlying factors from data. Again, the foundation behind these methods is the same as multivariate statistics, but they will be performed at a larger scale with much larger datasets.

Figure 2.6 provides a diagram that allows us to categorize those methods based on supervised learning and unsupervised learning categories. We won't cover all methods in this book, since some of them are very advanced. I focus on the methods commonly used in practice. Don't worry, you have enough methods from standard to advanced to build predictive models for any project.

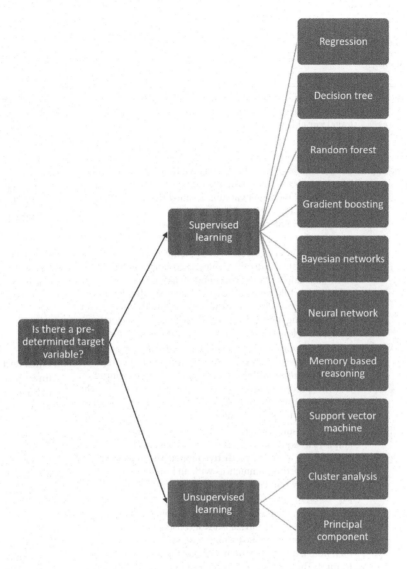

FIGURE 2.6
Classification of machine learning methods.

Descriptions and Characteristics of Machine Learning Methods

Table 2.3 provides brief descriptions of primary supervised learning algorithms, and Table 2.4 describes some primary unsupervised learning algorithms. Note that these are the methods that are actually covered in this book. Don't worry if some of them do not make much sense to you. These tables just give us some quick introduction to these methods. The characteristics, advantages, disadvantages, and the modeling and analysis process of each algorithm will be described in the subsequent chapters. We will have one chapter for each method.

TABLE 2.3

Supervised Learning Methods

Machine Learning Algorithms	Description	Characteristics
Linear regression	Linear regression is a prediction method used when the target variable is continuous. The relationship between the target variable and predictors is linear.	• Statistic-based • Linear relationships • Multiple assumptions
Classification regression (logistic regression)	Classification regression predicts the probability of a binary or nominal target variable based on a function of multiple predictors. If the target variable is binary, it is called logistic regression; if the target variable is categorical, it is called multinomial logit regression. Note that SAS Enterprise Miner uses the term *logistic regression* for both cases. Hence, in this book, I do the same.	• Statistic-based • Linear relationships between predictors and odds ratio of the target variable
Decision tree	Decision tree is a logical rule-based method that illustrates a hierarchical structure of variables, encompassing the root node (also known as the parent node) along with its subsequent child nodes. The root node is subdivided into two or more branches, employing the optimal condition for distinguishing individuals within each class. Decision tree can be used for both association and classification models.	• Rule-based • Can detect non-linear relationships
Neural network	A neural network model is characterized by its composition of several layers, with each layer comprising individual units or neurons. Within a layer, each unit receives input from the preceding layer and computes its own output. The resulting outputs from neurons within one layer then serve as inputs for the subsequent layer in the sequence of layers.	• Math-based • Can detect non-linear relationships • Can handle complex model structure
Gradient boosting	Gradient boosting is an ensemble learning method that employs a sequence of decision trees, collectively constructing a unified predictive model. The process of gradient boosting commences with an initial model and subsequently refines it by utilizing the residuals from the preceding model as the new target.	• Rule-based • Can detect non-linear relationships • Can handle complex model structure
Random forest	Random forest method is an ensemble learning technique used in machine learning and statistics. It constructs a multitude of decision trees during the training process, where each tree is built from a different random subset of the training data and features. This diversity in trees helps reduce overfitting and increases the model's robustness. In the case of classification models, the random forest output corresponds to the mode of the classes predicted by the individual trees. When dealing with association models, the random forest output represents the average prediction derived from the individual trees.	• Rule-based • Can detect non-linear relationships • Can handle complex model structure
Bayesian networks	Bayesian network is a probabilistic method founded on Bayes' theorem, enabling the prediction of future events through the consideration of prior evidence. It employs a directed acyclic graph to visually illustrate causal connections between predictors and the target variable. Additionally, a Bayesian network is characterized by a collection of conditional probabilities, facilitating causal inference and probabilistic reasoning. It serves as a valuable tool for modeling and understanding complex systems by representing and analyzing relationships among variables in a probabilistic manner.	• Math-based • Can detect non-linear relationships • Can handle complex model structure • Can infer causation

TABLE 2.4

Unsupervised Learning Methods

Machine Learning Algorithms	Description	Characteristics
Cluster analysis	Cluster analysis is an effective pattern discovery method. This method groups cases into clusters (or segments) based on their characteristics, aggregating them according to their similarities. Identified clusters can be applied to new data to classify new cases. Two common methods in cluster analysis include hierarchical and non-hierarchical clustering.	• Statistics based • Grouping cases into segments
Principal components	Principal component analysis is a method widely used to reduce the dimensionality of data while retaining its essential information. It accomplishes this by transforming the original correlated variables into a new set of uncorrelated variables called principal components. These components are linear combinations of the original variables and are ordered by the amount of variance they capture. Principal component analysis helps uncover underlying patterns, simplifies data interpretation, and aids in visualizing high-dimensional data by focusing on the most significant sources of variation.	• Statistics based • Data reduction (underlying constructs)

How to Choose the Right Machine Learning Methods? Selection Guidelines

Selecting the right machine learning methods is one of the most difficult decisions we need to make in data mining projects. Using the wrong methods results in unusable outcomes, or, even worse, incorrect outcomes, which leads to wrong business decisions. You should notice that different authors and resources tend to provide inconsistent or even contradictory suggestions for this decision, which makes it hard for us to know how and why to choose the right methods. I will provide you with specific criteria and steps which guide you through this selection process. I will also lay out scenarios, along with examples, to make it easier for you to follow.

The most useful guidelines

The method of selection should be based on the purpose of the study and the variable scales. More specifically, we need to have information about the target variable, predictors, and specific purposes of the analysis. I describe various decision scenarios in Figure 2.7 so you can use them to choose the right machine learning method for your project. In order to make this decision, we need to know the purpose of the analysis, type and size of data we have, variables, and their scales. If we move from left to right of the table and answer the questions in that order, we can decide the right methods to select.

Guidelines to Choose the Right Machine Learning Methods

I use two examples below as a demonstration of how to use the guidelines for method selection.

Guidelines to choose the right machine learning methods

Decision Order

Pre-determined target variable?

YES	SUPERVISED LEARNING METHODS							
	Categorical target variable?	Interval target variable?	Linear relationships?	Nonlinear relationships?	Interrelationships among predictors?	Causal inference?	Model complexity?	Methods
	No	Yes	Yes	No	No	No	No	Linear regression
	Yes	No	Yes	No	No	No	No	Classification regression
	Yes	Yes	Yes	Yes	Yes	No	No	Decision tree
	Yes	Yes	Yes	Yes	Yes	No	Yes	Neural Network
	Yes	Yes	Yes	Yes	Yes	No	Yes	Random Forest
	Yes	Yes	Yes	Yes	Yes	No	Yes	Gradient Boosting
	Yes	Yes	Yes	Yes	Yes	Yes	Yes	Bayesian Networks

NO	UNSUPERVISED LEARNING METHODS				
	Data reduction?	Social or market segmentation?	Group variables into a small number of variables (underlying factors)?	Group observations to distinct clusters or segments by similarities?	Methods
	Yes	No	Yes	No	Principal Components
	No	Yes	No	Yes	Cluster Analysis

FIGURE 2.7
Guidelines on how to select the right machine learning methods.

Case 1

Suppose we want to predict passengers' recommendations of an airline based on the passenger survey data. *Recommendation* is a non-metric target variable with two levels: Yes and No. Using this variable as the starting point, we will start with the first column on the left.

- Is there a pre-determined target variable? Yes, it is the recommendation. Hence, we should focus on **supervised learning** methods only.
- Is it categorical? Yes, it is binary. Hence, we must skip linear regression and select logistic regression.
- Are we expecting linear or non-linear relationships? Not sure. So we could expect both. Thus, we still keep logistic regression in the selection but keep in mind its limitation here (as mentioned before, while technically, logistic regression shows non-linear relationships in the form of a logarithm curve, the relationships between the odds ratio of the target variable and predictors is still linear).
- Do we want to examine interrelationships among predictors? If we answer yes, then we have to skip logistic regression. If we are not sure, we can keep it. Let's assume we do NOT want to examine interrelationships, as it makes the model more complex.
- Do we want to make causal inferences? Let's assume we answer No. Technically, Bayesian networks can be used even if we do not intend to make any causal inference. So, we keep it open.
- Final question: Do we want model complexity? Note that model complexity means the method can produce a complex structural model, but it also means the model is hard to understand and interpret. Let's say we answer No because we want an

easy interpretation of results, especially the effects of predictors on the target variable. In this case, we should skip neural networks, random forests, gradient boosting, and Bayesian networks. With this answer, we will have two choices: logistic regression and decision trees.

- In conclusion, in this scenario, we need to use supervised learning and focus on two methods: logistic regression and decision trees. In order to find meaningful and good predictive models, we need to build multiple models using those two methods with various configurations. By comparing these models, we will find the champion model.

Case 2

Suppose we want to identify different groups of citizens in terms of shopping modes during the COVID-19 pandemic. The goal is to see how many distinct groups exist in society based on their common shopping behaviors during the pandemic. Let's use the guidelines to select the right machine learning method in this case.

- Is there a pre-determined target variable? No. We do not intend to predict a certain decision or behavior. Then, we should focus on **unsupervised learning** methods in the second half of the table.

- Is data reduction the purpose of this study? No. Hence, we will skip the Principal Component method.

- Is social or market segmentation the purpose of this study? Yes. Hence, it confirms that Cluster analysis is still a possible choice.

- Do we intend to group variables into a small number of variables? No. Hence, we keep Cluster analysis as the option.

- Do we want to group observations (citizens) into distinct clusters or segments based on their similarities of certain perspectives? Yes, we want to group them into segments based on their common shopping behaviors during the pandemic. Thus, the final choice is Cluster analysis.

As you can see, the guidelines are quite easy to follow without complicated diagrams with boxes and arrows. Keep in mind there will be cases where we end up with four or five possible choices, while in other cases we have only one choice. In the former, we can develop multiple models using those different learning methods with different configurations. In the latter, when we have only one choice, we should still develop several models using different configurations to find the best model.

In SAS Enterprise Miner, unsupervised learning methods are not included in the Model step. Specifically, cluster analysis is a part of the Explore step, and principal components analysis is a part of the Modify step. It is set up that way because all methods in the Model step are supervised learning with a pre-determined target variable, and they are all used to make predictions. These prediction outcomes can be compared in the next step, the Assess step, which requires evaluating the prediction accuracy and predictive power. Nonetheless, we can still run cluster analysis and principal components analysis if it fits our analysis purpose. We can also run cluster analysis and use the outcomes as data exploration or run principal components analysis and use new variables as inputs for the Model step.

Ensemble

In data mining, there is an important approach that is worth mentioning, *ensemble modeling*. Ensemble models combine predictions from multiple models to create a single consensus prediction. This is a common practice in data mining when individual models disagree with each other. The ensemble model is typically more accurate than the individual models composing it. We cannot guarantee the ensemble model will work better than all others. But performing an ensemble would allow us to explore the possibility of a combined model from other individual models and compare them. It is a very useful approach in data mining. We will cover the details of ensemble modeling in Chapter 10.

Data Mining Software Comparison

As mentioned before, machine learning algorithms are usually constructed and configured by using specialized software. As machine learning continues to grow, data mining software also continues to improve. In this chapter, I review and compare some top software applications for data mining. These are applications that are widely used in the industry or academia. It means they have been validated and are capable of providing robust machine learning algorithms and configurations for analysis. There is a long list of software apps that claim to be able to perform data mining or big data analytics. We want to be careful with applications created only for learning purposes because while they may be easy to use, they tend to work only for projects at a small scale and have minimal algorithms and features. When we aim to analyze actual large data and intend to establish multiple configurations for our models, we will face the real limitations of those apps. Furthermore, the new software apps in the market also need to be validated as they may have errors in the algorithms. Last but not least, having skills and experience with well-recognized software would add value to your resume regarding analytics skills since companies and organizations you apply for may have already used that software. These software vendors always provide certificate programs, training courses, workshops, and extensive technical support.

I include several popular software applications (see Table 2.5), including the ones requiring coding and the ones not requiring coding. Keep in mind that this book primarily serves non-programmer audiences, so I focus my discussion more on the non-coding applications. Common coding software, including R and Python, are discussed for comparison purposes. Some hardcore programming software, such as MATLAB, are not included since they are more suitable for students with computer science backgrounds.

In this book, I cover five major data mining software apps: SAS Enterprise Miner, Rapid Miner, SPSS Modeler, R, and Python. These are the top data mining software apps in the market. SAS Enterprise Miner and Python are highly recognized in both industry and academia, but they seem to be dominant in the industry. Many organizations currently use SAS and Python for their applications, and analytics employees are usually required to have certificates to prove their skills. SAS and Python have very large certificate programs

TABLE 2.5

Data Mining Software Comparison

Criteria	SAS Enterprise Miner	Rapid Miner	SPSS Modeler	R	Python
Common users	Industry & Academia	Academia	Academia	Academia	Industry & Academia
Certification programs	Extensive; offered by SAS	Moderate; offered by Rapid Miner Academy	Moderate; offered by IBM	Extensive; offered by third parties	Extensive; offered by third parties
Coding and user interface	User-friendly; no coding required	User-friendly; no coding required	User-friendly; no coding required	Programming language; coding required	Programming language; coding required
Workspace diagram	Yes; intuitive; easy to view and follow	Yes; not intuitive; getting crowded with many models	Yes; getting crowded with many models	No workspace diagram	No workspace diagram
Algorithms	Robust ML algorithms; robust text mining	Robust ML algorithms	Improved ML algorithms	Improved ML algorithms	Robust ML algorithms
Connections of nodes and steps	Intuitive; connection is easy	Not intuitive; connections are confusing; easy to make mistakes	Intuitive	Coding required	Coding required
Configurations	Easy to use the property panel; too many choices	Easy to use the property window	Easy to use the property window	Coding required	Coding required
Variable importance feature	Built-in; easy to use and interpret	Requiring extra steps	Built-in; easy to use and interpret	Requiring extra steps	Requiring extra steps
Outputs graphs	Included in the output window	Requiring extra steps	Requiring extra steps	Coding required	Coding required
Performance evaluation	Included in the output window	Requiring extra steps	Included in the output window	Coding required	Coding required
Pricing	Free education version	Free education version	Expensive	Open source; free	Open source; free
Challenges	Cloud-based; slow; cumbersome file & folder management; not designed for data preparation	Confusing diagram & model comparison; confusing terms	Confusing diagram & model comparison; confusing results	Steep learning curve; cumbersome visualization	Steep learning curve; cumbersome visualization

that are accepted by many companies in different industries. On the other hand, Rapid Miner, SPSS Modeler, and R are more popular in academia. Instructors and researchers use these software apps in teaching or research. That is why we see more journal publications using these software apps.

I will go over the primary criteria and compare those software apps. I try to highlight their pros and cons, so you can see both sides of each software.

User Interface

One of the important criteria for software comparison is the user interface and the level of coding required. For students, instructors, and researchers in the field of math, science, and engineering, who have a strong foundation and skills in programming languages, coding is not an issue and is even preferred. But for users in the field of business management or social sciences, coding is a major obstacle. If you never coded before, learning a new programming language takes a lot of time with a steep learning curve. And I get it; not everyone is made for coding. But that should not prevent us from doing data mining. From that perspective, SAS Enterprise Miner, Rapid Miner, and SPSS Modeler are the ones with more user-friendly interfaces and tools. Basically, with those software apps, we can perform data mining with just point and click. Nonetheless, they still allow us to integrate codes or write codes to perform data mining if we want. They also allow us to integrate the codes with Python through various code libraries and tools. I like the flexibility these software apps provide us. For example, as non-programmers, you can build predictive models without having to code, and you are still able to convert your predictive algorithm into codes, which allows other programmers to integrate the algorithm into another platform to develop a complete application that makes real-life predictions.

On the other hand, R and Python are programming languages, and we have to write codes for every step in the data mining process, including visualization. As mentioned before, if you are new to programming, it will be a steep learning curve, and a lot of practice is required to use the software before we can even perform any actual analysis. You may also know that in programming, missing a comma or a period will result in programming errors. Hence, all coding lines must be done precisely. But if you are good at programming, these apps can provide you with a lot of flexibility and resources in writing the algorithms. Python has very rich libraries of codes that users can access and use for their modeling. Additionally, R and Python are widely accepted by the industry and are among the required skills for data scientists.

Workspace

The next item is the workspace diagram. Basically, the data mining process involves many steps and many models, so it is not easy to track the steps and models in our analysis. A workspace diagram is a visual tool that allows us to incorporate all steps and models in diagrams. Typically, we create such a workspace diagram by dragging and dropping nodes into the workspace and connecting them as appropriate. Steps like importing data files, sampling, partitioning, exploring, transforming data, modeling, and assessing can be done easily with this diagram. I usually build many models using different algorithms or using the same algorithms with different configurations, so I find this tool extremely useful. I can easily make a comparison, track the steps, make the modifications, run a part of the diagram, and review the final results. Data mining is an exploratory and iterative process, so it is not possible to get the result on the first try. The diagram makes the work easier to handle.

Among those software apps, SAS Enterprise Miner, Rapid Miner, and SPPS Modeler all provide the workspace diagram. On the other hand, R and Python do not have this feature due to the programming language nature of these apps. Among the three apps with this feature, I have tried all three and found the diagram by SAS Enterprise Miner is the easiest one to use. Figure 2.2 shows us an example of a diagram in this software. I have built many models using SAS Enterprise Miner diagrams, including some fairly complicated ones, and I have never encountered any confusion or difficulties. Besides, this software integrates its nodes in the SEMMA process, which makes it easier to find the node you need. SPSS

Modeler is not too bad, but the arrangement of the nodes makes it hard to find the right one. In addition, the way it handles multiple models and outputs could be more intuitive, and if we do not follow the steps correctly, we may get some vague error messages. In addition, you need additional nodes to collect the results, unlike in SAS Enterprise Miner, which produces results within each node. Finally, Rapid Miner diagram shares similar challenges, and figuring out how to put multiple models in the diagram is a challenging task. We also need to connect inputs separately from outputs when connecting two steps. Besides, I found that Rapid Miner uses very unusual names for operators in the diagram, which could be confusing to new users. For example, they use *label* instead of *target variable*, *example* instead of *dataset*, etc. And in the diagram, they use acronyms of these names, which even makes it harder to follow. As a matter of fact, there are so many unusual operator names that they have to create a glossary to provide definitions for these names.

Machine Learning Algorithms

As for the machine learning algorithms provided by these software apps, I find SAS Enterprise Miner, Rapid Miner, and Python have more robust algorithms that allow us to perform more complex modeling with different levels of configurations. Regardless, SPSS Modeler and R are improving their algorithms, and we have started seeing more features in these apps. I want to note that all software apps provide text analytics tools, but SAS Text Miner is easier to use when we deal with textual data. The steps of text parsing, text filtering, text topic, and text cluster are well organized and connected. On the other hand, Python offers a versatile collection of natural language processing (NLP) tools and libraries that enable developers to handle different NLP tasks, including sentiment analysis, POS tagging, document classification, topic modeling, word vectors, and more.

Pricing

Now we get into a sensitive topic of pricing. Among these apps, R and Python are fully open-source, so they are free. Rapid Miner is also an open-source app and is free for academics. It is not free for enterprises, though, and developers using it for commercialized purposes have to pay for the license. SPSS Modeler is also not free. It is quite expensive for enterprises and is still expensive for academics. I believe IBM is finally making SPSS Modeler free for educational purposes, which makes it a good choice for us. Finally, SAS Enterprise Miner is also expensive for enterprises. For universities, it is included in SAS packages for campuses, so if your university is a SAS campus, it is free. If not, they have a free cloud-based version, SAS On Demand for Academics. Note that at this time, this version only works with the Windows OS.

Challenges

I also want to summarize some key weaknesses of these apps. As mentioned above, R and Python are programming languages, so there will be a steep learning curve for new users. They both lack the workspace diagram, and visualization is cumbersome with these apps. Both SPSS Modeler and Rapid Miner have a confusing workspace design, hard-to-perform-model-comparison, and confusing nodes and operator names. In both SPSS Modeler and Rapid Miner, in order to view the output graphs, we have to go through some extra steps, especially with SPSS Modeler. SAS Enterprise Miner has an advantage here since all results, either in table or graph formats, are presented in the same node.

Additionally, SAS Enterprise Miner, especially the free cloud-based version, also has weaknesses. The first weakness is the way SAS handles folders and files. Unlike other software such as SPSS and Excel, SAS manages folders through libraries. That means folders containing files must be connected to a library, and SAS Enterprise Miner must be connected to the same library to allow us to access the files in that folder. It is certainly cumbersome and requires several steps to open a file. But this is how SAS always manages folders, as it is a more efficient way to manage data for SAS projects, especially when you have many different folders with numerous files. Note that SAS Enterprise Miner is not designed to upload files, change the file name, or move files between folders. These actions must be done using SAS Studio, which is free. It will take some time to get used to it, and it will be easier once we understand the process.

If we use the free cloud-based version for academics, we will also be limited to the software speed since it depends on the Internet connection and the server performance. Since it is free for all instructors, researchers, and students, there will be a time when many people access the server at the same time, which may cause slow processing time. Additionally, as mentioned before, at this time, the cloud-based version for academics only works with the Windows OS. Furthermore, international students and researchers may face difficulties in accessing shared folders if they log in from other countries. From my experience with SAS Enterprise Miner, everything seems to work smoothly, and I rarely encountered any delay in running my models. Note that the cloud-based SAS Enterprise Miner has full features as the commercial version for enterprises, including High-Performance nodes and Text Miner.

Finally, it is important to note that data mining software is not designed for easy data preparation or modification. They are data mining software apps, and they are dedicated to that task. Software apps like Rapid Miner and SAS Enterprise Miner do not even allow us to make changes to the data. The reason is that we are working with a lot of datasets, and such features may cause accidental changes to the data without us knowing about it. It would be a disaster since the output would become invalid, and there would be no way for us to find where the errors are. Hence, do not be surprised if you find out that you are not able to change the data or even variable names in those apps. Accordingly, data preparation should be done prior to using the data mining software. So how do we prepare the dataset? Typically, each vendor has other tools for that purpose. However, if you want to avoid learning another software, I find MS Excel is a good tool to code, merge, and clean the data. After we download raw datasets, we can use Excel to recode data, merge data from various sources, and clean the data. Excel has many useful features for these tasks, and we are all familiar with this app. Once we have the clean dataset, we just need to convert it into SAS or SPSS format, and then we can use our data mining software for modeling.

In conclusion, there is no perfect data mining software since all of them have pros and cons, and they serve different audiences. We should choose the software based on our needs, our background, and the project's purpose. Programming software like Python and R are favorable to science and engineering students and researchers in these fields due to their versatility and adaptability. They are also among the required skills for some data scientists' jobs. On the other hand, it does not mean we cannot do data mining if we do not have programming skills. Software like SAS Enterprise Miner, SPSS Modeler, and Rapid Miner can get the jobs done without coding requirements. As the data mining software market continues to advance, students in the field of business management and social sciences should take advantage of these technologies. Skills acquired with these software apps allow us to perform data mining projects well without a programming background. In this book, I chose SAS Enterprise Miner for its robustness and easy-to-use diagram. Its cloud-based version is also free with full features. I do plan to use SPSS Modeler and Rapid Miner in other books, so look out for them.

Summary

Data mining is an advanced analytic topic, and it requires some fundamental understanding of terminologies, statistics, variable scales, and the analytic process. Data mining process is critical for developing and testing predictive models. In this chapter, we discuss two primary data mining processes that are widely used in academia and industry: SEMMA and CRISP-DM. In this book, we mainly use the SEMMA process because it is robust and easy to follow. We also define some key terminologies to ensure they are used consistently throughout the book. In order to select the right machine learning methods, it is important to understand how they are categorized. We learn the differences between supervised learning and unsupervised learning. The chapter also includes a list of key machine learning methods, their descriptions, and characteristics. I designed guidelines that help you select the right method based on the purpose of the study, target variable, variable scales, and data size. It is easy to understand and follow. Finally, we compare five popular data mining software applications in the market, and their pros and cons. Keep in mind that there is no such thing as a perfect software app. Each user must choose the app suitable for their needs and skills. Regardless, since the intended audience of this book is non-programmers, I chose SAS Enterprise Miner as the primary software used in this book. Don't worry if you never used SAS Enterprise Miner before. I will provide step-by-step guidelines with screenshots to make them easier to follow.

CHAPTER DISCUSSION QUESTIONS

1. What is data mining process? Why is it important to follow a valid data mining process?
2. Describe all steps of the SEMMA process.
3. Compare SEMMA with CRISP-DM. What are the similarities and differences between these processes?
4. Explain the differences between prediction, predictive model, association model, and classification model.
5. What are primary variable measurement scales? In which case should we treat Likert scale variables as interval?
6. Differentiate between supervised learning and unsupervised learning? Give examples of these types of learning.
7. What are common machine learning methods for supervised learning and unsupervised learning?
8. What is ensemble modeling? In which case should we use ensemble modeling?
9. How do you select the appropriate machine learning method for a data mining project?
10. Compare data mining software applications. Search on the Internet and find the most current usage statistics for data mining software.

Exercises

Exercise 1: Set up an account for SAS OnDemand for Academics and register for the data mining course

Follow the process below.

1. As a first step, create your account for SAS OnDemand for Academics. To register, visit https://welcome.oda.sas.com/ and click on *Don't have a SAS Profile?* (See the instructions for account registration here https://support.sas.com/content/dam/SAS/support/en/products-solutions/ondemand/registration-sas-studio.pdf)
2. After you have successfully created your account, follow these steps:
   a. Log on the SAS OnDemand for Academics at https://odamid.oda.sas.com.
   b. Look for the **Enrollments** tab on the right panel. Click it to start the enrollment.
   c. Click the + sign to add a new enrollment. Enter the course code (provided by the Instructor)
   d. Click **Continue**.
   e. Confirm that this is the correct course and then click the button **Enroll in Course** to finish enrolling.

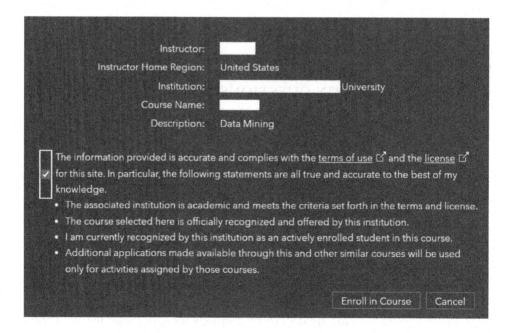

3. You should see a message confirming your enrollment.

Exercise 2: Install SAS Enterprise Miner

Follow the process below.

1. Log on SAS OnDemand for Academics at https://welcome.oda.sas.com/
2. On the right panel, click the icon 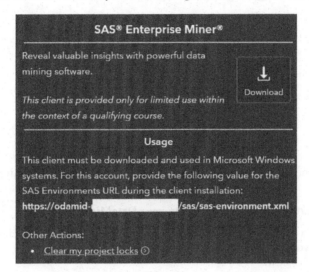 to open the instructions for SAS Enterprise Miner. Copy your SAS Enrollments URL (*Note*: each user has a unique URL; using the incorrect URL may result in being denied to software access)

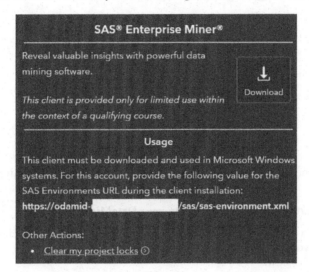

3. Click **Download** to download **SAS Enterprise Miner Client.** It is a. exe file, so at this time, it only works for Windows. Find the system requirements for SAS Enterprise Miner here https://support.sas.com/documentation/installcenter/ en/ikdminesr/75519/HTML/default/index.html
4. Run the file SASEnterpriseMiner152.exe on a Windows computer to install the software. When asked for **SAS Environments URL**, enter the URL you copied in Step 4.
5. Complete the installation process.
6. Run the software SAS Enterprise Miner 15.2 from the computer. Log on using your SAS username and password.

Exercise 3: Upload data files using SAS Studio

Follow the process below.

1. Log on SAS OnDemand for Academics at https://welcome.oda.sas.com/
2. Open SAS Studio from the SAS OnDemand Dashboard window (make sure to enable pop-ups on your browser).

3. Under Server Files and Folder, select Files (Home). Then right-click and select New/Folder to create a new folder. Name it DataMining.

4. Upload the data file *airlinerecommendation.sas7bdat* to the DataMining folder.

Exercise 4: Create a library and link it to your DataMining folder

You can create a new library and link it to your folder that contains all data files. Thus, whatever files you add to that folder will appear in that library.
Follow the steps below.

1. Open SAS Enterprise Miner software and log in to your account.
2. Select New Project to create a new project, and click Next. Name the project AirlineProject (*note: no space or special characters*).

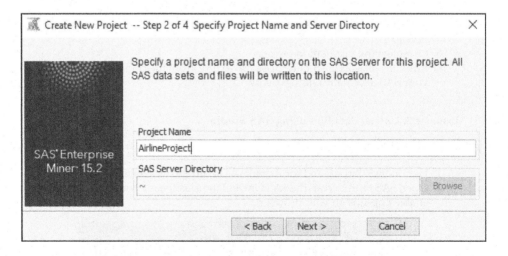

3. Click Next twice and click Finish. The project AirlineProject has been created.
4. In the File menu, select New/Library. The New Library Wizard will open.
5. Select Create New Library, and click Next.

6. Name the library PROJECT (*note: the library name should not have more than 8 characters and should not include space or special characters*).
7. To find the path for the folder DataMining, the easiest way is to use SAS Studio. Open SAS Studio, find the DataMining folder, right-click, and select Properties. You should find the path in the Location box. Highlight it and use Ctrl+C to copy this path.

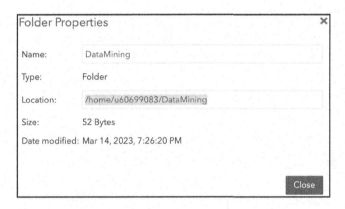

8. Go back to SAS Enterprise Miner, use Ctrl+V to paste this path to the Path box in the Library Wizard.

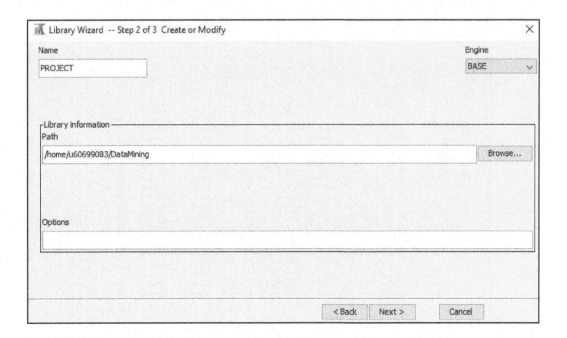

9. Click Next twice. The new library has been created. All data files in the Data Mining folder will appear under this library.

Exercise 5: Open the data file in SAS Enterprise Miner and identify the target variable

Follow the steps below.

1. Open SAS Enterprise Miner.
2. Open the project AirlineProject.
3. In the File menu, select New/Data Source.
4. The Data Source Wizard will open.
5. Click Next. In Step 2, select Browse to find your library. You should see the library PROJECT created before and the datafile *airlinerecommendation* in that library.

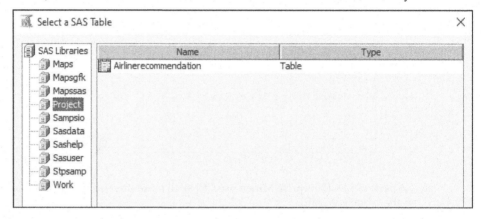

6. Select the data file and click OK.
7. Click Next until we get to Step 5. You should see the full list of variables in this dataset.

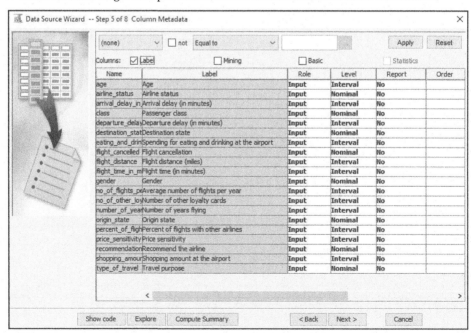

8. For the variable *recommendation*, change the role to T*arget* and the level to B*inary*.
9. Click Next until Step 8. Change the data name to Airline.
10. Click Next and then Finish. You have successfully added the dataset to your project and identified the target variable.

3

Data Sampling and Partitioning

LEARNING OUTCOMES

Upon the completion of this chapter, you will be able to

1. Define data sampling.
2. Explain the importance of data sampling.
3. Differentiate between population, sampling frame, and sample.
4. Compare probability sampling and non-probability sampling.
5. Identify sampling bias.
6. Evaluate and select the appropriate sampling method.
7. Sample a subset of the full dataset using SAS Enterprise Miner.
8. Determine the right sample size for a data mining project.
9. Describe the issue of an imbalanced dataset and overfitting.
10. Evaluate various strategies to address the imbalanced dataset.
11. Define oversampling and undersampling.
12. Explain the importance of data partitioning.
13. Determine the proper split ratio in data partitioning.
14. Implement data partitioning using SAS Enterprise Miner.

Introduction

In this chapter, we cover the first step in the SEMMA process, sampling. It is a necessary step to select a subset of the full dataset, so we can analyze it. Sampling must be done correctly to minimize the sampling bias. As mentioned before, the model can only be as good as the data. We need quality data to produce an effective predictive model. We also cover data partitioning, a process of splitting the dataset into several sub-samples. The training sample is used to train the model, and the validation sample is used to validate the model. Furthermore, the test sample is used to complete the final testing of the model before using it for actual predictions. This

DOI: 10.1201/9781003162872-4

chapter includes numerous concepts and terminologies in data sampling, which are necessary to understand various sampling methods. We need to differentiate between population, sampling frame, and sample. Our goal in sampling is to ensure that the sample is representative of the population. Since our predictive model is trained with the training sample, we want to make sure our model is generalized to other datasets. In other words, the model can make good predictions with any new dataset, indicating the usability of the model.

Sampling the Data

Essentially, sampling is the process of selecting a subset of the whole data set (sample) for analysis purposes. The goal of sampling is to gather representative and reliable information from a population, especially when it is impractical or impossible to collect data from every individual or element within that population. Sampling is a very important step in any research project to ensure the

> **DEFINITION**
>
> Sampling is the process of selecting a portion of the whole data set (sample) for analysis purposes.

data is sufficient and representative. Proper sampling would allow us to have a quality dataset with adequate size and representative of the target population, which enables us to produce a valid and generalizable model. In order to understand better the sampling process and how to sample data, I will describe the concepts of population, sampling frame, sampling strategy, and sample size from the data mining perspective. These concepts are described and discussed deeply in the research methodology books on survey, experiment, and interview designs, which are common methods for collecting primary data. In data mining studies, we apply these concepts in slightly different ways because, in data mining, we use secondary data, which has been collected prior to the project. Hence, we assume that the data have been collected by either marketing companies, industrial organizations, or governmental organizations. Since these databases are typically very large, it is not practical to analyze the full dataset. We need to have a strategy to sample a subset from the large dataset correctly and use it for analysis.

Figure 3.1 illustrates the differences between population, sampling frame, and sample. We will go into their details, how they are related, and the sampling methods we can choose.

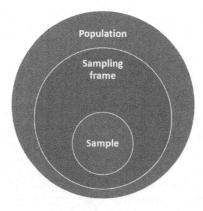

FIGURE 3.1
Population, sampling frame, and sample.

Population

Population is the primary target audience of which we want to examine the patterns of the data and make conclusions. The population of our study could be individuals, objects, cases, or a specific industry sector. The target population should be large enough to ensure the contributions of our findings but should be focused enough to ensure the feasibility of the study.

For example, our project aims to predict passengers' airline recommendations. U.S. airline passengers are an appropriate target population, which covers U.S. residents who use air transportation for travel. If we target worldwide residents, then it would be difficult to collect data that can capture this very large population. In addition, when we focus on residents of all countries, then there are questions about confounding variables, which are variables specific to countries that have effects on the target variables, but we do not have data for them. For

> **DEFINITION**
>
> **Population** is the primary target audience of which we want to examine the patterns of the data and make conclusions.
>
> **Sampling frame** is the actual list of units or sources from which a sample is drawn.
>
> **Sample** is a subset of the population.
>
> **Sampling method** refers to the procedure that we use to select participants and collect the data.

example, cultural, political, educational, or economic variables are potential confounding variables. Neglecting the effects of these variables may raise questions about the validity of our findings. By focusing on the U.S. market, we can find the data and also make valid conclusions about U.S. air travelers' decisions. We can accept residents of all ages or focus on residents with age 18 or older, depending on the scope of the study. In this book, I use a passenger survey dataset with a focus on predicting airline recommendations. I chose to focus on adult passengers only since they are the ones who could purchase tickets.

Another example of a population is all highway transportation incidents in Canada. By focusing on this population, we can build predictive models to predict the risk of injuries in a traffic incident in that country. For this project, we do not want to combine different modes of transportation, such as transport by air, road, and water, because incidents for these transportation modes have very different characteristics and contributing factors. We may end up with noisy data, which will lead to an invalid predictive model. By focusing on highway transportation, we should be able to build an effective and usable model that accurately predicts highway incidents.

Sampling Frame

Once we decide on the right population for our study, we need to determine the sampling frame. Note that it is not practical or recommended to survey or collect data from all individuals in our population. The obvious reason is that it is impossible to get responses from all individuals since it is very difficult to reach all of them, and some individuals may refuse to provide information or respond to surveys. This type of participation is voluntary, and individuals have the right to decline such a request from the data-collecting organization. Second, it is not necessary to have the data for the whole population to make valid conclusions about them. Statistically speaking, we only need to study a sample of the population, and if we perform sampling properly, the analysis results from this sample can be generalized to the whole population. The key is that we should have a representative sample with an adequate sample size. In order to achieve a representative sample, we need to have the right sampling frame. Simply put, *sampling frame* is the actual list of units or sources from which a sample is drawn. The sampling frame should have similar characteristics as the population to ensure representativeness.

For example, in the airline recommendation project, since our population is U.S. adult residents who travel by air, we could collect data from residents in six states: New York, Minnesota, Florida, Texas, California, and Washington. These states are our sampling frame, and they represent states from different regions, Northeast, Southeast, Midwest, Southwest, and Northwest, thus ensuring the representativeness of the sample. Let's say we only collect data for residents in California, a state in the West; then, it is likely that our sample is underrepresented since residents of that state have some unique characteristics and behaviors of the Western region and cannot represent our population. Hence, this discrepancy between the sampling frame and population will cause sampling bias, and our analysis results will not provide sufficient evidence to conclude about the population. That is the reason why we need to identify the sampling frame very carefully before sampling the data.

Sample

Sample is a small subset of a population. We use the sample for data analysis and make inferences about the population. In order to make sure our conclusions about the population are valid, the sample must be representative. To do so, we need to have a good sampling frame and then draw a sample from that sampling frame. For example, in the airline recommendation project, we have selected a sampling frame consisting of six states (NY, MN, FL, TX, CA, and WA). Then, we collect data from qualified residents in these states. The qualification requires that these residents must be 18 years or older and have used air transportation for travel in the past. It is to ensure we cover the individuals who have used air travel and are the ones who can purchase the ticket. Thus, their recommendation of an airline will be beneficial for the airlines to predict the travel demand. A sample is considered representative if it shares the same attributes and characteristics as the population. Hence, the analysis results based on this sample can be used to make inferences about the population.

Sampling Methods

Even if we have a good sampling frame, we may still end up with a biased sample if we do not have the appropriate sampling strategy. *Sampling* method refers to the procedure that we use to select participants and collect the data. For example, if an organization conducts the survey, they send the invitation to residents in the sampling frame (the six states above) and request their responses. However, how they select those participants is key to ensuring a representative sample. In data mining, suppose the full data have been collected by another organization, such as an airline or a government agency, and we, as data scientists, need to decide how to select individuals from that full dataset for our sample. We call it the sampling method. Selecting the right sampling method is the key to ensuring the quality of the data. I will describe common sampling methods in detail in the next section.

Basic Concepts in Data Sampling

Data sampling is a fundamental technique used in statistics and data mining to make inferences about a larger population based on a smaller subset of data, known as a sample. The sample is chosen carefully to ensure that it accurately represents the characteristics and diversity of the population. By studying the sample, data analysts can draw conclusions or make predictions about the entire population. Table 3.1 presents basic concepts in data sampling that are essential for understanding and conducting sampling methods accurately.

TABLE 3.1

Basic Concepts in Data Sampling

Terms	Description
Population	Population is the primary target audience of which we want to examine the patterns of the data and make conclusions.
Sampling frame	Sampling frame is the actual list of units or sources from which a sample is drawn.
Sample	Sample is a subset of the population. We use the sample for data analysis and make inferences about the population.
Sampling method	Sampling method is the procedure that we use to select participants and collect the data.
Sample size	Sample size refers to the number of individuals or subjects included in the sample. It should be determined based on statistical considerations.
Representative sample	Representative sample is a sample that accurately reflects the characteristics and diversity of the population.
Sampling bias	Sampling bias occurs when the selected sample does not accurately represent the population, leading to skewed or inaccurate results.
Probability sampling	Probability sampling is the method of selecting individuals randomly in such as way each individual in the sampling frame has an equal probability of being chosen.
Non-probability sampling	Non-probability sampling is the method of selecting individuals based on non-random criteria, and not every individual in the sampling frame has a chance of being included.
Margin of error	The margin of error is a measure of the uncertainty or variability in the estimates obtained from the sample.
Confidence level	The confidence level represents the degree of certainty or confidence we have in the estimates obtained from the sample.
Imbalanced dataset	An imbalanced dataset refers to a dataset where the number of samples in different classes significantly varies, resulting in an unequal representation of the classes. In an imbalanced dataset, one class (the minority class) typically has significantly fewer instances than the other classes (majority classes).
Oversampling	Oversampling is a technique that balances the data by incrementing the size of the minority (rare events) to the same size as the majority.
Undersampling	Undersampling is a technique that balances the data by reducing the size of the majority class to the same size as the minority class.

Sampling Methods

There are many different sampling methods, but typically, they are categorized into two primary types, probability sampling and non-probability sampling.

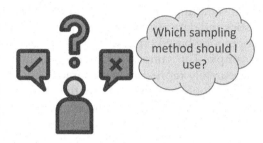

- **Probability sampling** is a random selection of participants. This method allows us to make strong statistical inferences about the whole population.

- **Non-probability sampling** is a non-random selection of participants based on convenience or other criteria. This method provides us with easier and cheaper ways to collect data, but there are questions about sampling bias.

Before we discuss these types of sampling methods, it is important to understand what sampling bias is and why we need to minimize it. *Sampling bias* is the bias in which a sample is collected in such a way that some members of a population are systematically

> Sampling bias occurs when some members of a population are systematically more likely to be selected in a sample than others, which limits the representativeness of the sample.
>
> Sampling bias is a serious issue since it poses a threat to external validity and limits the generalizability of the findings.

more likely to be selected in a sample than others. If sampling bias occurs, our findings, which are based on the data analysis of this sample, cannot be generalized to the whole population. In other words, there is a threat to external validity, which limits the generalizability of the findings. In this case, we can only make conclusions about our particular sample, which is very limited, but not about the intended population. In most cases, it is difficult to completely eliminate sampling bias, but we should do our best to minimize it. Some sampling methods are better than others at reducing sampling bias.

Probability Sampling

Probability sampling is the recommended method because it allows us to ensure the quality of the data and minimize sampling bias. Essentially, we select the individuals in the sampling frame randomly. Thus, each individual in the sampling frame has an equal

> **DEFINITION**
>
> Probability sampling is the method of selecting individuals randomly in such as way each individual in the sampling frame has an equal probability of being chosen.

probability of being chosen. This method is capable of producing an unbiased representation of the total population. There are four common probability sampling methods being used in research. I will describe them briefly with some examples. Figure 3.2 illustrates these sampling methods visually.

1. *Simple random sampling*: This method allows every member of the population to have an equal chance of being selected. A common way to do that is to assign a number for each individual in the sampling frame and then use a random number generating tool (e.g., RAND() function in Excel) to select the number of participants we need. Thus, the selection is completely based on chance, and there is no sampling bias.

FIGURE 3.2
Probability sampling methods.

For example, we want to select a simple random sample of 5,000 students of high schools in a county. To do so, we assign a number to every student in the student database, from 1 to 5,000. Then we use a random number generator to generate 500 random numbers. The 500 students with matching numbers will be selected.

2. *Systematic sampling*: Systematic sampling is a form of random sampling where a random generator is not employed. Instead, each individual is assigned a number, and we select these numbers at consistent intervals. It's crucial to emphasize that we must ensure the absence of any hidden patterns in the list that could potentially bias the sample. For instance, if the database arranges students by grade and lists them in ascending order of test scores, there exists a risk that our chosen intervals might inadvertently miss students with lower scores, leading to a sample that is skewed toward higher-scoring individuals.

Let's continue with our example of high school students. We have a total of 5,000 students in the county. First, we list these students in alphabetical order. Then, we select every 10th person on the list, which will give us a sample of 500 individuals.

3. *Stratified sampling*: This method requires us to divide the population into subgroups, called strata, based on the relevant characteristics (e.g., gender, age range, grade, score range). Based on the sample size needed, we calculate how many individuals should be selected from each subgroup. Then we use the systematic sampling method described above to select individuals from each subgroup. This method allows us to draw more precise conclusions by ensuring that every subgroup is properly represented in the sample.

For example, high schools in the county have 2,000 female students and 3,000 male students. We want to ensure that the sample reflects the gender balance of the schools, so we divide the student population into two strata based on gender. Then we use random sampling on each group, selecting 200 female students and 300 male students, which gives us a representative sample of 500 students.

4. *Cluster sampling:* Cluster sampling involves dividing the population into subgroups, each of which should possess similar characteristics to the entire population. These subgroups are called clusters. Instead of sampling individuals from each cluster, we randomly select several clusters and use all individuals in the clusters. When dealing with sizable clusters, it is possible to sample individuals within each cluster using one of the previously mentioned techniques, a method known as multistage sampling. Cluster sampling proves effective in handling extensive and widely dispersed populations. However, ensuring that the sampled clusters genuinely represent the entire population can be challenging.

> Probability sampling is recommended because it allows us to minimize sampling bias.

We will use high school students as an example of cluster sampling. For example, there are 20 high schools across the state, and we don't have the capacity to travel to every school to collect our data. Assuming these schools have similar demographics and characteristics, so we could use random sampling to select eight schools, and these are our clusters. As you see, if those schools have different demographics and characteristics, some of them may not be representative of the population, and we may not be able to get a good sample. It is the main disadvantage of cluster sampling.

Non-probability Sampling Methods

In non-probability sampling, individuals are selected based on non-random criteria, and not every individual in the sampling frame has a chance of being included. Non-probability sampling is easier and cheaper to conduct, but we face a higher risk of sampling bias, which results in a less representative sample. Consequently, our inferences about the pop-

> **DEFINITION**
>
> Non-probability sampling is the method of selecting individuals based on non-random criteria, and not every individual in the sampling frame has a chance of being included.

ulation are weaker and more limited than the ones we make with probability samples. Hence, if we choose to use a non-probability sample for any reason, we should still aim to make it as representative of the population as possible. Non-probability sampling methods are often used in exploratory and qualitative research with a smaller sample size using interviews. Since it is very difficult to randomly select a large sample for interview purposes, researchers need to use non-probability sampling and a much smaller sample size. In these types of research, the goal is not to make conclusions about a large population but to develop an initial understanding of a small or under-researched population. Another type of research that may use this method is experimental studies. The focus of experiments is to examine the causal effect of a treatment on outcomes of interest rather than to study a large population. Experiments tend to require participants to spend long hours in the lab or a controlled environment, such as a semester of a class. Hence, it is difficult to recruit a large sample randomly. Researchers need to rely on volunteers to have enough experimental participants, so they have to use non-probability sampling.

For data mining research, in which we work with large data and intend to produce a predictive model that is generalizable to other datasets, I would not recommend using non-probability sampling. With the amount of data we have, we should be able to select a large sample and use probability sampling. Nonetheless, I will briefly describe some typical non-probability sampling methods so you know what they are and how they work.

1. *Convenience sampling*: Convenience sampling involves selecting individuals who are readily accessible to the researcher. While it offers a straightforward and cost-effective means of collecting initial data, it falls short in producing results that can be generalized to the broader population. For instance, in a scenario where we're researching opinions on employee services within our organization, asking only colleagues working at the same level to complete a survey is a convenient approach. However, this limits the sample's representativeness as it doesn't encompass all employees at all levels within the organization.

2. *Voluntary response sampling*: Voluntary response sampling relies predominantly on accessibility. In this context, individuals volunteer to participate rather than being actively selected and contacted by the researcher. It's important to note that voluntary response samples tend to carry at least some degree of bias, as certain individuals are naturally more inclined to volunteer than others, potentially leading to non-representative results. For example, we send out a survey to all employees at the organization regarding health insurance benefits, and a lot of them decide to complete it. While this approach can provide us with some insights into the subject, it's worth noting that the respondents are more likely to hold strong opinions about the services. Therefore, we cannot definitively assert that their viewpoints accurately reflect those of all employees.

3. *Purposive sampling*: Purposive sampling, also known as judgment sampling, requires us to use our expertise to select a sample that is most useful for the purposes of the research. It is often employed in qualitative research, especially when the researcher seeks in-depth insights into a specific phenomenon rather than making statistical generalizations. It is particularly useful when dealing with a small and specific population. To ensure the effectiveness of purposive sampling, it's essential to establish clear criteria and a rational basis for inclusion. For example, if our goal is to gain a deeper understanding of the opinions and experiences of disabled employees within the organization, we deliberately select several employees with diverse support needs. This deliberate selection allows us to gather a wide range of data regarding their experiences with employee services.

> Non-probability sampling is easier and cheaper, but there is a higher risk of sampling bias.
>
> For data mining research, we should use probability sampling methods to ensure our findings are generalizable.

4. *Snowball sampling*: Snowball sampling can be used to recruit participants via other participants. Basically, we contact some people we know and ask them to contact people they know. As we get in contact with more people, the number of participants "snowballs"; hence, the term "snowball." For example, we are researching the experiences of the LGBTQ+ community in our city. Since there is no list of all LGBTQ+ people in the city, probability sampling isn't possible. So, we meet one person who agrees to participate in the research, and they put us in contact with other people that they know in the area.

As you can see, all of these non-probability sampling methods are easier and cheaper to do, but there is a higher risk of sampling bias, and it is likely that the sample is not representative of the population. Thus, we cannot generalize our findings to a larger population. In data mining research, we work with larger data than other types of study, so probability sampling should be used to ensure the representativeness of the data. As a result, the predictive model we develop can be more generalizable and applied to other datasets from the same population.

Secondary Data and Sample Representativeness

When we are the ones who collect data, we can select the sampling frame and use one of the sampling methods described above to ensure the representativeness of the sample. However, in many data mining projects, we use data that have been collected by other organizations or parties, secondary data. In this case, we consider the whole dataset a sampling frame and use one of these sampling methods to draw a sample from the whole dataset. Since we do not know how the data provider sampled and collected the data, how do we know if we have a representative sample?

To answer this question, I recommend an effective approach, which is to analyze the demographic information of the sample and compare it with the population. Essentially, we show that our sample shares similar demographic attributes and characteristics with the population. In that case, we can conclude that we have a representative sample, even if we do not know how the data was collected. This approach can also be used even if we collect data ourselves. The reason is that even if we choose the sampling frame and use probability sampling, there are uncertainties in the data collection process that may be out of our control, which may still cause sampling bias. For example, the individuals we collect data from may not be actually as representative as we have thought. In this case, to be sure, we should still compare the demographic information between the sample and the population.

> Comparing the demographics between the sample and the target population allows us to show the representativeness of the sample.

Table 3.2 shows an example of comparing demographics between the sample and the target population. In most cases, we could find the demographics for our population via online sources, such as the U.S. Census Bureau or other organizations' publications. As shown in the table, while these characteristics between the sample and population are not exactly the same, the difference is minimal and the data distributions are very similar. This comparison indicates the similarity between the sample and the population. In other words, our sample is representative of the population, and our findings in the sample can be applied to the population.

Sample Size

What Is Sample Size? Why Is It Important?

Sample size refers to the number of individuals or subjects included in the sample. Sample size is an important topic in data mining since an adequate sample is critical to ensuring the quality of the findings.

DEFINITION

Sample size refers to the number of individuals or subjects included in the sample.

TABLE 3.2

Example of a Comparison between Sample and Target Population

Demographic Characteristics	Sample (%)	Population (%)
Gender		
• Male	45%	48%
• Female	43%	42%
• Other	12%	10%
Age ranges		
• 18–30	20%	18%
• 31–40	38%	40%
• 41–50	30%	28%
• >50	12%	14%
Income ranges		
• <$40,000	38%	40%
• 40,000–99,999	29%	30%
• 100,000–200,000	24%	20%
• >200,000	9%	10%
Education		
• High school	23%	20%
• Bachelor	48%	50%
• Graduate degree	29%	30%
Marital status		
• Married	43%	45%
• Single	57%	55%
Region		
• Northeast	15%	17%
• Southeast	23%	21%
• Southwest	17%	18%
• Midwest	19%	20%
• West	26%	24%

Below are some key reasons highlighting the importance of sample size.

1. Representative patterns: Data mining aims to discover meaningful patterns and relationships in data. A larger sample size provides a more representative subset of the population, increasing the likelihood of capturing accurate and reliable patterns. With a larger sample size, we can achieve more accurate and representative results of the population being studied.

2. Increased generalizability: A larger sample size enhances the generalizability of research findings. When the sample is more diverse and includes a larger number of individuals or cases, the results are more likely to apply to the broader population from which the sample is drawn. This improves the external validity of the study.

3. Reliable model building: Data mining often involves building predictive models or classifiers. A larger sample size allows for more robust and accurate model building. With a larger sample, the model can capture a wider range of variations and complexities in the data, leading to more reliable and generalizable predictions.

4. Increased statistical power: Statistical power refers to the ability to detect true effects or relationships in the data. A larger sample size increases the statistical power of a study, making it more likely to detect significant differences or associations if they exist. It is particularly important in drawing meaningful conclusions from the data. Additionally, with a larger sample, data mining algorithms can detect patterns and relationships that might remain hidden in smaller samples, leading to more robust and significant findings.

5. Enhanced accuracy and confidence: A larger sample size reduces the variability and uncertainty in the prediction. Confidence intervals become narrower, providing a more accurate range within which the true population parameter is likely to fall. This improves the accuracy and reliability of the study findings.

6. Subgroup analysis: Researchers can conduct more robust subgroup analyses with a larger sample size. Subgroup analysis allows for investigating the effects or relationships within specific subgroups of the population. Adequate sample sizes within each subgroup ensure more reliable conclusions about those particular groups.

7. Increased stability: A larger sample size provides more stability to the results, reducing the influence of random fluctuations or outliers. Outliers or extreme values have lower impacts on the prediction when the sample size is large, ensuring more robust and reliable findings.

8. Account for variability: Many phenomena in real-world settings exhibit inherent variability. A larger sample size allows for capturing a broader range of variability, providing a more comprehensive understanding of the phenomenon under investigation.

9. Handling complex and rare patterns: In certain cases, data mining aims to discover complex or rare patterns that occur infrequently. A larger sample size increases the chances of encountering such patterns, making it easier to identify and understand these less common phenomena.

10. Validating results: Data mining often involves testing and validating the discovered patterns or models on unseen data. With a larger sample size, there is more confidence in the generalizability and reliability of the results during the validation process.

Sample Size for Traditional Statistical Research

Given the importance of sample size, the obvious question is: How large a sample size is sufficient for a project?

Typically, for traditional research, there are two ways to determine the needed sample size, based on the population size and based on the statistical techniques we use for analysis. First, the sample size must be adequate to represent the population size. In this case, the sample size is determined based on the size

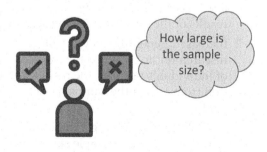

of the population, confidence level, and margin of error. Qualtrics provides a useful sample size calculator for this case. I included the mathematical formula below as the reference.

$$Sample\ size = \frac{(z\_score)^2 \times StdDev \times (1 - StdDev)}{(margin\ of\ error)^2}$$

Link to Qualtrics' sample size calculator: https://www.qualtrics.com/blog/calculating-sample-size/

The confidence level tells you how confident you are of this result. It is expressed as a percentage of times that different samples (if repeated samples were drawn) would produce this result. The common value for the confidence interval is 95%. A margin of error is a statistical measurement that accounts for the difference between actual and projected results. The common value for the margin of error is 5%.

For example, if we use a 95% confidence level, a margin of error of 5%, with a population size of 100,000, the calculated sample size is 383. If I increase the population size to 100 million, the needed sample size is still 385. The reason is that the population size is used to calculate the z-score, and the z-score saturates when the population size reaches a certain number. Hence, even if our population size is 300 million, the sample size needed is still 385. I understand this method may raise some further questions. For example, does the population size matter at all? Hence, we need to look at the second approach.

In the second approach, the sample size must be adequate to ensure the statistical test power and effect size for the statistical analysis. The formula is different depending on the statistical technique selected for analysis. I will not go into the details of those methods since there are many different formulas for calculating the sample size for different statistical methods. Two useful sources that I highly recommend using for this purpose are as follows.

- **Sample size calculators by Daniel Soper** (https://www.danielsoper.com/statcalc/): This site provides many useful statistical calculators, including sample size calculators, effect size calculators, and beta (Type II error rate) calculators. It provides all formulas and academic references for these calculators. The most useful sample size calculators include the ones for multiple regression, hierarchical multiple regression, and structural equation modeling. The site also provides all formulas and references they used to develop the calculators, which ensure the validity of these calculations.

- **G*Power software:** It is an open-source software application that allows us to calculate the sample size for many statistical methods, including t-test, ANOVA, MANOVA, repeated measures, logistic regression, and multiple regression. It is widely used in academic research studies. While this software is very capable, using it is not easy for everyone. Some features require reading the manuals carefully to avoid miscalculations.

  Link to download the software and the manual: https://www.psychologie.hhu.de/arbeitsgruppen/allgemeine-psychologie-und-arbeitspsychologie/gpower

The key in using these sample size calculators is to determine the primary parameters that we expect, including effect size, desired test power, significance level, number of independent variables (predictors), and number of dependent variables. Once we select the right statistical method and expected values for these parameters, the tools will determine the minimum sample size we need to ensure these statistical parameters. I won't go into details about these parameters since they are covered in-depth in statistics materials.

The rule of thumb is that we should use both methods and calculate the sample size needed for the population size and the sample size needed for the test power and effect size. Then, we pick the higher number between these two.

> Calculate two sample size numbers: one for the population size, and one for the test power and effect size. Then select the higher number between those two.

Sample Size for Data Mining Research

In data mining studies, the above approaches may not be very useful since they only apply to traditional statistical research, while many machine learning methods are not statistics-based. In addition, these calculations usually end up with a sample size within a range of 50–500 responses. While any of these numbers are more than sufficient for traditional statistical analysis purposes, they do not capture well the scope of data mining studies that focus on discovering unknown patterns from large data.

As mentioned in Chapter 1, when we talk about data size, we talk about both the number of variables in the data (variety) and the number of records (volume). In order to detect useful patterns in the data in terms of relationships among variables without a theoretical foundation, we need to have a large number of variables in the model. The reason is that only limited patterns (relationships) can be discovered with limited variables. In addition, if we exclude important input variables, the predictive model derived from the data may have a good model fit from a modeling perspective but have no practical implications.

When we include more variables in the model, the explanatory power of the model tends to decrease. I will get into more detail about the explanatory power in Chapter 6. Basically, it shows how well our model can explain the target variable. More specifically, it indicates the model's ability to explain variance in the target variable based on the variance in the predictors. Hence, as we add more variables, the model's explanatory power may decrease. In order to maintain the explanatory power with a large number of variables, we need more data points to train the model, meaning a larger sample size. Additionally, we also need to split the data (data partitioning) for validation purposes, which requires an even larger sample size.

So, how large a sample size is sufficient for data mining projects? It is a hard question to answer because there is no straight answer to it. Some authors say the more, the better, while some others say 10,000 data points are sufficient. I could not find consistent guidelines on this topic. It also depends on the data source because we cannot use more than what we have. Some data providers collect hourly operational data, and they should be able to provide millions of records. On the other hand, the organizations collecting accident data may only provide thousands of records. Essentially, we need enough data for training and validating models and to ensure the generalizability of the results. But we also need to be mindful of the computing power needed to process a very large dataset, as it may take much longer to train a complex model, such as a neural network, with a lot of data. I will give you my own recommendations based on my evaluation and experience with data mining projects.

Another important factor in sampling is the response ratio, the rate of the events we want to predict. For example, if our target variable is flight delays, then the response ratio is the ratio of the number of flight delays over the total number of flights. The events are delayed flights, and non-events are on-time flights. It is important to have a balanced dataset to make sure we have a valid and generalized predictive model. If the response ratio is too low or too high, we have an imbalanced dataset. For example, if the response ratio is 0.1, then 10% of the data are events, and 90% are non-events. When we train the model with this dataset, the model may estimate that all cases are non-events, leading to a high rate of false negatives. Thus, even though the overall prediction accuracy may seem high (90%), the model fails to predict the events (flight delays), which makes it invalid and unusable. On the other hand, if the response ratio is too high, we have a very large number of events vs. non-events, and we may end up with a predictive model with a very high rate of false positives, which also leads to the same issue. One common solution for an imbalanced dataset is to resample the data to gain an achievable response ratio. We will get into this solution later in this chapter.

In conclusion, when selecting a sample size for data mining, we need to look at both the number of records and the response ratio. For example, a sample size of 100,000 records with a response ratio of 0.4–0.6 should be considered sufficient, while a sample size of 1 million cases with a response ratio of 0.03

> For data mining projects, aim to get a sample size of at least 100,000 records with a response ratio of 0.4–0.6.

may still not be enough. In the perfect scenario, a response ratio of 0.5 represents a perfect balance between events and non-events. However, in reality, we usually do not have that perfect balance. My recommendation is to get a sample size of at least 100,000 cases with a response ratio of 0.4–0.6.

SAS ENTERPRISE MINER GUIDELINES

Sample Node Train Properties
(https://documentation.sas.com)

Default – When the Default method is selected, if the target variable is a class variable, then the sample is stratified on the target variable. Otherwise, random sampling is performed.

Cluster – When Cluster sampling is selected, samples are drawn from a cluster of observations that are similar in some way. For example, a data miner might want to get all the records of each customer from a random sample of customers. If you select Cluster Sampling as your method, you must use the Sample Node Variables Table to set the Sample Role and specify a cluster variable. If you perform cluster sampling, the Sample node creates a data set. Cluster sampling cannot be used to create a data view.

First N – When First N sampling is selected, the first n observations are selected from the input data set for the sample. You must specify the quantity n either as a percentage or as an absolute number of observations, by using the respective properties Observations and Percentage. To enable these options, set the Type property to Number of Observations or Percentage.

NOTE: The First N method of sampling can produce a sample that is not representative of the population, particularly if the input data set is not in random order.

Random – When random sampling is selected, each observation in the data set (population) has the same probability of being selected for the sample, independently of the other observations that happen to fall into the sample. For example, if observation 1345 is randomly drawn as the first member of the sample, we know that each member of the data set still has an equal chance of being the second member of the sample.

Stratify – When stratified sampling is selected, you choose nominal, binary, or ordinal variables from the input data set to form strata (or subsets) of the total population. Within each stratum, all observations have an equal probability of being selected for the sample. Across all strata, however, the observations in the input data set generally do not have equal probabilities of being selected for the sample. You perform stratified sampling to preserve the strata proportions of the population within the sample. This may improve the classification precision of fitted models.

Systematic – When systematic sampling is selected, the percentage of the population that is required for the sample is computed based on the number that you specify in the Observations or Percentage property. The tool divides 100 by the number in the Percentage property value field to come up with a number. The random sample process selects all observations that are multiples of this number for the sample.

Example: Sampling

In this section, we learn how to sample data using SAS Enterprise Miner. Suppose we have a very large dataset for data mining purposes, and we do not plan to use all data points. The main reason is that such as large dataset is unnecessary for modeling and can slow down the computing process, which affects the model training time. For example, we have a dataset with 10 million data points, but we decided to use 100,000 data points for the modeling purpose. So, how do we sample these 100,000 data points from a total of 10 million data points without sacrificing the quality and generalizability of the data? I will demonstrate how to do it using SAS Enterprise Miner.

The first step is to decide on the sampling method. As mentioned before, in data mining projects, we should use probability sampling methods. SAS Enterprise Miner provides these sampling methods for us. SAS Enterprise Miner's guidelines on sampling methods are presented on the previous page. In most cases, when we have a balanced dataset, we should use random sampling unless we have a specific reason to choose other methods. Random sampling allows us to draw a sample randomly while maintaining the response ratio. For example, if we have a response ratio of 0.45 in the full dataset and want to sample 10% of the data, random sampling will provide us with 10% of the data and maintain the response ratio of 0.45.

Once we choose the appropriate sampling method, believe it or not, drawing a sample from the full dataset is rather simple. Most data mining software applications have built-in sampling features that allow us to sample the data without any challenges. I will demonstrate how to do data sampling in SAS Enterprise Miner. Suppose we decided to use the random sampling method to sample data. In SAS Enterprise Miner, we have two ways to do the sampling: when we create a new data source or use the Sample Node. I will show you how to use the Sample Node since it has more setting properties, allowing us to configure our sampling process and change the configurations whenever we want.

We use an example dataset, *airline recommendation*. If you completed Chapter 2 exercises, you should have uploaded this dataset to your library and opened it in SAS Enterprise Miner. In Chapter 4, I will provide a detailed explanation of the dataset and variables. In this chapter, we only need to know that the target variable is *recommendation*, indicating passengers' recommendation of the airline for air travel. It is a binary variable with two levels: Yes – recommend the airline (events); No – not recommend the airline (non-events). The total dataset has 124,464 data points. The response ratio is 0.475 (or 47.5%), which is considered a balanced ratio. Our goal is to sample 50% of the data using random sampling.

Follow the steps below in SAS Enterprise Miner.

1. Run SAS Enterprise Miner.
2. Open the project AirlineProject.
3. Right-click on Diagrams and select Create Diagram. Name it Airline.

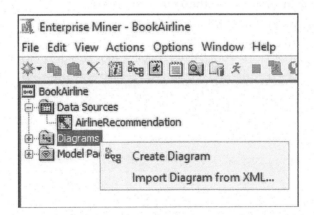

4. Double-click the Airline diagram to open it in the workspace.
5. Drag the data file AirlineRecommendation from Data Sources to the workspace.

6. From the Sample tab, drag the icon Sample to the workspace. Connect the Sample node to the AirlineRecommendation node. We should see a diagram as follows.

7. Click the Sample node, which will show the Property panel on the left.

.. Property	Value
General	
Node ID	Smpl2
Imported Data	...
Exported Data	...
Notes	...
Train	
Variables	...
Output Type	Data
Sample Method	Default
Random Seed	12345
⊟ Size	
⊢ Type	Percentage
⊢ Observations	.
⊢ Percentage	10.0
⊢ Alpha	0.01
⊢ PValue	0.01
Cluster Method	Random
⊟ Stratified	
⊢ Criterion	Proportional
⊢ Ignore Small Strata	No

General

General Properties

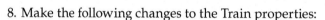

8. Make the following changes to the Train properties:
   - Set Sample Method to Random.
   - Set Percentage to 50%.

General	
Node ID	Smpl2
Imported Data	...
Exported Data	...
Notes	...
Train	
Variables	...
Output Type	Data
Sample Method	Random
Random Seed	12345
⊟ Size	
⊢ Type	Percentage
⊢ Observations	.
⊢ Percentage	50.0
⊢ Alpha	0.01
⊢ PValue	0.01
Cluster Method	Random

9. Run the Sample node.
10. When the run is complete, open the Results window.

```
23
24   Sampling Summary
25
26                                Number of
27   Type         Data Set       Observations
28
29   DATA         EMUS2.Ids_DATA    124464
30   SAMPLE       EMUS2.Smpl_DATA    62233
31
32
33   *---------------------------------------------------*
34   * Score Output
35   *---------------------------------------------------*
36
37
38   *---------------------------------------------------*
39   * Report Output
40   *---------------------------------------------------*
41
42
43
44   Summary Statistics for Class Targets
45   (maximum 500 observations printed)
46
47   Data=DATA
48
49                 Numeric    Formatted    Frequency
50    Variable      Value       Value        Count      Percent        Label
51
52   recommendation    .          No         59167     47.5374    Recommend the airline
53   recommendation    .          Yes        65297     52.4626    Recommend the airline
54
55
56   Data=SAMPLE
57
58                 Numeric    Formatted    Frequency
59    Variable      Value       Value        Count      Percent        Label
60
61   recommendation    .          No         29584     47.5375    Recommend the airline
62   recommendation    .          Yes        32649     52.4625    Recommend the airline
```

FIGURE 3.3
Results of the sampling.

The Results of the Sample node are a text file. Figure 3.3 shows the primary outputs. Note that in this example, I present the screenshot of the output text so you see what it looks like. For the remaining chapters, I will convert the outputs into table form for easy review.

Some important outputs we should focus on are as follows.

- Actual data size based on the target variable: recommended: 59,167 cases (47.54%); not recommended: 65,297 (52.46%).
- Sample data size based on the target variable: recommended: 29,584 cases (47.54%); not recommended: 32,649 (52.46%).

As you can see, the software randomly selects 50% of the data for the sample. In that process, it maintains the same response ratio as the full data (47.54%).

Imbalanced Dataset

As discussed before, we expect a balanced dataset to be able to produce a valid and useful predictive model. An imbalanced dataset poses a high risk of prediction error. A balanced dataset should have a response ratio close to 0.5; i.e., we have a similar number of events

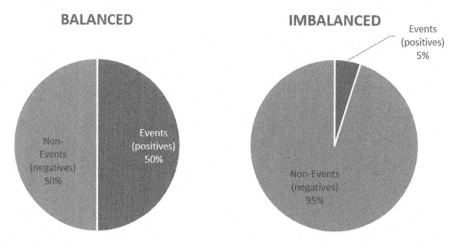

FIGURE 3.4
Balanced vs. imbalanced datasets.

(positives) as the number of non-events (negatives). Figure 3.4 shows an example of a balanced dataset and an imbalanced dataset. The balanced dataset has 50% of events and 50% of non-events or a response ratio of 50%. The imbalanced dataset has 5% of events and 95% of non-events or a response ratio of 5%. In the imbalanced dataset, we call the events a *minority class* (only 5% of the data) and the non-events a *majority class* (95% of the data).

Why does a very imbalanced dataset become a problem in predictive modeling? If we use this example, we have a dataset with 5% of the data being events (positives) and 95% of the data being non-events (negatives). When we train our model with this dataset, due to the data imbalance, the algorithm treats all cases are non-events because it tries to find the model with the highest prediction accuracy. Remember that the algorithm cannot tell the meaning of the variable or data. It only sees the numbers and tries fitting the data into a model. In this case, we have an overall prediction accuracy of 95%, which is considered very high. However, if we look deeply into the results, we notice that the model fails to predict any events (positives), which makes it practically useless because we built this model to predict that particular event.

So why does it happen? If we break down the prediction into positive and negative predictions, we see that the true positive rate is 0%, while the false negative rate is 100%. This is because the algorithm treats all cases as non-events (negatives) to receive the most accurate prediction. So, you see, the overall prediction accuracy could be misleading, and we need to examine other model fit metrics as well, such as specificity, sensitivity, F1-score, Gini coefficient, ROC chart, and Lift chart. We will get into these details in Chapter 6. In this case, due to the imbalanced dataset with a very low response ratio, the model is invalid.

> Be very careful when we build predictive models for imbalanced data. The overall prediction accuracy could be misleading.

Now we understand why an imbalanced dataset poses a high risk to our modeling. It is important to know approaches we can use to address that problem because it is not as uncommon as you may have thought. In projects like predicting credit frauds, aviation accidents, or cyberattacks, the events tend to be very rare (a very low response ratio), but it is really important to predict that risk. If our model fails to predict the target variable of interest, it is useless to us. There are several approaches to address this issue, as follows.

Using Multiple Model Fit Metrics

As we have seen in the example above, when we have an imbalanced dataset, training a good model is a challenge, and often we have a model with a good overall prediction accuracy yet invalid.

Misclassification rate = 1-prediction accuracy

Hence, it is imperative that we should not just rely on the prediction accuracy or misclassification rate to evaluate the model performance since it could be misleading. Note that the misclassification rate is basically one minus prediction accuracy. We need to use multiple model fit metrics to evaluate models. In addition to prediction accuracy and misclassification rate, some typical metrics include sensitivity, specificity, F1-score, Lift chart, ROC chart, and Gini coefficient. By using multiple metrics, we can evaluate the performance of a model from various perspectives and capture a whole picture of the model's performance. We will cover the details of these metrics in Chapter 6.

Data Partition and Model Validation

One primary concern with predictive modeling is overfitting. It means we may overtrain the model and achieve high prediction accuracy. However, since the model is overtrained with the training data, it only works well with this specific dataset. When we apply the same model to a new dataset, it does not work anymore; i.e., the model is not generalizable and, therefore, unusable. Hence, in addition to using multiple model fit metrics, we should also partition the data into training and validation samples. The training sample is used to train the model, while the validation sample is used to validate the model. This method allows us to detect any issues with our model when comparing the training and validation sample results. Model validation is a vital step when we build models with an imbalanced dataset. We will discuss the details of data partition later in this chapter.

Cost-Sensitive Learning

Another approach for addressing the imbalanced dataset is cost-sensitive learning. Basically, when we train models, we do not compare models based on the original prediction accuracy or misclassification rate but rather consider the costs of misclassification. In other words, we want a model that can minimize the total cost of misclassification. In order to do so, we need to create a payoff table for the target profile, showing the cost of misclassification for each level. It is also called a *decision matrix*.

I will focus mainly on the Cost-Sensitive Learning (CSL) approach since it is widely used in data mining. We could use the same approach for maximizing the total profit of accurate predictions, except we define the profit matrix for accurate predictions and aim to maximize the total profit.

CSL is a popular method to enhance the predictive model's performance with an imbalanced dataset. It is a subset of machine learning that takes into account the misclassification costs. Typically, the costs of misclassification (false negatives or false positives) are not equal. Therefore, by defining misclassification costs for all levels, we can train and select the model that minimizes the total cost.

In the case of an imbalanced dataset with a very low or very high response ratio, the cost of false negatives is usually much higher than the cost of false positives, so the mistake for the minority class (rare cases) should be strongly penalized. An example is a prediction of a serious health issue. False negatives lead to potential delays in treatment and could cause severe consequences. When we compare models, we select the one with the lowest total cost rather than the lowest misclassification rate. Thus, cost-sensitive learning optimizes the model's performance by considering the costs involved in different types of classification mistakes. It helps address class imbalance issues and improves the model's performance in real-world scenarios where the consequences of errors can vary significantly.

On the other hand, if we prefer focusing on the profits rather than the costs, we just need to define a profit matrix with detailed profits for accurate predictions. When comparing between models, we select the one with the highest total profit. In this book, we will use examples with the cost focus. I will go into the details of CSL and how to conduct it in Chapter 6.

Resampling – Oversampling and Undersampling

One common approach to address an imbalanced dataset is to resample the data and create a balanced dataset. This approach should be used if there is a threat to the model validity caused by the imbalanced dataset. In other words, if the above choices do not address the data imbalance issues, and there is a possibility that our models are invalid, then we should consider this option.

> **DEFINITION**
>
> **Oversampling**: Balance the data by incrementing the size of the minority (rare events) to the same size as the majority.
> **Undersampling**: Balance the data by reducing the size of the majority class to the same size as the minority class.

Basically, by resampling, we modify the imbalanced dataset to balance data between events and non-events. In order to do so, there are two primary methods: oversampling and undersampling. Figure 3.5 shows the differences between these two methods.

Oversampling (upsampling) is the technique to balance the data by incrementing the size of the minority (rare events) to the same size as the majority. By oversampling, we increase the number of records of the minority class in the training sample by duplicating the cases. The primary advantage of this method is there is no loss of information from the

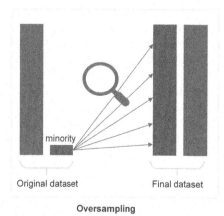

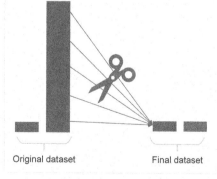

FIGURE 3.5
Oversampling and undersampling.

original dataset, and we can keep all records from the minority and majority classes. On the other hand, with duplicated data, our models are prone to overfitting. Additionally, we may end up with a very large dataset that could increase the computing time.

The most common technique for oversampling is random oversampling, which replicates minority class records randomly. This technique is simple but tends to lead to overfitting because the model learns from the same data points. A more advanced technique is the Synthetic Minority

The Oversampling option in SAS Enterprise Miner actually performs undersampling as we described above.

Oversampling Technique (SMOTE), which uses the k-nearest neighbor method to select cases that are close in the feature space. We won't cover it in this book.

Undersampling (down-sampling) is the technique to balance the data by reducing the size of the majority class to the same size as the minority class. A typical method to undersample is stratified sampling. The primary advantage of this method is the improved training time since we end up with a smaller size. On the other hand, by deleting numerous records in the majority class, we may lose some critical information.

Note that resampling is not a random sampling, so there may be questions about sampling bias. Hence, we need to address the sampling bias issues by comparing the demographics between the sample and the population to ensure the representativeness of the sample, as shown before.

SAS ENTERPRISE MINER GUIDELINES

Sample Node Train Properties

(https://documentation.sas.com)

SAMPLE NODE TRAIN PROPERTIES: SIZE

Type – Use the Type property to specify the method you want to use to determine the sample size.

- **Computed** – SAS computes the sample size that is required to capture rare events with the probability that you enter in the p-value field.
- **Number of Observations** – the sample size is determined by the number that you enter in the Observations property value field.
- **Percentage** – (default setting) the sample size is determined by the percentage number that you enter in the Percentage property value field.

Observations – When the Type property is set to **Number of Observations**, use the Observations property to specify the sample size n, where n is the number of observations to use from the input data set. Permissible values are nonnegative integers.

Percentage – When the Type property is set to **Percentage**, use the Percentage property to specify the sample size as a proportion of the input data set observations. Permissible values for the Percentage property are real numbers greater than zero. The default value for the Percentage property is 10.0.

Alpha – When the Type property is set to **Computed**, use the Alpha property to specify the alpha value that you want to use when calculating the final number n of observations in a sample. Permissible values are nonnegative real numbers. The default alpha value is 0.01.

P-value – When the Type property is set to **Computed**, use the p-value property to specify the p-value that you want to use when calculating the final number of observations for a sample. Permissible values are nonnegative real numbers. The default p-value is 0.01.

Cluster Method – When the Sample Method property is set to Cluster, use the Cluster Method property to specify the cluster sample building method that you want to use.

- **First N** – Using First N clusters sampling, the Sample node includes the first sequential n clusters that are associated with the specified cluster variable.

- **Random** – (default setting) Using simple random cluster sampling, every cluster that is associated with the cluster variable has the same probability of being selected in the sample, independently of the other clusters that are associated with the same cluster variable.

- **Systematic** – Using systematic cluster sampling, the Sample node computes the percentage of the variable-specified clusters that are required for the sample. The Sample node selects for the sample all matching variable clusters that are multiples of this number.

SAS ENTERPRISE MINER GUIDELINES

Sample Node Train Properties

(https://documentation.sas.com)

SAMPLE NODE TRAIN PROPERTIES: STRATIFIED

Criterion – Use the Criterion property to specify the sampling criterion that you want to use during stratified sampling.

Proportional – In proportional stratified sampling, the proportion of observations in each stratum is the same in the sample as it is in the population.

Equal – The equal property requires the Sample node to sample the same number of observations from each stratum. That is, the total sample size is divided by the number of strata to determine how many observations to sample from each stratum.

Optimal – With optimal allocation, both the proportion of observations within strata and the relative standard deviation of a specified variable within strata are the same in the sample as in the population. Usually, the within-strata standard deviations are computed for the target variable.

Level Based – If Level Based is selected, then the sample is based on the proportion captured and sample proportion of a specific level. When the Criterion property is set to Level Based, use the Level Based Options properties to specify parameters for the proportion captured, sample proportion, and the level of interest.

Ignore Small Strata When the Sample Method property is set to Stratify, and the Ignore Small Strata property is also set to**Yes**, any stratum that has a population less than the value n that is specified in the Minimum Strata Size property is excluded from the sample. The default setting for the Ignore Small Strata property is **No**. This option is ignored when using the Level Based stratification criterion.

Minimum Strata Size – When the Method property is set to **Stratify**, use the Minimum Strata Size property to specify the value n for the minimum number of observations that are required to construct a valid stratum. Permissible values are integers greater than or equal to 1. The default value for the Minimum Strata Size property is 5. This option is ignored when using the Level Based stratification criterion.

SAS ENTERPRISE MINER GUIDELINES

Sample Node Train Properties

(https://documentation.sas.com)

SAMPLE NODE TRAIN PROPERTIES: LEVEL BASED OPTIONS

You can configure Level Based Options when the Criterion property in the Stratified properties group is set to Level Based. The Level Based properties specify the Level Based stratification criterion when a single stratification variable is used. If more than one stratification variable is used, the Level Based Options settings are ignored, and the Criterion property in the Stratified properties group is automatically set to Proportional.

- **Level Selection** – Use the Level Selection property to specify the level of interest. The available choices are **Event** and **Rarest Level**. If **Event** is selected, then the level is based on the variable ordering. The default ordering is ascending for input variables and descending for target variables.

- **Level Proportion** – Use the Level Proportion property to specify the proportion of the selected level of interest to be included in the sample.

- **Sample Proportion** – Use the Sample Proportion property to specify what proportion of the sample should contain the selected level of interest.

SAMPLE NODE TRAIN PROPERTIES: OVERSAMPLING

The following properties configure Stratified Random Sampling (*oversampling*) properties. Oversampling is used most often to create models to predict rare events. Random sampling often does not provide enough targets to train a predictive model for rare events.

Oversampling biases the sampling to provide enough target events to effectively train a predictive model.

- **Adjust Frequency** – Set the Adjust Frequency property to **Yes** to adjust the frequency for oversampling and create a biased stratified sample. The biased stratified sample uses a frequency variable that contains the sampling weights to adjust the target level proportions. If you configure the Sampling node for oversampling and no frequency variable exists, Enterprise Miner creates one. Oversampling is only performed when the Adjust Frequency option is set to **Yes**. The extent of the adjustment depends on how biased your sample is with respect to the input data source.

- **Based on Count** – Set the Based on Count property to **Yes** if you want to base your frequency variable adjustment on counts. When the Based on Count property is set to **No**, frequency variable adjustments are based on percentages. The default setting for the Based on Count property is **No**.

- **Exclude Missing Levels** – Set the Exclude Missing Levels property to **Yes** if you want to exclude strata where the stratification variables contain missing values. When Exclude Missing Levels is set to **Yes**, the frequency variable for excluded strata is set to 0. The default setting for the Exclude Missing Levels property is **No**.

Example: Resampling Data

I will demonstrate how to perform resampling data using SAS Enterprise Miner. For example, in the airline recommendation case, suppose we have a very imbalanced dataset with an 8.35% response ratio; i.e., 8.3% of passengers do not recommend the airline, while 91.7% recommend it. Please note that I created this hypothetical scenario for our demonstration only (Table 3.3).

SAS Enterprise Miner uses stratified sampling to balance the dataset. Note that the oversampling option in this software actually performs undersampling as we described before.

Follow the steps below in SAS Enterprise Miner.

1. Run SAS Enterprise Miner.
2. Open the project Airline.
3. Open the Airline diagram.

TABLE 3.3

Hypothetical Imbalanced Dataset

Variable	Formatted Value	Frequency Count	Percent
recommendation	No	5,916	8.31%
recommendation	Yes	65,297	91.69%

4. Click the Sample node, which will show the Property panel on the left.

5. Make the following changes to the properties:

- Under Train tab: Set Sample Method to Stratify.
- Under Size tab: Set Type to Percentage.
- Set Percentage to 100%.
- Under Stratified tab: Set Criterion to Equal.
- Under Oversampling tab: Set Adjust Frequency to Yes.

.. Property	Value
Random Seed	12345
⊟Size	
⋮Type	Percentage
⋮Observations	.
⋮Percentage	100.0
⋮Alpha	0.01
⋮PValue	0.01
Cluster Method	Random
⊟Stratified	
⋮Criterion	Equal
⋮Ignore Small Strata	No
⋮Minimum Strata Size	5
⊟Level Based Options	
⋮Level Selection	Event
⋮Level Proportion	100.0
⋮Sample Proportion	50.0
⊟Oversampling	
⋮Adjust Frequency	Yes
⋮Based on Count	No
⋮Exclude Missing Levels	No

6. Run the Sample node.

7. When the run is complete, open the Results window.

Table 3.4 shows the detailed results. The Sample Node results in a balanced dataset with 50% of passengers recommending the airline and another 50% not recommending the airline. The output of this node is the new balanced dataset, and we can use it to train the models. It is an example of balancing data using undersampling in SAS Enterprise Miner.

TABLE 3.4

Results of the Undersampling

Data	Variable	Formatted Value	Frequency Count	Percent
Full data	recommendation	No	5,916	8.31%
	recommendation	Yes	65,297	91.69%
Sample	recommendation	No	5,916	50%
	recommendation	Yes	5,916	50%

Data Partition

In data mining, a popular strategy for assessing the quality of model generalization is to partition the data source. As mentioned before, overfitting in data mining may occur if we overtrain the model to achieve high accuracy. The trained model may not perform well with a new dataset, which raises questions about the generalizability of the model. In other words, the model only works well with the training sample and will likely fail when we apply it to different datasets. In order to avoid this situation, we partition the data into multiple datasets. The training sample is used for preliminary model fitting. The rest is reserved for empirical validation and is often split into two parts: validation sample and test sample. The validation sample is used to validate the model and prevent overfitting. We can conclude whether the model is generalizable by comparing the results between training and validation samples. The test sample is used for a final assessment of the model.

Figure 3.6 illustrates how data partitioning works. Why do we need three subsamples for data mining purposes? First, the training sample is used to train the model and find the one with a good model fit. Then, we run that model with the validation sample to validate the model. If the model is not validated, we reconfigure the model, retrain it, and validate the new one. It is an iterative process, and it may take some trials and errors until we find a good and validated model. Finally, we test this final model with the test sample to ensure its generalizability.

Split Ratio

A common question in data partitioning is about the split ratio; i.e., how many percent of the data should go to the training sample, and how many percent should go to the validation and test samples? For example, a split ratio is 60–40 typically means 60% of the data

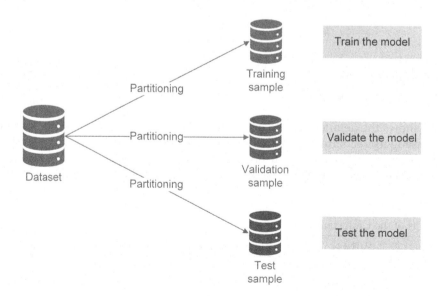

FIGURE 3.6
Data partition.

goes to the training sample, and 40% goes to the other two. In this case, we usually split 40% of the data evenly for validation and test samples. Hence, we will use 20% of the data for validation and another 20% for the final test.

There is no standard rule for split ratio. Literature shows various suggestions, ranging from 50–50, 60–40, 70–30, 80–20, to even 90–10. In order to determine the right split ratio, we will need to see how much data we have. The rule of thumb is that those three samples must share similar data trends with the original dataset. Otherwise, we will have sampling bias, and we may end up training the model with the biased dataset, which results in an invalid predictive model. We also need to make sure we have enough data points in each sample for modeling purposes. Typically, we want to use more data for training the model to achieve a good model fit, but the other two samples should have adequate data points to validate and test the model. Hence, data size is an important factor.

For example, suppose our original dataset has 100,000 data points. In that case, we can use a split ratio of 60–40, which will give us 60,000 records for training, 20,000 records for validation, and 20,000 records for final testing. Additionally, if we have more than 1 million data points, then a split ratio of 80–20 should work because it will give us 800,000 records for training, 100,000 records for validation, and 100,000 records for final testing. On the other hand, if we have a very small sample size, with fewer than 1,000 data points, we should use a split ratio of 60–40 but without the test sample. The reason is that we want to have enough data in the validation sample to validate the model.

I provide my recommended split ratio for different data sizes in Table 3.5. Note that it is a general recommendation, and depending on the machine learning method we use, we may need to make adjustments to the split ratio as needed.

TABLE 3.5

Recommended Split Ratio Based on the Sample Size

Sample Size	Recommended Split Ratio
Fewer than 1,000 data points	60–40 with no test sample (train: 60%; validation: 40%)
1,000–1 million data points	60–40 (train: 60%; validation: 20%; test: 20%)
1–10 million data points	80–20 (train: 80%; validation: 10%; test: 10%)
More than 10 million data points	90–10 (train: 90%; validation: 5%; test: 5%)

SAS ENTERPRISE MINER GUIDELINES

Data Partition Node Train Properties

(https://documentation.sas.com)

Partitioning Method – Use the Partitioning Method property to specify the sampling method that you want to use when you are partitioning your data.

- **Default** – When Default is selected, if a class target variable or variables is specified, then the partitioning is stratified on the class target variables. Otherwise, simple random partitioning is performed. Note that if additional stratification variables are specified in the Variables Editor, they will be used in addition to the target variables.

- **Simple Random** – When Simple Random is selected, every observation in the data set has the same probability of being written to one of the partitioned data sets.

- **Cluster** – Using simple cluster partitioning, you allocate the distinct values of the cluster variable to the various partitions using simple random partitioning. Note that with this method, the partition percentages apply to the values of the cluster variable, and not to the number of observations that are in the partition data sets. If you select cluster partitioning as your method, you must use the Variables property of the Data Partition node to set the Partition Role of the cluster variable (which can be the target variable) to cluster.

- **Stratified** – Using stratified partitioning, you specify variables to form strata (or subgroups) of the total population. Within each stratum, all observations have an equal probability of being written to one of the partitioned data sets. You perform stratified partitioning to preserve the strata proportions of the population within each partition data set. This might improve the classification precision of fitted models. If you select Stratified partitioning as your method and no class target variables are defined, then you must set the Variables window to set the partition role and specify a stratification variable.

Example: Partitioning Using SAS Enterprise Miner

This section demonstrates how to partition data in SAS Enterprise Miner. We use the *airline recommendation* dataset. The software sets the default values of 40–30–30 for three sub-samples. Since we have more than 100,000 data points, we will partition our dataset into three sub-samples using a split ratio of 60–40. Thus, we use 60% of the data for training, 20% for validation, and 20% for final testing.

Follow the steps below in SAS Enterprise Miner.

1. Run SAS Enterprise Miner.
2. Open the project Airline.
3. Open the Airline diagram.
4. From the Sample tab, drag the icon Data Partition 🖾 to the workspace. Connect the Data Partition node to the Sample node. We should see a diagram as follows.

5. Click Data Partition node, which will show the Property panel on the left.
6. Under Train properties: Keep Default for Partition Method.

7. Under Data Set Allocations tab, make the following changes:
   - Set Training to 60.0.
   - Set Validation to 20.0.
   - Set Test to 20.0.

Train	
Variables	
Output Type	Data
Partitioning Method	Default
Random Seed	12345
⊟ Data Set Allocations	
Training	60.0
Validation	20.0
Test	20.0
Report	
Interval Targets	Yes
Class Targets	Yes

8. Run the Data Partition node.
9. When the run is complete, open the Results window.

The results are presented in Tables 3.6 and 3.7. As you can see, the software has split the original data into three sub-samples, train, validate, and test, as we expected. An important thing that we need to keep in mind is that the response ratio is maintained at 52.5%, as with the original dataset. Thus, these three sub-samples share the response ratio as the original dataset. We also have enough data to train the model (more than 37,000 data points) and to validate and test the model (about 12,000 data points each). In other words, it is safe to train and validate our model with these sub-samples.

TABLE 3.6

Data Partitioning Results – Number of Observations by Sample

Type	Data Set	Number of Observations
Full sample	EMWS2.Smpl_DATA	62,233
Training sample	EMWS2.Part2_TRAIN	37,337
Validation sample	EMWS2.Part2_VALIDATE	12,447
Test sample	EMWS2.Part2_TEST	12,449

TABLE 3.7

Data Partitioning Results – Number of Observations by Class by Sample

Type	Variable	Formatted Value	Frequency Count	Percent
Full sample	recommendation	No	59,167	47.54%
	recommendation	Yes	65,297	52.46%
Training sample	recommendation	No	35,497	47.54%
	recommendation	Yes	39,175	52.46%
Validation sample	recommendation	No	11,834	47.54%
	recommendation	Yes	13,060	52.46%
Test sample	recommendation	No	11,836	47.54%
	recommendation	Yes	13,062	52.46%

Summary

In this chapter, we cover the first step in the SEMMA process, sampling. Sampling is vital to data mining since proper sampling provides us with a good dataset for analysis. By using the right sampling method, we are able to get a generalized dataset, which allows us to develop a good predictive model. A model with good predictive power should work for all datasets, not just the training sample. I provided some recommendations for the sample size and response ratio to ensure data adequacy. We also need a balanced dataset because an imbalanced dataset may create an overfitting issue, which results in an invalid and unusable predictive model. In order to address the data imbalance issue, there are several strategies, such as using multiple model fit criteria, partitioning data, resampling, and cost-sensitive learning. Resampling is a common technique that allows us to balance the imbalanced dataset. Finally, data partitioning is an important step to split the dataset into sub-samples. Typically, the training sample is used to train the model, the validation sample is used to validate the model, and the test sample is used to test the final model for generalizability. I provided some recommendations for the split ratio with different sample sizes. In this chapter, I also demonstrated how to use SAS Enterprise Miner to perform data sampling, resampling, and data partitioning.

CHAPTER DISCUSSION QUESTIONS

1. What is the purpose of sampling, and why is it important in data mining?
2. Describe the differences between population, sampling frame, and sample. How are they related? Give some real-life examples of population, sampling frame, and sample.
3. What is sampling bias? Give some examples of sampling bias.
4. Compare probability sampling and non-probability sampling. Which methods would allow us to minimize sampling biases?
5. Provide an example of a data mining project in your business and choose the right sampling method for this project. Justify your decision.
6. What are the methods of calculating the needed sample size? Use Daniel Soper's sample size calculator and G*Power to calculate a sample size for your project.
7. What is overfitting and how does it affect the validity of a predictive model?
8. Describe the main concerns with an imbalanced dataset. What are the primary strategies to address the imbalanced dataset?
9. What are the differences between oversampling and undersampling? Give some specific examples.
10. What is the purpose of data partitioning? How do we determine the right split ratio in data partitioning?

Exercises

Exercise 1: Data partitioning for the *Boston Housing* dataset

1. Upload the *boston* dataset to your server.
2. Open the dataset in SAS Enterprise Miner.
3. Create a new diagram *Partition*, and add the data source to the workspace.
4. Add a Data Partition to the workspace and connect it to the data source.
5. Partition the data using the split ratio 60–40: train sample: 60%; validation sample: 40%; test sample: 0%. Use the Simple Random method.
6. Run the Data Partition node and report the results.

Note: We will continue to use the *boston* dataset in the next chapters. We will assume that the data partitioning is already completed. Refer to this exercise if you need to redo the data partitioning.

Exercise 2: Data sampling for the *Try Buy* dataset

1. Upload the *try_buy* dataset to your server.
2. Open the dataset in SAS Enterprise Miner. Change the Role of BuyReturn to Target, and change the Level to Binary.
3. Create a new diagram *Sampling*, and add the data source to the workspace.
4. Add a Sample node to the workspace and connect it to the data source.
5. Sample 80% of the full dataset using two different sampling methods: (1) Random; and (2) Stratified.
6. Run the Sample node and report the results.

Exercise 3: Data resampling for the *Try Buy* dataset

1. Open the *try_buy* dataset in SAS Enterprise Miner.
2. Open the diagram *Sampling* created in Exercise 2, run the Sample node, and report the response ratio for the target variable, BuyReturn. Is it imbalanced?
3. Perform resampling to balance the data by reconfiguring the Sample node as follows.
   - Under Train: Set Sample Method to Stratify
   - Under Size: Set Percentage to 80.0
   - Under Stratified: Set Criterion to Equal
   - Under Oversampling: Set Adjust Frequency to Yes
4. Run the Sample node and report the results.
5. Is there a balance in this new sample?

Exercise 4: Data sampling and partitioning for the *Passenger* dataset

1. Upload the *passengers* dataset to your server.
2. Open the dataset in SAS Enterprise Miner. Change the Role of *return* to Target, and change the Level to Binary.
3. Create a new diagram *Sampling*, and add the data source to the workspace.

4. Add a Sample node and connect it to the data source.
5. Sample 20% of the full dataset using two different sampling methods: (1) Random and (2) Stratified.
6. Run the Sample node and report the results.
7. Add a Data Partition node and connect it to the Sample node.
8. Partition the data using the split ratio 60–40: train sample: 60%; validation sample: 20%; test sample: 20%. Use the Simple Random method.
9. Run the Data Partition node and report the results.

Note: We will continue to use the *passenger* dataset in the next chapters. We will assume that the sampling and data partitioning are already completed. Refer to this exercise if you need to redo the sampling and data partitioning.

4

Data Visualization and Exploration

Introduction

In this chapter, we cover the second step in the SEMMA process, Explore. Data exploration is a vital step in data mining since we need to have a thorough understanding of the data focusing on the parameters, characteristics, trends, and potential concerns. This understanding allows us to take appropriate actions to clean, prepare, and transform the data as needed. It also allows us to select the right machine learning method and analytic configurations to develop a good predictive model.

In this step, we use visualization and descriptive statistics to explore and understand the data, variables, and any potential concerns with the data, such as missing values or

DOI: 10.1201/9781003162872-5

outliers. Visualization is a powerful tool for exploring data, and there are many visualization tools. I will demonstrate those tools with examples.

Data Understanding

Before conducting any data analysis, it is important to understand the data, its parameters, and its quality. The quality of the inputs determines the quality of the outputs. "Garbage in, garbage out." This step is necessary for any type of data analysis, but it is particularly important for data mining since we deal with large, noisy data. When we are given a large dataset with many variables and many records, it is challenging to get a big picture of the dataset, given the size of the data. Without a thorough understanding of the data, we may use invalid or irrelevant variables as predictors in the modeling step or neglect relevant variables. It could also be challenging to identify the right machine learning method without understanding the characteristics and limitations of the data. Moreover, we may also receive a poor model fit because the dataset has excessive missing values or outliers. Accordingly, we need to thoroughly explore the data, focusing on what type of information we have, what variables exist in the data, the measurement scales of those variables, and any trends in the data. As discussed in Chapter 2, the selection of a machine learning method depends on the data, the scale of the target variable, and the purpose of our project.

Data exploration is one of the most important steps in data mining as it allows us to see what data look like and any potential concerns with the data, based on which we can decide the necessary strategy for data modifications and transformations. We can only achieve a good predictive model with quality inputs. The model can only be as good as the data. Imagine you are an airport executive and need to know the probability of flight delays/cancellations at your airport at certain times of the day or certain days of the year. Suppose due to poor inputs, such as missing values or excessive noises, the predictive model produced an inaccurate prediction that the likelihood of delays or cancellation today is very low (false negatives). Hence, based on this poor prediction, you decided not to take any action and later observed the big chaos in your airport due to excessive flight cancellations. This situation could be diverted if you took some mitigation actions before it happened. Of course, the poor prediction could also be caused by other factors, but poor inputs are usually one primary cause. Remember, "Garbage in, garbage out." Table 4.1 highlights some key points on why data exploration is important in data mining.

There are two ways to explore the data, visualization and statistical exploration. Visualization allows us to view the data trends and patterns and collect useful information from data through different types of graphs. This method is easy to use and can be incorporated into a business intelligence dashboard for managers or executives. The patterns or trends can be very quickly observed with visualization. There are many visualization tools that are available in the market, such as Tableau, Power BI, and SAS Viya. These applications allow us to add and customize charts and graphs based on our needs. If we have big data, the data can be fed through the dashboard in real-time, and we can see the patterns of the variables of interest at different times or over time. These tools provide dynamic visualization tools that show up-to-date information. In this book, I mainly focus on some charts we could use to explore the data for analysis purposes. These charts are semi-dynamic since some chart tools allow us to rotate the charts and see them from different angles. They provide us with needed information that allows us to develop good

TABLE 4.1

Importance of Data Exploration in Data Mining Projects

Items	Importance of Data Exploration
Understanding data characteristics	Data exploration helps us gain insights into the characteristics of the dataset. It allows us to understand the data distribution, range, variability, and potential data quality issues. By exploring the data, we can identify outliers, missing values, data inconsistencies, or other anomalies that may impact the quality and validity of data.
Variable selection	Understanding the data allows us to identify relevant variables for the data mining task. By analyzing the relationships between variables, their distributions, and their potential impact on the target variable, we can make informed decisions about which variables to include or exclude in the modeling process.
Data preprocessing and cleaning	Data exploration is useful in identifying and addressing data quality issues. We can detect and handle missing values, outliers, duplicates, or inconsistent data. Data treatment tasks, such as imputation, outlier detection, or data transformation, can be performed based on the insights gained during the exploration phase. Effective data cleaning and preparation lead to improved model performance and more reliable results.
Identifying patterns and relationships	Exploring the data allows us to identify potential patterns, trends, or relationships between variables. By visualizing the data, applying statistical measures, or conducting exploratory data analysis techniques, we can uncover meaningful insights and understand the underlying structure of the data. These insights guide the selection of appropriate machine learning methods and help us improve the predictive power of the predictive model.
Requirements and limitations	By exploring the data, we can identify any violations of assumptions required by specific machine learning algorithms. This awareness enables us to make informed decisions about the suitability of certain techniques and avoid potential pitfalls or biases in the modeling process.
New discoveries	Data exploration can inspire the generation of new discoveries. By observing patterns or trends in the data, we may come up with new potential relationships to investigate further. These initial insights gained during exploration can guide subsequent modeling and analysis, leading to new discoveries and research directions.

predictive models. Essentially, data visualization is one step in the data mining process. More extensive data visualization tools can be discussed in another book.

For data mining purposes, visualization alone may not be enough. Statistics exploration can provide us with useful information in the form of quantitative outputs. They include descriptive statistics of variables, which allow us to understand the characteristics of the variables in the data. Additionally, statistics exploration also provides preliminary information regarding correlations between the target variable and predictors. Combining visualization with statistics gives us the best of both worlds. I will show you how to use both methods to explore and understand data.

> It is recommended to use both data visualization and statistical exploration.

Data Description

One important thing to remember in data exploration is that we cannot just jump in and build charts and graphs without knowing what variables we have in the data and their attributes. The reason is that we will not know what types of graphs to use and how to interpret the outputs. Hence, before we run any visualization, we need to first get some basic information about the dataset, especially the number of variables, variable descriptions, and variable scales. That information would help us decide what types of graphs we should use to make sense of the data.

In this chapter, I have used our example of the *airline recommendation* data to demonstrate various types of visualizations that we could use using SAS Enterprise Miner. First, let's look at the parameters and characteristics of this dataset.

Case Study – Airline Recommendation

In this case study, a large-scale survey was conducted with passengers from multiple airlines in the United States. Passengers flying a specific airline from one origin to another destination were asked to answer the survey about their flight experience and whether they would recommend that airline to others. They provided demographic information and their flight experience, including the origin and destination states, number of flights in the past, travel purposes, spending amount at the airport, and price sensitivity. The passenger survey data were consolidated with airline status and flight variables, including flight distance, flight time, departure and arrival delays, and flight cancellation. This project aims to predict the target variable, which is passengers' airline recommendations. We want to determine which model best predicts this target variable and which variables are important predictors. The prediction would help airline executives develop strategies to improve their operations and services and attract more passengers.

Due to the number of variables in the data, we must first look at the variables, their roles, and their scales. Table 4.2 describes the variable names, descriptions, and scales in this dataset.

TABLE 4.2

Data Description

Variable Name	Label/Description	Scale	Role
recommend	Recommend the airline to others	Binary (Yes/No)	Target
airline_st	Airline status	Nominal	Input
age	Age	Interval	Input
gender	Gender	Binary (Male/Female)	Input
price_sensitivity *	Price sensitivity	Interval	Input
no_years_flying	Number of years flying	Interval	Input
no_flt_pa	Average number of flights per year	Interval	Input
pct_ flt_other_airline	Percent of flights with other airlines	Interval	Input
type_of_travel	Travel purpose	Nominal	Input
no_other_lty_cards	Number of other loyalty cards	Interval	Input
shopping_amt_airpt	Shopping amount at the airport	Interval	Input
eat_drink_airpt	Spending for eating and drinking at the airport	Interval	Input
class	Passenger class	Nominal	Input
origin_state	Origin state	Nominal	Input
destin_state	Destination state	Nominal	Input
depart_delay_in_minutes	Departure delay (in minutes)	Interval	Input
arrival_delay_in_minutes	Arrival delay (in minutes)	Interval	Input
flt_cancel	Flight cancellation	Binary (Yes/No)	Input
flt_time	Flight time (in minutes)	Interval	Input
flt_distance	Flight distance (miles)	Interval	Input

* Likert scale, treated as interval scale

Variable names: Since variable names are used in actual analyses and results, they should be clear but concise. A variable name should be clear enough so we can recognize the variable. At the same time, it should also be brief so the name does not get cut off in the output. Many software applications set the length limit for variable names. I would highly recommend NOT using spaces or special characters (@#$%^&*) in variable names. The reason is that software like SAS Enterprise Miner does not allow

Variable name requirements:
- Make it clear and concise
- Keep it short
- Don't use special characters
- Don't use a blank space

spaces and special characters and will give us error messages if it detects these issues in variable names. It is the same requirements for programming software, such as R or Python. Some other software may be more flexible, but it will create more errors if we want to integrate our models with the Python platform. In order to separate words in the variable name, we should use an underscore (_) instead of a space.

Variable labels/descriptions: The details of the variable can be provided in the description. In some applications, it is called *labels*. The description or label is to provide users with a more detailed description of the variables. As you see in Table 4.2, the labels clearly explain each variable and also include the measurement units, such as years, minutes, or miles. The labels help users understand more clearly the variables since the variable names tend to be short or use acronyms. There are no limits to variable descriptions. Nonetheless, we should try to be clear and concise to avoid confusion or misleading. Software applications with user interface (UI), like SAS Enterprise Miner, SPSS Modeler, or Rapid Miner, usually allow us to choose to show the labels next to the variable names. Hence, we can always refer to the label to fully understand the variable in case the variable name is not clear enough. In addition, we can also choose to show the labels instead of variable names in the outputs for reporting purposes. In this case, lengthy labels may create issues with the reports since they could enlarge the output tables and make it hard to fit them in the report. In addition, the lengthy labels also create challenges for presenting graphs. Accordingly, we need to choose the labels carefully.

Scales: Scales for measuring variables are very important for our analysis, especially when we need to determine the appropriate machine learning algorithms to use in the modeling step. Chapter 2 describes in detail the different variable scales we have. Basically, they include nominal, binary, ordinal, or interval. As described in Table 4.2, there are one binary target variable, seven nominal/binary predictors, and eleven interval predictors. Note that *price_sensitivity* uses the Likert scale, and we assume that the gaps between levels are equal in this variable. Hence, we chose to treat it as an interval variable (see Chapter 2 for a more detailed discussion on the Likert scale).

Role: The last important piece of information is the role of the variable. Basically, there are two primary roles for variables: Target and Input. We need to identify which variable is the target variable (the one we want to predict) and which variables are inputs (also called predictors, which are the ones we use to make a prediction). In our example, *recommendation* is the target variable with a binary scale, while others are predictors. Additionally, there are some additional roles, including ID (an indicator variable), Time ID (a time identifier), Rejected (a variable that is excluded from the analysis), Text (a variable that contains the text of documents), and some others. For now, we mainly focus on the Target role and Input role.

Data Visualization

With big data that we collect every day, visualization is a powerful tool to review the data trends and patterns without looking into the raw data and some descriptive statistics with numbers. Data visualization is easy for users to view and understand the data even if they have no background in data analytics or statistics. In many industries, organizations develop business intelligence dashboards, which allow users to quickly choose the key variables or key performance indicators (KPIs) they want to view and generate the charts representing the data trends or patterns. Operators use these tools to monitor daily operational activities. Decision-makers use visualization to form strategies and make business decisions. Nonetheless, the importance is what to look for (KPIs or metrics) and how to interpret the outcomes.

Visual analytics applications such as Tableau, Spotfire, SAS Visual Analytics, and Microsoft Power BI offer many features for users. Regardless of the tools we use, they typically use several common types of charts for visualization. I will cover some common chart types, how to create them, and how to interpret the results. I will show you how to create charts using SAS Enterprise Miner. However, note that you could use other tools that you feel comfortable with to explore the data. As mentioned before, in this book, data visualization is just one step in the SEMMA process. Hence, we will use those charts in a semi-dynamic mode rather than a full dynamic mode as you usually see in an intelligent dashboard.

I will use two primary visualization tools in SAS Enterprise Miner: Graph Explorer node and MultiPlot node. They are both listed under the Explore Tab on the top menu bar since data visualization is the Explore step in the SEMMA process.

SAS ENTERPRISE MINER GUIDELINES

Graph Explorer and MultiPlot Nodes
(https://documentation.sas.com)

GRAPH EXPLORER NODE

The Graph Explore node is an advanced visualization tool that enables you to explore large volumes of data graphically to uncover patterns and trends and reveal extreme values in the database. The node creates a run-time sample of the input data source. You use the Graph Explore node to interactively explore and analyze your data using graphs. Your exploratory graphs are persisted when the Graph Explore Results window is closed. When you re-open the Graph Explore Results window, the persisted graphs are re-created.

You can analyze univariate distributions, investigate multivariate distributions, create scatter and box plots, constellation and 3D charts, and so on. If the Graph Explore node follows a node that exports a data set in the process flow, then it uses either a sample (default) or the entire data set as input. The resulting plot is fully interactive – you can rotate a chart to different angles and move it anywhere on the screen to obtain different perspectives on the data. You can also probe the data by positioning the cursor over a particular bar within the chart. A text window displays the values that correspond to that bar. You can also use the node downstream in the process flow to perform tasks, such as creating a chart of the predicted values from a model developed with one of the modeling nodes.

MULTIPLOT NODE

With MultiPlot you can graphically explore large volumes of data, observe data distributions, and examine relationships among the variables. MultiPlot reveals extreme values in the data and helps you discover patterns and trends. The MultiPlot node creates the charts of each input grouped by the target variable.

- Bar Charts:
  - Histogram of each input and target.
  - Bar chart of each input versus each class target.
  - Bar chart of each input grouped by each interval target.
- Scatter Plots:
  - Plot of each interval input versus the target.
  - Plot of each class input versus the target.

You can annotate the interval input by interval target scatter plots with a regression line and 90% confidence intervals for the mean.

The Results window contains several tool icons for managing the graphs, shown below. You can select a graph from a list of all graphs, manually navigate through all the graphs, or automatically scroll through all the graphs. The drop-down menu, displaying **age** in the image below, enables you to select the variable that you want to graph.

The Graph Explorer or MultiPlot node must be connected to a predecessor node that exports one or more data sets, such as the Input Data, Data Partition, or Regression nodes.

Bar Charts and Histograms

Bar charts and histograms are the most common graphical tools used in data visualization. They both present the results using bars, either vertically or horizontally. So, what are the differences between them? Table 4.3 summarizes some key differences between these two graphical tools. Bar charts are suitable for categorical variables, while histograms are used for continuous variables. We will get into the details of these chart types and learn when to use which ones.

TABLE 4.3

Differences between Bar Charts and Histograms

Items	Bar Charts	Histograms
Data type	Bar charts are used to display categorical data. The categories or groups are displayed on the x-axis, while the height or length of the bars represents the frequencies or percentages associated with each category.	Histograms are suitable for continuous data. The data is divided into intervals or bins, and the height of the bars represents the frequency of data points falling within each interval.
X-axis representation	In a bar chart, the x-axis represents discrete categories or groups. Each category is usually represented by a separate bar.	In a histogram, the x-axis represents the range of values or intervals for the continuous variable being measured. The intervals are continuous and adjacent, forming a continuous scale.
Data presentation	Bar charts are effective for comparing data across different categories. They show distinct categories and compare their frequencies.	Histograms display the distribution of values within a continuous variable. They provide insights into the shape, central tendency, and spread of the data.
Bar placement	In a bar chart, the bars are usually separated from each other with gaps to emphasize the distinction between categories.	In a histogram, the bars are typically placed adjacent to each other without gaps since the intervals are continuous and form a continuous scale.
Axis labels	Bar charts use a label for each category on the x-axis to indicate a specific group or category.	Histograms use labels on both the x-axis and y-axis. The x-axis label represents the measured variable, while the y-axis label represents the frequency of data points within each interval.

Bar Charts

Basically, bar charts are used for categorical variables and present the frequency or percentage for each category or each level. It is fairly simple to understand and interpret. Note that percentage works better for comparison purposes, while the frequency can show us the number of cases in each category.

I use the Graph Explorer node to create bar charts for our *airline recommendation* dataset. Note that this approach allows us to choose and customize the charts as we want, but we have to create one chart at a time. There is a way to create charts for all variables in the dataset much quicker. I will show you that approach later.

> Bar charts are used for categorical variables.
>
> Histograms are used for interval variables.

Follow the steps below in SAS Enterprise Miner.

1. Open the project AirlineProject.

2. Create a new Diagram and name it Explore.

3. From the Explore tab, drag a Graph Explorer node to the workspace and connect it to the data source node.

4. Run the Graph Explorer node.

5. Open Results.
6. Select the Plot icon 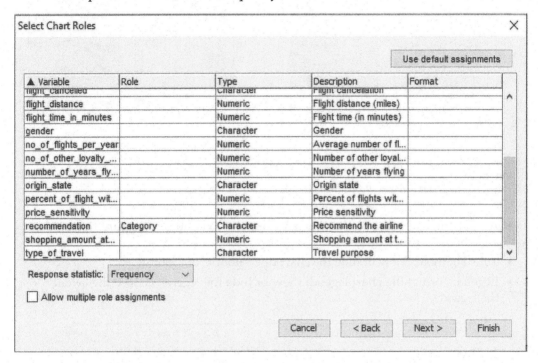 or go to View/Plot.
7. Select Bar, and click Next.
8. Select the variable *recommendation*, and change Role to Category.
9. For Response statistics, select Frequency.

Select Chart Roles ✕

Use default assignments

▲ Variable	Role	Type	Description	Format
flight_cancelled		Character	Flight cancellation	
flight_distance		Numeric	Flight distance (miles)	
flight_time_in_minutes		Numeric	Flight time (in minutes)	
gender		Character	Gender	
no_of_flights_per_year		Numeric	Average number of fl...	
no_of_other_loyalty_...		Numeric	Number of other loyal...	
number_of_years_fly...		Numeric	Number of years flying	
origin_state		Character	Origin state	
percent_of_flight_wit...		Numeric	Percent of flights wit...	
price_sensitivity		Numeric	Price sensitivity	
recommendation	Category	Character	Recommend the airline	
shopping_amount_at...		Numeric	Shopping amount at t...	
type_of_travel		Character	Travel purpose	

Response statistic: Frequency ⌄

☐ Allow multiple role assignments

Cancel   < Back   Next >   Finish

10. Click Next three times.
11. Click Finish. The bar chart will be generated. This bar chart shows the frequency. To show the percentage, you just need to select Percentage in Step 9.

Figure 4.1 shows the bar charts for the target variable, *recommendation,* in both frequency and percentage. Note that in these charts, the label is used instead of the variable name. That is why you see *Recommend the airline* instead of *recommendation*. Since the target variable is a binary variable (Yes/No), the charts show the frequencies and percentages of those two levels. As we can see, 52.7% of passengers recommend the airline, while 47.3% do not recommend it.

Graph Formatting

In order to change the graph properties, such as colors, format, title, axes, values, or legends, we use Graph Properties. Simply right-click anywhere on the chart and select Graph Properties. A new window opens and allows us to configure the chart. Basically, you can change the following.

- Graph: Select the chart style with different backgrounds and color tones.
- Bar: Change the color options for the bars in the bar chart; set the bar width; display the bar index (for levels of the variable); show the response statistics in the bar.

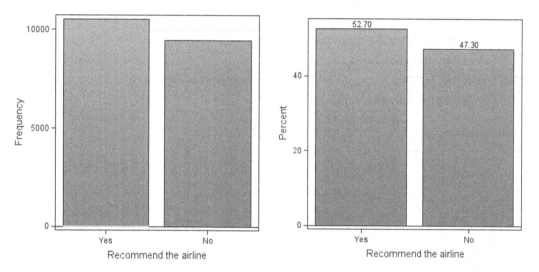

FIGURE 4.1
Bar charts for the target variable "Recommend the airline".

- Axes: Format vertical and horizontal axes; add axis titles; configure tick marks; and choose the axis range.
- Title/Footnote: Show or hide the chart title, subtitle, or footnote.
- Legend: Format the chart legend; show or hide the legend; choose the layout for the legend.

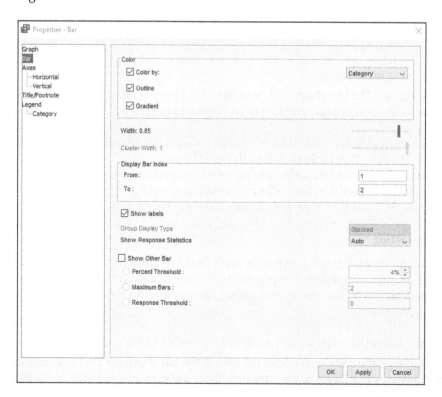

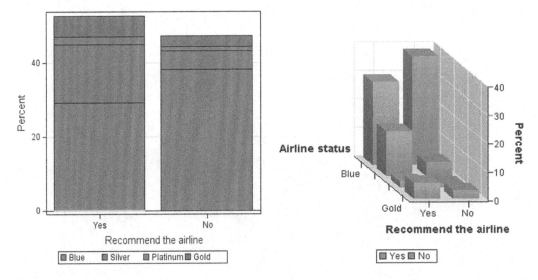

FIGURE 4.2
2D and 3D bar charts for two variables.

2D or 3D Bar Charts for Two Variables

If we want to graph two categorical variables and how they are related, we could use either a 2D bar chart or a 3D bar chart. For example, we want to see the airline recommendation by passengers' airline status.

To create a bar chart for two variables:

- Follow the same steps in the previous section.
- For 2D bar chart: In Step 8, change the Role to Category for *recommendation* and select Group for *airline_status*.
- For 3D bar chart: In Step 8, change the Role to Category for *recommendation* and select *Series* for *airline_status*.

Figure 4.2 shows the 2D and 3D bar charts for two variables: *recommendation* and *airline_status*. As you can see, those bar charts break down the percentage of the target variable by categories of the airline status. In this case, the 3D bar chart presents the data at a 3-dimensional angle, which is easier to compare across categories. We can interpret that among passengers recommending the airline, the majority are Blue class (30%), followed by Silver class (15%). However, a lot more passengers with Blue memberships do not recommend the airline (40%), while only about 5% of Silver passengers do not recommend that airline. In other words, the Blue class passengers are more likely not to recommend the airline, while the Silver passengers are more likely to recommend the airline.

Histograms

For continuous variables, bar charts may not be the best choice. Given the continuous scale, we receive very large and noisy charts, which are spread out across the x-axis. For example, Figure 4.3 shows a bar chart for age. While we still can see the distribution of

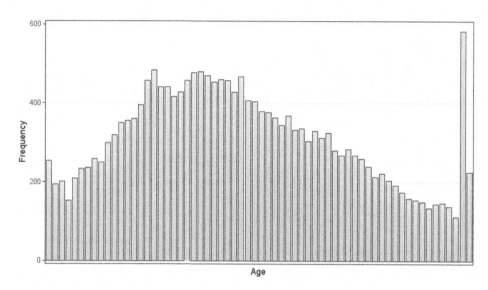

FIGURE 4.3
Bar chart for age.

age, it is harder to make any interpretation of the age ranges since age is interval, and the age years are spread out across the x-axis. More specifically, it has 63 bars of each age year.

Another example is a bar chart for the departure delay time in minutes (Figure 4.4). This bar chart uses 309 bars in total, which makes it very hard to see the data trend. Basically, it is meaningless and does not give us the information we need. Hence, we must find a different way to present this type of data.

FIGURE 4.4
Bar chart for departure delay in minutes.

For continuous variables, histograms are a better choice. Basically, histograms present the frequency distribution of continuous variables. A histogram divides the values into bins and calculates the frequency for each bin. Each bar in the histogram shows the frequency for that bin. Note that in histograms, there are no gaps between bars, given the continuous scale of the variable. Technically, we can identify the bins for histograms ourselves, but it will be a time-consuming process. We just need to specify the number of bins we need, and the software can automatically divide data into bins and construct the histogram.

For example, we want to create a histogram for age. Follow the steps below in SAS Enterprise Miner.

1. Run the Graph Explorer node.
2. Open Results.
3. Select the Plot icon 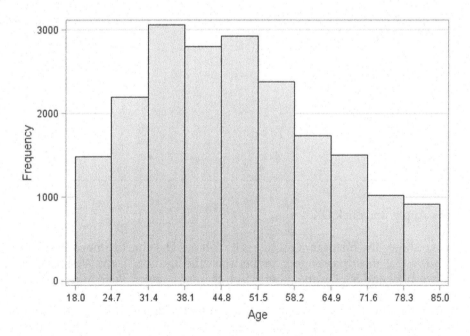 or go to View/Plot.
4. Select Histogram, and click Next.
5. Select the variable Age, and change Role to X.
6. Choose Frequency for Response statistic.
7. Click Next three times, and click Finish. The histogram chart will be generated.

Note that the above steps create a histogram with 10 bins, which are automatically decided by the software (Figure 4.5). As we can see, the chart shows the frequency for each range of age. It does give us an idea about the age distribution, which is close enough to a normal distribution.

FIGURE 4.5
Histogram for age with 10 bins.

Suppose we want a histogram for age with 5 bins to make the age chart easier to interpret. How do we change the number of bins?

In order to do so, follow the steps below.

1. Right-click on the chart and select Graph Properties.
2. In the Properties window, make the following changes:
   - Change the number of X bins to 5.
   - Check the box Ends Labels.

3. Click Apply, and click OK.

Figure 4.6 shows the histogram for age with 5 bins. The chart is much easier to follow now. It shows that most passengers are between the ages of 31 and 49, followed by the range between 49 and 58. On the other hand, there are fewer older passengers between 72 and 85 years.

We follow the same process to create a diagram for the departure delay time. But in this case, we choose to present the percentage instead of frequency. So in Step 6 of the process described on page 109, we change the Response statistic to Percent. As shown in Figure 4.7, the histogram shows the departure delay time is very right-skewed with missing values *(note: to*

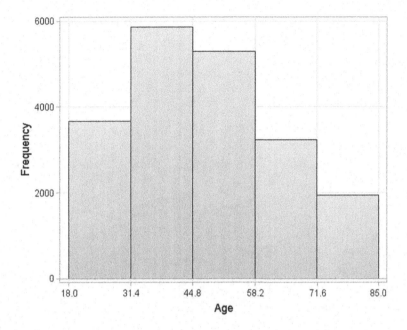

FIGURE 4.6
Histogram for age with 5 bins.

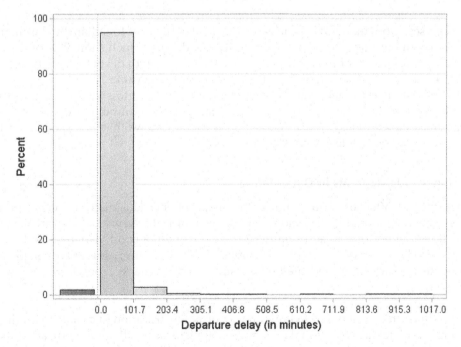

FIGURE 4.7
Histogram for departure delay with 10 bins.

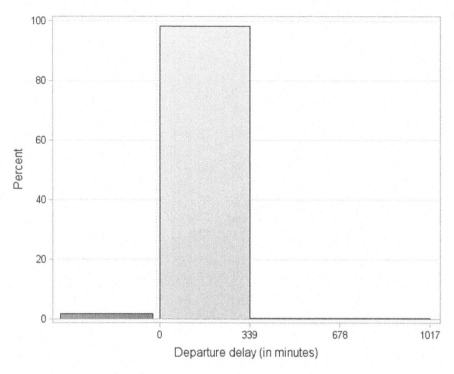

FIGURE 4.8
Histogram for departure delay with 3 bins.

show missing values in the histogram, check the box Showing Missing Bin in the Graph Properties).
As we can see, more than 90% of the cases have delay times of less than 101.7 minutes. If
we move our mouse over the chart, we will see the details, which show 95% of the cases
with delay times less than 101.7 minutes, followed by 2.6% with delay times between 101.7
and 203.4 minutes. In addition, 1.7% of the cases are missing values.

Since the data is extremely right-skewed, suppose we want to show a histogram with
only 3 bins to further examine the trend. By changing the number of bins, we have the
histogram as shown in Figure 4.8. In this case, the result shows that 98% of the cases have
departure delay times of less than 339 minutes.

Importance of Histograms in Data Mining

Histograms are often used to evaluate the shape of the data distributions, especially
whether they are normal distributions, left-skewed, or right-skewed. They can also show
us any potential outliers. In addition to providing us with a good visualization tool, histograms also have some important implications in data mining, especially in supervised
learning using statistics-based methods. I summarize some key points regarding this
chart as follows.

- The linear regression method requires a normal distribution to be able to produce
  a good model fit. The normal distribution appears as a bell curve, indicating that
  the data points are symmetric around the mean. It means data near the mean are
  more frequent in occurrence than data far from the mean.

- If a histogram shows skewed data, either left or right, we will need to consider transforming efforts to normalize the data.

- Histograms can show us outliers. Extensive outliers indicate noise in the dataset, and it may affect the predictive power of our model. By examining the extent of outliers, we can decide to keep them or remove cases with extreme outliers.

Box Plots

In addition to histograms, we have another graphical tool that allows us to indicate the skewness of the data and potential outliers. It is the box plot, also called the whisker plot. The box plot is a graph depicting the five-number summary of the dataset, which consists of the minimum, lower quartile (Q1), median, upper quartile (Q3), and maximum. In addition, the box plot indicates which observations, if any, are considered outliers.

Figure 4.9 presents two box plots related to the airline status. The first one shows the age distribution by airline status. As we can see, the median and the interquartile range (the box) are close enough to the center, indicating the symmetry of the data. The interquartile range (the box) seems consistent across four airline statuses. We only notice one outlier for the Silver passenger (the data point outside of the whisker).

The second plot shows the distribution of the flight number per year by airline status. The plot shows that the data are quite skewed. You may notice that the medium and the box are very off-center, indicating the asymmetry of the data. The box for Blue passengers is a little bigger than other statuses, showing the difference in the variance of the data. Finally, we can see that in all four statuses, there are multiple outliers.

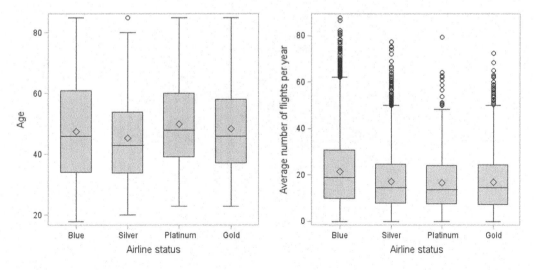

FIGURE 4.9
Box plots for age and average number of flights per year by airline status.

In order to create a box plot, follow the steps below.

1. Run the Graph Explorer node.
2. Open Results.
3. Select the Plot icon 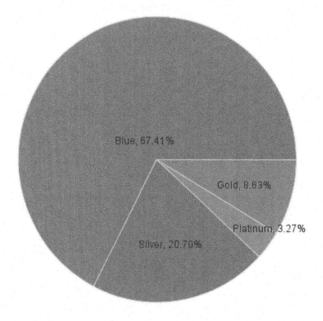 or go to View/Plot.
4. Select Box, choose the first icon, and click Next.
5. Select the variable *airline_status*, and change Role to X.
6. Select the variable *age*, and change Role to Y.
7. Click Finish. The box plot will be generated.

Pie Charts

If we want to present data for categorical variables as percentages, pie charts are a good choice since they provide us with the proportion of each category as a slide of a pie. It is visually easy to understand and interpret. For example, Figure 4.10 shows a pie chart presenting the percentage of the passenger airline status. The pie chart shows that 67% of passengers are Blue passengers, followed by Silver passengers (20.7%), Gold (8.63%), and Platinum (3.27%). Note that for pie charts, the total percentage must be 100% for it to make sense.

In order to create a pie chart, follow the steps below.

1. Run the Graph Explorer node.
2. Open Results.
3. Select the Plot icon or go to View/Plot.

FIGURE 4.10
Pie chart for airline status.

4. Select Pie, and click Next.

5. Select variable airline_status, and change Role to Category.

6. Choose Percent for Response statistic.

7. Click Next three times.

8. Click Finish. The pie chart will be generated.

Line Charts – Trend Analysis

When we have data collected over time, we would want to see the trend of the events or incidents. In this case, line charts are a good choice. Essentially, a line chart produces a line plot that connects a series of data points using a line. This chart type presents sequential values to help us identify trends. The x-axis represents a sequential progression of values.

For example, Figure 4.11 shows the trend of domestic and international flights from January 1, 2020, until March 1, 2022. As we can see in early 2020, when the COVID-19 pandemic hit us, the number of flights reduced significantly in both cases. As we move toward the end of 2021, when vaccination was provided nationwide, the travel demand increased, leading to more daily flights. The demand continues to increase in 2022, and we see more flights in the first half of 2022. Using the line charts allows us to examine the trend of the data over time, examine the changes in the events or incidents, and observe the noise in the data as well. In this example, I put two variables in the same chart for comparison. International flights are obviously lower than domestic flights, and there is less fluctuation in the data over time.

Note that line charts require two variables, one for the X axis, and another one for the Y axis. In this example, time is the X axis, and the number of flights (domestic and international) is the Y axis.

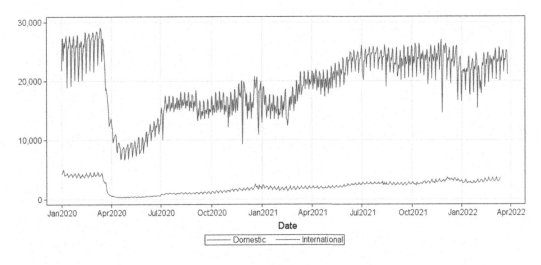

FIGURE 4.11
Line chart for domestic and international flights over time.

For the *airline recommendation* dataset, since the data are not presented by date or year, the application of a line chart is limited to the types of variables we have. I will show you two examples of line charts with this dataset.

Line Chart for Shopping Amount by Age

In order to create a line chart, follow the steps below.

1. Run the Graph Explorer node.
2. Open Results.
3. Select the Plot icon 🪣 or go to View/Plot.
4. Select Line, choose the second icon 〽, and click Next.
5. Select the variable *age*, and change Role to Category.
6. Select the variable *shopping_amount_at_airport*, and change Role to Responses.
7. Choose Sum for Response statistic.
8. Click Finish. The line chart will be generated.

The chart is shown in Figure 4.12. This line chart plots the values of y against each value of x and connects them with a line. This figure shows that passengers between 34 and 50 years old spend the most money on shopping at airports. Younger passengers and passengers older than 70 years tend to spend less. However, we can also notice a spike in shopping amounts for passengers 80 years old.

Line Chart for Flight Time against Flight Distance

In a second example, we use the line chart to graph the correlation between flight time (in minutes) and flight distance (miles). In order to create a line chart, follow the steps below.

1. Run the Graph Explorer node.
2. Open Results.
3. Select the Plot icon 🪣 or go to View/Plot.

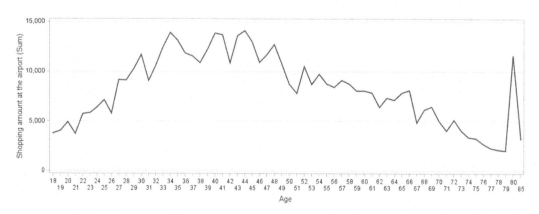

FIGURE 4.12
Line chart for the shopping amount by age.

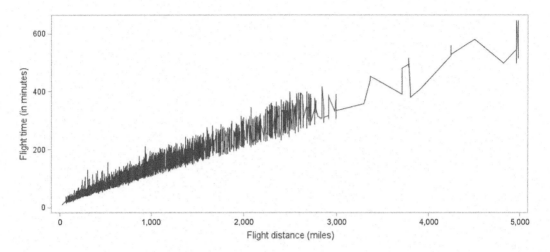

FIGURE 4.13
Line chart for flight time against flight distance.

4. Select Line, choose the first icon , and click Next.
5. Select the variable *flight_distance*, and change Role to X.
6. Select the variable *flight_time_in_minutes*, and change Role to Y.
7. Click Finish. The line chart will be generated.

Figure 4.13 shows this line chart. As you can see, the trend is linear and positive, meaning the longer the distance, the longer the flight, which makes sense. What is interesting is that there is a lot of noise in the data for fights under 300 miles, while the noise is much less from 3,000 miles above. That means for a flight distance of 3,000 miles or shorter, the flight time fluctuates for some reason.

Density Plots and Scatter Plots

When we plot one variable against another variable, there are two other graphical tools that may work very well. They are density plots and scatter plots. Both of them have options for two-dimensional distributions of data points. Density plots use small dots with different levels of opacity to capture data points to ensure the smoothness of the visual. It is useful to show the density of the data in different regions or ranges. On the other hand, scatter plots use bigger markers to plot data points. It shows how scattered the data points are.

For example, we want to explore the relationship between departure delay time and arrival delay time. I use both density and scatter plots for this purpose. As presented in Figures 4.14 and 4.15, both charts show the same information. Arrival delay time has a positive correlation with departure delay time. Essentially, when a flight takes off later, it will arrive late. The charts show that this correlation is stronger with delay times of 400 minutes or less based on the density of the data. You may notice the smoothness of the visualization in the density plot in comparison to the scattered data points in the scatter plot.

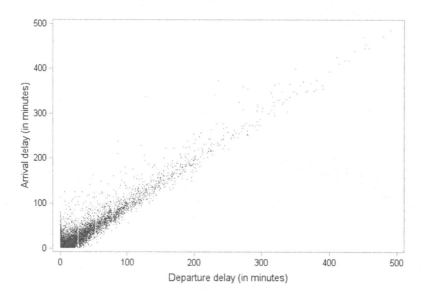

FIGURE 4.14
Density plot for arrival delay time against departure delay time.

In order to create a density plot or a scatter plot, follow the steps below.

1. Run the Graph Explorer node.
2. Open Results.
3. Select the Plot icon 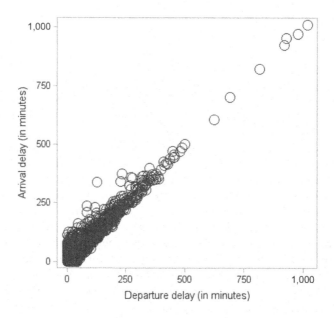 or go to View/Plot.

FIGURE 4.15
Scatter plot for arrival delay time against departure delay time.

4. For the Density plot: Select Density, choose the third icon 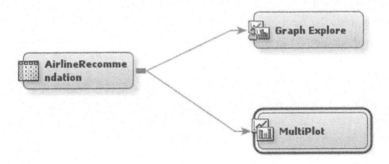, and click Next.
5. For the Scatter plot: Select Scatter, choose the first icon, and click Next.
6. Select the variable *departure_delay_in_minutes*, and change Role to X.
7. Select the variable *arrival_delay_in_minutes*, and change Role to Y.
8. Click Finish. The density chart will be generated.

MultiPlots

The graphic tools above are some typical ones we can use to explore the data. But as you can see, in those cases, we must create each graph manually. If we deal with big data (many variables and data points), how do we quickly generate multiple charts for exploratory purposes? SAS Enterprise Miner has a tool for just that purpose, MultiPlot.

The MultiPlot node serves as a valuable tool for visualizing data from various angles. Utilizing MultiPlot enables you to visually explore extensive datasets, observe data distributions, and analyze relationships between variables. MultiPlot also aids in identifying outliers within the data and uncovering underlying patterns and trends.

The MultiPlot node creates the following types of charts.

Bar Charts:

- Histograms for each input and target.
- Bar charts illustrating the relationship between each input and each class target.
- Bar charts displaying each input grouped according to each interval target.

Scatter Plots:

- Scatter plots depicting the relationship between each interval input and the target.
- Scatter plots illustrating the relationship between each class input and the target.

Follow the steps below in SAS Enterprise Miner to create MultiPlots.

1. Open the diagram Explore.
2. From the Explore tab, drag a MultiPlot node to the workspace and connect it to the data source node

3. In the property panel, make the following changes.
   - Set Type of Charts to Both to use bar charts and scatter charts.
   - Set Graph Orientation to Vertical.
   - Set Statistic to Percent.

General		
Node ID	Plot	
Imported Data		...
Exported Data		...
Notes		...
Train		
Variables		...
Type of Charts	Both	
⊟ Bar Chart Options		
├ Graph Orientation	Vertical	
├ Include Missing Values	Yes	
├ Interval Target Charts	Mean	
├ Show Values	Yes	
├ Statistic	Percent	
└ Numeric Threshold	20	
⊟ Scatter Options		
├ Confidence Interval	Yes	
├ Regression Equation	Yes	
└ Regression Type	Linear	

4. Run the MultiPlot node.
5. Open Results window.

The results of this node include a window that shows us all created graphs (bar charts and scatter plots) with all combinations, and we can move forward and backward to see the graph we want to investigate (Figure 4.16). We can also zoom in or out as desired. This tool can be used to explore large data in a meaningful way.

At the bottom of the Graphs window, the following buttons are displayed and can be used to move between charts.

- **First** – Displays the first graph.
- **Previous** – Displays the previous graph.
- **Play** – Starts an automatic slide show of all the plots.
- **Next** – Displays the next graph.
- **Last** – Displays the last graph.

> Note: If you only want the bar charts and histograms of all variables without connection to the target variable, then you will have to go back to the data source and change the role of the target variable to Input. In this case, SAS Enterprise Miner will generate charts for single individual variables.

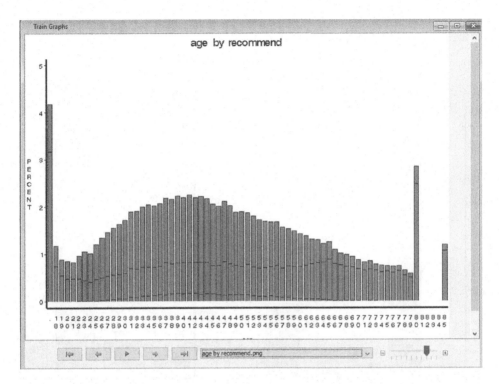

FIGURE 4.16
MultiPlot node results.

Figure 4.17 presents two bar charts extracted from the MultiPlot graph window. The first one shows the airline recommendation by airline status. We can see the differences in airline recommendation among Bule, Silver, Gold, and Platinum passengers. The second one shows the airline recommendation by class, business, eco plus, or eco.

Quick Chart Explorer

One question you may have is: What if we want to view the distributions of variables in the dataset all at once to examine their distributions and missing values? Instead of creating those charts manually one by one, as shown before, there is a way in SAS Enterprise Miner to generate all these charts at once.

Follow the steps below in SAS Enterprise Miner.

1. Open the diagram Explore.
2. Right-click on the data source, AirlineRecommendation, and select Edit Variables.
3. Highlight all variables using your mouse and select Explore. The Explore Results window will open.
4. Expand the Sample Properties window and make the following changes.
   - Set Sample method to Random.
   - Set Fetch size to Max to use the maximum data points allowed.
5. Click Apply.

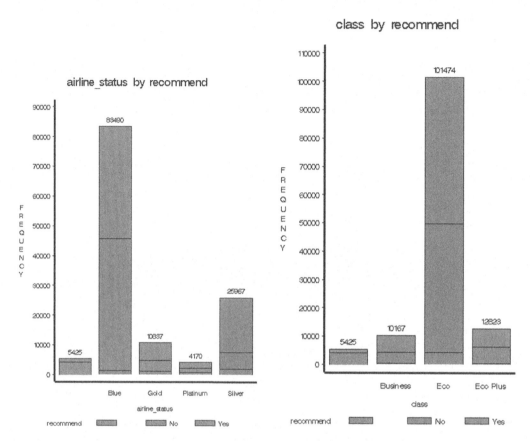

FIGURE 4.17
Airline status and passenger class against airline recommendation.

SAS Enterprise Miner produces the histograms and bar charts for all variables for a maximum of 20,000 rows, which are randomly sampled from the dataset. It is a very effective way to view the distributions of all variables all at once. Figure 4.18 shows the results of those multi charts for our *airline recommendation* dataset. We can see all histograms and bar charts for our variables in multiple windows. Expand each window to see the detailed chart for that variable. Remember that bar charts are for categorical variables, while histograms are for interval variables.

Statistics Exploration

Data visualization provides us with numerous graphical tools to visualize data trends and patterns. In order to select the appropriate machine learning method and determine the right configurations for predictive modeling, we also need to explore the statistics of

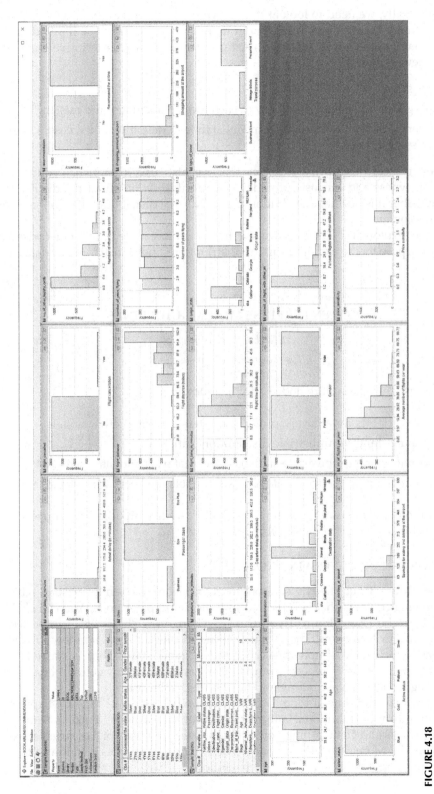

FIGURE 4.18
Results of the quick chart explorer.

our data. Basically, we need to look at the descriptive statistics of all variables to understand their characteristics and determine if there are any concerns or if any data transformation may be needed in the Modify step. Some primary descriptive statistics we want to review include.

- Sample size.
- For categorical variables: frequency of each level, percentage, and missing values.
- For interval variables: min, max, mean, standard deviation, skewness, kurtosis, and missing values.

These are typical descriptive statistics that we also use in statistics courses. As a reminder, skewness and kurtosis provide us with information about the distribution of data and whether it is normal distribution or not. Normal distribution is necessary for the linear regression method.

For statistics exploration purposes, we use the StatExplore node in SAS Enterprise Miner. It is a multipurpose tool to examine variable distributions and statistics in our datasets.

SAS ENTERPRISE MINER GUIDELINES

StatExplore Node
(https://documentation.sas.com)

We can use the StatExplore node to do the following:

- Select variables for analysis, profiling clusters, and predictive models.
- Compute standard univariate distribution statistics.
- Compute standard bivariate statistics by class target and class segment.
- Compute correlation statistics for interval variables by interval input and target.

We can combine the functions of the StatExplore node with other Enterprise Miner node functions to perform data-mining tasks.

STATEXPLORE NODE TRAIN PROPERTIES

- **Variables** – Click the ellipsis icon (three-dot icon) to open a variables table showing the data that is imported into the StatExplore node. You can click cells in the Use column if you want to change the status of an imported variable to **No** or **Yes**. The Default setting in the Variables window for the StatExplore node simply preserves the variable status that is passed to StatExplore by the predecessor node. You can click on any column heading to toggle between ascending and descending table sorts.

  You can select one or more variable rows in the table and click the Explore button to view additional information about the variables, such as Sample Properties and Details, tables of variable values, and plots of the variable distribution. More detailed information on exploring variables is in the section on the StatExplore node's Variables window.

STATEXPLORE NODE TRAIN PROPERTIES: DATA

- **Number of observations** – Specifies the number of observations to use for generating various reports. When **ALL** is selected, the entire data set is used. When a number n is specified, the first n observations are used.
- **Validation** – Specify **Yes** if you want summary and association statistics to be generated for the validation data set.
- **Test** – Specify **Yes** if you want summary and association statistics to be generated for the test data set.

STATEXPLORE NODE TRAIN PROPERTIES: STANDARD REPORTS

- **Interval distributions** – Specify **Yes** if you want to generate distribution reports for interval variables. These reports include overall summary statistics of all selected interval input variables and across all levels of class target variables. They also include the Interval Variable plots that display the scaled mean deviations across all levels of the class target variables.
- **Class distributions** – Specify **Yes** if you want to generate distribution reports for class variables. These reports include summary statistics of all segment, target, and selected class input variables, plus summary statistics across all levels of class target variables. The reports include the Class Variables plots that display the distribution selected class variables for all levels of the class target variables. The reports also include the Chi-Square plot that identifies the selected variables that are most highly associated with the class target variables.
- **Level summary** – Specify **Yes** if you want to generate the level summary report. The level summary report displays the number of distinct levels for ID, segment, and class target variables.
- **Use Segment Variables** – Set the Use Segment Variables property to **Yes** if you want to generate summary and association statistics for all segment variables in the data set that you submitted to the StatExplore node. The default setting for the Segment Variables property is **No**.
- **Cross-tabulation** – Click the ellipsis icon to open a dialog box that enables you to specify the cross-tabulation variables.

STATEXPLORE NODE TRAIN PROPERTIES: CHI-SQUARE STATISTICS

- **Chi-Square** – Set the Chi-Square property to **No** if you want to suppress the generation of Chi-Square statistics for the data set that you submitted to the StatExplore Node. The default setting for the Chi-Square property is **Yes**.
- **Interval Variables** – set the Interval Variables property of the StatExplore node to **Yes** if you want to generate Chi-Square statistics for the interval variables by binning the variables. If you set the Interval Variables property to **Yes**, you must specify N, the number of bins with the Number of Bins property. The default setting for the Interval Variables property is **No**.

- **Number of Bins**—When you set the StatExplore node Interval Variables property to **Yes**, you must use the Number of Bins property to specify N, the number of bins that you want to generate for the interval variables in your data set. The StatExplore node uses the binned values to calculate Chi-Square statistics for the interval variables in your data set. Permissible values for the Number of Bins property are integers ranging from 2 to 10. The default value is 5.

STATEXPLORE NODE TRAIN PROPERTIES: CORRELATION STATISTICS

- **Correlations** – Set the Correlations property to **No** if you want to suppress the generation of correlation statistics for the data set that you submitted to the StatExplore node. The default setting for the Correlations property is **Yes**.

- **Pearson correlations** – Set the Pearson correlations property to **No** if you want to suppress the generation of Pearson correlation statistics for the data set that you submitted to the StatExplore node. The default setting for the Pearson property is **Yes**.

- **Spearman correlations** – Set the Spearman property to **Yes** if you want to generate Spearman correlation statistics for the data set that you submitted to the StatExplore node. The default setting for the Spearman property is **No**.

Example: Statistics Exploration

We will use the StatExplore node to explore our *airline recommendation* dataset. Follow the steps below.

1. Open the diagram Explore.
2. From the Explore tab, drag a StatExplore node to the workspace and connect it to the data source node.

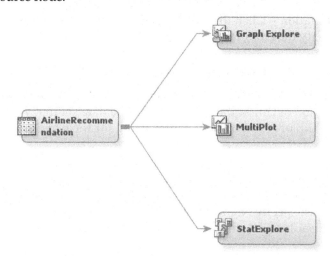

3. In the Train properties, make the following changes.
   - Set Interval Distributions to YES
   - Set Class Distributions to YES
4. Run the StatExplore node and open the Results window.

Descriptive Statistics Results

The StatExplore node produces multiple results. Tables 4.4–4.6 present the summary statistics of the target variable, categorical variables, and interval variables, respectively. I summarize some key findings as follows.

- The frequency and percentage of two levels of the target variable show a relatively balanced dataset, in which 52.46% of the data are Yes (recommend) and 47.54% are No (not recommend).
- Missing values: There are no missing values in categorical variables. For interval variables, there are missing values for three variables: *arrival delay time, departure delay time,* and *flight time.* Other interval variables do not seem to have missing values. However, if we look deeply into the *price sensitivity* variable, we notice something unusual. This variable has a minimum value of zero. However, since price sensitivity is Likert scale, it should not have a value of 0 (a 5-point Likert scale has a range from 1 to 5). Hence, the zero values indicate missing values. We will need to recode this value as a missing value. We will discuss how to handle missing values in Chapter 5.

TABLE 4.4

Target Variable Statistics

Variable Name	Role	Level	Frequency	Percent
recommendation	Target	Yes	65,297	52.46%
recommendation	Target	No	59,167	47.54%

TABLE 4.5

Descriptive Statistics for Categorical Variables

Variable Name	Role	Number of Levels	Missing	Mode 1	Mode 1 Percentage	Mode 2	Mode 2 Percentage
airline_status	INPUT	4	0	Blue	67.08	Silver	20.86
class	INPUT	3	0	Eco	81.53	Eco Plus	10.3
destination_state	INPUT	52	0	California	12.74	Texas	12.41
flight_cancelled	INPUT	2	0	No	98.19	Yes	1.81
gender	INPUT	2	0	Female	56.8	Male	43.2
origin_state	INPUT	52	0	California	12.87	Texas	12.61
type_of_travel	INPUT	3	0	Business travel	62.56	Personal Travel	30.14
recommendation	TARGET	2	0	Yes	52.46	No	47.54

TABLE 4.6

Descriptive Statistics for Interval Variables

Variable	Mean	Standard Deviation	Non Missing	Missing	Min	Median	Max	Skewness	Kurtosis
age	47.5	16.50	124,464	0	18	46	85	0.316	−0.711
arrival_delay_in_minutes	15.38	38.84	121,899	2565	0	0	1,584	6.663	95.221
departure_delay_in_ minutes	15.00	38.45	122,263	2201	0	0	1,592	6.817	100.767
eating_and_drinking_at_ airport	68.84	52.60	124,464	0	0	60	895	1.997	9.948
flight_distance	793.87	592.10	124,464	0	31	630	4,983	1.510	2.778
flight_time_in_minutes	111.51	71.77	121,899	2565	8	92	669	1.484	2.688
no_of_flights_per_year	20.09	14.40	124,464	0	0	17.36	100	0.851	0.468
no_of_other_loyalty_cards	0.84	1.12	124,464	0	0	0	12	1.357	1.867
number_of_years_flying	6.78	2.98	124,464	0	2	7	11	−0.072	−1.291
percent_of_flight_with_ other_air	9.44	8.87	124,464	0	1	7	110	2.346	7.625
price_sensitivity	1.27	0.54	124,464	0	0	1	5	0.783	1.189
shopping_amount_at_ airport	26.87	53.16	124,464	0	0	0	879	3.309	15.935

- Descriptive statistics for categorical variables: Table 4.5 presents variable name, role, number of levels, mode 1, mode 1 percentage, mode 2, and mode 2 percentage. Due to the space limitation, the table does not provide the mode and percentage beyond level 2. As you can see, most variables have two levels (binary). There are two levels with three levels, and two variables with 52 levels (they represent 52 U.S. states). These results provide us with information about each level of the variable. For example, Blue passengers account for 67.08% of total passengers, while Eco class accounts for 81.53% of total passengers.

- Descriptive statistics for interval variables: Table 4.6 presents variable name, min, max, mean, median, standard deviation, skewness, and kurtosis values. These are typical descriptive statistics results we have from most statistics software applications. We can notice that only several variables have distributions close to normal, with the skewness and kurtosis values close to zero. They include *age, number of flights per year, number of loyalty cards, price sensitivity,* and *number of years flying. Flight distance* and *flight time* are not normal but close enough. On the other hand, other variables have high skewness and kurtosis values, indicating that their distributions are skewed and far from normal. Depending on the machine learning methods we choose to use for modeling, we can decide if data normalization and transformation are needed.

Chi-Square and Variable Worth Plots

The StatExplore Results window also produces two charts that are very useful for exploration purposes.

- A Chi-Square plot that orders the top categorical variables by their Chi-Square statistics measuring their association with the target variable (Figure 4.19).
- A variable worth plot that orders the top variables by their worth in predicting the target variable (Figure 4.20).

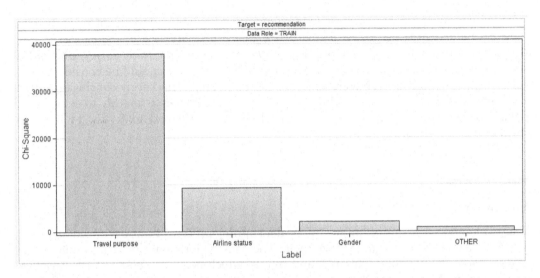

FIGURE 4.19
Chi-Square plot.

Note that the Chi-Square plot is only for categorical variables, while the variable worth plot includes all variables. SAS Enterprise Miner calculates variable worth using the worth statistics based on the decision tree method. We will get into the details of the decision tree method later in Chapter 8.

Both charts give us a preliminary idea of what variables may play an important role in predicting the target variable, the airline recommendation. The Chi-Square plot indicates

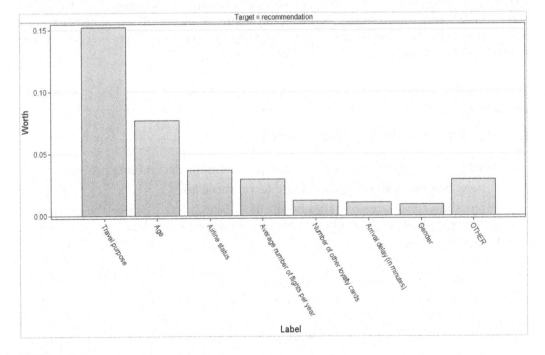

FIGURE 4.20
Variable worth plot.

travel purpose, airline status, and *gender* are important variables. The variable worth plot indicates *travel purpose, age, airline status, average number of flights per year,* and *number of other loyalty cards* are among important predictors. We should note that *travel purpose* and *airline status* show up as the top variables in both charts. Hence, they should be considered the preliminary top predictors. Nonetheless, we should not try to make any conclusion at this time since these are just some preliminary results, and this step is mainly to explore the data. In order to build a good predictive model, there is more work to do, and I will get to them in the next chapters.

Summary

Data exploration is an important step in the data mining process because we need to understand the data before we can analyze them. The data exploration provides us with information about the variables, patterns, and trends, which helps us decide which variables and which methods to use in the modeling step. We cover two methods of data exploration, visualization and descriptive statistics. Visualization is a popular method to explore large data because the outputs are easy to understand and follow. We can use multiple types of graphs to create data visualization, including bar charts, histograms, box plots, pie charts, line charts, density plots, scatter plots, and multiplot. SAS Enterprise Miner has dynamic visual features that allow us to move and review charts from different angles. The MultiPlot tool creates charts for all variables and also enables users to move between charts or start a slide show. In addition to visualization, we also need to review descriptive statisics, which show us statistical information on all variables, such as frequency, missing values, min, max, standard deviation, skewness, and kurtotis. Additionally, Chi-Square and variable worth plots identify potential important predictors. These statistics results help us decide the next step in the data mining process, specifically whether we need to impute missing values or transform the data.

CHAPTER DISCUSSION QUESTIONS

1. What is data exploration and why is it important in the data mining process?
2. Differentiate between categorical and interval variables.
3. Discuss the advantages of data visualization. Search and describe the primary software applications that provide visualization tools for big data.
4. What is the main difference between bar charts and histograms? When should we use histograms?
5. Describe the purpose of box plots. Give some examples.
6. Give examples of how pie charts and line charts are used to explore data trends and patterns.
7. What is MultiPlot? What are the applications of MultiPlot features in the industry?
8. Describe the primary descriptive statistics for interval variables. How do we use descriptive statistics to improve data mining?

Exercises

Exercise 1: Graph Explore for the *Bank* dataset

1. View the variable description of the *bank* dataset (see Appendix A.1).
2. Open the *bank* dataset in SAS Enterprise Miner.
3. Create a new diagram Explore, and add the data source to the workspace.
4. Add a Graph Explore node to the workspace and connect it to the data source.
5. We are interested in plotting the following pair of variables against each other. Select the right graph types to create the graphs for those variables. Explain the results.
   - *Income* vs. *Age*
   - *Saving balance* vs. *Credit card balance*
   - *IRA balance* vs. *Age*
   - *Line of credit balance* vs. *Income*
   - *Credit card purchase* vs. *Mortgage*
6. Use the Multiplot tool to create charts for all variables. Run the chart slideshow and explain the results.

Exercise 2: Graph Explore and MutiPlot for the *Passengers* dataset

1. View the variable description of the *passengers* dataset (see Appendix A.2).
2. Open the *passengers* dataset in SAS Enterprise Miner.
3. Create a new diagram Explore, and add the data source to the workspace.
4. Add a Graph Explore node to the workspace and connect it to the data source.
5. Create histograms for all interval variables. Report and explain the results regarding the distributions of those variables.
6. Create bar charts for all binary and nominal variables. Report and explain the results.
7. Identify variables with missing values.
8. Add a MultiPlot to the workspace and connect it to the data source.
9. Create MultiPlot charts using *return* as the category. Run the slideshow of all charts. Explain the results.
10. Create MultiPlot charts using *customer type* as the category. Run the slideshow of all charts. Explain the results.

Exercise 3: Stat Explore for the *Passengers* dataset

1. Open the *passengers* dataset in SAS Enterprise Miner.
2. Open the diagram Explore.
3. Add a StatExplore to the workspace and connect it to the data source.
4. Run the StatExplore node and present descriptive statistics results for all variables. Identify variables with missing values. Report the number of missing values.
5. Explain the descriptive statistics results. Identify any issues or concerns with the data. (Note: Variables using the Likert scale should not have zero values. Hence, zero values for those variables must be re-coded as missing values.)

Exercise 4: Graph Explore for the *Boston* dataset

1. View the variable description of the *boston* dataset (see Appendix A.3).
2. Open the *boston* dataset in SAS Enterprise Miner.
3. Create a new diagram Explore, and add the data source to the workspace.
4. Add a Graph Explore node to the workspace and connect it to the data source.
5. Create histograms for five variables: *Imv, AgePre40, CrimePC, and Tax*. Explain the results regarding the distributions of those variables.
6. Create a scatter plot for *LogDistance* against *Imv*. Explain the results. Create a density plot for the two variables. Compare the results.
7. Use the quick graph explorer approach to create histograms for all variables at once.

Exercise 5: Graph Explore for the *Try Buy* dataset

1. Open the *try_buy* dataset in SAS Enterprise Miner.
2. Create a new diagram Explore, and add the data source to the workspace.
3. Add a Graph Explore node to the workspace and connect it to the data source.
4. Create a 2D bar chart and a 3D bar chart for *BuyReturn* against *Promotion Type*. Explain the results.
5. Create pie charts for *Promotion Type* and *Market Seg*ment. Explain the results.

Exercise 6: MultiPlot for the *Cardiac* dataset

1. Open the *cardiac* dataset in SAS Enterprise Miner.
2. Create a new diagram Explore, and add the data source to the workspace.
3. Add a MultiPlot node to the workspace and connect it to the data source.
4. Create three box plots for *Age, Height,* and *Weight* using *BodyType* as the category. Explain the results.
5. Create MultiPlot charts using *BodyType* as the category. Run the slideshow of all charts. Explain the results.

Exercise 7: StatExplore for the *Boston* dataset

1. Open the *boston* dataset in SAS Enterprise Miner.
2. Create a new diagram Explore, and add the data source to the workspace.
3. Add a StatExplore node to the workspace and connect it to the data source.
4. Run the StatExplore node and present descriptive statistics results for all variables. Are there any missing values? Evaluate the normality of the data based on skewness and kurtosis values.
5. Create histograms for all variables. Evaluate the distributions and compare them with the descriptive statistics results in Step 4.
6. Create the variable worth plot. Evaluate the important predictors based on this plot.

5

Data Modification

LEARNING OUTCOMES

Upon the completion of this chapter, you will be able to

1. Explain the important role of data modification in the data mining process.
2. Provide examples of when data modification is needed.
3. Explain the advantages and disadvantages of data modification techniques.
4. Compare replacement, imputation, and transformation techniques in data modification.
5. Select the appropriate data modification techniques.
6. Evaluate various replacement methods and their applications.
7. Perform data replacement using SAS Enterprise Miner.
8. Evaluate various imputation methods and their applications.
9. Perform data imputation using SAS Enterprise Miner.
10. Evaluate various normalization methods and their applications.
11. Evaluate various discretization methods and their applications.
12. Perform data normalization and discretization using SAS Enterprise Miner.

Introduction

In the previous chapter, we discussed how to use data visualization to present the patterns and trends of the data. Additionally, descriptive statistics results also provide us with the detailed characteristics of each variable. Hence, we are able to evaluate the information we have in the data and the information that is missing. We can also identify any incorrect information, noise in the data, and any other concerns that may affect the modeling process. What if we find issues with the data? The simple answer is that any concerns with the quality of the data must be addressed before the modeling step.

This chapter focuses on the next step in the SEMMA process, Modify. More

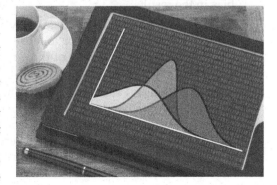

specifically, we will cover the reasons why data modification is important and the techniques we can use to prepare and modify the data. Primary topics include replacement, imputation, and transformation. I will show you how to perform data modification using SAS Enterprise Miner. Remember, our predictive models can only be as good as the data we use to train them. Preparing and transforming data allow us to address any data quality concerns and produce an effective and accurate predictive model.

Importance of Data Modification

Data modification, also known as data preprocessing, is a critical step in machine learning that involves preparing and transforming the raw data to make it suitable for training our predictive models. The goal of data modification is to improve the quality and relevance of the data, which enables us to perform more robust model training. As a result, we can achieve more accurate and useful predictive models.

> **DEFINITION**
>
> Data modification involves preparing and transforming the raw data to make it suitable for training our predictive models.

There are many reasons why data modification is important in data mining. Following are some key points.

1. Data quality improvement: Data modification techniques, such as data cleaning and replacement, help improve the quality of the dataset. By identifying and correcting errors, inconsistencies, and missing values, we can enhance the data quality. High-quality data is essential for valid and reliable predictive modeling, as it reduces the risk of misleading or invalid results. Remember, "garbage in, garbage out."

2. Noise reduction: Raw data often contains noise or irrelevant information that can negatively impact the accuracy of the predictive model. By using techniques like outlier detection and data replacement, we can effectively reduce the impact of noisy data points, leading to reliable and valid models.

3. Handling missing data: In real-world datasets, missing data is a common issue due to the data collection process. Imputation techniques help address missing data by filling the gaps with estimated values. Proper handling of missing data ensures that valuable information is not lost during the analysis and minimizes bias in the results.

4. Variable selection and dimensionality reduction: These techniques help identify the relevant variables for analysis. Removing irrelevant or redundant variables reduces the complexity of the data, enhances computational efficiency, and improves model performance by focusing on the most informative parameters.

5. Normalization and standardization: These techniques ensure that different variables are on a comparable scale. It is particularly useful when applying algorithms that are sensitive to the scale of the data. Normalizing and standardizing the data enable fair comparisons and prevent certain features from dominating the analysis. For certain machine learning algorithms, normalized and standardized data can improve the model fit.

6. Handling heterogeneous data: In many cases, data from different sources or in different formats need to be combined for analysis. Data modification techniques such as data integration and aggregation allow for harmonizing heterogeneous data. This integration provides a more comprehensive view of the problem, facilitates analysis, and enables the discovery of valuable patterns that may be hidden within individual datasets.

7. Preparing data for specific algorithms: Different machine learning algorithms have specific requirements and assumptions about the input data. Data modification helps prepare the data to meet these requirements. For example, discretization may be necessary for algorithms that require categorical inputs, while normalization is an important assumption for the multiple regression method.

Overall, data modification is vital in data mining as it helps ensure the accuracy, reliability, and efficiency of predictive modeling. By enhancing data quality, reducing noise, handling missing data, selecting relevant features, and preparing the data for specific algorithms, data modification techniques allow us to produce an effective and accurate predictive model.

Data Modification Techniques

There are many different techniques that can be used to modify data. They can be grouped into three primary categories, as follows.

- Data cleaning: Data cleaning is the process of identifying and correcting errors in the data. It can be done by identifying and removing duplicate data, correcting typos, and filling in missing data.
- Data transformation: Data transformation is the process of changing the format or structure of the data. Several transformation practices we can do include converting categorical data to numerical data, normalizing the data, and aggregating the data.
- Data reduction: Data reduction involves reducing the size of the data without losing important information. We can use techniques for tasks such as dimensionality reduction, variable selection, and sampling.

Data modification is an essential part of data mining. It is a complex process that requires careful planning and execution. However, the benefits of data modification can be significant, including improved accuracy, efficiency, and interpretability of data mining results. When we perform data modification, there are several important things we need to consider, as follows.

- Use a variety of techniques: There is no single technique that is best for all data sets. It is important to use a variety of techniques to ensure that the data is properly modified.
- Be careful not to overfit the data: Overfitting occurs when the data modification process is too aggressive and the data no longer represents the target population. It can lead to inaccurate data mining results.

- Test the results: It is important to test the results of the data modification process to ensure that they are accurate and useful. Cross-validation is a useful technique for this purpose.

In this chapter, I do not cover all data modification techniques. The sampling and resampling techniques have been covered in-depth in Chapter 3. Additionally, the dimension reduction methods will be covered later in Chapters 12 and 13, when we discuss unsupervised methods, including principal component analysis and cluster analysis. This chapter is focused on the common techniques in data modification, including data cleaning and transformation. More specifically, we cover three primary techniques: replacement, imputation, and transformation. I will explain their differences and when we should use which technique. I find these techniques easy to use and very useful in most projects. These techniques are available in SAS Enterprise Miner, so we will go over some specific examples of how to implement them using this software.

In this chapter, we focus on three primary data modification techniques: replacement, imputation, and transformation.

Replacement, Imputation, and Transformation

As mentioned above, in this book, we cover three primary data modification techniques available in SAS Enterprise Miner: replacement, impute, and transformation. These techniques are provided as separate nodes in the Modify group. Table 5.1 summarizes the differences between them and when they should be used.

- **Replacement node:** The replacement technique allows us to clean the data by re-coding or correcting data to ensure the accuracy of the analysis. In data mining fields, replacement is often considered a part of data transformation. In this book, we separate replacement from transformation to avoid confusion since we

TABLE 5.1

Replacement, Imputation, and Transformation

	Replacement	Imputation	Transformation
What does it do?	Recode, correct, or reassign values for categorical or interval variables in the data.	Replace missing values in datasets with estimated values.	Create new variables that are transformations of existing variables in datasets or create interaction variables. It can be used to standardize and normalize data, convert data, or aggregate data.
When to use this tool?	Replacement node should precede the Impute node.	Impute node should precede the Transformation node.	Transformation node should precede the machine learning algorithm node in the Model step.

need to use replacement to clean the data or reassign values before handling missing values and transforming variables. The Replacement node should precede the Imputation node so we have the correct information and codes for missing values.

- **Impute node**: Imputation is a common technique to handle missing values. When we have missing values, our first instinct is to remove them. However, the removal of missing values may result in losing important information and even potentially increase bias in the data. Hence, researchers tend to choose to fill missing values with estimated values. The challenge is to determine the appropriate imputation method to ensure the quality of the data and avoid causing bias. The Imputation node should precede the Transformation node so we have all the data points for the transformation.

- **Transformation node**: This technique enables us to change the format or structure of the data to meet the requirements for data analysis. We can use it to convert data, normalize data, or aggregate data. Some machine learning algorithms work better with standardized and normalized data, such as linear regression. In this case, when the data distribution of a certain variable is not normal, we can use this technique to convert the data to normally distributed data. Additionally, in some other cases, we may want to convert a continuous variable to a categorical variable or aggregate two variables into one variable for analysis purposes. The Transformation node allows us to perform these tasks without any difficulties. The Transformation node should precede the machine learning algorithm node in the Model step to ensure that we have the necessary data to train the model.

Advantages and Disadvantages of Data Modification

Data modification is an important step in the data mining process with many benefits. However, there are some challenges we may have to face when applying these techniques. In this section, we discuss the primary advantages and disadvantages of data modification.

Advantages

1. Improved data quality: Data cleaning enhances the quality and reliability of the dataset. They improve data quality by addressing errors, inconsistencies, and missing values, which leads to more accurate and reliable results.

2. Enhanced model performance: Dimensionality reduction and data transformation are useful techniques to identify the most relevant and informative variables for model training. These techniques allow us to reduce irrelevant or redundant features and create new meaningful variables, which improves the model performance, resulting in better predictive accuracy and generalization.

3. Handling missing data: Data imputation ensures that valuable information is not lost during analysis, reducing potential bias, and improving the representativeness of the data.

4. Efficient computation: Techniques like dimensionality reduction and data sampling can significantly reduce the computational complexity of the analysis. They help reduce the number of variables or the size of the dataset, which significantly reduces the training time of machine learning models.

5. Addressing data imbalance: Data sampling techniques, including oversampling and undersampling, help address the data imbalance issue where one class is significantly underrepresented. By rebalancing the class distribution, model performance on minority classes can be improved, leading to more accurate predictions.

Disadvantages

1. Information loss: Changing data can result in information loss since removing certain variables or reducing the dimensionality of the data may discard valuable information that could have been useful for the analysis.

2. Overfitting risks: Oversampling can introduce synthetic or duplicated instances, which may lead to overfitting. Overfitting occurs when a model performs well on the training data but fails to generalize to new, unseen data.

3. Subjectivity and bias: Data modification often involves making subjective decisions about how to handle missing values, outliers, or feature selection. If not done correctly, these decisions could introduce bias into the analysis, potentially impacting the validity of the results.

4. Increased complexity: Data modification techniques add complexity to the data preprocessing stage, requiring additional time and effort. Selecting appropriate techniques and optimizing their parameters can be challenging, especially for large and complex datasets.

5. Sensitivity to assumptions: Some data modification techniques, such as imputation or transformation, rely on certain assumptions about the data distribution or relationships. If these assumptions are violated, the modified data may not accurately represent the underlying patterns, leading to biased results.

It is important to carefully consider the advantages and disadvantages of data modification techniques in the context of the specific project and dataset. The choice of techniques should be guided by the study purpose, requirements, and limitations of the analysis, as well as a thorough understanding of the data characteristics.

Replacement

As mentioned before, replacement is a useful data modification technique for data cleaning. We can use this technique to remove incorrect information or correct errors in the dataset by reassigning values to certain variables to ensure the accuracy of the data. SAS Enterprise Miner has a dedicated node for this tool. I outline below some typical scenarios, in which we must use the Replacement node to clean the data.

- **Remove incorrect information**: We tend to assume that collected data are always correct. However, you may be surprised that datasets often include errors due to flaws in data collection instruments, data collection processes, or misentered information by participants. We can detect those errors in the Explore step by reviewing data using visualization and descriptive statistics of variables, as described in Chapter 4. For example, when exploring the age data using a histogram, we notice there are some cases with an age of zero. Obviously, these are incorrect information since age cannot be zero. Similarly, we may see cases with ages under 18 years even though the data description clearly indicated that only adults were surveyed. There are several reasons for these situations. First, the age information was entered incorrectly by the participants, making it unusable for analysis. Second, it was a missing value (the participant decided to keep it blank) and was coded as zero by the software or the survey instrument. In either case, we should treat those values as missing values but not zero to avoid misanalyzing data. Using the Replacement node, we can remove the incorrect information, and the software will treat these values as missing data.

> **DEFINITION**
>
> Replacement is a process of recoding, correcting, or reassigning values in the datasets to ensure all information is correct.

- **Correct errors**: In some cases, when the incorrection information is obvious, we can make corrections in the dataset. For example, when exploring the income information using a histogram, we found several cases with negative salaries. Let's say that after examining the survey forms, we found that it is possible that the salary was entered incorrectly as a negative value when it should be positive. This incorrect information can lead to incorrect prediction in the modeling step. In this case, we can use the Replacement node to correct the error by removing the negative sign. Another example is some typos showing up in categorical variables, creating several new levels and causing misinformation. For example, the job title "Manaer" should be treated the same as "Manager" due to the typo, but the software thought they were two different classes. Using the Replacement node, we can make the correction for this data.

- **Reassign values**: One common application of the Replacement node is to reassign missing values. You may be surprised to find that data providers code missing values very differently, depending on the way they collect data or the standards they use to archive the data. I have seen missing values coded as blank, zero, or 99. As default, SAS Enterprise Miner codes a missing value with a dot (.). Hence, if we notice missing values coded differently, we need to reassign those values with (.) to make sure the software detects missing values correctly. In some cases, when we have extreme outliers, we do not want to use them in the analysis since it may cause bias in modeling, but we do not want to remove the entire data row. In this case, we can also replace these outliers with missing values.

These are some examples to show when the Replacement node can be used in data mining. Depending on the issues you run into in your project, you should be able to leverage this tool to clean your data. I will demonstrate some examples using SAS Enterprise Miner.

SAS ENTERPRISE MINER GUIDELINES

Replacement Node Train Properties
(https://documentation.sas.com)

REPLACEMENT NODE TRAIN PROPERTIES: INTERVAL VARIABLES

- **Replacement Editor** – Click the ellipsis button ⬚ to open the Interactive Replacement Interval Filter Window for the associated data set.

  The interactive window is especially useful if you want to specify different limits methods for individual variables instead of applying the default limits method to all interval variables. You can use the Interactive Replacement Interval Filter table to filter an interval variable for a single value by setting both the Upper Limit and Lower Limit columns for that variable to the desired variable value.

- **Default Limits Method**

  - **Mean Absolute Deviation (MAD)** – The Mean Absolute Deviation method eliminates values that are more than n deviations from the median. You specify the threshold value for the number of deviations, n, in the Cutoff for MAD property.

  - **User-Specified Limits** – The User-Specified Limits method specifies a filter for observations that are based on the interval values that are displayed in the Lower Limit and Upper Limit columns of your data table. You specify these limits in the Interactive Replacement Interval Filter window.

  - **Metadata Limits** – Metadata Limits are the lower and upper limit attributes that you can specify when you create a data source or when you are modifying the Variables table of an Input Data node on the diagram workspace.

  - **Extreme Percentiles** – The Extreme Percentiles method filters values that are in the top and bottom p-th percentiles of an interval variable's distribution. You specify the upper and lower threshold value for p in the Cutoff Percentiles for Extreme Percentiles property.

  - **Modal Center** – The Modal Center method eliminates values that are more than n spacings from the modal center. You specify the threshold value for the number of spacings, n, in the Cutoff for Modal Center property.

  - **Standard Deviations from the Mean** – (Default) The Standard Deviations from the Mean method filter values that are greater than or equal to n standard deviations from the mean. You must use the Cutoff for Standard Deviation property to specify the threshold value that you want to use for n.

  - **None** – Do not filter interval variables.

SAS ENTERPRISE MINER GUIDELINES
Replacement Node Train Properties
(https://documentation.sas.com)

REPLACEMENT NODE TRAIN PROPERTIES: CLASS VARIABLES

- **Replacement Editor** – Use the Interactive Class Variables Replacement Editor Window to specify new values for specific class levels of variables in the data imported to the Replacement node.

  Click the ellipsis button [...] to open the Replacement Editor window for the associated data set. The Replacement Editor is a table that lists the levels of all class variables. The level "_UNKNOWN_" enables you to specify a replacement value to use at scoring time when encountering levels not in the training data. The Replacement Editor contains read-only columns for Variable (name), Level, Frequency, Type (character, numeric), Character Raw Value, and Numeric Raw Value. The Replacement Value column can be edited.

- **Unknown Levels** – Use the Unknown Levels property to specify the way that unknown levels for a variable should be handled during scoring. Unknown levels are levels that do not occur in the training data set.

The Unknown Levels property has the following options:

- **Ignore** – Variable observations that contain unknown levels are not modified. This is the default setting.
- **Missing Value** – Variable observations that contain unknown levels are replaced with SAS missing value notations.
- **Mode** – Variable observations that contain unknown levels are replaced by the most frequent class level, or mode.

Imputation for Missing Values

In data mining, missing values refer to the absence or lack of data for certain variables or observations in a dataset. Missing values can occur due to various reasons, such as data entry errors, incomplete data collection, or intentional omission by the data source. Missing values can be represented in different ways depending on the dataset format and context:

- Blank or empty cells: In most datasets, missing values are often denoted by blank or empty cells. These cells have no value or information recorded for the corresponding variable and observation.

- Null or NA values: Some datasets use specific codes or markers, such as "null" or "NA," to indicate missing values. These codes are typically assigned to indicate the absence of data for a particular variable or observation.
- Placeholder values: In certain cases, missing values may be represented using specific placeholder values that are distinct from the valid values of the variable. For example, using "–1" or "9999" to denote missing values in a numeric variable. SAS Enterprise Miner uses "." To indicate missing values.

Handling missing values is an essential step in data mining, as it can create biases in the data and impact the quality and validity of the results. Following are some typical cases showing the impacts of missing values in data mining.

DEFINITION

Missing values refer to the absence or lack of data for certain variables or observations in a dataset.

1. Bias in data analysis: When missing values are present in a dataset, excluding or ignoring these observations can lead to biased results. If the missing values are not handled properly, the remaining data may not accurately represent the population, leading to inaccurate predictions and ungeneralized models.

2. Reduced sample size: Missing values can reduce the effective sample size needed for data mining. It results in decreased statistical power and may affect the performance of machine learning algorithms, especially those that rely on large amounts of data to learn meaningful patterns.

3. Distorted relationships: Missing values can introduce distortion or bias in the relationships between variables. Correlations and patterns within the data may be influenced by the absence of data points, leading to incorrect interpretations of the underlying relationships. This issue can impact the performance of predictive models, as they rely on accurate relationships between features.

4. Algorithm compatibility: Some machine learning algorithms, such as linear regression, cannot directly handle missing values. Other algorithms expect complete data as input and may fail to train the model or produce incorrect results if missing values are present.

5. Loss of information: Missing values represent lost information, such as relevant variables in the data. Depending on the extent and pattern of missing data, valuable information may be lost, potentially leading to decreased predictive accuracy.

To mitigate these issues, it is essential to apply appropriate techniques for handling missing values, such as imputation (replacing missing values with estimated values) or exclusion (removing observations or variables with excessive missingness). The choice of technique depends on the specific dataset, the nature of missing data, and the project purpose. Removing missing values can be done using the Replacement node. The challenge is to decide whether the removal would lead to any server issues in predictive modeling. I will focus on imputation, the most common strategy in handling missing values.

Basically, imputation is a process of estimating or filling in missing values in a dataset with estimated values. It is a technique used to handle data with missing values, ensuring that the dataset is complete before conducting further analysis. There are many methods of imputation. When we decide on the imputation method, there are some important considerations as follows.

DEFINITION

Imputation is a process of estimating or filling in missing values in a dataset with estimated values.

- The choice of imputation method should be guided by the characteristics of the dataset, the nature of the missing data, and the purpose of the analysis. Different methods have different assumptions and may lead to varying results.
- Imputation introduces uncertainty into the dataset since the filled-in values are estimated based on available data. It is important to account for this uncertainty when performing subsequent modeling.
- Imputation should be performed cautiously, as it may introduce bias if the missing data is not completely random. It means there may be some specific reasons behind missing data, making them systematic missing data instead of random missing data. It is essential to understand the reasons for missing data and consider potential biases in the imputed values.
- It is a good practice to document the imputation process, including the method used and any assumptions made, to ensure transparency and replicability of the analysis.

Overall, imputation is a widely used technique in data modification to handle missing values and ensure completeness in the dataset. The choice of imputation method should be carefully considered based on the characteristics of the missing data and the purpose of the analysis. It is important to understand the limitations and potential biases associated with imputation. Table 5.2 presents some common imputation methods and their characteristics. For each method, I include a brief description, assumptions, how the imputed value is calculated, and when we can use this method. You don't have to worry about calculating those values since

Some machine learning methods, such as decision trees or neural networks, can handle missing values very well in training the model. In those cases, imputation is not needed since it may introduce biass into the data, distort the real data distribution, and make it more difficult to detect real patterns.

the software takes care of this task automatically. But we need to know when to use which method. Note that these methods are mainly used for interval variables since they require quantitative calculations. The imputation methods for categorical variables are limited due to their non-metric nature.

TABLE 5.2

Common Imputation Methods

Imputation Methods	Description	When to Use
Mean	It replaces missing values with the mean of the available values. It assumes that the missing values are similar to the average of the observed values. *Imputed value = Mean (available data)*	*For interval variables.* It is a good choice for data sets that are normally distributed and that contain a small number of missing values.
Median	It replaces missing values with the median of the available values. It is less sensitive to outliers compared to mean imputation. *Imputed value = Median (available data)*	*For interval and ordinal variables.* It is a good choice for data sets that are not normally distributed (skewed) and that contain a small number of missing values. It is also a good choice for ordinal data.
Mid-range	It replaces the missing values with the midpoint between the minimum and maximum values of the available data for that variable. The midrange is a rough measure of central tendency. *Imputed value = (max + min)/2*	*For interval variables.* It is a good choice for normally distributed datasets.
Distribution	It uses the distribution of the data to fill in missing values. This method is based on the assumption that the missing values are randomly distributed and that they can be estimated from the values of the observed data. The estimated values are determined based on the probability distribution of the non-missing observations.	*For interval and categorical variables.* It is a good choice if missing values are randomly distributed. This method typically does not change the distribution of the data very much.
Tree-based	Also known as predictive mean matching, it uses decision trees to impute missing values in a dataset. It is particularly useful for imputing missing values in variables with both continuous and categorical data types. Since the imputed value for each input variable relies on the values of other input variables, this method of imputation could potentially offer greater accuracy compared to a straightforward replacement of missing tree values with the variable's mean or median.	*For interval and categorical variables.* This method should be used for nonlinear relationships or multiple imputations (when multiple imputed datasets are created).
Tree imputation with surrogate split	It is an extension of tree-based imputation that incorporates surrogate variables when imputing missing values. Surrogate splits are additional split rules created in decision trees to handle missing values in predictor variables.	*For interval and categorical variables.* This method is a good choice if we have a high rate of missing values, complex dependencies, or interaction effects among predictors.

(Continued)

TABLE 5.2 *(Continued)*

Common Imputation Methods

Imputation Methods	Description	When to Use
Mid-minimum spacing	It uses the median and the minimum value of the observed data to impute missing values. It specifies the proportion of the data to be contained in the spacing. It assumes that the missing values would fall within the range defined by the adjacent minimum values. There are two steps in calculating this statistic: (1) trim the data using N percent of the data (e.g. 10%); (2) the mid-minimum spacing value is calculated as the maximum plus the minimum (of the trimmed data) divided by two. *Imputed value = [max(trimmed data) + min(trimmed data)]/2* 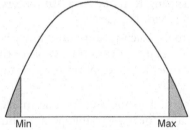 Min　　　　　Max	*For interval variables.* It is useful when the minimum values in a time series have meaningful significance or represent some kind of lower limit.
Robust M-estimators of location	Robust M-estimators of location are statistical estimators used to estimate the central location or location parameters of a. They are less sensitive to outliers. There are three primary M-estimators: (1) Turkey's Biweight; (2) Huber; (3) Andrew's Wave. 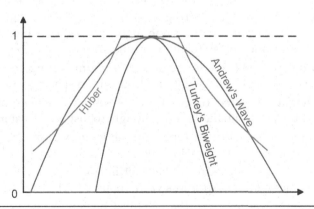	*For interval variables.* They are particularly useful when dealing with datasets that contain outliers or data points that deviate significantly from the majority of the data.

SAS ENTERPRISE MINER GUIDELINES

Impute Node Train Properties

(https://documentation.sas.com)

IMPUTE NODE TRAIN PROPERTIES: INTERVAL VARIABLES

Default Input/Target Method – Use the Method Interval property of the Impute node to specify the imputation statistic that you want to use to replace missing interval variables. The choices are:

- **Mean** – Use the Mean setting to replace missing interval variable values with the arithmetic average, calculated as the sum of all values divided by the number of observations.
- **Maximum** – Use the Maximum setting to replace missing interval variable values with the maximum value for the variable.
- **Minimum** – Use the Minimum setting to replace missing interval variable values with the minimum value for the variable.
- **Median** – Use the Mean setting to replace missing interval variable values with the 50th percentile, which is either the middle value or the arithmetic mean of the two middle values for a set of numbers arranged in ascending order.
- **Midrange** – Use the Midrange setting to replace missing interval variable values with the maximum value for the variable plus the minimum value for the variable divided by two.
- **Distribution** – Use the Distribution setting to replace missing interval variable values with replacement values that are calculated based on the random percentiles of the variable's distribution.
- **Tree** – Use the Tree setting to replace missing interval variable values with replacement values that are estimated by analyzing each input as a target.
- **Tree Surrogate** – Use the Tree Surrogate setting to replace missing interval variable values by using the same algorithm as Tree Imputation, except with the addition of surrogate splitting rules.
- **Mid-Minimum Spacing** – Use the Mid-Minimum setting to replace missing interval variable values with mid-minimum spacing.
- **Tukey's Biweight** – Use the Tukey's Biweight setting to replace missing interval variable values with the Tukey's Biweight robust M-estimator value.
- **Huber** – Use the Huber setting to replace missing interval variable values with the Huber's robust M-estimator value.
- **Andrew's Wave** – Use the Andrew's Wave setting to replace missing interval variable values with the Andrew's Wave robust M-estimator value.
- **Default Constant Value** – Use the Default Constant Value setting to replace missing interval variable values with the value that you enter in the **Default Character Value** property.
- **None** – Specify the None setting if you do not want to replace missing interval variable values.

SAS ENTERPRISE MINER GUIDELINES

Impute Node Train Properties

(https://documentation.sas.com)

IMPUTE NODE TRAIN PROPERTIES: CLASS VARIABLES

- **Default Input/Target Method** – Use the Default Input/Target Method property of the Impute node to specify the imputation statistic that you want to use to replace missing class variables. The choices are
  - **Count** – Use the Count setting to replace missing class variable values with the most frequently occurring class variable value.
  - **Default Constant Value** – Use the Default Constant setting to replace missing class variable values with the value that you enter in the **Default Character Value** property.
  - **Distribution** – Use the Distribution setting to replace missing class variable values with replacement values that are calculated based on the random percentiles of the variable's distribution
  - **Tree** – Use the Tree setting to replace missing class variable values with replacement values that are estimated by analyzing each input as a target.
  - **Tree Surrogate** – Use the Tree Surrogate setting to replace missing class variable values by using the same algorithm as Tree Imputation, except with the addition of surrogate splitting rules.
  - **None** – Missing class variable values are not imputed under the None setting.
- **Normalize Values** – When the Normalize property is set to **Yes**, the Impute node uses normalized values. The default setting for the Normalize property is **Yes**.

Transformation

In data mining, transformation is the process of creating new variables that are transformations of existing variables. It can be used to standardize and normalize data, convert data, or aggregate data.

As mentioned before, sometimes replacement and imputation are considered parts of the transformation. Since we already covered those methods, in this section, we will focus on two primary transformation techniques, data normalization and variable discretization.

> In this book, we cover two primary data transformation tools: normalization and variable discretization.

Normalization

Data normalization, also known as variable scaling, is a preprocessing step in machine learning that converts the variables of a dataset to a similar range. It is one of the most popular transformation techniques. First, let's discuss the differences between un-normalized data and normalized data and why it is important to normalize data in some cases. Table 5.3 highlights the differences between un-normalized data and normalized data. Figure 5.1 illustrates these differences using scatter plots and histograms.

> **DEFINITION**
>
> Data normalization, also known as variable scaling, is a preprocessing step in machine learning that converts the variables of a dataset to a similar range.

Normalization provides great benefits in data mining but also poses some challenges. Following are some key advantages and disadvantages of data normalization.

Advantages

- Improved performance of machine learning algorithms: By bringing data into a consistent range, normalization prevents certain variables from dominating others and ensures that all variables contribute equally to the learning process.

- Mitigation of the impact of outliers: Data normalization can reduce the effect of outliers by scaling the data, making it less sensitive to extreme values.

TABLE 5.3

Normalized and Un-normalized Data

Items	Un-normalized Data	Normalized Data
Range	Unnormalized data can have different ranges across different variables. The values can span a wide range, making it difficult to compare or interpret them directly.	Normalized data is transformed to have a consistent range. It typically falls within a predefined range, such as [0, 1] or [−1, 1], making it easier to compare values across features.
Bias	Unnormalized data may exhibit biases due to the inherent differences in ranges. Variables with larger values might dominate the analysis or have a disproportionate impact on models.	Normalization helps to eliminate biases caused by different ranges. By scaling the data, all variables contribute more equally to the modeling process.
Outliers	Outliers in unnormalized data can have a significant influence on the overall modeling process.	Depending on the normalization method used, outliers might have less impact on the overall data representation. Certain normalization techniques, like robust scaling, can handle outliers more effectively.
Interpretation	Interpreting the magnitude of unnormalized data might be challenging since the range of each variable varies.	Normalized data allows for a more intuitive interpretation and comparison. The values are transformed to a standardized range, enabling comparisons and assessments based on relative magnitudes.

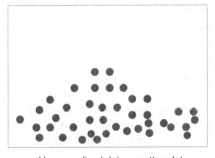

Un-normalized data - scatter plot

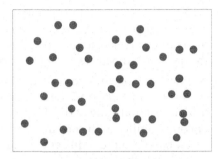

Normalized data - scatter plot

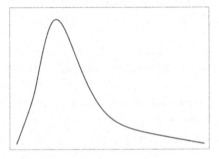

Un-normalized data - histogram

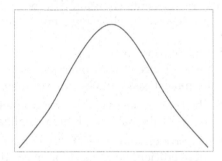

Normalized data - histogram

FIGURE 5.1
Un-normalized data and normalized data.

- Simplified interpretation and visualization: Normalizing data allows for easier interpretation and visualization of the data. When data is scaled to a common range, patterns and trends become more apparent, and it becomes simpler to compare and understand different variables.

- Accelerated convergence in optimization algorithms: Some machine learning methods require search optimization. Optimization algorithms can converge faster when working with normalized data.

Disadvantages

- Loss of original data distribution: Normalization alters the original distribution of the data, compressing or stretching it to fit within a specific range. This can potentially lead to the loss of some information about the data distribution, which may be relevant in certain analysis scenarios.

- Increased complexity in interpretation: While normalization can simplify interpretation in some cases, it can also introduce complexity. Transformed values need to be converted back to their original scale for meaningful interpretation, which can be challenging, especially when dealing with multiple normalization techniques or complex data transformations.

- Sensitivity to outliers during normalization: Although normalization can help miti-gate the impact of outliers, certain normalization techniques, such as min-max nor-malization, are sensitive to extreme values. Outliers can disproportionately affect the normalized data, leading to potential distortions or loss of information.
- Application-specific considerations: The suitability of data normalization depends on the specific data and the machine learning methods. In some cases, maintain-ing the original scale of the data might be necessary for meaningful interpretation or compatibility with certain algorithms. Normalization should be carefully eval-uated based on the requirements and characteristics of the data and the intended modeling techniques.

Table 5.4 presents common data normalization methods. There are several factors we must consider when choosing a normalization method.

- The purpose of normalization: Are you normalizing your data to improve the performance of your machine learning model? Or are you normalizing your data to make it easier to visualize or interpret?
- The type of data you are working with: Are you working with numerical data or categorical data? Note that normalization only works with interval variables.
- The size of your dataset: If you have a large dataset, then you may want to use a more efficient normalization method.

TABLE 5.4

Common Data Normalization Methods and When to Use Them

Normalization Methods	Descriptions	When to Use
Min-Max normalization (also known as rescaling)	Formula: $$X' = \frac{X - X_{min}}{X_{max} - X_{min}}$$ Range: [0, 1]	When you want to scale the data to a specific range, particularly when the distribution is known to be bounded.
Z-score normalization (also known as standardization):	Formula: $$X' = \frac{X - X_{mean}}{SD}$$	When you want to standardize the data to have a mean of 0 and a standard deviation (SD) of 1. This method is commonly used when the distribution of the data is unknown or not normally distributed.
Robust scaling (also known as median and MAD scaling):	Formula: $$X' = \frac{X - X_{median}}{MAD}$$	When you have data with outliers or a skewed distribution, and you want to scale the data based on the median and median absolute deviation (MAD) instead of the mean and standard deviation.
Log transformation:	Formula: $$X' = \log(X)$$	When the data is highly skewed or contains exponential growth patterns, applying a logarithmic transformation can help normalize the distribution.
Power transformation:	Formula: $$X' = X^n$$	When the data has a specific power-law relationship, a power transformation can help normalize the distribution. Common power values include: n = 0.5 (square root), n = 2 (square), and n = −1 (inverse).

Note: X' = new value; X = current value

- The algorithms you are using: Some algorithms, such as k-nearest neighbors and artificial neural networks, are more sensitive to the scale of your data than others. Additionally, linear regression works best with normally distributed data. If you are using one of these algorithms, then you should use normalization to ensure that all of your variables are on the same scale.
- The performance of your model. You can try different normalization methods and see which one gives you the best performance on your model.

Not all machine learning methods require normalization. In this case, using the original scales may improve the model performance.

In addition, some advanced machine learning tools, such as the Neural Network node in SAS Enterprise Miner, has built-in standardization and normalization features. In this case, we do not need to perform normalization separately.

Variable Discretization

Variable discretization is a process of converting a continuous variable into a categorical variable. It is a common preprocessing step in data mining when you want to transform a variable with a continuous scale into discrete categories. As mentioned before, I will use the term *interval variable* to ensure consistency. This conversion can be useful in certain

> **DEFINITION**
>
> Variable discretization is a process of converting a variable with continuous scale (interval variable) into discrete categories (a categorical variable).

scenarios, such as when you want to capture non-linear relationships or when the original variable needs to be treated as a categorical variable for a specific data mining algorithm. Figure 5.2 illustrates the concept of discretization. The input is a continuous variable, and the output is a categorical variable with discrete levels.

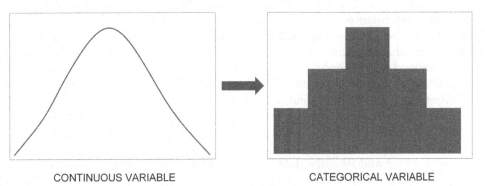

CONTINUOUS VARIABLE   CATEGORICAL VARIABLE

FIGURE 5.2
Data discretization.

A general approach to converting an interval variable into categorical variables can be described as follows.

1. **Determine the number and range of categories**: Decide on the desired number of categories or groups you want to create for the new variables. This number represents the number of levels that you need for the categorical variable. This decision may depend on the specific dataset, the nature of the variable, and the analysis purpose. You can also consider using domain knowledge or statistical techniques to guide your decision.

2. **Partition the range of values**: Divide the range of values of the interval variable into distinct intervals or bins. Each bin represents a category or level. The intervals should be defined in a way that captures meaningful distinctions in the data while maintaining a balance between the number of categories and the information contained within each category.

3. **Assign categories to data points**: Map each data point from the original interval variable to its corresponding category based on its value falling within the defined intervals. This mapping can be achieved using if-else statements, mathematical functions, or specialized functions available in data mining software.

4. **Encode categories into the new categorical variable**: Once the data points are assigned to categories, represent each category as a separate level of the new categorical variable. This step can be done differently depending on the software.

For example, let's consider converting an interval variable *age* into a categorical variable. We define categories such as *young, middle-aged,* and *elderly* based on specific age ranges. Three distinct bins are created based on pre-defined ranges for those bins. Then, continuous age values are assigned to those bins accordingly. Finally, the new categorical variable, let's call it *r_age* is created and encoded with three levels: *young, middle-aged,* and *elderly.*

It's important to note that converting interval variables into categorical variables introduces some loss of information by discretizing the data. Additionally, the specific approach and number of categories chosen can impact the data mining results. I strongly recommend experimenting with different categorization schemes and evaluating their impacts on the model performance.

Table 5.5 describes common methods for variable discretization. The choice of method depends on the characteristics of the data and the analysis purpose. I highlight when to use which method for reference.

The selection of a method depends on the characteristics of the data, underlying data distributions, the presence of outliers, and requirements of the machine learning method. Exploring the data using visualization, descriptive statistics, and domain expertise is valuable for understanding the data and selecting an appropriate method. It's important to note that converting an interval variable to a categorical one involves making decisions about how to group and label the data. These decisions can impact subsequent modeling steps, so it's essential to evaluate the implications and assess the trade-offs associated with each method.

TABLE 5.5

Common Variable Discretization Methods and When to Use Them

Discretization Methods	Description	When to Use
Fixed-width/binning (equal-width binning)	This method divides the range of the interval variable into a predetermined number of equal-width bins and assigns category labels based on which bin each value falls into.	When you want to perform a simple discretization without considering the distribution of the data. This method is less sensitive to outliers but may not capture the underlying patterns in the data.
Quantiles/binning (equal-frequency binning)	This method divides the data into bins based on equal-frequency or equal-sized subsets to ensure that each bin contains an equal number of data points. Then, it assigns category labels based on the bin each value belongs to.	When you want to ensure an equal representation of data points in each category and capture the distribution of the data. This method can be helpful for handling skewed data, but it may result in uneven bin sizes if the data contains outliers or extreme values.
Clustering*	This method applies a clustering algorithm like k-means to group similar values together and then assigns category labels based on the cluster assignments.	When you want to let the data determine the category boundaries based on the similarity between the records. This method is useful when the natural clusters in the data correspond to meaningful categories. However, you need to specify the number of clusters in advance.
Domain-specific thresholds	This method defines predefined thresholds based on domain knowledge or specific requirements and assigns category labels based on those thresholds.	When there are well-established thresholds or standards in the field that define categorical boundaries. This method is suitable when there are clear and meaningful cut-off points for categorization.

We will get into the details of cluster analysis later in Chapter 14

SAS ENTERPRISE MINER GUIDELINES

Transform Variable Node Train Properties

(https://documentation.sas.com)

Interval Inputs/Targets – Use the Interval Inputs property to specify the default transformation method that you want to apply to interval input/target variables.

- **Best** – Performs several transformations and uses the transformation that has the best Chi-Square test for the target.
- **Multiple** – Creates several transformations intended for use in successor Variable Selection nodes.
- **Log** – Transformed using the logarithm of the variable.
- **Log 10** – Transformed using the base-10 logarithm of the variable.
- **Square Root** — Transformed using the square root of the variable.

- **Inverse** – Transformed using the inverse of the variable.
- **Square** – Transformed using the square of the variable.
- **Exponential** – Transformed using the exponential logarithm of the variable.
- **Centering** – Centers variable values by subtracting the mean from each variable.
- **Standardize** – Standardizes the variable by subtracting the mean and dividing by the standard deviation.
- **Range** – Transformed using a scaled value of a variable equal to (x - min) / (max - min), where x is current variable value, min is the minimum value for that variable, and max is the maximum value for that variable.
- **Bucket** – Buckets are created by dividing the data into evenly spaced intervals based on the difference between the maximum and minimum values.
- **Quantile** – Data is divided into groups with approximately the same frequency in groups.
- **Optimal Binning** – Data is binned in order to maximize the relationship to the target.
- **Maximum Normal** – A best power transformation to maximize normality.
- **Maximum Correlation** – A best power transformation to maximize correlation to the target. No transformation occurs if used on data sets with non-interval targets.
- **Equalize** – A best power transformation to equalize spread with target levels.
- **Optimal Max. Equalize** – An optimized best power transformation to equalize spread with target levels.
- **None** – (Default) No transformation is performed.

Treat Missing as Level – Use the Treat Missing as Level property to indicate whether missing values should be treated as levels when creating groupings. If the Treat Missing as Level property is set to Yes, a group value will be assigned to the missing values of the variable. If the Treat Missing as Level property is set to No, the group value will be set to missing for each variable.

Examples of Data Modification Using SAS Enterprise Miner

Airline Recommendation Dataset

The first example is for the *airline recommendation* dataset. For this dataset, we use two data modification tools in SAS Enterprise Miner: **Replace node** and **Imputation node**.

Before we perform those modification tasks, it is important to explore the data to see what kind of issues we have. By using the Stat Explore node, as described in Chapter 4, we

TABLE 5.6

Brief Descriptive Statistics for Categorical Variables

Variable Name	Role	Number of Levels	Missing
airline_status	INPUT	4	0
class	INPUT	3	0
destination_state	INPUT	51	0
flight_cancelled	INPUT	2	0
gender	INPUT	2	0
origin_state	INPUT	51	0
type_of_travel	INPUT	3	0
recommendation	TARGET	2	0

can get the descriptive statistics information we need for the variables in the dataset. Since this dataset has two groups of variables, interval and categorical, I present the descriptive statistics for them separately in Tables 5.6 and 5.7. Note that I do not provide the full descriptive statistics as shown in Chapter 4 because, in this step, we focus on missing values and any issues with the data. The results show no missing values for categorical variables (Table 5.6). Hence, we are good with these variables. However, Table 5.7 shows three interval variables with missing values: *arrival delay time, departure delay time,* and *flight time*. In addition, we also notice one issue with *price sensitivity*. As stated in Chapter 4, this variable uses the Likert scale with a range from 1 to 5. But the descriptive statistics results show that this variable has a minimum value of 0, which does not make sense. A valid reason for this issue is that 0 was used to code missing values. Since SAS Enterprise Miner uses blank spaces or dots to represent missing values, it may misinterpret the zeros for this variable as actual zero values. This misinformation will result in invalid predictive modeling results. Hence, we need to make the correction by using the Replacement node to correctly code these missing values. After that, we use the Impute note to handle missing values for this dataset.

TABLE 5.7

Brief Descriptive Statistics for Interval Variables

Variable	Mean	Standard Deviation	Non Missing	Missing	Min	Median	Max
age	47.5	16.50	124,464	0	18	46	85
arrival_delay_in_minutes	15.38	38.84	121,899	2565	0	0	1,584
departure_delay_in_minutes	15.00	38.45	122,263	2201	0	0	1,592
eating_and_drinking_at_airport	68.84	52.60	124,464	0	0	60	895
flight_distance	793.87	592.10	124,464	0	31	630	4,983
flight_time_in_minutes	111.51	71.77	121,899	2565	8	92	669
no_of_flights_per_year	20.09	14.40	124,464	0	0	17.36	100
no_of_other_loyalty_cards	0.84	1.12	124,464	0	0	0	12
number_of_years_flying	6.78	2.98	124,464	0	2	7	11
percent_of_flight_with_other_air	9.44	8.87	124,464	0	1	7	110
price_sensitivity	1.27	0.54	124,464	0	0	1	5
shopping_amount_at_airport	26.87	53.16	124,464	0	0	0	879

Replacement Example for the Airline Recommendation

The purpose of this example is to recode the zero values for the *price sensitivity* variable as missing values to correct the information in the data. We continue from the Data Partition and Explore steps completed in Chapters 3 and 4. To use the Replacement node, from the Modify tab, drag a Replacement node to the workspace and connect it to the Data Partition node as follows.

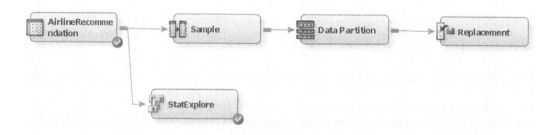

Follow the steps below to configure the Replacement node.

1. Under the Train properties: Set Default Limits Method to User-Specified Limits.
2. Under the Score properties: Set Replacement Values to Missing.
3. Under Interval Variables: Click the ellipsis button (the three-dot button) next to Replacement Editor. The Interactive Replacement Interval Filter window opens.
4. For the *price sensitivity* variable:
   - Set Limit Method to User-Specified.
   - Set Replacement Lower Limit to 1 (i.e., any values lower than this lower limit are considered missing values).

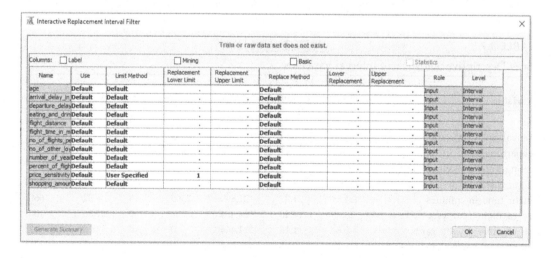

Name	Use	Limit Method	Replacement Lower Limit	Replacement Upper Limit	Replace Method	Lower Replacement	Upper Replacement	Role	Level
age	Default	Default	.	.	Default	.	.	Input	Interval
arrival_delay_in	Default	Default	.	.	Default	.	.	Input	Interval
departure_delay	Default	Default	.	.	Default	.	.	Input	Interval
eating_and_drin	Default	Default	.	.	Default	.	.	Input	Interval
flight_distance	Default	Default	.	.	Default	.	.	Input	Interval
flight_time_in_m	Default	Default	.	.	Default	.	.	Input	Interval
no_of_flights_pe	Default	Default	.	.	Default	.	.	Input	Interval
no_of_other_lo	Default	Default	.	.	Default	.	.	Input	Interval
number_of_yea	Default	Default	.	.	Default	.	.	Input	Interval
percent_of_fligh	Default	Default	.	.	Default	.	.	Input	Interval
price_sensitivity	Default	User Specified	1	.	Default	.	.	Input	Interval
shopping_amou	Default	Default	.	.	Default	.	.	Input	Interval

5. Click OK.
6. Run the Replacement node and open the Results window.

```
Limits and Replacement Values for Interval Variables


                                                 Lower                    Upper
                                      Lower    Replacement    Upper    Replacement
        Variable       Replace Variable    limit      Value      Limit       Value

price_sensitivity    REP_price_sensitivity     1         .          .           .



*--------------------------------------------------------------*
* Report Output
*--------------------------------------------------------------*




Replacement Counts

Obs      Variable            Label        Role     Train    Validation    Test

 1    price_sensitivity   Price sensitivity    INPUT     1184        391        368
```

FIGURE 5.3
Replacement results.

The results output shows that a new variable named REP_price_sensitivity was created for this task. Additionally, 1,943 values were replaced with missing values (Figure 5.3). If we break it down by samples, we will have 1,184 (train), 391 (validation), and 368 (test). The new variable (REP_price_sensitivity) will be used in the next step of the process.

Imputation Example for the Airline Recommendation

In this example, we use the Impute node to replace missing values with mean values. We chose the mean method for imputation because the percentage of missing values is low (about 2%) and it is the most common imputation method.

We continue with the Replacement node that we did previously. To use the Impute node, from the Modify tab, drag an Impute node to the workspace and connect it to the Replacement node (see below).

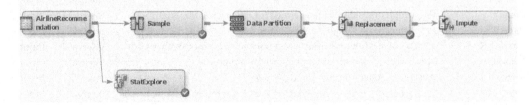

Follow the steps below to configure the Impute node.

- Under Train properties:
  - For Interval Variables: Set Default Input Method to Mean (i.e., replacing missing values for interval input variables with the mean values of the available data).
- Run the Impute node and open the Results window.

TABLE 5.8

Imputation Results

Variable Name	Impute Method	Imputed Variable	Imputed Value	Label	Missing for TRAIN
REP_price_sensitivity	MEAN	IMP_REP_price_sensitivity	1.308	Replacement: Price sensitivity	1,184
arrival_delay_in_minutes	MEAN	IMP_arrival_delay_in_minutes	15.201	Arrival delay (in minutes)	779
departure_delay_in_minutes	MEAN	IMP_departure_delay_in_minutes	14.82	Departure delay (in minutes)	669
flight_time_in_minutes	MEAN	IMP_flight_time_in_minutes	112.543	Flight time (in minutes)	779

The results presented in Table 5.8 show the variables with missing values (note the new name *REP_price_sensitivity* created after the Replacement step), imputation method, new imputed variables (IMP is added to all variable names to indicate the imputation), imputed values label, and number of missing values replaced for the training sample. These new variables will be used to train predictive models in the next step. Note that the software performs imputation for the training sample only because this is the data that will be used to train models.

Boston Housing Dataset

In the second example, we use the *Boston Housing* dataset to perform imputation and normalization tasks. See the data description in Table 5.9. First, let's run the Stat Explore node and see what we have with this dataset. Table 5.10 shows the descriptive statistics for variables (all of them are interval). As you can see, only one variable has missing values, the target variable *(Imv)* with 54 missing values.

TABLE 5.9

Boston Housing Data – Variable Descriptions

Variable Name	Description	Scale	Role
CrimePC	Crime rate per capita	Interval	Input
ZonePr	Proportion of residential land zoned for lots over 25,000 sq.ft.	Interval	Input
IndustPr	Proportion of non-retail business acres.	Interval	Input
Charles_River	Charles River dummy variable (1 if tract bounds river; 0 otherwise)	Interval	Input
NiOxSQ	Nitric oxides concentration (parts per 10 million)	Interval	Input
RmSQ	Average number of rooms per dwelling	Interval	Input
AgePre40	Proportion of owner occupied units built prior to 1940	Interval	Input
LogDisstance	Weighted distances to five Boston employment centers	Interval	Input
LogAccess	Index of accessibility to radial highways	Interval	Input
Tax	Full value property tax rate per $10,000	Interval	Input
PtRatio	Pupil-teacher ratio	Interval	Input
B	1,000 (Bk - 0.63)^2 where Bk is the proportion of blacks by town	Interval	Input
Lstat	% lower status of the population	Interval	Input
Imv	Median value of owner-occupied homes in $ 1,000's	Interval	Target

TABLE 5.10

Descriptive Statistics Results – Boston Housing

Variable	Role	Mean	Standard Deviation	Non Missing	Missing	Min	Median	Max
AgePre40	INPUT	58.74	33.10	506	0	1.14	65.20	100.00
B	INPUT	332.79	125.32	506	0	0.32	390.64	396.90
Charles_River	INPUT	0.14	0.31	506	0	0.00	0.00	1.00
CrimePC	INPUT	1.27	2.40	506	0	0.00	0.14	9.97
IndustPr	INPUT	9.21	7.17	506	0	0.00	6.96	27.74
LogAccess	INPUT	78.06	203.54	506	0	1.00	5.00	666.00
LogDistance	INPUT	6.17	6.48	506	0	1.13	3.92	24.00
Lstat	INPUT	11.54	6.06	506	0	1.73	10.36	34.41
NiOxSQ	INPUT	1.10	1.65	506	0	0.39	0.54	7.31
PtRatio	INPUT	42.61	87.59	506	0	2.60	18.90	396.90
RmSQ	INPUT	15.68	27.22	506	0	3.56	6.32	100.00
Tax	INPUT	339.32	180.67	506	0	20.20	307.00	711.00
ZonePr	INPUT	13.30	23.05	506	0	0.00	0.00	100.00
Imv	TARGET	23.75	8.81	452	54	6.30	21.90	50.00

Imputation Example for the Boston Housing

Since the missing values account for just about 11% of the data, we chose to use the mean imputation method. Open the Boston Housing project. We continue from Data Partition and Explore steps completed in Chapters 3 and 4. To use the Impute node, from the Modify tab, drag an Impute node to the workspace and connect it to the Data Partition node (see below).

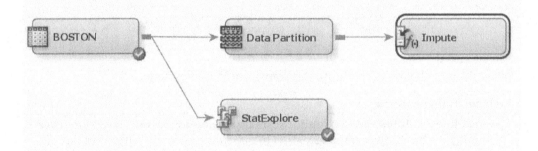

Follow the steps below to configure the Impute node.

1. Under Train properties:
   - For Interval Variables: Set Default Target Method to Mean (i.e., replacing miss-ing values for interval target variables with the mean values of the available data).
2. Run the Impute node and open the Results window.

The results in Figure 5.4 output show the new variable, *IMP_Imv*, impute method, imputed value, role, level, and label. There are 28 values imputed for the training sample. This new variable will be used for the next step.

```
Imputation Summary
Number Of Observations



                                                                     Number of
Variable   Impute     Imputed     Impute               Measurement    Missing
  Name     Method    Variable      Value     Role         Level       Label   for TRAIN

  Imv       MEAN     IMP_Imv      23.3120   TARGET      INTERVAL       Imv        28
```

FIGURE 5.4
Imputation results.

Normalization Example for the Boston Housing

If you have done the data exploration for the *Boston Housing* dataset in the Chapter 4 exercise, you find that variables in the data are not normally distributed. Suppose we plan to use the linear regression method to analyze this data, and this method usually works best with normally distributed data. For that reason, we decide to normalize all interval variables in this dataset.

We continue with the Impute node completed previously. To normalize data using SAS Enterprise Miner, we use the Transform Variables node. From the Modify tab, drag a Transform Variables node to the workspace and connect it to Impute node (see below).

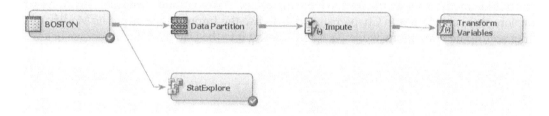

Follow the steps below to configure the Transform Variables node.

1. Under Train properties:
   - Set Interval Inputs to Maximum Normal. This option lets the software determine the best power transformation to maximize normality. It makes our task easier since we do not have to decide which normalization methods to use for which variables.
2. Run the Transform Variables node and open the Results window.

The results output shows the normalization functions selected by SAS Enterprise Miner (Table 5.11). As you can see, the software determines the best normalization functions for each variable. Common functions used include logarithm and square root functions. New variables are created with the function added to the variable names. These new variables will be used for predictive modeling in the next step. This tool is very useful for data mining purposes when we have many variables. It is not feasible for us to examine each variable individually to decide which function to use for normalization.

Table 5.12 shows the comparison between the original data and normalized data. If we review the mean and standard deviation values, we can notice that before normalization,

TABLE 5.11

Normalization Functions

Variable Name	New Variable Name	Formula
AgePre40	EXP_AgePre40	exp(max(AgePre40-1.137, 0.0)/98.863)
B	LOG_Charles_River	log(max(Charles_River-0, 0.0) + 1)
Charles_River	LOG_CrimePC	log(max(CrimePC-0, 0.0)/9.96654 + 1)
CrimePC	LOG_LogAccess	log(max(LogAccess-1, 0.0)/665 + 1)
IndustPr	LOG_LogDistance	log(max(LogDistance-1.1296, 0.0)/22.8704 + 1)
LogAccess	LOG_NiOxSQ	log(max(NiOxSQ-0.385, 0.0)/6.583 + 1)
LogDistance	LOG_PtRatio	log(max(PtRatio-7.68, 0.0)/389.22 + 1)
Lstat	LOG_RmSQ	log(max(RmSQ-3.561, 0.0)/96.439 + 1)
NiOxSQ	LOG_ZonePr	log(max(ZonePr-0, 0.0)/100 + 1)
PtRatio	PWR_B	(max(B-2.52, 0.0)/394.38)**4
RmSQ	SQRT_IndustPr	sqrt(max(IndustPr-0, 0.0)/27.74)
ZonePr	SQRT_Lstat	sqrt(max(Lstat-2.47, 0.0)/28.34)

variables have different ranges with mean values from 0.13 to 337. After the normalization, these variables have much more consistent ranges, which helps the interpretation and comparison of the results. Regarding the normal distribution, by comparing the skewness and kurtosis values (they are expected to be closer to zeros), we can see that only seven variables with improved skewness and kurtosis after normalization (I highlighted them in the table). This output indicates that finding the right normalization method to ensure normal distributions is not an easy task. It requires an iterative process of trial and error.

You may ask: Why don't we use normalization for interval variables in the *airline recommendation* dataset? It is a good question. Let me explain. Normal distribution is a common requirement for methods based on ordinal least square (OLS) such as linear regression. These algorithms work best with normalized data since it helps us achieve good model fit. The *boston* dataset has an interval target variable, so linear regression is the appropriate choice. That is why normalizing data is recommended. However, other methods such as logistic regression, decision trees, or random forest, are based on different foundations, and normal distribution is not a requirement. Hence, normalizing data may not

TABLE 5.12

Comparison between Original and Normalized Data

Variable Name	Mean	Standard Deviation	Skewness	Kurtosis	New Variable Name	Mean	Standard Deviation	Skewness	Kurtosis
AgePre40	60.00	31.84	−0.45	−1.10	EXP_AgePre40	1.90	0.56	−0.13	−1.37
B	337.26	122.29	−2.05	2.45	LOG_Charles_River	0.10	0.22	1.93	1.92
Charles_River	0.13	0.31	2.01	2.34	LOG_CrimePC	0.11	0.19	1.89	2.26
CrimePC	1.36	2.52	2.09	3.22	LOG_LogAccess	0.07	0.20	2.82	6.02
IndustPr	9.18	6.86	0.55	−0.79	LOG_LogDistance	0.17	0.18	2.12	3.56
LogAccess	68.68	190.71	2.83	6.05	LOG_NiOxSQ	0.08	0.17	2.86	6.51
LogDistance	5.83	6.11	2.37	4.43	LOG_PtRatio	0.07	0.15	3.73	12.30
Lstat	11.60	5.77	0.84	0.49	LOG_RmSQ	0.09	0.19	2.84	6.15
NiOxSQ	1.02	1.53	2.93	6.97	LOG_ZonePr	0.10	0.18	1.78	2.32
PtRatio	39.70	82.95	3.80	12.89	PWR_B	0.78	0.34	−1.56	0.81
RmSQ	14.55	25.93	2.85	6.23	SQRT_IndustPr	0.52	0.25	−0.39	−0.44
ZonePr	12.92	23.26	2.09	3.67	SQRT_Lstat	0.54	0.18	0.01	−0.30

produce any advantages for those algorithms. In the *airline recommendation* dataset, we have a binary target variable, which makes logistic regression the right choice for predictive modeling. Among advanced machine learning methods, neural networks also do not require normally distributed data but may require data standardization to help achieve better model fit. The neural network tool in SAS Enterprise Miner has built-in data standardization options, which allow us to try different methods in a more dynamic way. That is why we do not need to normalize interval variables in this dataset.

Discretization Example for the Boston Housing

In order to show you an example of variable discretization, let's consider a hypothetical scenario. Assuming we want to convert the target variable (*IMP_Imv*), which is interval, to a categorical variable for prediction purpose. To meet this goal, we need to perform variable discretization. We use the Transform Variables node for this task.

We continue with the Transform Variables node completed before. In order to perform discretization, from the Modify tab, drag another Transform Variables node to the workspace, change its name to "Discretization," and connect it to the Impute node (see below).

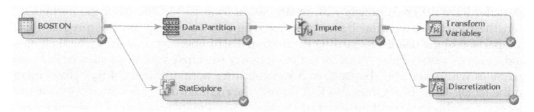

Follow the steps below to configure the Discretization node.

1. Under Train properties:
   - For Default Methods: Set Interval Targets to Quantile (i.e., it divides the date into groups with approximately the same frequency in groups).
2. Run the Discretization node and open the Results window.

The results outputs show the original variable (IMP_Imv), role (target), original level (interval), new name (PCTL_IMP_Imv), new level (nominal), and discretization method (quantile with four levels) (Table 5.13).

In order to see the new levels of *IMP_Imv* after discretization, from the Explore tab drag a Graph Explore node to the workspace and connect it to the Discretization node (see below). Run the Graph Explore node and open the Results window.

Figure 5.5 shows that we have a new categorical target variable with four levels, decided by the quantile formula, as follows.

- Level 1: <19
- Level 2: 19–22.45

TABLE 5.13

Discretization Results

Name	Role	Level	Name	Level	Formula
IMP_Imv	TARGET	INTERVAL	PCTL_IMP_Imv	NOMINAL	Quantile(4)

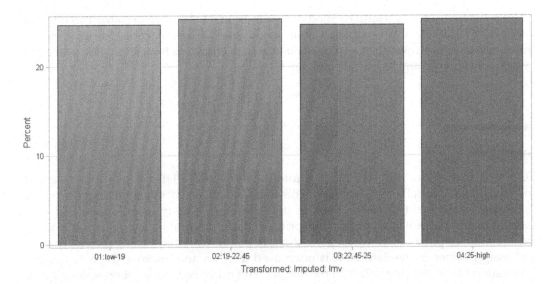

FIGURE 5.5
Discretization results – Quantile method.

- Level 3: 22.45–25
- Level 4: > 25

As you can see, the quantile formula divides the data into four levels with approximately the same frequency (about 25% each). Now we can use this new target variable as a categorical variable for predictive modeling.

If we change the discretization method to Bucket (it divides the data into evenly spaced intervals based on the difference between the maximum and minimum values) and repeat the process, we have a new categorical target variable with four levels but with different frequencies (see Figure 5.6).

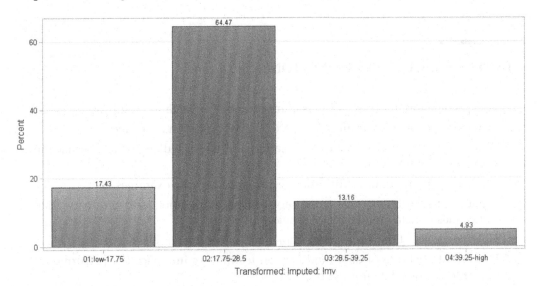

FIGURE 5.6
Discretization results – Bucket method.

Discretization is a very useful method in data mining if we choose to convert an interval variable into a categorical variable for analysis purposes. SAS Enterprise Miner provides this tool within the Transform Variables node, which allows us to perform discretization tasks easily without any technical challenges.

Summary

Data modification is a process in data mining that involves altering the original dataset to enhance its quality, completeness, or compatibility for predictive modeling purposes. It consists of various techniques such as data cleaning, data transformation, and data reduction. In this chapter, we cover three primary data modification techniques, including replacement, imputation, and transformation. Replacement allows us to recode, correct, and assign values in the dataset. It is often used to clean and improve the data quality. Imputation fills in missing values in the dataset with estimated values. It provides us with a complete dataset and avoids loss of information. Transformation is the process of creating new variables that are transformations of existing variables. It can be used to standardize and normalize data, convert data, or aggregate data.

In this chapter, I introduce multiple methods for imputation, normalization, and discretization. The selection of the right method depends on the specific characteristics of the dataset, the machine learning method, and the purpose of the data mining project. It requires careful consideration of the potential impact on the data, such as the introduction of bias during imputation or the loss of certain information during normalization or aggregation. Data modification in data mining is a dynamic and iterative process, often involving multiple iterations of preprocessing steps to refine and optimize the dataset for predictive modeling. We also learn how to perform various data modification techniques using SAS Enterprise Miner with two different datasets.

CHAPTER DISCUSSION QUESTIONS

1. What is data modification? Why is it important in the data mining process?
2. Provide some practical examples where data modification is needed.
3. What are the benefits of data modification and what challenges we may face in using data modification techniques?
4. What are primary data modification techniques? Provide examples.
5. What are the differences between replacement, imputation, and transformation techniques in data modification? Provide examples.
6. How do we select the appropriate data modification techniques?
7. How can the choice of data modification techniques influence the performance and outcome of a data mining project?
8. Provide examples in which replacement techniques can be used to clean the data.

9. What are missing values and how do they impact the data mining?

10. What are the trade odds of data imputation? How do we balance between improving data completeness and preserving the quality and representativeness of the original data? Provide examples.

11. What are common imputation methods and how to select the right one for our project?

12. What are the main purposes of data normalization? In which case should we use normalization?

13. What are the potential challenges when we normalize data?

14. What are common normalization methods, and when to use them?

15. What are the main purposes of variable discretization? Describe the steps of the discretization process. Provide examples.

16. What are common discretization methods and their applications?

Exercises

Exercise 1: Imputation for the *Bank* dataset

1. View the variable description of the *bank* dataset (Appendix A.1).
2. Open the *bank* dataset in SAS Enterprise Miner.
3. Create a new diagram Modify, and add the data source to the workspace.
4. Add a StatExplore node to the workspace and connect it to the data source.
5. Run the StatExplore node and report the descriptive statistics. Report variables with missing values.
6. Add an Impute node and connect it to the data source node.
7. Replace missing values using the mean imputation method.
8. Report the Impute results showing the new variables, imputed values, and replaced missing values.

Exercise 2: Normalization for the *Bank* dataset

1. Continue from Exercise 4.
2. Add a Transform Variables node to the workspace and connect it to the data source.
3. Normalize data using Maximum Normal setting for these variables: *acctage, ddabal, dep, checks, teller, cdbal, income,* and *hmval*.
4. Report the normalization results showing the new variables and normalization functions.
5. Compare the mean, standard deviation, skewness, and kurtosis between original data and normalized data. Explain the results.

Exercise 3: Normalization for the *Cardiac* dataset

1. Open the *cardiac* dataset in SAS Enterprise Miner.
2. Create a new diagram Modify, and add the data source to the workspace.
3. Add a Transform Variables node to the workspace and connect it to the data source.
4. Normalize all interval variables using Maximum Normal setting.
5. Report the normalization results showing the new variables and normalization functions.
6. Compare the mean, standard deviation, skewness, and kurtosis between original data and normalized data. Explain the results.

Exercise 4: Discretization for the *Cardiac* dataset

1. Continue from Exercise 3.
2. Add another Transform Variables node to the workspace and connect it to the data source.
3. Convert the *bmi* variable into a categorical variable using the Bucket method. Report the results.
4. Convert the *bmi* variable into a categorical variable using the Quantile method. Report the results.
5. Compare the results between Steps 3 and 4.

Exercise 5: Replacement for the *Passengers* dataset

1. View the variable description of the *passengers* dataset (Appendix A.2).
2. Open the *passengers* dataset in SAS Enterprise Miner.
3. Create a new diagram Modify, and add the data source to the workspace.
4. Add a Sample node to the workspace and connect it to the data source. Sample 20% of the full dataset using the Random method.
5. Add a Data Partition node and connect it to the Sample node.
6. Partition the data using the split ratio 60–40: train sample: 60%; validation sample: 20%; test sample: 20%. Use the Simple Random method.
7. Refer to Exercise 6 in Chapter 4 to identify Likert scale variables with zero values.
8. Add a Replacement node and connect it to the Data Partition node. Replace the zero values for the above variables with missing values. This step is to correct the information in the dataset.
9. Report the Replacement results showing the number of zero values replaced by missing values for each variable.

Exercise 6: Imputation for the *Passengers* dataset

1. Continue from Exercise 1.
2. Add an Impute node to the workspace and connect it to the Replacement node.
3. Replace missing values using the mean imputation method.
4. Report the Impute results showing the new variables, imputed values, and replaced missing values.

Part II

Data Mining Methods

6

Model Evaluation

LEARNING OUTCOMES

Upon the completion of this chapter, you will be able to

1. Explain the purpose and importance of model evaluation.
2. Compare model fit and predictive power.
3. Describe overfitting problems and potential root causes.
4. Discuss possible solutions to avoid overfitting.
5. Differentiate between model reliability and validity.
6. Evaluate the reliability and validity of predictive models.
7. Define the champion model and explain the importance of model comparison.
8. Explain the purpose and importance of model fit metrics.
9. Select the appropriate model fit metrics for association and classification models.
10. Calculate model fit metrics for association models.
11. Define confusion matrix and describe its components.
12. Calculate model fit metrics for classification models.
13. Describe cost-sensitive learning.

Introduction

Evaluating the performance of predictive models is important in the data mining process. As mentioned before, there is no such thing as a perfect predictive model, and there is always a margin of error in any predictive modeling. If we know how well a model can predict the target variable, we can decide whether to use it for actual predictions and the level of prediction errors that we need to accept. Model performance in data mining is always a challenging task since there are so many different concepts,

processes, and metrics. In addition, they are not presented consistently in books or online resources, which often causes confusion for the readers. If we follow an incorrect process or use inappropriate metrics, we may end up with an invalid predictive model. That is why I want to cover this topic carefully before we start working with machine learning methods.

In this chapter, we focus on some key concepts of model performance evaluation, the evaluation process, and key metrics we should use to evaluate the model fit. As mentioned in Chapter 2, a common practice in data mining is to build multiple models using different machine learning methods and then compare their performance to select the champion model. Before we compare the models, we need to decide the metrics for model fit. In this topic, there are some interchangeable terminologies, which could cause confusion. So I provide standard definitions and explanations for those terms and when to use them. This foundational understanding plays a vital role in selecting the right metrics for evaluation and following the process. You should note that the metrics we use for model evaluation in this chapter only apply to supervised learning; i.e., there is a pre-defined target variable, and our purpose is to predict this target variable. These metrics do not apply to unsupervised learning since there is no prediction involved. In addition, model fit metrics for the association model (with a continuous target variable) are different from the ones for the classification model (with a categorical target variable). Hence, we need to pay attention to the scale of the target variable to be able to select the correct metrics.

Basic Concepts

Before we go deeper into the topic of model evaluation, I present key basic concepts of this topic with descriptions in Table 6.1. These concepts allow you to understand the terms I use in this chapter. Use the table as a reference. I will describe and explain those concepts in detail, and you can always return to this table if you need to refresh your mind when you need to check the definition of a concept.

Model Fit and Predictive Power

First, let's clear out some terminologies. *Model fit* and *predictive power* are two terms commonly used in data mining, but the differentiation between them is never clearly explained and addressed. You may notice that in many books or online materials, authors use them as interchangeable terms. Those terms certainly overlap, which could cause a great deal of confusion. Model fit is more commonly used in traditional statistical analyses, while predictive power is used

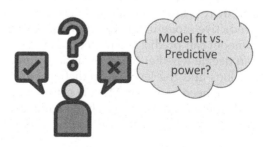

TABLE 6.1

Basic Concepts in Model Performance Evaluation

Terms	Descriptions
Model fit	Model fit measures how well the model fits the data.
Predictive power	Predictive power is the ability of a model to accurately capture and represent the underlying patterns, relationships, or trends present in the data and generalize the results to other datasets.
Overfitting	Overfitting is the situation in which the model is overtrained to the training sample and not generalized to other datasets. Hence, the model is invalid and unusable.
Model reliability	Model reliability refers to the internal consistency of a model. It means the model produces consistent results with different runs using different data sets.
Model validity	Model validity refers to the accuracy of the model. It means the model consistently produces an accurate prediction of the target variable.
Champion model	Champion model is the model with the best performance among the models we train and validate.
Prediction errors	Errors measure the extent to which the trained model misfits the data. The lower the error, the more accurate the model.
Sum of Squared Error (SSE)	SSE measures unexplained variance, which is how far the data are from the model's predicted values.
Sum of Squared Regression (SSR)	SSE measures explained variance, which is how far the mean is from the model's predicted values.
Sum of Squared Total (SST)	SST measures total variance, which is how far the data are from the mean.
Root Mean Squared Error (RMSE)	RMSE is a common metric for association models. It measures the average difference between the predicted values and the actual values in a dataset, expressed in the same units as the predicted variable.
Mean Absolute Percentage Error (MAPE)	MAPE is a common metric for association models. It measures the percentage difference between the predicted values and the actual values in a dataset.
Relative Squared Error (RSE)	RSE is a common metric for association models. It measures the relative improvement of the model's predictions compared to a simple baseline model that always predicts the mean of the actual values.
Explanatory Power (EP)	EP refers to the ability of a predictive model, especially association model, to explain or predict the variability observed in the data. It measures how well the model captures the underlying relationships between the input variables (predictors) and the target variable.
Actual by predicted chart	The *actual by predicted chart* compares the actual values with the predicted values, showing us how well the trained model fits the data.
Residuals	Residuals measure the difference between actual values and predicted values in a dataset.
Residual by predicted chart	The residual by predicted chart presents not only how close the actual values are to the predicted values but also indicates any patterns in the residuals.
Confusion matrix	Confusion matrix, also called the classification matrix, is the table that summarizes the performance of a classification algorithm.
True Positive (TP)	TP is the prediction that correctly indicates the presence of the event.
True Negative (TN)	TN is the prediction that correctly indicates the absence of the event.
False Positive (FP)	FP is the prediction that wrongly indicates the presence of the event.
False Negative (FN)	FN is the prediction that wrongly indicates the absence of the event.
Misclassification Rate (MR)	MR is a measure of how often a model misclassifies (makes incorrect predictions) the target variable (including actual positives and actual negatives).
Prediction Accuracy (ACC)	ACC is a measure of how accurately a model predicts the target variables (including actual positives and actual negatives).
Sensitivity, Recall, or True Positive Rate (TPR)	Sensitivity is the probability of a positive result (event) or how well a model can predict true positives (events).

(Continued)

TABLE 6.1 (*Continued*)

Basic Concepts in Model Performance Evaluation

Terms	Descriptions
Specificity, Selectivity, or True Negative Rate (TNR)	Specificity is the probability of a negative result (non-event) or how well a model can predict true negatives (non-events).
F1-score	F1-score is the harmonic mean of the sensitivity (recall) and precision (positive predicted value); a high F1 score means low false positives (FP) and low false negatives (FN).
Receiver Operating Characteristic (ROC) chart	The ROC chart shows the values of the true positive fraction on the vertical axis and the false positive fraction on the horizontal axis. it reflects the tradeoff between sensitivity and specificity.
Lift chart	Lift is a measure of the effectiveness of a predictive model calculated as the ratio between the results obtained with and without the predictive model. The Lift chart, or Lift curve, presents the graphic representation between the lift values and response rates.
Gini coefficient	Gini coefficient is a measure of the model's discriminatory power, which is the effectiveness of the model in differentiating between positives and negatives. The Gini coefficient measures how equal the positive rates are across the attributes of a characteristic.
Cost-sensitive learning	Cost-sensitive learning is a method to evaluate and select a model based on the costs of misclassification.
Decision matrix	Decision matrix is the table that presents the costs of misclassifications, including costs of false positives and costs of false negatives.

exclusively in the context of predictive modeling. Predictive power is certainly less precise than model fit, but it is an important concept in data mining. I will differentiate those terms based on their purposes rather than how they are measured since overlaps exist in this perspective.

Model Fit

What is the model fit? Imagine we have a model, represented either by mathematical expressions, logic, or rules, which presents relationships between the target variable and predictors. Thus, this model can be used to predict the target variable value. It could be developed based on a theoretical foundation or derived from a machine learning algorithm. What we

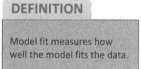

DEFINITION

Model fit measures how well the model fits the data.

need to know is how well this model fits actual data; it is called model fit. The difference between the model and actual data is called residuals, for association models, or misclassification, for classification models. The lower the residuals or misclassification, the better the model fit.

Model fit is measured by goodness-of-fit indices, which estimate how well our model can predict the target variable based on predictors. There are universal goodness-of-fit indices, which can be used for all models, and there are more unique goodness-of-fit indices that only apply to specific machine learning methods. For example, we can use prediction accuracy, misclassification rate, sensitivity, specificity, Lift-chart, and ROC chart for all classification models. Additionally, we can use Root Mean Squared Error, Mean Absolute Percent Error, and residual by predicted chart for all association models. However, we can only use F-test and R^2 to measure the model fit for linear regression models and -2LL difference and pseudo R^2 for logistic regression models. Accordingly, we need to keep in mind both general model fit metrics and specific model fit metrics. Of course, general model fit metrics are more common and more widely used since not all machine learning methods have their specific metrics.

Note that the term *goodness-of-fit* is used in other statistics books and materials as well. I know the new terminology may cause further confusion for readers. Essentially, goodness-of-fit indices are specific metrics we use to evaluate model fit. Since I will use the term *model fit* a lot more in this book, it may be a good idea to ensure consistency and simplicity. Accordingly, throughout the book, I will use the term *model fit* instead of *goodness-of-fit* to make it easier for you to follow. And *model fit metrics* will also be used in place of *goodness-of-fit indices*.

> We use the term *model fit* throughout the book to ensure the consistency. This term is considered the same as *goodness-of-fit*.

One important note is that model fit is usually evaluated in the model training step with the training sample. Hence, achieving a good model fit for the training sample does not guarantee the predictive model will work. Why? Let's discuss predictive power.

Predictive Power

In terms of measurement, predictive power uses the same measures as model fit metrics, which measure how well the model fits the data. However, evaluating predictive power goes beyond the model fit of the training sample. We must evaluate the predictive power of a model by testing it with a new set of samples, such as validation and test samples. Confusing? I understand. Let's examine an example. Suppose we

DEFINITION

Predictive power is the ability of a model to accurately capture and represent the underlying patterns, relationships, or trends present in the data and generalize the results to other datasets.

built and trained a predictive model with the training sample and received a good model fit, indicating a good fit between that model and the training data. Now we want to see if that model will work with a new data set. So we run the same model with the validation sample to validate the model and later with the test sample for the final model assessment. Do we still have a good model fit? If yes, that means our model is generalizable and can make a good prediction of the target variable with real-life data. We say it has good predictive power. If not, our model does not have good predictive power since it is not generalizable and cannot be used for different datasets, which makes it unusable. It is likely that we have an overfitting issue. We will get to that in a moment.

In short, model fit and predictive power use very much the same model fit metrics, but they serve different purposes. Model fit is used to evaluate the model performance with one particular dataset, such as the training model. Predictive power is used to evaluate the model performance in the validation step with new data samples. Predictive power is to ensure the model has a good model fit with other datasets; i.e., it is generalizable and can be used to predict the target variable with real-life data. Essentially, predictive power is broader than model fit since it requires a good model fit for all datasets. Achieving good predictive power should be our goal.

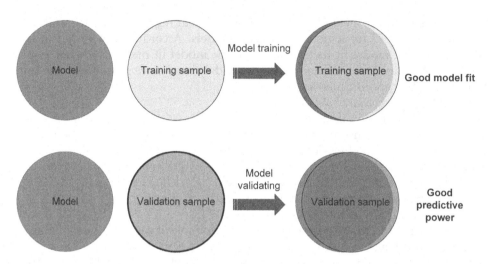

FIGURE 6.1
Model fit and predictive power.

Figure 6.1 illustrates how model fit and predictive power are measured. In order to keep the concept simple, I only use training and validation samples in the figure. In the first case, we have a good model fit with the train-ing sample (the model fits well the data). But it does not guarantee predictive power because we still need to ensure the same model fits the validation sample, meaning it is generalized to other datasets. On the other hand, before we evaluate predictive power, we must first have a good model fit with the training sam-ple because if the trained model does not fit the data (poor model fit), it will likely not fit other datasets (poor predictive power).

> Model fit guarantees the model fits one particular dataset.
>
> Predictive power indicates the model fits all datasets.

Overfitting

Overfitting is a big concern in both statistical analyses and predictive modeling because it affects the predictive power of a model. It is a common issue caused by the large data we use in data mining. But it is a confusing concept that needs to be carefully explained. In some materials, authors tend to use this terminology inconsistently, which causes a great deal of confusion for readers. The primary reason is that they do not provide a clear defini-tion or explanation of this issue.

What Is Overfitting?

The previous differentiation on model fit and predictive power helps us understand this concept easier. Regardless, I break down the overfitting issue into several steps so you can

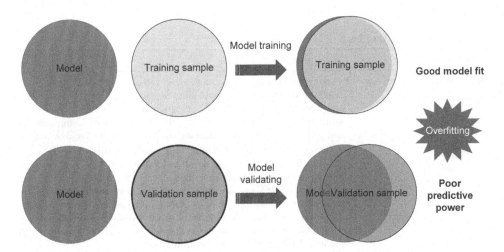

FIGURE 6.2
Overfitting illustration.

follow them. Figure 6.2 illustrates this problem using graphics. By following these steps, we should be able to identify the overfitting problem in our data mining project.

> **DEFINITION**
>
> Overfitting is the situation in which the model is overtrained to the training sample and not generalized to other datasets. Hence, the model is invalid and unusable.

1. We used the training sample to train our model. We achieved a very good model fit, indicating a great fit between the model and this data set.

2. We tested this model with a new data set, the validation sample. Unfortunately, the model fit was very poor in this case. What happened?

3. We tried again with a different data set, the test sample. The result was not good. Model fit was still poor.

4. What does it mean? It means our model is biased to the training sample, and it only works well with that data set. It is not generalizable since it does not work with new datasets. Thus, it does not have good predictive power, which makes it unusable. Accordingly, we cannot deploy this model to make the prediction of the target variable with real-life data.

5. What is the reason? We overtrained the model with the training sample, and we have the overfitting issue. It could be due to the imbalanced dataset that was used to train the model. It could also be caused by sampling bias in the training sample. Or it could be due to the configurations of the machine learning algorithm we used.

How to Address Overfitting?

Now we are able to identify an overfitting problem. When we have overfitting, our model is invalid and unusable. So, what can we do to prevent this problem from happening or to solve the problem? There is no standard solution, but there are several options that we can try. Table 6.2 describes common solutions for preventing and addressing overfitting.

TABLE 6.2

Solutions for the Overfitting Issue

Solutions for Overfitting	Description
Perform data sampling correctly	By using the correct sampling method, we can obtain a dataset that is generalizable to the target population; i.e., our dataset shares the same trends and characteristics as the target population. If we use a biased training sample with biases, then our model will be biased as well. Using a quality and generalizable dataset to train the model allows us to avoid overfitting.
Get a large dataset	Training predictive models require large data, especially since some machine learning algorithms require a lot of data to work properly. A dataset with a small sample size may lead to a poor model fit. Having a sufficient sample size can increase the model's explanatory power, especially when we have many variables in the model. Having a large dataset also allows us to split the dataset into multiple sub-samples for validation purposes. However, we should be careful not to overtrain the model, which could lead to overfitting.
Clean the data well	A clean dataset is needed to train the model. Remember, "garbage in, garbage out." Our predictive model can only be as good as the input data. Data with too much noise and irrelevant information may lead to poor model training since the machine learning algorithm tries to account for all the noise and misinformation as well, which results in poor predictive power. We should examine the data carefully, correct any errors, and remove excessive noises and irrelevant predictors. We should also handle missing values and outliers, and remove predictors with excessive missing values or outliers if needed. Data cleaning is the most time-consuming step in data mining. It may account for 60–80% of the project time.
Partition data properly	It is essential to partition the dataset into several sub-samples to train and validate the model. By using the right partition method, we can ensure those sub-samples share the same trends and characteristics as the original dataset. Thus, we can minimize biases in the model training and validation process, which allows us to avoid overfitting.
Maintain the balance in the data	As we discussed before, a highly imbalanced dataset often leads to overfitting since the machine learning algorithm may mistake all cases as negative cases. While the prediction accuracy seems high enough, the model actually fails to predict the event, which makes it invalid. Using an imbalanced dataset is one of the primary causes of overfitting. If the dataset is imbalanced, we need to perform resampling to balance the response ratio.
Use multiple model fit metrics	There are multiple model fit metrics, each of them measures one aspect of the model fit. If we rely on one metric, the result could be misleading. By using multiple metrics, we can evaluate the model fit collectively and correctly and have strategies to improve it.
Use cost-sensitive learning	In reality, the costs of misclassification are often not the same. In most cases, the cost of false negatives is much higher than the cost of false positives. Therefore, we should not choose a model simply based on the prediction accuracy. By incorporating the weights of the misclassification costs in the model evaluation, we can select the model that minimizes the total costs. This approach allows us to find the model that works best for the real-life situation, which allows us to minimize overfitting.
Use an ensemble model	Sometimes, we cannot find one single model that works best for our data even if we try various machine learning methods. Additionally, these models may even disagree with each other. In this case, we should try using an ensemble model, which combines predictions from multiple models to create a single consensus prediction. The ensemble model is typically more accurate than the individual models composing it.

Model Reliability and Validity

An important question we usually receive is about the quality of our model. More specifically, do we have a reliable and valid predictive model? So what is the difference between model reliability and validity? The concept of reliability and validity seems simple, and those terms are often used in statistics and research methodology materials. However, they are rarely described and explained clearly, especially in the field of data mining. It is vital to understand the differences between them, which allows us to measure and evaluate them correctly. I will explain those concepts in a simple way in the context of data mining so you understand why they are important.

Essentially, reliability reflects the internal consistency of a model, and validity indicates the accuracy of the model. In a simpler way, a reliable model should provide consistent results when we run it with different data sets. And a valid model should produce an accurate prediction of the target variable. Both of them are important. But reliability does not guarantee validity. Hence, we have to evaluate both. Still confused? Let's use a fairly simple example of using a scale to measure the weight of a 25 lb bag of rice. A reliable scale would give us consistent weight numbers in multiple measurements. But it does not mean the scale is valid. For example, we use the scale to measure the weight of that rice bag ten times, and each time the scale gives us a very consistent reading ranging between 22.1 and 22.8 lbs. As you can see, the scale is very reliable but inaccurate because it is off about 2 lbs. Thus, we have reliability but not validity. We want a reliable scale that also gives us an accurate reading of 25 lbs.

> **DEFINITION**
>
> **Model reliability** refers to the internal consistency of a model. It means the model produces consistent results with different runs using different data sets.
>
> **Model validity** refers to the accuracy of the model. It means the model consistently produces an accurate prediction of the target variable.

You may say: Does it mean a valid scale should imply reliability as well? The answer is Yes. However, we don't know it until we measure the weights multiple times. For example, we buy a brand new scale, and the first measurement gives us an accurate reading of 25 lbs. Sounds great, right? But to be sure, we must repeat the measurements several more times. If it keeps producing accurate readings multiple times, then it is a good scale. On the other hand, if we keep receiving inconsistent readings, then the scale is neither reliable nor valid. In data mining, it is the case of overfitting that we have discussed before when a model produces a good prediction with the training sample but fails to do so with other datasets. Accordingly, it is vital to evaluate both model reliability and validity. We cannot confirm the overall model validity until we achieve reliability. In other words, in order to achieve model validity, the model must consistently produce an accurate prediction of the target variable. Essentially, model validity is the same as predictive power. Figure 6.3 illustrates the case where we have model reliability but not validity.

With a clear understanding of the difference between reliability and validity, the next step is to learn how to assess the reliability and validity of a predictive model. Note that

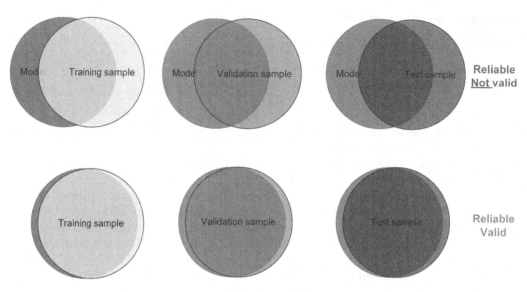

FIGURE 6.3
Model reliability and validity.

we cannot do it in two separate processes since model fit metrics are used for both pur-poses. Reliability and validity must be done in the same process, even though we need to provide separate evidence for reliability and validity.

Model Reliability and Validity Assessment Process

Follow the steps below to evaluate the reliability and validity of a predic-tive model.

1. Split the sample into sub-samples, including training, validation, and test samples. The recommended split ratio is 60:40, meaning 60% for training, 20% for validation, and 20% for final testing.
2. Configure a predictive model based on the selected machine learning methods (we will go into the details of each method in the next chapters).
3. Train the model with the training sample. Then validate the model with the vali-dation sample. Most data mining programs run this step automatically.
4. Evaluate the model fit of the training sample using pre-determined appropriate metrics (the next sections provide details on model fit metrics). If the model fit is satisfactory, then move to Step 5. If not, go back to Step 2 to reconfigure the models.
5. Compare the model fit metrics between the training and validation samples using the metrics.
6. If the comparison shows consistency between training and validation samples, then we can conclude that we have model reliability. Note that the level of consis-tency is subject to the context of the study and the justification of the researchers. Nonetheless, if the discrepancy is less than 5%, we can consider acceptable reli-ability. **Conclusion: Model reliability is achieved.**

7. If the model reliability is not achieved, make adjustments to the sampling and modeling processes in Steps 1 and 2 to address the problem. Solutions may include resampling data, reconfiguring the model, using alternative machine learning methods, or using an ensemble model. Repeat Steps 2–5 until we achieve reliability.

8. Evaluate the full model fit metrics for the validation sample to confirm the overall model fit (more metrics can be added for this purpose). If the model fit is satisfactory, go to Step 9. If not, further adjustments are needed to improve the model's performance.

9. Evaluate the model fit for the test sample as the final assessment. If the model shows a good fit with this sample, then we achieve model validity. **Conclusion: Model validity is achieved.**

How to Report the Model Reliability and Validity Results?

Suppose we completed the predictive modeling process and achieved both model reliability and validity. How do we report the results effectively? Since the above process is iterative, presenting the results for all steps is not recommended since it may make the results more complicated than they should be and cause confusion to the readers. I recommend the following steps to present the results clearly and effectively. Note that these steps apply to the project in which we train multiple models.

1. If there are multiple models, present the model comparison results. Use key model fit metrics for the validation sample in this comparison and explain whether the model fit is satisfactory and why. Note that while we need to evaluate the model fit for the training sample first, as mentioned in the process above, it is not necessary to report the results separately. Since the validation sample is used to validate the model, the validation results are important for the readers to understand the validated model fit metrics.

2. Identify the preliminary champion model based on the model comparison results. Confirm this selection by using multiple model fit metrics.

3. Present the comparison of model fit metrics between the training, validation, and test samples and explain whether the results are reliable between those samples and why. In this step, focus on the champion model only. If we have consistent results, we can conclude that the model reliability is achieved.

4. Present additional model fit metrics to perform a complete evaluation of model fit. Confirm the champion model has a good model fit.

5. With satisfactory model fit metrics for the validation sample and the model reliability, we can conclude that the model validity is achieved. Overall, the champion model has good predictive power.

> I will use this process to present the results of predictive modeling in most chapters.

6. Report and explain the model structure, relationships among variables, and variable importance of the champion model.

Model Comparison

In data mining, we aim to discover unknown patterns from large and noisy data. That means we mine the data and see what they tell us. The patterns we uncover from the data are usually new relationships among variables that do not exist in the current literature or new predictors. For that purpose, it is hard to predetermine which machine learning methods and which model configurations will work best. The best machine

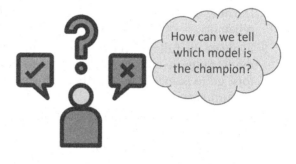

learning model essentially depends on the data. Our goal is to find the model that best fits the data. Accordingly, using a complicated or advanced method does not guarantee we have the best model.

Let's take a look at a hypothetical scenario presented in Figure 6.4. Suppose we build two models for a given dataset. One model uses an advanced machine learning method, for instance, neural networks (the one on the right). This model produces nonlinear relationships between predictors and the target variable and seems to fit the data very well. Another model uses a simple method, linear regression, which shows a linear relationship between predictors and the target variable (the one on the left). In the model training process, the linear regression model may not show a good model fit as the neural network model, based on the prediction accuracy. However, if we visually review the data with a scatter plot, we can easily detect that the data follow a linear pattern. That means while being much simpler, the linear regression model captures the pattern much better than the neural network model. When we run both models with the validation sample, we find that the regression model consistently produces a good model fit. On the other hand, the neural network's model fit is much lower for the validation sample in comparison with the training results. What happens here? The reason is that the neural network model has an overfitting issue because it tries to account for noises in the data

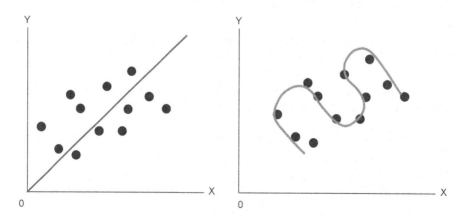

FIGURE 6.4
Simple linear model and a complex, non-linear model – A hypothetical scenario.

and incorporate those noises in the model in the training process without thinking they are mainly noises. That is why it receives a near perfect model fit for the training model, but when we run this model with the validation sample, it does not make an accurate prediction. Thus, the complex non-linear pattern derived from this model does not capture the actual pattern in the data. We can conclude that

There is no such thing as a perfect data mining method. But there is the best method for a specific set of data.

this model is not generalizable, meaning it has poor predictive power. In this particular case, the linear regression model is a better one.

This example tells us that it is hard to predetermine or speculate which machine learning method is the best without applying various methods to the actual data. Otherwise, we could just go straight to the most advanced method all the time and not have to bother with less advanced ones. Similarly, even with the same method, we can establish numerous analytical configurations to find a model with good predictive power. For instance, in the example above, we could reconfigure our neural network model appropriately to capture the linear pattern

DEFINITION

Champion model is the model with the best performance among the models we train and validate.

instead of the non-linear one. The simplest form of the neural network is very much the same as linear regression.

With that note in mind, in order to find a predictive model with good predictive power, the best practice is to build multiple models with different methods and different configurations. Then, we compare the performance of these models based on model fit metrics to find the model with the best performance. This model is called

Build and train multiple models and compare them to find the champion model.

the *champion model* and can be used as the final predictive model for a real-life prediction. Note that it is only the champion model among the models we train and validate with the given data. Therefore, there is still a chance that the champion model does not have the expected predictive power. This situation occurs when all models we train do not have a good model fit, so the best one among them is not necessarily mean a good model. We can say, it is a relative best. Hence, we still have to evaluate this champion model and decide whether further adjustments are needed or additional models should be trained.

Model Comparison Steps

Follow the steps below to build and compare models.

1. Develop and train multiple predictive models using different machine learning methods and analytical configurations, appropriate for the given data.
2. Run those models with the training and validation samples.
3. Select model fit metrics for model selection.
4. Compare the models using the identified metrics and select the champion model.
5. Examine the model fit of the champion model to see if it is satisfactory. If not, make adjustments to configurations of existing models or consider adding new models.

6. Repeat Steps 1–5 until a satisfactory champion model is achieved.

7. Evaluate the model fit of the champion model with the test sample to confirm its predictive power.

> The champion model is only the best model among the models we train and validate with the given data. There is no guarantee it has good predictive power. We need to examine it carefully to determine whether more models need to be trained.

Model Fit Metrics

We have talked about model fit and predictive power. So how do we evaluate them? In other words, what specific model fit metrics should we use to assess model fit? As mentioned before, in order to avoid confusion, I use the term *model fit* instead of *goodness-of-fit* and *model fit metrics* instead of *goodness-of-fit indices*. Again, the same metrics are used to evaluate predictive power. These metrics are also used to compare models and identify the champion model. Keep in mind that we have different metrics for association models and classification models because they have different types of target variables. As a reminder, association models have continuous target variables, and classification models have binary or nominal target variables. Hence, I break down the model fit metrics for these types of models. Table 6.3 summarizes those metrics. Note that in this chapter, we focus on general model fit metrics that apply to all machine learning methods in that category. Each method may have its own specific model fit metrics, and they will be described in detail in the chapters for those methods (not all machine learning methods have their own specific metrics).

TABLE 6.3

Model Fit Metrics Summary

	Association Models	**Classification Model**
Target Variable	*Continuous*	*Binary or Nominal*
General model fit metrics	• Root Mean Squared Error (RMSE) • Mean Absolute Percent Error (MAPE) • Relative Squared Error (RSE) • Explanatory Power (EP) • Actual by predicted chart • Residual by predicted chart	• Misclassification rate • Prediction accuracy • Specificity • Sensitivity • F1-score • ROC chart (only available for the model with binary target variable) or ROC index • Lift chart or Lift value • Gini coefficient
Machine learning method specific model fit metrics	Additional model fit metrics are decided depending on the machine learning method (we will cover them in the next chapters). Note that not all machine learning methods require additional metrics.	

Model Fit Metrics for Association Models

Model fit metrics are used to evaluate how well our trained model fits the data. It is measured by either the accuracy or error of the prediction. For association models with continuous target variables, we can categorize those metrics into error measures and charts. The error measures allow us to perform a numeric evaluation of model fit, while charts allow us to visually examine the model fit.

Prediction Error Measures

Errors measure the extent to which our trained model misfits the data. Typically, the lower the error, the more accurate the model. There are numerous error measures in statistics, ranging from simple ones to more complicated ones. Using all of them is overkilling and unnecessary since some of them are quite similar to one another. I describe a few common measures and recommend the most useful ones. The following formulas show these common measures for errors and how to calculate these errors using actual values, predicted values, and mean values.

Sum of Squared Error (SSE)

$$SSE = Sum \ of \ (Actual - Predicted)^2$$

Sum of Squared Regression (SSR)

$$SSR = Sum \ of \ (Predicted - Mean)^2$$

Sum of Squared Total (SST)

$$SST = Sum \ of \ (Actual - Mean)^2$$

Mean Absolute Error (MAE)

$$MAE = \frac{Sum \ of \ |Actual - Predicted|}{sample \ size}$$

Mean Squared Error (MSE)

$$MSE = \frac{Sum \ of \ (Actual - Predicted)^2}{sample \ size}$$

Root Mean Squared Error (RMSE)

$$RMSE = \sqrt{\frac{Sum \ of \ (Actual - Predicted)^2}{sample \ size}}$$

Mean Absolute Percent Error (MAPE)

$$MAPE = \frac{Sum\ of\ \left|\dfrac{Actual - Predicted}{Actual}\right|}{sample\ size}$$

Relative Squared Error (RSE)

$$RSE = \frac{Sum\ of\ (Actual - Predicted)^2}{Sum\ of\ (Actual - Mean)^2} = \frac{SSE}{SST} = \frac{Unexplained\ Variance}{Total\ Variance}$$

Model's Explanatory Power (EP)

$$EP = 1 - RSE = \frac{Explained\ Variance}{Total\ Variance}$$

We can notice that SSE, SSR, and SST are the essential components of other error measures, even though they are not used as the final model fit metrics. Hence, I describe what they mean as follows.

- Sum of Squared Error (SSE) – unexplained variance: How far the data are from the model's predicted values.
- Sum of Squared Regression (SSR) – explained variance: How far the mean is from the model's predicted values.
- Sum of Squared Total (SST) – total variance: How far the data are from the mean.

Note that in these measures, the mean value is the average of actual values in the dataset, and it represents the expected prediction if we do not use any model. Figure 6.5 illustrates the relationship between SSE, SSR, and SST for linear regression as an example.

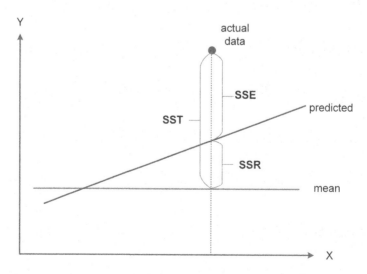

FIGURE 6.5
SSE, SSR, and SST for linear regression.

Note that the relat ionship among SSE, SSR, and SST in Figure 6.5 is only accurate for linear regression. It may be different when we have nonlinear patterns. Hence, we should use SSE and SST to calculate RSE and EP.

Let's discuss some popular model fit metrics. Mean Absolute Error (MAE) is the average of all absolute errors, representing the average distance between the actual values and predicted values. MAE is easy to interpret since it tells us about the average absolute error in the same scale as the target variable. The main drawback of MAE is that it treats all errors the same way and does not punish large errors. Mean Squared Error (MSE) is similar to MAE, except that we use the square of errors instead of absolute errors. MSE is the average of all squared errors. The key difference between MAE and MSE is that MSE punishes large errors to a greater extent because the error is squared. In some cases, punishing large errors may be important because we can prioritize models with smaller errors. Hence, MSE can better capture the model fit. A drawback of MSE is that it uses the squared value of errors, which is not the same scale as the data. Root Mean Squared Error solves this problem by using the square root of MSE, which makes RMSE the same scale as the data. For that reason, I recommend using RMSE.

RMSE is scale-dependent, and it can be used to compare the prediction errors across models with the same target variable with the same scale. It eliminates the effect of sample size by using the average score and the effect of the sign by using the squared value instead of the actual difference. It is important to note that RMSE is scale-dependent and does not tell us the prediction accuracy because they are not presented in percentage. For example, we have two models, one with an RMSE of 24.12 and another one with an RMSE of 29.36. In this case, we can conclude that the first model has a better model fit because its RMSE is lower. However, we cannot make any conclusion about the model fit of this model in terms of prediction accuracy because 24.12 is the Root Mean Squared Error, which is hard to interpret.

In this context, Mean Absolute Percent Error (MAPE) is a better measure because it represents the percent error. In other words, MAPE is scale-independent, and it does tell us the percent error. The lower the MAPE, the higher the prediction accuracy. It also eliminates the effect of sample size by using the mean value and the effect of the sign by using the absolute value. There is no standard cutoff value for MAPE. But my rule of thumb is that a MAPE of 0.05 or lower means a great model fit, and a MAPE of 0.10 or lower means a good model fit.

In addition to MAPE, Relative Squared Error (RSE) is another scale-independent metric that is presented in percentage. As shown in the formula above, RSE is SSE divided by SST, indicating the rate of unexplained variance in the model. RSE allows us to calculate the Explanatory Power (EP). EP is SSR divided by SST, indicating the rate of explained variance in the model. EP is 1 minus RSE. EP is an important metric because it represents how well the model can explain the variance in the target variable based on the variance in the predictors. In simpler terms, it shows us how well our model can explain the target variable. For example, an EP of 92% means the model can explain 92% of the variance in the target variable based on the variance in the predictors. I highly recommend using RSE and EP to evaluate model fit.

TABLE 6.4

Recommended Model Fit Metrics for Association Models

Metrics	Descriptions	Recommended Cutoff Values
RMSE	Scale-dependent; a measure of the average difference between the predicted values and the actual values in a dataset	None; depending on the scale of the data
MAPE	Scale-independent; a measure of the percentage difference between the predicted values and the actual values in a dataset.	MAPE = 0.05 or lower: Great MAPE = 0.05–0.1: Good MAPE = 0.1–0.15: Acceptable
RSE	Scale-independent; a measure of the relative improvement of the model's predictions compared to a simple baseline model that always predicts the mean of the actual values.	RSE = 0.1 or lower: Great RSE = 0.1–0.3: Good RSE = 0.3–0.5: Acceptable
EP	Scale-independent; a measure of how well the model captures the underlying relationships between the input variables (predictors) and the target variable.	EP = 90% or higher: Great EP = 70–90%: Good EP = 50–70%: Acceptable

Again, there is no standard rule for EP. My rule of thumb is that an EP of 90% or higher is considered a great fit, and an EP between 70% and 90% is considered a good fit. In most cases, an EP of 50–70% can be considered acceptable, especially if we have numerous predictors in the model. Table 6.4 presents my recommended model fit metrics and cutoff values.

While all software apps produce MSE, RMSE values, they usually to not produce RSE and EP directly in the output. In this case, we need to export the output data to Excel and do the calculation using the formula.

Actual by Predicted Chart and Residuals by Predicted Chart

In addition to these error measures, there are two important charts we can build to evaluate the model fit for association models: *actual by predicted chart* and *residuals by predicted chart*. These charts provide us with visualization capturing how well the model fits the data. They can be used to evaluate the model fit of a predictive model.

The *actual by predicted chart* compares the actual values with the predicted values, showing us how well the trained model fits the data. This chart is conducted by plotting the actual values on the Y-axis and predicted values on the X-axis. Essentially, the closer the dots in this chart are to the diagonal line, the better the model fit because the residuals between actual and predicted values are relatively small (see Figure 6.6 for an example). If the dots are scattered around and far from the line, then the model fit may not be satisfactory.

Residuals are measured by the difference between actual values and predicted values. The *residual by predicted chart* is a very important chart because it presents not only how close the actual values are to the predicted values but also indicates any patterns in the residuals. This chart is conducted by plotting the residuals on the Y-axis and predicted values on the X-axis. The distance between the point and the line captures the accuracy

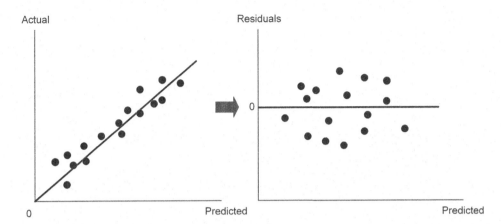

FIGURE 6.6
Actual by predicted chart and residual by predicted chart – An example of a good model fit.

of the prediction. We would expect this distance not to be too large to ensure the accuracy of the prediction. Additionally, we need to examine this chart to see if there is any clear pattern. A non-random pattern in this chart indicates a correlation between residuals and predicted values, implying potential confounding variables. In other words, the predictors in the model do not capture some explanatory information that is revealed in the residuals. Typically, we would expect a chart with no clear pattern, also called a random pattern. In other words, there is only white noise. In order to meet this requirement, points should be symmetrically distributed and cluster toward the middle of the plot (see Figure 6.6).

Note that not all software apps produce those charts automatically. We will need to create charts from the output data.

Figure 6.7 shows several examples of the scatter plot with non-random patterns, such as uneven distribution of the plot (Chart A), clear shapes (Charts B and C), and outliers (Chart D). In these cases, we conclude that the model does not achieve a satisfactory model fit and should be further improved. The solution may include reconfiguring the model, using an ensemble model, adding more data points by resampling or adding additional predictors.

Overall, I recommend using RMSE, MAPE, RSE, and EP to compare models and using MAPE, RSE, EP, actual by predicted chart, and residual by predicted chart to evaluate the model fit of a model.

Example: Model Fit Metrics for an Association Model

Let's review an example of an association model and see how these metrics are calculated and interpreted. For example, we built and trained a predictive model to predict the number of tickets sold for a boat tour in

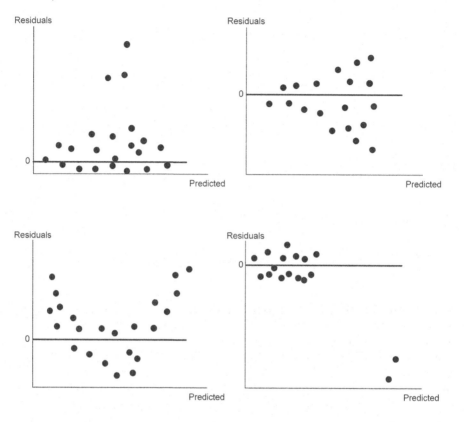

FIGURE 6.7
The residual by predicted charts with non-random patterns.

a city at nighttime. Table 6.5 shows the actual values and the predicted values as a result of the predictive modeling process. The residuals are essentially the prediction errors and are measured by the difference between actual and predicted values. The squared errors are the square values of the errors.

Using the formulas presented before, we calculate the model fit metrics as follows.

- SSE = 68,037
- SST = 220,908.95
- MSE = 68,037/20 = 3,401.85
- RMSE = $\sqrt{3,401.85}$ = 58.33
- MAPE = 0.066
- RSE = SSE/SST = 0.308
- EP = 1- RSE = 0.692

As you can see, MSE and RMSE are scale-dependent, so they must be interpreted with the scale of the target variable in mind, which is the number of tickets. MSE is an average squared error and is 3,401.85 squared tickets. RMSE is a Root Mean Squared Error and is 58.33 tickets. MSE and RMSE certainly punish large errors, as shown in cases 2, 5, 7, 11, and 15, where the absolute errors are higher than 80 tickets. RMSE is a great metric to compare between models, but it is not easy to determine the prediction accuracy with this metric.

TABLE 6.5

Actual and Predicted Values

No.	Actual Values	Predicted Values	Residuals (Errors)	Squared Errors
1	779	750	29	841
2	958	878	80	6,400
3	860	850	10	100
4	882	821	61	3,721
5	606	508	98	9,604
6	766	813	−47	2,209
7	669	761	−92	8,464
8	856	847	9	81
9	686	652	34	1,156
10	887	829	58	3,364
11	995	907	88	7,744
12	779	724	55	3,025
13	953	995	−42	1,764
14	771	726	45	2,025
15	804	886	−82	6,724
16	992	1,034	−42	1,764
17	895	951	−56	3,136
18	843	858	−15	225
19	752	799	−47	2,209
20	738	797	−59	3,481

On the other hand, MAPE is scale-independent and measured by percentage. In this case, we have a MAPE of 0.066, or 6.6%, indicating the model has a prediction error of 6.6%, or the prediction accuracy is 1–0.066 = 0.934 or 93.4%, which is considered a good model fit.

We can also look at RSE and EP to evaluate the model's explanatory power. In this example. We have an RSE of 0.308 or an EP of 0.692. In other words, the model has an explanatory power of 69.2%, which is considered acceptable.

To further evaluate the model fit, we want to look at the *actual by predicted chart* and the *residual by predicted chart.* As shown in Figure 6.8, in the *actual by predicted chart,* data points are relatively close to the diagonal line, and there are no outliers. It indicates a good model fit. In addition, in the *residuals by predicted chart,* the residual points seem to be random and symmetrically distributed on both sides of the centerline. They do not form any patterns or outliers, as shown in Figure 6.9, and they are not too far from the centerline. Accordingly, we can conclude that this model has a good model fit.

> Use Excel to construct these charts using the data presented in Table 6.5.

Model Fit Metrics for Classification Models

Classification models have either binary target variables or nominal target variables. Binary target variables are more common cases since, most of the time, we aim to predict the occurrence of an event. The target variable has two levels: occurrence (events) and non-occurrence (non-events). For example, the risk of credit fraud, aviation accidents, flight cancellations,

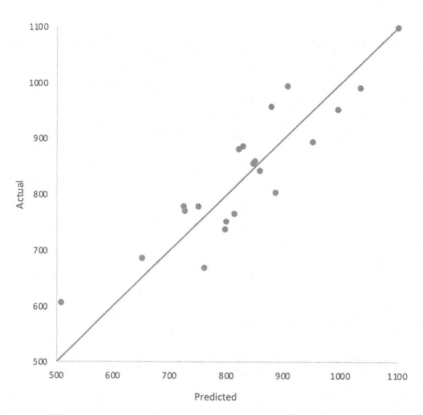

FIGURE 6.8
Actual by predicted chart.

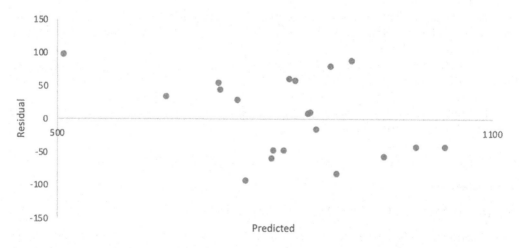

FIGURE 6.9
Residual by predicted chart.

or customers' decision to buy a product or service. Hence, we focus mainly on models with binary target variables. Models with nominal target variables (more than two levels) use the same model fit metrics with some calculation differences, which I will explain later.

Binary Target Variables

Confusion Matrix Metrics

When we have a binary target variable, there are several important model fit metrics to be used to evaluate the model performance. In order to calculate those metrics, we need to have the confusion matrix. Confusion matrix, also called the classification matrix, is the table that summarizes the performance of a classification algorithm. It presents all results of the prediction, including correct and incorrect predictions. More specifically, it presents the number of True Positives (TP), True Negatives (TN), False Positives (FP), and False Negatives (FN). Table 6.6 shows the format of a confusion matrix. The values of TP, TN, FP, and FN are extracted from the results at the modeling step. See the definitions of these terms in the definition box.

DEFINITION

Confusion matrix, also called the classification matrix, is the table that summarizes the performance of a classification algorithm.

True Positive (TP): the prediction that correctly indicates the presence of the event.
True Negative (TN): the prediction that correctly indicates the absence of the event.
False Positive (FP): the prediction that wrongly indicates the presence of the event.
False Negative (FN): the prediction that wrongly indicates the absence of the event.

Typically, in most data mining projects, we intend to predict an event and a non-event. In this case, we usually have a binary target variable with values of 1 (event) or 0 (non-event). We consider events (1) as positives and non-events (0) as negatives. For example, we want to predict the risk of flight cancellation, so 1 means *cancellation* and 0 means *no cancellation*. In this case, the cancellation cases are positives, and the non-cancellation cases are negatives. There are several model fit metrics calculated based on the confusion matrix. The most common metrics include misclassification rate, prediction accuracy, sensitivity, specificity, and F-1 score. The following are formulas for calculating the metrics based on the confusion matrix. In addition, Table 6.7 provides descriptions of these metrics.

$$Misclassification\ rate\ (MR) = \frac{FP+FN}{Total} = \frac{FP+FN}{TP+TN+FP+FN}$$

$$Accuracy\ (ACC) = \frac{TP+TN}{Total} = \frac{TP+TN}{TP+TN+FP+FN} = 1-MR$$

TABLE 6.6

Classification Matrix or Confusion Matrix

	Predicted YES	Predicted NO
Actual YES	TP (true positive)	FN (false negative)
Actual NO	FP (false positive)	TN (true negative)

TABLE 6.7

Model Fit Metrics and Descriptions

Model Fit Metrics	Description
Misclassification Rate (MR)	How often a model misclassifies (makes incorrect predictions) the target variable (including actual positives and actual negatives)
Prediction Accuracy (ACC)	How accurate a model predicts the target variables (including actual positives and actual negatives) ACC = 1 - MR
Sensitivity, Recall, or True positive rate (TPR)	The probability of a positive result (event) or how well a model can predict true positives (events)
Specificity, Selectivity, or True negative rate (TNR)	The probability of a negative result (non-event) or how well a model can predict true negatives (non-events)
F1 score	Alternative accuracy metric; it is the harmonic mean of the sensitivity (recall) and precision (positive predicted value); a high F1 score means low false positives (FP) and low false negatives (FN)

$$Sensitivity,\ Recall,\ or\ True\ positive\ rate\ (TPR) = \frac{TP}{TP + FN}$$

$$Specificity,\ Selectivity,\ or\ True\ negative\ rate\ (TNR) = \frac{TN}{TN + FP}$$

$$F1\ score = \frac{2TP}{2TP + FP + FN}$$

It is vital that we examine multiple metrics rather than just one. The reason is that while the accuracy rate (ACC) shows us the overall accuracy of the model, it does not tell us whether we have any issues with false negatives (FN) or false positives (FP). For example, we have an accuracy rate of 90%, meaning a misclassification rate of 10%. At a glance, it looks like we have a good predictive model since the model can accurately predict the target variable 90% of the time. However, suppose we look at other metrics and note that the sensitivity (recall) is only 50%, then we need to investigate further. Sensitivity is also called the true positive rate, and it tells us how well our model can predict the positives (events).

Rule of thumb:
- MR= 5% or lower: Great
- MR = 5-10%: Good
- ACC, TPR, TNR, F1 = 95% or higher: Great
- ACC, TPR, TNR, F1 = 90-95%: Good

The low sensitivity means we have high false negatives. So, why do we still have a good overall prediction accuracy? As we discussed in Chapter 3, one primary reason is that we may have a very imbalanced dataset with the rarest events. For example, the response ratio is 5%. In our example of flight cancellation, it means only 5% of the dataset are cancellation cases. Accordingly, if the model treats all cases as negatives (no cancellation), it still achieves an accuracy of 95%. However, by examining the sensitivity, we realize that the model fails to predict the events (cancellation), which is the main purpose of the project. Hence, the model is not valid, usable, and generalizable. In this case, we can say that the misclassification rate and accuracy rate results are misleading. That is why we do not want to rely on one metric to choose the model. We need to evaluate multiple metrics.

There are no standard cut-off values for these metrics. Ultimately, in the industry, the decision depends on the answer to this question: As the decision maker, which margin of error is considered acceptable for your business? 1%, 5%, or 10%? My rule of thumb is similar to what we have in the previous section. A misclassification rate (MR) of 5% or lower is considered great, and an MR between 5% and 10% is considered good. On the other hand, for accuracy rate, sensitivity, specificity, and F1 score, a value of 95% or higher is considered great, while a value between 90% and 95% is considered good.

Example: Model Fit Metrics for a Classification Model

This example demonstrates how to calculate model fit metrics for a classification model. For example, we have a confusion matrix for a house-buying prediction, as presented in Table 6.8.

Using the formulas above, we calculate our model fit metrics as follows.

$$Misclassification\ rate\ (MR) = \frac{53+17}{982+864+53+17} = 0.037\ or\ 3.7\%$$

$$Accuracy\ (ACC) = \frac{982+864}{982+864+53+17} = 0.963\ or\ 96.3\%$$

or ACC = 1 − MR = 1 − 0.037 = 0.063

$$Sensitivity,\ Recall,\ or\ True\ positive\ rate\ (TPR) = \frac{982}{982+17} = 0.983\ or\ 98.3\%$$

$$Specificity,\ Selectivity,\ or\ True\ negative\ rate\ (TNR) = \frac{864}{864+53} = 0.942\ or\ 94.2\%$$

$$F1\ score = \frac{2*982}{2*982+53+17} = 0.966\ or\ 96.6\%$$

Overall, our misclassification rate is 3.7%, or the accuracy rate is 96.3%, which is great. Further examination shows the sensitivity, or a true positive rate, of 98.3%, which is great, and the specificity, or a true negative rate, of 94.2%, which is good. Finally, F1 score is 96.6%, which is great. In conclusion, our model has a great model fit, and all model fit metrics show consistent results.

TABLE 6.8

Example of a Confusion Matrix for a House-Buying Prediction

	Predicted Buying	Predicted Not buying
Actual Buying	TP = 982	FN = 17
Actual Not buying	FP = 53	TN = 864

Additional Model Fit Metrics

In addition to these metrics, we should evaluate several additional metrics to further confirm the model fit. These are not the metrics based on the confusion matrix, but they show the model fit from different perspectives, which is how well the model explains the target variable. They include the ROC chart, Lift chart, and Gini coefficient.

Receiver Operating Characteristic (ROC) Chart

The ROC chart or Receiver Operating Characteristic chart shows the values of the true positive fraction on the vertical axis and the false positive fraction on the horizontal axis. Basically, an ROC chart reflects the tradeoff between sensitivity and specificity. We have discussed sensitivity and specificity in detail above. The straight diagonal line is the baseline, while the vertical line on the left and the horizontal line on the

> **DEFINITION**
>
> The ROC chart shows the values of the true positive fraction on the vertical axis and the false positive fraction on the horizontal axis. it reflects the tradeoff between sensitivity and specificity.

top represent the perfect classification. The larger the area between the ROC chart of the model and the diagonal line, the better fit the model. Figure 6.10 illustrates the ROC chart and some scenarios for model fit evaluation. Note that we can only produce an ROC chart

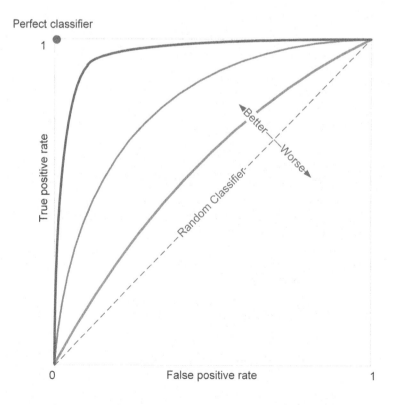

FIGURE 6.10
ROC chart.

with a binary target variable because this chart has two dimensions. For nominal target variables with more than two levels, we can only have the ROC index. An ROC index of 0.9 or higher is considered a good fit.

Lift Chart

Lift chart is another common metric to evaluate the model performance for classification models. Lift is a measure of the effectiveness of a predictive model calculated as the ratio between the results obtained with and without the predictive model. The Lift chart, or Lift curve, presents the graphic representation between the lift values and response rates. At a given response rate, the model with a higher lift value performs better.

> **DEFINITION**
>
> Lift is a measure of the effectiveness of a predictive model calculated as the ratio between the results obtained with and without the predictive model. The Lift chart presents the graphic representation between the lift values and response rates.

Basically, the X-axis shows the percentile, and the Y-axis shows the lift values. Basically, for any given number of cases (X-value), the lift value represents the expected number of positives we would predict. Keep in mind that the baseline (no model) is a horizontal line intersecting the Y-axis at 1. For example, if we select 10% of the data without any predictive model, we would expect to be able to predict 10% of the positives by default; i.e., we do not have any model and just simply select cases at random. This is what we mean by no lift (or Lift = 1).

The Lift chart shows us that given selected cases, by building a predictive model, we are able to predict more positive cases, indicating how effective the model is. Figure 6.11 shows us an example of a Lift chart. The chart indicates if we select 20% of the cases by using the predictive model, we should be able to predict 2.5 (20%) or 50% of the positive cases because the lift value is 2.5. That is 2.5 times as many as if we use no model. The higher the lift value, the better the model. Again, we need to compare this Lift chart with other models to decide which model is better.

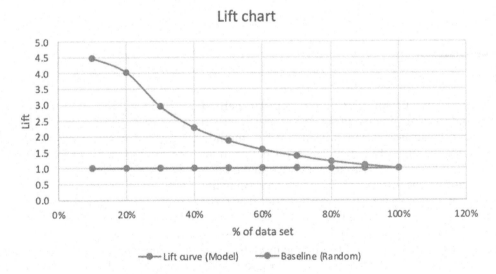

FIGURE 6.11
Lift chart

Gini Coefficient

Gini coefficient is a metric measuring the model's discriminatory power, the effectiveness of the model in differentiating between positives and negatives. In the context of machine learning, the Gini coefficient is used to measure how equal the positive rates are across the attributes of a characteristic. It ranges from 0 to 1. The higher the Gini coefficient, the better the model. Essentially, a Gini coefficient indicates how close our model is to being the perfect model and how far it is from being a random model.

> **DEFINITION**
>
> Gini coefficient is a measure of the model's discriminatory power, which is the effectiveness of the model in differentiating between positives and negatives. The Gini coefficient measures how equal the positive rates are across the attributes of a characteristic.

There are several ways to calculate a Gini coefficient, but a common method is to use the area under the ROC curve (AUROC). Most software provides AUROC value. Once we find out the AUROC for our ROC chart, we can calculate the Gini coefficient, also called Somers' D Gini, as follows. Somers' D is named after Robert H. Somers, who proposed this metric in 1962.

$$Gini = 2*AUROC - 1$$

There is no standard cut-off value for the Gini coefficient, but the rule of thumb is that a

> ROC chart and Lift chart are two dimensional and are only available for binary target variable. The workaround is to create those charts for each level separately. Alternatively, we can also use ROC index and Lift value.

Gini coefficient of 0.6 or high is considered a good model fit.

Cost-Sensitive Learning (CSL)

As introduced in Chapter 3, CSL is a popular method that allows us to evaluate and select a model based on the costs of misclassification. It is an effective method to enhance the predictive model's performance in an imbalanced dataset. Essentially, when we make business decisions, the misclassification rate alone may not be the best way to select a predictive model. The costs

> **DEFINITION**
>
> Cost Sensitive Learning is a method to evaluate and select a model based on the costs of misclassification.

of misclassification must be taken into account because in the business world, typically, the cost of false negatives and the cost of false positives are not equal.

Let's look at an example of predictive modeling for fraudulent credit card transactions. The cost of accurate classification is zero (the model is doing a good job). On the other hand, the misclassification cost for false negatives differs from the cost for false positives. Missing a fraudulent transaction (false negatives) causes a loss directly to the customers but also to further fraudulent uses of the card and the company's reputation. At the same time, blocking legitimate transactions (false positives) causes inconvenience to customers and generates useless investigation costs. Typically, the cost of false negatives is higher than the cost of false positives.

When we define misclassification costs, we need to keep in mind that costs are not always measured by monetary loss. An example is terminal disease prediction. False negatives could result in a serious health condition for the patient, while false positives tend to lead

When predicting a risk:
Cost of false negatives > Cost of false positives

to unnecessary treatment and medical charges. Hence, the executives need to define and quantify misclassification costs properly to allow us to build useful predictive models. We use the cost matrix to present misclassification costs.

After defining misclassification costs for all levels in a table (it is called a decision matrix), we can train and select the model that minimizes the total cost. Table 6.9 explains the decision matrix using misclassification costs.

$$Total\ cost = FN*C(FN) + FP*C(FB)$$

C(FN) is the cost of a false negative, and C(FP) is the cost of a false positive. Keep in mind that C(FN) is often higher than C(FP). Most software has a feature that allows us to enter the decision matrix and set the minimization of the total cost as the model selection metric. I will demonstrate how to perform the CSL in SAS Enterprise Miner in later chapters.

In the case of an imbalanced dataset with a very low response ratio, if the cost of false negatives is usually much higher than the cost of false positives, then the mistake for the minority class (rare cases) will be strongly penalized. When we compare models, we will select the one with the lowest total cost rather than the lowest misclassification rate. Thus, CSL improves their importance during the training step and pushes the decision boundaries away from these instances, allowing us to improve the generalization on the minority class.

On the other hand, in some cases, we can choose to focus on the profits of the accurate prediction. For example, by accurately predicting customers' decisions to buy our products, we can have an effective strategy for the supply chain, distribution, logistics, and shipment, which allows us to reduce operational costs and increase revenue. Thus, the accurate prediction will result in a higher profit margin. In this example, it is safe to say the profit of true positives (buying) is higher than the profit of true negatives (not buying). Of course, there are no profits for misclassification.

TABLE 6.9

Decision Matrix – Costs of Misclassification

	Predicted Event	**Predicted Non-event**
Actual Event	True Positive Cost = 0	False Negative Cost = C(FN)
Actual Non-event	False Positive Cost = C(FP)	True Negative Cost = 0

TABLE 6.10

Decision Matrix – Profits of Accurate Classification

	Predicted Event	Predicted Non-event
Actual Event	True Positive Profit = P(TP)	False Negative Profit = 0
Actual Non-event	False Positive Profit = 0	True Negative Profit = P(TN)

If we prefer focusing on the profits, then we just need to define a decision matrix with detailed profits for accurate predictions. When comparing between models, we set the maximization of the total profit as the model selection metric and use it to choose the best model. Table 6.10 shows a decision matrix for the profits of accurate classifications.

$$Total \ profit = TP^*P(TP) + TN^*P(TN)$$

P(TP) is the profit of a true positive, and P(TN) is the profit of a true negative. Keep in mind that P(TP) is often higher than P(TN).

What if we want to include both profits and costs? For example, in the case of buying decisions, what if we decide that misclassification actually may result in higher operational costs due to ineffective planning? In this case, we can define a decision matrix that consists of both profits of accurate classifications and costs of misclassifications. My suggestion is to define a decision matrix in terms of profits. For costs of misclassifications, we assign negative profit margins. Thus, we can still set the objective of maximizing the total profit to select the best model. Table 6.11 illustrates this matrix.

$$Total \ profit = TP^*P(TP) + TN^*P(TN) - FN^*C(FN) - FP^*C(FB)$$

Nominal (Multi-Class) Target Variables

In most data mining projects, we deal with binary target variables because we often aim to predict the occurrence of events vs. non-events. In some cases, we have nominal target variables with multiple levels. They are also called multi-class target variables.

So, how do we measure model fit in this case? Essentially, we use the same metrics we described for binary target variables with some modifications. The most significant difference is that the confusion matrix for multi-class target variables has more levels and,

TABLE 6.11

Decision Matrix with Profits and Costs

	Predicted Event	Predicted Non-event
Actual Event	True Positive Profit = P(TP)	False Negative Profit = - C(FN)
Actual Non-event	False Positive Profit = - C(FP)	True Negative Profit = P(TN)

TABLE 6.12

Confusion Matrix for a Three-Class Target Variable

	Predicted 1	Predicted 2	Predicted 3
Actual 1	a	l	m
Actual 2	x	b	n
Actual 3	y	z	c

therefore, is more complex. Table 6.12 shows a confusion matrix for a target variable with three levels (1, 2, and 3). For example, we want to predict residents' shopping behaviors during the COVID-19 pandemic. They have three choices: 1 – Online shopping; 2 – Curbside pickup; or 3 – In-store shopping. The confusion matrix has actual and predicted values for all three levels. The challenge is how we can calculate the model fit metrics, which require TP, TN, FP, and FN. With three classes of the target variable, we need to find a way to calculate these values.

I explain below a method to calculate TP, TN, FP, and FN for a multi-class target variable. Basically, we need to do it separately for these three classes. For each class, we treat that class as positive and the other two classes as negative. The following formulas allow us to calculate these values for each class.

For Class 1

- TP = a
- TN = b + c + n + z
- FP = x + y
- FN = l + m

For Class 2

- TP = b
- TN = a + c + m + y
- FP = l + z
- FN = x + n

For Class 3

- TP = c
- TN = a + b + l + x
- FP = m + n
- FN = y + z

Once we calculate TP, TN, FP, and FN for each class, we can calculate model fit metrics using the same formulas as presented for binary target variables. Note that when we calculate model fit metrics, we have to do it for each class separately. It is different from the case with a binary target variable, where we only need to do it once. For example, in this example, we need to calculate the following metrics for all three classes.

Class 1:

- MR (Class 1)
- ACC (Class 1)
- TPR (Class 1)
- TNR (Class 1)
- F1 score (Class 1)

1. Calculate TP, TN. FP, and PN separately for each class.
2. Calculate model fit metrics separately for each class.
3. Use metrics for all classes to evaluate the model performance

Class 2:

- MR (Class 2)
- ACC (Class 2)
- TPR (Class 2)
- TNR (Class 2)
- F1 score (Class 2)

Class 3:

- MR (Class 3)
- ACC (Class 3)
- TPR (Class 3)
- TNR (Class 3)
- F1 score (Class 3)

When we evaluate the model fit and compare between models, we need to use the model fit metrics for all three classes.

As for the ROC chart and Lift chart, these charts can only be constructed for a binary target variable since they are two-dimensional. However, most software provides the following metrics for us to use instead.

- AUROC (area under the ROC curve): To measure the area between our model and the baseline model.
- Lift value: To measure the Lift of our model in comparison with the baseline (no model).
- Gini coefficient.

Summary

Evaluation of predictive model performance is not an easy task, given the variety of variables and modeling methods we have. In this chapter, we cover many important concepts and terminologies related to model fit. We also learn the difference between model fit and predictive power. Essentially, model fit measures how well our model fits the actual data for one particular sample, such as the training sample. Predictive power measures how well the model fits all datasets consistently. In other words, predictive power tells us if our model is generalizable. A model that fits well the training sample but does not make good predictions with other datasets does not have good predictive power. In this case, we may have overfitting. We discuss various strategies to avoid or minimize overfitting. We also differentiate between model reliability and model validity and why we need to assess both of them.

The second half of the chapter focuses on how to measure model fit metrics for association models and classification models. I introduce multiple metrics and recommend the appropriate metrics we should use, along with some rules of thumb. Depending on the scale of the target variable, we need to select the right metrics to measure model fit. It is vital to use multiple model fit metrics since they will allow us to capture the whole picture of the model fit. We will use these metrics in the next few chapters when we work on actual predictive modeling. Finally, CSL is an effective approach for evaluating and selecting a model based on the costs of misclassification. I will demonstrate how to use this approach in Chapter 8.

CHAPTER DISCUSSION QUESTIONS

1. What is the purpose of model evaluation, and why is it important in data mining?
2. What is model fit? Explain the difference between model fit and predictive power. How do they overlap? Give examples.
3. What is overfitting, and how does it affect the validity of a predictive model?
4. What are the primary root causes for overfitting? What are strategies to address the overfitting issues?
5. Differentiate between model reliability and validity. Provide some specific examples.
6. Why do we need to evaluate both model reliability and validity? List the steps for evaluating the reliability and validity of predictive models.
7. What is the purpose of model comparison in data mining?
8. What is the champion model? Is the champion model the best model overall? Why do we need it?
9. What are recommended model fit metrics for association models? Why?
10. Define confusion matrix.
11. Describe recommended model fit metrics for classification models. Why do we need to evaluate multiple metrics instead of using only one metric?
12. Describe Cost Sensitive Learning. In which scenario should we conduct Cost Sensitive Learning?

Exercises

Exercise 1: Model fit metrics for an association model

1. Download Excel file *resp_training.xlsx*. It contains the training results of the *boston* dataset, which include actual values and predicted values.
2. Add new columns and calculate the residuals (errors) for all cases.
3. Add new columns and calculate the squared errors for all cases.
4. Use the formulas in this chapter to calculate several model fit metrics: RMSE, MAPE, RSE, and EP.
5. Evaluate the model fit based on those metrics. Do we have a good model fit?
6. Construct two charts: Actual by predicted chart and residual by predicted chart.
7. Evaluate these charts and confirm the model fit evaluation in Step 5.

Exercise 2: Model fit metrics for a classification model with a binary target variable

We have the following confusion matrix for a binary target variable (1 = accident; 0 = no accident).

	Predicted Accident	Predicted No accident
Actual Accident	TP = 1685	FN = 158
Actual No accident	FP = 212	TN = 956

1. Use the formulas in this chapter to calculate the following model fit metrics:
   - Misclassification rate (MR).
   - Accuracy (ACC).
   - Sensitivity (Recall).
   - Specificity (Selectivity).
   - F1-Score.
2. Evaluate the model fit based on those metrics.

Exercise 3: Model fit metrics for a classification model with a nominal target variable

We have the following confusion matrix for a multi-class target variable with three classes: A, B, and C.

	Predicted A	Predicted B	Predicted C
Actual A	856	125	79
Actual B	111	425	98
Actual C	69	75	327

1. Calculate TP, TN, FP, and FN for all three classes.
2. Use the formulas in this chapter to calculate the following model fit metrics for those three classes (A, B, C) separately:
   - Misclassification rate (MR).
   - Accuracy (ACC).
   - Sensitivity (Recall).
   - Specificity (Selectivity).
   - F1-Score.
3. Evaluate the model fit based on those metrics.

7

Regression Methods

Introduction

We have covered the first three steps in the SEMMA process: Sample, Explore, and Modify. All of these efforts are to prepare us for the most important step in this process, Model. In this step, researchers select machine learning methods, build and configure multiple models, train the models with data, and validate the models. The results of these steps are predictive models that produce a prediction of the target variable. So,  you can see the importance of this step in data mining and why we need to do it right. Any mistakes in this step result in invalid predictive models. In order to complete the modeling step correctly and effectively, it is essential that we understand the underlying foundation of the machine learning methods we select and make appropriate configurations.

DOI: 10.1201/9781003162872-9

I will kick off the Model step with the most popular data mining method, regression. This chapter describes two regression methods, linear regression and logistic regression. They are widely used in many fields of study because the analysis process is standardized and straightforward, and the results are easy to interpret. These methods allow us to derive a regression equation reflecting the relationship between predictors and the target variable. For example, these methods can be used to predict the customer purchase of a product or the risk of flight delays.

Essentially, linear regression is an association method used when the target variable is continuous. The relationship between the target variable and predictors is linear. On the other hand, logistic regression is a classification method used when the target variable is binary (logistic regression) or categorical (multinomial logistic regression). This type of regression presents a nonlinear relationship between predictors and the target variable in the form of a logit function. Since regression methods are covered in most statistics books and courses, this chapter provides a brief description of the statistical foundation and focuses more on how the methods are used for data mining purposes. I will use some practical examples to demonstrate and explain the data mining process and how to interpret the results. If you are interested in learning the statistical foundation of these methods, I include some references that you can use.

> **DEFINITION**
>
> Regression is a method that estimates the relationship between one dependent variable (target variable) and multiple independent variables (predictors).
>
> Dependent variable = Target variable
> Independent variable = Predictor

What Is the Regression Method?

Regression is a popular method that estimates the relationship between one dependent variable (target variable) and multiple independent variables (predictors). The goal of regression is to find a mathematical function or model that can predict the values of the dependent variable based on the values of the independent variables. Note that in most statistics books, the authors use the terms *dependent variable* and *independent variable*. I will stick with our terms in this book, *target variable* and *predictor*, to ensure consistency. But you should remember that in this chapter, *target variable* is the same as *dependent variable*, and *predictor* is the same as *independent variable*.

Let's examine an example. Suppose we want to predict whether customers choose to go to a restaurant for dinner. So the target variable is the dining decision (Yes or No). Predictors may include gender, race, age, education, income, diet preference, and health condition. The

> **Inputs of the regression model:** target variable and all predictors.
> **Output of the regression model:** regression equation showing the relationship between the target variable and significant predictors.

regression model derived from data can identify predictors that have significant relationships with the dinner decision and estimate mathematical relationships between these predictors and the target variable. More specifically, the regression method estimates the coefficients (weights) of the predictors in the model to minimize the difference between the predicted values and the actual values of the target variable.

The primary advantage of the regression method is that it is easy to understand, use, and interpret. The mathematical foundation of regression is the same as the one we see in statistics courses, so it is fairly easy to find resources and materials that explain the method algorithm in detail. In fact, most statistics books or quantitative analysis books provide very detailed explanations of this method and how the regression equation is estimated. In this book, I will focus more on the purpose of the method and how to use it rather than repeating the mathematical and statistical foundation. Nonetheless, I will repeat and explain key terminologies and important points in the data analysis process as needed.

Linear Regression and Logistic Regression

There are two primary types of regression: linear regression and logistic regression. Both of them are regression methods, but there are some fundamental differences. Linear regression is a regression method in which the target variable is continuous. Thus, it is an association model. In many cases, a target variable with a Likert scale can be used with linear regression as long as the gaps between the levels are equal. As covered in Chapter 3, in this case, we can treat Likert scale variables as interval variables.

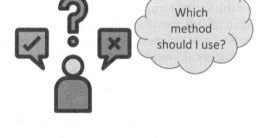

On the other hand, logistic regression is a regression method in which the target variable is categorical (binary or nominal). It is a classification model. Binary variables have two levels, and nominal variables have more than two levels (multi-class). Usually, when we have a nominal target variable, we call the model multinomial logistic regression. In data mining, the term difference has become less

> **DEFINITION**
>
> Linear regression: Target variable is interval
> Logistic regression: Target variable is binary
> Multinomial logistic regression: Target variable is nominal (multi-class)

concerning since we focus more on the model performance. To avoid confusion, I use *logistic regression* for both of those cases, binary and nominal target variables, and specify the target variable scale for clarification. Table 7.1 presents two examples of linear and logistic regression, which allows you to see the practical difference between them.

TABLE 7.1

Examples of Linear Regression and Logistic Regression

Regression Methods	Examples
Linear regression example	The target variable is the students' SAT scores; it is a continuous variable with a range from 0 to 1,600. Predictors include age, gender, race, high school GPA, and family income.
Logistic regression example	The target variable is the student's decision to select one particular major, marketing. It is a binary variable (Yes or No). Another example is the student's decision to choose one of four majors: marketing, accounting, finance, or management. In this case, the target variable is nominal with four levels: 1 (marketing), 2 (accounting), 3 (finance), or 4 (management). Predictors include age, gender, race, high school GPA, and family income.

Due to the difference in the target variable, these methods use two different estimation methods, which lead to differences in assumptions, outputs, and result interpretation. More specifically, linear regression uses the Ordinal Least Square (OLS) method to estimate the regression equation. On the other hand, logistic regression uses the Maximum Likelihood (ML) method for estimation.

> **How to choose the right regression method?**
> If the target variable is continuous or Likert scale, then use linear regression.
> If the target variable is binary or nominal, then use logistic regression.

The regression equations for these methods look like the following. I try to avoid using typical mathematical notations to make the equations easier to understand, so I name the variables and coefficients using a more ordinal way than using Greek characters.

For linear regression:

$$target = int + coe_1 * predictor_1 + coe_2 * predictor_2 + coe_3 * predictor_3 + \ldots + error$$

And for logistic regression:

$$logit(target) = int + coe_1 * predictor_1 + coe_2 * predictor_2 + coe_3 * predictor_3 + \ldots + error$$

Where
target is the target variable
predictor is the predictor variable
int is intercept
coe is the regression coefficient for the corresponding predictor
error is the error terms

You can notice that in logistic regression, we do not estimate directly the target variable but rather the logit value of that variable. Of course, it is hard to understand what it means by the logit value. Hence, when we interpret the results for logistic regression, we will use odds ratios rather than correlation coefficients. I will get into that soon.

The charts in Figure 7.1 show how the linear regression equation differs from the logistic regression equation. As you can see, linear regression can only detect the linear relationship between the target variable (Y) and

> **Linear regression:** linear relationship between the target variable and all predictors.
> **Logsitic regression:** non-linear relationship, in a form of a logit function, between the target variable and all predictors.

predictors (X). On the other hand, logistic regression can detect the non-linear relationship, in the form of a logit function, between the target variable (Y) and predictors (X). In logistic regression, the target variable is binary (0 or 1), so Y can only be one of those two values. However, note that the relationship between logit(Y) and X is still linear, as indicated in the equation above. Thus, the ability of logistic regression to detect non-linear relationships is limited to the logit function and the linear effect of correlation coefficients. This is a key difference between logistic regression and other non-linear methods, such as decision trees, neural networks, or random forests, which can detect more complex forms of nonlinearity.

Table 7.2 presents some key differences between linear regression and logistic regression. In the next sections, we will get into the details of these two methods and how to configure models with these methods.

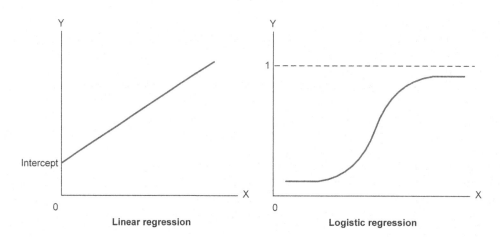

FIGURE 7.1
Linear regression and logistic regression.

TABLE 7.2

Differences between Linear Regression and Logistic Regression

Items	Linear Regression	Logistic Regression
Measurement scale of the dependent variable	The target variable in linear regression is continuous and numeric, representing a range of real numbers. The model aims to establish a linear relationship between the predictors and the continuous outcome.	The target variable in logistic regression is binary or categorical, representing two or more discrete outcomes. The model predicts the probability of an event in one category.
Output and range	The output of linear regression is a continuous value, and the predicted values can be any real number. The range of predictions is not constrained.	The output of logistic regression is a probability score between 0 and 1, representing the likelihood of the event occurring.
Model function	The model function in linear regression is a linear equation that represents the weighted sum of the predictors plus an intercept term. The relationship between the variables is assumed to be linear.	The model function in logistic regression is the logistic (sigmoid) function, which represents the weighted sum of the predictors to a probability score. It models the odds of an event occurring. Note that the relationship between the odds of an event and predictors is assumed to be linear.
Applications	Linear regression is used for predicting and modeling continuous outcomes, such as predicting house prices, temperature, or sales volume based on various factors.	Logistic regression is used for binary or multinomial classification tasks, such as predicting whether an email is spam or not or classifying images into multiple categories.
Evaluation metrics	Linear regression uses common model fit metrics for association models plus F-test and R-squared (coefficient of determination).	Logistic regression uses common model fit metrics for classification models.
Optimization method	The model parameters in linear regression are typically estimated using methods like Ordinary Least Squares (OLS) to minimize the sum of squared errors.	The model parameters in logistic regression are typically estimated using Maximum Likelihood Estimation (MLE) to maximize the likelihood of the observed outcomes.

Advantages and Disadvantages

Note that in data mining, there is no such thing as a perfect machine learning method, regardless of its complexity. Every method has pros and cons. Hence, it is important for us to understand their advantages and disadvantages, so we can choose the right method and make the correct interpretation of the results. Regression methods are based on statistical foundations, so they are relatively easier to implement and understand. However, the linearity nature of these methods and the assumptions limit the extent of our predictive modeling. Table 7.3 summarizes the advantages and disadvantages of these regression methods.

TABLE 7.3

Advantages and Disadvantages of Regression Methods

Regression Methods	Advantages	Disadvantages
Linear regression	• Simple to implement. • Works best to detect linear patterns. • The outputs are easy to understand and interpret (regression coefficients, direction, significance value). • Produces a good model fit with a small number of predictors. • Does not require a lot of data to work. • Less susceptible to overfitting. • Short computing time.	• Subject to normality assumption. • Requires the linearity between the target variable and predictors. • Requires continuous variables. • Sensitive to missing values. • Sensitive to outliers. • Unable to detect non-linear relationships. • May not produce a good model fit with a large number of predictors. • Prone to multicollinearity, which limits us from analyzing big data.
Logistic regression	• Simple to implement and efficient to train. • Provides regression coefficients, direction, and significance value for interpretation. • Provides probabilistic output. • Does not require normal distribution. • Can be extended to multiple classes (multinomial regression). • Works with both continuous and categorical predictors. • Able to detect non-linearity in the form of logit function. • Less susceptible to overfitting. • Short computing time.	• Requires a categorical target variable. • Requires the linearity between the logit value of the target variable and predictors. • Unable to detect all forms of non-linear relationships. • Unable to detect complex patterns. • Prone to multicollinearity, which limits us from analyzing big data. • Regression coefficients are harder to understand and interpret. • Lack of interpretability for a nominal target variable with multi-levels. • Requires more data to provide a good model fit.

Linear Regression

Linear Regression Equation

We start with a linear regression equation to understand the components of this method. As stated before, the regression equation shows the mathematical relationships between the target variable and predictors. Linear regression only works with an interval target variable. Let's use the linear regression equation in a more traditional way here for reference purposes. It helps you understand the outputs provided by different software apps. You can always refer to the equation presented in a more ordinal way, as shown before.

$$Y = \beta_0 + \beta_1 x_1 + \beta_2 x_2 + \ldots + \beta_n x_n + \varepsilon$$

Where
  Y is the target variable
  x_1 to x_n are predictor variables *1- n*
  β_0 is intercept
  β_1 to β_n are regression coefficients for the corresponding predictors
  ε is the residual or error

Estimation Approach

Essentially, an estimation approach is the statistical method used to calculate the values for all components of the regression equation, including intercept, regression coefficients, and error terms. The Ordinal Least Square (OLS) is the estimation approach for linear regression. It is a common method to estimate the intercept and regression coefficients that minimize the sum of squared errors. The mathematical foundation for OLS is explained in many statistics books, so I do present them here. What I want to emphasize is that using this method does lead to some strict assumptions for linear regression.

Assumption Requirements

Linear regression for traditional statistical studies is subject to very strict assumptions to ensure the validity of the results, including normality, homoscedasticity, linearity, non-multicollinearity, continuous variables, and no missing values. In other words, when we violate the assumptions, the software still runs the analysis and produces outputs. However, we cannot be sure whether the results are valid, and therefore, we cannot make

> Linear regression has strict assumptions, but we have some flexibility in data mining projects since we use large datasets.

valid conclusions based on them. Note that in traditional statistical studies, we often have a small number of predictors (independent variables) and use a very small sample size. For example, if we have 5 predictors and use an effect size of 0.25, the required sample size is 57 records. With 10 predictors, we only need a sample size of 75 records.

In data mining, we use a very large dataset with many predictors and a very large sample size. Accordingly, we have more flexibility with the linear regression in terms of assumptions; i.e., we do not have to fully meet all assumptions to run the analysis as with traditional statistical studies. The primary reason is that according to the Central Limit Theorem, when we have a large enough sample size, the distribution of the sample can be assumed approximately normal. Thus, when we use linear regression as a machine learning algorithm with large data, we do not have to test and meet all assumptions. Nonetheless, it is still recommended to check several key items and make data transformations or modifications on some level since it would help improve the performance of the regression model. For example, linear regression works better with a complete dataset, so handling and imputing missing values are highly recommended. In addition, since normality is an important assumption for this method, normalizing the data allows us to achieve a better model fit. Finally, handling outliers would reduce noise in the data, which results in a better fit model.

You may ask: **Should we be concerned about the validity of the results if we do not meet the test assumptions?** It is a good question since we should always pay attention to the reliability and validity of the results. In data mining studies, we use more rigorous steps to ensure the quality of the results. As mentioned in Chapter 3, we usually split the sample into training, validation, and test samples. The training sample is used to train the model, and the validation sample is used to validate the model. It is to ensure the trained model is valid for samples other than just the training sample; i.e., we do not have the overfitting issue. By comparing the model results across those three samples, we can evaluate the performance of the model and ensure the model's reliability and validity. Thus, even when we do not meet all assumptions, these steps still allow us to guarantee the validity of our predictive model.

I list a few key assumptions required for linear regression and the level of flexibility in data mining projects as follows.

- *The target variable must be continuous*: This assumption is important to establish the association model. Nonetheless, the target variable with the Likert scale is acceptable as long as the gaps between levels are equal.

- *Predictors must be continuous*: There is more flexibility with this requirement. While having continuous predictors is still preferable since it ensures the interpretability of the regression coefficients and improves the model fit, it is OK to have categorical (binary or nominal) predictors in linear regression. Basically, we can dummy code those variables to convert them to interval variables. For example, we have a nominal variable, *education level*, with three levels: 1 – high school, 2 – bachelor, and 3 – graduate. We dummy code this variable by creating three separate variables: high school, bachelor, and graduate; each has two levels, 1-yes, and 0-no. Unlike traditional statistics software, in which we have to take some extra steps to dummy code these variables, most data mining software apps take care of this process automatically, making the analysis more efficient. Regardless, we still need to be careful when interpreting the regression coefficients of these predictors because it is not as straightforward as with interval variables.

- *Normality*: It is one of the most common assumptions for parametric statistical methods, especially with the OSL method. As mentioned, since we have a large sample size in data mining studies, fully satisfying the normality assumption is not required. However, if the data is too skewed, it still affects the model performance and results in a poor model fit. Hence, it is recommended to review the histogram of variables and make transformations as much as we can to normalize the data. Extreme outliers also skew the data, so we need to review our histograms and box plots to identify outliers and remove excessive ones. We do not have to achieve full normality but getting closer to a normal distribution allows us to achieve a better model fit.

- *Non-multicollinearity*: Linear regression assumes that predictors are independent. It is an important assumption for regression analysis in traditional statistical studies. Multi-collinearity indicates inter-correlation among independent variables, and we need to prove that multi-collinearity does not exist before we run the regression analysis. However, several research studies show that by increasing the sample size, we can reduce the presence of multi-collinearity. Since we use a large sample size in data mining projects, multi-collinearity is not a big concern.

- *No missing values*: For traditional statistical studies, regression analysis requires a complete dataset. Hence, all missing values must be handled, either by imputing or elimination. Some software applications give an error message if missing values are detected. However, in data mining, the software can still run analyses with missing values. If missing values are not excessive, the model performance is not significantly affected. Regardless, if we detect a considerable percentage of missing values (more than 15%), imputation is recommended. Having a complete dataset may allow us to build a regression model with a better fit.

Linear Regression Model Fit Evaluation

In the OLS process, it is important to evaluate the model fit. So what is the model fit? We have covered it in detail in Chapter 6. Basically, on the one hand, we have our theoretical regression model represented by the regression equation. On the other hand, we have data for the target variable and all predictors. Now we need to fit the data to that theoretical model and see if they fit well. Model fit measures how well our model fits the data.

$$Residuals = Actual\ data - Predicted\ data$$

I have described the general model fit metrics for association models in Chapter 6, including RMSE, MAPRE, RSE, Ethe P, actual by predicted chart, and the residuals by predicted chart. In this chapter, I focus on the metrics specific to the linear regression method. More specifically, when we use linear regression, we also need to evaluate the F-test and R^2. Table 7.4 explains these metrics and how to use them.

In linear regression, when we review materials for F-test and R^2, we may see some terminologies, notations, and formulas. I included them in Table 7.5 for quick reference. Following are the formulas showing how to calculate SST and R^2 using SSR and SSE.

$$SST = SSR + SSE$$

$$R^2 = \frac{SST - SSE}{SST} = \frac{Explained\ variance}{Total\ variance}$$

As explained in Chapter 6, these formulas apply only to linear regression but not to other methods. As you can see, in linear regression, R^2 is essentially the same as the explanatory power that we discussed in Chapter 6.

TABLE 7.4

Model Fit Metrics Specific to Linear Regression

Metrics	Description
F-test	F-test is used to test the significance of the overall model. In other words, a significant F-test indicates that our regression model fits the data better than the model without any predictors. We would expect a significant F-test.
R^2 or coefficient of determination	R^2 is a common model fit metric for linear regression models. It measures the percentage of the variance in the target variable that is explained by variance in predictors collectively. There is no standard cut-off value for a good R^2 since it depends on the number of predictors in the model. However, my rule of thumb is as follows. • R^2 higher than 0.7: good model fit • R^2 between 05–0.7: acceptable model fit • R^2 lower than 0.5: poor model fit Note that R^2 should be interpreted based on the number of predictors in the model since the more predictors, the lower the R^2. Accordingly, a lower R^2 can be acceptable for a model with many predictors, which is often the case in data mining projects.
Adjusted R^2	It is a modified version of R^2 that considers only predictors that have an effect on the model's performance. It is recommended to use adjusted R^2. Use the same thresholds as suggested above.

Model Selection Process

In the regression modeling process, model selection is the key step in training the model. It describes how predictors are entered into the regression analysis. We may think that we can enter all variables at once, and the analysis tells us which predictors are significant. However, entering all variables at once in the analysis increases the computing time and makes it harder to fit the model. It may surprise you that there are more ways to decide how variables are entered into the model. By selecting the right variable selection method, we may be able to improve the model fit.

Basically, the regression literature shows three primary variable selection methods in linear regression: backward, forward, and stepwise. I will explain them in a simple way with some diagrams for easy understanding. Then I will show you the exact methods used in SAS Enterprise Miner because we use this software for our analysis.

TABLE 7.5

Key Terminologies and Notations in Linear Regression

Terminologies	Notations	Descriptions
Target variable	y	Actual value of the target variable (dependent variable).
Predictor	x	Actual value of the predictor (independent variable).
Mean of target variable	$\bar{y}$	Mean value of the target variable.
Predicted value	$\hat{y}$	Predicted value of the target variable is estimated by the model.
Error	e	Error (residual) is the difference between the actual and predicted values of the target variable.
Sum of Squared Error	SSE	How far the data are from the model's predicted values.
Sum of Squared Total	SST	How far the data are from the mean.
Sum of Squared Regression	SSR	How far the mean is from the model's predicted values.

There is one important note I want to make here is that all these three methods are essentially stepwise methods. Stepwise method is an iterative variable selection method used in data mining to identify the most relevant subset of variables for a predictive model. Hence using the term *stepwise* to refer to a specific stepwise process may cause confusion.

Hence, I rename them as *forward stepwise, backward stepwise,* and *adaptive stepwise.* For each method below, I describe the steps of variable selection and demonstrate them in the diagrams (Figures 7.2–7.4). As you can imagine, each of these methods results in numerous models, and the last one is usually the best one.

> Stepwise method is an iterative variable selection method used in data mining to identify the most relevant subset of variables for a predictive model. There are three primary stepwise methods: forward stepwise, backward stepwise, and adaptive stepwise.

- **Forward Stepwise** (Figure 7.2)
    1. The process begins with a model without any predictors (null model).
    2. The most significant variables are added to the model, one after the other. Significant variables are the ones significantly associated with the target variable. Typically, the most significant predictor is the one with the smallest p-value or provides the highest increase in R^2.

FORWARD STEPWISE

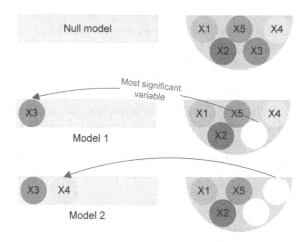

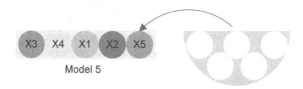

FIGURE 7.2
Forward stepwise method.

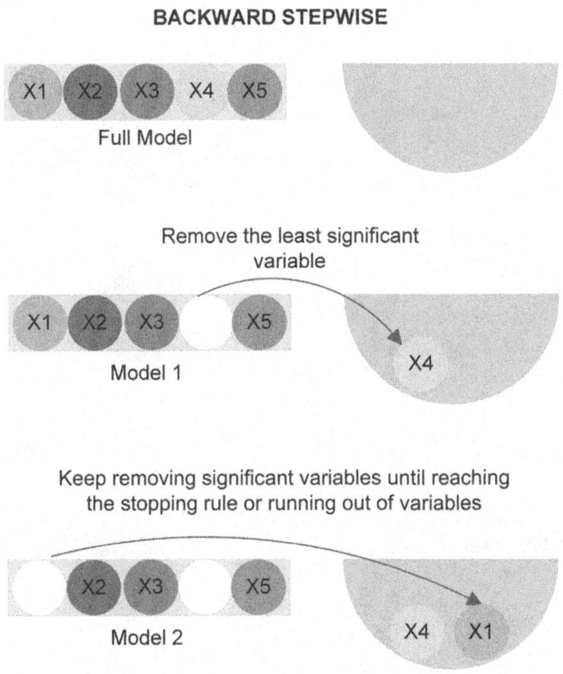

BACKWARD STEPWISE

FIGURE 7.3
Backward stepwise method.

3. The selection will stop when all variables under consideration are added or a pre-determined stopping rule is met.

- **Backward Stepwise** (Figure 7.3)

    1. The process begins with a model with all predictors (full model).

    2. The least significant variables are removed from the model, one after the other.

    3. The selection will stop when no variables are left or a pre-determined stopping rule is met.

- **Adaptive Stepwise** (Figure 7.4): This method is actually forward stepwise with one key difference. After adding an additional variable to the model, it can remove a variable currently in the model but no longer significant. In other words, it is adaptive. In some cases, *adaptive stepwise* is also known as *bidirectional stepwise*.

    1. The process begins with a model without any predictors (null model).

    2. The most significant variables are added to the model, one after the other.

    3. After adding an additional variable, the variable already in the model but non-significant will be removed.

    4. The selection will stop when all variables under consideration are added or a pre-determined stopping rule is met.

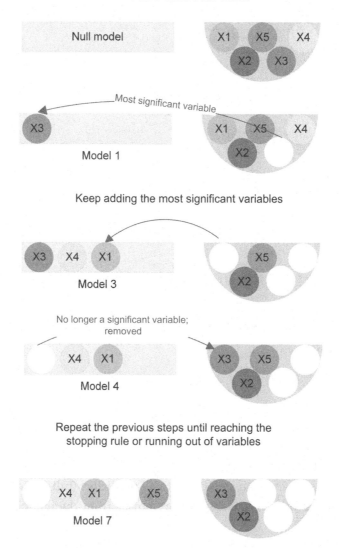

FIGURE 7.4
Adaptive stepwise method.

The important question is, which stepwise method should we use? Table 7.6 describes the scenarios in which each method should be used. As explained above, adaptive stepwise seems to be capable of selecting predictors that best predict the target variable. Unlike forward and backward stepwise, in which the process is linear and sequential, adaptive stepwise allows us to add and remove variables in such a way that we achieve the best model fit. In other words, it can

> **Rule of thumb:**
> Start with the adaptive stepwise method
> as it allows us to achieve the best model fit.

TABLE 7.6

When to Use Stepwise Methods?

When to Use Forward Stepwise?	When to Use Backward Stepwise?	When to Use Adaptive Stepwise?
Large number of predictors When dealing with a large number of potential predictors, forward stepwise is computationally more efficient, as it starts with an empty model and incrementally adds variables.	**Multicollinearity concerns** If there are concerns about multicollinearity (high correlation) between predictors, backward stepwise helps identify and remove redundant predictors.	**Exhaustive search** Adaptive stepwise allows for an exhaustive search of significant predictors without becoming overly computationally intensive.
Exploratory analysis Forward stepwise is a good starting point for exploratory analysis, as it allows us to gradually build a model by adding variables that have a significant impact on the target variable.	**Well-founded theoretical basis** When there is a strong theoretical basis or domain knowledge for what predictors are more important than others, backward stepwise is useful in eliminating less significant variables from the model.	**Data exploration and model building** Adaptive stepwise is useful at the initial stages of data exploration and model building as it allows for a comprehensive examination of various predictor subsets and their impact on the model.
No prior knowledge When there is no strong prior knowledge or theory about which predictors are likely to be relevant, forward stepwise helps identify potentially important predictors.	**Complex models** Backward stepwise is particularly useful in complex models, where removing less relevant variables can improve the model's interpretability and generalization.	**Model fit improvement** Since adaptive stepwise considers all possible combinations of predictors, it provides more robust results and improves the model fit.
		Variable interaction analysis When interactions between predictors are essential, adaptive stepwise helps identify relevant interaction terms that might not be captured by individual forward or backward selection.

choose the best combination of predictors for model-fitting purposes. Thus, this method is recommended for data mining. The disadvantage of this method is that it may require more computing time and, in some cases, may overfit. Nonetheless, by cross-validation with subsamples, we can evaluate the predictive power and avoid overfitting.

Since SAS Enterprise Miner uses the terms for these methods a little differently, I put the term comparison in Table 7.7 to avoid any confusion.

TABLE 7.7

SAS Enterprise Miner's Terms and Equivalent Terms

SAS Enterprise Miner's Terms	Equivalent Terms
Forward	Forward stepwise
Backward	Backward stepwise
Stepwise	Adaptive stepwise

SAS ENTERPRISE MINER GUIDELINES

Regression Node Train Properties
(https://documentation.sas.com)

CLASS TARGETS

Regression Type – Use the Regression Type property of the Regression node to specify the type of regression that you want to run.

- **Logistic Regression** – The default regression type for binary or ordinal targets. Logistic regression attempts to predict the probability that a binary or ordinal target will acquire the event of interest as a function of one or more independent inputs. For binary or ordinal targets, the default type is Logistic Regression.
- **Linear Regression** – The default regression type for interval targets. Linear regression attempts to predict the value of a continuous target as a linear function of one or more independent inputs. For interval targets, the default type is Linear Regression.

MODEL SELECTION METHODS

Backward – Begins, by default, with all candidate effects in the model and then systematically removes effects that are not significantly associated with the target until no other effect in the model meets the **Stay Significance Level** or until the **Stop Variable Number** that you specified is met. This method is not recommended when the target is binary or ordinal and there are many candidate effects or many levels for some classification input variables.

Forward – Begins, by default, with no candidate effects in the model and then systematically adds effects that are significantly associated with the target until none of the remaining effects meet the Entry Significance Level or until the Stop Variable Number criterion is met.

Stepwise – As in the Forward method, Stepwise selection begins, by default, with no candidate effects in the model and then systematically adds effects that are significantly associated with the target. However, after an effect is added to the model, Stepwise can remove any effect already in the model that is not significantly associated with the target.

This stepwise process continues until one of the following occurs:

- No other effect in the model meets the Stay Significance Level.
- The Max Steps criterion is met. If you choose the Stepwise selection method, then you can specify a Max Steps to put a limit on the number of steps before the effect selection process stops. The default value is set to the number of effects in the model. If you add interactions via the Interaction Builder, the Max Steps is automatically updated to include these terms.
- An effect added in one step is the only effect deleted in the next step.

None – (default) all candidate effects are included in the final model. If you choose **None** as the selection method, then the properties related to the selection method have no effect.

Stepwise selection of inputs requires more computing time than Forward or Backward selection, but it has an advantage in terms of the number of potential subset models checked before the model for each subset size is decided.

How to Read and Understand the Regression Equation and Results?

After running the regression analysis, we examine the model fit using all recommended metrics, including R^2, F-test, RMSE, MAPE, RSE, EP, actual by predicted chart, and residuals by predicted chart. Suppose all criteria are met, indicating a good model fit. The next step is to report and explain the regression analysis outputs. How do we make sense of these outputs, and what conclusions can we make?

These are common questions when we conduct any type of data analysis, and it is even more important in data mining, given the large number of predictors we have in our model. We now look at some simple hypothetical regression equations to learn how to read and understand the prediction results. I limit the number of predictors to simplify the interpretation. We will look at some actual regression results in the data mining example with SAS Enterprise Miner later in this chapter.

For linear regression, the estimation results typically include the following information:

- Intercept
- Unstandardized regression coefficient (B)
- Standard error for B
- Standardized regression coefficients (beta)
- t-value
- Significance value (p-value)
- 95% confidence interval for B

In order to interpret the regression results correctly, we focus on significance values, unstandardized coefficients, and standardized coefficients. Table 7.8 provides the descriptions of these terms and how they are used in interpreting regression results.

TABLE 7.8

Significance Value, Unstandardized Regression Coefficient, and Standardized Regression Coefficient

Terms	Description
Significance value (p-value)	The significance value (p-value) is a statistical measure for assessing the significance of the estimated coefficients (also known as the regression weights or beta values) of the predictors in the regression. It determines whether the relationship between each predictor and the target variable is statistically significant or if it could have occurred by chance.
Significance level (alpha)	Significance level (alpha) refers to the significance level or the threshold used for hypothesis testing when evaluating the statistical significance of the estimated coefficients.
Unstandardized regression coefficient (B)	Unstandardized regression coefficient is a measure used in linear regression to quantify the relationship between a predictor and the target variable in its original units of measurement.
Standardized regression coefficient (beta)	Standardized regression coefficient is a measure used in linear regression to quantify the relationship between a predictor and the target variable after standardizing both variables to a common scale. Standardized coefficients range between 0 and 1 and are measured using the same scale in all cases via standard deviation.

Significance Value (p-Value)

The significance value (p-value) is a statistical measure for assessing the significance of the estimated coefficients (also known as the regression weights or beta values) of the predictors in the regression. It determines whether the relationship between each predictor and the target variable is statistically significant or if it could have occurred by chance. The threshold used to evaluate the statistical significance is called significance level (or alpha). The most commonly used significance level is 0.05 (5%). If the calculated p-value is less than or equal to the significance level ($p \leq \alpha$), it indicates that the coefficient is statistically significant. Let's go back to the previous example for linear regression, with the target variable being the students' SAT scores. Suppose after the data mining analysis, we find GPA and family income are the two predictors with p-values lower than 0.05, indicating that these are significant predictors.

Unstandardized Regression Coefficients (B)

After determining the significant predictors, we need to explain their relationships with the target variable. In order to do that, we use unstandardized regression coefficients (B). Basically, an unstandardized regression coefficient is a measure used in linear regression to quantify the relationship between a predictor and the target variable in its original units of measurement. In our SAT prediction example, suppose the regression results show the unstandardized coefficients for GPA and family income are 120 and 0.01, respectively. In addition, the intercept is 105. With that output, we can write our regression equation as follows.

$$SAT \ score = 105 + 120 * GPA + 0.01 * family\_income$$

In this equation, we have the intercept and unstandardized coefficients. The equation indicates that, hypothetically, family income and GPA are two significant predictors of SAT scores, and both of them have positive correlations with SAT scores. These predictors capture the student's academic performance via GPA and the family's resources for education and SAT tutoring via income. Thus, if we know the values of these predictors of a student, we can predict the student's SAT score based on that equation. More importantly, we know how changing each predictor will change the target variable based on the coefficient correlations. In other words, we can see the importance of these predictors in predicting the SAT score and the extent of that effect, also called effect size. For example, the coefficient correlation for GPA is 120; i.e., if the GPA increases by one point, the SAT score increases by 120 points. Similarly, if the family income increases by $1, the SAT score increases by 0.01 point. To make more sense of this one, we can say if the family income increases by $10,000, the SAT score will improve by 0.01*10,000 or 100 points.

Note that I do not include the error term in this equation because we already use the error in evaluating the model fit. The error represents the difference between the predicted SAT scores and actual scores, and since we have a good model fit, the error is considered acceptable. In addition, in this step, we use the above equation to predict the changes in SAT scores based on the changes in these two significant predictors. Thus, the error is irrelevant.

Standardized Regression Coefficients (beta)

One thing you may notice is that the unstandardized coefficients depend on the unit of the predictor. In other words, they are scale-dependent. For example, we can conclude that GPA has a higher regression coefficient than family income, but it is not possible for us to determine how much more because they have different scales (points for GPA vs. USD for income). In order to make a meaningful comparison, we need to use standardized coefficients.

A standardized regression coefficient is a measure used in linear regression to quantify the relationship between a predictor and the target variable after standardizing both variables to a common scale. Standardized coefficients range between 0 and 1 and are measured using the same scale in all cases via standard deviation. In other words, they are scale-independent. So, they are directly comparable. For example, if the standardized coefficients for GPA and family income are 0.68 and 0.34, respectively. In this case, we can conclude that GPA has a higher effect size than family income, with a twice higher coefficient. Thus, we can also conclude that family income is twice as important as GPA in predicting SAT scores.

Thus, in order to identify and rank important predictors, it is recommended to use the standardized coefficients and rank them from high to low. A more generic term commonly used in data mining to capture the importance of predictors is "relative importance."

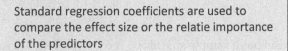

Unstandardized regression coefficients and the intercept are used in the regression equation to calculate the target variable value based on the predictors.

Standard regression coefficients are used to compare the effect size or the relatie importance of the predictors

Example: Linear Regression

In this example, we perform a linear regression analysis with the *boston* dataset using SAS Enterprise Miner. In the Chapter 3 exercise, you had a chance to explore the data. In this chapter, we build a predictive model using linear regression.

Data Description

The Boston Housing dataset provides the housing data in the area of Boston, MA, which was collected by the U.S. Census Bureau. The dataset has 14 variables, as described in Table 7.9. As you see, all variables are interval (*Charles_River* was originally a binary variable but has been dummy coded into interval). The target variable is *Imv*, which represents the median house values in the area. The purpose of this analysis is to predict the median values of the housing in Boston. Hence, linear regression is the appropriate method.

We follow the SEMMA process in this example. I do not describe the general purpose of each step in this step in detail since we already covered that in previous chapters. Instead, I explain the steps we take in each of these steps, along with the outputs and decisions we make and why. Note that in the next chapters, the steps Sample, Explore, and Modify are the same. Hence, I won't repeat these steps again. You can always return to this chapter to see the details.

TABLE 7.9

Boston Housing Data Description

Variable	Description	Scale	Role
CrimePC	Crime rate per capita	Interval	Input
ZonePr	Proportion of residential land zoned for lots over 25,000 sq.ft.	Interval	Input
IndustPr	Proportion of non-retail business acres.	Interval	Input
Charles_River	Charles River dummy variable (1 if tract bounds river; 0 otherwise)	Interval	Input
NiOxSQ	Nitric oxide concentration (parts per 10 million)	Interval	Input
RmSQ	Average number of rooms per dwelling	Interval	Input
AgePre40	Proportion of owner occupied units built prior to 1940	Interval	Input
LogDisstance	Weighted distances to five Boston employment centers	Interval	Input
LogAccess	Index of accessibility to radial highways	Interval	Input
Tax	Full value property tax rate per $10,000	Interval	Input
PtRatio	Pupil-teacher ratio	Interval	Input
B	1000(Bk - 0.63)^2 where Bk is the proportion of blacks by town	Interval	Input
Lstat	% lower status of the population	Interval	Input
Imv	Median value of owner-occupied homes in $1000's	Interval	Target

Sample

The dataset has a sample size of 506 records. Since it is a relatively small dataset, we use all of the records for analysis. Hence, I do not use the Sample node here. The primary task in this step is data partition, and we use the Data Partition node to partition the data (see the diagram below). Since the sample size is smaller than 1,000, as recommended in Chapter 3, we partition the data into training and validation samples using the split ratio of 60:40. No test sample is created. The details of the Data Partition node are covered in Chapter 3. Follow the steps below.

1. From the Sample tab, drag a Data Partition node to the workspace and connect it to the data source.
2. Under the Data Set Allocations tab, make the following changes:
   - Set Training to 60
   - Set Validation to 40
3. Run the Data Partition node.

Explore

We explore the descriptive statistics of the data first. To do so, we use the StatExplore node. To get the statistics using all records, follow the steps below.

1. From the Explore tab, drag a StatExplore node to the workspace and connect it to the data source (see below).

2. Run the StatExplore node and open the Results window.

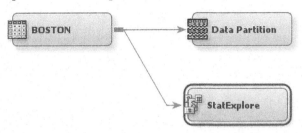

Below are the results of the StatExplore node showing the detailed descriptive statistics of all variables (Table 7.10). Those parameters are selected because they are commonly used to explore the data.

As you can see, we have 54 missing values for the target variable and no missing values for the predictors. We need to impute these missing values since linear regression works better with a complete dataset. We also notice that most variables do not have normal distributions based on the skewness and kurtosis values (these values should be between −0.5 and 0.5 for the data to be considered normal distributions). We will review the histograms for confirmation.

Remember that in order to get the histograms for all variables at once, we use the Variable option in the data node rather than the Graph Explore node. Follow the steps below.

1. Click the BOSTON data node, which will show the Property panel on the left.

2. Under the Columns tab, click the Ellipsis button for Variables.

3. The Variables window opens. Highlight all variables with the computer mouse.

4. Click Explore.

5. SAS Enterprise Miner will generate the histograms for all variables.

I rearranged the histograms for easy review, as shown in Figure 7.5. We can see that some variables are just slightly skewed, including *Imv, Lstat,* and *Tax,* with some outliers, while

TABLE 7.10

Descriptive Statistics of Boston Housing Variables

Variable	Missing	Min	Max	Mean	Median	Standard Deviation	Skewness	Kurtosis
LogAccess	0	1.00	666.00	78.06	5.00	203.54	2.55	4.53
Charles_River	0	0.00	1.00	0.14	0.00	0.31	1.90	1.95
PtRatio	0	2.60	396.90	42.61	18.90	87.59	3.53	10.82
CrimePC	0	0.00	9.97	1.27	0.14	2.40	2.20	3.78
RmSQ	0	3.56	100.00	15.68	6.32	27.22	2.60	4.88
ZonePr	0	0.00	100.00	13.30	0.00	23.05	2.07	3.63
NiOxSQ	0	0.39	7.31	1.10	0.54	1.65	2.65	5.29
LogDistance	0	1.13	24.00	6.17	3.92	6.48	2.14	3.26
IndustPr	0	0.00	27.74	9.21	6.96	7.17	0.59	−0.79
AgePre40	0	1.14	100.00	58.74	65.20	33.10	−0.39	−1.22
Tax	0	20.20	711.00	339.32	307.00	180.67	0.37	−0.07
Lstat	0	1.73	34.41	11.54	10.36	6.06	0.90	0.65
B	0	0.32	396.90	332.79	390.64	125.32	−1.95	2.04
Imv	54	6.30	50.00	23.75	21.90	8.81	1.30	1.67

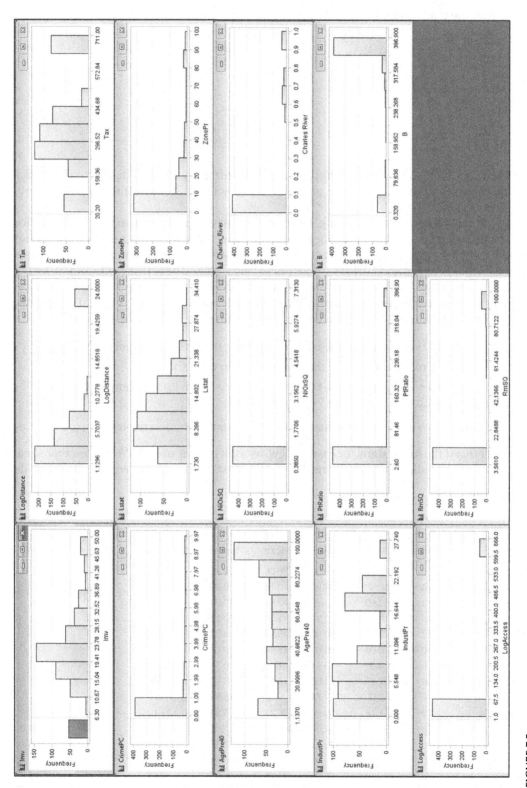

FIGURE 7.5
Histograms of all variables in the Boston Housing dataset.

other variables are highly skewed. They need to be normalized. We also noticed that the target variable, *Imv*, has some missing values, as discussed before, and they need to be imputed.

In order to build more graphs for these variables, refer to Chapter 3, which explains various graphical tools for data visualization.

Modify

As mentioned above, since we have non-normal distributions for most variables and missing values for the target variable, in this step, we perform data imputation and normalization.

Imputation: Follow the steps below to impute missing values.

1. From the Modify tab, drag an Impute node to the workspace and connect it to the Data Partition node.

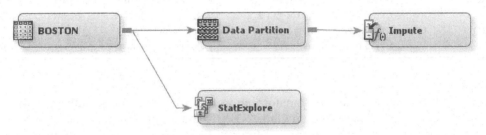

2. In the Train properties for the Impute node, under the Interval Variables tab, set Default Target Method to Mean.
3. Run the Impute node.
   The output shows that there are 28 missing values in the training sample, and they are imputed with a mean value of 23.31.

Normalization: Follow the steps below to normalize the data.

1. From the Modify tab, drag a Transform Variables node to the workspace and connect it to the Impute node.

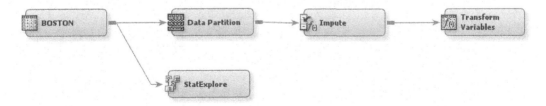

2. In the Train properties, under the Default Methods, set Interval Inputs to Maximum Normal. As a reminder, the Maximum Normal option uses the Maximize Normality Power Transformation method to normalize the data. We do not transfer the target variable since it is close enough to normality. Since we only have interval variables, we do not have to worry about Class Inputs.
3. Run the Transform Variables node.

TABLE 7.11

Transformation Results and Comparison

Variables	Transformation Formulas	After Transformation		Before Transformation	
		Skewness	**Kurtosis**	**Skewness**	**Kurtosis**
AgePre40	exp(max(AgePre40-1.137, 0.0)/98.863)	−0.12902	−1.36828	−0.44752	−1.09681
B	(max(B-2.52, 0.0)/394.38)**4	−1.56234	0.814982	−2.05444	2.454467
Charles River	log(max(Charles_River-0, 0.0) + 1)	1.92926	1.921266	2.005914	2.341274
CrimePC	log(max(CrimePC-0, 0.0)/9.96654 + 1)	1.89155	2.262801	2.09322	3.220161
IndustPr	sqrt(max(IndustPr-0, 0.0)/27.74)	−0.39259	−0.44335	0.55102	−0.79487
LogAccess	log(max(LogAccess-1, 0.0)/665 + 1)	2.819711	6.024658	2.82744	6.051484
LogDistance	log(max(LogDistance-1.1296, 0.0)/ 22.8704 + 1)	2.116489	3.559006	2.370935	4.428196
Lstat	sqrt(max(Lstat-2.47, 0.0)/28.34)	0.013377	-0.3022	0.838316	0.486698
NiOxSQ	log(max(NiOxSQ-0.385, 0.0)/6.583 + 1)	2.863824	6.507101	2.933305	6.966952
PtRatio	log(max(PtRatio-7.68, 0.0)/389.22 + 1)	3.729146	12.30244	3.801598	12.88777
RmSQ	log(max(RmSQ-3.561, 0.0)/96.439 + 1)	2.841287	6.151051	2.85256	6.225376
ZonePr	log(max(ZonePr-0, 0.0)/100 + 1)	1.780932	2.316695	2.091902	3.671935

The results show the selected transformation formulas, skewness, and kurtosis values before and after transformation (Table 7.11). To make the comparison, I copied and pasted the results from SAS Enterprise Miner to Excel, so I could combine the outputs for comparison purposes. As we can see, while transformations do not fully normalize all variables, these values show improvement. Hence, we will use the transformed values for our regression analysis in the next step. Note that the *Tax* variable is not shown here because it is already normally distributed, indicating that it does not need to be normalized.

Model

In this step, we build a linear regression model. Follow the steps below.

1. From the Model tab, drag a Regression node to the workspace and connect it to the Transform Variables node (see below).

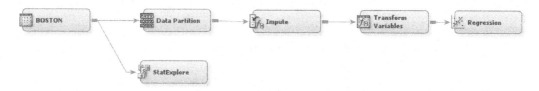

2. In the Train properties, make the following changes.
   - Under the Class Targets tab, set Regression Type to Linear Regression.
   - Under the Model Selection tab, Set Selection Model to Stepwise.
   - Set the Selection Criterion to Default.
3. Run the Regression node and open the Results window.

```
              Summary of Stepwise Selection

              Effect                 Number
   Step      Entered          DF      In    F Value   Pr > F

    1        SQRT_Lstat        1       1     323.88    <.0001
    2        LOG_Charles_River 1       2      13.69    0.0003
    3        LOG_LogDistance   1       3       8.39    0.0041
    4        SQRT_IndustPr     1       4      39.41    <.0001
    5        LOG_RmSQ          1       5      15.66    <.0001
    6        LOG_ZonePr        1       6      13.65    0.0003
    7        LOG_LogAccess     1       7       5.35    0.0215


The selected model is the model trained in the last step (Step 7). It consists of the following effects:

Intercept  LOG_Charles_River  LOG_LogAccess  LOG_LogDistance  LOG_RmSQ  LOG_ZonePr  SQRT_IndustPr  SQRT_Lstat
```

FIGURE 7.6
Stepwise selection summary.

Assess

In the last step, we evaluate the performance of the regression model. SAS Enterprise Miner presents many outputs. As discussed in Chapter 6, we focus on two primary outputs for model performance: (1) model fit; (2) significant predictors. As shown in Figure 7.6, the stepwise process identifies seven steps. In the end, seven predictors are entered into the model, and they are significant predictors (they have significant correlations with the target variable). Figure 7.7 shows us the iteration of the stepwise steps and the corresponding

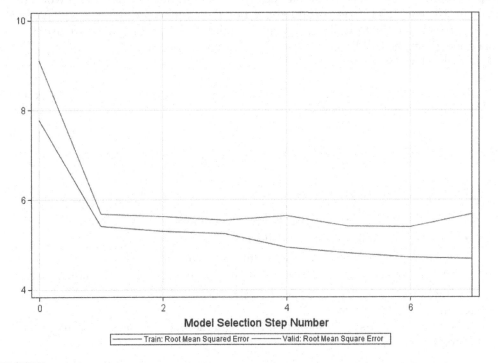

FIGURE 7.7
Model selection step comparison.

TABLE 7.12

Model Fit Metrics from SAS Enterprise Miner

Statistics Label	Train	Validation
Mean Square Error	21.33	32.26
Root Mean Squared Error	4.62	5.68
Sum of Squared Errors	6484.63	6516.11
F-test	77.19 ($p<0.001$)	
R^2	0.646	
Adjusted R^2	0.638	

RMSE. As we can see, as we add predictors, the RMSE decreases. For the training, Step 7 has the lowest RMSE, and for the validation, Step 6 has the lowest RMSE. But the stepwise modeling is determined by the training sample. The results between the training and validation are not the same but they are close enough.

In order to evaluate the model fit, we collect the model fit metric for an association model (see the details in Chapter 6). From SAS Enterprise Miner outputs, we can identify the following model fit metrics for our linear regression model (note that the software only provides F-test and R^2 values for the training sample), as shown in Table 7.12.

These metrics give us some initial evaluation of the model and the differences between the training and validation samples. We also need some additional model fit metrics to gain the full picture of the model performance, including MAPE, RSE, EP, MAPE, actual by predicted chart, and residual by predicted chart. Unfortunately, SAS Enterprise Miner does not produce these metrics automatically in the outputs. But we have a workaround for them. The solution is to export the prediction data into an Excel file and then produce these metrics using the formulas and graphs. In order to export the data, we use the Save Data node under the Utility tab.

Follow the steps below.

1. From the Utility lab, drag a Data Node to the workspace and connect it to the Regression node (see below).

2. In the Train properties, make the following changes:
   • Set File Format to Excel Spreadsheet.
   • Enter the directory path of your folder to Directory. All files will be saved to your selected folder. (*Hint*: Copy and paste the directory path from SAS Studio).
3. Run the Save Data node.
   The results of this node show that two data files have been saved in that folder, as follows.
   • em_save_TRAIN.xlsx: prediction data for the training sample (total observations = 304).

TABLE 7.13

Complete Model Fit Metrics

Model Fit Metrics	Train	Validation
RMSE	4.62	5.68
MAPE	0.148	0.161
RSE	0.354	0.393
EP	0.646	0.607
F-test	77.19 (p<0.001)	
R^2	0.646	
Adjusted R^2	0.638	

- em_save_VALIDATE.xlsx: prediction data for the validation sample (total observations = 202).

Then, download these Excel files to your computer and use the formulas described in Chapter 6 to calculate the metrics we need. Specifically, we calculate MAPE, RSE, and EP for both training and validation samples. In Table 7.13, I combine them with the metrics we extracted from SAS Enterprise Miner above. We can say that MAPE, RSE, and EP are close enough between the training and validation samples, while there is a slight difference between the two samples in RMSE. Keep in mind RMSE is scale-dependent, while others are scale-independent. Hence, we can consider the model's reliability acceptable.

Additionally, from the model fit perspective, a significant F-test indicates the significance of the overall model. An adjusted R^2 of 0.638 indicates that the model can explain 63.8% of the variance in the target variable by the variance in the predictors, which is considered acceptable. We will evaluate the model fit based on the validation results as well. As explained before, in linear regression, R^2 is practically the same as EP, but we can only get R^2 for the training sample. The RSE and EP give us similar information for the validation results. Specifically, the validation results show that the model's explanatory power is 60.7%. The MAPE of 0.161 means the model has a prediction accuracy of 1–0.161 = 0.839 or 83.9%. This accuracy level is considered marginally acceptable but not great. It is up to the decision-maker to decide if it is acceptable or not. Generally, we can say the accuracy is marginal but could be better. In the next chapters, we will use other methods to build additional predictive models.

In order to further examine the model fit, we look at the charts for validation results. These charts are constructed in MS Excel using the files we received from the Save Data node. I compared the charts between training and validation samples, and they are close enough. I won't present all of them here and focus more on the validation results for our model fit evaluation purpose because, as described in Chapter 6, we use the validation sample to validate the model.

The actual by predicted chart shows that the data points are scattered around the diagonal line, with some outliers (Figure 7.8). Additionally, the residual by predicted chart indicates that there is no pattern of residuals, as they are randomly distributed on both sides of the zero line (Figure 7.9). However, we do notice some outliers in the chart, especially above the zero line. In conclusion, the model's predictive power is considered acceptable but not great.

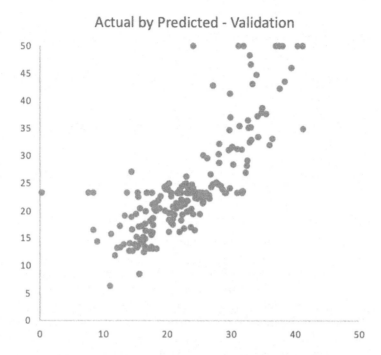

FIGURE 7.8
Actual by predicted chart for the validation sample.

Regression Equation Interpretation

Let's assume that the model fit discussed above is acceptable. Then, we need to interpret the regression equation to explain the effects of significant predictors. For this purpose, we use the regression output from SAS Enterprise Miner. It does show us some model fit metrics, as shown above, including F-test and R^2. In this section, we pay more attention

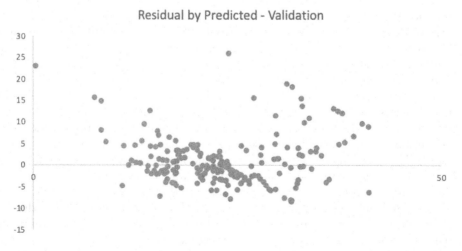

FIGURE 7.9
Residual by predicted chart for the validation sample.

to the Analysis of Maximum Likelihood Estimates portion since it provides us with the detailed correlation coefficients of the significant predictors.

Figure 7.10 presents a screenshot of the SAS Enterprise Miner's regression output so you know what it looks like and where to find it. Henceforth, I will present the output in a table form. As shown in Figure 7.10, we have seven significant predictors in the final model (their p-values are less than 0.05). Using the unstandardized coefficients, we can write the regression equation as follows (to avoid confusion, I do not include the prefix LOG or SQRT, which indicates the transformation we did).

$$Imv = 45.86 + 5.99 * Chalers\_River - 45.59 * LogAccess - 44.37 * LogDistance$$

$$+ 73.89 * RmSQ + 7.77 * ZonePR - 12 * IndustPr - 24.94 * Lstat$$

Using this equation, we can interpret the effects of those predictors on the target variable. For example, in terms of *LogDistance*, we can say that if the weighted distance to Boston employment centers increases by one point, the medium value of the house will decrease by 44.37*1000 or $44,370. Additionally, if the index of accessibility to radial

Analysis of Variance					
Source	DF	Sum of Squares	Mean Square	F Value	Pr > F
Model	7	11837	1691.031080	77.19	<.0001
Error	296	6484.632980	21.907544		
Corrected Total	303	18322			

Model Fit Statistics				
R-Square	0.6461	Adj R-Sq	0.6377
AIC	946.2895	BIC	948.6355
SBC	976.0257	C(p)	9.5486

Analysis of Maximum Likelihood Estimates					
Parameter	DF	Estimate	Standard Error	t Value	Pr > |t|
Intercept	1	45.8619	1.9914	23.03	<.0001
LOG_Charles_River	1	5.9977	1.5164	3.96	<.0001
LOG_LogAccess	1	-45.5943	19.7191	-2.31	0.0215
LOG_LogDistance	1	-44.3729	5.6755	-7.82	<.0001
LOG_RmSQ	1	73.8932	21.3034	3.47	0.0006
LOG_ZonePr	1	7.7748	2.1757	3.57	0.0004
SQRT_IndustPr	1	-12.0053	2.3300	-5.15	<.0001
SQRT_Lstat	1	-24.9453	1.8841	-13.24	<.0001

FIGURE 7.10
Linear regression outputs.

highways increases by one point (*LogAccess*), the medium value of the house will increase by $45,590. On the other hand, if the average number of rooms per dwelling (*RmSQ*) increases by one room, then the medium value of the house will increase by 73.89*1000 or $73,890. Furthermore, if the proportion of residential land (*ZonePr*) increases by 1%, the medium housing price will increase by $7,770. That is how we interpret the effects of the predictors.

If we want to compare the effects of the predictors, note that SAS Enterprise Miner does not directly produce standardized regression coefficients (some codes can be written to achieve these coeffi-cients, but it is not the purpose of this book). We can still make a comparison to decide which predictor has a higher unstandard-ized coefficient, but the comparison may not be as meaningful as using standardized

> SAS Enterprise Miner does not directly produce standardized coefficients. Hence, we can still use the absolute coefficient chart to make a comparison, but we need to interpret the results with caution because it does not provide us with the relative importance due to scale differences.

coefficients. Figure 7.11 shows the absolute coefficient chart, presenting the absolute values of regression coefficients of all predictors. The chart indicates that *RmSQ* has the highest coef-ficient, followed by *LogAccess*, *LogDistance*, and *Lstat*. *ZonePr* and *Charles_River* have the low-est regression coefficients. Keep in mind that we need to interpret the results with caution because this chart does not provide us with the relative importance due to scale differences.

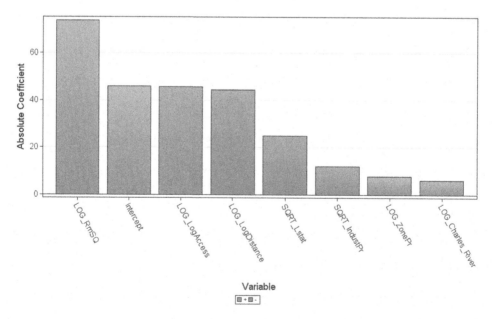

FIGURE 7.11
Absolute coefficient chart.

Model Comparison

In order to show how the model comparison works, let's add another regression model to the diagram. We use the same configurations for this model. The only difference is that this second model, Regression (2), does not use the normalized variables. We are interested in knowing which model has a better model fit.

Follow the steps below.

1. From the Model tab, drag a second Regression node into the workspace and connect it to the Impute node. Name it Regression (2).

2. Use the same configurations for this model: Linear Regression for Regression Type, Stepwise for Selection Model.

3. Add the Model Comparison node and connect it to Regression and Regression (2).

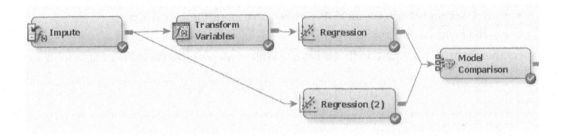

4. In the Train properties, make the following changes.
   - Set Selection Statistic to Average Square Error.
   - Selection Table to Validation (we select the best model based on the validation results).
5. Run the Model Comparison node and open the Results window.

Table 7.14 presents the comparison result in terms of model fit. We use MSE and RMSE for comparison purposes. As we can see, the model using the normalized variables, Regression, has a lower MSE and RMSE than the one using untransformed variables, Regression (2). This result shows that by normalizing the data, we achieved a better fit model.

TABLE 7.14

Model Fit Comparison

Model Fit Metrics	Regression	Regression (2)
Mean Squared Error	32.26	40.38
Root Mean Squared Error	5.68	6.35

Logistic Regression

Logistic Regression Equation

Logistic regression works with the target variable, which is binary or nominal. Following is the logistic regression equation in the traditional way

$$Logit(Y) = log\left(\frac{p}{1-p}\right) = \beta_0 + \beta_1 x_1 + \beta_2 x_2 + \ldots + \beta_n x_n + \varepsilon$$

Where

- Y is the target variable
- p is the probability of the event in the target variable
- x_1 to x_n are predictor variables *1- n*
- β_0 is intercept
- β_1 to β_n are regression coefficients for the corresponding predictors
- ε is the residual or error

Another form of this equation that is easier to interpret presents the odds ratio as follows.

$$Odds(Y) = \left(\frac{p}{1-p}\right) = e^{(\beta_0 + \beta_1 x_1 + \beta_2 x_2 + \ldots + \beta_n x_n + \varepsilon)}$$

Don't feel intimidated by those equations. We do not actually use them in the analysis or results interpretation. I will explain the results in a simpler way.

Estimation Approach

Logistic regression estimates the target variable and regression coefficients in a different way compared to linear regression. The estimation method is called maximum likelihood estimation (MLE). In simple terms, first, we need to assume the probability distribution of the target variable. Then, we use a likelihood function to calculate the probability of the outcome based on the predictors. This method can estimate the probability of an event and is not subject to strict assumptions as with OLS.

Assumption Requirements

As explained, due to the nature of the MLE method, logistic regression does not require strict assumptions like normality, homoscedasticity, and linearity. Typically, logistic regression has the following assumptions.

- **Binary target variable**: The target variable must be binary, meaning it has two distinct levels. For example, 1 – accident; 0 – no accident.
- **Multiple predictors:** Logistic regression requires multiple predictors. However, it does not require continuous predictors and can work well with binary or nominal predictors. Basically, there are no restrictions to the scales of predictors. It is a great advantage since we often analyze large data with predictors with different scales.
- **Non-multicollinearity**: It is a similar assumption to linear regression. Basically, predictors must be independent of each other. Similar to the discussion with

linear regression, with a large sample size, the effect of multicollinearity is considered tolerable.

- **Linearity**: There needs to be a linear relationship between predictors and the logit value of the target variable. As shown in the equation before, we have a linear regression equation between the logit of the target variable and predictors.

In conclusion, there is more flexibility in assumptions for logistic regression, which makes it a robust data mining method for any type of data.

Model Fit Evaluation

Logistic regression is a classification model. Hence, we use the model fit metrics for a classification model, as described in Chapter 6. They include misclassification rate, accuracy rate, sensitivity, specificity, F1-score, Gini coefficient, ROC chart, and Lift chart.

In addition, logistic regression has some specific model fit metrics pertaining to this method. They are somewhat similar to model fit metrics for linear regression. Table 7.15 summarizes model fit metrics between these regression methods. Thus, we can see the equivalent model fit metrics between these methods.

Chi-Square test and pseudo R^2 are the method-specific metrics for logistic regression. In order to understand the Chi-Square test for the −2LL difference, we need to understand −2LL. Hence, I include the description of -2LL in Table 7.16.

TABLE 7.15

Method-Specific Fit Metrics for Linear Regression and Logistic Regression

Linear Regression	Logistic Regression
Sum of Squares Total (SST)	−2LL of the base model
Sum of Squares Error (SSE)	−2LL of the proposed model
Sum of Squares Regression (SSR)	Difference of -2LL between the base and proposed models
F-test of model fit	Chi-Square test of -2LL difference between the base and proposed models
Coefficient of determination (R^2)	Pseudo R^2 measures

Source: Hair et al., 2019

TABLE 7.16

Recommended Method-Specific Metrics for Logistic Regression

Logistic Regression Metrics	Description
−2LL (−2 Log Likelihood)	A measure of how well the model fits the likelihood. A good model is characterized by a high likelihood of the observed results or a low −2LL. In the ideal scenario where a model fits perfectly the data, the likelihood attains a value of 1, and the -2LL score becomes 0).
Chi-Square test of −2LL difference	Difference of −2LL between two models in the stepwise process. We would expect a significant Chi-Square test, which indicates the improvement in the modeling step.
Pseudo R^2	A measure of how well the model fits the data, compared to a model that always predicts the mean. The two most common pseudo R^2 are • McFadden's R^2 • Cox & Snell R^2 Note that pseudo R^2 does not range from 0 to 1 since it has a much lower upper bound. Hence, the general rule of thumb is that a pseudo R^2 between 0.2 and 0.4 is considered a good fit.

Model Selection Methods

In logistic regression, we also have three stepwise methods, as described before. They include for-ward stepwise, backward stepwise, and adaptive stepwise. While logistic regression has a binary target variable instead of a continuous variable, it

> Start with adaptive stepwise method.

also uses the same types of stepwise methods. Accordingly, I recommend starting with the adaptive stepwise for variable selection since it allows us to find the best combination of the predictors that produces a good model fit.

How to Read and Understand the Logistic Regression Results?

Again, before we try to interpret the logistic regression results, we need to make sure we have a good model fit. Suppose we have checked the model fit metrics for logistic regression, including -2LL, Chi-Square test for -2LL, pseudo R^2, RMSE, RSE, EP, misclas-sification rate, accuracy, sensitivity, specificity, F1-score, Gini coefficient, LOC chart, and Lift chart, and we found a satisfactory model fit. The next step is to interpret the logistic regression results to identify the significant predictors and their effects on the target variable.

Typically, the logistic regression estimation results include:

- Logistic coefficient (B)
- Standard error
- Wald statistic: test for significance of the coefficients
- Degree of freedom
- Significance value (p-value)
- Exp(B) or odds ratio
- 95% confidence interval for Exp(B)

We focus on the important outputs that help us interpret the results. Logistic regres-sion results are harder to read and understand due to the use of the logit function. In order to understand the estimation results, we will focus mainly on the significance values, logistic coefficients, and odds ratio. For example, suppose we find the following regression equation for the example with the target variable being students' decision to choose major A.

$$Logit\left(majorA_{choice}\right) = 0.5 - 0.3 * gender + 0.4 * age$$

In this equation, 0.5 is the intercept, −0.3 is the logistic coefficient for gender, and 0.4 is the coefficient for age. The sign of the coefficient does show us the sign of the effect. In this case, based on the results, we can say that gender has a negative effect on the major A selection, while age has a positive effect on the major A selection.

The coefficients are supposed to allow us to interpret the effect size. However, the cor-relation coefficients in this equation relate to the logit value instead of the actual target variable, making it very hard to interpret. In order to overcome this challenge, we will use the odds ratio instead of the logit function. For that purpose, we can transform that equation into an equivalent one as follows.

$$Odds\left(majorA\_choice\right) = e^{(0.5\ -0.3^{*}gender\ +0.4^{*}age)}$$

Most analytic software gives us the odds ratio for each predictor and the correlation coefficient. We use the sign of the coefficients to determine the sign of the effect and use the odds ratio to interpret the effect of the predictor on the target variable. For example, the regression equation shows that two significant, important predictors for major A choice are gender and age.

Additionally, gender has a positive correlation, and age has a negative correlation with the major choice. Suppose we find the odds ratios for those two predictors as follows.

Odds ratio for gender $= 0.74$

Odds ratio for age $= 1.49$

So, how do we interpret these numbers? First, let's look at gender. Note that gender is, supposedly, in this case, a binary variable (Male and Female), and Male is used as the reference (we need to set one level as the reference to interpret the relationship in logistic regression). Thus, we can say switching from Male to Female reduces the odds of choosing major A by 26% (we take the odds ratio minus 1 and convert it to a percentage $0.74-1=-0.26$). In other words, the chance of a male student choosing major A is $1/0.74 = 1.35$ times more likely than a female student. On the other hand, as the age increases by one year, the odds of a student choosing major A will increase by 49% ($1.49-1 = 0.49$). As you can see, the interpretation of logistic regression results is more challenging than the linear regression results. But if we follow that process, we should be able to do it right. We will get into actual analysis results in an example later.

Example: Logistic Regression

In order to illustrate how logistic regression works in data mining, we use the *airline recommendation* dataset, as described in the previous chapters. For convenience, I included the variable description in Table 7.17. You can find the details of this dataset in Chapter 4.

We follow the SEMMA process. Note that the Sample, Explore, and Modify steps have been completed in the previous chapters. Hence, I won't repeat them and just summarize the outcomes of those steps.

Sample

As described in Chapter 3, we used the following strategies for sampling.

- Use random sampling to sample 50% of the full dataset.
- Partition data into three sub-samples: 60% training, 20% validation, and 20% test.

TABLE 7.17

Airline Recommendation Data Description

Variable Name	Description	Scale	Role
recommend	Recommend the airline to others	Binary (Yes/No)	Target
airline_st	Airline status	Nominal	Input
age	Age	Interval	Input
gender	Gender	Binary (Male/Female)	Input
price_sensitivity*	Price sensitivity	Interval	Input
no_years_flying	Number of years flying	Interval	Input
no_flt_pa	Average number of flights per year	Interval	Input
pct_ flt_other_airline	Percent of flights with other airlines	Interval	Input
type_of_travel	Travel purpose	Nominal	Input
no_other_lty_cards	Number of other loyalty cards	Interval	Input
shopping_amt_airpt	Shopping amount at the airport	Interval	Input
eat_drink_airpt	Spending for eating and drinking at the airport	Interval	Input
class	Passenger class	Nominal	Input
origin_state	Origin state	Nominal	Input
destin_state	Destination state	Nominal	Input
depart_delay	Departure delay (in minutes)	Interval	Input
arrival_delay	Arrival delay (in minutes)	Interval	Input
flt_cancel	Flight cancellation	Binary (Yes/No)	Input
flt_time	Flight time (in minutes)	Interval	Input
flt_distance	Flight distance (miles)	Interval	Input

Table 7.18 presents the result of the data partition step.

Since we have a relatively balanced dataset, with 52.46% recommending the airline and 47.53% not recommending the airline, resampling is not needed.

Explore

Refer to Chapter 4 for the detailed results of this step.

Modify

We have completed this step in Chapter 5. In summary, in the Modify step, we performed the following tasks.

- Use the Replacement node to recode the missing value for *price_sensitivity*.
- Use Impute node to impute the missing values with mean values.

TABLE 7.18

Sampling and Partition Results

Sample	Target: Airline Recommendation			
	Yes	Yes (percentage)	No	No (percentage)
Training	19.510	52.25%	17.827	47.75%
Validation	6.504	52.25%	5.943	47.75%
Test	6.505	52.25%	5.943	47.75%
Total	**32.519**	**52.25%**	**29.713**	**47.75%**

TABLE 7.19

Imputation Results

Variable Name	Imputed Variable	Impute Value	Label	Number of Missing for TRAIN
REP_price_sensitivity	IMP_REP_price_sensitivity	1.308	Replacement: Price sensitivity	1181
arrival_delay_in_minutes	IMP_arrival_delay_in_minutes	15.189	Arrival delay (in minutes)	778
departure_delay_in_minutes	IMP_departure_delay_in_minutes	14.811	Departure delay (in minutes)	669
flight_time_in_minutes	IMP_flight_time_in_minutes	112.554	Flight time (in minutes)	778

The results show the number of cases that are coded with missing values for price_sensitivity as follows.

- Train: 1,181 records.
- Validation: 394 records.
- Test: 368 records.

There are four variables with missing values: *price_sensitivity, arrival_delay_in_minutes, departure_delay_in_minutes,* and *flight_time_in_minutes.* The results of the Impute node show how variables with missing values are imputed using mean values (Table 7.19).

Model

In order to build a predictive model using logistic regression, follow the steps below.

1. From the Model tab, drag a Regression node to the workspace and connect it to the Impute node. It is to make sure we use the dataset with imputations.

2. In the Train properties panel, make the following changes:
   - Set Regression Type to Logistic Regression.
   - Set Selection Model to Stepwise
   - Set Selection Criterion to Validation Misclassification. It is to inform the model to use the validation sample's misclassification rate to decide when to stop the stepwise process.
3. Run the Regression node and open the Results window.

Assess

In this step, we evaluate the model performance. Since the Regression node does not provide us with all the model fit metrics we need, we use the Model Comparison node to get those metrics. For that reason, I add the Model Comparison node to the Regression node and run it. I will specify which outputs we receive from the Regression node and which ones we receive from the Model Comparison node.

Results

Number of Steps in the Stepwise Process

Before we evaluate the model fit, we want to see how many steps that take the algorithm to come up with the final model. Table 7.20 shows the results of the stepwise process from SAS Enterprise Miner (Regression Node Results). It takes 14 steps to get to the final model. As we move from one step to another, with the addition of an additional predictor, the mis-classification rate (MR) decreases. The process steps at Step 14, when the MR reaches the lowest value of 0.2304. As shown in Figure 7.12, the step information between the training and validation samples is very close.

Model Fit Evaluation

Now, we know it takes 14 steps to find the final model. Let's evaluate the model fit. First, we look at logistic regression's specific model fit metric, -2LL difference. Figure 7.13 presents the SAS Enterprise Miner output (Regression Node Results), showing the -2LL difference Chi-Square test is significant ($p < 0.01$). It indicates that the final model has improved significantly from the base model.

Next, we examine the general model fit metrics for classification models, as described in Chapter 6. Using the Regression Node Results, we can combine the classification results into the confusion matrix for training and validation samples as follows (Table 7.21). We use the validation sample for validating the model and will look at the test sample later.

TABLE 7.20

Steps in the Stepwise Process

Step	Entered	Number In	Score Chi-Square	Pr > ChiSq	Validation Misclassification Rate
1	type_of_travel	1	11165.530	<0.0001	0.239
2	airline_status	2	2521.032	<0.0001	0.238
3	IMP_arrival_delay_in_minutes	3	280.583	<0.0001	0.232
4	age	4	189.426	<0.0001	0.234
5	gender	5	140.010	<0.0001	0.232
6	no_of_flights_per_year	6	152.744	<0.0001	0.232
7	class	7	58.081	<0.0001	0.232
8	IMP_REP_price_sensitivity	8	29.081	<0.0001	0.232
9	IMP_departure_delay_in_minutes	9	19.850	<0.0001	0.232
10	no_of_other_loyalty_cards	10	17.353	<0.0001	0.232
11	flight_cancelled	11	13.557	0.0002	0.232
12	number_of_years_flying	12	10.992	0.0009	0.230
13	flight_distance	13	4.546	0.033	0.231
14	shopping_amount_at_airport	14	4.362	0.0367	0.230

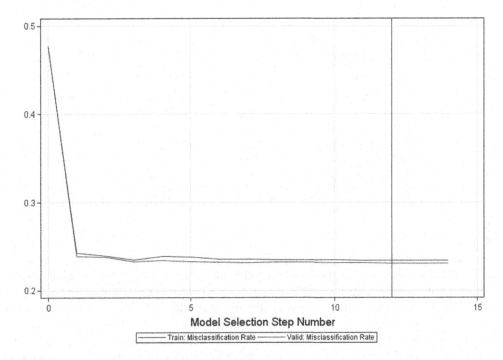

FIGURE 7.12
Model selection step number (regression node results).

```
   Likelihood Ratio Test for Global Null Hypothesis: BETA=0

   -2 Log Likelihood              Likelihood
 Intercept      Intercept &         Ratio
     Only       Covariates       Chi-Square      DF      Pr > ChiSq

 51684.184        35842.008       15842.1763      16        <.0001
```

FIGURE 7.13
Chi-Square test for -2LL difference.

TABLE 7.21

Confusion Matrix for Training and Validation Samples

	Training Sample			Validation Sample	
	Predicted YES	**Predicted NO**		**Predicted YES**	**Predicted NO**
Actual YES	TP=17,336	FN = 2,174	Actual YES	TP=5,811	FN = 693
Actual NO	FP = 6,566	TN = 11,261	Actual NO	FP = 2,175	TN = 3,768

TABLE 7.22

Model Fit Metrics for Training and Validation Samples

Metrics	Train	Validation
MR	0.234	0.230
ACC	0.766	0.770
Sensitivity	0.889	0.893
Specificity	0.632	0.634
F1 Score	0.799	0.802
Gini Coefficient*	0.67	0.66

* Extracted from the Model Comparison node results.

Using the formulas described in Chapter 6, we calculate the model fit metrics, as shown in Table 7.22 (the Gini coefficients are extracted from the Model Comparison node results). We should notice that the difference in these metrics between the training and validation samples is very small, indicating the reliability of the model. We do not see any overfitting issues in this case.

As for model fit, based on the validation results, the prediction accuracy seems a little low, about 77% (MR is around 23%). Looking further into sensitivity and specificity, we see that the sensitivity is relatively good, with a rate of 89.3%, indicating that the model can predict the positives well (recommendation). On the other hand, the specificity is just moderate at 63.4%, showing that the model struggles to predict the negatives (no recommendation). From the confusion matrix, we can tell the false positives (FP) are quite high compared to false negatives (FN). The F-1 score, which balances sensitivity and precision, shows a marginally acceptable value of 80.2%. Finally, the Gini coefficient is 0.66, which is considered acceptable. Overall, while MR and ACC alone may indicate a moderate model fit, further looking into other metrics gives us more insights into the model performance.

Before making the final conclusion about model fit, we should review the ROC chart and Lift chart for confirmation. Again, we use the charts for the validation sample. The ROC chart (Figure 7.14) shows that our model is between the baseline (the diagonal line) and the perfect fit model (upper left corner). Hence, the model is not considered a good fit. If we look at the ROC index in the Model Comparison Results, it is 0.83, which is marginally acceptable (ROC index of 0.9 or higher indicates a good model fit).

We also need to review the Lift chart (Figure 7.15). The chart shows that if we use 20% of the dataset, the Lift value is 1.6, indicating that our model can capture 1.6*20% = 32% of the positive cases, which is 1.6 times as many as if we use no model. It is considered a moderate lift.

Overall, these charts confirm the results we got before. If our objective is to predict the airline recommendation cases (positives), then we can use this model (sensitivity of 89.3%). However, the model does a poorer job of predicting the non-recommendation cases (negatives).

Let's compare the model fit across three samples: training, validation, and test (Table 7.23). We can extract the following outputs from the Model Comparison node results. As you can see, the metrics (MR, ACC, Gini coefficient, ROC index, and Cumulative Lift) are very

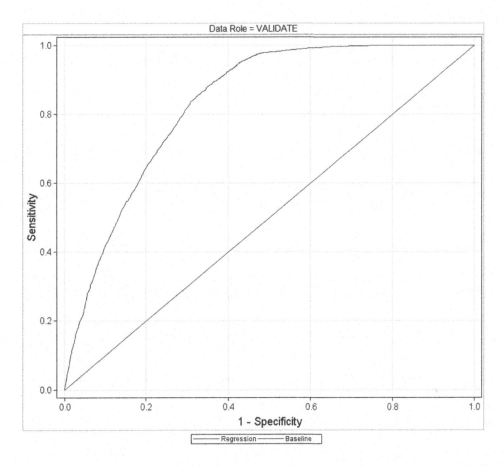

FIGURE 7.14
ROC chart.

consistent across those sub-samples. Thus, we have validated our model with the validation sample and completed the final testing with the test sample. There are no overfitting issues, and the model is very reliable. However, some model fit metrics are marginal, indicating further modeling using other methods is needed. We will continue to build predictive models for this dataset in the next chapters with different methods.

TABLE 7.23

Model Fit Comparison (From Model Comparison Node Results)

Metrics	Train	Validation	Test
Misclassification rate	0.233	0.230	0.236
Accuracy	0.767	0.77	0.764
Gini Coefficient	0.67	0.66	0.67
ROC index	0.83	0.83	0.83
Cumulative Lift	1.67	1.65	1.65

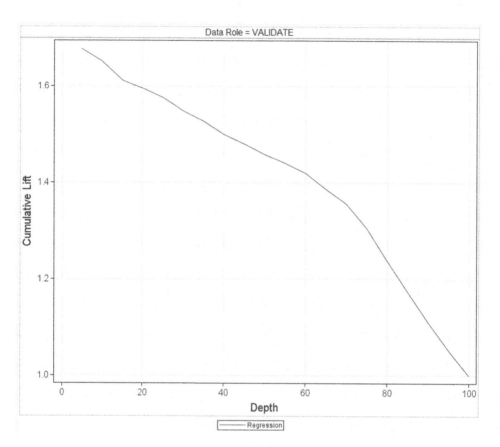

FIGURE 7.15
Lift chart.

Logistic Regression Result Interpretation

Assuming the model fit is acceptable, we need to interpret the regression results. Table 7.24 shows the detailed logistic regression results (Analysis of Maximum Likelihood Estimates) extracted from the Regression Node Results. First, we review the p-value for the Wald Chi-Square test. These p-values are lower than 0.01, indicating the predictors are significant in predicting the target variables. The Estimate column shows us the logistic coefficients and the Standardized Estimate column shows us the standardized coefficients.

As stated before, the Estimate sign shows us the sign of the effect, negative or positive. For example, price sensitivity has a negative effect on airline recommendation, while airline status has a positive effect. However, the effect size should be interpreted with the odds ratio to make sense of the results. In this result, Exp(Est) is the odds ratio. But we will not use this odds ratio since it does not show the reference level. We need to know the reference level for interpreting the effect of nominal or binary predictors. In order to do so, we use the Odds Ratio Estimates output in Table 7.25 (from the Regression node results). As you can see, this output shows us the reference level for nominal and binary predictors. The information for interval predictors is the same as the results above.

There are many predictors with different results, so it is hard to explain all of them in detail. I summarize the result interpretation for those predictors in a summary table (Table 7.26).

TABLE 7.24

Analysis of Maximum Likelihood Estimates

Parameter		Estimate	Standard Error	Wald Chi-Square	Pr > ChiSq	Standardized Estimate	Exp(Est)
Intercept		1.318	0.095	192.95	<0.0001		3.737
IMP_REP_price_ sensitivity		−0.155	0.027	32.96	<0.0001	−0.042	0.856
IMP_arrival_delay_ in_minutes		−0.012	0.001	85.64	<0.0001	−0.237	0.989
IMP_departure_ delay_in_minutes		0.006	0.001	20.32	<0.0001	0.115	1.006
age		−0.013	0.001	170.67	<0.0001	−0.116	0.987
airline_status	Blue	−0.746	0.025	862.67	<0.0001		0.474
airline_status	Gold	0.194	0.039	24.39	<0.0001		1.214
airline_status	Platinum	−0.385	0.053	51.83	<0.0001		0.681
class	Business	0.237	0.035	46.9	<0.0001		1.268
class	Eco	−0.130	0.023	32.02	<0.0001		0.878
flight_cancelled	No	0.183	0.050	13.49	0.0002		1.201
gender	Female	−0.172	0.013	163.4	<0.0001		0.842
no_of_flights_per_year		−0.013	0.001	156.12	<0.0001	−0.099	0.988
no_of_other_loyalty_ cards		−0.052	0.013	17.15	<0.0001	−0.032	0.949
number_of_years_flying		−0.015	0.004	10.99	0.0009	−0.024	0.986
type_of_travel	Business travel	1.104	0.021	2821.7	<0.0001		3.016
type_of_travel	Mileage tickets	0.640	0.030	450.74	<0.0001		1.897

TABLE 7.25

Odds Ratio Estimates

Effect		Point Estimate
IMP_REP_price_sensitivity		0.856
IMP_arrival_delay_in_minutes		0.989
IMP_departure_delay_in_minutes		1.006
age		0.987
airline_status	Blue vs. Silver	0.186
airline_status	Gold vs. Silver	0.476
airline_status	Platinum vs. Silver	0.267
class	Business vs. Eco Plus	1.411
class	Eco vs. Eco Plus	0.977
flight_cancelled	No vs. Yes	1.443
gender	Female vs. Male	0.709
no_of_flights_per_year		0.988
no_of_other_loyalty_cards		0.949
number_of_years_flying		0.986
type_of_travel	Business travel vs. Personal Travel	17.257
type_of_travel	Mileage tickets vs. Personal Travel	10.85

TABLE 7.26

Logistic Regression Result Interpretation

Predictors	Sign of Effect	Level	Odds Ratio	Interpretation
price_sensitivity	-	Interval	0.856	As price sensitivity increases by one unit, the odds of airline recommendation decrease by 1–0.856 = 0.144 or 14.4%
arrival_delay_in_minutes	-	Interval	0.989	As arrival delay increases by one minute, the odds of airline recommendation decrease by 1–0.989 = 0.011 or 1.1%
departure_delay_in_minutes	+	Interval	1.006	As departure delay increases by one minute, the odds of airline recommendation increase by 1.006–1 = 0.006 or 0.6%
age	-	Interval	0.987	As age increases by one year, the odds of airline recommendation decrease by 1–0.986 = 0.013 or 1.3%
no_of_flights_per_year	-	Interval	0.988	As flight numbers increases by one flight per year, the odds of airline recommendation decrease by 1–0.988 = 0.012 or 1.2%
no_of_other_loyalty_cards	-	Interval	0.949	As the loyalty cards increase by one per year, the odds of airline recommendation decrease by 1–0.949 = 0.051 or 5.1%
number_of_years_flying	-	Interval	0.986	As the years flying increase by one year, the odds of airline recommendation decrease by 1–0.986 = 0.014 or 1.4%
airline_status	-	Blue vs. *Silver*	0.186	The odds of Silver passengers recommending the airline is 1/0.186 = 5.38 times more likely than Blue passengers.
airline_status	-	Gold vs. *Silver*	0.476	The odds of Silver passengers recommending the airline is 1/0.476 = 2.1 times more likely than Gold passengers.
airline_status	-	Platinum vs. *Silver*	0.267	The odds of Silver passengers recommending the airline is 1/0.267 = 3.75 times more likely than Platinum passengers.
class	+	Business vs. *Eco Plus*	1.411	The odds of Business class passengers recommending the airline is 1.411 times more likely than Eco Plus class passengers.
class	-	Eco vs. *Eco Plus*	0.977	The odds of Eco Plus class passengers recommending the airline is 1/0.977 = 1.02 times more likely than Business class passengers.
flight_cancelled	+	No vs. *Yes*	1.443	The odds of passengers without flight cancellation experience recommending the airline is 1.443 times more likely than the one with delay experience.
gender	-	Female vs. *Male*	0.709	The odds of male passengers recommending the airline is 1/0.709 = 1.41 times more likely than female passengers.
type_of_travel	+	Business Travel vs. *Personal Travel*	17.257	The odds of business travel passengers recommending the airline is 17.257 times more likely than personal travel passengers.
type_of_travel	+	Mileage tickets vs. *Personal Travel*	10.85	The odds of mileage ticket passengers recommending the airline is 10.85 times more likely than personal travel passengers.

Note: underlined =reference level

TABLE 7.27

Variable Importance

Parameter	Standardized Estimate
IMP_arrival_delay_in_minutes	−0.2373
age	−0.116
IMP_departure_delay_in_minutes	0.115
no_of_flights_per_year	−0.0991
IMP_REP_price_sensitivity	−0.0419
no_of_other_loyalty_cards	−0.0324
number_of_years_flying	−0.0239

Basically, we use the interpretation method as described before for each predictor (we will not interpret the effect of the intercept since it does not have any practical implication, even though it is needed for the regression equation). I group interval predictors together and nominal/binary predictors together for easy interpretation. Note that an odds ratio greater than 1 indicates a positive effect, while an odds ratio lower than 1 indicates a negative effect. As you can see, the interpretation of interval predictors is rather straightforward, while the interpretation of nominal and binary predictors is a little more tricky. In addition, the odds ratio greater than 1 is easier to interpret than the odds ratio lower than 1.

Variable Importance

One important question is how important are the significant predictors, and which one is more important than the others? In order to answer this question, we use the standardized estimates in Table 7.27. I extracted the information and ranked the predictors by their importance using the absolute values of the standardized estimates. Note that standardized coefficients are provided for the primary predictors but not the specific levels.

The results show that *arrival delay time* is the most important predictor, followed by age and *departure delay time*. On the other hand, *the number of years flying* and *the number of other loyalty cards* are among the least important predictors. As you can see, the standardized estimates range from 0 to 1 and are scale-independent, which provides us with useful insights into the relative importance of each predictor. These findings help airline executives establish marketing and promotion strategies to improve their services and attract more passengers.

Summary

Regression is considered one of the most popular machine learning algorithms due to its simplicity in implementation and result interpretation. Regression methods allow us to predict the value of the target variable based on multiple predictors. Linear regression is an association model with a continuous target variable, while logistic regression is a classification model with a binary target variable. The key characteristic of regression methods is the linear relationship. The linear regression equation presents a linear relationship between the target variable and the predictors. The logistic regression equation represents a linear relationship between the logit value of the target variable and the predictors. Regression analysis is widely used in various fields, including economics, finance, healthcare, aviation, and social sciences, to make predictions and gain insights from data.

This chapter covers the fundamental knowledge and concepts of regression methods, equations, estimation methods, model selection methods, assumptions, model fit metrics, and outputs. We also learn how to perform linear regression and logistic regression with actual datasets using SAS Enterprise Miner. The process of training models, presenting results, comparing models, selecting the champion model, and explaining the regression equation is thoroughly described with hands-on examples.

The regression method has both advantages and limitations. On the positive side, it provides a straightforward approach for making predictions when relationships between variables are well-defined. It is also interpretable, allowing users to understand the impact of each predictor on the target variable. However, regression assumes a linear relationship between variables, and if this assumption is violated, it may lead to inaccurate predictions. Additionally, regression is sensitive to outliers and missing values, which may affect the model fit. Overall, regression is a valuable tool in data mining for understanding and predicting numerical relationships between variables, but it is essential to carefully assess its assumptions and limitations for reliable results.

CHAPTER DISCUSSION QUESTIONS

1. Define regression. What are the primary characteristics of regression methods?

2. Compare linear regression and logistic regression. Can logistic regression detect non-linear patterns? Explain.

3. Provide practical examples for using linear regression and logistic regression in real life.

4. Explain the advantages and disadvantages of regression methods in data mining.

5. What are the assumptions for linear regression and logistic regression? In data mining projects, must we meet all assumptions to be able to use those methods? Why?

6. Which estimation methods are used for linear regression and logistic regression? What is the key difference between these methods?

7. What is the purpose of model selection methods? Compare forward stepwise, backward stepwise, and adaptive stepwise. Which method should we use?

8. What are specific model fit criteria for linear regression and logistic regression?

9. How do we interpret the coefficients of significant predictors in linear regression?

10. How do we interpret the coefficients of significant predictors in logistic regression?

Exercises

Exercise 1: Linear regression model for the Bank dataset

1. Open the *bank* dataset in SAS Enterprise Miner.
2. Sample the entire dataset. See the variable names and descriptions in Appendix A.1.
3. Partition the data using a split ratio of 60:40 (train: 60%; validation: 20%; test: 20%)
4. Create visualization for variables to explore the data trends.
5. Explore the data to identify
   - Missing values.
   - Outliers.
   - Variables with skewed data.
6. Perform data modification as needed:
   - Impute missing values.
   - Normalize variables with skewed data distribution.
7. Set *CRSCORE* (credit scores) as the target variable.
8. Run a linear regression model using the adaptive stepwise method.
9. Evaluate the model fit using both general and regression-specific model fit metrics.
10. Present the results, including significant predictors and coefficients.
11. Interpret the regression coefficient for each significant predictor and explain how it predicts the target variable.

Exercise 2: Logistic regression model for the Passengers dataset

1. Open the *passengers* dataset in SAS Enterprise Miner.
2. Sample 20% of the full data. Set *return* (decision to return to the airline) as the target variable and change its role to binary. See the variable names and descriptions in Appendix A.2.
3. Evaluate the balance of the dataset regarding the target variable (balance between 1 – Yes and 0 – No).
4. Partition the data using a split ratio of 60:40 (train: 60%; validation: 20%; test: 20%)
5. Explore the data to identify
   - Missing values.
   - Outliers.
   - Variables with skewed data.
6. Perform data modification as needed:
   - Replace zero values for Likert scale variables with missing values.
   - Impute missing values.
   - Normalize variables with skewed data distribution.
7. Run a linear regression model using the adaptive stepwise method.
8. Evaluate the model fit using both general and regression-specific model fit metrics.
9. Present the results, including significant predictors, coefficients, and odds ratios.
10. Interpret the odds ratio for each significant predictor and explain how it predicts the target variable.
11. Compare the standardized estimates of the significant predictors and interpret the relative importance of each predictor.

8

Decision Trees

Introduction

This chapter focuses on the decision tree method. This method presents the hierarchical structure of variables in the tree form using logical rules. The tree consists of nodes, which split into two or more branches, using the condition that best separates the individuals of each class. It is one of the most popular machine learning methods because it is easier to implement and understand. The tree structure shows relationships among variables through nodes and branches. This

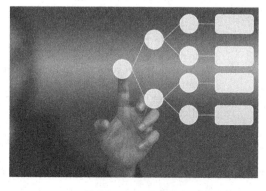

DOI: 10.1201/9781003162872-10

method is also capable of detecting non-linear relationships. In this chapter, we discuss the advantages and disadvantages of decision trees, so we can compare them with other methods. The two common types of decision trees are CART (Classification and Regression Tree) and CHAID (Chi-Squared Automatic Interaction Detector). We will learn their characteristics and differences, and I will show you how to build these two types of trees using SAS Enterprise Miner, including the tree pruning process. Since this method is non-parametric and logical rule-based, the theoretical foundation is quite different from regression methods. We follow the branches of the tree to see how predictors correlate with the target variable rather than relying on mathematical equations. It still includes some mathematical algorithms used to determine how the tree hierarchy is built, and some of them may be quite complicated. But don't worry. I do not get into the detailed algorithms. Instead, I try to explain the method in a simpler way so you can understand how it works.

What Is a Decision Tree? How Does It Work?

Decision tree is a very popular machine learning method. It is often used in a decision-making process, and it has become a popular algorithm in data mining projects. It is a non-parametric and non-linear method. Decision tree models offer notable advantages due to their inherent simplicity in conceptualization while remaining highly adaptable to

> **DEFINITION**
>
> Decision tree is a logical rule-based method that presents a hierarchical structure of variables, including the root node, parent nodes, and child nodes.

capturing non-linear relationships between predictor variables and the target variables. The tree is presented as a flow chart showing the relationships among variables visually, which makes it easy to understand and explain, even with a complex process. It is a big advantage because we cannot say the same thing for other machine learning algorithms.

Let's look at a simple example of a decision tree in Figure 8.1. Suppose we want to predict the likelihood of passengers purchasing an airline ticket for a trip. We assume that

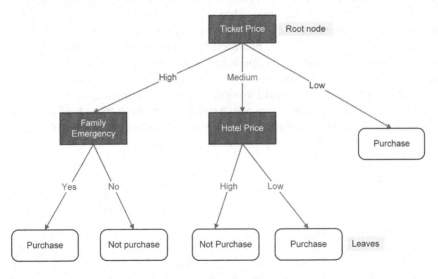

FIGURE 8.1
An example of a decision tree.

this decision depends on several factors, ticket price, family emergency, and hotel price. The flowchart presents the decision-making process or the rules capturing the relationship between the passenger decision (target variable) and those factors (predictors). Let's examine the tree structure.

- The primary factor is the ticket price; hence, it is the root node. The flowchart shows that if the ticket price is high, the next factor that should be considered is the family emergency. If there is a family emergency, then the passenger will decide to purchase the ticket, even if it is high. If there is no emergency, there will be no ticket purchasing since the trip can wait.
- If the ticket price is medium, then the next considered factor is the hotel price. If the hotel price is high, then the passenger will not purchase the ticket and perhaps wait for another time. But if the hotel price is low, it would be a good deal for the trip, and the passenger will purchase the ticket.
- Finally, if the ticket price is low, it is a good deal, and the passenger will purchase the ticket and take the trip without considering other factors.

As you can see, the decision tree presents the decision-making process in a rather straightforward and logical way. It is easy to follow and understand the relationships among variables in the model based on those rules. The tree provides us with a set of rules that can be used to make the prediction. Hence, decision tree is a logical rule-based method, not a statistical or mathematical method. The flowchart allows us to create a model that predicts the ticket purchasing decision based on those predictors, and when we train and validate the model properly with enough data, the model can predict the purchasing decision (purchase vs. not purchase) with good predictive power.

A decision tree represents a hierarchical structure of variables, including the root node, parent nodes, child nodes, and leaf nodes. The root node is the one on the top of the tree and contains the entire dataset. A parent node is a node split into child nodes, forming branches. Parent nodes and child nodes are relative terms depending on which one we are interpreting. Any node that falls under another node is a child node, and any node preceding these child nodes is a parent node. That means one node is a child node to a parent node and can also be a parent node to other child nodes. The final nodes of the decision tree are called leaf nodes, or leaves. For each leaf, a decision is made and applied to all observations in the leaf. In predictive modeling, the decision is the predicted value.

In our previous example, the hierarchy is the tree. Ticket price is the root node, Family emergency and Hotel price are child nodes, and each of these nodes is split into two branches. Hence, Family Emergency is also a parent node with two child nodes, Purchase and Not Purchase. The rounded rectangle nodes are the leaves, representing the final classification decision (Purchase or Not purchase).

Basic Concepts in the Decision Tree Method

Given the number of new terms we have in this chapter, Table 8.1 presents basic concepts in the decision tree methods and their descriptions.

TABLE 8.1

Basic Concepts in Decision Trees

Terms	Descriptions
Decision tree	Decision tree is a logical rule-based method that presents a hierarchical structure of variables, including the root node, parent nodes, and child nodes.
Root node	A root node is at the beginning of a tree. It represents the initial decision based on a specific feature that has the most significant impact on the target variable. Starting from the root node, the dataset partitioned based on different features, and subsequently, these subgroups are further divided at each decision node located beneath the root node.
Splitting	Splitting is a process of dividing a node into two or more sub-nodes.
Splitting criterion	Splitting criterion is a measure used to evaluate and select the best predictor to split the data at each node of the tree. It is a measure of impurity or variance reduction.
Decision node	When a sub-node splits into additional sub-nodes, it is referred to as a decision node.
Leaf node	Nodes that do not split are called leaf nodes. They represent the output or the predicted value/class for the specific subgroup of data that reaches that node.
Pruning	The process of eliminating the sub-nodes of a parent node is known as pruning. It is a technique used to simplify the decision tree by removing nodes that do not significantly improve its performance on the validation set. A tree is expanded by splitting and reduced in size through pruning.
Branch or sub-tree	A branch or a sub-tree is a sub-section of a decision tree.
Parent node and child node	These are relative terms. Any node that falls under another node is a child node or sub-node, and any node that precedes these child nodes is called a parent node.
Recursive partitioning	Recursive partitioning denotes an iterative process procedure involving the division of data into partitions, followed by further splitting along each branch.
Classification and Regression Tree (CART)	CART is a binary tree, which uses an algorithm to split a parent node into TWO child nodes repeatedly. CART can be used for both classification and association models.
Chi-Squared Automatic Interaction Detection (CHAID)	CHAID is a non-parametric method used for creating decision trees by recursively splitting the data into homogeneous subgroups based on the categorical predictor variables, using the Chi-Square test to assess the independence between variables and find significant splits.

How Does Node Splitting Work?

From the example above, we see how a tree is structured based on the hierarchy of decisions made by the passengers. We can also see that how those nodes are split is the key to constructing that tree. So, how does node splitting work?

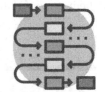

Node splitting is a key process in constructing a tree's hierarchical structure, as it determines how the data should be segregated at each level of the tree. In this procedure, the algorithm chooses a variable, and the corresponding node is divided into two or more branches. The criterion for division is the one that optimally separates individuals within each class. If the variable is categorical, the branches represent distinct classes within the node. Conversely, if the variable is continuous, the branches indicate specific intervals within the node. At each split, a separation condition is applied how to divide the parent node into child nodes. This process persists until a predefined stopping criterion is met. This procedure is referred to as *recursive partitioning*.

Recursive involves recursively dividing the dataset into smaller and more homogenous subsets (nodes) based on the splitting criterion. The goal is to create a hierarchical tree-like structure that represents the underlying relationships in the data, making it easy to interpret and make decisions. This process includes the following steps.

> **DEFINITION**
>
> Recursive partitioning is an iterative process of splitting the data into partitions, and then splitting it up further on each of the branches.

1. **Selecting a splitting criterion**: At each node of the tree, the algorithm selects a variable and a corresponding splitting criterion to partition the data into child nodes. The selection of the splitting criterion is determined based on the scale of the target variable and may include measures such as F-test, Chi-Square test, Gini impurity, or Entropy.

2. **Splitting the data**: The selected splitting criterion is used to split the node into two or more child nodes. Each child node represents a branch from the current node in the tree.

3. **Stopping criteria**: The algorithm checks if any stopping criteria are met. Common stopping criteria include reaching a maximum tree depth, having a minimum number of samples per leaf, or achieving a specific level of impurity reduction.

4. **Recursive process**: If the stopping criteria are not met, the process continues recursively for each branch. The child nodes become new parent nodes, and the process continues.

5. **Leaf nodes**: When a stopping criterion is met or there are no further meaningful splits, the process stops, and the final nodes of the tree are called leaf nodes. Leaf nodes represent the final predictions of the target variable.

The recursive partitioning process continues until all the stopping criteria are satisfied or until the tree becomes fully grown. However, a fully grown tree may lead to overfitting, where the model captures noise and specific details of the training data, resulting in poor predictive power. In order to mitigate overfitting, tree pruning can be used to simplify the tree. We will cover pruning techniques in this chapter.

Overall, recursive partitioning in decision trees is a top-down approach, starting with the entire dataset and recursively dividing it into smaller subsets. This process is efficient and allows decision trees to handle both categorical and continuous variables, making them powerful and interpretable models for data mining.

Do Missing Values Have Effects on Decision Trees?

In traditional statistical studies, missing values are a big concern as they may show missing information in the data and can affect the results. Regression methods are sensitive to missing values since they tend to require a complete dataset to build models with a good model fit. In addition, missing values result in a loss of information and may create biases in the data. However, decision tree is a non-parametric method and is based on logical rules. Since the tree is constructed by splitting parent nodes into multiple child nodes, missing values have a less significant impact on the process of constructing a tree since this method has a very effective way of handling missing values.

Essentially, decision trees handle missing values naturally in their splitting process. Below are some typical ways of handling missing values in decision trees.

Splitting Criteria with Missing Values

Decision trees can use different splitting criteria, such as Gini impurity or Entropy, to determine the best variable and threshold for splitting the data at each node. When a variable has missing values for a particular data point, the algorithm typically treats the missing values as a separate category or group. The data point with the missing value traverses down both branches of the split, and the algorithm calculates the impurity or error for each branch based on the available data. This allows the decision tree to take advantage of the information from non-missing values to make decisions even when some values are missing.

Using Imputation

Some decision tree implementations may support imputation of missing values. We have covered this topic in Chapter 5.

Creating Multiple Branches

If a data point has missing values for multiple variables, the decision tree creates multiple branches from the current node to account for the combinations of missing and non-missing values. The algorithm evaluates each branch separately and considers the available values for each data point.

Missing Value Handling during Prediction

When making predictions for new data, if a variable has missing values, the decision tree will still be able to make a prediction by following the appropriate branches based on the available values. If a data point has missing values for multiple variables, the tree will traverse down multiple paths to reach the leaf nodes, and the predictions from these paths are combined to make the final prediction.

It is important to note some data mining software applications may have built-in support for handling missing values more efficiently for decision tree mod-

- Decision tree can naturally handle missing values.
- It is recommended to use software with built-in algorithms, such as SAS Enterprise Miner, to handle missing values in the decision tree modeling.

eling. It is recommended to use those built-in algorithms. SAS Enterprise Miner has such built-in algorithms to handle missing values (see the details on the next page).

SAS ENTERPRISE MINER GUIDELINES

Decision Trees – Missing Values

(https://documentation.sas.com)

HOW DOES SAS ENTERPRISE MINER HANDLE MISSING VALUES FOR DECISION TREES?

- If the value of the target variable is missing, the observation is excluded from training and evaluating the decision tree model.

- The search for a split on an input uses observations whose values are missing on the input (provided that you did set the Missing Values property to Use in search). All such observations are assigned to the same branch. The branch might or might not contain other observations. The resulting branch maximizes the worth of the split.

- For splits on a categorical variable, this amounts to treating a missing value as a separate category. For numerical variables, it amounts to treating missing values as having the same unknown non-missing value.

- One advantage of using missing data during the search is that the worth of the split is computed with the same number of observations for each input. Another advantage is that an association of the missing values with the target values can contribute to the predictive ability of the split.

- When a split is applied to an observation in which the required input value is missing, surrogate splitting rules can be considered before assigning the observation to the branch for missing values.

- A surrogate splitting rule is a backup to the main splitting rule. If several surrogate rules exist, each surrogate is considered in sequence until one can be applied to the observation. If none can be applied, the main rule assigns the observation to the branch that is designated for missing values.

SAS ENTERPRISE MINER GUIDELINES

Decision Tree Node Train Properties

(https://documentation.sas.com)

DECISION TREE NODE TRAIN PROPERTIES: SPLITTING RULE

Missing values – Specifies how splitting rules handle observations that contain missing values for a variable. The default value is **Use in search**.
Select from the following available missing value policies:

- **Use in search** – Uses missing values in the calculation of the worth of a splitting rule. This consequently produces a splitting rule that assigns the missing values to the branch that maximizes the worth of the split.

This is a desirable option when the existence of a missing value is predictive of a target value.

- **Largest branch** – Assigns the observations that contain missing values to the largest branch.
- **Most correlated branch** – Assigns the observation to the branch with the smallest residual sum of squares among observations that contain missing values.

Advantages and Disadvantages of Decision Tree Methods

Decision tree is a very popular method in data mining. It is a non-parametric method that can detect non-linear relationships. It can be used with various measurement scales and is not sensitive to missing values or outliers. The tree structure is logical and easy to understand and interpret. Since we use a strategy that requires developing multiple models using different methods and configurations, it is important to understand the advantages and disadvantages of decision trees, which allows us to compare this method with the regression methods we covered in Chapter 7 and other more advanced methods we will cover later. I summarize the key advantages and disadvantages of this method as follows.

Advantages of decision trees

- **Interpretability:** Decision trees provide a transparent and intuitive representation of the decision-making process. The tree's hierarchical structure is easy to understand and interpret, making it a valuable tool for explaining the predictions to non-experts.
- **Handling non-linearity and complex relationships:** By using decision trees, researchers can effectively capture non-linear relationships and complex interactions between variables through the hierarchical structure.
- **Flexibility with data types:** Decision trees can be used to build either association models or classification models, making them versatile and suitable for a wide range of applications. They can also work with both continuous and categorical predictors.
- **Irrelevant features:** Decision trees are useful to model irrelevant variables in the data since they focus on variables that are more informative for splitting the data.
- **Scalability:** Large datasets are handled more efficiently in decision trees, which do not require high computing power.
- **Handling missing values:** Due to the nature of the recursive partitioning process, decision trees are able to handle missing values effectively through the splitting process.
- **Ensemble methods:** Decision trees can be combined using ensemble methods like Random Forests and Gradient Boosting, which often lead to improved predictive performance and reduced overfitting.
- **Providing variable importance**: Relative variable importance plot is available in a decision tree's output, which makes it easier for us to identify important predictors.

Disadvantages of decision trees

- **Overfitting:** Decision trees are sensitive to overfitting, especially when the tree is deep and complex.
- **Instability and variance:** Small changes in the data can lead to significantly different tree structures, which results in high variance in the predictions.
- **Bias towards dominant classes:** In classification models with imbalanced datasets, decision trees may be biased toward the majority class, which leads to suboptimal performance in minority classes.
- **Difficulty handling numeric outliers:** Decision trees are sensitive to the scale of continuous variables, and outliers can have a disproportionate influence on the tree's structure and predictions.
- **Global optimum vs. local optimum:** The greedy nature of the decision tree algorithm may lead to suboptimal splits at individual nodes, even though they contribute to the overall best split.
- **Lack of coefficients:** Unlike regression, the output of a decision tree model does not provide coefficients for evaluating the effects of predictors on the target variable. These effects must be evaluated through the tree structure and the probability values, which could be challenging to understand.

Despite their limitations, decision trees remain a valuable and widely used machine learning method, especially for data mining projects that require interpretability, handling non-linear relationships, and dealing with both categorical and continuous variables. However, to address some of the drawbacks, techniques like pruning, ensemble methods, and careful hyperparameter tuning are often applied to improve the model performance.

Two Different Types of Decision Trees

As we can see from the previous example, how to split a node is the key to developing a good decision tree model. In data mining, the tree will be derived from the data, not from our common-sense rules or business rules. Hence, having valid splitting rules is very important to produce a decision tree model with good predictive power. Splitting algorithms allow us to categorize different types of trees.

The two primary types of decision trees are Classification and Regression Tree (CART), CHAID (Chi-Squared Automatic Interaction Detection). I introduce some general descriptions of these trees and when to use which one. As usual, I avoid mathematical formulation and focus on practical applications.

> In SAS Enterprise Miner, there are no dedicated nodes for CART and CHAID trees. Those two types of tree can be created using the same Decision Tree node. I will show how to configure the exact CART and CHAID trees in SAS Enterprise Miner.

Classification and Regression Tree (CART)

CART is a popular decision tree method developed by Breiman et al. (1984). If you are interested, you can read the details of this method in their book *Classification and Regression Trees.* I skip the mathematical details of this method. Basically, CART is a binary tree, which uses an algorithm to split a parent node into TWO child nodes repeatedly. CART can be used for both categorical and continuous target variables. The Regression tree is used for the continuous target variable, while the Classification tree is used for the categorical target variable. More specifically,

- Association models: A Regression tree relies on assessing the impurity of a node through the measure of least-squared-deviation (LSD), which effectively quantifies the variance within the node.
- Classification models: In a Classification tree, the basis for evaluation is the Gini index of equality. A Gini score of 0 signifies perfect equality among classes, while a score of 1 indicates highest level of inequality.

Nonetheless, most data mining software applications have both trees in the same CART tree feature, so we do not have to worry about separating them. Essentially, CART uses the so-called binary split; i.e., the algorithm splits a parent node into two child nodes repeatedly. That is why CART is called a binary tree. We do not get into the details of the splitting process due to its complexity. Essentially, the process searches for the best splitting algorithm based on the splitting criterion, and the splitting process stops when the stopping criterion is met. As long as we understand the binary split nature of CART, we will be fine. As for missing values, they are taken as a separate group and only be combined with any other category if there is actually a high similarity between the two categories.

A CART tree looks like the following example in Figure 8.2. As shown in the figure, each parent node is split into **two** child nodes, no more than that.

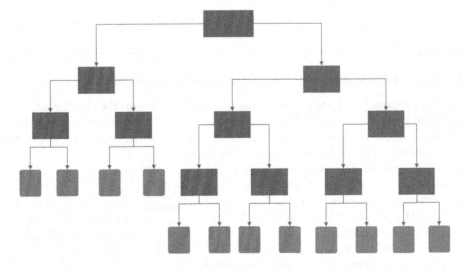

FIGURE 8.2
An illustration of CART.

SAS ENTERPRISE MINER GUIDELINES

Decision Tree node Train Properties

(https://documentation.sas.com)

CART TREE CONFIGURATION

For nominal targets, do the following:

- Set the **Nominal Criterion** property to **Gini**.

For interval targets, do the following:

- Set the **Interval Criterion** property to **Variance**.

For nominal or interval targets, do the following:

- Set the Maximum Branch property to 2.
- Set the Missing Values property to Largest Branch.
- Set the Number of Surrogates Rules property to 5.
- Set the Node Sample property to a number greater than or equal to all observations or whatever setting is deemed appropriate for the methodology of BFOS.
- Set the Exhaustive property to a very large number to enumerate all possible splits. For example, 2,000,000,000 (2 billion) might suffice.
- When using prior probabilities and misclassification losses, the BFOS method incorporates these into the split search. The Decision Tree incorporates them the same way when the property "incorporate priors/profits in the split search" is selected. SAS Enterprise Miner does not specify equal priors by default. You must use the Decision Tree Properties Panel to specify equal priors.

Chi-Squared Automatic Interaction Detection (CHAID)

CHAID was proposed by Kass in 1980. This method is based on the Chi-Square statistic. A Chi-Square is a non-parametric test that is used to examine the differences between categorical variables. The test produces a probability value between 0 and 1. A Chi-Square value closer to 0 indicates that there is a significant difference between the two variables. Similarly, a value closer to 1 indicates that there is not any significant difference between the variables. Unlike CART, CHAID tends to split a parent node into *more* than two child nodes.

Typically, CHAID can be used for both the association model (a continuous target variable) and the classification model (a categorical target

> **DEFINITION**
>
> CHAID is a non-parametric method used for creating decision trees by recursively splitting the data into homogeneous subgroups based on the categorical predictor variables, using the chi-squared test to assess the independence between variables and find significant splits.

variable), but it requires categorical predictors, either ordinal or nominal. However, many software applications accept interval inputs and automatically group the values into ranges before growing the tree. The CHAID algorithm has evolved significantly since Kass' algorithm and now can handle continuous target variables by using the p-value of the F-test.

CHAID uses two statistical tests to determine the next best split

- Association models (with a continuous target variable): F-Test (p-value).
- Classification models (with a categorical target variable): Chi-Square test (p-value).

Again, I do not get into the detailed splitting process of CHAID, which is a complex stepwise process. Essentially, the process searches for the best splitting algorithm based on the adjusted p-value for the F-test or Chi-Square test, and the splitting process stops when the stopping criterion is met. Keep in mind that CHAID splits a node into two or more child nodes, which is a key difference from CART. Figure 8.3 shows an illustration of a CHAID tree. As for missing values, a missing value is treated as a separate value. More specifically, it is considered a new category (for nominal predictors) or free of any order restrictions (for ordinal predictors).

As mentioned before, SAS Enterprise Miner does not have a dedicated node for the CHAID tree. We can build a CHAID tree by setting specific configurations for the Decision Tree node.

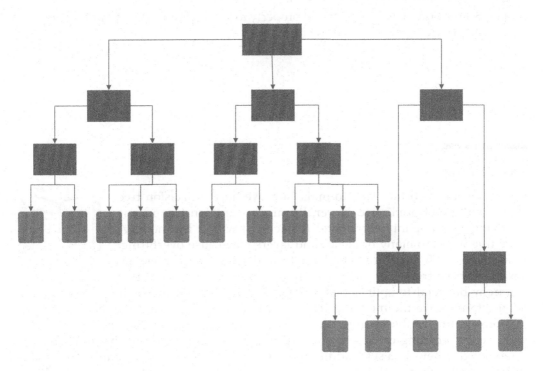

FIGURE 8.3
An illustration of a CHAID tree.

SAS ENTERPRISE MINER GUIDELINES

Decision Tree Node Train Properties
(https://documentation.sas.com)

CHAID TREE CONFIGURATION

For nominal targets, do the following:

- Set the **Nominal Criterion** property to **PROBCHISQ**.

For interval targets, do the following:

- Set the **Interval Criterion** property to **PROBF**.

For either nominal or interval targets, do the following:

- Set the Chi-Square or F test **Significance Level** to 0.05 (or whatever significance level seems appropriate).
- Set the **Maximum Branch** property to the maximum number of categorical values in an input.
- Set the **Number of Surrogate Rules** property to 0.
- To force a heuristic search, set the **Exhaustive** property to 0.
- Set the **Leaf Size** to 1.
- Set the **Split Size** property to 2.
- Set the **Bonferroni Adjustment** property to **Yes**, and the **Time of Bonferroni Adjustment** property to **After**.

Tree Pruning

Pruning is an important step to make sure we have a decision tree model with good predictive power. Pruning a decision tree means removing a redundant subtree and replacing it with a leaf node. A large tree with too many branches and layers may cause overfitting. In addition, such trees are very hard to understand and interpret. Basically, these trees use the same predictors to construct the tree  hierarchy but tend to split nodes multiple times to create many different branches, hoping to improve the model fit. However, that process may create very large trees that only work for the training sample and cause overfitting. Pruning a tree helps to prevent overfitting caused by overtraining the training data so that our model is generalized to new data sets. Additionally, it can provide us with a simpler tree that is easier to understand and interpret without scarifying the model fit. Figure 8.4 shows an illustration of decision tree pruning.

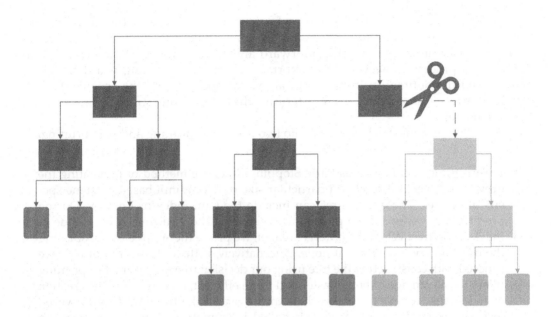

FIGURE 8.4
Decision tree pruning.

The process of tree pruning has six steps as follows.

1. *Growing the full tree*: The first step is to grow the decision tree to its maximum depth or until a specified stopping criterion is met. During this stage, the algorithm recursively partitions the data and creates branches and nodes based on the selected splitting criterion.

2. *Evaluating node importance*: After growing the full tree, we assess the importance of each node in improving the model performance. Nodes that contribute little to the overall predictive accuracy or are not statistically significant are candidates for pruning.

3. *Cost-complexity pruning*: Cost-complexity pruning (also known as minimal cost-complexity pruning) is a popular method used for decision tree pruning. It involves adding a complexity parameter (alpha) that balances the model's accuracy and complexity. The algorithm evaluates the impact of removing each node and calculates a cost-complexity score for the subtree rooted at that node.

4. *Selecting the optimal pruning level*: The algorithm iteratively prunes nodes with the smallest cost-complexity score while evaluating the model performance on a validation set. The pruning continues until further pruning results in a significant drop in predictive performance. The optimal pruning level corresponds to the subtree that achieves the best balance between accuracy and simplicity.

5. *Pruning the tree*: Once the optimal pruning level is determined, the decision tree is pruned by removing the nodes and branches that correspond to the subtrees above the selected level. The resulting pruned tree is a simplified version of the full tree.

Pruning helps control overfitting by reducing the complexity of the decision tree, which improves the model's predictive power. It also enhances the interpretability of the model by creating a more straightforward and concise representation of the decision-making process. However, it is important to note that pruning is a data-driven process, and the optimal pruning level may vary depending on the specific dataset. Regular validation should be used to determine the best pruning strategy for each decision tree model.

Decision tree pruning can be divided into two types: pre-pruning and post-pruning.

- **Pre-pruning**, also known as Early Stopping Rule, is a method of preventing the growth of a tree if it reaches a particular size or depth limit based on some specific measures. These measures can include the Gini index or Entropy. During pre-pruning, we assess the pruning criteria using the measures at each node in the decision tree. When the criteria are met, we prune the subtree by substituting the decision node with a leaf node. Alternatively, if the criteria are not met, we proceed with constructing the tree using our decision tree algorithm. Pre-pruning offers the advantage of being faster and more efficient, as it prevents the creation of excessively complex subtrees that tend to overfit the training data. However, in pre-pruning, the tree's growth is halted is prematurely due to our stopping conditions.

- **Post-pruning** involves the process of pruning after the entire tree has been constructed. In this approach, we first grow the tree to its full extent and then systematically prune the subtrees from the bottom upwards, one at a time. We initiate the process at the lowest decision node, and using measures such as Gini Impurity or Information Gain, we determine whether to retain this decision node or substitute it with a leaf node.

Manual or Auto-pruning

Manual pruning is typically not recommended for data mining projects since it is subject to the researcher's interpretation and decision, which could be biased. It also requires a clear ground and justification for removing a subtree. For example, how do we know which branches are redundant to remove, and how do we justify that decision? A mistake in this process could result in a tree with a poorer model fit or even a useless tree. Additionally, manual pruning may be feasible for simple trees with a simple hierarchy. However, when we have a very large tree with a large number of nodes and branches, it is not possible to prune the tree manually. It also defeats the purpose of mining larger datasets.

The pruning method I recommend is Automatic pruning. Basically, we set specific assessment requirements for the tree development and subtree selection and then let the software do the pruning based on those configurations. Typically, we tell the software how to select the subtree, the subtree assessment method, and whether we want to do cross-validation. The software uses the search algorithm to find the best tree satisfying these criteria and requirements. Typically, for association models, we use mean squared error (MSE) as the assessment method, and for classification models, we use misclassification rate (MR) as the assessment method. The software will select the tree that minimizes MSE or MR.

SAS ENTERPRISE MINER GUIDELINES

Decision Tree node Train Properties

(https://documentation.sas.com)

AUTO PRUNING AND SUB-TREE SELECTION

After the sequence of subtrees is established, the **Decision Tree** node uses one of three methods to select which subtree to use for prediction. You set the desired subtree method by using the **Method** property. The **Method** property can be set to **Assessment, Largest,** or **N.**

If the **Method** property under Subtree grouping is set to **Assessment,** then the **Decision Tree** node uses the smallest subtree with the best assessment value. This smallest subtree in turn depends on the **Assessment Measure** property value. The assessment uses the validation data when available. (There are instances where only the training data is used to determine the sequence of subtrees.)

Use the **Assessment Measure** property to specify the method that you want to use to select the best tree, based on the **validation data**. If no validation data is available, training data is used. The available assessment measurements are Decision, Average Square Error, Misclassification, and Lift. The default setting of Decision selects the tree that has the largest average profit and smallest average loss if a profit or loss matrix is defined. If no profit or loss matrix is defined, the value of model assessment measure will be reset in the training process, depending on the measurement level of the target. If the target is interval, the measure is set to Average Square Error. If the target is categorical, the measure is set to Misclassification. The **Average Square Error** method selects the tree that has the smallest average square error. The **Misclassification** method selects the tree that has the smallest misclassification rate. The **Lift** method evaluates the tree based on the prediction of the top n% of the ranked observations. Observations are ranked based on their posterior probabilities or predicted target values. For an interval target, it is the average predicted target value of the top n% observations. For a categorical target, it is the proportion of events in the top n% data. When you set the Measure property to Lift, you must use the fraction property to specify the percentage for the top n% of cases.

If the **Method** property under Subtree grouping is set to **Largest,** then the **Decision Tree** node uses the largest subtree after it prunes the nodes that do not increase the assessment based on the training data. For nominal targets, the largest subtree in the sequence might be much smaller than the original unpruned tree. This is because a splitting rule might have a significant split but not have an increase in the number of observations that are correctly classified.

Differences between CART and CHAID

I summarize some key differences between CART and CHAID trees in Table 8.2. In general, these two types of trees are fairly similar. Some differences come from the way a node is split. As a reminder, CART uses the binary split algorithm, while CHAID uses the multi-split algorithm. Both trees allow

TABLE 8.2

Differences between CART and CHAID Trees

Tree Types	CART	CHAID
Target variable	Works with both continuous and categorical target variables	Works with both continuous and categorical target variables
Predictors	Continuous or ordinal predictors are preferred	Categorical predictors are preferred
Number of splitting branches	Two branches only	Two or more branches
Splitting rules	Binary split only: Gini, Entropy, or variance	Multiway split: F-test or Chi-square test
Tree size	Smaller, taller tree	Larger, shorter trees
Pruning recommendation	Yes	Yes
Effect of outliers	No	No
Effect of missing values	No	No
Data requirement	Does not require large data	Requires large data
Sensitive to overfitting	Yes	Less

us to build either association models or classification models. However, CART prefers continuous or ordinal predictors, while CHAID prefers categorical predictors. Nonetheless, most data mining software applications allow us to use a combination of predictors.

Additionally, due to the splitting differences, CART tends to produce a smaller (skinner) but taller tree (binary split), while CHAID tends to produce a larger but shorter tree (multisplit). CHAID may require more data than CART to train the model, but it is less susceptible to overfitting than CART. Some authors note that pruning is not needed for CHAID, but I would recommend pruning for both types to avoid very large trees. We will examine some examples later.

It is hard to tell which type of tree works better because they both have strengths and weaknesses. The selection depends on the data. My recommendation is to build multiple trees using both types with different configurations and compare them to determine which tree works best for the data.

Example: Classification Model Using Decision Trees

In this example, we build classification models for the *airline recommendation* data using decision trees. The target variable is the airline recommendation, a binary variable (1 – recommend; 0 – not recommend). We will build two decision tree models, one using CART and another one using CHAID. Since decision trees have effective methods to handle missing values, we do not impute the missing data but use SAS Enterprise Miner's built-in algorithm to handle them.

Sample-Explore-Modify

1. Open the Airline project.
2. Create a new diagram and name it Decision Trees.

3. Follow the same steps as in Chapters 3, 4, and 5 to complete the Sample, Explore, and Modify steps. We use the Sample node, Data Partition node, and Replacement node.

Model

In the Model step, we build two models using CART and CHAID. From the Model tab, drag two Decision Tree nodes to the workspace and connect them to the Replacement node as follows. Name the first tree node CART Tree and name the second one CHAID Tree.

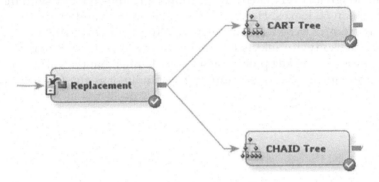

Use the following configurations to set up those two tree models. We use auto pruning for them.

CART Tree

Below are the configurations for the CART tree.

1. Click the CART Tree node. In the Train properties, make the following changes.
   Under Splitting Rules
   - Set the Nominal Target Criterion to Gini.
   - Set the Maximum Branch to 2.
   - Set the Missing Values to Largest Branch.
   Under Node
   - Set the Number of Surrogates Rules property to 5.
   Under Split Search
   - Set the Node Sample property to 100,000.
   - Set the Exhaustive property to 2,000,000,000 (2 billion).
     Under Subtree (Auto pruning configuration)
   - Set Method to Assessment.
   - Set Assessment Measure to Misclassification (The misclassification method selects the tree that has the lowest misclassification rate).
   Under P-Value Adjustment
   - Set Bonferroni Adjustment to Yes.
2. Run the CART Tree node.
3. Open the Results window.

Assess

We review several key results to understand and interpret the tree. Note that SAS Enterprise Miner, like other software applications, tends to produce many results outputs. I do not use and explain all of them. Instead, I show you which ones are important to use and review. The first result we need to review is the subtree assessment plot. This plot describes the depth of the tree in terms of the number of leaves in the final tree and how it is selected. Figure 8.5 shows the subtree assessment plot for the CART tree. As shown in the plot, the tree with 17 leaves is selected when the misclassification rate (MR) of 0.208 is achieved (to see the exact number, hover your mouse over a specific point in your chart). As you can see, that is not the tree with the lowest MR for the training sample, even though it is very close. In the training results, the tree with the lowest MR requires more than 60 leaves. However, if we look at the validation results, trees with leaves ranging from 17 to 54 leaves have almost the same MR, which is the lowest one (0.208). Hence, the software selects the tree with the lowest validation MR with fewer leaves or 17 leaves. So, the key point to remember here is that the validation MR is used to select the tree during the tree pruning. Essentially, it is the tree-pruning decision process.

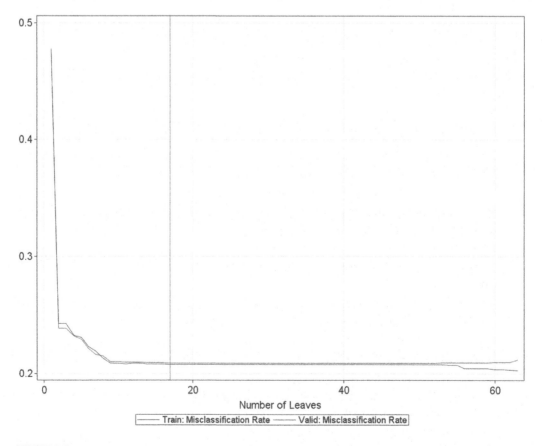

FIGURE 8.5
Subtree assessment for the pruned CART tree.

To get the subtree assessment plot:

- On the Results window: View -> Model -> Subtree assessment plot

A common question is: What if we do not prune this CART tree? I show you how to do it in SAS Enterprise Miner and why we need to prune the tree. Basically, if we do not prune the tree, then the algorithm constructs the full tree. Let's see what tree we get if we build the full CART tree without pruning.

To build the full tree, follow the steps below to make adjustments to the tree properties.

1. Under Subtree: Set the Method to Largest. This selection will allow us to build the full tree (no pruning).
2. Run the CART tree node and open the Results window.

Figure 8.6 presents the subtree assessment plot for the full CART tree. As you notice, a tree with 63 leaves is selected. This tree has a lower training MR but a little higher validation MR. Remember that the tree is selected based on the validation results.

So how are these two trees different in the hierarchical structure? Figure 8.7 shows the differences in the tree structure of the full CART tree versus the pruned CART tree. As you can see, the full tree is very large, with many branches and leaves. It would be hard to go through each branch and each node to understand the tree. On the other hand, the pruned tree is skinnier and easier to interpret.

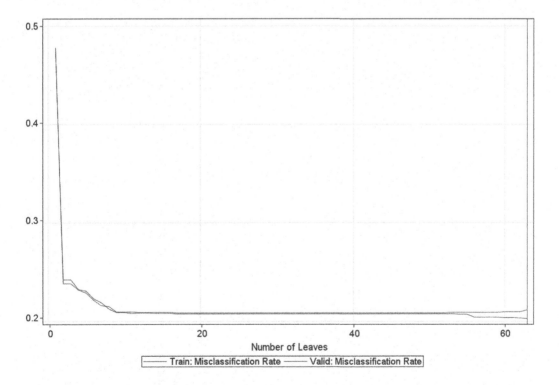

FIGURE 8.6
Subtree assessment plot for the full CART tree.

(a)

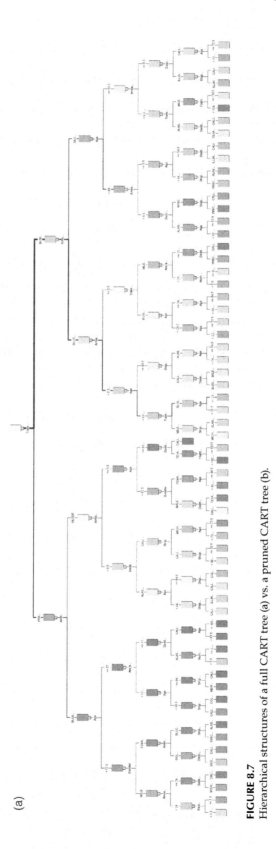

FIGURE 8.7
Hierarchical structures of a full CART tree (a) vs. a pruned CART tree (b).

(b)

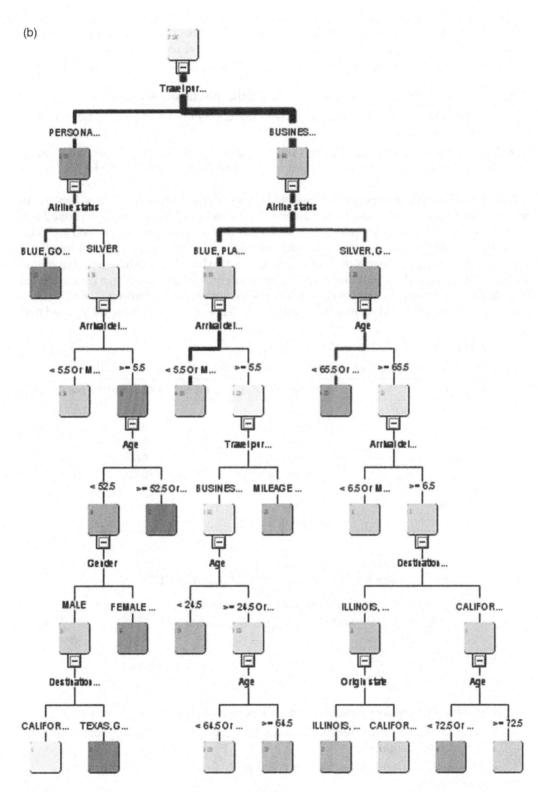

FIGURE 8.7
(*Continued*)

We compare the model fit metrics between these two trees using the validation results to examine the differences between them. As a reminder, we use the following outputs to extract or calculate those metrics (see Chapter 6 for the details).

- Use the output of the CART tree node to get the misclassification rate.
- Use the output of the Model Comparison node to get the ROC index, Lift value, and Gini coefficient.
- Extract the confusion matrix from the output of the CART tree node. Then use this confusion matrix to calculate Accuracy, Sensitivity, Specificity, and F1-Score.

Table 8.3 presents the comparison of model fit metrics between these two trees. As you can see, these metrics are fairly close between the full tree and the pruned tree. The pruned tree actually has a better accuracy and misclassification rate. In addition, the pruned tree also has better sensitivity and F1 score, while its specificity is a little lower. The full tree has a slightly better Gini coefficient, ROC index, and cumulative lift. Overall, these trees have similar model fit metrics. Thus, building a full tree does not present any advantage over a pruned tree. On the other hand, the full tree is much larger to understand and interpret, it may take a longer computing time, and we may risk overfitting. Hence, it is logical to use the pruned tree.

TABLE 8.3

Model Fit Metrics for the Full CART Tree and the Pruned CART Tree

Statistics	Full CART Tree (63 Leaves)	Pruned CART Tree (17 Leaves)
Misclassification Rate	0.212	0.209
ACC	0.788	0.791
Sensitivity	0.930	0.958
Specificity	0.633	0.608
F1-Score	0.821	0.827
Gini coefficient	0.68	0.66
ROC index	0.84	0.83
Lift	1.67	1.61

SAS ENTERPRISE MINER GUIDELINES

Decision Tree Node Results

(https://documentation.sas.com)

TREE PLOT

A decision tree contains the following items:

- **Root node** – the top node of a vertical tree that contains all observations.
- **Internal nodes** – non-terminal nodes that contain the splitting rule. This includes the root node.
- **Leaf nodes** – terminal nodes that contain the final classification for a set of observations.

A default decision tree has the following properties:

- It is displayed in vertical orientation.
- The nodes are colored by the proportion of a categorical target value or the average of an interval target.
- The line width is proportional to the ratio of the number of observations in the branch to the number of observations in the root node.
- The line color is constant.

You can select one or more nodes in a tree plot by doing one of the following:

- Clicking or holding down the Ctrl key and clicking the nodes.
- Pressing the left mouse button and dragging the mouse to define a rectangle that contains the node or nodes that you want to select.

When you move your mouse pointer over a node of a tree, a text box displays information about the node. To display node text in the nodes of a tree, right-click in the tree and select **View -> Node Text**.

The node text that is displayed in a tree depends on the target variable. For a categorical target variable, the text box contains separate rows for each target value and each decision. It provides information about the percentage of observations in a node for each target value. If the target is interval, the text box displays the number of observations in a node and the average value of the model assessment measure.

To zoom in or zoom out in the tree, right-click in the tree, select **View**, and then select the percentage that you want.

Figure 8.8 shows our pruned tree with 17 leaves. I remove some of the labels in each node so the tree fits on the page. To change the tree properties:

- Right-click on the tree and select Graph Properties.
- Select Nodes tab, under Text change to Show Values Only (this option will remove the labels and only shows values in the nodes, which makes the nodes smaller).

In order to interpret the tree plot, we use the instructions from SAS Enterprise Miner on the previous page.

I extracted three top nodes to illustrate the detailed texts in each node and what they mean (Figure 8.9). Basically, each node consists of the following components.

- Node ID
- Statistics for all levels of the target variable in the training and validation samples. More specifically,
  - Percentage of the training sample and validation sample that do NOT recommend the airline (NO).
  - Percentage of the training sample and validation sample that DO recommend the airline (YES).
  - Count of the records (observations) for the training and validation sample.

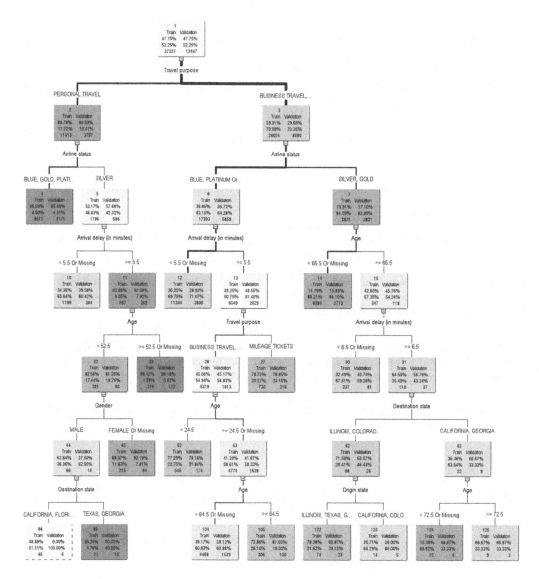

FIGURE 8.8
The pruned CART tree plot.

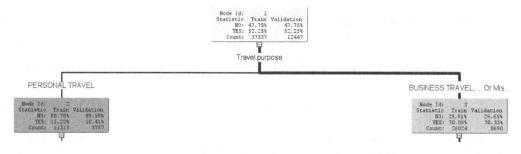

FIGURE 8.9
Detailed node texts.

For example, in Figure 8.9, if we select the node *Personal Travel*, we can interpret that for passengers who travel for personal purposes, we have the following statistics.

- There are 11,313 records in the training and 3,757 records in the validation sample.
- A total of 88.78% of the passengers in this group (training sample) do NOT recommend the airline (89.59% of the validation sample).
- Only 11.22% DO recommend the airline (10.41% of the validation sample).

How to Interpret a Tree Plot?

The tree has many nodes and branches. Naturally, you may feel confused and not know where to start. If we are not careful, we can get lost in the tree structure and confuse ourselves with the plot. The easiest way to explain and interpret the tree plot is to follow the tree hierarchy from top to bottom and the branches. For this example, I break the tree plot down by nodes and branches following the tree hierarchy. I also create a hierarchy for the bullets to match the tree hierarchy. It makes it easy to explain the outputs and minimizes errors. Note that I only use the validation percentages for this purpose.

- Follow the tree hierarchy and create a bullet hierarchy that matches the tree hierarchy.
- Use the validation results.

Tree Plot Interpretation

- Travel Purpose – *Personal Travel*: 89.59% do not recommend the airline; 10.41% recommend it.
  - Airline status – Blue, Gold, Platinum: 95.49% do not recommend the airline; 4.51% recommend it.
  - Airline status – Silver: 57.68% do not recommend the airline; 42.32% recommend it.
    - Arrival delay – less than 5.5 minutes: 39.58% do not recommend the airline; 60.42% recommend it.
    - Arrival delay – 5.5 minutes or more: 92.08% do not recommend the airline; 7.92% recommend it.
      - Age – 52.5 years or more: 99.18% do not recommend the airline; 0.82% recommend it.
      - Age – less than 52.5 years: 81.25% do not recommend the airline; 18.75% recommend it.
        - Gender – Female: 92.19% do not recommend the airline; 7.81% recommend it.
        - Gender – Male: 37.5% do not recommend the airline; 62.5% recommend it.
          - Destination state – CA, FL: 0% do not recommend the airline; 100% recommend it.
          - Destination state: TX, GA: 60% do not recommend the airline; 40% recommend it.

- Travel Purpose – *Business Travel*: 29.65% do not recommend the airline; 70.35% recommend it.
    - Airline status – Blue, Platinum: 35.72% do not recommend the airline; 64.28% recommend it.
        - Arrival delay – less than 5.5 minutes: 28.93% do not recommend the airline; 71.07% recommend it.
        - Arrival delay – 5.5. minutes or more: 48.55% do not recommend the airline; 51.45% recommend it.
            - Travel purpose – Mileage tickets: 76.85% do not recommend the airline; 23.15% recommend it.
            - Travel purpose – *Business Travel*: 45.17% do not recommend the airline; 54.83% recommend it.
                - Age – less than 24.5 years: 78.16% do not recommend the airline; 21.84% recommend it.
                - Age – 24. 5 years or more: 41.67% do not recommend the airline; 58.33% recommend it.
                    - Age – less than 64.5 years: 39.12% do not recommend the airline; 60.88% recommend it.
                    - Age – 64.5 years or more: 81% do not recommend the airline; 19% recommend it.
    - Airline status – Silver, Gold: 17.1% do not recommend the airline; 82.9% recommend it.
        - Age – less than 65.5 years: 15.85% do not recommend the airline; 84.15% recommend it.
        - Age – 65.5 years or more: 45.76% do not recommend the airline; 54.24% recommend it.
            - Arrival delay – less than 6.5 minutes: 40.74% do not recommend the airline; 59.26% recommend it.
            - Arrival delay – 6.5 minutes or more: 56.76% do not recommend the airline; 43.24% recommend it.
                - Destination state – IL, CO, TX: 53.57% do not recommend the airline; 46.43% recommend it.
                    - Origin state – IL, TX, GE: 60.87% do not recommend the airline; 39.13% recommend it.
                    - Origin state – CA, CO: 20% do not recommend the airline; 80% recommend it.
                - Destination state – CA, GE: 66.67% do not recommend the airline; 33.33% recommend it.
                    - Age – less than 72.5 years: 66.67% do not recommend the airline; 33.33% recommend it.
                    - Age – 72.5 years or more: 66.67% do not recommend the airline; 33.33% recommend it.

As you can see, it is not too hard if we make sure the bullet hierarchy matches the tree hierarchy. Typically, in data mining reports, we just need to present the tree plot and explain some key nodes and branches. There is no need to cover all nodes and branches because it could result in many pages of details. Nonetheless, I provide a full interpretation here as a demonstration so you can refer back to this page to learn how to interpret the tree plot.

You can also notice some nodes, such as age, travel purpose, or destination state are presented multiple times in the tree. That selection is determined by the splitting algorithm to maximize the model fit. In the case of age, this node needs to be split multiple times because CART only uses the binary split.

How to Interpret Leaf Nodes?

The above is a way to interpret the tree plot, more specifically, the tree hierarchy. We also need to understand and interpret the leaf nodes, which present the decisions. Fortunately, SAS Enterprise Miner provides such outputs using the Node Rules. These rules explain the output for leaf nodes in a tree model.

To get the node rules

- On the Results window: View -> Model -> Node Rules

Below is the snapshot of the node rules, explaining three leaf nodes, 4, 10, and 12, as examples. I don't present all of them as they are quite long. Since we know our tree has 17 leaves, we have rules for 17 leaf nodes.

Leaf Nodes Interpretation

```
*----------------------------------------------------------------*
Node = 4
*----------------------------------------------------------------*
if Travel purpose IS ONE OF: PERSONAL TRAVEL
AND Airline status IS ONE OF: BLUE, GOLD, PLATINUM or MISSING
then
 Tree Node Identifier = 4
 Number of Observations = 9517
 Predicted: recommendation=Yes = 0.04
 Predicted: recommendation=No = 0.96


*----------------------------------------------------------------*
Node = 10
*----------------------------------------------------------------*
if Travel purpose IS ONE OF: PERSONAL TRAVEL
AND Arrival delay (in minutes) < 5.5 or MISSING
AND Airline status IS ONE OF: SILVER
then
 Tree Node Identifier = 10
 Number of Observations = 1199
```

```
Predicted: recommendation=Yes = 0.66
Predicted: recommendation=No = 0.34
*-------------------------------------------------------------*
Node = 12
*-------------------------------------------------------------*
if Travel purpose IS ONE OF: BUSINESS TRAVEL, MILEAGE TICKETS or MISSING
AND Arrival delay (in minutes) < 5.5 or MISSING
AND Airline status IS ONE OF: BLUE, PLATINUM or MISSING
then
 Tree Node Identifier = 12
 Number of Observations = 11344
 Predicted: recommendation=Yes = 0.70
 Predicted: recommendation=No = 0.30
*-------------------------------------------------------------*
```

Variable Importance

Another important output of a decision tree model is the variable importance table (see Table 8.4). Essentially, the variable importance table presents the relative importance of the predictors in predicting the target variable. It is calculated using some complicated formulas involving the sum of squared errors. I won't explain the mathematical calculation of this score here. What we need to know is that this score presents the relative importance of the predictors in predicting the target variable, and it ranges from 0 to 1. The closer the

TABLE 8.4

Variable Importance for CART Tree

Variables	Training Importance	Validation Importance
Travel purpose	1.000	1.000
Age	0.917	0.919
Average number of flights per year	0.852	0.852
Percent of flights with other airlines	0.825	0.829
Airline status	0.432	0.375
Flight distance (miles)	0.365	0.340
Arrival delay (in minutes)	0.317	0.303
Departure delay (in minutes)	0.294	0.280
Flight time (in minutes)	0.260	0.250
Destination state	0.186	0.185
Origin state	0.183	0.188
Shopping amount at the airport	0.162	0.135
Spending for eating and drinking at the airport	0.147	0.143
Gender	0.044	0.061
Number of other loyalty cards	0.034	0.037
Number of years flying	0.028	0.000

score to 1, the more important the predictor is. This table is an important output since it tells us which predictors are important to predicting the target variable and the rank of those predictors. Table 8.4 shows us the importance scores for the training and validation samples. As you can see here, the results are very consistent, indicating the reliability of the model.

The results show that *travel purpose* is the most important predictor, followed by *age*, *average number of flights per year*, *percent of flights with other airlines*, and *airline status*. On the other hand, *number of years flying* and *number of other loyalty cards* seem to be the least important predictors. The predictors not included in this list are insignificant ones, meaning they do not play any role in predicting the target variable (airline recommendation).

CHAID Tree

Use the configurations below to set up the CHAID tree.

1. Click the CHAID tree node. In the Train properties, make the following changes.
   Under Splitting Rules

   - Set the Nominal Target Criterion to PROBCHISQ.
   - Set the Significance Level to 0.05.
   - Set the Missing Values to Use in search.
   - Set the Maximum Branch property to 20.

   Under Node

   - Set the Number of Surrogate Rules property to 0.
   - Set the Leaf Size to 1.
   - Set the Split Size to 2.

   Under Split Search

   - Set the Exhaustive to 0 to force a heuristic search.

   Under Subtree (Auto pruning configuration)

   - Set the Method to Assessment.
   - Set the Assessment Measure to Misclassification.

   Under p-Value Adjustment

   - Set the Bonferroni Adjustment property to Yes.
   - Set the Time of Bonferroni Adjustment property to After.
2. Run the CHAID tree node.
3. Open the Results window.

Go to View -> Model -> Subtree assessment plot to get the chart. Figure 8.10 shows the subtree assessment plot for the pruned CHAID tree. Remember that we use auto-pruning for this tree. As shown in the figure, the tree has 23 leaves with the minimum

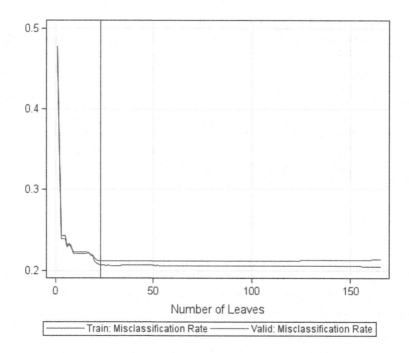

FIGURE 8.10
Subtree assessment plot for the pruned CHAID tree.

validation MR. For comparison purposes, if we build the full CHAID tree, we will have a tree with 165 leaves, a significantly larger tree (I won't show the detail of this full tree here). In this example, we use the pruned CHAID tree since it is smaller and easier to understand and interpret.

The tree plot is shown in Figure 8.11. Note that since this tree is shorter but much wider, I must present it horizontally so it fits on the page. I also need to remove the labels as before to keep the node size small.

To change the tree properties

- Right-click on the tree and select Graph Properties.
- Select Tree, and under Orientation, select Horizontal.
- Select the Nodes tab, and under Text change to Show Values Only (this option will remove the labels and only shows values in the nodes, which makes the nodes smaller).

I won't explain the CHAID tree plot here. You can use the same approach above to interpret this tree hierarchy. Similarly, we can also use Node Rules to interpret the information of the leaf nodes.

The variable importance for this CHAID tree is presented in Table 8.5. The results show that travel purpose is the most important predictor, followed by airline status, arrival delay, and age. This variable importance matches the tree plot in Figure 8.11 very well and

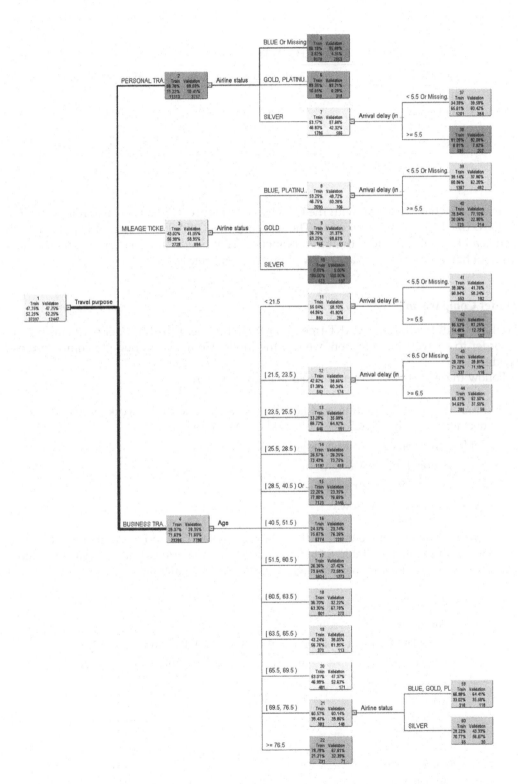

FIGURE 8.11
The pruned CHAID tree plot.

TABLE 8.5

Variable Importance for the CHAID Tree

Variables	Training Importance	Validation Importance
Travel purpose	1.000	1.000
Airline status	0.375	0.320
Arrival delay (in minutes)	0.308	0.286
Age	0.302	0.270

is also somewhat consistent with the CART tree in Figure 8.8. You can also notice that the CHAID tree is short by rather wide. The reason is that CHAID allows multi-splits, so each node can be split into more than two branches. That is why the tree can model the data without having to split a node into two branches repeatedly.

Model Comparison

We have built two trees, a CART tree and a CHAID tree. Which model performs better? In order to answer this question, we use the Model Comparison node to compare those models.

Follow the steps below to set up the model comparison.

1. From the Assess tab, drag a Model Comparison node to the workspace and connect it to both the CART tree node and CHAID tree node.
2. Set Selection Statistic to Misclassification rate.
3. Set Selection Table to Validation.
4. Run the Model Comparison node.
5. Open the Results window.

We use the same steps we used in the CART tree to extract and calculate model fit metrics for both models (see Table 8.6). Again, some metrics are extracted from the Model Comparison node's Results window, while others require calculation using the confusion

TABLE 8.6

Model Fit Metrics Comparison between the CART Tree and CHAID Tree

Model Fit Metrics	Pruned CART Tree	Pruned CHAID Tree
Misclassification Rate	0.209	0.211
Accuracy	0.791	0.789
Sensitivity	0.958	0.939
Specificity	0.608	0.624
F1-Score	0.827	0.823
Gini coefficient	0.66	0.64
ROC index	0.83	0.82
Lift	1.61	1.52

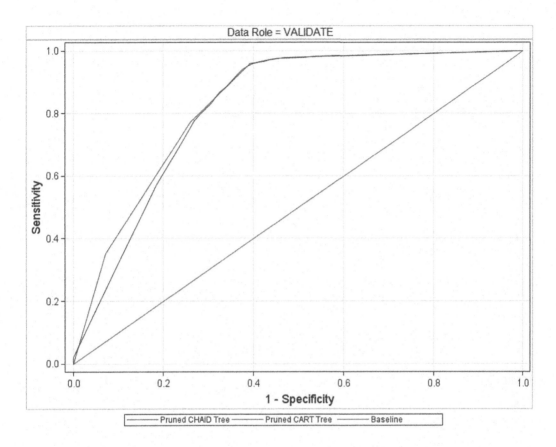

FIGURE 8.12
ROC chart.

matrix. I won't show the detailed calculations here to avoid repetitive information. Refer to Chapter 6 for detailed formulas and examples.

As you can see, the model fit metrics are fairly close between the two models. You can notice that, except for specificity, the CART tree has better fit metrics than the CHAID tree. We further confirm that with the ROC chart (Figure 8.12) and Lift chart (Figure 8.13). The ROC chart shows that the CART tree is a little farther from the baseline than the CHAID tree. Similarly, the CART tree has a slightly higher lift score than the CHAID tree. Since their fit metrics are very close, we can use either tree for prediction purposes. But if we have to pick the champion model, the CART tree is a better choice. While the CART tree is the champion model, it does not necessarily mean it has very good predictive power. The accuracy rate is 79.1%, which is slightly better than the logistic regression model we built in Chapter 7 (that model has an accuracy of 77.7%). The reason is that while the sensitivity is quite good (0.958), the specificity is rather low (0.608). This is due to the high rate of false positives. Regardless, it does show that the CART tree has improved the model fit a little bit. We will continue to build other models for this dataset and compare them with this model.

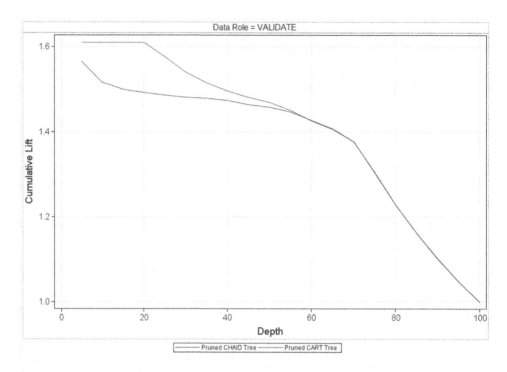

FIGURE 8.13
Lift chart.

Example: Association Model Using Decision Trees

In this example, we build decision tree models for the *Boston housing* dataset. As a reminder, our target variable is an interval variable, *lmv*, the median home value in the Boston area. Since decision trees work with continuous target variables as well, we build a CART tree and a CHAID tree for this dataset. As usual, we follow the SEMMA process and have the diagram as follows.

To add the Decision Tree nodes, from the Model tab, drag two Decision Tree nodes to the workspace and connect them to the Data Partition. Name them CART Tree and CHAID Tree.

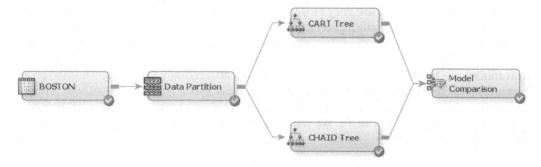

Sample-Explore-Modify

We have completed these three steps in Chapters 3–5. However, you may notice that we do not use the Impute node and Transform node. The reason is that decision trees can handle missing values well, and we use the software's built-in algorithm for missing values. Additionally, it is a non-parametric method, so it does not require normal distribution. Hence, imputing missing values and normalizing the data are not needed.

Model

In the Model step, we build one CART tree and one CHAID tree using auto-pruning.

CART Tree: Follow the steps below to configure a CART tree.

1. Click the CART Tree node. In the Train properties, make the following changes.
   Under Splitting Rules
   - Set the Interval Target Criterion to Variance.
   - Set the Maximum Branch property to 2.
   - Set the Missing Values property to Largest Branch.
   Under Node
   - Set the Number of Surrogates Rules property to 5.
   Under Split Search
   - Set the Node Sample property to 100,000.
   - Set the Exhaustive property to 2,000,000,000 (2 billion).
   Under Subtree (Auto pruning configuration)
   - Set the Method to Assessment.
   - Set the Assessment Measure to Average Squared Error (The Average Squared Error method selects the tree that has the smallest ASE).

CHAID Tree: Follow the steps below to configure a CHAID tree.

2. Click the CHAID Tree node. In the Traini properties, make the following changes.
   Under Splitting Rules
   - Set the Interval Criterion property to PROBF.
   - Set the Significance Level to 0.05.
   - Set the Maximum Branch property to 20.
   - Set the Missing Values to Use in search.
   Under Node
   - Set the Number of Surrogate Rules property to 0.
   - Set the Leaf Size to 1.
   - Set the Split Size property to 2.
   Under Split Search
   - Set the Exhaustive property to 0 to force a heuristic search.

Under Subtree (Auto pruning configuration)
- – Set the Method to Assessment.
- – Set Assessment Measure to Average Squared Error.

Under P-Value Adjustment
- – Set the Bonferroni Adjustment property to Yes.
- – Set the Time of Bonferroni. Adjustment property to After.

3. From the Assess tab, drag a Model Comparison node to the workspace and connect it to both the CART tree node and CHAID tree node.
4. Set Selection Statistic to Average Squared Error.
5. Set Selection Table to Validation.
6. Run the Model Comparison node.
7. Open the Results window.

Assess

We make a comparison between the two models. Using the Results for the Model Comparison node, we are able to extract the Mean Squared Error (MSE) and Root Mean Squared Error (RMSE), and we use these two metrics for the model comparison. Table 8.7 shows those model fit metrics for the validation sample. As you can see, the CART tree has a lower MSE and a lower RMSE than the CHAID tree. It means the CART tree can produce a more accurate prediction. To further confirm this finding, we calculate additional model fit metrics, including MAPE, RSE, and EP (see Chapter 6 for more details on these metrics).

As mentioned in Chapter 7, SAS Enterprise Miner does not produce those metrics, and we need to calculate them using the prediction data. To do that, we use the Save Data node to export the prediction data to Excel files.

Follow the steps below.

1. From the Utility tab, drag a Save Data node to the workspace and connect it to the CART tree.
2. Drag another Save Data node to the workspace and connect it to the CHAID tree.
3. In the Train properties, under Output Format make the following changes:
   - Set File Format to Excel Spreadsheet.
   - Enter the directory path to your folder to Directory. All files will be saved to your selected folder.

TABLE 8.7

Model Fit Comparison

Model Fit Metrics	CART Tree	CHAID Tree
Average Squared Error	21.23	23.81
Root Mean Squared Error	4.608	4.879

4. Run the Save Data node (since we have two Save Data nodes, run one of them at a time, download the Excel files to the computer, then run another Save Data node).

Run one Save Data node at a time, then download the data files to your computer before running the second one. While SAS Enterprise Miner does create two different files, doing that would avoid confusion or file mixed-up.

As a result, two data files are saved to our server.

- em_save_TRAIN.xlsx: prediction data for the training sample.
- em_save_VALIDATE.xlsx: prediction data for the validation sample.

We use the validation data file to calculate the model fit metrics for both CART and CHAID trees (see Chapters 6 and 7 for detailed instructions). As a result, we have the model fit metrics as shown in Table 8.8. I also include the metrics for the logistic regression model we built in Chapter 7 for

Since we do not impute missing data, the actual data have missing values. We have to remove the cases with missing values before calculating those metrics.

reference. As you can see, the CART tree also has better fit metrics, including MAPE, RSE, and EP, than the CHAID tree. The MAPE of 0.129 shows that the model can predict the median house values with an accuracy of 1−0.129 = 87.1%, which is considered acceptable. The EP of 0.774 indicates that this model can explain 77.4% of the variance in the target variable based on the variance in the predictors. As indicated in Chapter 6, an EP of 0.7 or more is considered a good model fit. If we compare the CART tree with the logistic regression tree we built before, we can see that the CART tree shows a significant improvement in model fit. Thus, we can conclude that among the two tree models, CART tree is the champion model.

CART Tree Interpretation

Let's dive deeper into the CART tree. Figure 8.14 shows the subtree assessment plot, which informs us of the pruning results. As you can see, the final tree has 22 leaves, decided by the ASE for the validation results. When we look at the same chart for the CHAID tree, we find out that the CHAID tree has 58 leaves, which makes it a much larger tree.

We can also notice as the number of leaves increases, the difference in ASE between the training and validation samples increases as well. This issue may hint that the

TABLE 8.8

Model Comparison Using Validation Metrics

Model Fit Metrics	CART Tree	CHAID Tree	Logistic Regression
RMSE	4.608	4.880	5.68
MAPE	0.129	0.136	0.161
RSE	0.226	0.253	0.393
EP	0.774	0.747	0.607

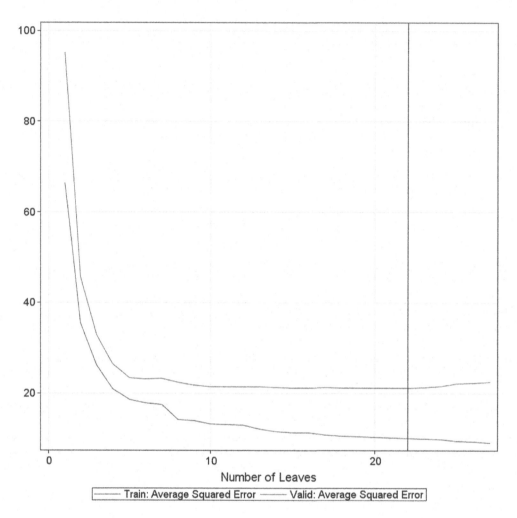

FIGURE 8.14
Subtree assessment plot for the CART tree.

model reliability is not great. However, keep in mind that ASE is the Average Squared Error, which is the same as MSE. The value is scale-dependent, so it is hard to interpret whether this difference is acceptable or not. By reviewing the RMSE, we see that the RMSE for training is 3.19, while the RMSE for validation is 4.61. These two values are not too far from each other. We also review the score distribution for the mean predicted values and mean target values for both samples (Figure 8.15). The distributions are very close between the two samples. You may also notice, in the validation sample, the mean target does not match the mean predicted values as in the training sample. It explains a little higher valida-tion RMSE. Overall, there is no major concern with model reliability.

To further review the CART tree performance, we also look at two charts, actual by predicted and residual by predicted charts, for final confirmation. These charts are con-structed using the Excel files we downloaded before. Figure 8.16 shows the actual by pre-dicted chart, while Figure 8.17 shows the residual by predicted chart.

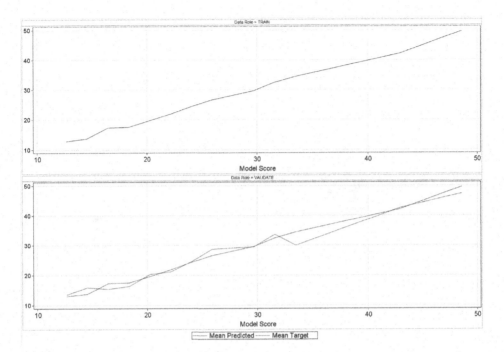

FIGURE 8.15
Score distribution for training and validation samples.

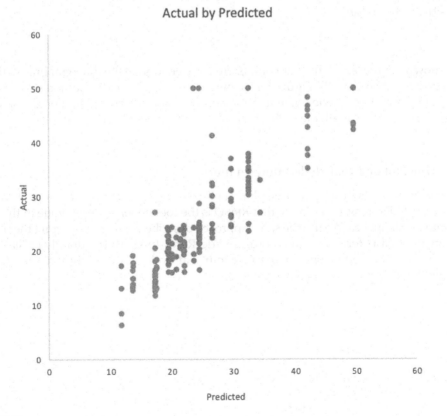

FIGURE 8.16
Actual by predicted chart.

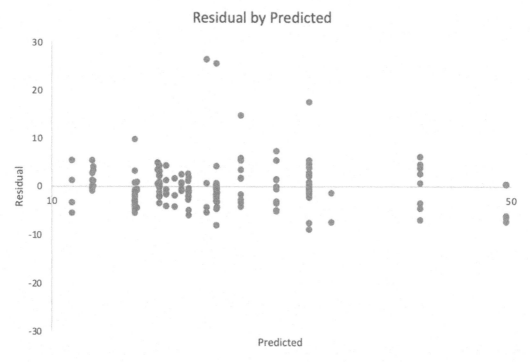

FIGURE 8.17
Residual by predicted chart.

As shown in Figure 8.16, the data points are close enough to the diagonal line, with some small outliers. Additionally, Figure 8.17 shows the residuals are distributed systematically between the zero line. We do not detect any non-random patterns, even though some small outliers are noted. Overall, these charts show no concerns with the model fit.

CART Tree Plot and Leaf Node Interpretation

Figure 8.18 shows the full CART tree plot. The tree is too large to show all node details. But based on the hierarchy, you can see that *RmSQ* is the root node, and each node in this tree is split into two branches. We use the same approach described before to interpret the tree plot.

As mentioned before, we can also use Node Rules to show the details of leaf nodes. Following are the node rules for the first four leaf nodes, explaining how *Imv* (median housing value) is predicted at each leaf node.

```
*------------------------------------------------------------*
Node = 6
*------------------------------------------------------------*
if RmSQ < 7.435 AND RmSQ >= 6.963 or MISSING
then
Tree Node Identifier = 6
Number of Observations = 24
Predicted: Imv = 32.458333333
```

```
*----------------------------------------------------------------*
Node = 9
*----------------------------------------------------------------*
if RmSQ < 6.963 or MISSING
AND Lstat < 9.95
AND Charles River >= 0.5
then
Tree Node Identifier = 9
Number of Observations = 7
Predicted: Imv = 34.385714286


*----------------------------------------------------------------*
Node = 14
*----------------------------------------------------------------*
if RmSQ >= 7.435
AND PtRatio < 14.8
then
Tree Node Identifier = 14
Number of Observations = 6
Predicted: Imv = 49.55


*----------------------------------------------------------------*
Node = 15
*----------------------------------------------------------------*
if RmSQ >= 7.435
AND PtRatio >= 14.8 or MISSING
then
Tree Node Identifier = 15
Number of Observations = 8
Predicted: Imv = 42.075


*----------------------------------------------------------------*
Node = 24
*----------------------------------------------------------------*
if RmSQ < 6.133
AND Lstat < 9.95
AND Charles River < 0.5 or MISSING
AND B < 388.12
then
Tree Node Identifier = 24
Number of Observations = 5
Predicted: Imv = 23.58
*----------------------------------------------------------------*
```

Variable Importance

As usual, the final important result is variable importance. Table 8.9 shows that the relative importance results are consistent between the training sample and the validation sample. The results indicate that *RmSQ* is the most important predictor, followed by *Lstat*, *IndustPr*, and *NiOxSQ*. On the other hand, *LogAccess*, *Tax*, and *Charles River* are among the least important predictors in the prediction of Imv. This finding would allow the decision maker to evaluate the housing market in the Boston area and develop appropriate strategies to improve the housing values.

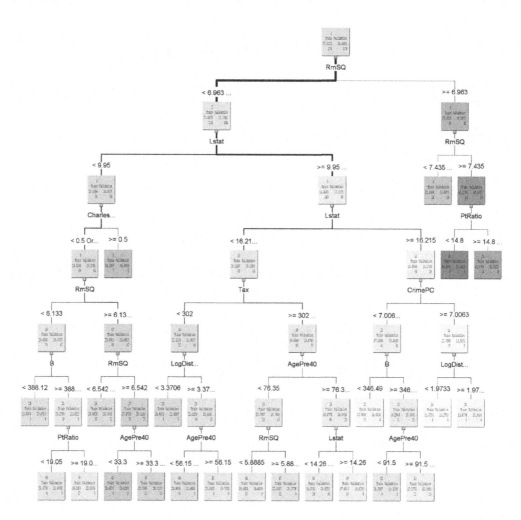

FIGURE 8.18
Full CART tree.

TABLE 8.9

Variable Importance

Variables	Training Importance	Validation Importance
RmSQ	1	1
Lstat	0.967	0.982
IndustPr	0.8846	0.9216
NiOxSQ	0.8459	0.8951
PtRatio	0.7585	0.8041
ZonePr	0.7374	0.7905
CrimePC	0.5342	0.4459
AgePre40	0.4852	0.4584
B	0.3664	0.296
LogDistance	0.3435	0.2348
Charles River	0.3397	0.2517
Tax	0.3326	0.2587
LogAccess	0.1399	0.0755

Example: CSL Using SAS Enterprise Miner

As explained in Chapters 3 and 6, CSL is a popular method to allow us to evaluate and select a model based on the costs of misclassification rather than misclassification rate. The assumption is that each misclassification may result in different costs, and our objective is not to minimize the misclassification rate but rather to minimize the total costs of misclassification.

I will demonstrate how to perform CSL using *the airline recommendation* dataset. The target variable is a binary variable with two levels: YES – recommend the airline and NO – not recommend the airline. The Decision node is used to perform the CSL, and these two levels represent the decisions in the CSL. I will demonstrate how to perform the CSL in two scenarios.

1. *Objective*: minimize the total costs of misclassification.
2. *Objective*: maximize the total profits of accurate classification.

CSL with the Cost Minimization Objective

Before we build our diagram, it is important to develop the decision matrix for this scenario. Table 8.10 presents the hypothetical matrix for this scenario. In this case, the goal is to predict the passenger recommendations of the airline, based on which the airline can establish an appropriate strategy to meet the demand. Let's assume that the false positives (predicting recommendations while they are actually non-recommendations) may end up costing the airline more than false negatives (predicting non-recommendations while they are actually recommendations). The reason is that false positives may lead to a misprediction that the demand will rise, and the airline decides to increase the number of flights and airplanes. The decision based on this misclassification will increase the airline's operating costs while the revenue will not improve. On the other hand, false negatives will incur some opportunity costs for the airline since they miss the golden opportunity to meet the rising demand. However, this cost is lower than the cost of false positives. We use a hypothetical scenario that the cost of false positives is then times the cost of false negatives. Instead of using an actual dollar amount, which we don't have, I use the unit cost of 200 units for false positives and 20 units for false negatives (Table 8.10). Our objective is to find the predictive model that minimizes the total cost of misclassification.

In order to enter this decision matrix in SAS Enterprise Miner diagram, from the Assess tab, drag a Decision node to the workspace and connect it to the Replacement node (see below).

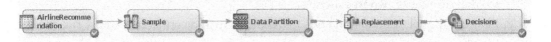

TABLE 8.10

Decision Matrix – Costs of Misclassification

	Predicted YES	**Predicted NO**
Actual YES	True Positive Cost = 0	False Negative Cost = 20
Actual NO	False Positive Cost = 200	True Negative Cost = 0

Run the Decision node (to get the information on the variables) and follow the steps below to configure the decision matrix.

1. In the Train properties:
   - Set Apply Decisions to Yes.
   - Set Decision to Custom.
2. Click the ellipsis button (three-dot button) next to Custom Editor. The Decision Processing – Decisions window will open.
3. Select the Decision tab and select Yes for "Do you want to use the decision?"
4. Select the Decision Weights tab:
   - Select Minimize.
   - Enter the cost units for false positives and false negatives (see below).

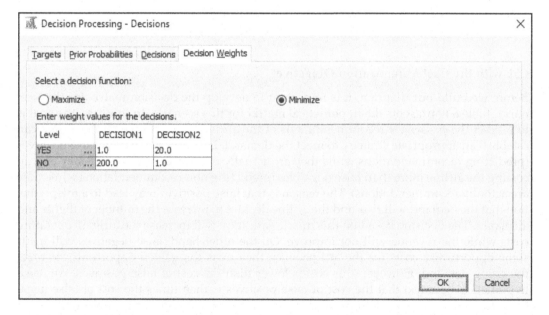

5. Click OK.
6. From the Model tab, drag two Decision Tree nodes to the diagram, connect them to the Decisions node, and name them Pruned CHAID Tree and Pruned CART Tree.
7. Use the configurations in the previous example for the *airline recommendation* data to configure those two tree models.
8. Drag the Model Comparison node to the diagram and connect it to these two tree nodes.
9. In the Train properties for the Model Comparison node:
   - Under Model Selection: Set the Selection Statistics to Average Profit/Loss.
10. Run the Model Comparison node and open the Results window.

The results output (Table 8.11) shows that the Pruned CHAID Tree is the better one with a lower total cost of 10.719. Thus, while the Pruned CART Tree has a lower validation misclassification rate, when we take into account the costs of misclassification, the Pruned CHAID Tree performs slightly better.

TABLE 8.11

CSL Results – Cost Minimization

Model Description	Valid: Average Loss for recommendation	Valid: Misclassification Rate
Pruned CHAID Tree	10.719	0.211
Pruned CART Tree	10.928	0.208

CSL with the Profit Maximization Objective

In this scenario, we focus on the profits of accurate predictions. We assume that the airline is experiencing some decrease in demand, and they need to make operational decisions in terms of the number of flights and investment in new airplanes. We can argue that the prediction of non-recommendations (true negatives) proves to be more useful for the airline than the prediction of recommendations (true positives). In other words, if the airline knows the correct number of passengers not recommending the airline, then they can establish the right strategy to adjust the flight volume, airplane capacity, and flight paths. These adjustments help them reduce the costs significantly, which results in increasing the total profits. Table 8.12 presents the decision matrix for this scenario, in which the unit profit of true negatives is 1,000, while the unit profit of true positives is 100. Our objective is to find the predictive model that maximizes the total profit of accurate classification.

Follow the same steps as before, except for the Decision Processing – Decisions window, in which we need to change the configurations for the Decision Weights tab as follows.

- Select Maximize.
- Add the profit units for true positives and true negatives.

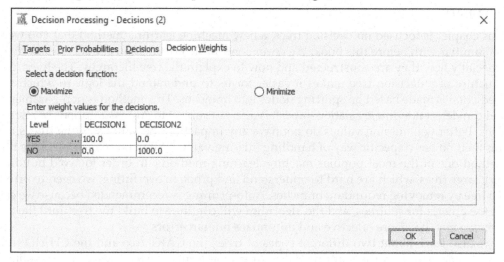

TABLE 8.12

Decision Matrix – Profits of Accurate Classification

	Predicted YES	**Predicted NO**
Actual YES	True Positive Profit = 100	False Negative Profit = 0
Actual NO	False Positive Profit = 0	True Negative Profit = 1000

TABLE 8.13

CSL Results – Profit Maximization

Model Description	Valid: Average Loss for Recommendation	Valid: Misclassification Rate
Pruned CHAID Tree	478.57	0.153
Pruned CART Tree	477.46	0.150

Once we run the Model Comparison node, the results output (Table 8.13) indicates that the Pruned CHAID Tree is the model with a higher total profit of 478.47. We also notice that while this model has a higher validation misclassification rate, when we account for the profits of accurate classification, it performs slightly better than the Pruned CART Tree.

As you can see, by using the Decisions node, we can perform CSL easily and can take into account the costs of misclassification or profits of accurate classification in our model comparison process and use cost minimization or profit maximization to select the champion model. In this book, in order to ensure consistency, I will continue to use the misclassification rate as the selection statistics in the consequent chapters. Nonetheless, if your project requires using costs or profits as the deciding factor, you can also return to this chapter and follow the same steps to incorporate the Decisions node in your diagram.

Summary

This chapter is focused on decision trees, a new machine learning method that you were not familiar with before this book. We cover some basic information about decision trees, especially how they are constructed and how to explain the tree hierarchy. The hierarchy structure of a decision tree makes it easier for us to understand the logic in which the prediction is made based on splitting nodes into branches. This method is non-parametric and can detect non-linear relationships. It is also not subject to any assumptions or restrictions. Better yet, missing values do not have any impact on the validity of the tree, since this method has a specific way of handling missing values. All of these reasons make this method one of the most popular machine learning methods. In order to avoid building very large trees, which are hard to understand and prone to overfitting, we need to prune the tree by removing redundant branches. Auto-pruning is recommended because we can set the criteria for subtrees, and the algorithm will continue to build the tree until the criteria are met. It is more effective and minimizes human errors.

We also learn about two different types of trees, the CART tree and the CHAID tree, determined based on the splitting rules. In simple terms, CART uses a binary split, in which a node is split into two branches only, while CHAID uses a multi-split, in which a node can be split into more than two branches. These two trees both have pros and cons. It is important to note that they can be used to build either association models or classification models. They can also work with continuous or categorical predictors. Basically, decision trees are very versatile. SAS Enterprise Miner does not have dedicated nodes for CART and CHAID; it only has a Decision Tree node. Nonetheless, we can configure a CART tree or a CHAID tree with specific configurations. The outputs of decision trees consist of the tree plot, which shows the full tree hierarchy, and leaf node rules, which explain how the prediction is made at each leaf node. Finally, the variable importance table provides us with a list of significant predictors and ranks them by relative importance. Thus, we can know which predictors are important to predicting the target variables. I continue to use examples of the airline recommendation dataset and the Boston housing dataset, so you can compare the decision trees with other models we build.

The CSL using the Decision node is also explained and demonstrated in this chapter. CSL is one of the popular methods for comparing models and selecting the champion model based on the costs of misclassification rather than the misclassification rate. Essentially, the algorithm selects the model with the minimum total costs of misclassification. CSL can also be used in case our goal is to minimize the total profits of accurate predictions. It is a useful method for profit/loss consideration and also could help address the overfitting issue.

CHAPTER DISCUSSION QUESTIONS

1. Explain the purpose of the decision tree method. How does the decision tree method work in machine learning?

2. What are the main components of a decision tree? Explain the tree's hierarchical structure.

3. Discuss the process of constructing a decision tree and the criteria used for splitting nodes.

4. What are the advantages and disadvantages of using decision trees compared to other machine learning algorithms?

5. Do missing values affect decision trees? How do decision tree algorithms handle missing values?

6. Decision trees can handle missing values by imputation or using surrogate splits. Compare and contrast these techniques, discussing their advantages, limitations, and potential impact on decision tree accuracy.

7. What are the purposes of tree pruning? Describe and explain different pruning approaches.

8. Compare Classification and Regression Tree (CART) tree and Chi-Squared Automatic Interaction Detection (CHAID) tree.

9. Interpretability is a key advantage of decision trees. How can the decision tree structure be interpreted to gain insights into the important predictors and their impact on the target variable? Discuss methods for visualizing and analyzing decision trees.

10. Decision trees are versatile and applicable to various domains. Give examples of real-world applications where decision trees have been successfully employed and discuss the advantages of using decision trees in those contexts.

11. Discuss the purposes and benefits of CSL. In which cases should CSL be used? Provide practical examples.

Exercises

Exercise 1: Decision tree model for the Bank dataset

1. Open the *bank* dataset in SAS Enterprise Miner.
2. Sample the entire dataset. See the variable names and descriptions in Appendix A.1.
3. Partition the data using a split ratio of 60:40 (train: 60%; validation: 20%; test: 20%)
4. Perform data modification as follows:
   - Impute missing values.
   - Normalize variables with skewed data distribution.
5. Set *CRSCORE* (credit scores) as the target variable.
6. Configure four decision tree models for this dataset as follows (using Auto Pruning).
   - Full CART tree.
   - Pruned CART tree.
   - Full CHAID tree.
   - Pruned CHAID tree.
7. Compare the model fit metrics between these four models using the validation results.
8. Select the champion model and justify this selection with the necessary evidence.
9. Present the results of the champion model.
10. Evaluate the reliability and validity of the champion model.
11. Present the variable importance information and interpret the results.

Exercise 2: Decision tree models for the Passengers dataset

1. Open the *passengers* dataset in SAS Enterprise Miner.
2. Sample 20% of the full data. Set *return* (decision to return to the airline) as the target variable and change its role to binary. See the variable names and descriptions in Appendix A.2.
3. Partition the data using a split ratio of 60:40 (train: 60%; validation: 20%; test: 20%)
4. Perform data modification as follows:
   - Replace zero values for Likert scale variables with missing values.
   - Impute missing values.
5. Configure four decision tree models for this dataset as follows (using Auto Pruning).
   - Pruned CART tree using the built-in missing value algorithm (under the Splitting rules, set the Missing Values to Largest Branch).
   - Pruned CART tree using imputation for missing values.
   - Pruned CHAID tree using the built-in missing value algorithm (under the Splitting rules, set the Missing Values to Use in search).
   - Pruned CART tree using imputation for missing values.
6. Compare the model fit metrics between those four models using the validation results.
7. Select the champion model and justify this selection with the necessary evidence.
8. Present the results of the champion model.
9. Evaluate the reliability and validity of the champion model.
10. Present the variable importance information and interpret the results.

Exercise 3: CSL model for the Passengers dataset

1. Repeat Steps 1-5 in Exercise 2.
2. Conduct the CSL model with the objective of minimizing the total costs of misclassification. Use the decision matrix below.

	Predicted YES	Predicted NO
Actual YES	True Positive Cost = 0	False Negative Cost = 150
Actual NO	False Positive Cost = 2000	True Negative Cost = 0

3. Compare the four decision tree models using the total costs of misclassification (use the validation results).
4. Select the champion model and present justify this selection with the necessary evidence.
5. Conduct the CSL model with the objective of maximizing the total profits of accurate predictions. Use the decision matrix below.

	Predicted YES	Predicted NO
Actual YES	True Positive Profit = 200	False Negative Profit = 0
Actual NO	False Positive Profit = 0	True Negative Profit = 2500

6. Compare the four decision tree models using the total profits of accurate predictions (use the validation results).
7. Select the champion model and present justify this selection with the necessary evidence.

9

Neural Networks

LEARNING OUTCOMES

Upon the completion of this chapter, you will be able to

1. Define neural networks.
2. Explain the importance of neural networks in data mining and provide practical examples.
3. Describe common types of neural networks
4. Explain the foundational concepts of neural networks, including the structure and function of artificial neurons, activation functions, and network architectures.
5. Compare forward propagation and backward propagation algorithms used in training neural networks.
6. Differentiate different activation functions.
7. Describe the multi-layer perceptron (MLP) method.
8. Demonstrate how to normalize data for neural network training.
9. Discuss the advantages and disadvantages of neural networks.
10. Apply neural network configurations in the model training using SAS Enterprise Miner.
11. Interpret the neural network results, including the model fit, network structure, and variable importance.

Introduction

In this chapter, we focus on neural networks. The neural network is a very popular method in the age of machine learning and AI, but it is a rather complex concept, and it is challenging to fully understand this method and how to implement it. It is not hard to find many resources, including videos, websites, blogs, or books on neural networks. Books tend to provide content on an advanced level requiring some strong

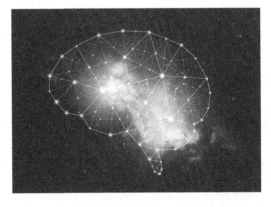

DOI: 10.1201/9781003162872-11

background in mathematics. We start seeing more fun videos explaining the concept of neural networks in a simple way to help the audience gain a basic understanding of this method. In this book, I intend to explain the neural network method in a simple way without showing mathematical expression, but I do not mean for it just to be fun. I want it to be practical, so you can perform actual neural network research.

Neural network is not a new concept, but it is a complex method, so in the past, very few scientists actually understood and could implement it. With the advancement of data mining and machine learning, we start seeing more actual applications using neural networks in real life, which makes this method more popular. Some examples we see very often in the media or in our daily activities include the Tesla autopilot, smartphone facial recognition, voice recognition, and Deep Fake. Deep Fake technology can put one person's face into another's face that can fool anyone. I do not intend to explain how those technologies  work since they use extensive neural network applications that require a lot of resources and teams of data scientists working for a long period of time. As mentioned before, my purpose is to provide a simple introduction and explanation of this method that helps you build predictive models using neural networks. So, the fundamental question is: How do we understand it in a simple way, without any mathematical formulas? Ok, let's get started.

What Is Neural Network?

Simply put, a neural network (NN) mimics the human brain's biological neural network. That explains the term *neural network* and also indicates the complexity of this concept because we all know the human brain is the most complex network. As we continue to explore this method, it gets more complex. It is like as we go to an intersection, we see more roads ahead, and the deeper we go, the bigger the network gets. Figure 9.1 shows some typical types of neural network architectures. The node, also called *cell or neuron*, represents one variable or unit in the network. These nodes can move forward, backward, back in time, or interact with other nodes. That is how complex the network can get. Neural networks are math-based, so each type of neural network consists of multiple mathematical expressions to capture the connections among those nodes.

SAS Institute defines neural networks as "computing systems with interconnected nodes that work much like neurons in the human brain. Using algorithms, they can recognize

> **DEFINITION**
>
> Neural networks are computing systems with interconnected nodes that work much like neurons in the human brain. Using algorithms, they can recognize hidden patterns and correlations in raw data, cluster and classify it, and, over time, continuously learn and improve (SAS Institute).

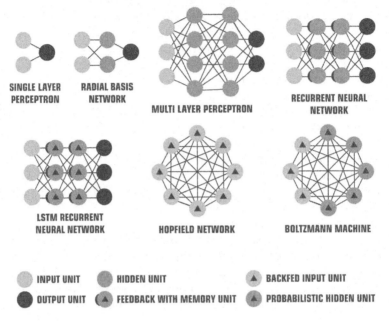

FIGURE 9.1
Various neural network architecture types.

hidden patterns and correlations in raw data, cluster and classify it, and, over time, continuously learn and improve." That is not hard to understand at all, right?

The diagram in Figure 9.2 presents a typical structure of a neural network. In a simple sense, a neural network consists of the input layer, hidden layers, and the output layer. The input layer includes predictors in our model, and the output layer includes the target variable(s) that we want to predict. Hidden layers include multiple hidden nodes that connect the input layer to the output layer in different ways. Hidden layers play an

DEFINITION

Neurons or cells represent nodes in a neural network architecture.

Neural network model is the same as neural network architecture.

Artificial Neural Network (ANN) is a neural network with more than one hidden layer.

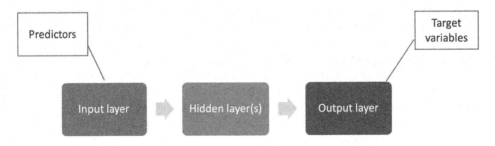

FIGURE 9.2
Simple diagram of a neural network.

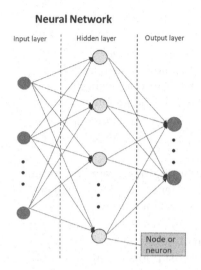

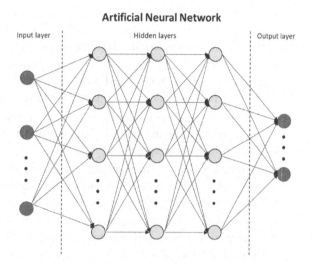

FIGURE 9.3
Neural network and artificial neural network.

important role in detecting the patterns from the data. So, one of the key decisions in neural network modeling is the number of hidden layers we need and the number of nodes in each layer. We will get to that later.

Let's look at two actual diagrams of neural networks in Figure 9.3. On the left, we have a typical neural network model with one hidden layer. Again, these nodes are called "cells" or "neurons." When we have more than one hidden layer, the network is called an **"Artificial Neural Network" (ANN).** You know it by a more common name, deep learning. Of course, an actual deep learning network will have much more than just two or three hidden layers.

The green nodes represent input nodes, which are predictors in our model. The blue nodes present output nodes, which are target variables in our model. Neural networks can be used for both categorical and continuous target variables, so they are very versatile. The yellow nodes represent hidden nodes, which connect input nodes with output nodes. These connections represent the **neural network architecture or model.**

Practical Applications of Neural Networks

Neural networks have wide applications across various domains due to their ability to learn complex patterns from data and make accurate predictions. Below are some practical applications of neural networks.

- **Image recognition and computer vision:** Neural networks, especially convolutional neural networks, excel in image recognition tasks. They can identify objects, faces, and scenes in images, enabling applications like facial recognition, object detection, and self-driving cars.

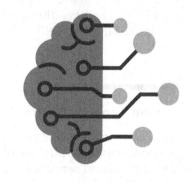

NEURAL NETWORK

- *Natural language processing (NLP)*: Recurrent neural networks and transformer networks have revolutionized NLP tasks. Neural networks can perform machine translation, sentiment analysis, text generation, speech recognition, and chatbots.
- *Healthcare*: Neural networks are used in medical image analysis, such as detecting abnormalities in X-rays and MRI scans. They also assist in diagnosing diseases and predicting patient outcomes based on medical records and genomic data.
- *Finance*: Neural networks are used for credit risk assessment, fraud detection, stock market prediction, and algorithmic trading to analyze financial data and make informed decisions.
- *Media and product recommendation*: The recommendation engines created by neural networks enable services provided to personalize content and product suggestions in streaming platforms, e-commerce sites, and social media.
- *Flight control systems*: Flight control systems use neural networks to optimize aircraft performance and improve stability. Neural networks can model complex flight dynamics, adapt to changing conditions, and assist pilots in handling critical situations.
- *Autonomous vehicles*: Neural networks are the key component in self-driving cars, enabling them to interpret sensor data and make real-time decisions to navigate safely.
- *Gaming and virtual environments*: Intelligent agents in gaming and virtual environments can be created by neural networks to learn and adapt to player behavior.
- *Flight path prediction*: Neural networks can predict flight paths and optimize flight trajectories for fuel efficiency and reduced emissions. Factors such as weather conditions, wind patterns, and air traffic congestion are often included in the prediction.
- *Airline passenger behavior analysis*: Airlines can use neural networks to analyze passenger data to understand behavior patterns, preferences, and customer satisfaction. This information can be used to personalize services and enhance the passenger experience.
- *Robotics*: Neural networks are used in robotics for perception, object recognition, grasping, and motion control.
- *Music and art generation*: Artists can use neural networks to generate music, create art, and produce visual content based on learned patterns and styles.

These are just a few examples of the diverse practical applications of neural networks. Their versatility and ability to handle complex data make them a crucial tool in modern machine learning and artificial intelligence, shaping various industries.

Common Types of Neural Networks

Neural networks come in various architectures and designs, each tailored to handle specific types of data and the purpose of the project. Common types of neural networks include feedforward neural network (FNN), convolutional neural network (CNN), recurrent neural network (RNN), long short-term memory (LSTM) network, and radial basis function network (RBFN). Table 9.1 describes these types of networks, their strengths, and weaknesses.

TABLE 9.1

Common Types of Neural Networks

Type of NN	Description	Strengths	Weaknesses
Feedforward neural network (FNN)	The simplest type of neural network. Data flows in a single direction from the input layer to the output layer.	• Easy to understand and implement. • Suitable for a wide range of tasks.	• Less accurate than other types of NNs for complex tasks. • Slower to train.
Convolutional neural network (CNN)	A type of FNN that is specifically designed for image processing. It uses convolution operations to extract features from images.	• Very good at image processing tasks. • High accuracy.	• Complex to understand and implement. • Requires a lot of data to train.
Recurrent neural network (RNN)	A neural network that can process sequential data. It has feedback loops, which allow it to remember past inputs and use that information to process future inputs.	• Good at tasks that involve sequential data. • Suitable for long-term dependencies.	• Complex to understand and implement. • Requires a lot of data to train.
Long short-term memory (LSTM) network	A variant of RNN that is specifically designed to handle long-term dependencies in sequential data.	• Very good at tasks that involve long-term dependencies. • High accuracy.	• Complex to understand and implement. • Requires a lot of data to train.
Radial basis function network (RBFN)	A neural network that uses radial basis functions to compute the output of the network.	• Good at regression tasks. • High accuracy.	• Complex to understand and implement. • Requires a lot of data to train.

> Note that in this book, I do not get into complex forms of neural networks. We mainly focus on a popular Feedforward Neural Network, *Multi-Layer Perceptron Feedforward (MLP)*.

Neural Network Training

Forward propagation and backward propagation are two fundamental processes in training FNNs. They work together to enable the network to learn from data and improve its predictions. Forward propagation is the fundamental mechanism used to process data and make predictions for a given input. It passes input data through a neural network to generate predictions or outputs. Backward propagation, also called backpropagation, is a learning algorithm used to train FNNs.

DEFINITION

Forward propagation is the process of passing input data through the neural network to generate predictions.

Backward propagation is a learning algorithm that computes the prediction error in term of loss function and then adjusts the network's parameters to minimize the errors during the training process.

It evaluates the difference between the predicted outputs and the actual target values (errors) and then adjusts the network's weights and biases to minimize the errors during the training process.

1. **Forward propagation:**
   - Input data is fed into the neural network, and it passes through the layers in a forward direction, from the input layer to the output layer.
   - At each layer, the input data is multiplied by the layer's weights and biases, and then an activation function is applied to the result to introduce non-linearity.
   - The output of each layer becomes the input to the next layer, and this process continues until the final output is generated at the output layer.
   - Forward propagation is essentially the process of making predictions based on the current weights and biases of the neural network, without considering the actual target values.

2. **Backward propagation:**
   - Backward propagation is the learning algorithm used to update the weights and biases of the neural network based on the prediction errors during the forward pass.
   - After the forward propagation and predictions, the prediction error is computed using a loss function, which quantifies how far off the predictions are from the true values and serves as a measure of the network's performance.
   - Backward propagation works by computing the gradients of the loss function. The gradients represent the sensitivity of the loss to changes in the network's parameters (weights and biases), indicating which direction and how much each parameter should be adjusted to reduce the error.
   - Using the computed gradients, the weights and biases are adjusted using an optimization algorithm to minimize the loss and improve the network's performance.

In summary, forward propagation is the process of passing input data through the neural network to generate predictions, while backward propagation is the process of computing the gradients of the loss function and using them to update the network's parameters during training. Together, these processes form the basis of training FNNs and are crucial for enabling the network to learn from data and improve its predictive power.

Advantages and Disadvantages of Neural Networks

Neural networks are a very powerful machine learning algorithm. This method has been used in many areas and plays a vital role in the research and development of artificial intelligence. Nonetheless, neural networks are not perfect and still have challenges. It is important for us to understand the advantages and disadvantages of this method, so we can decide when it is the right time to use neural networks for our data mining projects.

Advantages of neural networks

- *Non-linear*: Neural networks can capture well non-linear relationships in data, which makes this method well-suited for complex problems where traditional linear models might fail.

- *Adaptive learning*: They can learn and adapt to new data in real time. Thus, they are quite effective for modeling dynamic environments where data is constantly changing.

- *Unlimited information*: This method is not limited to input data since it uses many hidden layers to create connections between layers. In the training process, more information is created to produce a good model.

- *Parallel processing*: Neural networks can process multiple inputs at the same time. Hence, they can be used for tasks requiring high efficiency, such as image recognition and natural language processing.

- *Fault tolerance*: This method is resilient to noise and errors in data. The network can still perform well even when some data is missing or corrupted because it stores information on the network instead of the database.

- *Variable extraction*: Relevant variables can be automatically extracted from raw data, eliminating the need for manual variable selection.

Disadvantages of neural networks

- *Black box*: A neural network is often considered a "black box" because it can be difficult to understand how the model works and how variables are correlated. In other words, we feed the input data to the model, and it predicts the values of output variables. But we do not really understand what is going on in the black box. This lack of interpretability can make the method less suitable for certain applications where transparency is required.

- *Overfitting*: Neural networks can be prone to overfitting, especially when we use a very large amount of data. It means they perform well on the training data but not on new, unseen data. In other words, the model is not generalizable.

- *Data requirements*: This method requires large amounts of labeled data to train effectively, which can be a significant bottleneck in some applications.

- *Computationally intensive*: The training process can be computationally intensive, requiring high computing power and longer training time.

- *Hyperparameter configuration*: Setting hyperparameters for a neural network can be challenging and must be done carefully to achieve optimal performance. Since there are no straightforward rules for determining the right configurations for the network architecture, the modeling process requires experimentation to achieve optimal performance.

Despite these disadvantages, neural networks are still a powerful machine learning method, and their applications are growing rapidly, especially deep learning methods. By understanding the strengths and weaknesses, we can have a good strategy to use this method for our research. Again, the purpose of this book is to provide a simple introduction and guidelines for implementing neural networks, a complex machine learning algorithm. So, we will not go deeply into the complex methods in neural network modeling.

Basic Concepts in Neural Networks

As mentioned before, the neural network method is a complicated machine learning method. Even if we focus on the simplest form of neural networks, it is still a challenge to understand how the model works. The following basic concepts form the foundation of neural networks and help you understand the architecture of a neural network and the training process (Table 9.2).

TABLE 9.2

Basic Concepts in Neural Networks

Terms	Description
Neuron (node)	A neuron, also called a node or unit, is a basic building block of a neural network. It receives inputs, processes them using an activation function, and produces outputs.
Connection (edge)	A connection connects neurons. Each connection has an associated weight that determines the level of the influence between connected neurons.
Activation function	An activation function is a function that determines the output of a neuron based on the weighted sum of its inputs. Common activation functions include sigmoid, ReLU (Rectified Linear Unit), and tanh (hyperbolic tangent).
Weight	Each connection between neurons is assigned a weight, which represents the strength or importance of that connection. These weights determine how much influence the input of one neuron has on the output of another.
Bias	A bias term is added to the weighted sum of inputs in each neuron. It allows the network to learn a bias toward certain values and improves the accuracy of the model.
Layers	Neurons are organized into layers in a neural network. The input layer receives the input data, the output layer produces the final output, and there can be one or more hidden layers in between.
Forward propagation	Forward propagation is the process of transmitting input signals through the network, layer by layer, to produce an output. Each neuron in a layer receives input from the previous layer, performs computations using its activation function, and passes the output to the next layer.
Backward propagation (or backpropagation)	Backward propagation is the process of adjusting the weights and biases in the network based on the prediction error. It involves calculating the gradients of the loss function and adjusting the parameters to minimize the error.
Training	Training a neural network involves iteratively adjusting the weights and biases using a training dataset. The goal is to minimize the error or loss function and improve the network's prediction accuracy.
Loss function	A loss function measures the discrepancy between the predicted output of the neural network and the actual target values. It quantifies the error and guides the adjustment of the parameters during training.
Optimization algorithm	The optimization algorithm is used during training to adjust the network's parameters based on the computed gradients. Gradient descent is a common optimization algorithm used for this purpose.

Neural Network Model Connections

Now, we have some basic understanding of what a neural network is. As shown before in Figure 9.3, neural network models consist of the connections between input nodes, hidden nodes, and output nodes. So, how do we express these connections without getting into complex math? To demonstrate it, I use the neural network architecture with one hidden layer. Figure 9.4 provides the connections between nodes in a simple way.

Network Connections

Basically, an output node is a function of hidden nodes connecting to that node and corresponding weights. In essence, each route from a hidden note to an output node has a weight, similar to regression weight. The weights capture the importance of that relationship in the model. Similarly, a hidden node is a function of input nodes connecting to that node and corresponding weights. In each equation, we also have a bias node. A bias is a learnable parameter associated with each node. The bias node allows us to shift the function left or right, which is important for training the model. The function we keep mentioning is called the **activation function**. The mathematical expressions of these connections are much more complex but trust me, that is all they mean. We will get into the details of some common activation functions soon.

So you may wonder why I do not present these equations as a linear regression equation with the intercept plus regression weight times input variable plus errors. The reason is that the activation function could be either linear or non-linear. This is the strength of neural networks since it can capture the non-linear relationships between input nodes, hidden nodes, and output nodes in a complex network architecture.

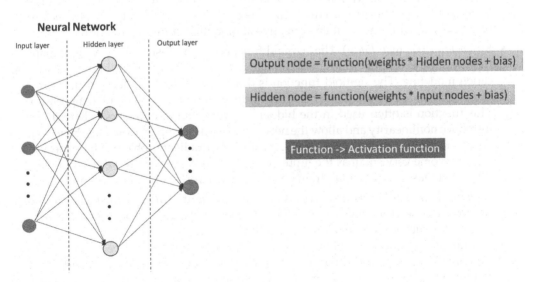

FIGURE 9.4
Connections between nodes in a neural network model.

Activation Functions

Again, an activation function is a function that determines the output node based on an input node or a set of input nodes. The activation function is an essential component of the network, as it introduces nonlinearity and enables the network to model complex, nonlinear relationships in the data. Selecting the right activation function may play a key role in building a good neural network.

As explained before, the activation function takes the weighted sum of the inputs to a node (neuron), adds a bias term, and then applies a nonlinear transformation to produce the output of a node. This output is then passed to the next layer of the network as input. In other words, these functions represent mathematically the connections between nodes, which form the neural network model. Selecting the function and configuring it is a primary task in neural network modeling.

There are many different types of activation functions that can be used in a neural network, each with its own advantages and disadvantages. Table 9.3 shows the common activation functions that are available in SAS Enterprise Miner. Without going into too much mathematic formulation, I present the function name, range, expression in terms of x as the input, and chat showing the graphical display of the function. I discuss some most common activation functions as follows.

- *Identity (linear)*: The identity function is a simple nonlinear function that is commonly used in neural networks. It returns the input value unchanged, which makes it useful in certain types of neural network architectures where the goal is to reconstruct the input from the output. This function is also used as the default activation function in the output layer of regression models, where the goal is to predict a continuous value. In this case, the output of the neural network is a linear combination of the inputs, which can be interpreted as a regression function. While the identity activation function is simple and easy to compute, it does not introduce any nonlinearity in the neural network. This constraint limits the power of the network and makes it less effective at modeling complex functions.

- *Sigmoid function (non-linear)*: The sigmoid function has an S-shaped curve that maps input values to output values between 0 and 1, which is useful for binary classification modeling. The sigmoid function is differentiable, which makes it useful for training neural networks using backpropagation, a popular optimization algorithm. This function is often used in the hidden layers of neural networks, where it can introduce nonlinearity and allow the network to model complex functions. However, the sigmoid function can suffer from the vanishing gradient problem, where the gradients become very small as the input values become very large or very small. This constraint makes it difficult to train deep neural networks with many layers.

- *Tanh function (non-linear)*: The hyperbolic tangent (tanh) function is similar to the sigmoid function but maps input values to a range between –1 and 1, which is useful for classification models where the output can take negative values. The tanh function is also differentiable, so it is useful for the backpropagation process. Like sigmoid, this function is often used in the hidden layers of neural networks and can introduce nonlinearity. Compared to the sigmoid function, the tanh function is symmetric around the origin, which can be useful in certain contexts. The tanh function also suffers from the vanishing gradient problem, especially when the

TABLE 9.3

Common Activation Functions (Available in SAS Enterprise Miner)

Function Name	Range	Expression in Terms of x	Chart
Identity	$(-\infty, \infty)$	x Efficient; linear	

Identity

| **Logistic (or Sigmoid)** | $(0, 1)$ | $1/(1+\exp(-x))$
Binary classification model | |

Logistic (sigmoid)

| **Hyperbolic Tangent (or Tanh)** | $(-1, 1)$ | $\tanh(x)=[1- [2/(1+\exp(2x)]$
Classification model with negative target values | |

Hyperbolic Tangent

(Continued)

TABLE 9.3   *(Continued)*

Common Activation Functions (Available in SAS Enterprise Miner)

Function Name	Range	Expression in Terms of x	Chart
Softmax	$(0, 1)$	$[\exp(x)/\text{Sum}(\exp(x))]$ Multiclass classification problems.	
Exponential	$(0, \infty)$	$\exp(x)$	
Reciprocal	$(0, \infty)$	$1/x$	

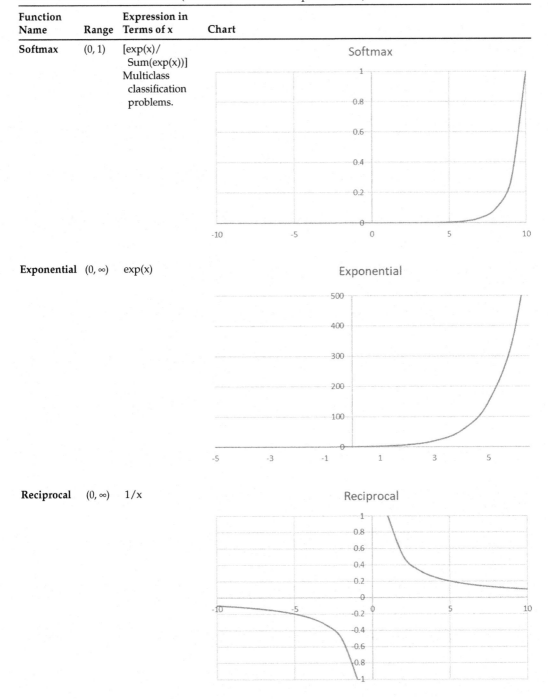

(Continued)

TABLE 9.3 *(Continued)*

Common Activation Functions (Available in SAS Enterprise Miner)

Function Name	Range	Expression in Terms of x	Chart
Sine	[-1, 1]	sin(x)	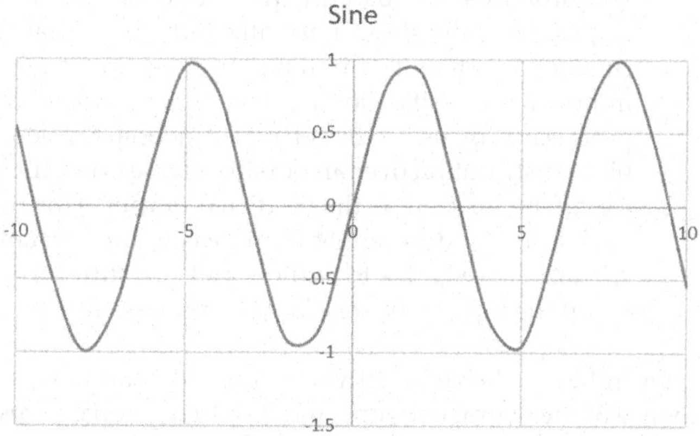

Sine

Square	$(0, \infty)$	x^2	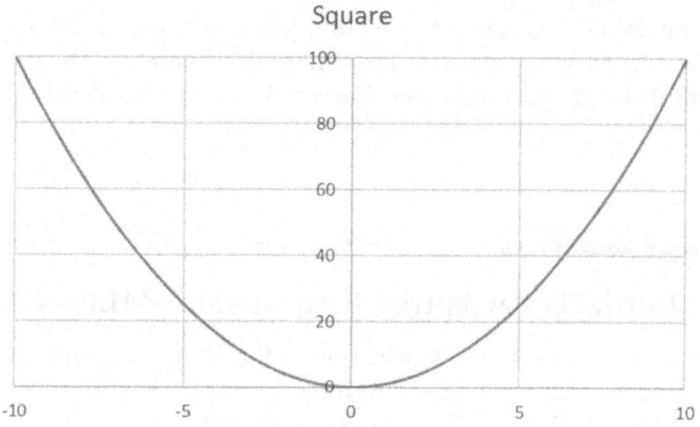

Square

Normal	$(0, \infty)$		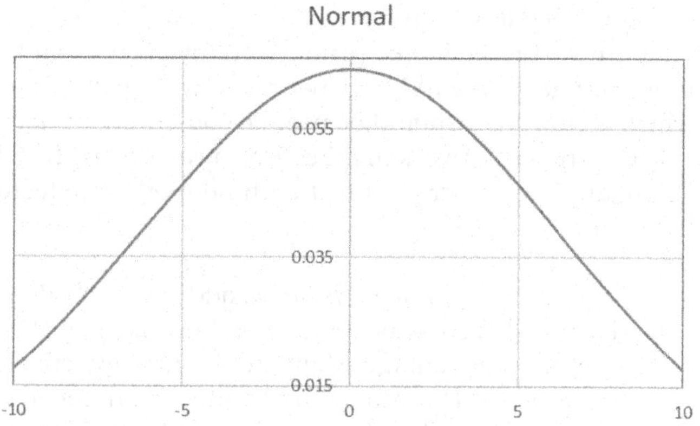

Normal

inputs are very large or very small. However, the tanh function is generally considered to be a better activation function than the sigmoid function, as it is able to model more complex functions due to its range being between –1 and 1.

- *Softmax function (non-linear)*: The softmax function takes real numbers as input and produces a probability distribution as output. Specifically, it maps the inputs to positive values and normalizes them so that they add up to 1. The softmax function is often used in the output layer of neural networks that are trained for multi-class classification models, such as image recognition or natural language processing. By using the softmax function, the neural network can output a probability distribution over all possible classes, and the class with the highest probability can be selected as the predicted output. This function has several advantages, such as being differentiable and easily interpretable as probabilities. However, it can also be sensitive to outliers and can suffer from the vanishing gradient problem if the inputs are very large or very small.

Overall, the choice of activation function can have a significant impact on the performance of the neural network, and it is often a topic of research and experimentation in the field of deep learning. A good activation function should be computationally efficient, be easily differentiable, and enable the network to model complex, nonlinear relationships in the data. There are several complex activation functions that are often used in deep learning, but I won't discuss them here. We focus on the ones that are commonly used in the multilayer perceptron feedforward (MLP) neural networks.

Multilayer Perceptron Feedforward (MLP) Network Architecture

As mentioned at the beginning of the chapter, neural networks have many types of architectures that can be used to model complex systems. However, in this book, we only focus on the MLP network. But even within this MLP network, there are multiple architectures we can select. Now you can understand the complexity of this machine learning algorithm and how deep it will go.

Figure 9.5 presents four primary architectures that SAS Enterprise Miner provides for us to use when we build MLP neural network models. In the modeling step, we can decide which architecture should be used to construct our neural networks.

These are the network architectures provided by SAS Enterprise Miner for users to use. Below are brief descriptions of each network architecture that allow you to understand the figure.

- In a *single hidden layer network*, additional hidden nodes are introduced sequentially, and their selection is based on the activation function that offers the most significant advantage. Many models can effectively fit with a single hidden layer. In a *funnel network*, new hidden nodes are incorporated in a funnel-like pattern, with their selection determined by the activation function that yields the greatest benefit.

- In a *block network*, new hidden nodes are appended as new layers within the network, and the choice of activation function is guided by the most beneficial one.

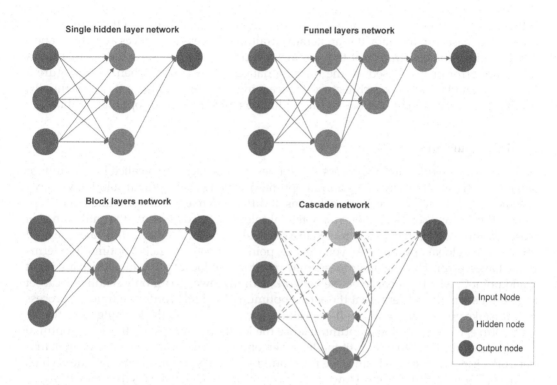

FIGURE 9.5
MLP network architectures.

- In a *cascade network*, new hidden nodes are introduced and interconnected with all existing input and hidden neurons. All previously trained weights and biases remain fixed. Each subsequent step focuses on optimizing the network's fit to the residuals of the preceding step.

> SAS Enterprise Miner offers another neural network along with MLP, which is Radial Basis Function (RBF) Network. It also provides multiple built-in architechtures for these two types of neural networks under the Neural Network node. However, in this book, we focus on MLP networks with those four basic architechtures.

Neural Network Searching

Neural network training is a process of finding a network structure (a network consists of nodes, layers, connections, weights, and activation functions) that best fits the data. Given the number of parameters (hyperparameter) and the number of possible networks we can configure in neural networks, the training process may be time consuming. It is not possible to figure out the best network manually based on our judgments due to the number of possible networks. Typically, most data mining software applications have an optimization learning feature that can find the optimal neural network based on the data. It is an iterative training process that solves an optimization problem given the constraints of the parameters and data to find the network that has a minimum error or loss based on the training dataset. That is why when we configure a large and complex network architecture, the learning time tends to increase exponentially, given the number of computations the algorithm has to do to find the optimal solution.

Local Optimum Situation

In the neural network training process, sometimes we may face the so-called local optimum situation. This situation describes a local optimum which is the optimal solution within a specific neighborhood of candidate solutions. It differs from a global optimum, which represents the optimal solution among all potential solutions, encompassing the entire range of feasible values, rather than being limited to a particular subset. Figure 9.6 illustrates the local optimum vs. global optimum. As you can see, point A shows the global optimum in terms of the lowest error. The training process may result in two local optimums, which are point B and point C, which appear to be the network with the lowest error only within a local set of solutions and do not represent the actual optimum. In other words, the training process may mistake point B or point C as the optimum due to the flaw in the learning algorithm.

Of course, we want a global optimum since the local optimum is not the actual optimal solution and may lead to a poor fit model. Overcoming local optimum problems in neural networks is not an easy task since we must build a very good optimization model, which is not in the scope of this book. However, a local optimum is not always the worst thing. In some cases, when we build larger neural networks, the local optimum with reasonably low error is acceptable. In the above example, we can consider point B acceptable even though it is not the global optimum because it has a reasonably low error. On the other hand, point C is not acceptable due to the high error.

> SAS Enterprise Miner provides three searching approaches under the AutoNeural node: Train, Increment, and Search (default)

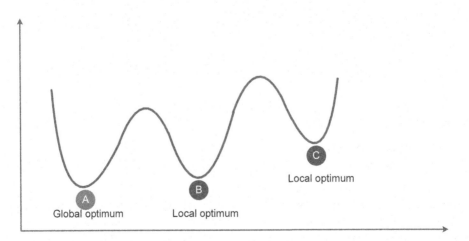

FIGURE 9.6
Global optimum and local optimum.

SAS Enterpriser Miner's Network Searching Methods

SAS Enterprise Miner provides three approaches under the AutoNeural node, as follows.

- *Train*: All chosen functions undergo training until a stopping condition is met.
- *Increment*: Nodes are added one at a time, with no reuse of activation functions. If a layer reduces the average error, it is retained; otherwise it is removed from the model.
- *Search* (*Default*): Nodes are added based on a predetermined architecture and the best-performing network becomes the final model.

As a part of the training process, the Termination property of the AutoNeural node is utilized to specify the termination method. Training always concludes when the maximum runtime is exceeded, and the model that has the best selection criteria is retained.

There are three termination methods as follows.

- *Overfitting* (*Default*): Training terminates when overfitting is detected.
- *Training Error*: Training terminates when the reduction in training data set error is less than 0.001.
- *Time Limit*: Training stops when the time specified in the **Total Time** property is exceeded.

SAS ENTERPRISE MINER GUIDELINES

AutoNeural Node Train Properties

(https://documentation.sas.com)

AUTONEURAL NODE TRAIN PROPERTIES: INCREMENT AND SEARCH

Adjust Iterations – When set to No, the Adjust Iterations property of the AutoNeural node suppresses adjustments that are made to the **Maximum Iterations** property value setting when **Train Action** is set to **Search** or **Increment**. If **Train Action** is set to **Search** or **Increment,** and Adjust Iterations is set to **Yes**, then the **Maximum Iterations** value is adjusted higher if the selected iteration equals the previously used **Maximum Iterations**. Similarly, the **Maximum Iterations** value can be adjusted lower if the selected iteration is significantly lower than the previously used **Maximum Iterations**. The default setting for the Adjust Iterations property is **Yes**.

Freeze Connections – Use the Freeze Connections property of the AutoNeural node to specify whether connections should be frozen. The default setting for the Freeze Connections property is **No**.

Total Number of Hidden Units – Use the Total Number of Hidden Units property of the AutoNeural node to specify the total hidden units ceiling when the Train Action is set to Search. When Search is performed, the total number of hidden units trained is calculated at each run. If the calculated number of total hidden units is greater than or equal to the value stored in Total Hidden, then training stops, and a final model is selected. Permissible values are 5, 10, 20, 30, 40, 50, 75, or 100. The default setting is 30.

Final Training – Use the Final Training property of the AutoNeural node to indicate whether the final model should be trained again to allow the model to converge. If the Final Training property is set to **Yes**, the number of iterations that are used will correspond to the value set in the Final Iterations property.

Final Iterations – Use the Final Iterations property of the AutoNeural node to indicate the number of iterations to use when the Final Training property is set to **Yes**. The Final Iterations property is unavailable if the Final Training property is set to **No**. The Final Iterations property accepts integers greater than zero.

Normalization

Before we start constructing and training a neural network model, there is one last thing we need to know, normalization. The primary purpose of normalization is to convert input and output variables to the same scale, which would help improve the model training efficiency and result interpretation. Many variables are on different scales; sometimes, the difference is very significant, which may cause longer training time and less accurate prediction. In addition, it is also harder to interpret the outputs. By normalizing these variables, we can improve the training efficiency and interpret the results since now all variables are on the same scale.

There are three common normalization approaches. Do not get intimidated by the formulas that I present below. They are quite simple. But I do not focus on them but rather on the ranges of values. The first one is to use z-score, a common approach in statistics. Z-scores, technically speaking, can be any number. But in reality, they usually range between –4 and +4. A more common range for z-score is between –3 and +3. Second, normalization uses max and min values, which produce values in the range from 0 to 1. This method is usually used with the sigmoid activation function. Third, adjusted normalization also uses max and min values with some adjustments, which produces values in the range from –1 to +1. This method is usually used with the hyperbolic tangent activation function. I provide the formulas for these three methods in simple terms as follows.

Z-score method

$$new\ value = \frac{actual\ value - mean\ value}{standard\ deviation}$$

Normalization method using max and min values

$$new\ value = \frac{actual\ value - \min\ value}{\max\ value - \min\ value}$$

Adjusted normalization method

$$new\ value = \frac{2 * \left(actual\ value - \min value\right)}{\max value - \min value} - 1$$

> SAS Enterprise Miner provides the Z-score method and adjusted normalization method (it is called Range in the software) under the HP Neural node.

SAS Enterprise Miner – DMNeural Node

SAS Enterprise Miner has a special node for neural networks, DMNeural. Basically, this node applies a principal components analysis to the training data set to obtain a set of principal components and then uses a small set of principal components for modeling. You can see the detailed description of the DMNeural training process provided by SAS Enterprise Miner below. I won't go into detail. The important thing to remember is that this node automatically configures all hyperparameters for us and finds the best network. We do not have to decide what to use for those parameters. The running time is also shorter. Of course, since it is almost fully automatically configured, there is no guarantee that it provides better models than other nodes. Nonetheless, it is worth adding this node to our modeling process because it does not require any special configurations. We will experiment with this node in our examples.

SAS ENTERPRISE MINER GUIDELINES

DMNeural Node Train Properties

(https://documentation.sas.com)

The DMNeural node enables you to fit an additive nonlinear model that uses the bucketed principal components as inputs to predict a binary or an interval target variable.

The algorithm that is used in DMNeural network training was developed to overcome the following problems of the common neural networks for data mining purposes. These problems are likely to occur especially when the data set contains highly collinear variables.

- **Nonlinear estimation problem** – The nonlinear estimation problem in common neural networks is seriously underdetermined, which yields highly rank-deficient Hessian matrices and results in extremely slow convergence of the nonlinear optimization algorithm. In other words, the zero eigenvalues in a Hessian matrix correspond to long and very flat valleys in the shape of the objective function. The traditional neural network approach has serious problems to decide when an estimate is close to an appropriate solution and the optimization process can be prematurely terminated. This is overcome by using estimation with full-rank Hessian matrices of a few selected principal components in the underlying procedure.

- **Computing time** – Each function call in common neural networks corresponds to a single run through the entire training data set; normally many function calls are needed for convergence of the nonlinear optimization. This requires a tremendous calculation time to get an optimized solution for data sets that have a large number of observations. In DMNeural network training of the DMNeural node, we obtain a set of grid points from the selected principal component and a multidimensional frequency table from the training data set for nonlinear optimization. In other words, segments of the data are trained instead of the entire data, and the computing time is reduced dramatically.

- **Finding global optimal solution** – For the same reason, common neural network algorithms often find local rather than global optimal solutions, and the optimization results are very sensitive with respect to the starting point of the optimization. However, the DMNeural network training can find a good starting point that is less sensitive to the results, because it uses well-specified objective functions that contain a few parameters and can do a very simple grid search for the few parameters.

In the DMNeural training process, a principal components analysis is applied to the training data set to obtain a set of principal components. Then a small set of principal components is selected for further modeling. This set of components shows a good prediction of the target with respect to a linear regression model with an R^2 selection criterion. The algorithm obtains a set of grid points from the selected principal component and a multidimensional frequency table from the training data set. The frequency table contains count information of the selected principal components at a specified number of discrete grid points.

In each stage of the DMNeural training process, the training data set is fitted with eight separate activation functions. The DMNeural node selects the one that yields the best results. The optimization with each of these activation functions is processed independently.

Example: A Classification Model Using Neural Networks

In this example, we will build neural network models for the *airline recommendation* dataset.

Dataset: airlinerecommendation.sas7bdat

Target variable: recommendation (binary): 1 – recommend the airline; 0 – do not recommend the airline.

Sample-Explore-Modify: Refer to previous chapters.

Model

In order to demonstrate different features provided by SAS Enterprise Miner, we build several neural network models using AutoNeural, HP Neural, and DMNeural nodes as follows.

- From the Model tab: AutoNeural and DMNeural nodes.
- From the HPDM tab: HP Neural node.

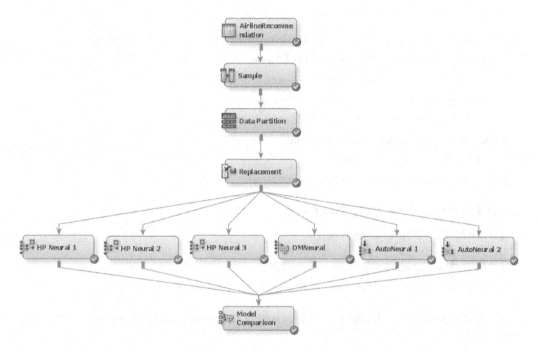

Note: to have the diagram on the vertical layout, right-click on the diagram space, select Layout, and choose Vertically.

Use the following configurations to set up these six neural network models:

Model 1 (AutoNeural 1) – Using Block Layers

In the AutoNeural 1 Train properties:

1. Under the Model Options tab, set the Architecture to Block Layers.
2. Set the Train Action to Search.
3. Set the Termination to Overfitting. Because we have a binary target variable, the misclassification rate of the Validation data set is used.
4. Set the Tolerance to Medium.
5. Set the Number of Hidden Units to 8.
6. Set the Maximum Iteration to 20.
7. Under the Activation Functions tab, set the Direct, Normal, Square, and Tanh properties to Yes. Set the remaining activation functions to No.

Model 2 (AutoNeural 2) – Using Funnel Layers

In the AutoNeural 2 Train properties:

1. Under the Model Options tab, set the Architecture to Funnel Layers.
2. Set other properties the same as Model 1 (AutoNeural 1).

Model 3 (HP Neural 1) – Using One Layer

In the HP Neural 1 Train properties:

1. Under the Network Options, set the Number of Hidden Neurons to 10.
2. Set Architecture to One Layer with Direct.
3. Set the Input Standardization to Z-score.
4. Set the Output Standardization to Z-score.
5. Set Target Activation Function to Identity.
6. Set Target Error Function to Normal.
7. Set the Number of Tries to 10.
8. Set the Maximum Iterations property to 50.

Model 4 (HP Neural 2) – Using Two Layers

In the HP Neural 2 Train properties:

1. Under the Network Options, set Architecture to Two Layers with Direct.
2. Set other properties the same as Model 3 (HP Neural 1).

Model 5 (HP Neural 3) – Using Two Layers with a Different Standardization Approach

In the HP Neural 2 Train properties:

1. Under the Network Options, set Architecture to Two Layers with Direct.
2. Set the Input Standardization to Range.
3. Set the Output Standardization to Range.
4. Set other properties the same as Model 4 (HP Neural 2).

Model 6 (DMNeural Model)

In the DMNeural Train properties:

1. Under the Model Criteria group, set the Selection to ACC.
2. Set the Optimization to ACC.
3. Keep all other properties as default by the software.

Assess

From the Assess tab, drag a Model Comparison node to the workspace and connect it to all neural network models (see the diagram above). The purpose is to compare these models and find out which model is the champion model.

TABLE 9.4

Model Fit Comparison (Validation Results)

Model Description	Misclassification Rate	Gini Coefficient	ROC Index	Lift
HP Neural 1	0.219	0.72	0.85	1.71
AutoNeural 2	0.222	0.69	0.84	1.66
DMNeural	0.231	0.65	0.82	1.62
HP Neural 3	0.232	0.66	0.83	1.65
HP Neural 2	0.233	0.68	0.84	1.67
AutoNeural 1	0.237	0.65	0.83	1.63

In the Model Comparison Train properties.

1. Under Model Selection, set Selection Statistics to Misclassification Rate.
2. Set Selection Table to Validation.

Run the Model Comparison node and open the Results window.

We use the standard result presentation process described in Chapter 6. The validation results are used for comparison. Table 9.4 compares the model fit metrics for all six neural network models. The misclassification rate indicates HP Neural 1 is the model with the highest accuracy (low misclassification rate). Other model fit criteria confirm this outcome since this model has the highest Gini coefficient, ROC index, and Lift value.

We also review the ROC chart and Lift chart to further confirm this result. As shown in Figures 9.7 and 9.8, HP Neural 1 has the best ROC chart (furthest from the baseline) and the best Lift chart (highest Lift value). Thus, we can conclude that among the six neural network models we built, HP Neural is the champion model. We should also note that these six models are very close. For example, HP Neural 1 and AutoNeural 2 have similar model fit. DMNeural is ranked third, which is also an interesting result.

HP Neural 1 Model Performance

Now, we have determined HP Neural 1 model is the champion model. Let's take a closer look at this model. Using the output of the HP Neural 1 node results, which provide the confusion matrix, we can calculate the model fit metrics for this model for training, validation, and test samples (Table 9.5). Again, Gini coefficient, ROC index, and Lift score are extracted from the results of the Model Comparison node. The sensitivity, specificity, and F1-score are calculated from the confusion matrix, extracted from the HP Neural 1 node results. The table indicates that the results for these three samples are very similar, indicating the reliability of the model.

TABLE 9.5

Model Fit Metrics for HP Neural 1 Model

Model Fit Metrics	Training	Validation	Test
Misclassification rate	0.216	0.219	0.218
Accuracy	0.784	0.781	0.782
Sensitivity	0.876	0.870	Not available
Specificity	0.684	0.683	Not available
F1-Score	0.809	0.806	Not available
Gini	0.710	0.720	0.70
ROC index	0.850	0.850	0.85
Lift	1.730	1.710	1.69

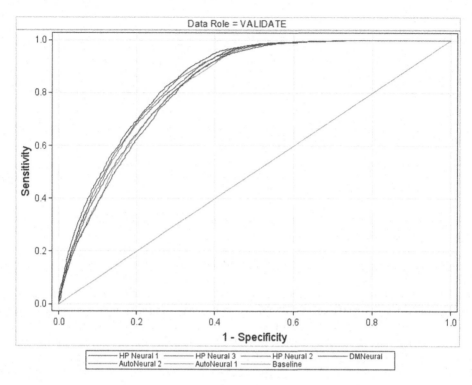

FIGURE 9.7
ROC chart.

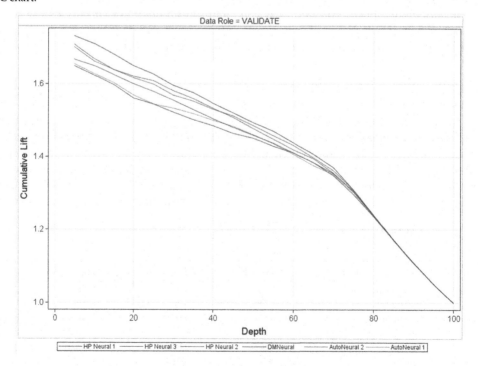

FIGURE 9.8
Lift chart.

Next, we evaluate the validity of the model via the metrics. Since ACC is lower than 80%, we want to look into other metrics as well. The sensitivity is considered acceptable since it is close to 90%, but the specificity is rather low, indicating high false positives. The F-1 score, which balances between sensitivity and specificity, is just about 80%, which is marginal. Finally, a Gini coefficient of 0.72 is considered a good fit, while an ROC index of 0.85 is considered acceptable. Overall, the model can be considered marginally acceptable.

> Note: SAS Enterprise Miner does not produce the confusion matrix for the test sample. While we can get this result by adding some SAS codes, it is not the purpose of this book. Regardless, the information is sufficient for us to compare the model fit across samples. In addition, we use the validation results for model review.

Suppose these model fit metrics are acceptable to the airline, and the model can be selected to make actual predictions. We want to review the neural network itself to understand its architecture and parameters. Figure 9.9 shows the network, predictors, hidden nodes, and weights used for this model. Essentially, the network has one hidden layer

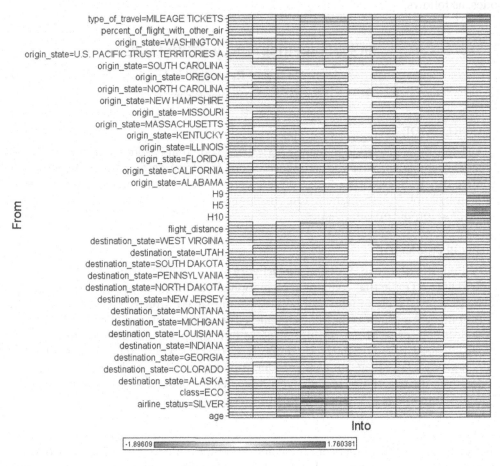

FIGURE 9.9
HP Neural 1 network, nodes, sign, and weights.

with ten hidden nodes. The figure uses color code to present the sign and weights of each input-output path in the network. Blues represent negative relationships, while red represents positive relationships. The darker the color, the higher the weight. However, it is not possible to explain the exact relationships between the predictors and the target variable via this complicated network structure. As you can see, it does look like a black box, which is very hard to interpret.

Variable Importance

Since the neural network looks like a black box, which is not interpretable, we examine the variable importance to review the relative importance of predictors. However, neural networks typically do not produce variable importance results directly as decision trees. Hence, in order to generate variable importance, we use two additional nodes in SAS  Enterprise Miner to do the trick: Score node (from the Assess tab) and Reporter node (from the Utility tab). SAS Enterprise Miner provides some brief descriptions of those nodes, as follows.

SAS ENTERPRISE MINER GUIDELINES

Score Node and Reporter Node

(https://documentation.sas.com)

SCORE NODE

The Score node is used to manage SAS scoring code that is generated from a trained model or models to save the SAS scoring code to a location on your client computer and to run the SAS scoring code. You can score a data set to generate predicted values that might not contain a target. You can also score a data set to create a segment variable or to impute missing values.

REPORTER NODE

The Reporter node uses SAS Output Delivery System (ODS) capability to create a single PDF or RTF file that contains information about the open process flow diagram. The PDF or RTF documents can be viewed and saved directly and are included in SAS Enterprise Miner report package files. The report contains a header that shows the SAS Enterprise Miner settings, process flow diagram, and detailed information for each node. Based on the Node property setting, each node that is included in the open process flow diagram has a header, property settings, and variable summary. Moreover, the report also includes results such as variable selection, model diagnostic tables, and plots from the Results browser.

Basically, by connecting a Score node and Reporter node to our neural network model and setting the right properties, the software can generate predictions, simulate the effects of predictors on the target variables, and produce the variable importance plot. In this case, since we need the variable importance for the HP Neural 1 model, I connect these two nodes to that model, as shown below. Alternatively, since HP Neural 1 is the champion model, we can also connect Score and Reporter nodes to the Model Comparison node, which produces the outcome of the champion model. Nonetheless, I want to show you the approach that you can use for any model.

Follow the steps below.

1. From the Assess tab, drag a Score node to the workspace and connect it to the HP Neural 1 node.
2. From the Utility tab, drag a Reporter node to the workspace and connect it to the Score node.
3. Keep all default settings for the Score node.
4. In the Reporter Train properties
   - Set Nodes to Summary.
   - Set Show All to Yes.
   - Under the Summary Report Options, set Yes to all options.
5. Run the Reporter node and open the Results.

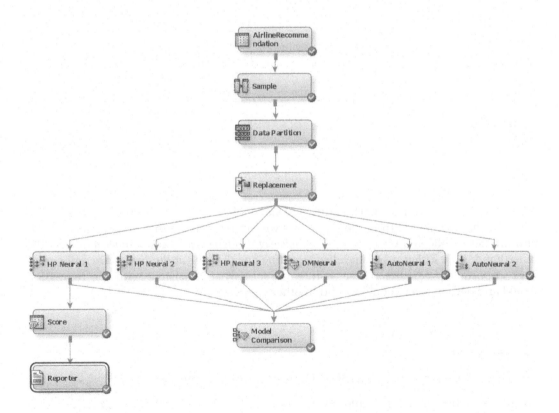

This node creates a report in PDF format. Click View to open the report. In the report, you should see a lot of useful information, including sample information, confusion matrix, model fit statistics, Lift chart, and prediction details. The information we need

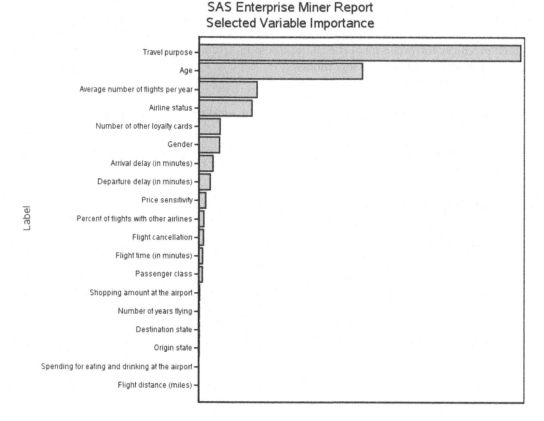

FIGURE 9.10
Variable importance.

is the variable importance chart. Figure 9.10 shows the variable importance chart for HP Neural 1 that I extracted from the report. As we can see, *travel purpose* is the most important predictor, followed by *age, average number of flights per year,* and *airline status.* On the other hand, *flight distance* and *spending for eating and drinking at the airport* are among the least important predictors. These results are somewhat consistent with the regression model and decision tree model we did in other chapters.

Example: An Association Model Using Neural Networks

For an association model, we build several neural network models for the *Boston Housing* dataset.

  Dataset: boston.sas7bdat

  Target variable: *Imv* – median housing value in the Boston area (interval)

  Sample-Explore-Modify: Refer to previous chapters.

Model

Since neural networks work the same way for both classification and association models, we build the exact six models as we did for classification models, using the same configurations. Please refer to the previous example for detailed configurations.

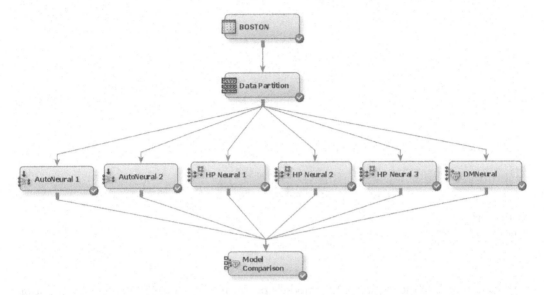

Assess

We use a Model Comparison node to compare those models. From the Assess tab, drag a Model Comparison node to the workspace and connect it to all neural network models.

In the Model Comparison Train properties:

- Under Model Selection, set Selection Statistics to Average Squared Error.
- Set Selection Table to Validation.

Run the Model Comparison node and open the Results window.

Using the output from the Results window, we can have the AVE and RMSE for validation results to compare across models. As shown in Table 9.6, AutoNeural 2 model has the lowest ASE and RMSE, meaning this model produces the most accurate prediction. Hence, we can conclude that among the six models, AutoNeural 2 is the champion model.

TABLE 9.6

Model Fit Comparison Using the Validation Results

Models	ASE	RMSE
AutoNeural 2	14.124	3.758
HP Neural 1	16.945	4.116
AutoNeural 1	21.988	4.689
HP Neural 2	22.824	4.777
DMNeural	25.295	5.029
HP Neural 3	25.917	5.091

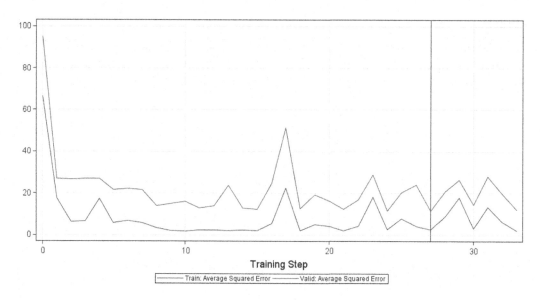

FIGURE 9.11
Iteration plot.

We will look into the details of this model's performance. Figure 9.11 shows the iteration plot based on ASE values. We can see that the training algorithm selects the final model after 27 iterations, where the ASE is the lowest. We can also notice some discrepancies between training and validation results, which is similar to what we have seen in Chapter 8. Keep in mind that the ASE is the average squared value, so the distance represents the squared difference instead of the actual difference.

To further examine the model reliability, we review the mean predicted chart between the training and validation samples (Figure 9.12). The chart shows similar patterns between training and validation samples, indicating that the model has acceptable reliability. It also shows the closeness between mean predicted values and mean target values, indicating the accuracy of the prediction.

In order to further examine the performance of this model, we need the full prediction dataset. As usual, we use the Save Data node to export the prediction data for this model. When we run this node, it will export the training and validation prediction data to our SAS server. Please refer to previous chapters on how to enter the server directory to this node properties and how to use SAS Studio to download the file in Excel. Using the formulas and procedures described in Chapter 6, we can calculate the three additional fit metrics for AutoNeural 2, including MAPE, RSE, and EP, as shown in Table 9.7.

The MAPE of 0.129 shows that the model can predict the median house values with an accuracy of 1–0.129 = 87.1%, which is considered acceptable. The EP of 0.85 indicates that this model can explain 85% of the variance in the target variable based on the variance in the predictors. As indicated in Chapter 6, an EP of 0.7 or more is considered a good model fit. For a comparison purpose, I add the model fit metrics for the CART tree (the best tree model described in Chapter 8) to the table. As you can see AutoNeural 2 has the same prediction accuracy (MAPE = 0.129) but much better explanatory power with RSE of 0.15 and EP of 0.85.

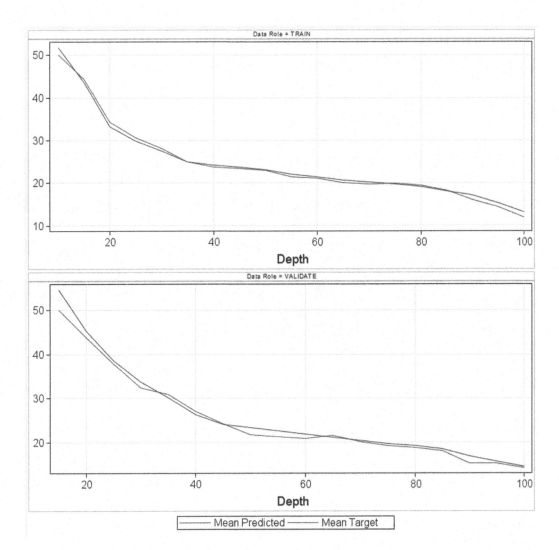

FIGURE 9.12
Mean predicted chart.

TABLE 9.7

AutoNeural 2 Model Fit Metrics

Model Fit Metrics	AutoNeural 2	CART Tree
RMSE	3.758	4.608
MAPE	0.129	0.129
RSE	0.150	0.226
EP	0.850	0.774

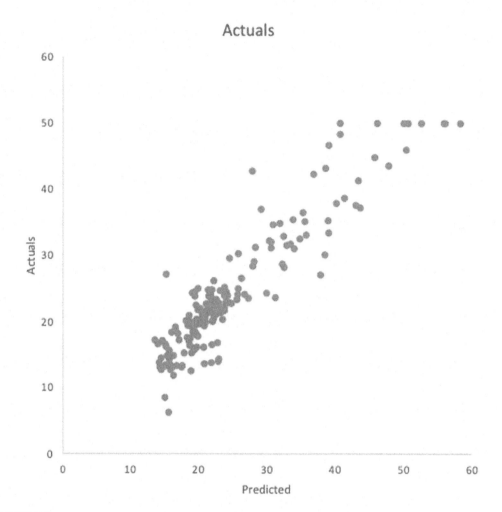

FIGURE 9.13
Actual by predicted chart.

We also review two charts, the actuals by predicted chart and the residuals by predicted chart, using the validation results. As shown in Figure 9.13, the data points are scattered closely to the diagonal line, indicating a good fit. Additionally, Figure 9.14 shows that the residuals seem to be random and show no patterns. Overall, these charts indicate that AutoNeural 2 has a good model fit.

Now, we have determined AutoNeural 2 is the champion model with a good model fit, we dive deeper into the model itself. Figure 9.15 shows the network, nodes, and weights. In order to get this chart, in the Results window, go to View/Model, and select Weights – Final.

As you can see, this network uses three hidden layers with a total of 24 hidden nodes. The figure is color-coded to show the sign of the relationship and weight for each input-output path in the network. Since the network structure is not interpretable, we look at the variable importance instead.

Using the same procedure as described before, we add two nodes (Score and Reporter) to AutonNeural 2. Then we run the Reporter node and receive the report (in PDF) from SAS

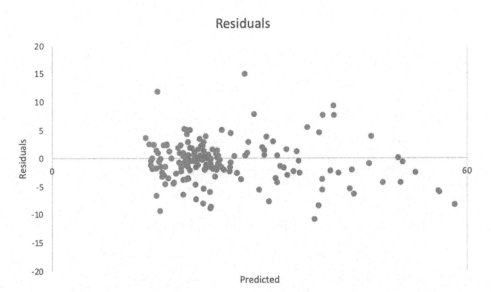

FIGURE 9.14
Residuals by predicted chart.

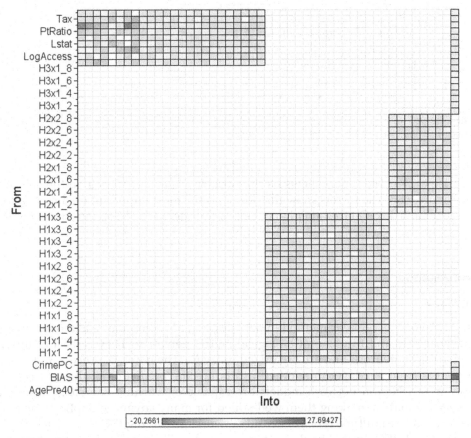

FIGURE 9.15
Neural network, nodes, and weights.

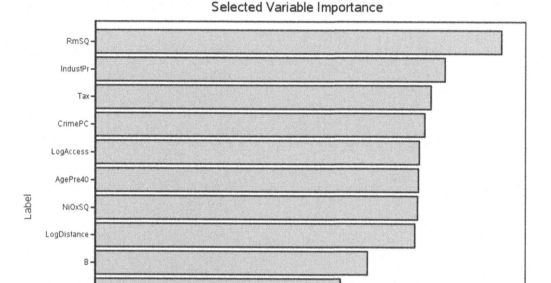

FIGURE 9.16
Variable importance chart.

Enterprise Miner. The report shows us the variable importance based on the neural network (Figure 9.16). The results show that RmSQ is the most important predictor, followed by IndustPr and Tax. On the other hand, Lsat is considered the least important predictor.

Summary

Neural networks, a popular method in data mining, are computational models inspired by the structure and function of biological neural networks. They consist of interconnected artificial neurons and are organized in layers. The network process and transmit information from one layer to another to produce the prediction of the outputs based on the inputs. Neural network models are capable of learning complex patterns and relationships in data, making them well-suited for many advanced applications in data mining. There are multiple types of neural networks, including FNN, CNN, RNN, LSTM network, and RBFN. In this book, we focus on the multi-layer feedforward perceptron (MLP) network.

In this chapter, we learn how the training process for neural networks works. The key idea behind neural networks is to iteratively adjust the weights and biases of the nodes based on input data, which allows the network to learn and make predictions. This learning process is typically achieved through the use of backward propagation, which computes the gradients of a chosen loss function with respect to the network's parameters. By updating the weights and biases that minimize the loss function, neural networks iteratively improve their predictive power.

One of the strengths of neural networks is their ability to model complex, non-linear relationships in data, making them suitable for a wide range of applications. They have achieved remarkable success in computer vision, natural language processing, aviation, finance, healthcare, robotics, and more. However, neural networks are not without challenges. They require a considerable amount of labeled training data to learn effectively and are computationally intensive, especially for deep learning. Overfitting can also be a concern since the model may be overtrained with the training data and fail to generalize to new data. Despite these challenges, the neural network method remains a cutting-edge technique in the field of artificial intelligence, driving innovation, and transforming various industries.

CHAPTER DISCUSSION QUESTIONS

1. What is a neural network, and how does it work?
2. What are the advantages and disadvantages of using neural networks?
3. Neural networks have been successful in various domains. Choose one domain and discuss the specific applications used to leverage neural networks effectively in that domain. What are the primary challenges?
4. How do neural networks differ from traditional machine learning algorithms?
5. What is deep learning, and how is it related to neural networks?
6. What are some common types of neural networks, and what are their strengths and weaknesses?
7. How do you train a neural network, and what are some common training processes?
8. What are the differences between forward propagation and backward propagation?
9. The choice of activation function plays a crucial role in neural network performance. What are common activation functions?
10. What is the multi-layer perceptron (MLP) method? Describe the primary MLP network architectures.
11. Why is Local Optimum Situation a concern? How do we address this issue?
12. Interpretability is a critical concern in neural network models. How can the predictions and decision-making process of a neural network be explained and interpreted?

Exercises

Exercise 1: Neural network models for the Bank dataset

1. Open the *bank* dataset in SAS Enterprise Miner.
2. Sample the entire dataset. See the variable names and descriptions in Appendix A.1.
3. Partition the data using a split ratio of 60:40 (train: 60%; validation: 20%; test: 20%)
4. Perform data modification as follows:
   - Impute missing values.
5. Set *CRSCORE* (credit scores) as the target variable.
6. Configure seven neural network models for this dataset as follows.
   - DMNeural model.
   - AutoNeural model (single layer)
     - Set the Number of Hidden Units to 4.
     - Set the Maximum Iteration to 10.
   - AutoNeural model (block layers)
     - Set the Number of Hidden Units to 8.
     - Set the Maximum Iteration to 20.
   - AutoNeural model (cascade)
     - Set the Number of Hidden Units to 8.
     - Set the Maximum Iteration to 50.
   - HP Neural model (one hidden layer with direct, z-score normalization)
     - Set the Number of Hidden Neurons to 8.
     - Set the Maximum Iteration to 20.
   - HP Neural model (two hidden layers with direct, range normalization)
     - Set the Number of Hidden Neurons to 10.
     - Set the Maximum Iteration to 50.
   - HP Neural model (three hidden layers – user-specified, range normalization)
     - Set the Number of Hidden Neurons to 20.
     - Set the Maximum Iteration to 50.

   Note: Refer to the examples in this chapter for other configurations
7. Compare the model fit metrics between those models using the validation results.
8. Select the champion model and justify this selection with the necessary evidence.
9. Present the results of the champion model.
10. Evaluate the reliability and validity of the champion model.
11. Present the variable importance information and interpret the results.

Exercise 2: Neural network models for the Passengers dataset

1. Open the *passengers* dataset in SAS Enterprise Miner.
2. Sample 20% of the full data. Set *return* (decision to return to the airline) as the target variable and change its role to binary. See the variable names and descriptions in Appendix A.2.
3. Partition the data using a split ratio of 60:40 (train: 60%; validation: 20%; test: 20%)
4. Perform data modification as follows:
   - Replace zero values for Likert-scale variables with missing values.
   - Impute missing values.

5. Configure seven neural network models for this dataset as follows.
   - DMNeural model.
   - AutoNeural model (single layer)
     - Set the Number of Hidden Units to 4.
     - Set the Maximum Iteration to 10.
   - AutoNeural model (block layers)
     - Set the Number of Hidden Units to 8.
     - Set the Maximum Iteration to 20.
   - AutoNeural model (cascade)
     - Set the Number of Hidden Units to 8.
     - Set the Maximum Iteration to 50.
   - HP Neural model (one hidden layer with direct, z-score normalization)
     - Set the Number of Hidden Neurons to 8.
     - Set the Maximum Iteration to 20.
   - HP Neural model (two hidden layers with direct, range normalization)
     - Set the Number of Hidden Neurons to 10.
     - Set the Maximum Iteration to 50.
   - HP Neural model (three hidden layers – user-specified, range normalization)
     - Set the Number of Hidden Neurons to 20.
     - Set the Maximum Iteration to 50.

   Note: Refer to the examples in this chapter for other configurations.
6. Compare the model fit metrics between those models using the validation results.
7. Select the champion model and justify this selection with the necessary evidence.
8. Present the results of the champion model.
9. Evaluate the reliability and validity of the champion model.
10. Present the variable importance information and interpret the results.

10

Ensemble Modeling

LEARNING OUTCOMES

Upon the completion of this chapter, you will be able to

1. Describe the principles and concepts of ensemble methods in machine learning.
2. Explain the concept of diversity in ensemble modeling.
3. Differentiate between the ensemble model and an individual model (base learner).
4. Discuss the advantages and disadvantages of ensemble modeling compared to individual models.
5. Compare different types of ensemble methods, including bagging, boosting, and stacking.
6. Describe aggregation techniques including averaging, voting, weighted voting, and maximum.
7. Develop and test ensemble models using SAS Enterprise Miner.
8. Evaluate the prediction accuracy of ensemble models.

Introduction

In this chapter, we learn about ensemble modeling, a powerful method in machine learning that can help improve the accuracy, robustness, and interpretability of models, while also providing insights into the underlying patterns in the data. The basic idea behind ensemble modeling is that if we have multiple models that have different levels of accuracy or errors on a given dataset, we can combine their predictions to reduce the overall error and increase the  predictive power. Ensemble modeling can be applied to a variety of machine learning models, including classification and association models. It is particularly useful for large and complex datasets where individual models may have difficulty capturing all of the patterns and relationships in the data.

DOI: 10.1201/9781003162872-12

Ensemble modeling can also be used to improve the interpretability of machine learning models by providing insights into the underlying patterns in the data. By combining the predictions of multiple models, we can identify which predictors are most important for making accurate predictions and gain a better understanding of how the models are working. In this chapter, we practice constructing ensemble models in data mining projects.

What Is Ensemble Modeling?

Ensemble modeling is a concept revolving around the idea that combining the predictions of multiple diverse models can lead to better overall performance than any single model in isolation. In simple terms, ensemble modeling is a machine learning method that involves combining the predictions of multiple individual models, called base learners, to produce a more accurate and robust prediction.

DEFINITION

Ensemble modeling is a machine learning method that involves combining the predictions of multiple models to produce a more accurate and robust prediction.

Concept of Diversity

Diversity is a critical concept in ensemble modeling and refers to the differences among the individual base learners that make up the ensemble. It is one of the key factors that contribute to the effectiveness of the ensemble model. The main goal is to ensure that the base learners' strengths and weaknesses complement each other, leading to improved overall performance and robustness. Below are some aspects of diversity in ensemble modeling.

- *Data diversity*: Data diversity refers to using different subsets of the training data to train each base learner. For instance, in bagging-based methods like Random Forest, subsets of the training data are randomly selected with replacement to train individual decision trees. This diversity helps reduce overfitting and allows the ensemble to capture various aspects of the data distribution.
- *Algorithm diversity*: Using different machine learning algorithms as base learners is another way to introduce diversity. Ensemble models often consist of a combination of classifiers or regressors with different underlying principles. For example, a Gradient Boosting Machine (GBM) can be combined with a Support Vector Machine (SVM) and a Neural Network, providing diverse perspectives to the ensemble.
- *Variable diversity*: Ensemble models benefit from variable diversity, which involves using different subsets of variables for training the base learners. This approach is commonly used in ensemble techniques like the Random Subspace Method and Random Patches.

- *Configuration diversity*: Each base learner can be trained with different configurations, such as stepwise, number of hidden units, or tree depth. The ensemble model then leverages a range of hyperparameter configurations, which lead to a more comprehensive exploration of the model's parameter space.
- *Model architecture diversity*: In deep learning ensembles, diversity can be achieved by using various architectures or network structures with different depths, widths, or skip connections. Each architecture captures different hierarchical features, enhancing the ensemble's performance.
- *Training diversity*: Diversity can be introduced during the training process by using different random seeds or initialization methods for each base learner. This ensures that each model starts from a different point in the parameter space and explores different regions during optimization.
- *Domain diversity*: In some cases, domain-specific models or models trained on different datasets can be combined in an ensemble. This is particularly useful in transfer learning scenarios, where knowledge from one domain is leveraged to improve performance in another related domain.

By combining diverse base learners, ensemble models can collectively address different aspects of the data mining process and reduce individual model biases. Diversity is crucial for avoiding the problem of "groupthink," where multiple models end up making similar errors due to similar biases or limitations. Instead, a diverse ensemble fosters a more robust and accurate decision-making process, making ensemble modeling a powerful tool for tackling complex real-world challenges.

Basic Concepts in Ensemble Modeling

Ensemble modeling is a powerful machine learning technique that combines the predictions of multiple individual models to improve overall performance and robustness. Table 10.1 summarizes fundamental concepts in ensemble modeling.

Ensemble Methods

Now, we understand the purpose of ensemble modeling. But, how do we combine the predictions created by multiple models? There are three primary methods for building ensemble models: bagging, boosting, and stacking.

Bagging

Bagging is the short form for bootstrap aggregating. Bootstrapping is a sampling technique where samples are derived from the whole dataset using the replacement

TABLE 10.1

Basic Concepts in Ensemble Modeling

Terms	Description
Ensemble	Ensemble is a machine learning method that involves combining the predictions of multiple models to produce a more accurate and robust prediction.
Diversity	The primary strength of ensemble models lies in the diversity of their individual models. By using different learning algorithms or training on different subsets of the data, the ensemble captures various patterns and reduces the risk of overfitting.
Base learners (individual models)	Base learners are the individual models that constitute the ensemble. Base learners can be any machine learning algorithm, such as decision trees, support vector machines, neural networks, etc.
Aggregation methods	Ensemble models combine the predictions of base learners using aggregation methods. Common aggregation methods include averaging, voting, and weighted voting. The aggregated result is often more accurate and reliable than the predictions of individual models.
Bagging	Bagging is an ensemble method that involves training multiple base learners independently on different random subsets of the training data (sampling with replacement). The final prediction is typically an average or voting over the predictions of all the base learners.
Boosting	Boosting is an iterative ensemble method where base learners are trained sequentially, and each learner focuses on correcting the mistakes made by its predecessors. Boosting assigns higher weights to misclassified instances, effectively giving more attention to challenging samples.
Stacking	Stacking (stacked generalization) is a more complex ensemble technique that combines the predictions of multiple base learners by training a meta-model on their outputs. The meta-model learns to weigh the predictions of individual models effectively.
Ensemble size	The number of base learners in an ensemble is an important consideration. Increasing the ensemble size can lead to better performance up to a point, after which the returns diminish, and the model may become computationally expensive.
Model selection and tuning	Ensemble models require careful selection and tuning of base learners and configurations. Different combinations of models and configurations can significantly impact the model's performance.

procedure, and aggregation combines all possible outcomes of the prediction and randomizes the outcome. In bagging, we create multiple models by training each one on a different subset of the training data. The subsets are created by randomly sampling the data with replacement. The predictions of these models are then averaged to produce a final prediction.

Bagging is particularly useful for reducing the variance in the model. Since the models in the ensemble are trained on different subsets of the data, they may have different biases and variances. By combining their predictions, the ensemble model can produce a prediction that has a lower variance than any individual model. Figure 10.1 shows how bagging works.

Boosting

Boosting is an ensemble technique that learns from previous predictor mistakes to make better predictions in the future. In boosting, we train multiple models sequentially. Each model in the sequence is trained on the residual error of the previous model. This approach helps correct the errors of the previous model and produce a more accurate prediction. The predictions of these models are then combined to produce a final prediction.

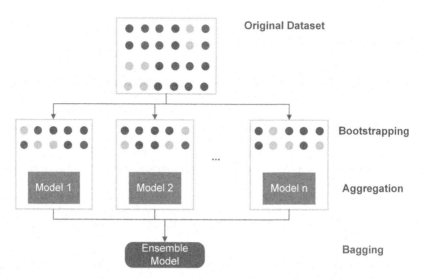

FIGURE 10.1
Bagging method.

Boosting is very useful for reducing bias in the model. Since each model in the sequence is trained on the residual error of the previous model, it helps to correct any biases in the previous model. This approach can lead to more accurate predictions, particularly in classification problems. Boosting is explained in Figure 10.2.

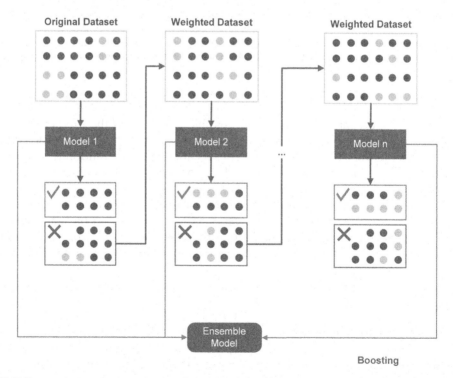

FIGURE 10.2
Boosting method.

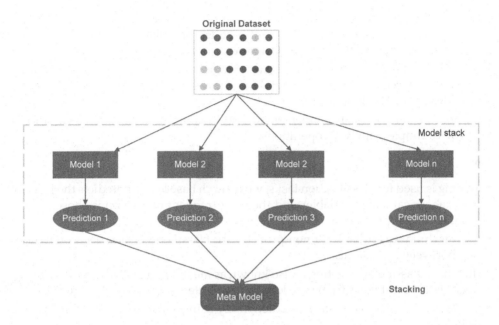

FIGURE 10.3
Stacking method.

Stacking

Stacking is often referred to as stacked generalization. In stacking, we train multiple models and use their predictions as input to another model (meta-model). In other words, these predictions from individual models are used as the training data for the meta-model. The new model learns how to weigh the predictions of each model to produce a final prediction (Figure 10.3).

Stacking is useful when the individual models in the ensemble have different strengths and weaknesses. By combining their predictions in a way that minimizes their weaknesses, the ensemble model can produce a more accurate prediction.

Aggregation Methods

Ensemble modeling involves combining the predictions of multiple base learners to obtain a more accurate and robust final prediction. In this process, aggregation methods are used to calculate or determine the final ensemble prediction from individual models. Some common aggregation methods used in ensemble modeling include averaging, voting, weighted voting, and maximum.

Averaging

- In averaging, the predictions of individual base learners are combined by taking their arithmetic mean (for regression) or their weighted mean (for classification).
- For regression tasks, the ensemble prediction is the average of the individual predictions, resulting in a smoother and more stable final prediction.

- In probabilistic classification, averaging the probabilities of the level (of the categorical target variable) from different base learners helps in obtaining a more confident estimate of the event probabilities.
- It is particularly effective in reducing variance and improving model stability since the aggregated predictions tend to be less sensitive to outliers or noisy predictions from individual models.
- Averaging can be easily implemented and is computationally efficient since it involves simple arithmetic operations.

Voting

- Voting is used for classification tasks, where each base learner predicts the level (of the categorical target variable), and the most frequent prediction is chosen as the final ensemble prediction.
- This technique is suitable for non-probabilistic classifiers, such as decision trees or support vector machines.
- In binary classification, voting is also known as majority voting, where the level that receives the most votes from base learners is selected as the ensemble prediction.
- It can handle ties or conflicting predictions by using a majority or weighted voting scheme.
- Voting ensembles work well when individual models are diverse and have complementary strengths in different regions of the feature space. This allows the ensemble to exploit different decision boundaries and improve overall classification accuracy.
- Voting is easy to interpret, and the final prediction corresponds to the most commonly agreed-upon level among the base learners.

Weighted Voting

- Weighted voting is an extension of the voting technique, where each base learner's prediction is assigned a weight based on its performance.
- The final ensemble prediction is a weighted combination of the individual base learners' predictions, with higher-performing models carrying more influence.
- Weighted voting allows the ensemble to emphasize the predictions of stronger models, potentially leading to improved overall accuracy.

Maximum

- In the maximum technique, the final ensemble prediction is obtained by selecting the maximum prediction from the individual models.
- It is commonly used when the ensemble models are non-probabilistic associations, such as decision trees or neural networks.
- For classification models, the maximum of the posterior probabilities (for categorical targets) is used as the final ensemble prediction.
- For association models, the maximum of the predicted values (for interval targets) from different models is used as the final ensemble prediction.
- The maximum technique is suitable for problems where the final prediction should be more conservative and tends to favor the most confident predictions from individual models.

These aggregation methods can be applied to various types of problems and base learners. Each of them has its strengths and applications in ensemble modeling. The choice of the appropriate method depends on the characteristics of the data, the nature of the individual models, and the desired properties of the ensemble model.

Advantages and Disadvantages of Ensemble Modeling

Ensemble modeling is a popular machine learning technique that combines multiple models to produce more accurate predictions. While ensemble modeling has several advantages, there are also some disadvantages that should be considered. In this section, we discuss both the advantages and disadvantages of ensemble modeling.

Advantages of ensemble modeling

- Increased accuracy: Ensemble modeling can improve the overall predictive accuracy of the model by combining the predictions of multiple models. By leveraging the strengths of each individual model while minimizing their weaknesses, ensemble modeling can produce more accurate predictions than any individual model.
- Improved generalization: By using ensemble modeling we can improve the generalization of the model by reducing overfitting. Since the ensemble model is made up of multiple models, it is less likely to be biased toward a particular type of data, making it more suitable for real-world applications where the data may be varied.
- Robustness: Ensemble modeling enhances the robustness of the model since it reduces the impact of noisy data. Since the models in the ensemble are trained on different subsets of the data, they may not be affected by the same noise in the data. This can help to produce more accurate predictions even when the data is noisy.
- Versatility: Ensemble modeling can be applied to a wide range of machine learning tasks, including association and classification models.

Disadvantages of ensemble modeling

- Increased complexity: Ensemble modeling can be more complex than training a single model. Since ensemble models involve multiple models, they may require more computing time to train.
- Overfitting: While ensemble modeling can reduce overfitting, it can also lead to overfitting if not done correctly. If the individual models in the ensemble are too similar or the ensemble is too complex, it may be prone to overfitting.
- Interpretability: Ensemble modeling can be less interpretable than individual models. Since the ensemble model is made up of multiple models, it is more difficult to interpret the contribution of each individual model to the final prediction.
- Data requirements: Ensemble modeling may require more data than individual models. Due to the combination of multiple models, we may need more data to train each individual model, which increases the data requirements for the overall model.

Overall, ensemble modeling is a powerful technique that can improve the accuracy and generalization of machine learning models. While there are some disadvantages to ensemble modeling, the benefits often outweigh the drawbacks, making it a popular choice for many machine learning applications.

SAS Enterprise Miner – Ensemble Node

SAS Enterprise Miner has an Ensemble Node, which allows us to aggregate results from multiple models. Keep in mind that the Ensemble Node in SAS Enterprise Miner does not actually have the specific three ensemble methods we described before (bagging, boosting, and stacking). However, it provides three methods for aggregating the results of multiple models: average, maximum, and voting. Before explaining these methods, I want to note that the prediction results are different for classification models (categorical target variables) from association models (interval target variables). More specifically,

- *Classification models*: The prediction results are posterior probabilities of the target variable.
- *Association models*: The prediction results are the predicted values of the target variable.

> SAS Enterprise Miner's Ensemble node does not offer explicitly three ensemble methods (bagging, boosting, and stacking). Instead, it provides three aggregation methods for combining results of multiple models.
>
> In order to create bagging and boosting models, we need to use Start Groups node and End Groups node.

With that in mind, SAS Enterprise Miner provides three aggregation methods as follows.

- *Average*: In this method, the prediction from the Ensemble node is determined by taking the average of the posterior probabilities (for categorical targets) or predicted values (for interval targets) from different models. This calculation is performed irrespective of the target event level.
- *Maximum*: The Maximum method selects the highest posterior probability (for categorical targets) or predicted value (for interval targets) from among the different models as the prediction from the Ensemble node.
- *Voting*: This method is specifically designed for categorical targets. When using the Voting method to compute posterior probabilities, there are two sub-methods available: Average and Proportion.
  - *Average*: When using the Average method for voting posterior probabilities, the Ensemble node calculates the posterior probabilities based on the models that predict the same target event. For example, if models M1, M2, and M3 predict event level J1, while model M4 predicts event level J2, the posterior probability for J1 in the Ensemble node would be computed by averaging the posterior probabilities of J1 from models M1, M2, and M3, and model M4 is not considered.
  - *Proportion*: In the Proportion method for voting posterior probabilities, individual model-generated posterior probabilities are disregarded. Instead, the

Ensemble node computes the posterior probability for a specific target value (e.g., J1) based on the proportion of individual models that predict the same event level. For instance, if models M1, M2, and M3 predict the target value J1, and model M4 predicts J2, the posterior probability for J1 in the Ensemble node would be calculated as 3/4.

SAS ENTERPRISE MINER GUIDELINES

Ensemble Node Train Properties

(https://documentation.sas.com)

ENSEMBLE NODE TRAIN PROPERTIES: INTERVAL TARGET

- **Predicted Values** – Use the Predicted Values property of the Ensemble node to specify the function that you want to use to combine models for interval targets. The function choices are **Average** and **Maximum**. The default setting is **Average**.

ENSEMBLE NODE TRAIN PROPERTIES: CLASS TARGET

- **Posterior Probabilities** – Use the Posterior Probabilities property of the **Ensemble** node to specify the method that you want to use to combine probabilities for class targets. The choices are **Average**, **Maximum**, and **Voting**. The default setting is **Average**.

- **Posterior Probabilities for Voting** – Use the Posterior Probabilities for Voting property of the **Ensemble** node to specify the method that you want to use to compute the posterior probabilities when the function to combine models is voting, with class targets (binary, ordinal, or nominal). The method choices are **Proportion** and **Average**. The default setting is **Average**.

SAS Enterprise Miner – Start Groups and End Groups Nodes

In order to build bagging and boosting ensemble models in SAS Enterprise Miner, we use two different nodes: Start Groups node and End Groups node.

- The Start Groups node is employed to process data iteratively, repeating the group processing part of the process flow diagram multiple times. It offers modes like bagging and boosting, though it doesn't directly provide the stacking method. The Target mode is the closely related option to the stacking method, and it can be utilized to construct an ensemble model.

- The End Groups node serves to delineate the boundaries of the group processing part within a process flow. It aggregates results, whether from bagging, boosting, or target models. It is important to note that the End Groups node can only be used in conjunction with the Start Groups node. Additionally, the End Groups node must follow the Start Groups node in the process flow diagram and should be succeeded by at least one other node after the Start Groups node.

SAS Enterprise Miner Guidelines

Start Group Node Train Properties

(https://documentation.sas.com)

Mode – Specifies the looping mode that you want the **Start Groups** node to use. Exceptions for the High-Performance Data Mining nodes are noted.

- **Index** – The index mode setting specifies the number of times to loop through the group processing portion of the process flow diagram. No additional sampling or model averaging is performed.
- **Bagging** – Unweighted resampling for bagging is the most straightforward method of resampling. Unweighted resampling uses random sampling with replacement to create the n-sample replicates. You set the number of samples (and in turn, models) that you want to create in the Index Count property in the General section of the Train properties. Unweighted resampling does not apply extra weight to the cases that were misclassified in the previous samples. When you specify the Bagging mode, you should specify settings for the Type, Percentage, and Random Seed properties in the Bagging properties section.
- **Boosting** – The boosting mode performs weighted resampling to create boosting models. Boosting models are a modification of bagging models. Boosting models use a frequency variable that has a value proportional to the model residual. Rows that are incorrectly sampled are given higher frequency values, so the next model will consider them more significantly.
- **Target** – The target mode loops for each target variable that is identified in the training data. The target looping mode creates similar models for a number of targets, such as modeling a competitive cross-sell scenario.
- **Stratify** – Use the Stratify mode to perform standard group processing. When you use the Stratify mode, the **Start Groups** node loops through each level of group variable when you run the process flow diagram. When you select the Stratify mode, the Minimum Group Size and Target Group properties are enabled.
- **Cross-Validation** – The cross-validation looping mode is a modification of the stratified mode. You use the cross-validation mode when you want to export the complement of the groups specified, as opposed to the groups themselves.

No Grouping – No looping is performed. You might want to suppress the node from looping to reduce the run time during preliminary model building.

Example: A Classification Model Using Ensemble Node

In this example, we build an ensemble model for the *airline recommendation* dataset using the Ensemble node.

Dataset: AirlineRecommendation.sas7bdat

Target variable: *Recommendation* (binary): 1 – recommend the airline; 0 – do not recommend the airline.

Sample-Explore-Modify: Refer to the previous chapters.

Model

In this step, we use the Ensemble node to combine three models we configured before, including the Regression model (Chapter 7), Pruned CART Tree (Chapter 8), and HP Neural 1 (Chapter 9). Then we also compare this ensemble model with those individual models to see which model performs better.

Follow the steps below to create an ensemble model.

- Add three previous models to the same diagram– Regression model (Chapter 7), Pruned CART Tree (Chapter 8), and HP Neural 1 (Chapter 9). See the diagram below.

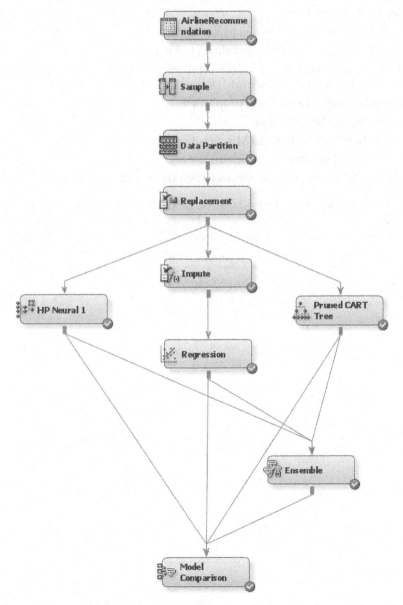

- Configure those models using the same configurations in the previous chapters.
- From the Model tab, drag an Ensemble node to the workspace and connect it to HP Neural 1, Regression, and Pruned CART Tree.

TABLE 10.2

Model Comparison Results

Model Description	Valid: Misclassification Rate	Valid: Gini	Valid: ROC	Valid: Lift
Pruned CART Tree	0.20889	0.66	0.83	1.61
Ensemble	0.21234	0.63	0.82	1.46
HP Neural 1	0.21909	0.7	0.85	1.71
Regression	0.23042	0.6	0.83	1.65

- In the Ensemble Train properties.
  - Under the Class Target:
    - Set Posterior Probabilities to Voting.
    - Set Voting Posterior Probabilities to Proportion.
- From the Assess tab, drag a Model Comparison node to the workspace and then connect it to Ensemble, HP Neural 1, Regression, and Pruned CART Tree.
- In the Model Comparison Train properties:
  - Under the Model Selection:
    - Set Selection Statistic to Misclassification Rate.
    - Set Selection Table to Validation.
- Run the Model Comparison node and open the Results window.

First, we compare the performance of those models. The comparison results are shown in Table 10.2 with four model fit metrics: misclassification rate, Gini coefficient, ROC index, and Lift value for the validation sample. Figures 10.3 and 10.4 present the ROC chart and

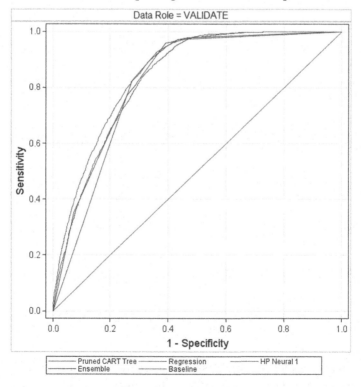

FIGURE 10.4
ROC chart.

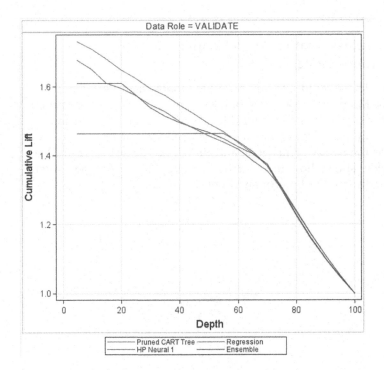

FIGURE 10.5
Lift chart.

Lift chart, respectively. The Pruned CART Tree appears to have the lowest misclassification rate of 0.2889, followed by the Ensemble model, HP Neural 1, and Regression. If we examine other metrics, HP Neural 1 seems to perform better with the highest Gini coefficient, ROC index, and Lift value. The Ensemble model seems to be in the middle. Figures 10.4 and 10.5 also incorporate this outcome, showing HP Neural 1 has a slightly better ROC curve and higher Lift than other models. Thus, in this example, the Ensemble model using the voting aggregation method does not perform better than the individual models. One explanation is that this node combines those three models using the voting option, and the outcome may be affected by the poor performance of the Regression model. Note that this ensemble model mainly aggregates the results from individual models using the voting method. Ensemble methods, such as bagging, boosting, and stacking are not used in this case.

Suppose we want to focus on the misclassification rate, we compare this rate across three samples. Table 10.3 provides the misclassification rates for three samples: training, validation, and test. As you can see, the results are consistent across those three samples, indicating the reliability of the models. The comparison also shows that the Pruned CART Tree has the highest accuracy, followed by Ensemble and HP Neural 1. Regression has the lowest prediction accuracy.

TABLE 10.3

Misclassification Rate for Three Samples

Model Description	Valid: Misclassification Rate	Train: Misclassification Rate	Test: Misclassification Rate
Pruned CART Tree	0.20889	0.20768	0.2056
Ensemble	0.21234	0.21354	0.214
HP Neural 1	0.21909	0.21601	0.2188
Regression	0.23042	0.23408	0.2358

Example: A Classification Model Using Start Groups and End Groups Nodes

In this example, we build several Ensemble models using three ensemble methods. More specifically, we build bagging, boosting, and target ensemble models for the Pruned CHAID Tree we developed in Chapter 8. Then, we compare and determine which model performs best. For this purpose, the Start Groups node and En Groups node are used. The diagram below shows how to construct bagging, boosting, and target ensemble models in SAS Enterprise Miner.

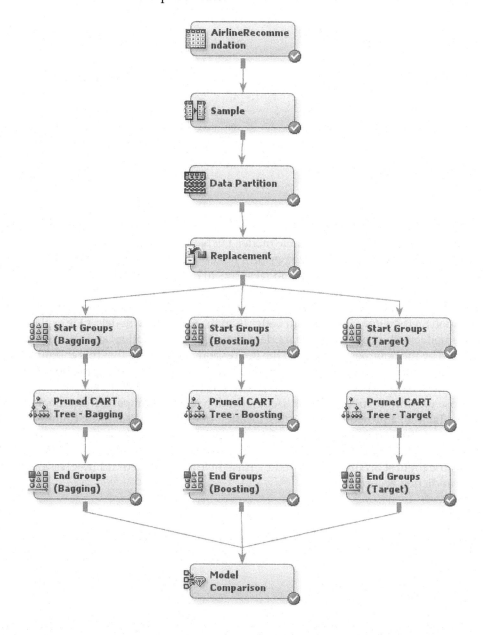

Follow the steps below to build those ensemble models:

- To build a bagging ensemble model for the Pruned CART tree:
  - From the Utility tab, drag a Start Groups node to the workspace and connect it to the Replacement node.
  - In the Start Groups Train properties:
    - Under General property, set Mode to Bagging.
    - Set Index count to 50.
    - Under Bagging, Set Type of Percentage.
    - Set Percentage to 100.
  - From the Model tab, drag a Decision tree node to the workspace and connect it to the Start Groups node. Configure the CART tree model using configurations described in Chapter 8 (you can also copy and paste this node from the Decision tree diagram). Name it Pruned CART Tree – Bagging.
    - From the Utility tab, drag an End Groups node and connect it to the Pruned CHAID Tree – Bagging node.
- To build a boosting ensemble node, follow the same steps, except for the Start Groups node, set Mode to Boosting, and set Index count to 50.
- To build a target ensemble node, follow the same steps, except for the Start Groups node, set Mode to Target, and keep the remaining properties as default.
- From the Assess tab, drag a Model Comparison node to the workspace and connect it to all three End Groups nodes.
- In the Model Comparison Train Properties:
  - For Model Selection:
    - Set Selection Statistic to Misclassification Rate.
    - Set Selection Table to Validation.
- Run the Model Comparison node and open the Results window.

First, we compare the three models. Table 10.4 shows the model comparison results with the misclassification rate, Gini coefficient, ROC index, and Lift value using validation results. Figures 10.5 and 10.6 present the ROC chart and Lift chart, respectively. The target model has the lowest misclassification rate, followed by the bagging model. The boosting model has the highest misclassification rate. If we examine other model fit metrics, we can notice that the bagging model has the highest ROC index, Gini coefficient, and lift value.

TABLE 10.4

Model Comparison Results

Model Description	Valid: Misclassification Rate	Valid: Gini	Valid: ROC	Valid: Lift
Target Model	0.20889	0.66	0.83	1.61
Bagging Model	0.21355	0.68	0.84	1.68
Boosting Model	0.43215	0.64	0.82	1.55

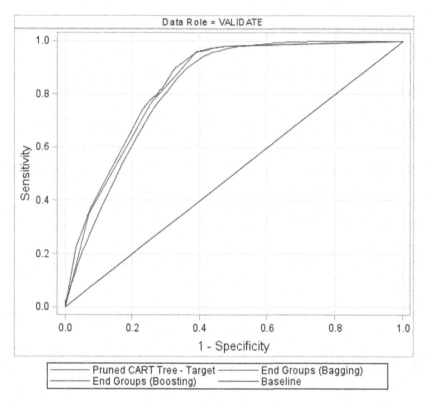

FIGURE 10.6
ROC chart.

Reviewing Figures 10.6 and 10.7 shows us a similar result that the bagging model has the best ROC chart and Lift chart. We should also note that the bagging model performs better than the best individual model in the previous example (pruned CART tree) in all metrics except for the misclassification rate.

To compare between samples, we present the misclassification rates for the three models in Table 10.5. The results show consistent outcomes between the samples, confirming the reliability of the models.

With these results, which model should be selected depends on the purpose of the project and the organization's strategy. As we have noticed, the bagging model works better than the target model, except for the misclassification rate. We also know that we should not rely solely on the misclassification rate. Hence, we need to look further into sensitivity, specificity, and F1-score. Table 10.6 compares those metrics between the target model and the bagging model.

TABLE 10.5

Misclassification Rate for Three Samples

Model Description	Valid: Misclassification Rate	Train: Misclassification Rate	Test: Misclassification Rate
Target Model	0.20889	0.20768	0.2077
Bagging Model	0.21355	0.21295	0.2129
Boosting Model	0.43215	0.42727	0.4272

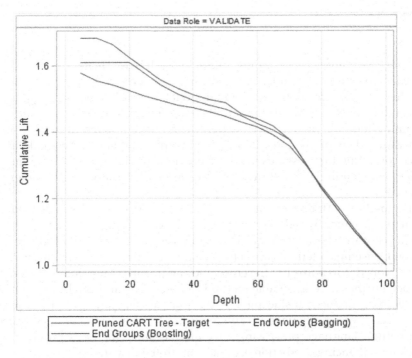

FIGURE 10.7
Lift chart.

The results indicate that the target model has a lower misclassification rate due to a higher sensitivity. However, the bagging model has a better specificity. The reason is that the target model has a higher rate of false positives. As a reminder, sensitivity measures how well the model predicts the true positives (events), and specificity measures how well the model predicts the true negatives (non-events). The target model has a slightly better F1-score. Thus, the decision-maker should make the decision based on the organization's priority and strategy. If predicting the true positives (passengers recommending the airline) is the main focus, then the target model is the best.

> I do not provide an example using the Boston dataset because the process and configurations are the same. You can practice with this dataset by following the guidelines.

However, if the priority is the true negatives (passengers not recommending the airline) and the decision-maker wants to consider multiple metrics, such as Gini coefficient, ROC index, and Lift value, then the bagging model should be selected.

TABLE 10.6

Comparison between the Target Model and the Bagging Model

Metrics	Target Model	Bagging Model
Valid: Misclassification rate	0.20889	0.21355
Valid: Sensitivity	0.95849	0.89929
Valid: Specificity	0.60794	0.66296
Valid: F1-score	0.82745	0.81485

Summary

Ensemble methods involve combining multiple models to create a more accurate and robust predictive model. The underlying principle is that the collective predictions of multiple models can outperform any individual model. Ensemble methods come in various forms, including bagging, boosting, and stacking. Bagging methods, create an ensemble by training multiple models independently on different subsets of the training data and aggregating their predictions. Boosting methods iteratively train weak learners and emphasize correcting the mistakes made by previous models. Finally, stacking combines the predictions of multiple models as input to a higher-level model, often referred to as a meta-learner.

Ensemble methods offer several advantages. First, they tend to provide improved generalization performance by reducing overfitting. By combining diverse models, ensemble methods can capture a broader range of data patterns and decrease the variance of predictions. Second, ensemble methods are robust against noise and outliers. Individual models may make errors due to noise, but the ensemble's aggregated predictions can help mitigate their impact. Furthermore, ensemble methods are versatile and can be applied to various machine learning projects, including classification, association, and anomaly detection. They have been successfully used in a wide range of domains, including finance, healthcare, and natural language processing. Overall, ensemble methods provide a powerful framework for enhancing prediction accuracy and reliability in data mining.

We also need to keep in mind that it is not a guarantee that the ensemble model always outperforms the individual models. It depends on the data and the purpose of data mining. As mentioned before, there is no such thing as a perfect method. There is always the best model for our data. Hence, we do not know if ensemble modeling is a good choice or not until we include it in our modeling process. Additionally, ensemble modeling still requires careful configuration tuning since we combine models based on different machine learning methods. Nonetheless, ensemble modeling is a viable option for us to consider when we build multiple predictive models.

CHAPTER DISCUSSION QUESTIONS

1. How do ensemble methods differ from individual models in terms of predictive performance and generalization capability?

2. What are the advantages and disadvantages of using ensemble methods compared to single models?

3. Can ensemble methods handle imbalanced datasets effectively? If yes, how do they address the issue of class imbalance?

4. Discuss the concept of model diversity in ensemble methods. How does diversity contribute to the overall performance of the ensemble?

5. What are some common methods for generating diversity in ensemble methods, such as bagging, boosting, and stacking? How do these techniques enhance the ensemble's predictive power?

6. In what scenarios would ensemble methods be particularly beneficial and suitable for a data mining project? Are there any specific domains or types of problems where ensemble methods have shown significant success?

7. Discuss the computational complexity of ensemble methods. Are there any techniques or optimizations that can be employed to improve their efficiency for large datasets?

8. Explain the concept of ensemble size and its impact on the performance of ensemble methods. How does the number of models in the ensemble affect prediction accuracy and computational resources?

9. What are some potential challenges or limitations of ensemble methods that researchers and practitioners should be aware of? How can these challenges be addressed or mitigated in practice?

Exercises

Exercise 1: Ensemble models for the Bank dataset

1. Open the *bank* dataset in SAS Enterprise Miner.
2. Sample the entire dataset. See the variable names and descriptions in Appendix A.1.
3. Partition the data using a split ratio of 60:40 (train: 60%; validation: 20%; test: 20%)
4. Perform data modification as follows:
   - Impute missing values.
   - Normalize the data.
5. Set *CRSCORE* (credit scores) as the target variable.
6. Build an ensemble model using the Ensemble node for four individual models. Configure it as follows:
   - Use the Average aggregation method for the Predicted value (under the Interval target).
   - Combine the results from four individual models: linear regression (Chapter 7 exercise), pruned CHAID tree (Chapter 8 exercise), DMNeural (Chapter 9 exercise), and HP Neural with two hidden layers with direct (Chapter 9 exercise).
7. Compare the ensemble model with the four individual models using the validation results. Which model has the best performance?
8. Build two ensemble models using the Start Groups node and End Groups node as follows.
   - Combine the results from four individual models: linear regression (Chapter 7 exercise), pruned CHAID tree (Chapter 8 exercise), DMNeural (Chapter 9 exercise), and HP Neural with two hidden layers with direct (Chapter 9 exercise).
   - Build a bagging model combining those four individual models.
   - Build a target model combining those four individual models.
9. Compare the model fit metrics between those two ensemble models using the validation results. Which model has the best performance?

Exercise 2: Ensemble models for the Passengers dataset

1. Open the *passengers* dataset in SAS Enterprise Miner.
2. Sample 20% of the full data. Set *return* (decision to return to the airline) as the target variable and change its role to binary. See the variable names and descriptions in Appendix A.2.
3. Partition the data using a split ratio of 60:40 (train: 60%; validation: 20%; test: 20%)
4. Perform data modification as follows:
   - Replace zero values for Likert scale variables with missing values.
   - Impute missing values.
5. Build an ensemble model using the Ensemble node for four individual models. Configure it as follows:
   - Use the Voting aggregation method for the Poster Probabilities (under the Class target). Select Proportion for the Voting Poster Probabilities.
   - Combine the results from four individual models: logistic regression (Chapter 7 exercise), pruned CHAID tree (Chapter 8 exercise), DMNeural (Chapter 9 exercise), and HP Neural with two hidden layers with direct (Chapter 9 exercise).
6. Compare the ensemble model with the four individual models using the validation results. Which model has the best performance?
7. Build three ensemble models using the Start Groups node and End Groups node as follows.
   - Combine the results from four individual models: logistic regression (Chapter 7 exercise), pruned CHAID tree (Chapter 8 exercise), DMNeural (Chapter 9 exercise), and HP Neural with two hidden layers with direct (Chapter 9 exercise).
   - Build a bagging model combining these four individual models.
   - Build a boosting model combining these four individual models.
   - Build a target model combining these four individual models.
8. Compare the model fit metrics between these three ensemble models using the validation results. Which model has the best performance?

11

Presenting Results and Writing Data Mining Reports

LEARNING OUTCOMES

Upon the completion of this chapter, you will be able to

1. Explain the importance of writing an effective data mining project report.
2. Differentiate between academic research reports, technical reports, and business reports.
3. Identify the target audience for your report and determine the right writing styles.
4. Outline a general structure of a data mining project report.
5. Describe the purpose and content of primary sections in a report.
6. Evaluate approaches for effective writing.
7. Implement various approaches to hook the audience and keep their interest in your report.
8. Write an effective title, abstract, introduction, literature review, methodology, results, discussions, and conclusions for a data mining report.

Introduction

In the previous chapters, we have covered the most important parts of data mining, prepared the data, and performed the data analysis. We have gone through all the steps in the SEMMA process, including sample, explore, modify, model, and assess. We have the data mining results, the champion model, and detailed structure and detailed patterns in this model. The next step is to write up the report. Sounds simple enough? Not really. Data mining is a complex process with many steps and many decisions

we made. It consists of machine learning algorithms, configurations, and results. The results include multiple diagrams, tables, and graphs. Given the overwhelming information, it is important to select and present the appropriate results and write the report in a well-organized format to avoid confusing the readers. We may have done some good

DOI: 10.1201/9781003162872-13

analyses and achieved useful results. But if we do not produce a quality report, the audience and stakeholders may not be able to understand what we did and what we achieved, or even worst, they may misunderstand our outcomes. Consequently, a poorly written report may lead to incorrect decisions that result in business failures or incidents.

In this chapter, I provide specific guidelines for writing a data mining report, with more emphasis on the result presentation. I will give you guidelines, tips, and specific examples as demonstrations. Just keep in mind that I use a hypothetical study of airline recommendations as an example. It is not an actual research study, so there are some parts of the report I can only provide recommendations on how to write them. Nonetheless, for some important sections, such as Introduction, Methodology, and Results, I will provide specific examples of how to write certain statements or explanations.

Note that I focus on technical writing skills, not writing in general. My assumption is that you already have good general writing skills and are familiar with standards such as APA. It is not the purpose of this chapter to show how to structure a sentence, form phrases, or write correct grammar. We focus on the technical aspects, with more emphasis on what content we should present in each section. Additionally, I keep the writing style mixed between scholarly writing and business report writing. Scholarly writing allows us to be objective in presenting the results. Thus, we can avoid inducing our own opinions or biases in the report. All statements and conclusions are substantiated by the data and analysis results. However, while scholarly writing is favored in academic research, it tends to be very formal, with extensive use of passive voice, which may not be suitable for professionals and industrial audiences. I assume this type of report may have a mixture of target audiences, including researchers, executives, business managers, consultants, project managers, and policymakers. Hence, I use more active voices in sentences and keep the tone less academic.

It would be best if you also practiced writing every day. No one can become a great writer in one day, especially technical writing, which requires a specific skill set. The more you write, the better writer you become. By writing every day, even just a little, you will feel more comfortable with technical writing and can fix any weaknesses.

What Are the Different Types of Reports?

Before we get into writing the report, we need to understand different types of reports and our audiences. Depending on the target audience and the purpose of the study, we can decide what type of report we need to write, structure requirements, and writing styles. We all have heard the saying, "Know your audience." It could not be any more true in this case. Table 11.1 describes three primary types of data mining reports and their key differences.

It's important to note that the characteristics and specific requirements of these reports may vary across different disciplines, industries, or organizations. The comparison above shows some characteristics of those types of reports, but it's always recommended to consult the specific guidelines or requirements provided by the respective institutions or organizations.

In this chapter, I provide general guidelines and tips without specifying any standards or specific requirements. You should read the guidelines provided by the organization, so you know the structure, standards, and styles they require for the report. Remember, they are the ones who will read your report.

TABLE 11.1

Different Types of Data Mining Reports

Items	Academic Research Reports	Technical Reports	Business Reports
Purpose	• The primary purpose of academic research reports is to present new knowledge, advance a particular field of study, and satisfy the requirements of academic institutions. • They aim to explore research questions, present findings, and make scholarly contributions.	• Technical reports are generally focused on presenting technical information related to a specific technical project, funded by an organization. • They are often used to communicate technical details, methodologies, and results within a specialized domain.	• Business reports are prepared to address specific business needs and objectives. • They provide information, analysis, and recommendations to support decision-making in a business context.
Audience	• The common audience of academic research reports is the academic community, including researchers, scholars, and students in a specific discipline or field of study.	• Technical reports are intended for technical professionals, engineers, project stakeholders, or individuals with a specific interest or expertise in the subject matter.	• Business reports are tailored for business professionals, stakeholders, executives, managers, or individuals involved in strategic decision-making within an organization.
Structure	• Academic research reports typically follow a standard structure, including sections such as abstract, introduction, literature review, methodology, results, discussion, and conclusion. • They may also include an extensive list of references and citations.	• Technical reports often include sections such as an abstract, introduction, problem statement, technical background, methodology, results, discussion, conclusions, and recommendations. • They may also contain technical diagrams, charts, or graphs specific to the subject matter.	• Business reports may vary in structure depending on the specific purpose, but they often include sections such as executive summary, introduction, business problem, business background, methodology, analysis, findings, recommendations, and conclusion. • They may also incorporate financial data, market analysis, or business strategy components.
Writing style	• Academic research reports typically adopt a formal and objective writing style. • They focus on providing a thorough analysis, using clear and concise language, and adhering to the conventions of academic writing. • All statements must be supported by references, and all sources must be cited properly in compliance with a specific standard.	• Technical reports are characterized by a precise and technical writing style. • They emphasize accuracy, clarity, and the use of technical terminology relevant to the subject matter. • Statements, interpretations, and conclusions must be substantiated by facts and analysis results.	• Business reports may vary in writing style depending on the intended audience and the project purpose. • They can range from formal and professional to more concise and business-oriented language. • The tone may be persuasive, informative, or analytical, depending on the report's objective.

General Structure of a Project Paper Using Data Mining

A good data mining research report should be well-organized, clearly written, and logically structured. It should provide sufficient details about the research problem, purpose of the study, background information, research process, data, methodology, and results to ensure reproducibility. Furthermore, it should effectively communicate the significance of the findings and their implications in the field of study.

Figure 11.1 shows the general structure of a data mining report. Typically, it consists of a project title, abstract, introduction, literature review, methodology, results, discussions and conclusions, references, and appendices. The literature review part is usually

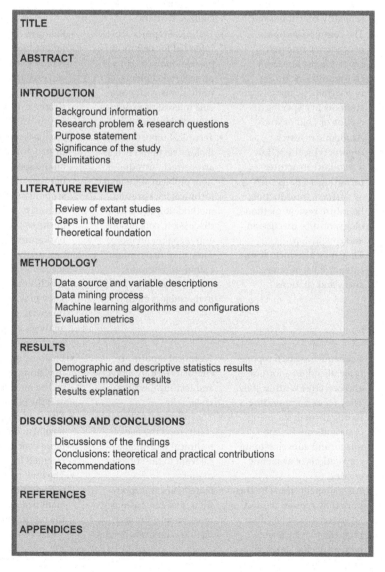

FIGURE 11.1
Structure of a data mining report.

the required section for academic reports. Nonetheless, for technical or business reports, this section can be replaced with background information describing existing technologies or systems and the foundation for our

> I use the structure and outline for academic research reports due to its standardized organization. This structure is logical for a data mininhg project and easy to follow. It can be adjusted easily for other types, such as technical reports or business reports with modifications in the Literature Review sections and Discussions and Conclusions section.

project framework or model. Additionally, appendices are optional, and we usually use this section to include full details, instruments, design, supplemental analysis, or results that we do not need to put in the main report, but we want to make available for the readers to view. The readers can refer to these details if they have further questions or need the details to replicate the study.

Table 11.2 explains each section in detail. Note that each main section usually comprises sub-sections. These sub-sections allow us to break down the content into categories, which makes it easier for the readers to follow.

How to Follow My Writing Guidelines?

In order to help you follow my guidelines and examples of report writing, I developed some specific color codes and formats as follows. Keep in mind that I use a hypothetical study of airline recommendations instead of an actual research study since we have been using the *airline recommendation* dataset in all chapters of this book. Hence, for some parts, I provide tips and recommendations rather than actual writing, which requires conducting an actual research study.

Hypothetical Research Project: Prediction of Passengers' Airline Recommendations

Figure 11.2 shows the format of my writing guidelines. Below are the instructions for using this format.

- *Bold and capitalized text* indicates the section of interest.
- *Texts in the white background* provide the purpose of the section and general guidelines and tips. Those guidelines are typically broken down into key points with specific recommendations.
- *Texts in light blue shade* are the actual examples of writing with full sentences and specifics. They provide you with demonstrations on how to phrase certain statements. Those statements are specific to the airline recommendation project and the data mining context. They would help you learn how to write an effective title, abstract, problem statement, purpose statement, research questions, and delimitations. More importantly, you learn how to

> In these examples, I do not use strictly scholarly writing styles for academic research papers. Instead I mix it with business report writing styles and use more active voices in sentences.

write statements for the methodology and results of a data mining study.

TABLE 11.2

Detailed Descriptions of the Report Sections

Sections	Description	Purpose
TITLE	A concise and descriptive summary of the research topic. It should be clear, informative, and capture the main focus of the study.	It attracts the attention of readers by informing the primary focus of the study.
ABSTRACT	A concise summary of the entire research paper. It briefly introduces the research problem, objectives, methodology, key findings, and conclusions.	It helps the readers quickly understand the essence of the study without having to read the entire paper.
I. INTRODUCTION	Providing an introduction on the topic, identifying the research problem or question, and explaining the significance and relevance of the study.	The introduction sets the stage for the research and communicates clearly the purpose of the study.
• Background information	An overview of the domain or problem being addressed, including relevant literature and prior research.	
• Research problem and research questions	Clear articulation of the research problem and the specific research questions being investigated.	
• Purpose statement	Specific objectives of the research.	
• Significance of the study	Explanation of why this research is important.	
• Delimitations	Scope of the study (what are included and what are excluded, and why).	
II. LITERATURE REVIEW	Providing an overview of the current knowledge in the field, identifying key theories and foundational frameworks, and highlighting any gaps or controversies in the literature.	It helps situate the study within the broader academic context and justifies the research objectives.
• Review of extant studies	Review of relevant literature and prior research in this field of study.	
• Gaps in the literature	Highlights of research gaps in the literature.	
• Theoretical foundation	Theories and foundations for the research framework or model.	
III. METHODOLOGY	Explaining the overall approach, including the study's research design, data sources, data collection methods, sample size, and any statistical or analytical techniques employed.	It allows the readers to replicate the methodology or assess the validity of the study.
• Data source and variable descriptions	Description of the data sources, sampling process, and any preprocessing steps performed.	
• Data mining process	Steps in the data mining process.	
• Machine learning algorithms and configurations	Explanation of the machine learning methods and specific configurations for the models in the study.	
• Evaluation metrics	Specification of the model fit metrics used to assess the model performance and compare models.	
IV. RESULTS	Presenting the findings of the study in a clear and organized manner.	It aims to objectively present the outcomes of the research without interpretation or discussion.

(Continued)

TABLE 11.2   (*Continued*)

Detailed Descriptions of the Report Sections

Sections	Description	Purpose
• Demographic and descriptive statistics results	Presentation of key demographic and descriptive statistics results using charts and tables. The results are used to justify the generalizability of the study.	
• Predictive modeling results	Clear and well-organized presentation of the results, using charts and tables. Key results include model evaluation and comparison, champion model, and important predictors and their rankings.	
• Result explanation	In-depth analysis and explanation of the findings, highlighting the key patterns, trends, or relationships discovered.	
V. DISCUSSIONS AND CONCLUSIONS	Discussing the implications, significance, and limitations of the findings; comparing them to previous research; offering explanations or theories to explain the outcomes; providing recommendations for the industry and future research.	It interprets the results in light of the research objectives and broader context and explains the contributions of the research.
• Discussions of the findings	Discussion of key findings and their implications in relation to the research objectives; explanations of the results in the context of the topic; comparison with existing literature; and highlight of new discoveries.	
• Conclusions	Theoretical and practical contributions; discussion of the novel insights, contributions, or advancements resulting from the research; acknowledgment of any limitations.	
• Recommendations	Suggestions for further research or potential areas of investigation based on the current findings.	
REFERENCES	Properly cited references to acknowledge prior work and support the claims made in the report (check with the publisher or funding organizations for the reference standard).	It provides the readers with reliable and valid sources used to support the study.
APPENDICES	Additional information, such as detailed descriptions of algorithms, data samples, supplementary analysis, full results, and full graphs that support the main findings.	It includes full details and supplemental analysis that are not presented in the main report.

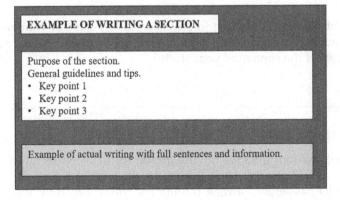

FIGURE 11.2
Format for the writing guidelines.

How to Write the Title?

When writing a title for a research paper, it is important to create a concise and informative statement that captures the essence of your study. Following are some useful guidelines for writing a good title:

1. *Be clear and specific*: Your title should clearly convey the main focus of your research. Avoid using vague or general terms. Instead, use specific and descriptive language that accurately represents the content of your paper.

2. *Keep it concise*: Aim for a title that is brief and to the point. Typically, research paper titles are around 8–15 words long. Avoid lengthy and convoluted titles that may confuse or lose the reader's attention.

3. *Use keywords*: Include relevant keywords that reflect the main concepts, methods, or variables of your research. These keywords will help readers quickly identify the topic and content of your paper. It can also improve the discoverability of your research in online databases or search engines.

4. *Be informative*: Your title should provide a clear idea of what the research paper is about. It should hint at the purpose, scope, or findings of your study, giving readers a preview of what they can expect from the paper.

5. *Consider the tone*: The tone of your title should align with the overall style and purpose of your research. It can be descriptive, objective, provocative, or even creative, depending on the nature of your study and the target audience.

6. *Spell the acronyms*: If you use an acronym in the title, make sure to spell it out since not all readers are familiar with the acronym. Typically, acronyms should only be used if they are absolutely necessary.

7. *Review existing titles*: Look for examples of titles from related research papers in your field. Analyze their structure, language, and effectiveness. This can provide you with inspiration and insights into how to craft your own title.

8. *Write the title last*: It is often helpful to write the title after you have completed the rest of the research paper. This way, you have a clearer understanding of the main findings and contributions of your study, making it easier to create a title that accurately represents your work.

Remember that the title is the first impression readers have of your research paper. It should be informative, engaging, and relevant to attract the attention of potential readers and accurately reflect the content of your study.

Example: Writing a Title

Below are examples of four titles we can use for the airline recommendation project. We should clearly communicate the purpose of the study, which is to predict passengers' airline recommendations. Secondly, the use of the data mining method should also be specified in the title.

Predicting Passengers' Airline Recommendations Using Data Mining Methods

Using Machine Learning Algorithms to Predict Passengers' Airline Recommendations

Predictive Modeling for Passengers' Airline Recommendations

How Do We Predict Passengers' Recommendations of the Airline Using Machine Learning?

How to Write an Abstract?

An abstract is the first thing that readers read about the paper. Hence, it plays a very important role in getting the readers' attention and interest. Most readers don't jump in and read the entire paper immediately. Usually, they read the abstract carefully first. Once they understand the purpose and findings of the **ABSTRACT** study, they will decide whether they should read the full paper. If they see the relevance, novelty, and usefulness of the study, they will dive into the details of the paper. A good abstract should get the readers' attention and interest, which convinces them to read the paper in detail. On the other hand, a poor abstract may confuse and lose the readers at the first read. Consequently, they may skip the whole thing.

Writing an abstract for a research paper involves summarizing the key elements of your study in a concise and engaging manner. Here are some steps to help you write an effective abstract:

1. *Understand the requirements*: Familiarize yourself with any specific guidelines or requirements provided by the target journal, conference, or publishing organization. Pay attention to word limits, formatting, and any specific sections or elements they expect to be included in the abstract.

2. *Identify the purpose*: Typically, abstracts aim to provide a concise overview of the research problem, objectives, methodology, key findings, and conclusions. Determine what information is most essential to convey and what aspects of your study are most important to highlight.

3. *Structure the abstract*: While the specific structure may vary depending on the requirements, most abstracts include the following elements:
   - *Context*: Start by providing a brief context of your research. Explain the research problem or question you aimed to address.

- *Purpose*: Describe the objectives of the study that allow you to find the answer to the research questions.

- *Methods*: Summarize the research design, methodology, and data collection procedures employed in your study. Include briefly any relevant details about the sample size, data analysis techniques, or experimental setup.

- *Results*: Present the key findings or outcomes of your research. Highlight the most significant and noteworthy results that directly address the research objectives.

- *Conclusions*: State the main conclusions or implications of your study. Explain the significance and relevance of your findings and how they contribute to the broader field of research.

4. *Be clear and concise*: Abstracts are typically limited in word count, so it's crucial to convey your information succinctly. Use clear and concise language and avoid unnecessary jargon or technical terms. Make every word count to effectively communicate the essence of your study.

5. *Add keywords*: Incorporate relevant keywords or phrases that reflect the main concepts, variables, method, or design of your research. It is a common practice to add keywords to the end of the abstract. These keywords can help index your abstract in databases and make it more discoverable to readers searching for related studies.

6. *Write and revise*: Start by drafting your abstract and ensuring that you cover all the necessary elements. Once you have a draft, review and revise it multiple times. Make sure each sentence contributes to the overall clarity and coherence of the abstract. Remove any unnecessary details or repetitions.

7. *Check the style and formatting*: Verify that your abstract adheres to any required style or formatting guidelines, such as font size, margins, or referencing style. Pay attention to any specific instructions provided by the target journal or conference.

8. *Proofread and edit*: Finally, proofread your abstract for grammar, typos, spelling, and punctuation errors. Edit for clarity and readability. Make sure that the abstract is well-written, engaging, and accurately represents the content and contributions of your research.

Remember, the abstract serves as a concise summary of your research, allowing readers to quickly grasp the key aspects and significance of your study. It should be engaging, informative, and well-crafted to capture the attention and interest of potential readers.

Example of Writing an Abstract

Following are some key points you should write in an abstract with specific writing demonstrations for the airline recommendation paper.

Brief introduction of the research problem.

The airline industry has faced some operational and business disruption challenges due to pilot shortages, lack of ground staff, flight delays and cancellations, and unstable services. Some airlines experienced losing passengers to other carriers and need to develop strategic actions to improve their competitive advantages. Their primary challenges are to find a way to predict passengers' airline recommendations and find out what variables are associated with the recommendations.

Describe the purpose of the study.

The purpose of this study is to build predictive models that predict passengers' airline recommendations and identify important predictors.

Describe the data and methodology.

The data mining method was selected, and various machine learning algorithms were used to develop predictive models. Data collected from the airline passenger survey provided by [*add the data source*] were used to train and validate the models with a sample size of 100,000 responses. Primary machine learning algorithms included logistic regression, decision trees, and neural networks.

Present the primary findings.

The results indicated that the high-performance neural network model with one layer was the champion model with the best predictive power. The output of this model showed travel purpose as the most important predictor, followed by age, average number of flights per year, and airline status.

Explain the contributions of this study.

These findings provide the airlines with useful information and a decision-supporting tool that they can use to predict the demand and establish appropriate strategies to enhance their competitive advantage in the competing market.

Keywords: Select keywords that not only capture the essence of the study but also help improve the index of the paper.

Keywords: airline industry; airline recommendation; data mining; machine learning; predictive modeling; neural network; decision tree; regression; predictive power; model fit

How to Write an Introduction Section?

The introduction section of a research paper serves as the opening statement, which sets the stage for your study and captures the reader's interest. The readers tend to read this section very carefully to understand the purpose of the study, why it is important to academia and industry, the scope of  the study, and any novel direction or method we took. By understanding those critical points, they can follow the rest of the paper easily. If the introduction is unclear or inconsistent, the readers may decide that this paper does not provide them with any useful information and will stop reading it.

It is not an exaggeration that the introduction section is the hardest section to write. There are some important steps you can follow to make sure you write a good introduction section, as follows.

1. *Hook the reader*: Begin your introduction with a captivating opening sentence or a compelling fact that grabs the reader's attention. You can use an anecdote, a relevant quote, a startling statistic, or a thought-provoking statement. The goal is to intrigue the reader with curiosity and make them want to continue reading.

2. *Provide context*: Give a brief overview of the study area and provide the necessary context information to help readers understand the relevance of your study. Explain why the topic is important and highlight any real-world implications or applications.

3. *State the research problem*: Clearly state the specific research problem or question that your study aims to address. Be concise and precise in formulating your research problem to avoid ambiguity or confusion. This statement should highlight the gap or limitation in the existing knowledge that your study seeks to fill.

4. *Review previous research*: Summarize the key findings and contributions of previous studies related to your research topic. This literature review should focus on the most relevant and recent research. Identify any gaps, controversies, or unanswered questions in the existing literature that your study aims to address.

5. *Outline objectives and scope*: Clearly state the research objectives or hypotheses that your study intends to achieve. These objectives should be specific and align with your research problem.

6. *Scope and limitations*: State the scope (delimitations) and limitations of your study to set appropriate expectations for the reader.

7. *Justify the research*: Explain why your study is important and necessary from both theoretical and practical perspectives. Discuss the potential benefits, advancements, or contributions that may arise from your research findings. Demonstrate the significance of your study in advancing the field of research or addressing a practical issue.

8. *Preview the methodology*: Provide a brief overview of the research design and methodology employed in your study. This includes mentioning the data collection methods, target population, or analytical techniques. However, save the detailed description of the methodology for the methodology section of your paper.

9. *Structure and organization*: Briefly outline the organization of your research paper by mentioning the main sections and their order. This helps readers understand the flow of your paper and locate specific information they may be interested in.

10. *Maintain clarity and conciseness*: Ensure that your introduction is clear, concise, and focused. Avoid unnecessary technical jargon, excessive details, or length sentences. Use simple and straightforward language to make it accessible to a wide range of readers.

11. *Include citations*: Provide appropriate citations for the sources you reference in the background section. This helps support the credibility of your research and allows readers to explore the referenced studies for more in-depth information.

12. *Write and revise*: Start by drafting the introduction section and incorporating the points discussed above. Once you have a draft, review and revise it multiple times. Make sure that the information flows logically, the tone is engaging, and the introduction effectively sets the stage for your research.

Again, the introduction section sets the stage for your study and captures key points in the research project. It should generate interest and motivate readers to continue reading your paper to learn more about your research findings and conclusions.

Example of Writing an Introduction Section

Before I break down the section into subsections for the airline recommendation paper, I want to show you a complete introduction section of a research paper I published in 2021 in the Journal of Air Transport Management. It provides you with a complete example of an actual introduction section in an actual research study published in a top-tier academic journal. This section follows the same format and guidelines I presented before. You can access the full paper via the reference below.

Figure 11.3 shows the introduction section of this paper. It is broken down by paragraph and shows how each paragraph describes each part of the introduction section.

- *Paragraph 1*: Hooks the reader to the topic of COVID-19 and how the travel restrictions and spread of the coronavirus have impacted individuals in their lives, personal trips, and transportation choices.

- *Paragraph 2*: Provides the context of the study by focusing on the air travel volume and why I chose to measure it by the number of domestic and international flights instead of the number of passengers.

- *Paragraph 3*: States the research problem by describing the challenges the airline industry was facing, especially the substantial losses they took due to the pandemic.

- *Paragraph 4*: States the research question: What will the air travel demand be during and post-pandemic?

- *Paragraph 5*: Reviews previous studies and highlights their shortcomings.

1. Introduction

The COVID-19 pandemic has significantly affected the airline industry. In order to reduce the spread of coronavirus, many countries have issued travel restrictions, especially air travel, to limit the travel volume. In the United States, many states limit air travel by mandating self-quarantine for people arriving from other states or countries by air. This requirement has affected many business and personal trips as it causes disruption in business operations or personal activities. Many organizations have moved to working from home and using Zoom meetings to avoid any interruption. People chose to travel by car whenever possible. As a result, travel has reduced significantly. Figs. 1 and 2 show the comparison of commercial flights between 2019 and 2020. It appears that the number of commercial flights, both domestic and international, has declined significantly amid the pandemic. Before the pandemic, there was an average of 25,000 domestic flights and 4300 international flights per day in 2019. Since early April 2020, when most states issued stay-home orders, the number of flights reduced significantly to less than 10,000 domestic flights and about 500 international flights per day. While these numbers started to rise again in early July 2020, they are still far below the number of flights in the same month in 2019. From July to December 2020, the number of daily domestic flights was about 15,000, whereas daily international flights ranged from 1000 to 1500 (BTS, 2020a).

In this study, air travel is measured by the number of domestic and international flights. While flights during the pandemic may not be full, this number is not too far off the actual travel demand. Fig. 3 shows the actual number of people checked in daily at U.S. airports for both domestic and international flights. We can note the similar trends of these numbers compared to the trends of domestic and international flights. There was a sharp fall in April 2020, followed by a slow gain from June to August 2020. Then, the demand gradually increased toward the end of December 2020. Thus, the number of flights does capture well the patterns of travel demand by U.S. residents. One advantage of using the number of flights is that it allows airlines to easily estimate their revenues and expenses in the future, which helps determine the timeline for the airline industry recovery.

The decreased air travel has had negative impacts on the airline industry. According to BTS (2020b), U.S. airlines reported substantial losses in three consecutive quarters in 2020, with a loss of $5.2 billion in the first quarter, $11 billion in the second quarter, and $11.8 billion in the third quarter in both domestic and international operations. Compared to high profits accumulated in 2019, with $4.5 billion profit in the third quarter and $3.4 billion profit in the fourth quarter, these losses pose a significant risk to the airline industry and its future. In order to cope with these losses, many airlines have furloughed or laid off many employees, which results in a bigger challenge for the economy in the near future. According to Mr. Calio, the CEO of Airlines for America, the airline industry will not fully rebound until 2024 (Blum, 2020). Given the uncertainty in the trend of the pandemic and the vaccine rollout timeline, the time it takes for the airline industry to come back to normal may even be more uncertain.

While it may take some time for the airline industry to fully recover, it is vital to understand what the industry will look like in the meantime. More specifically, the overarching question that needs answers is what will be air travel during and post COVID-19. Air travel will certainly continue to be on the low side during the pandemic and may start growing after the pandemic. But to what extent? What will air travel be in different COVID-19 remediation scenarios? What will air travel be after the pandemic? The answers to these questions can provide useful information about the status of the airline industry in the medium and long term.

The traditional literature in air travel prediction tends to focus on macro factors, such as population demographics, location, economic, consumption expenditure, and deregulation, and micro factors, including airlines' service, pricing, and quality (Wang and Song, 2010; Valdes, 2015). While these factors still play an important role in determining air travel demand, they do not reflect how the demand changes amid a pandemic, especially an unprecedented one like COVID-19. The airline industry has never experienced anything like this before, including the September 11 event. The impact of COVID-19 on society and transport behavior is dynamic and unpredictable with a high uncertainty level. Thus, a good prediction needs a capability to capture the dynamism of the pandemic and the change in people's travel behavior. The literature on COVID-19's impact on air transportation is rather limited and focused primarily on the impact differences between regions and how airlines reacted to travel restrictions. A specific model that can predict air travel during and post COVID-19 is still missing.

The purpose of this paper is to predict air travel in the U.S. during and post COVID-19 using novel variables. These novel variables are U.S. residents' daily trips by distance since their daily travel decisions change dynamically according to their risk perception of COVID-19. Research shows that the more trips people make amid the pandemic, the safer they feel in their travels (Beck and Hensher, 2020). In addition, the trip distance does play an important role in their travel behavior in responding to changes in COVID-19 cases and deaths. More specifically, the residents tend to make short trips right after they notice the decrease in COVID-19 cases and deaths, while it takes them more time to decide to make medium and long trips (Truong and Truong, 2021). Thus, it is possible that residents' daily travel behavior can capture the dynamism of the transport pattern during and post pandemic. Finding whether these novel variables can predict air travel is the purpose of this study. Other input variables include the economic index, COVID-19 variables, and travel restrictions in order to capture the spread and severity of the pandemic and the economic condition. Neural network and Monte Carlo simulation are appropriate methods to find a pattern of relationship between input variables and air travel and to perform what-if-scenarios to predict the air travel volume during and post COVID-19. This paper's findings add value to the air transportation literature by examining the effects of novel variables, daily trips by distance, and modeling the air travel under uncertainty. The sensitivity analysis results provide a prediction of air travel in various scenarios, which can help the government and airlines make informed decisions to formulate policies and strategies to survive this crisis. It is important to note that this paper does not aim at performing time series forecast, as this method assumes temporal dependency of the air travel. Given the rapidly changing situation of COVID-19 and unclear patterns in the past, time series forecast models may need to be updated frequently to be meaningful (Truong and Truong, 2021). Accordingly, the simulation results in this paper can provide more useful information to run several what-if scenarios to examine how air travel will be during and post pandemic.

The paper is organized as follows. Section 2 reviews the existing literature in air travel prediction and COVID-19's impacts on air transportation. Research gaps are discussed, along with the explanation for the contributions of this study. Section 3 describes the data sources, variables, and research methodologies, including neural network and Monte Carlo simulation. Section 4 provides detailed results of the neural network models, simulation results, and sensitivity analysis results. Finally, Sections 5 and 6 discuss the research findings, implications of the study, and recommendations for future research.

FIGURE 11.3
Example of an Introduction Section (Truong, 2021a).

- *Paragraph 6*:
  - Describes the objectives of the study, which is to predict air travel during and post-COVID-19 using novel variables. The novelty of the study is the focus on the daily trips by distance. Further references are provided to justify the selection of these variables.
  - States the methodology, which is the use of machine learning and Monte Carlo simulation methods.
  - Justifies the importance of the study and how the findings would benefit the airlines and government.
  - Describes the scope of the study and its limitations. Specifically, this study focuses on building simulations based on the relationships between input variables and air travel volume. Time series forecasts are not used.
- *Paragraph 7*: Describes the organization of the paper and the purpose of each section.

As you can see, writing an introduction section requires a lot of effort since you need to present a lot of important information concisely and informatively in one or two pages. Now, let me show you how we can write the introduction for the airline recommendation paper.

Introduction for the Airline Recommendation Paper

Since it is not an actual research study and I use this dataset for the examples of machine learning in this book, I am not able to show you how to write a full research paper on this topic. Nonetheless, I provide you with specific guidelines and tips on how to write each sub-section and how to get the attention of the reader. I provide specific writing demonstrations for the problem statement, research questions, and purpose statement.

How to Hook the Reader?

Write about some recent incidents occurring in the airline industry. Describe and elaborate on one or two incidents, such as flight delays or cancellations, that caused passengers' dissatisfaction with a certain airline. Provide statistics on airlines losing passengers and suffering business losses.

How to Provide the Context of This Paper?

Focus on the context of airline recommendations for airlines and why it is an important topic for the airline industry. It is important to define airline recommendations of an airline to make sure the readers understand what you are examining. You can also provide some studies or statistics showing how airline recommendations may lead to the success or failure of an airline.

How to State the Research Problem and Research Questions?

Describe clearly the new challenges that the airline industry is facing and why it is important to understand how passengers decide to recommend an airline to other passengers.

It is important to note that if there are many studies addressing this issue, it is not a good research problem anymore, even if it still exists. The point is that you want to tackle a new problem that has yet to be addressed in the literature since it allows you to justify the originality of your study. If other researchers have addressed the same problem, then the topic is no longer original.

Below is an example of a short problem statement. Keep in mind that you need to build up to this statement through the context information above.

> The recurring flight delays and cancellations in the past few years have caused serious concerns among passengers regarding airlines' operational efficiency and service quality. Due to multiple venues for communication and feedback, passengers tend to share their recommendations of an airline with other passengers, such as their family, friends, colleagues, or other passengers, via social networks. Positive recommendations lead to successful travel businesses, while negative recommendations result in losing passengers and increasing business losses. Understanding airline recommendations is critical for airlines to be able to establish appropriate strategies and make informed decisions on improving their flight plans, operations, and service quality…

Add a research question to this paragraph to highlight the important unanswered question.

> … The primary question is: How to find the right tool to predict passengers' airline recommendations accurately? Misprediction can lead to poor business decisions that result in the airline's failures. Additionally, airlines also need to know what they need to do to increase their positive recommendations and decrease negative ones. Hence, the second question is: What are the important factors associated with the recommendations?

How to Review Previous Studies?

In order to convince the readers that this problem has yet to be addressed or addressed adequately in the literature, you need to conduct a comprehensive literature review. In this paragraph, briefly summarize the literature review, the findings of the previous research, and their shortcomings. For example, you can show evidence that machine learning methods have not been used to predict passengers' airline recommendations in the past, and most existing studies tend to use traditional statistical methods via surveys with a small sample size, which limits the generalizability of their findings and leaves out many relevant variables. Save the details for the literature review section. If written well, you can justify why it is essential to do this research.

How to Write a Purpose Statement?

For data mining papers, especially supervised learning studies, there are typically two primary objectives: (1) find the champion model using machine learning algorithms, and

(2) identify important predictors and rank them. As you can see, these objectives also align with the two research questions we stated above. Hence, we can write a purpose statement as follows.

> The purpose of this study is twofold. First, we aim to develop predictive models and find a champion model that predicts the passengers' airline recommendations accurately. Second, based on the champion model, we identify important predictors and rank them by order.

How to Briefly State the Methodology?

This statement is to inform the readers of the methodology we use, especially if we deploy a novel analytic method, and why it is the appropriate method. For example, you can write a statement as follows.

> In order to meet those objectives, the data mining method is selected. Given the large number of variables and the data size, data mining is the appropriate method to discover unknown patterns from the data using machine learning algorithms. The airline survey dataset provided by *[add data source]* in 2021 is used to train and validate the predictive models.

How to Justify the Significance of the Study?

Clearly explain how this study adds value to the airline management literature (theoretical implications) and how the findings benefit the airline industry (practical implications). For example, you can state that by developing predictive models using novel variables, including a mixture of flight operations and efficiency, such as flight delays, cancellations, flight durations, travel purposes, and flight path, this study sheds new light on airlines' decision models in the changing world (theoretical). Including demographic variables allows us to capture a big picture of passengers' behaviors. Additionally, the findings enable the airlines to estimate the patterns of passengers' airline recommendations, and airline executives can use the prediction results to establish appropriate strategies to improve their competitive advantage (practical).

How to Describe the Delimitations and Limitations?

You should describe the scope (delimitations) of this study, such as the study is focused on U.S. airlines and domestic flights only. The target population is U.S. adults who have been flying for at least one year. Additionally, the variables in the analysis are mainly focused on flight operations, flight delays, cancellations, travel purposes, and passengers' demographics. Then, you need to clarify the limitations of this study. For example, this study does not consider the impact of the pandemic, competition of international airlines, and security concerns. I also recommend explaining how these limitations would not affect the validity of the study.

How to Describe the Organization of the Paper?

Typically, this part is relatively easy since you only need to explain the remaining sections of the paper, such as the literature review, methodology, results, and discussions and conclusions. It is fairly straightforward. My only suggestion is to avoid repeating phrases to make the writing more professional.

> The paper is organized as follows. Section 2 reviews extant studies in airline management and highlights the research gaps related to passengers' airline recommendations. The foundational framework for variable selection and predictive modeling is also explained in this section. Section 3 describes why the data mining method is selected, the data mining process, data collection and sampling, and the machine learning algorithms used in the study. Detailed results of the data mining are presented and explained in Section 4, showing the model comparison, the champion model, and variable importance. Finally, Section 5 provides discussions of the findings, implications of the study, limitations, and recommendations for future research.

How to Write a Literature Review Section?

When writing a literature review section for a research paper that focuses on data mining, you need to review and summarize existing research and scholarly works specifically related to the focused topic, applications of data mining techniques in this area in the literature, and any advancements.

Following are some tips to help you write an effective literature review section.

1. *Define the scope*: Determine the scope and boundaries of your literature review. Use the research questions and study objectives to guide your review within the field of the focused topic and data mining. This helps you focus your search and analysis on relevant literature.

2. *Identify relevant sources*: Conduct a comprehensive search to identify relevant sources specifically related to the scope identified above. Use library databases, academic journals, conference proceedings, and reputable organizations that specifically cover relevant topics. Include recent and seminal works to ensure the review is up-to-date and comprehensive.

3. *Categorize the literature*: Organize the literature based on different categories or themes on the topic of interest. Additionally, if your paper involves developing advancement in data mining methods, include topics such as data preprocessing techniques, algorithm development, or any other relevant subfields or applications within data mining.

4. *Summarize key findings*: Summarize the key findings and contributions of each source within the relevant categories or themes. Provide a concise summary of each work, including the research objectives, methodologies, datasets used, sample, sample size, and main results or conclusions. Highlight any unique or innovative approaches, algorithms, or applications discussed in the literature. If you have a

large number of studies to review, I highly recommend using a table to summarize these key findings. It is easier to follow than details in the text, and it saves space.

5. *Identify gaps and limitations*: Identify any gaps, limitations, or unresolved issues in the existing literature related to the topic of this paper. Discuss areas where further research is needed or where conflicting results or opinions exist. This highlights the need and rationale for your own research within the field.

6. *Compare and contrast*: For data mining literature, compare and contrast the different approaches, algorithms, or techniques discussed in the literature. Analyze the strengths and weaknesses of each approach, considering factors such as accuracy, scalability, interpretability, or applicability. Identify trends, similarities, and differences in the findings across the reviewed studies.

7. *Synthesize the literature*: Synthesize the information regarding theories or foundational frameworks by integrating the findings and conclusions across the reviewed sources. Look for common themes, patterns, or emerging trends. Provide a coherent and well-structured narrative that connects the literature to your own research objectives. This synthesis helps you identify the right theoretical foundation for your study.

8. *Describe the theoretical foundation for the study*: This part is usually required for theory-driven research. Since data mining studies are data-driven, exploratory rather than theory-driven confirmatory research, we do not need to present any theory to support our model. However, we still need to provide a theoretical foundation for selecting variables in the analysis. Usually, this theoretical foundation or framework is derived from the literature synthesis above.

9. *Discuss the novelty of this study*: Explain why this study is original and important, how it helps fill the research gaps, and what novel variables you add to the study. This part is to answer the "so what" question from the readers.

10. *Write and revise*: Start by drafting the literature review section and incorporating the points discussed above. Once you have a draft, review and revise it multiple times. Ensure that the information flows logically, the sources are appropriately cited, and the review provides a comprehensive understanding of the literature.

The literature review section should provide an overview of the current state of knowledge and advancements in the topic of interest. It should demonstrate your understanding of the existing literature and how it informs and supports your own research objectives. By critically analyzing and synthesizing the literature, you establish the context and rationale for your research within the field of data mining.

Since this section requires a deep review of existing studies in the literature, I don't provide any detailed suggestions or writing examples since airline recommendation is not an actual research study. Nonetheless, if you follow the above steps, you should be able to write an effective literature review section to inform the readers of the current knowledge in the field of airline management, gaps in the literature, and how this study adds value to the body of knowledge.

Note that for technical and business reports, this section usually is much lighter and less focused on peer-reviewed literature but more focused on case studies, other technical reports, or managerial reports that have been published by organizations in the same field. In addition, these types of reports do not require extensive justification of the novelty of the study and theoretical contributions but focus more on the practical contributions of the study. Hence, depending on the type of report, you can decide how to adjust the literature review section appropriately.

How to Write a Methodology Section

Methodology is an important section since it provides the readers with the details on the research method and process used in the study. The information allows them to evaluate the validity of your study and helps them replicate the methodology in their future research. When writing a methodology section for a research paper using data mining, you need to outline the specific steps and techniques involved in extracting knowledge from large datasets. I summarize a few tips for writing a good methodology section as follows.

1. *Research design*: Explain the overall research design and objectives of your study. Justify why data mining is an appropriate method to address the research question(s).

2. *Data collection*: Describe the datasets used in your study. Specify the sources of data, including any public repositories, proprietary databases, or data obtained through surveys or experiments. Provide details about the sample size of the dataset, variables, and their scales.

3. *Data preprocessing*: Explain the steps taken to preprocess the data before applying data mining techniques. This may involve data cleaning, imputing missing values, handling outliers, data transformation, normalization, variable selection, or dimensionality reduction. Describe any specific methods and functions used in the preprocessing stage.

4. *Machine learning method selection*: Specify the machine learning method selected for the study. For example, specify whether you build a classification or association model and which methods you select, such as logistic regression, decision tree, neural network, or random forest. Justify your selection based on their suitability for your research objectives and dataset characteristics.

5. *Configurations*: Provide details about the parameter settings and configurations used for each machine learning method. It is common to build multiple models using the same method but with different configurations. Explain how you determined the optimal parameter values. Include any specific software and tools used for implementing the algorithms.

6. *Evaluation metrics*: Describe the evaluation metrics used to evaluate the model performance and compare the models. For example, common model fit metrics for classification models include misclassification rate, accuracy, sensitivity specificity, F1 score, Gini coefficient, ROC chart, and Lift chart. Justify your choice of evaluation metrics based on the type of predictive models and data characteristics.

7. *Ethical considerations*: Discuss any ethical considerations related to data mining, such as data privacy, confidentiality, or potential biases. Explain how you addressed these considerations, such as by de-identifying sensitive information, obtaining informed consent, or complying with relevant regulations.

8. *Write and revise*: Start by drafting the methodology section and incorporating the points discussed above. Once you have a draft, review and revise it multiple times. Ensure that the information is presented in a clear, logical, and structured manner. Clarify any technical terms or procedures to make it accessible to readers.

Remember to provide enough detail for readers to understand and replicate your data mining approach. Explain the rationale behind your choices and justify the suitability of the techniques used. By transparently describing your methodology, you enhance the credibility and reproducibility of your research.

Example of Writing a Methodology Section

As you can see, I have covered all those details in the previous chapters when I used the *airline recommendation* dataset in those chapters' examples. Hence, I won't repeat all the details here to avoid unnecessarily duplicated content. Nonetheless, I summarize the key points we must cover in each part, some writing examples, and which chapter you can revisit for the details. You should also keep this section well organized and concise rather than making it too long.

Below are some key points to write in the methodology section with writing examples.

Justify the Use of the Data Mining Method

> The main purpose of this study is to find the best model to predict the passengers' airline recommendations from large data and identify important predictors. To address these objectives, data mining is the appropriate method since it is a data-driven, exploratory method. Data mining allows researchers to analyze large data and discover unknown patterns from the data, based on which business decisions can be made.

Data Source and Variable Descriptions

> In this study, the airline passenger survey data in 2021 was used. The data was collected from *[add the data source]*. The organization sent out a survey to adults living in the United States who had been flying for at least one year. The participants responded to the survey regarding their experience with domestic flights within the time period and whether they recommend the airline to others. The survey data was collected, validated, and coded by the data provider. Unusable data were removed to ensure the quality of the data. The data provider also de-identified any personal or identification information in order to avoid potential harm to human subjects before it was processed, archived, and shared with the public. Hence, there are no ethical concerns, and the Institutional Review Board (IRB) review is not required.

[Note that since this is not actual research, I present those points hypothetically. In your paper, you must provide the correct data source and how the data was actually collected.]

The dataset consists of one target variable and 19 predictors. Table 11.3 presents variable names, labels, descriptions, scales, and roles. The target variable is *recommendation* (passenger's airline recommendation), and it is binary (Yes- recommend; No- not recommend). The predictors have various scales, including interval, binary, and nominal. Price sensitivity is a 5-point Likert scale variable, but it is treated as an interval variable since the gaps between levels are equal.

TABLE 11.3

Data Description

Variable Name	Label/Description	Scale	Role
recommend	Recommend the airline to others	Binary (Yes/No)	Target
airline_st	Airline status	Nominal	Input
age	Age	Interval	Input
gender	Gender	Binary (Male/Female)	Input
price_sensitivity *	Price sensitivity	Interval	Input
no_years_flying	Number of years flying	Interval	Input
no_flt_pa	Average number of flights per year	Interval	Input
pct_ flt_other_airline	Percent of flights with other airlines	Interval	Input
type_of_travel	Travel purpose	Nominal	Input
no_other_lty_cards	Number of other loyalty cards	Interval	Input
shopping_amt_airpt	Shopping amount at the airport	Interval	Input
eat_drink_airpt	Spending for eating and drinking at the airport	Interval	Input
class	Passenger class	Nominal	Input
origin_state	Origin state	Nominal	Input
destin_state	Destination state	Nominal	Input
depart_delay_in_minutes	Departure delay (in minutes)	Interval	Input
arrival_delay_in_minutes	Arrival delay (in minutes)	Interval	Input
flt_cancel	Flight cancellation	Binary (Yes/No)	Input
flt_time	Flight time (in minutes)	Interval	Input
flt_distance	Flight distance (miles)	Interval	Input

* 5-point Likert scale, treated as interval scale

[Refer to Chapter 4 for the details of the dataset.]

Data Mining Process

In this section, you need to specify and justify the use of the SEMMA process. Then, describe briefly what was done in each step of SEMMA. Remember that you do not just present the general process but must explain what was done in each step with enough specifics so the readers can follow your decision-making process. Below is an example.

In this study, we follow the Sample-Explore-Modify-Model-Assess (SEMMA) process as recommended by SAS. This process fits the purpose of this research as it guides us through all the necessary steps to build predictive models, find the champion model, and identify important predictors. Since it is not the purpose of this study to deploy the model in real-life business operations, the model deployment step is not needed. SAS Enterprise Miner was used for data mining. One advantage of this software is that its tools follow the SEMMA process.

In the Sample step, since we have a large dataset, we randomly sampled 20% of the entire dataset and used this sample for the analysis. This step results in a sample size of 62,233 responses, which is sufficient for the data mining purpose. Within this sample, there are 29,584 cases of "recommend" (47.54%) and 32,649 cases of "not recommend" (52.46%). Since the dataset has a relative balance between the two levels, re-sampling was not needed.

Then, the data was partitioned into three samples using the split ratio of 60:40: training sample (60%), validation sample (20%), and test sample (20%). This partition provides us with enough data to train the models, and we still have enough data to validate the models and perform the final test.

[Refer to Chapter 3 regarding details of the Sample step.]

In the Explore step, both visualization and descriptive statistics were used to explore data. We noticed three interval variables with missing data: *arrival delay in minutes, departure delay in minutes,* and *flight time in minutes.* In addition, while *price sensitivity* is a Likert scale variable, the descriptive statistics indicated cases with zero values, which does not make sense since Likert scale variables do not take zero values. It was concluded that these zero values actually were missing values. This error needed to be addressed.

[Refer to Chapter 4 regarding details of the Explore step.]

In the Modify step, several efforts were conducted to correct errors in the data and handle missing values. *Price sensitivity* values were re-coded using the Replacement node to replace zeros with missing values. Thus, we have four variables with missing values. All missing values in these four variables were imputed using the mean value via the Impute node in SAS Enterprise Miner. The mean method for imputation was chosen because the percentage of missing values is low (about 2%) and the mean is the most common imputation method. The imputed values for these four variables were used for the modeling step.

[Refer to Chapter 5 regarding details of the Modify step.]

In the Model step, multiple classification models were developed since the target variable is binary. Three primary machine learning methods were selected, including logistic regression, decision trees, and neural networks. They are appropriate methods for this study because they are well known for building robust and valid classification models. They all can handle large datasets and are not subject to strict assumptions. Those methods are different in nature, which allows us to capture various kinds of relationships in the model. Logistic regression is statistics-based and can capture well a linear relationship between the odds ratio of the target variable and predictors. On the other hand, decision trees are the rule-based method and can capture well non-linear relationships. Finally, neural networks are able to model complex, non-linear relationships using multiple hidden layers. Decision trees and neural networks are also less impacted by the missing values. The detailed configurations of these models will be presented later.

[Refer to Chapters 7–9 regarding the details of these methods.]

In the last step, Assess, all models were evaluated for model fit and predictive power. These models were also compared to determine the champion model. The output of the champion allows us to identify important predictors and their ranks. Evaluation metrics are provided in the next section.

[Refer to Chapter 6 regarding model evaluation and comparison.]

Machine Learning Algorithms and Configurations

In this part, you need to provide detailed configurations for all models you build. The easiest way to do that is to summarize the configurations in a table. I extracted the key model configurations presented from Chapter 7 (Regression), Chapter 8 (Decision Trees), and Chapter 9 (Neural Networks), and put all of them in Table 11.4 as an example. Since we built six neural network models in Chapter 9, I chose only two for this example to avoid excessive information.

In this study, we built multiple predictive models using three primary methods: logistic regression, decision trees, and neural networks. Table 11.4 presents the detailed configurations for each model.

TABLE 11.4

Predictive Model Configurations

Predictive Models	Configurations
Model 1: Logistic regression	• *Model selection method*: stepwise • *Selection criterion*: validation misclassification
Model 2: CART Tree	• *Splitting rule*: Variance. • *Maximum branch*: 2. • *Number of surrogates rules*: 5. • *Split search: node sample*: 100,000; exhaustive search: 2,000,000,000 (2 billion). • Auto pruning configuration, using misclassification as an assessment measure.
Model 3: CHAID Tree	• *Splitting rule*: PROBCHISQ. • *Chi-Square significance level*: 0.05. • *Maximum branch*: 20. • Heuristic search. • *Leaf size*: 1. • *Number of rules*: 5. • *Split size*: 2 • Auto pruning configuration, using misclassification as an assessment measure. • Bonferroni Adjustment
Model 4: Neural Network model with 1 layer	• Number of hidden neurons: 10. • One layer with direct links. • *Input standardization*: z-score. • *Output standardization*: z-score. • *Target activation function*: identity. • *Target error function*: normal. • *Number of tries*: 10. • *Maximum iterations*: 50.
Model 5: Neural Network model with 2 layers	• *Number of hidden neurons*: 10. • Two layers with direct links. • *Input standardization*: range. • *Output standardization*: range. • *Number of tries*: 10. • *Maximum iterations*: 50.

[Refer to Chapters 7–9 regarding the explanation of those configurations.]

Evaluation Metrics

Describe the key metrics for evaluating model fit and comparing models. We have covered them in detail in Chapter 6. Depending on the audience, you can decide how much detail you should get into. Typically, for the academic audience, you can just describe the metrics without providing all the details because they are already familiar with these metrics. For professional or business audiences, it is also not necessary to go into the details since they care more about the purposes of these metrics rather than the scientific background. Below is an example of the statement.

> Several metrics were used to evaluate the model fit and compare the models. More specifically, model fit metrics include misclassification rate, accuracy, sensitivity, specificity, F1-score, Gini coefficient, ROC chart, and Lift chart. These are common model fit metrics for classification models. First, we compared all models using the misclassification rate for the validation sample to identify the champion model, which is the one with the lowest misclassification rate. Then we used Gini coefficient, ROC chart, and Lift chart to confirm that result. Once the champion model was identified, we further evaluated the performance of this model to make sure it met the predictive power expectation. In this step, sensitivity, specificity, and F-score were also evaluated along with the above metrics. Next, the detailed structure of the champion model was reviewed to examine the relationships between predictors and the target variable. Finally, the variable importance result was provided to identify the important predictors and rank them in order of importance.

[Refer to Chapter 6 regarding the explanation of model fit metrics.]

How to Write a Results Section?

The results section is the second important section that the readers focus on because they want to know what you have found. In this section, you need to present and explain the findings derived from your data mining analysis. This section tends to be rather straightforward but also requires more careful writing to ensure the accuracy of the results and avoid interpreting and discussing the findings. Your goal is to present the results clearly and objectively without influencing the readers. The key is to review the analysis results carefully and understand them thoroughly before writing this section. Following are some useful tips for writing an effective results section.

1. *Organize the presentation*: Start by organizing the presentation of your results in a logical and coherent manner. Consider the research objectives and the structure of your analysis to determine the most appropriate way to present the findings.
2. *Provide demographic information*: Provide key demographic information on the data. These results help the reader understand the characteristics of individuals, cases, or organizations in the dataset. Demographic information allows you to justify the representativeness of your sample, which ensures the generalizability of the study.
3. *Provide descriptive statistics*: Provide descriptive statistics results of the data. It includes measures such as frequency, mean, median, mode, standard deviation, minimum, maximum, or any other relevant statistical measures that help describe the characteristics of the dataset.
4. *Present data mining results*: Present the main results of your data mining analysis. This part should include the outcomes of all predictive models that you trained and validated. Report the specific model fit metrics for each model, model comparison, and the champion model. Present and explain the predictive power of

the champion model, its detailed structure, and data patterns detected by this model. Finally, present the variable importance results to show which predictors are important and rank them by order.

5. *Visualize the results*: Use visualizations such as tables, charts, graphs, or diagrams to enhance the understanding of your results. Choose visual representations that are appropriate for the type of data and the research objectives. Include captions or labels to provide clear explanations of the visualizations. Visualization is usually easier to understand and follow than just texts.

6. *Explain the findings*: Explain the findings of your data mining analysis objectively in the context of your research objectives. It is to help the readers follow and understand the findings. Don't assume that they can understand everything just by looking at tables or graphs. Explain the patterns, relationships, or insights that emerge from the analysis and avoid interpreting and discussing the findings. The objective of this section is to present the results objectively without influencing the readers.

7. *Highlight new discoveries*: Compare your results with the findings from existing literature in the field of data mining. If your results show any new discoveries, such as new significant predictors, new relationships, or new patterns, highlight them.

8. *Provide supplementary analysis*: Consider providing additional supplementary analysis if relevant to support or clarify your main findings. This could include sensitivity analyses, subgroup analyses, or additional exploratory data mining techniques that help deepen the understanding of the results.

9. *Write and revise*: Start by drafting the results section and incorporating the points discussed above. Once you have a draft, review and revise it multiple times. Make sure that the information is presented clearly, concisely, and in a well-structured manner. Use appropriate terminology and provide sufficient context for readers to understand and follow the results.

The results section should provide a comprehensive and clear presentation of the findings derived from your data mining analysis. It should be supported by appropriate statistical measures, visualizations, and interpretation. By effectively communicating the results, you contribute to the overall credibility and impact of your research.

Example of Writing a Results Section

I provide some specific examples of how to write the results section for the airline recommendation paper. The results are extracted from the findings in previous chapters.

Demographic Information

This section provides the readers with some important information about the demographic characteristics of the individuals, cases, or organizations in your dataset. The demographic information allows the readers to understand the characteristics of the sample and connect it to the data mining outcomes later. In addition, the demographic information also helps justify the representativeness of the sample, which results in the generalizability of the study.

Depending on the data availability, you can decide which demographic information to present. In Chapter 4, we explored the data and built multiple charts for the *airline recommendation* dataset. Since passengers' survey responses are the data point, you should present their primary demographic characteristics. Graphs are an effective method for this purpose, so I use bar charts and pie charts. Based on the data description (Table 4.2), you can present the information for demographic variables such as age, gender, airline status, and travel purposes. Chapter 4 shows us various ways to present the information using visualization. In this section, I choose the most relevant ones for the demonstration purposes.

It is important to remember that the graphs already show all the details of the demographic information. Hence, you should not repeat the same details in the report because the readers can view them in the graphs. Instead, you should try to explain and elaborate the results in a different way to show the readers any important pattern that they should focus on.

Here is an example of the demographic information results.

Figures 11.4–11.7 show the information about passengers' age, gender, travel purposes, and airline class, respectively. The results indicate that most passengers (about 55%) are in middle age, ranging from 31 to 58 years old. We can also see a reasonable number of young passengers (aged 18–31 years) in the sample. On the other hand, about 26% of passengers are older than 58 years old. Overall, there are wide ranges of ages in the sample. As for gender, there are slightly more female passengers than male passengers, but the ratio is relatively balanced and similar to the nation's demographics. The travel purposes show some interesting information, with the majority of passengers traveling for business purposes, followed by personal purposes. There is only a small percentage of passengers traveling for mileage tickets. Finally, most passengers have blue status (about 65%), which reflects the actual market. The remaining 35% have silver, gold, and platinum statuses. Overall, the sample shows a wide range of demographic characteristics of the passengers. The results are similar to national data of airline passengers, which allows us to generalize the results of this study to the entire population of U.S. passengers.

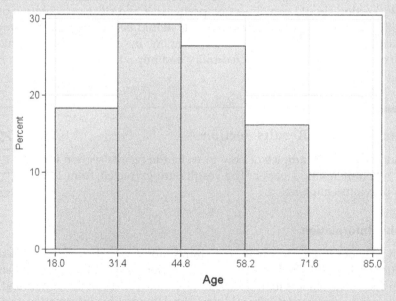

FIGURE 11.4
Age.

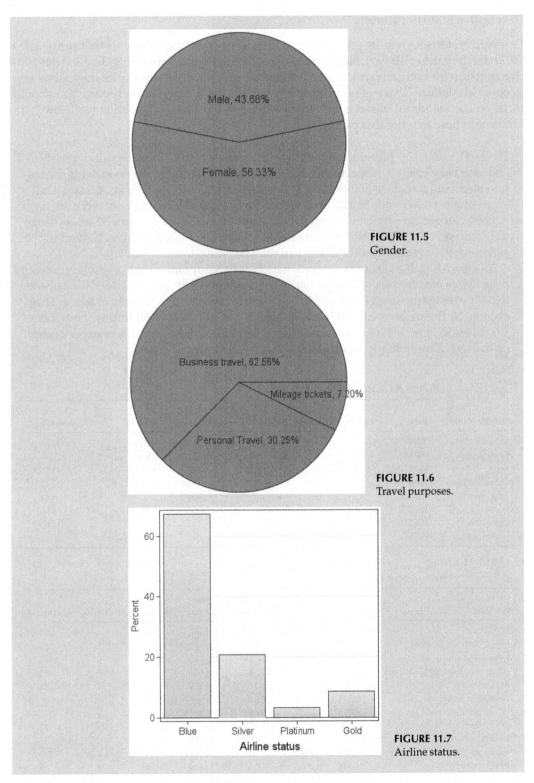

FIGURE 11.5
Gender.

FIGURE 11.6
Travel purposes.

FIGURE 11.7
Airline status.

[Refer to Chapter 4 for detailed results.]

Descriptive Statistics Results

Descriptive statistics results provide the readers with statistical measures that summarize the characteristics of all variables in the dataset. I recommend presenting detailed descriptive statistics for both categorical and interval variables using tables since they allow you to cover all details. There is no need to explain all the details in the report. You should focus on any stand-out observations that the readers need to pay attention to. Below is an example of how to write this part.

Tables 11.5 and 11.6 present the descriptive statistics results for categorical variables and interval variables, respectively. The results show that there are no missing values for categorical variables (Table 11.5). The target variable is binary with a relative balance between two levels: 52.46% (Yes – recommend) and 47.54% (No – not recommend). Among categorical predictors, *original states* and *destination states* have 52 levels since they represent 52 U.S. states. *Airline status* has four levels, while *passenger class* and *travel purpose* both have three levels. Other variables have two levels (binary).

As shown in Table 11.6, three interval variables have missing values, including *arrival delay time in minutes, departure delay time in minutes,* and *flight time in minutes.* We can see that the average passenger age is 47.5 years, with an average of 6.78 years of flying. They average 20 flights per year, with an average of 111 minutes of flight time and about 793 miles of flight distance. An interesting result is that these passengers experienced, on average, 15 minutes of departure delays as well as arrival delays.

TABLE 11.5

Descriptive Statistics for Categorical Variables

Variable Name	Role	Levels	Missing	Mode 1	Mode 1 Percentage	Mode2	Mode 2 Percentage
recommendation	TARGET	2	0	Yes	52.46	No	47.54
airline_status	INPUT	4	0	Blue	67.08	Silver	20.86
class	INPUT	3	0	Eco	81.53	Eco Plus	10.3
destination_state	INPUT	52	0	California	12.74	Texas	12.41
flight_cancelled	INPUT	2	0	No	98.19	Yes	1.81
gender	INPUT	2	0	Female	56.8	Male	43.2
origin_state	INPUT	52	0	California	12.87	Texas	12.61
type_of_travel	INPUT	3	0	Business travel	62.56	Personal Travel	30.14

TABLE 11.6

Descriptive Statistics for Interval Variables

Variable	Role	Mean	Standard Deviation	Non Missing	Missing	Minimum	Maximum
age	INPUT	47.50	16.50	124,464	0	18	85
arrival_delay_in_minutes	INPUT	15.38	38.84	121,899	2,565	0	1,584
departure_delay_in_minutes	INPUT	15.00	38.45	122,263	2201	0	1,592
eating_and_drinking_at_airport	INPUT	68.84	52.60	124,464	0	0	895
flight_distance	INPUT	793.87	592.10	124,464	0	31	4,983
flight_time_in_minutes	INPUT	111.51	71.77	121,899	2565	8	669
no_of_flights_per_year	INPUT	20.09	14.40	124,464	0	0	100
no_of_other_loyalty_cards	INPUT	0.84	1.12	124,464	0	0	12
number_of_years_flying	INPUT	6.78	2.98	124,464	0	2	11
percent_of_flight_with_other_air	INPUT	9.44	8.87	124,464	0	1	110
price_sensitivity	INPUT	1.31	0.50	120,488	3976	1	5
shopping_amount_at_airport	INPUT	26.87	53.16	124,464	0	0	879

[Refer to Chapter 4 for detailed results. The only thing I changed here is that I updated the descriptive statistics for *price sensitivity* since we re-coded the zero values as missing values. To do that, connect the Replacement node directly to the data source node. Then, connect the StatExplore node to the Replacement node. That gave me the descriptive statistics for the new price sensitivity with the whole dataset.]

Data Mining Results

This part is important because all data mining results are presented here. Typically, you begin with the model comparison to identify the champion model. Then, present the details of the champion model, its predictive power, its structure, and variable importance. Again, you should not repeat the details of tables and charts in the text but rather explain what they mean and what details the readers need to pay attention to. You also must explain the decisions you made in this process and provide justification for those decisions.

First, let's present the model comparison results. Typically, I use both tables and charts to show the comparison between models using various model fit metrics. You may remember that the ROC chart and Lift chart are two common metrics. However, in this example, since I have not put all of those models in the same diagram, I do not have the Model Comparison node that can produce the ROC chart and Lift chart. Hence, I present the metrics in a table format so the comparison can be made, and I use ROC index and Lift value instead. They essentially give us the same outcomes. In addition, as you have seen in other chapters since the models are quite close to each other the curves seem to overlap and it is hard to tell which model is better from the charts. Presenting results in the table allows us to see more clearly the comparison.

Below is an example of how to write the model comparison results in this hypothetical scenario.

In order to determine the champion model, all five predictive models were compared using four model fit metrics: misclassification rate, Gini coefficient, ROC index, and Lift value. Table 11.7 presents the model comparison using validation results. The results indicate that those five models are quite close in performance. Based on the misclassification rate, Model 2 (CART Tree) has the lowest misclassification rate of 0.209, equivalent to the highest overall prediction accuracy (79.1%), followed by Model 3 (CHAID Tree) and Model 4 (Neural Network with 1 layer). Models 1 and 5 have relatively higher misclassification rates (above 0.23), so we do not consider them. Since the misclassification rate alone is not a good indicator for model fit, other metrics need to be examined. It appears that Model 4 becomes superior with the highest Gini coefficient, the highest ROC index, and the highest Lift. Based on the comparison of those four metrics, it is concluded that Model 4 is the champion model.

TABLE 11.7

Model Comparison – Results for the Validation Sample

Model Description	Misclassification Rate	Gini Coefficient	ROC Index	Lift
Model 1: Logistic Regression	0.230	0.67	0.83	1.65
Model 2: CART Tree	0.209	0.66	0.83	1.61
Model 3: CHAID Tree	0.211	0.64	0.82	1.52
Model 4: Neural Network with 1 layer	0.219	0.72	0.85	1.71
Model 5: Neural Network with 2 layers	0.232	0.66	0.83	1.65

[Refer to Chapters 7–9 for those detailed results.]

Now you have identified the champion model, in the next part, you must further examine the performance of this model to make sure the results are reliable and valid, and we have the model with good predictive power.

Below is an example of how to write this part.

The model fit metrics for the champion are presented in Table 11.8. In this table, more metrics are added, including accuracy, sensitivity, specificity, and F-1 score. Comparing the results between the training sample and validation sample, we can see the results are very similar, indicating the model's reliability. In other words, the model produces consistent results between the training and validation samples.

Since model accuracy is lower than 80%, it is recommended to look into other metrics as well. The sensitivity is considered acceptable since it is close to 90%, but the specificity is rather low (68.3%), indicating high false positives. The F-1 score, which balances between sensitivity and specificity, is just about 80%, which is marginal. Finally, a Gini coefficient of 0.72 is considered a good fit, while an ROC index of 0.85 is considered acceptable. Overall, the model's predictive power is considered acceptable.

TABLE 11.8

Model Fit Metrics for the Champion Model
(Neural Network Model with One Layer)

Model Fit Metrics	Training	Validation
Misclassification rate	0.216	0.219
Accuracy	0.784	0.781
Sensitivity	0.876	0.870
Specificity	0.684	0.683
F1-Score	0.809	0.806
Gini	0.710	0.720
ROC index	0.850	0.850
Cumulative Lift	1.730	1.710

[Refer to Chapter 9 for those detailed results.]

After evaluating the model performance, you should present the detailed model structure to inform the readers of the relationships between predictors and the target variable. Here is an example.

Figure 11.8 shows the structure of the final Neural Network, which consists of predictors, hidden nodes, and weights used in the neural network. Essentially, the network has one hidden layer with ten hidden nodes. The sign and weight of each input-output path in the network are color-coded. In the SAS Enterprise Miner outputs, blues represent negative relationships, while red represents positive relationships. The darker the color, the higher the weight. Given the complex nature of neural networks, it is not expected to show clear relationships between predictors and the target variable.

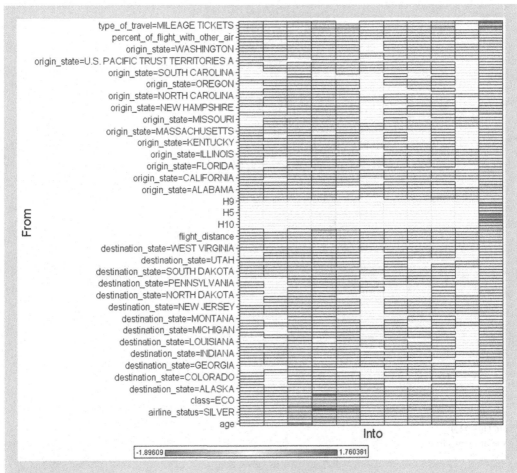

FIGURE 11.8
Neural network structure.

The effects of predictors on the target variable (airline recommendation) can be examined via the variable importance chart. Figure 11.9 presents the variable importance chart, which ranks significant predictors by order of importance. As we can see, *travel purpose* is the most important predictor, followed by *age, average number of flights per year,* and *airline status.* They are considered significant and important predictors that predict passengers' airline recommendations. Other less important predictors include *the number of other loyalty cards, gender, arrival delay time, departure delay time,* and *price sensitivity.* The remaining predictors are considered non-significant.

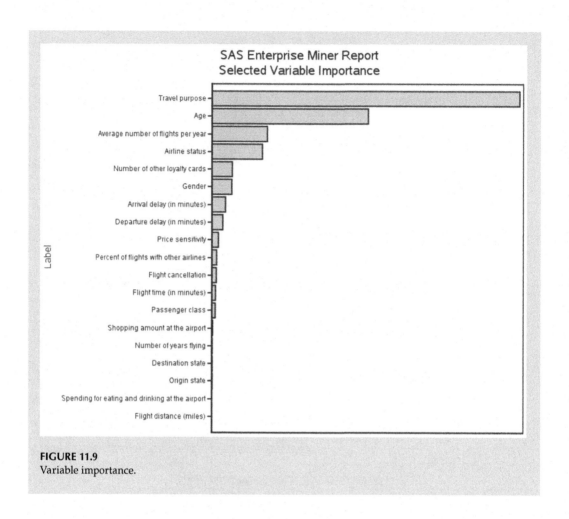

FIGURE 11.9
Variable importance.

[Refer to Chapter 9 for those detailed results.]

How to Write Discussion and Conclusion Sections?

The discussion and conclusion sections of a research paper are crucial for interpreting the findings, discussing their implications, and summarizing the key takeaways from your study. In some cases, the discussion and conclusion are written as two separate sections. And in other cases, they are included  in the same section. It depends on the structure requirements set by the publisher, businesses, or funding organizations. Nonetheless, the strategies for writing the discussion and conclusion sections are the same regardless of the format. Below are some guidelines to help you write these sections effectively.

Discussion Section

1. *Recapitulate the findings*: Begin the discussion section by summarizing the main findings of your data mining analysis. Provide a concise overview of the significant results and patterns that emerged from your study.

2. *Revisit research objectives*: Restate the research objectives or questions that guided your study. Evaluate whether the objectives were met and to what extent the research questions were answered based on your findings.

3. *Interpret the findings*: Interpret the results in the context of your research objectives and the existing literature. Discuss the implications of the findings and explain their relevance to the research questions or problem you investigated.

4. *Compare with existing literature*: Compare your results with previous studies in the same field. Identify similarities, differences, or contradictions between your findings and those reported in the literature. Discuss potential explanations for any discrepancies and highlight the contributions of your study.

5. *Address unexpected results*: If you encounter unexpected or contradictory results, discuss possible reasons behind them. Explore alternative explanations, potential confounding factors, or limitations of the methods employed. This demonstrates critical thinking and adds depth to your discussion. It is also the opportunity to discuss any new discoveries in the study, such as new significant predictors, new relationships, or new patterns. Discuss how the new discoveries add value to the body of knowledge and literature.

6. *Explore methodological implications*: Discuss the methodological implications of your study. Evaluate the effectiveness and suitability of the data mining techniques used and suggest potential improvements or alternative approaches. Address any challenges or limitations in the implementation of the methods and provide recommendations for future research.

Conclusion Section

1. *Summarize key findings*: Begin the conclusion section by summarizing the main results and their significance in a concise manner.

2. *Emphasize theoretical contributions*: Highlight the theoretical contributions of your findings to the field of the study and data mining. Explain how your research fills gaps in existing knowledge, provides new insights, or advances the knowledge in the domain of interest.

3. *Explain practical applications*: Discuss the practical applications and real-world implications of your findings. Explore how the insights gained from your data mining analysis can be applied in relevant domains or industries. Highlight potential benefits, challenges, and considerations for implementing the findings in practice.

4. *Provide recommendations to the target audience*: Offer recommendations to the target audience, especially the government, industry, or private organizations, on how to use the results of this study to enhance their operations or performance. All recommendations should be substantiated by the analysis results to avoid bias.

5. *Discuss limitations*: Acknowledge and discuss the limitations of your data mining analysis. This may include constraints in the dataset, assumptions made during the analysis, or potential biases. Explain how these limitations may affect the generalizability or validity of your findings.

6. *Discuss implications and future directions*: Discuss the broader implications of your findings and their potential impact. Highlight any new research avenues that have emerged from your study and suggest future directions for further investigation.

7. *End on a strong note*: Conclude your research paper with a strong and concise statement that summarizes the key takeaways from your study. Emphasize the significance of your findings and their potential contributions to the field of data mining.

Remember to provide a clear and logical flow of information in both the discussion and conclusion sections. Maintain a balance between summarizing the findings and providing critical analysis. By effectively discussing the implications and summarizing the key findings, you ensure that your research paper concludes on a strong note, leaving a lasting impression on the reader.

Examples of Writing Discussion and Conclusion Sections

As stated before, airline recommendation is not an actual research study but rather a hypothetical one. Hence, I am unable to provide actual writing of discussions and conclusions, which require discussing the theoretical and practical implications of the results. Instead, I will show you the complete discussion and conclusion sections in the article I published (it is the same one I used in the Introduction section). I break them down by paragraph, so you can see how the content flows. Then, I will provide recommendations on key points you should write for the airline recommendation case.

Discussion Section

Figures 11.10 and 11.11 show the actual discussion section in my article, with four paragraphs, as follows.

- *Paragraph 1*: Restates the purpose of the study and summarize the primary findings, focusing on domestic air travel. More specifically, the factors that predict domestic air travel volume during the pandemic are identified. The new discovery is also mentioned here.

- *Paragraph 2*: Discusses the findings for international travel, focusing on the factors affecting international air travel volume. The results are explained in the context of travel behaviors.

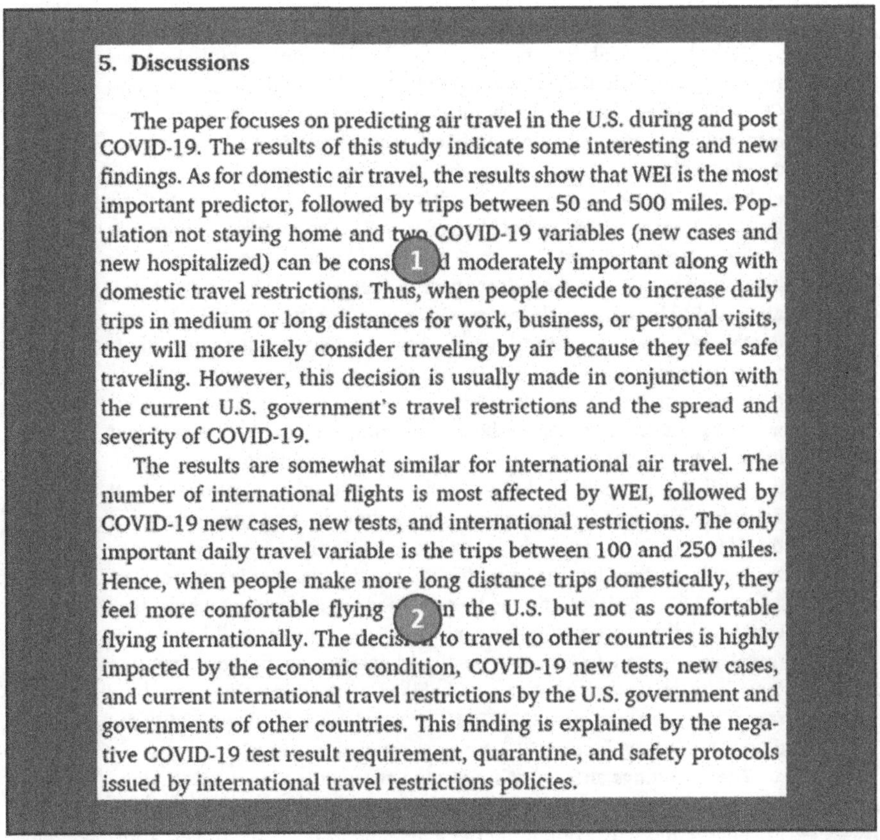

5. Discussions

The paper focuses on predicting air travel in the U.S. during and post COVID-19. The results of this study indicate some interesting and new findings. As for domestic air travel, the results show that WEI is the most important predictor, followed by trips between 50 and 500 miles. Population not staying home and two COVID-19 variables (new cases and new hospitalized) can be considered moderately important along with domestic travel restrictions. Thus, when people decide to increase daily trips in medium or long distances for work, business, or personal visits, they will more likely consider traveling by air because they feel safe traveling. However, this decision is usually made in conjunction with the current U.S. government's travel restrictions and the spread and severity of COVID-19.

The results are somewhat similar for international air travel. The number of international flights is most affected by WEI, followed by COVID-19 new cases, new tests, and international restrictions. The only important daily travel variable is the trips between 100 and 250 miles. Hence, when people make more long distance trips domestically, they feel more comfortable flying within the U.S. but not as comfortable flying internationally. The decision to travel to other countries is highly impacted by the economic condition, COVID-19 new tests, new cases, and current international travel restrictions by the U.S. government and governments of other countries. This finding is explained by the negative COVID-19 test result requirement, quarantine, and safety protocols issued by international travel restrictions policies.

FIGURE 11.10
Example of a discussion section (part 1) (Truong, 2021a).

- *Paragraph 3*: Discusses the simulation results that predict the travel volume in the medium and long term. Explanations of the findings are also provided. The new discoveries are specified here.
- *Paragraph 4*: Discusses the overall implications of the findings in practice.

Conclusion Section

Figures 11.12 and 11.13 present the actual conclusion section, with six different paragraphs, as follows.

- *Paragraph 1*: Restates the importance of this study and explain specific theoretical contributions of the findings. More specifically, how the findings fill the research gaps and add value to the body of knowledge, especially in the literature on COVID-19's impacts on air travel. The discovery of novel predictors is mentioned here.

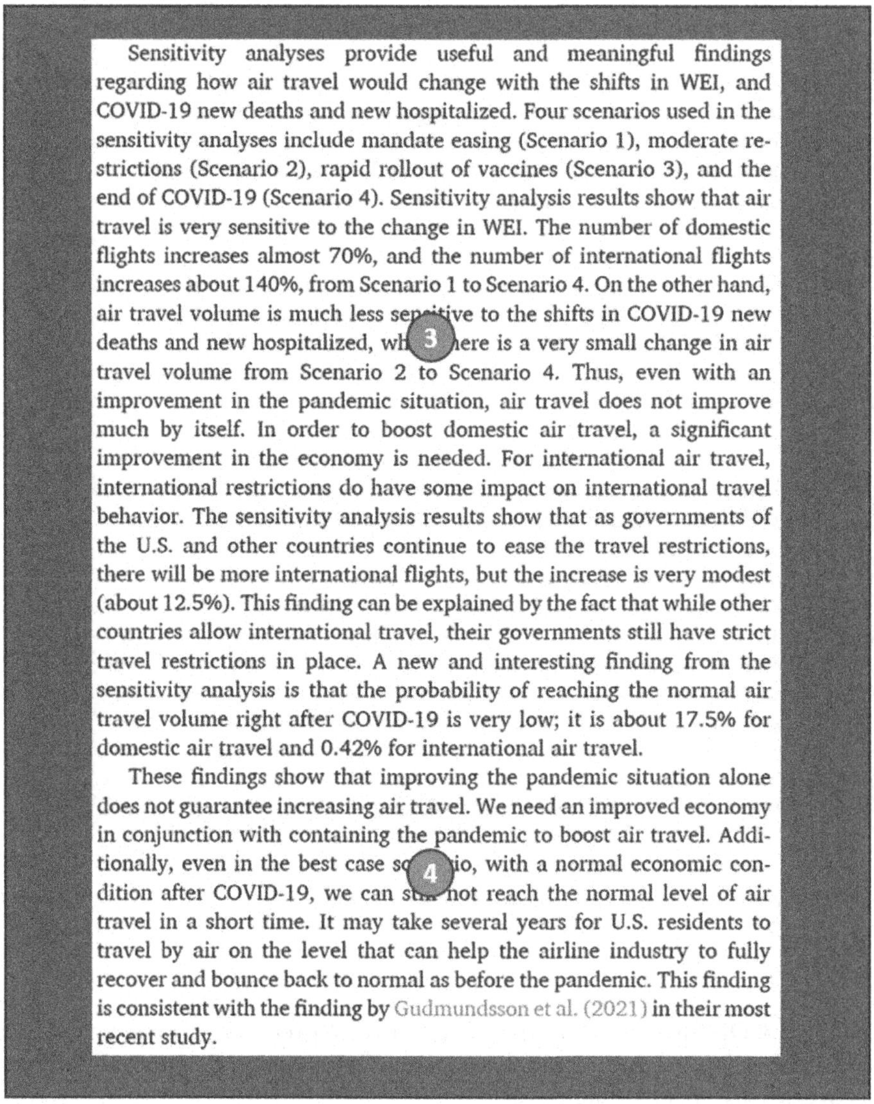

Sensitivity analyses provide useful and meaningful findings regarding how air travel would change with the shifts in WEI, and COVID-19 new deaths and new hospitalized. Four scenarios used in the sensitivity analyses include mandate easing (Scenario 1), moderate restrictions (Scenario 2), rapid rollout of vaccines (Scenario 3), and the end of COVID-19 (Scenario 4). Sensitivity analysis results show that air travel is very sensitive to the change in WEI. The number of domestic flights increases almost 70%, and the number of international flights increases about 140%, from Scenario 1 to Scenario 4. On the other hand, air travel volume is much less sensitive to the shifts in COVID-19 new deaths and new hospitalized, where there is a very small change in air travel volume from Scenario 2 to Scenario 4. Thus, even with an improvement in the pandemic situation, air travel does not improve much by itself. In order to boost domestic air travel, a significant improvement in the economy is needed. For international air travel, international restrictions do have some impact on international travel behavior. The sensitivity analysis results show that as governments of the U.S. and other countries continue to ease the travel restrictions, there will be more international flights, but the increase is very modest (about 12.5%). This finding can be explained by the fact that while other countries allow international travel, their governments still have strict travel restrictions in place. A new and interesting finding from the sensitivity analysis is that the probability of reaching the normal air travel volume right after COVID-19 is very low; it is about 17.5% for domestic air travel and 0.42% for international air travel.

These findings show that improving the pandemic situation alone does not guarantee increasing air travel. We need an improved economy in conjunction with containing the pandemic to boost air travel. Additionally, even in the best case scenario, with a normal economic condition after COVID-19, we can still not reach the normal level of air travel in a short time. It may take several years for U.S. residents to travel by air on the level that can help the airline industry to fully recover and bounce back to normal as before the pandemic. This finding is consistent with the finding by Gudmundsson et al. (2021) in their most recent study.

FIGURE 11.11
Example of a discussion section (part 2) (Truong, 2021a).

- *Paragraph 2*: Discusses the implications of the simulation results, which allow us to predict air travel volume in the medium and long term.
- *Paragraph 3*: Explains the practical implications of the study. More specifically, how airlines can use the model and the prediction results to establish effective business strategies and how the government can use the results to evaluate the impact of policies on the economy.
- *Paragraph 4*: Discusses the limitations of the study due to the data availability.
- *Paragraph 5*: Discusses the method not used in the study since it is not the purpose of this study to examine causal relationships.
- *Paragraph 6*: Recommendations for future research.

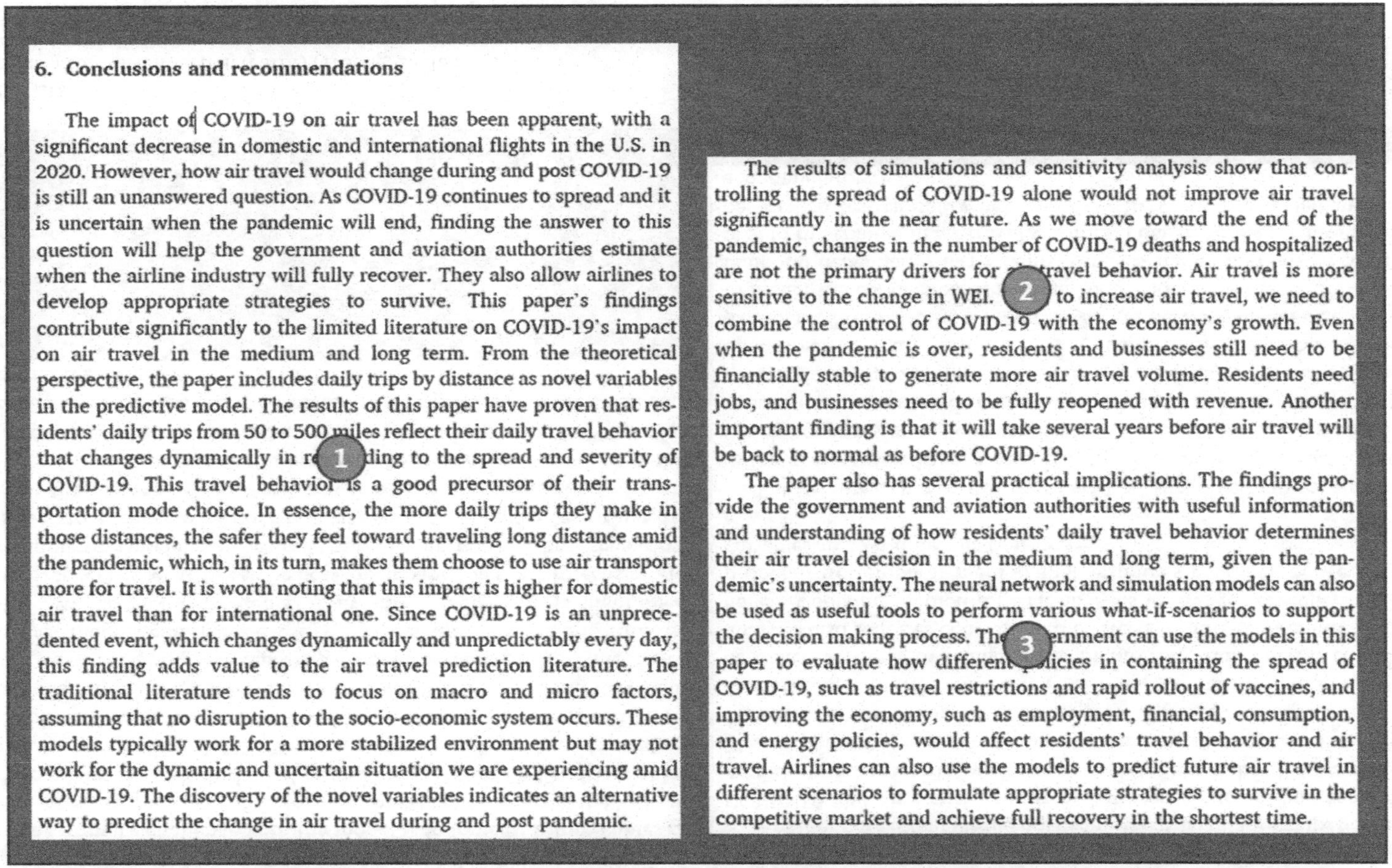

6. Conclusions and recommendations

The impact of COVID-19 on air travel has been apparent, with a significant decrease in domestic and international flights in the U.S. in 2020. However, how air travel would change during and post COVID-19 is still an unanswered question. As COVID-19 continues to spread and it is uncertain when the pandemic will end, finding the answer to this question will help the government and aviation authorities estimate when the airline industry will fully recover. They also allow airlines to develop appropriate strategies to survive. This paper's findings contribute significantly to the limited literature on COVID-19's impact on air travel in the medium and long term. From the theoretical perspective, the paper includes daily trips by distance as novel variables in the predictive model. The results of this paper have proven that residents' daily trips from 50 to 500 miles reflect their daily travel behavior that changes dynamically in r **①** ding to the spread and severity of COVID-19. This travel behavior is a good precursor of their transportation mode choice. In essence, the more daily trips they make in those distances, the safer they feel toward traveling long distance amid the pandemic, which, in its turn, makes them choose to use air transport more for travel. It is worth noting that this impact is higher for domestic air travel than for international one. Since COVID-19 is an unprecedented event, which changes dynamically and unpredictably every day, this finding adds value to the air travel prediction literature. The traditional literature tends to focus on macro and micro factors, assuming that no disruption to the socio-economic system occurs. These models typically work for a more stabilized environment but may not work for the dynamic and uncertain situation we are experiencing amid COVID-19. The discovery of the novel variables indicates an alternative way to predict the change in air travel during and post pandemic.

The results of simulations and sensitivity analysis show that controlling the spread of COVID-19 alone would not improve air travel significantly in the near future. As we move toward the end of the pandemic, changes in the number of COVID-19 deaths and hospitalized are not the primary drivers for **②** ravel behavior. Air travel is more sensitive to the change in WEI. **②** to increase air travel, we need to combine the control of COVID-19 with the economy's growth. Even when the pandemic is over, residents and businesses still need to be financially stable to generate more air travel volume. Residents need jobs, and businesses need to be fully reopened with revenue. Another important finding is that it will take several years before air travel will be back to normal as before COVID-19.

The paper also has several practical implications. The findings provide the government and aviation authorities with useful information and understanding of how residents' daily travel behavior determines their air travel decision in the medium and long term, given the pandemic's uncertainty. The neural network and simulation models can also be used as useful tools to perform various what-if-scenarios to support the decision making process. The **③** rnment can use the models in this paper to evaluate how different licies in containing the spread of COVID-19, such as travel restrictions and rapid rollout of vaccines, and improving the economy, such as employment, financial, consumption, and energy policies, would affect residents' travel behavior and air travel. Airlines can also use the models to predict future air travel in different scenarios to formulate appropriate strategies to survive in the competitive market and achieve full recovery in the shortest time.

FIGURE 11.12
Example of a conclusion section (part 1) (Truong, 2021a).

The primary challenge with the model is to forecast future values of predictors. The forecast values for WEI can be extracted from the Federal Reserve Bank of New York, and forecast values for COVID-19 variables can be extracted by IHME. These organizations have been providing reliable and valid forecasting based on rich data and robust analytical methods. In addition, Maryland Transportation Institute and CATT lab have been collecting the daily travel data automatically. Time series forecast models can also be used 4 detect the patterns and forecast future values of the residents' travel behavior. As mentioned above, specific scenarios can be developed based on these forecasts, and the simulation models can be used to predict air travel in these scenarios. Furthermore, the model does not take into account the lead time between the change in residents' travel behavior and the time of their flights. The challenge with this option is the lack of available data on the individual level since the lead time varies from one to another. Data for actual travel decisions can be obtained by conducting large-scale surveys nationwide.

Another note is that we did not examine causal relationships between COVID-19 and air travel volume or between air travel and economic growth. In other words, we focus on correlations rather than causality. The reason is that this paper aims at examining the impacts of multiple variables in predicting air travel, while a causality study focuses on establishing a causal relationship 5 ween two variables of interest or causality between two time series in the long run. Such a causality analysis also requires controlling the effects of other confounding variables. A popular method for that analysis is Granger causality, a non-probabilistic temporal method that examines causality between two variables in two different time series (Baker et al., 2015; Hakim and Merkert, 2016).

Future research can use the model to run sensitivity analyses in different countries. Then, a cross-country comparison can be made to see which countries or regions can achieve full recovery of air travel in a shorter time. A new study can expand the model to include more factors such as time, states of residents' travel behavior, and changes in airlines' operations to fully capture the dynamism of the economy post pandemic. Additionally, a recurrent neural network model can be used to model the connection of neurons in a sequential order to reflect the temporal dependency in residents' travel behavior and how it contributes to the change in air travel volumes. Finally, Granger causality can be used to test causality between COVID-19, air travel demand, and economic growth.

FIGURE 11.13
Example of a conclusion section (part 2) (Truong, 2021a).

Discussions and Conclusions for the Airline Recommendation Paper

Below are some key points that you should present in these sections for the airline recommendation paper.

Discussions

- Restate the purpose of this study, which is to build a good predictive model that predicts accurately the passengers' airline recommendations and identifies important predictors.
- Discuss detailed findings related to each of these two objectives and explain what these mean. In this case, five predictive models were trained and validated. The model comparison indicated the higher-performance neural network model with one layer is the champion model with acceptable predictive power. Secondly, the output of this champion model shows that *travel purpose* is the most important predictor, followed by *age, average number of flights per year,* and *airline status.*
- Interpret these findings to provide the readers with more insights into what these results mean in the airline business. You can also provide explanations for the important predictors.
- Compare these results with the existing literature and highlight similarities and differences. Discuss any new findings, such as new predictors or new relationships.
- Discuss the implications of these findings in practice.

Conclusions

- Restate concisely the importance of the study and primary findings (keep it at the high level because the findings have been discussed in detail in the discussion section).
- Provide detailed theoretical contributions of the findings and how they add value to the body of knowledge, especially how they help fill the research gaps.
- Discuss the practical contributions, such as how the airline industry can use the predictive model to make predictions, based on which they can establish a business strategy for success. In addition, discuss how the identified important predictors can help the airlines improve their operations, services, and passengers' satisfaction.
- Address any limitations in the study. For example, factors such as on-ground services, customer services, and on-board services are not included in the study due to the data availability. In addition, the study is focused on U.S. passengers flying from and to the United States only. Discuss how these limitations affect the generalizability of the findings.
- Provide specific recommendations for future research.

Summary

Writing an effective data mining report is a crucial step in a data mining project, in which the results and insights obtained from mining large datasets are documented and communicated effectively. The first step in writing the report involves identifying the target audience, understanding the report requirements, and selecting the appropriate writing styles. In the report, you need to start by identifying the research problem and then defining the scope and objectives of the project and justifying why the study is important. The background information is to inform the readers of the existing projects in the field and any gaps, which helps justify the originality of the study. The literature synthesis also provides the foundational framework for the models in the study. The methodology section plays a crucial role in helping the readers to evaluate the validity of the findings and replicate the methodology in their future studies. This section includes describing the dataset, variables, specific machine learning methods, configurations, and evaluation metrics.

The next stage of writing a data mining report is the presentation of results and analysis. This section presents the discovered patterns, associations, or correlations found in the data. Visualizations, charts, and graphs are commonly used to illustrate the patterns and make the information more accessible to the readers. The report should not only present the outcomes of the data mining process but also provide explanations and insights into the significance of the results in the context of the research objectives.

The final part of the data mining report is the discussion and conclusion. This section summarizes the key findings and their implications. It may discuss the practical applications of the results and suggest potential areas for further research. If applicable, the report may also propose actionable recommendations based on the data analysis outcomes.

Overall, writing an effective data mining report requires careful planning, diligent data collection and analysis, and effective communication of findings. It is a journey that demands perseverance, critical thinking, and adherence to ethical guidelines to contribute meaningfully to the community and advance knowledge in a particular field. A well-written data mining report should be structured, concise, and tailored to the target audience, enabling stakeholders to make informed decisions based on the extracted knowledge from the data.

CHAPTER DISCUSSION QUESTIONS

1. What is the main purpose of a data mining report?
2. Why is it important to an effective report for a data mining project?
3. What are the primary differences between academic research reports, technical reports, and business reports? Discuss in detail those differences.
4. Select one data mining project and identify the target audience. What are the expectations of that audience for your data mining report?
5. What is the effective writing style for that audience? Why? Describe the pros and cons of that writing style.

6. What are the primary sections of a data mining report? Describe the purpose and content of each section.

7. What are different ways to hook the audience and keep their interest in your report?

8. How do you tell if a report title is effective? What are strategies to write a good title?

9. What are the key strategies for writing each section of the report?

Exercises

Exercise 1: Writing the report for the Bank dataset

1. Prepare an outline for a business report of the bank customer project. The purpose is to build a predictive model that accurately predicts a customer's credit scores based on their demographic variables and banking information.
2. Write a project title.
3. Write an abstract.
4. Write a brief introduction section, including the problem statement, research questions, purpose statement, significance of the study, and delimitations.
5. Write a methodology section, including data source, variable description, data mining process, machine learning methods and configurations, and model evaluation metrics.
6. Choose the results of the following linear regression and decision tree models you completed for the exercises in Chapters 7 and 8.
   - Linear regression using stepwise.
   - Pruned CART tree.
   - Pruned CHAID tree.
7. Write a results section to present the results, including:
   - Demographic information.
   - Descriptive statistics results.
   - Model comparison results.
   - Champion model identification.
   - Evaluating the reliability and validity of the champion model.
   - Detailed structure and relationships in the champion model.
   - Variable importance explanation.
8. Write a brief discussion section, including discussions of the findings, their implications, and limitations of the analysis.

Exercise 2: Writing the report for the Passengers dataset

1. Prepare an outline for a business report of the airline passengers project. The purpose is to build a predictive model that accurately predicts a passenger's decision to return to the same airline based on their demographic variables, flight information, and their evaluation of the airline services.
2. Write a project title.
3. Write an abstract.
4. Write a brief introduction section, including the problem statement, research questions, purpose statement, significance of the study, and delimitations.

5. Write a methodology section, including data source, variable description, data mining process, machine learning methods and configurations, and model evaluation metrics.
6. Choose the results of the neural network models you completed for the exercises in Chapter 9.
   - DMNeural model.
   - AutoNeural model (block layers).
   - HP Neural model (one hidden layer with direct, z-score normalization).
   - HP Neural model (two hidden layers with direct, range normalization).
7. Write a results section to present the results, including:
   - Demographic information.
   - Descriptive statistics results.
   - Model comparison results.
   - Champion model identification.
   - Evaluating the reliability and validity of the champion model.
   - Detailed structure and relationships in the champion model.
   - Variable importance explanation.
8. Write a brief discussion section, including discussions of the findings, their implications, and limitations of the analysis.

12

Principal Component Analysis

LEARNING OUTCOMES

Upon the completion of this chapter, you will be able to

1. Describe the concepts of Principal Component Analysis (PCA) as a dimensionality reduction technique in data mining.

2. Explain the principles and algorithms used in PCA for extracting the principal components from a dataset.

3. Discuss the advantages and disadvantages of PCA in the context of data mining.

4. Describe how PCA captures the variance and correlation structure of data through eigenvalues and eigenvectors.

5. Select the proper number of principal components to retain using the scree plot, cumulative eigenvalue, and explained variance.

6. Explain component rotation methods used in PCA to align principal components with the original variables in order to improve interpretability.

7. Conduct PCA to reduce the number of variables using SAS Enterprise Miner.

Introduction

When we deal with big data, we often have a dataset that includes a large number of variables, like a hundred variables. It is called a high-dimensional dataset. In order to build our predictive models, researchers tend to try to include all of them in the analysis. Sometimes it works, and sometimes, it does not. As described in the previous chapters, the number of variables included in the modeling process may affect the model's explanatory power. The more variables in the model, the lower the explanatory power because the algorithm has to account for the variance in all variables in the model. Consequently, our model may not achieve satisfactory predictive power. The large number of variables may also increase the computing time.

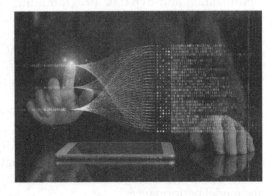

DOI: 10.1201/9781003162872-14

So, how do we reduce the number of variables in the data without affecting the validity of the model? Essentially, it depends on the characteristics of our data. Suppose in the explore step, we find out some variables may not be relevant to the target variable, which means they do not contribute to the prediction. In this case, we can use the variable selection tool to choose the most significant variables and use them as predictors for the modeling step. In other cases, what if our variables are relevant, but some of them may be highly correlated to each other? It means we have subsets of correlated variables in the data. If we only keep the most significant variables and reject others, we may end up losing information in the data. In this case, a solution is to combine those correlated variables into a smaller number of new variables. In simple terms, we replace our original variables with a set of new variables; each of them is a composite of correlated original variables. Thus, we end up with a dataset with a much smaller number of variables. This practice is called dimensionality reduction. The challenge is that this process changes the original data. Hence, the question is, how do we reduce the data dimensionality while retaining the information of the original variables?

Principal Component Analysis (PCA) is a commonly used technique in machine learning for dimensionality reduction. Essentially, PCA is a statistical technique that allows us to summarize the variation in a high-dimensional dataset by identifying the most important variables or combinations of variables, known as principal components. PCA is widely used in various fields like computer vision, image processing, data mining, bioinformatics, and many more. In this chapter, we cover the basic concepts of PCA, its applications, and the steps involved in implementing PCA in machine learning.

Curse of Dimensionality

Before getting into the details of dimensionality reduction and PCA, I want to describe one common issue in data mining, *the curse of dimensionality*. It is a term used to describe problems that arise when we deal with high-dimensional data, a dataset with a large number of variables. The term was introduced by Richard Bellman in the context of optimization and dynamic programming. In general, as the number of dimensions of a dataset increases, the amount of data needed to  ensure that the data is representative and informative grows exponentially. In simpler terms, when we have many variables in the dataset, we need a very large sample size. This requirement makes it increasingly difficult to model or analyze the data, and many techniques that work well in low dimensions become infeasible or less effective in high dimensions.

One of the main issues with high-dimensional data is that it becomes increasingly sparse as the number of dimensions increases. This means that the available data becomes less and less representative of the overall distribution, making it difficult to accurately model or make predictions. Additionally, high-dimensional data often contain redundant or irrelevant features, which can further complicate the modeling process and decrease the model performance.

The curse of dimensionality can also have a significant impact on computational efficiency. Many machine learning algorithms require a large amount of computation, and as the number of dimensions increases, the amount of computation required can quickly become unmanageable. This can result in long training time, increased memory usage, and reduced scalability.

To mitigate the curse of dimensionality, techniques such as dimensionality reduction, variable selection, and regularization can be used. These techniques aim to reduce the number of dimensions in the data while preserving important information, making it easier to model and analyze. In this chapter, we focus on one of the most popular dimensionality reduction techniques, PCA. It allows us to reduce the data dimensionality and, at the same time, retain information in the original data.

Basic Concepts of Principal Component Analysis

PCA is a method that seeks to identify patterns and structure in high-dimensional data by reducing the dimensionality of the data while retaining the most important information in the data. In other words, this method allows us to combine a large number of variables into a smaller number of variables without losing information. It is done by transforming the original variables into a new set of variables, called principal components, which are linearly uncorrelated and capture the maximum amount of variance in the data. In other words, principal components are distinctive variables and can explain well the variance in the data. Figure 12.1 presents an illustration of this dimensionality reduction process.

> **DEFINITION**
>
> PCA is a method that seeks to identify patterns and structure in high-dimensional data by reducing the dimensionality of the data while retaining the most important information.

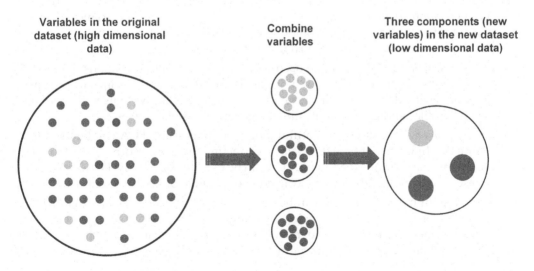

FIGURE 12.1
Illustration of the dimensionality reduction.

Principal Components

The principal components are linear combinations of the original variables, and each principal component represents a new dimension in the reduced dimensional space. The first principal component captures the largest amount of variance in the data, and each

subsequent component captures the next largest amount of variance, subject to the constraint that it is uncorrelated with the previous components.

Eigenvalue

The importance of each principal component can be measured by its eigenvalue, which represents the amount of variance in the data captured by that component. The eigenvalue of each principal component is equal to the squared length of its corresponding eigenvector, which is a vector that defines the direction of the component. I won't get into the mathematical details of eigenvalue calculation. The key point is that the eigenvalue allows us to determine the right number of components in our dataset. There are several basic concepts in the PCA. Table 12.1 presents these key concepts along with detailed descriptions.

Practical Applications of PCA in the Industry

PCA has many practical applications in various fields. Below are some examples of PCA applications.

- *Image compression*: PCA can be used to compress images by reducing the dimensionality of the image data while preserving the essential features. For example, in facial recognition systems, PCA can be used to reduce the number of dimensions in the image data to improve recognition accuracy.
- *Finance*: In finance, PCA can be used to identify the underlying factors that drive the correlation structure of asset returns. By decomposing the covariance matrix of asset returns into principal components, portfolio managers can better understand the sources of risk and return in their portfolios.
- *Genetics*: In genetics, PCA can be used to identify the genetic variations that contribute to the differences between individuals. By analyzing the principal components of genetic data, researchers can identify groups of individuals with similar genetic profiles and gain insights into the genetic basis of diseases.
- *Natural language processing*: In natural language processing, PCA can be used to reduce the dimensionality of text data by extracting the most informative features. For example, in sentiment analysis, PCA can be used to identify the keywords and phrases that are most strongly associated with positive or negative sentiment.
- *Marketing*: In marketing, PCA can be used to identify the key factors that drive consumer preferences and behavior. By analyzing the principal components of customer data, marketers can identify the segments of customers that are most similar and tailor their marketing strategies accordingly.

These are just a few examples of the many applications of PCA. PCA is a versatile and widely used technique that can help to simplify complex datasets and reveal the underlying structure and patterns in the data.

TABLE 12.1

Basic Concepts of PCA and Descriptions

Concepts	Description
Variance	Variance of a variable measures how much the values of that variable vary from their mean. In PCA, the goal is to find the directions in the data with the highest variance, as these directions contain the most information about the data.
Covariance	Covariance between two variables measures how much they vary together. If two variables have a high covariance, it means they are positively correlated, while a low covariance indicates no correlation. In PCA, we choose the principal components with the expectation that they are uncorrelated.
Eigenvectors and eigenvalues	PCA seeks to identify the directions of maximum variability in the data. Eigenvectors are the directions in the data that are not affected by a linear transformation, while eigenvalues indicate how much variance is captured by each eigenvector. In PCA, the principal components are the eigenvectors of the covariance matrix, sorted by their corresponding eigenvalues.
Principal components	Principal components are the eigenvectors that correspond to the highest eigenvalues of the covariance matrix. They are ordered in terms of their importance, where the first principal component explains the maximum variance in the dataset, followed by the second principal component, and so on.
Explained variance	The proportion of variance explained by each principal component is crucial for understanding the importance of each component in the data. It helps us determine how many principal components to retain for dimensionality reduction while preserving significant information.
Scree plot	A scree plot is a graphical tool used in PCA to visualize the eigenvalues associated with each principal component. It is a simple line segment plot that shows the eigenvalues for each individual principal component. The scree plot helps determine the number of principal components based on the amount of variance they explain.
Component rotation	Component rotation is used to transform the principal components to align those components with the original variables, which achieves a more interpretable and meaningful representation of the data.
Orthogonal rotation	Orthogonal rotation is the rotation method, in which the rotated components are constrained to be orthogonal to each other, meaning they are independent and uncorrelated.
Oblique rotation	Oblique rotation is the rotation method, in which the rotated components are allowed to be correlated with each other.
Varimax	Varimax is an orthogonal rotation method that aims to maximize the variance of the squared loadings on each component, leading to a simple and sparse structure where each variable has a high loading on one component and close to zero loadings on other components.
Oblimin	Oblimin is an oblique rotation method that allows for correlation or obliqueness between the rotated components. The main objective of Oblimin rotation is to achieve a simpler structure by minimizing the number of variables with high loadings on a component.
Promax	Promax is an oblique rotation method that extends the advantages of Varimax rotation while also accounting for possible correlations between the rotated components. It is considered a compromise between the simplicity of orthogonal rotation and the flexibility of oblique rotation.
Dimensionality reduction	Once the principal components have been identified, PCA can be used to transfer the high-dimensional data into lower-dimensional data, while still retaining as much of the original variation as possible. The number of principal components retained determines the dimensionality of the new data.
Reconstruction	PCA allows the inverse transformation of the lower-dimensional data back into the original high-dimensional space. Although some information is lost during dimensionality reduction, the reconstruction can still be useful for interpretation or other downstream tasks.

Applications of PCA in Data Mining

In the context of data mining and predictive modeling, PCA can be used for two purposes, as follows.

- In the Modify step of supervised learning, PCA is used to transfer a large number of predictors into a smaller number of predictors using the principal components. These components are used as new predictors in the Model step to develop predictive models that predict the target variable.

- In unsupervised learning, PCA is used to explore and detect underlying theoretical factors from the data. The principal components represent these underlying factors, and these factors can be used to build a theoretical research model to examine the relationships among them.

Advantages and Disadvantages

PCA is a popular technique used in machine learning for dimensionality reduction. It has many important advantages but also has challenges. Understanding the advantages and disadvantages of PCA can help data scientists make informed decisions about whether to use this technique in their data mining projects.

Advantages of PCA

- *Reduces dimensionality*: One of the primary advantages of PCA is that it reduces the dimensionality of a dataset, which makes it easier to analyze and visualize the data.

- *Retains the maximum amount of information*: PCA retains the maximum amount of information from the original dataset, while still reducing the dimensionality. It helps minimize the loss of information during the dimensionality reduction process.

- *Eliminates correlated features*: PCA identifies the most important variables or combinations of variables, known as principal components, that capture the most variation in the data. These principal components are uncorrelated, meaning that they eliminate the redundant information present in correlated variables.

- *Improves accuracy*: PCA can improve the accuracy of machine learning models by removing noise and irrelevant variables from the dataset.

- *Speeds up computation*: PCA reduces the number of variables in a dataset, which can speed up the computation time of machine learning algorithms.

Disadvantages of PCA

- *Interpretability*: PCA transforms the original variables into a new set of principal components, which is difficult to interpret. It may be challenging to understand the underlying factors driving the variation in the data.

- *Information loss*: While PCA retains the maximum amount of information, there is still some loss of information during the dimensionality reduction process. The amount of information loss depends on the number of principal components.
- *Sensitivity to outliers*: PCA is sensitive to outliers in the data. Outliers can significantly affect the calculation of the principal components, leading to inaccurate results.
- *Assumes linearity*: A key assumption in PCA is that variables are linearly correlated. If the data has a non-linear relationship, PCA may not be the best technique for dimensionality reduction.
- *Scalability*: PCA may not be scalable to large datasets. The computation time and memory requirements increase with the size of the dataset, which can make it difficult to implement in some situations.

Steps of Principal Component Analysis

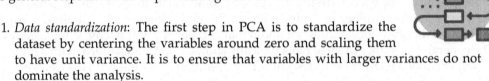

The general steps involved in performing PCA are described as follows.

1. *Data standardization*: The first step in PCA is to standardize the dataset by centering the variables around zero and scaling them to have unit variance. It is to ensure that variables with larger variances do not dominate the analysis.

2. *Compute the covariance matrix*: Once the data is standardized, the covariance matrix is calculated. This matrix captures the relationships between the variables in the dataset.

3. *Compute the eigenvectors and eigenvalues*: The next step is to compute the eigenvectors and eigenvalues of the covariance matrix. The eigenvectors represent the directions of maximum variability in the data, while the eigenvalues represent the amount of variability explained by each eigenvector.

4. *Rank eigenvectors by eigenvalues*: The eigenvectors are ranked according to their corresponding eigenvalues. The eigenvector with the highest eigenvalue is the first principal component.

5. *Select the principal components*: In this step, the number of principal components is determined. It is usually based on a threshold of variance explained. There is no standard threshold for variance explained, but 70% or more is typically acceptable. Scree plot is also a common method that is used to select the number of components.

6. *Transform the data*: The selected principal components are used to transform the data into a lower-dimensional space. This results in a new set of variables that capture most of the variability in the original data.

7. *Interpret the results*: Finally, the transformed data can be analyzed to understand the underlying patterns and structure in the data.

In SAS Enterprise Miner, most of those steps are handled by the software, and we just need to set the right configurations. However, there is one step that requires us to have a good understanding of it to be able to make the right decision, which is the selection of the number of components. Typically, we select the number of components that can capture the high percentage of the total variance without using too many components since it defeats the purpose of dimensionality reduction. The rule of thumb is that we should stop when adding an additional component does not significantly reduce the eigenvalue, meaning it does not help us explain better the variance in the data. The common method used in this case is scree plot. I will discuss this method in the next section.

Scree Plot and Number of Components

A scree plot is a graphical tool used in PCA to visualize the eigenvalues associated with each principal component. The scree plot helps determine the number of principal components based on the amount of variance they explain.

A scree plot is a simple line segment plot that shows the eigenvalues for each individual principal component. It shows the eigenvalues on the y-axis and the number of components on the x-axis (Figure 12.2). It always displays a downward curve since adding an additional component will decrease the eigenvalue. The general appearance of scree plots typically shows a common pattern, with a high start on the left, followed by a swift descent before eventually leveling off. This trend emerges because the initial component typically accounts for a substantial portion of the variance, while the subsequent few components contribute moderately, and the later components

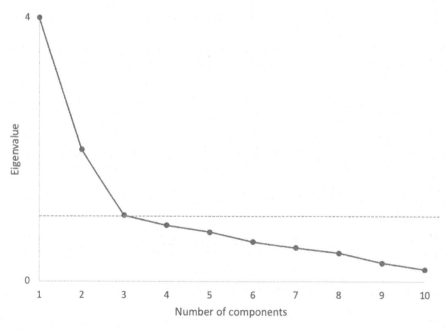

FIGURE 12.2
Example of a scree plot.

only explain a minor portion of the overall data variability. The rule of thumb is to look for the *elbow* in the curve and select all components just before the line flattens out. For example, in this example, we notice an elbow with three components. Hence, we select three components for the PCA.

Component Rotation Methods in PCA

The principal components extracted by PCA are linear combinations of the original variables. They are arranged in descending order of variance, and they are orthogonal to each other, meaning they are uncorrelated. However, the principal components obtained from PCA are not always aligned with the original variables, and their interpretation may not be straightforward. PCA rotation is used to transform the principal components in order to achieve a more interpretable and meaningful representation of the data. The goal of the rotation is to obtain a simpler and more structured representation of the relationships between the variables.

The two common rotation methods in PCA are orthogonal and oblique rotations. These methods aim to achieve different goals in terms of maximizing variance, minimizing the number of variables with high loadings on a component, or allowing for correlation between components. Figure 12.3 illustrates the differences between these two methods.

> **DEFINITION**
>
> Orthogonal rotation is the rotation method, in which the rotated components are constrained to be orthogonal to each other, meaning they are independent and uncorrelated.
>
> Oblique rotation is the rotation method, in which the rotated components are allowed to be correlated with each other.

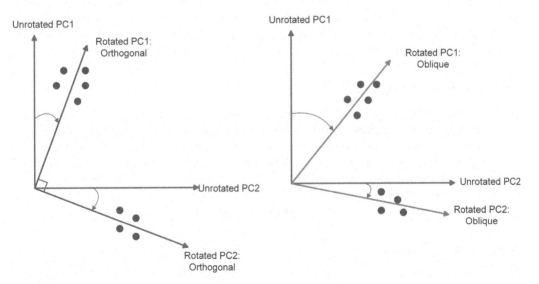

ORTHOGONAL ROTATION

Unrotated PC1

Rotated PC1: Orthogonal

Unrotated PC2

Rotated PC2: Orthogonal

OBLIQUE ROTATION

Unrotated PC1

Rotated PC1: Oblique

Unrotated PC2

Rotated PC2: Oblique

FIGURE 12.3
Orthogonal and oblique rotations.

Orthogonal rotation is the rotation method, in which the rotated components are constrained to be orthogonal to each other, meaning they are independent and uncorrelated. Orthogonal rotation is particularly useful when the components are assumed to be uncorrelated, as it provides simpler and more interpretable solutions.

On the other hand, oblique rotation is the rotation method, in which the rotated components are allowed to be correlated with each other. This means that the components can have shared variance, and they are no longer independent. Oblique rotation is suitable when the factors are assumed to be correlated or when there are theoretical reasons to allow for such correlation among the factors.

By applying a rotation method, the principal components are transformed to have a more interpretable structure, which allows us to identify the underlying factors or patterns in the data. The rotated components may align more closely with the original variables, making it easier to understand the relationships between the variables and interpret the results.

It's important to note that PCA rotation is an optional step in the PCA analysis and is not always necessary. The decision to perform rotation depends on the specific goals of the analysis and the complexity of the data. If the principal components obtained from PCA are already interpretable and aligned with the original variables, rotation may not be required. However, if the components are complex and difficult to interpret, rotation can be useful to simplify and clarify the results.

Common Rotation Methods

Varimax, Oblimin, and Promax are popular rotation methods used in PCA to achieve a more interpretable and meaningful representation of the extracted components. Below are descriptions of those rotation methods.

Varimax Rotation (Orthogonal)

Varimax rotation is a widely used orthogonal rotation method. It aims to maximize the variance of the squared loadings on each component, leading to a simple and sparse structure where each variable has a high loading on one component and close to zero loadings on other components. This rotation method helps in achieving component interpretability by reducing cross-loadings and emphasizing clear relationships between variables and components.

Oblimin Rotation (Oblique)

Oblimin rotation is a popular oblique rotation method. Unlike Varimax, Oblimin allows for correlation or obliqueness between the rotated components. The main objective of Oblimin rotation is to achieve a simpler structure by minimizing the number of variables with high loadings on a component. It allows for correlation between components, which can be useful when there are underlying factors that are not completely independent. Oblimin rotation provides a more flexible approach by allowing components to be correlated and can result in a more realistic representation of the data.

Promax Rotation (Oblique)

Promax rotation is an oblique rotation method that extends the advantages of Varimax rotation while also accounting for possible correlations between the rotated components. It is considered a compromise between the simplicity of orthogonal rotation and the flexibility of oblique rotation. Promax rotation includes a parameter (kappa) that controls the degree of orthogonality, which allows varying levels of correlation between components. By adjusting the kappa value, Promax rotation can be tuned to emphasize orthogonality (similar to Varimax) or allow for more correlation (similar to Oblimin).

These rotation methods provide different approaches to achieve a more interpretable and structured representation of the components obtained from PCA. The choice of rotation method depends on the specific goals of the analysis, the underlying assumptions about the relationships between variables, and the desired interpretability of the components. It's worth noting that there is no universally "best" rotation method, and the selection depends on the specific characteristics of the data.

Principal Component Analysis in SAS Enterprise Miner

In SAS Enterprise Miner, PCA is listed under the Modify group instead of the Model group. The reason is that in data mining, PCA is often used to reduce the data dimensionality for predictive modeling purposes. In other words, when we have a very large number of variables, we can use PCA to combine these variables into a smaller set of components and then use these components as predictors for the predictive modeling.

SAS Enterprise Miner preconfigures the PCA steps, so we do not have to perform each step in the PCA process as we must when using other statistics software, such as SPSS. It makes the process of running PCA easier but also decreases our controllability in the analysis process. However, we should keep in mind that in data mining, we need to automate the process to reduce the analysis time since we are analyzing large data. SAS Enterprise Miner still allows us to make certain changes in PCA configurations, which enables us to produce good principal components for dimensionality reduction. I will show you some key configurations in SAS Enterprise Miner that we could change.

SAS ENTERPRISE MINER GUIDELINES

Principal Component Node Train Properties

(https://documentation.sas.com)

The Principal Components node belongs to the Modify category in the SAS data mining process of Sample, Explore, Modify, Model, Assess (SEMMA). The Principal Components node calculates eigenvalues and eigenvectors from the uncorrected covariance matrix, corrected covariance matrix, or the correlation matrix of input variables.

Principal components are calculated from the eigenvectors and can be used as inputs for successor modeling nodes in the process flow diagram. Since interpreting principal components is often problematic or impossible, it is much safer to view them simply as a mathematical transformation of the set of original variables.

Eigenvalue Source – Use the Eigenvalue Source property of the Principal Components node to specify the type of source matrix that you want to use to calculate eigenvalues and eigenvectors. You can choose from:

- Covariance – Use the covariance matrix to calculate eigenvalues and eigenvectors.
- Correlation (Default) – Use the correlation matrix to calculate eigenvalues and eigenvectors.
- Uncorrected – Use the uncorrected matrix to calculate eigenvalues and eigenvectors.

Interactive Selection – Once the Principal Components node has successfully run, you can interactively view and select the principal components that you want to export to the successor node. Select the Ellipses Selector button to the right of the Interactive Selection property to open the Interactive Principal Components Selection table. You use the Plot list to select the y-axis Eigenvalue display. The y-axis display options are:

- Eigenvalue
- Proportional Eigenvalue
- Cumulative Proportional Eigenvalue
- Log Eigenvalue
- Eigenvalue Table

Example: Principal Component Analysis

In this example, we build a PCA model for the *airline recommendation* dataset.

Dataset: AirlineRecommendation.sas7bdat

Target variable: recommendation (binary): 1 – recommend the airline; 0 – do not recommend the airline.

Variables for PCA: Table 12.2 shows variables used for PCA. Note that since PCA is unsupervised learning, only input variables are used for the analysis. The target variable, *recommend*, will be omitted in the analysis process. We also reject the input variables with binary or nominal scales because it is less likely that they represent a subset of correlated variables.

Sample-Explore-Modify: Refer to the previous chapters. Since we have missing values for interval variables, we impute them with mean values.

TABLE 12.2

Airline Recommendation Data Description – Input Variables for PCA

Variable Name	Label/Description	Scale	Role
recommend	Recommend the airline to others	Binary (Yes/No)	Target
airline_st	Airline status	Nominal	Rejected
age	Age	Interval	Input
gender	Gender	Binary (Male/Female)	Rejected
price_sensitivity *	Price sensitivity	Interval	Input
no_years_flying	Number of years flying	Interval	Input
no_flt_pa	Average number of flights per year	Interval	Input
pct_ flt_other_airline	Percent of flights with other airlines	Interval	Input
type_of_travel	Travel purpose	Nominal	Reject
no_other_lty_cards	Number of other loyalty cards	Interval	Input
shopping_amt_airpt	Shopping amount at the airport	Interval	Input
eat_drink_airpt	Spending for eating and drinking at the airport	Interval	Input
class	Passenger class	Nominal	Rejected
origin_state	Origin state	Nominal	Rejected
destin_state	Destination state	Nominal	Rejected
depart_delay	Departure delay (in minutes)	Interval	Input
arrival_delay	Arrival delay (in minutes)	Interval	Input
flt_cancel	Flight cancellation	Binary (Yes/No)	Rejected
flt_time	Flight time (in minutes)	Interval	Input
flt_distance	Flight distance (miles)	Interval	Input

Principal Components Node

Follow the steps below to configure the Principal Components node.

1. From the Modify tab, drag a Principal Components node to the workspace and connect it to the Impute node.
2. In the Principal Components Training properties, set Eigenvalue Source to Covariance.
3. Keep other settings as default values.
4. Run the Principal Components node and open the Results window.

Number of Principal Components

First, we take a look at the number of principal components determined by the software first and then make the necessary adjustments to produce more meaningful outcomes. The easiest way to view this result is to use the scree plot (in SAS Enterprise Miner, it is called

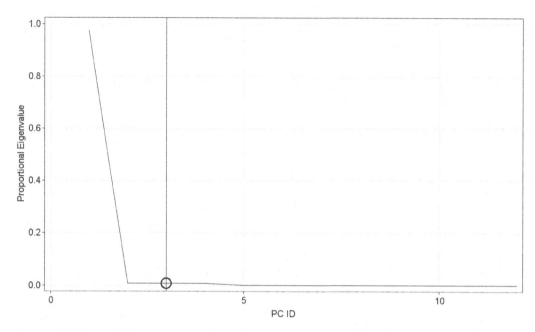

FIGURE 12.4
Eigenvalue plot (scree plot).

an eigenvalue plot). The initial results show that we have three components (Figure 12.4). However, as we can see that the three-component point is not the elbow of this plot. That means using three components does not improve the variance explained significantly, which may lead to irrelevant components. Using the elbow technique described above, we can see that the elbow appears at the two component points in the plot.

Thus, two components seem to be a better choice to capture variance in the data, and using three components may lead to irrelevant components. With that observation, we need to change the number of components to 2.

In order to do so, follow the steps below.

1. Close the Results window and go back to our PCA diagram.
2. In the Principal Components Train properties, click the ellipsis button (three-dot button) for Interactive Selection to open the Interactive Principal Components Selection window (see Figure 12.5). This window allows us to choose the number of components based on our evaluation.
3. Change the Number of Components to be exported to 2, and we will see the eigenvalue plot adjust to select three components.
4. Click OK.
5. Run the Principal Components node again.
6. Once the run is completed, open the Results window.

In the Results window, we clearly see three principal components derived from data based on our selection above. Let's review some key PCA outputs.

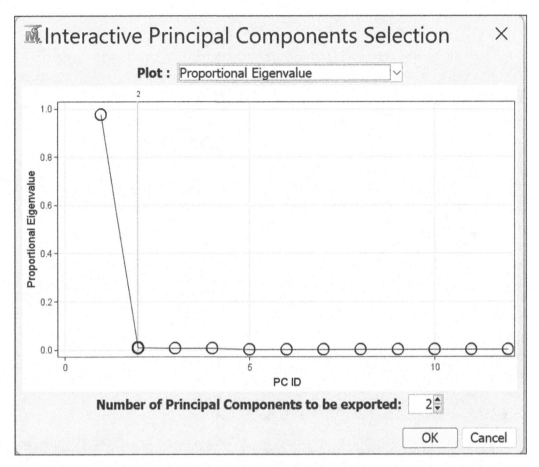

FIGURE 12.5
Interactive principal components selection.

Principal Components Matrix Plot

This visualization shows scatter plots for every possible pair of the designated principal components. By default, the initial matrix plot presents scatter plots featuring the first five principal components. Each data point is assigned a specific color corresponding to the value of the target variable.

Figures 12.6 and 12.7 show the Principal Components Matrix plots for our PCA model with two components at two levels of the target variable: Yes = recommend= and No = not recommend. We can see the relationship between two principal components for these two cases. These plots are certainly not easy to understand. We should not try to explain all the details of the plots but rather should focus on the pairwise scatter plot between each pair of the principal components. As you can see, we have two principal components, which results in two pairwise plots: PC1-PC2 and PC2-PC1. They are particularly the same, just in different directions. The key takeaway is that those scatter plots are random and do not show any pattern, meaning those principal components are uncorrelated. Other outputs will give us more information about those components.

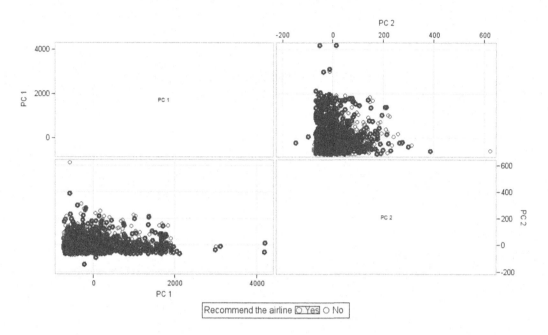

FIGURE 12.6
Principal Components Matrix plot (target = Yes).

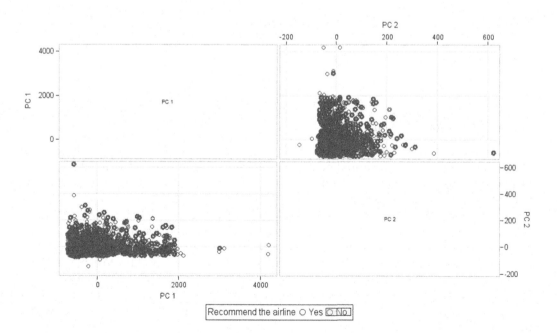

FIGURE 12.7
Principal Components Matrix plot (target = No).

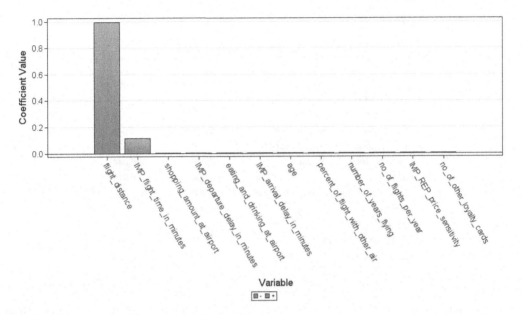

FIGURE 12.8
Principal component coefficient – component 1.

The next output that we review is the principal component coefficients for those two components. Figures 12.8 and 12.9 show the coefficients for Component 1 and Component 2, respectively. I use a cutoff value of 0.1 to identify the relevant variables for each component. The results in Figure 12.8 show that Component 1 consists of two primary variables, *flight distance* and *flight time*. We can see that these two variables are correlated

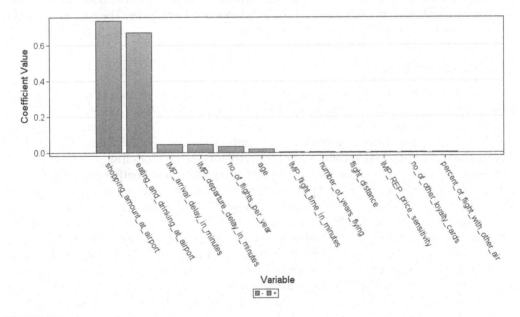

FIGURE 12.9
Principal component coefficient – component 2.

TABLE 12.3

Principal Components Coefficients for Two Components

Variables	PC1	PC2
flight_distance	0.993	−0.001
flight_time_in_minutes	0.115	0.002
shopping_amount_at_airport	0.001	0.738
departure_delay_in_minutes	0.000	−0.044
eating_and_drinking_at_airport	0.000	0.671
arrival_delay_in_minutes	0.000	−0.044
age	0.000	0.019
percent_of_flight_with_other_air	0.000	0.000
number_of_years_flying	0.000	0.001
no_of_flights_per_year	0.000	−0.033
REP_price_sensitivity	0.000	−0.001
no_of_other_loyalty_cards	0.000	0.000

since they both measure the duration of a flight. Additionally, Figure 12.9 shows that Component 2 consists of two variables, *shopping amount at airports* and *eating and drinking spending at airports*. Both of them refer to the passenger's spending at the airport. For this component, we do not consider *departure delay time* and *arrival delay time* because their coefficients are lower than 0.1, and they a clearly not correlated with the other two variables.

Based on these component coefficients, we can conclude that two components are a good choice for this data as they capture the variance in the data and also produce meaningful principal components for the dimensionality reduction purpose. These principal components can also be seen clearly in Table 12.3. In this table, we present the coefficients for two components and mark the variables with coefficients of 0.1 or higher. The results show the same component structure as we observed above.

Dimensionality Reduction

So, what does it mean for data dimension reduction with those two principal components? Basically, the findings inform us that *flight distance* and *flight time* can be combined into one new variable (PC1), and *shopping amount at the airport* and *eating and drinking spending at the airport* can be combined into another variable (PC2). Thus, PC1 and PC2 replace these four original variables as new predictors in the modeling step. Other input variables are still being used as potential predictors. Their low coefficients do not mean we should remove them but rather mean these variables are exclusive and they cannot be reduced to principal components. Table 12.4 shows the input variables we use as predictors for predictive modeling. PC1 and PC2 are new variables as the results of the PCA. We give PC1 the name *flight duration* as it captures the flight time and distance and give PC2 the name *spending at airport* since it captures the amount of spending on food, drink, and shopping at the airport. As you can see, originally, we use 19 input variables for predictive modeling. By using PCA to combine some variables, we can reduce the number of predictors to 17 predictors. This small dimensionality reduction is just an example in this case. If we have a large dataset with many correlated variables, we are able to reduce the data dimension further.

TABLE 12.4

Airline Recommendation Data – New Input Variables for Predictive Modeling

No	Variable Name	Label/Description	Scale	Role
1	recommend	Recommend the airline to others	Binary (Yes/No)	Target
2	airline_st	Airline status	Nominal	Input
3	age	Age	Interval	Input
4	gender	Gender	Binary (Male/Female)	Input
5	price_sensitivity	Price sensitivity	Interval	Input
6	no_years_flying	Number of years flying	Interval	Input
7	no_flt_pa	Average number of flights per year	Interval	Input
8	pct_flt_other_airline	Percent of flights with other airlines	Interval	Input
9	type_of_travel	Travel purpose	Nominal	Input
10	no_other_lty_cards	Number of other loyalty cards	Interval	Input
11	shopping_amt_airpt	Shopping amount at the airport	Interval	Rejected
12	eat_drink_airpt	Spending for eating and drinking at the airport	Interval	Rejected
13	class	Passenger class	Nominal	Input
14	origin_state	Origin state	Nominal	Input
15	destin_state	Destination state	Nominal	Input
16	depart_delay	Departure delay (in minutes)	Interval	Input
17	arrival_delay	Arrival delay (in minutes)	Interval	Input
18	flt_cancel	Flight cancellation	Binary (Yes/No)	Input
19	flt_time	Flight time (in minutes)	Interval	Rejected
20	flt_distance	Flight distance (miles)	Interval	Rejected
21	PC1 (flight duration)*	Flight distance and time	Interval	Input
22	PC2 (spending at airport)*	Amount of spending at the airport	Interval	Input

* New variables

Summary

PCA is a widely used dimensionality reduction technique in data mining that aims to transform high-dimensional data into lower-dimensional data while preserving the most important information. PCA achieves this goal by identifying the principal components, which are new variables that capture the maximum variance in the data. The first principal component explains the largest amount of variability, followed by subsequent components in descending order. By selecting a subset of principal components that capture a significant portion of the total variance, PCA enables the reduction of data dimensionality while retaining meaningful information.

PCA offers several advantages in data mining. It simplifies the data representation by reducing the number of variables, making it easier to visualize and interpret. It also helps to eliminate redundant or irrelevant variables, thereby improving computational efficiency and mitigating the risk of overfitting. PCA can uncover hidden patterns and relationships within the data, as the principal components represent linear combinations of the original variables. Additionally, PCA can be used as a preprocessing step before building predictive models to reduce the number of variables using principal components that capture maximum variance in the data.

However, it is important to note that PCA relies on the assumption of linearity and is sensitive to outliers. Furthermore, interpreting the meaning of the principal components might be challenging, as they are combinations of multiple original variables. Nonetheless, PCA remains a valuable tool in data mining, enabling effective dimensionality reduction, variable selection, and exploratory data analysis.

CHAPTER DISCUSSION QUESTIONS

1. What is PCA and how does it enable dimensionality reduction?
2. Discuss the advantages and potential limitations of using PCA to reduce the number of variables in a dataset.
3. How does PCA capture and quantify the variability in the data through the concept of principal components?
4. Explain the role of eigenvalues and eigenvectors in determining the importance and direction of each principal component.
5. In what scenarios would PCA be particularly useful in data mining tasks? Discuss specific applications where PCA has been successfully applied.
6. What techniques can be used to determine the optimal number of principal components to retain in a given dataset?
7. Discuss the interpretation of the principal components obtained from PCA. How can the relationships between the original variables and the principal components be understood and analyzed?
8. What is the purpose of the component rotation in CPA? Discuss primary rotation methods.
9. Discuss the trade-off between dimensionality reduction achieved by PCA and the potential loss of information. How can the impact of dimensionality reduction on model performance or data analysis outcomes be assessed and evaluated?

Exercises

Exercise 1: PCA for the Bank dataset

1. Open the *bank* dataset in SAS Enterprise Miner.
2. Sample the entire dataset. See the variable names and descriptions in Appendix A.1.
3. Partition the data using a split ratio of 60:40 (train: 60%; validation: 20%; test: 20%)
4. Perform data modification as follows:
   - Impute missing values.
   - Normalize interval variables.

5. Reject *CRSCORE* (the target variable) and all categorical variables (binary and nominal) in the dataset.
6. Conduct a PCA for all interval input variables.
   - Set Eigenvalue Source to Covariance.
   - Check the number of principal components using the eigenvalue plot and make the adjustment as needed.
7. Present the PCA results.
8. Identify the principal components and the significant variables composing each component.
9. Validate the results for those components with the principal component coefficients.
10. Interpret the dimensional reduction with those principal components and give them names and descriptions.

Exercise 2: PCA for the Passengers dataset

1. Open the *passengers* dataset in SAS Enterprise Miner.
2. Sample 20% of the full data. Set *return* (decision to return to the airline) as the target variable and change its role to binary. See the variable names and descriptions in Appendix A.2.
3. Partition the data using a split ratio of 60:40 (train: 60%; validation: 20%; test: 20%)
4. Perform data modification as follows:
   - Replace zero values for Likert scale variables with missing values.
   - Impute missing values.
   - Normalize interval variables.
5. Reject *recommend* (the target variable) and all categorical variables (binary and nominal) in the dataset.
6. Conduct a PCA for all interval input variables.
   - Set Eigenvalue Source to Covariance.
   - Check the number of principal components using the eigenvalue plot and make the adjustment as needed.
7. Present the PCA results.
8. Identify the principal components and the significant variables composing each component.
9. Validate the results for these components with the principal component coefficients.
10. Interpret the dimensional reduction with these principal components and give them names and descriptions.
11. Evaluate the reliability and validity of the champion model.
12. Present the variable importance information and interpret the results.

13

Cluster Analysis

LEARNING OUTCOMES

Upon the completion of this chapter, you will be able to

1. Describe the concept and principle of cluster analysis.
2. Differentiate between cluster analysis and Principal Component Analysis.
3. Discuss the advantages and disadvantages of cluster analysis.
4. Explain how cluster analysis groups object by similarity.
5. Compare hierarchical and partitioning cluster algorithms.
6. Describe the key steps involved in the cluster analysis process.
7. Explain the role of distance measures in cluster analysis and describe common measures.
8. Describe the two-step cluster analysis. Discuss its advantages and limitations.
9. Conduct cluster analysis using SAS Enterprise Miner.

Introduction

In this book, we cover two unsupervised learning methods. In Chapter 12, we have learned about Principal Component Analysis (PCA). Another unsupervised learning method that I want to introduce is cluster analysis. Even though it is also unsupervised learning like PCA, cluster analysis serves a very different purpose. Suppose we have a large dataset, and each record in the data represents a specific case or a specific individual. When we have a dataset with a  million records of cases or individuals, in some cases, we want to find out if these cases or individuals share similar characteristics, and if yes, how we can group them into different groups. These groups must represent distinct segments of cases or individuals in the sector of interest. Based on this segmentation, we can choose the right strategies to make informed business decisions, either to address the safety issues for these segments of cases or to market a product or service to those segments of customers. These groups or segments are also called clusters; hence, the term *cluster analysis*.

424

DOI: 10.1201/9781003162872-15

Cluster analysis is a powerful technique used in machine learning for identifying groups of data points that share similar characteristics. It is a type of unsupervised learning, which means that it does not require labeled data to identify the patterns in the data. Instead, it uses a clustering algorithm to group similar data points together based on their distance from each other. This chapter provides an introduction to cluster analysis, including its definition, applications, and types of clustering algorithms.

Definition of Cluster Analysis

Cluster analysis is an unsupervised learning method that groups similar data points together into clusters based on their similarity. The similarity between two data points is measured by their distance from each other. The goal of cluster analysis is to identify the underlying structure of the data and group similar data points into clusters or segments. Clusters are expected to be distinct from each other, and the dissimilarity between clusters is measured by the distance between each pair of clusters. Figure 13.1 shows an illustration of cluster analysis.

> **DEFINITION**
>
> Cluster analysis is an unsupervised learning method that groups similar data points together into clusters based on their similarity.

These clusters are distinct from each other and represent exclusive groups of individuals or cases. By examining the characteristics and attributes of these clusters based on the demographic and relevant variables, we can differentiate between them. This step is called cluster profiling. The profiles identified from cluster profiling allow decision-makers to establish effective strategies targeting each cluster. Cluster analysis is widely used in various fields, such as biology, finance, marketing, and social sciences.

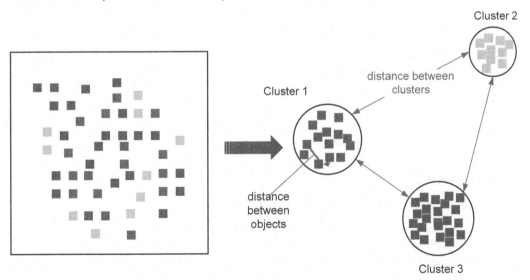

FIGURE 13.1
Illustration of cluster analysis.

Practical Applications of Cluster Analysis

Cluster analysis is a useful technique for grouping similar objects or observations together based on their attributes or characteristics. It is applied in many domains. Some practical applications of cluster analysis are as follows.

- *Customer segmentation*: In marketing, companies use cluster analysis to group customers based on their demographic, geographic, and behavioral characteristics. This clustering helps them identify customer segments that have similar needs and preferences and allows marketers to tailor their marketing strategies accordingly.
- *Image segmentation*: Cluster analysis is used to segment images into regions with similar color or texture characteristics. This application can be useful for object detection, image recognition, and other image processing tasks.
- *Fraud detection*: Financial companies use this method to detect fraudulent activity by identifying groups of transactions that are similar in nature. Then, they can identify potential fraudsters who are attempting to avoid detection by spreading their activity across multiple transactions.
- *Medical diagnosis*: In healthcare, cluster analysis is used to group patients based on their symptoms and medical history. Doctors can use it to diagnose diseases and develop personalized treatment plans for each patient.
- *Natural language processing*: In this field, researchers use cluster analysis to group similar documents or words together. This tool can be useful for information retrieval, topic modeling, and other text processing tasks.
- *Crime analysis*: By using cluster analysis, law enforcement can identify areas with high crime rates by grouping together crimes that are similar in nature. Police departments use the cluster profiles to allocate resources more efficiently and reduce crime rates in high-risk areas.

These are just a few examples of how cluster analysis can be applied in different domains. The technique is widely applicable and can be used in any situation where there is a need to group similar objects together based on their characteristics and attributes.

Differences between PCA and Cluster Analysis

PCA and cluster analysis are two different unsupervised machine learning methods. However, both involve grouping objects in the dataset based on their covariance or similarities. It is easier to get confused between them, which may lead to misuse of the technique. Hence, it is important to understand the differences between these methods so we can select

TABLE 13.1

Comparison between PCA and Cluster Analysis

Items	Principal Component Analysis (PCA)	Cluster Analysis
Purpose	To identify the most important variables or combinations of variables that explain the variation in the data and to reduce the dimensionality of the data.	To group objects or observations together based on their similarity or dissimilarity of specific characteristics and attributes.
Goal	To simplify the data and identify the underlying structure in the data, rather than to group or cluster similar objects together.	To identify natural groupings in the data and to understand the characteristics of each group.
Objects of analysis	Variables	Observations (cases or individuals)
Output	A set of principal components that summarize the information in the original data.	A set of clusters, where each cluster is a group of similar objects.
Methodology	PCA involves creating a new set of variables, called principal components, which are linear combinations of the original variables. The principal components are ordered based on their importance, with the first principal component explaining the largest amount of variation in the data.	Cluster analysis involves partitioning the data into a set of groups, called clusters, such that objects within a cluster are as similar as possible to each other, while objects in different clusters are as dissimilar as possible from each other.
Application	PCA is often used in data visualization, variable selection, and dimensionality reduction.	Cluster analysis is used in market segmentation, customer profiling, and anomaly detection.
Similarity and dissimilarity measures	PCA does not involve any similarity or dissimilarity measures.	Cluster analysis requires a similarity or dissimilarity measure to group similar objects together.

the right one based on the analysis purpose. Table 13.1 provides a comparison between PCA and cluster analysis.

Basic Concepts in Cluster Analysis

Cluster analysis is a data exploration and unsupervised machine learning technique used to group similar objects or observations together based on their characteristics. There are some fundamental concepts in cluster analysis. Understanding these concepts is crucial for effectively applying clustering techniques and interpreting the results. Table 13.2 presents these concepts and descriptions.

TABLE 13.2

Basic Concepts in Cluster Analysis and Descriptions

Terms	Descriptions
Clustering	A process of grouping objects or observations into clusters (segments) based on their similarity or proximity. The goal is to create clusters that are internally homogeneous (objects within the same cluster are similar) and externally heterogeneous (objects from different clusters are dissimilar).
Cluster or segment	A cluster, also known as a segment, refers to a group of data points or objects that are similar to each other based on certain characteristics or attributes.
Distance or similarity measures	A distance, also known as a similarity measure, quantifies the similarity or dissimilarity between pairs of objects. These measures are used to determine the proximity between objects and form the basis for clustering algorithms. Common distance measures include Euclidean distance, Manhattan distance, and cosine similarity.
Centroids	Centroids are the mean values of the attributes for the objects in a cluster. They are used to represent the cluster and are often used as the basis for assigning new objects to a cluster.
Dendrograms	A dendrogram is a tree-like diagram that shows the hierarchical relationship between clusters in hierarchical clustering. The height of each branch represents the distance between clusters at that level.
Clustering algorithms	A clustering algorithm determines the number of clusters and assigns observations to clusters. Cluster algorithms can be categorized into hierarchical clustering and partitioning clustering.
Hierarchical clustering	Hierarchical clustering builds a hierarchy of clusters, forming a tree-like structure called a dendrogram.
Partitioning clustering	Partitioning clustering divides the data into non-overlapping partitions or clusters. It directly assigns each data point to a specific cluster.
K-means clustering	K-means is a partitioning clustering algorithm that partitions the data into K distinct clusters by iteratively updating the cluster centroids and assigning data points to the nearest centroid. The objective is to minimize the sum of squared distances between data points and their respective cluster centroids.
Cluster assignment	Cluster assignment is a process of assigning each object to a specific cluster based on its similarity to the cluster centroids. The assignment is usually done by comparing the distance or similarity of the object to the centroids.
Cluster validation	Cluster validation is a process of assessing the quality and reliability of the clusters obtained. It involves evaluating the internal cohesion and separation of the clusters, as well as their stability and meaningfulness.
Cluster profiling	Cluster profiling involves analyzing the characteristics of each cluster, such as the mean value of the attributes or the distribution of the objects within the cluster.

Advantages and Disadvantages of Cluster Analysis

Cluster analysis is a powerful unsupervised technique for identifying patterns in data sets, but it also has its limitations. We should carefully consider this method's strengths and weaknesses when using it in machine learning.

Advantages

- *Pattern recognition*: Cluster analysis helps identify patterns in large data sets that may not be apparent to humans.

- *Unsupervised learning*: It is an unsupervised learning method, which means that it does not require a target variable and labeled data to identify patterns. This makes it useful in situations where labeled data is scarce or expensive to obtain.
- *Data reduction*: Cluster analysis reduces the size of large data sets by grouping similar data points together. It makes it easier to analyze and visualize data. Instead of dealing with individual data points, we have the data represented by the clusters, reducing the complexity and dimensionality of the dataset.
- *Decision making*: It helps with decision-making by identifying groups of similar objects or data points that can be used to inform decisions.
- *Anomaly detection*: Clustering identifies outliers or anomalies that deviate significantly from the typical patterns observed in clusters. These anomalies could represent errors, unusual behaviors, or novel observations that necessitate further investigation.

Disadvantages

- *Difficulty with the number of clusters*: One of the main challenges of cluster analysis is determining the optimal number of clusters. If the number of clusters is too small, important patterns may be overlooked. If it is too large, the results may be difficult to interpret.
- *Sensitivity to initial conditions*: This method is sensitive to the initial conditions such as cluster centers. Different starting points can lead to different results. Multiple runs with different initializations might be necessary to achieve more robust results.
- *Outliers*: Cluster analysis is also sensitive to outliers, and outliers can skew the results of the clustering analysis.
- *Difficulty with high-dimensional data*: As the dimensionality of the data increases, the distance measures may become less meaningful, and the curse of dimensionality can impact the clustering results.
- *Interpretability*: While clustering can reveal clusters or segments in the data, the meaning and interpretation of the clusters often require further analysis and domain knowledge. The clusters themselves may not have clear labels or explanations, limiting their direct utility in some applications.
- *Scalability*: This method can be computationally intensive and may not be scalable to very large data sets. This can make it difficult to use in situations where real-time analysis is required.

Steps of Cluster Analysis Process

In order to conduct cluster analysis, there are typically eight steps as follows.

1. *Data preprocessing*: This step involves data cleaning, data transformation, and variable selection. The goal of data preprocessing is to ensure that the data is in a suitable format for clustering.
2. *Variable selection for clustering*: Clusters are formed based on similarity. In this step, we select the variables that are used to determine the similarity between objects.

3. *Distance measure selection*: The next step is to select an appropriate distance measure to quantify the similarity or dissimilarity between pairs of objects. This is an important step, as the choice of distance measure can affect the clustering results. In this book, we cover some most common distance measures in cluster analysis.

4. *Clustering algorithm selection*: There are two primary types of clustering algorithms, hierarchical clustering and partitioning clustering. It is important to select an appropriate clustering algorithm based on the characteristics of the data and the purpose of the clustering analysis.

5. *Selection of the number of clusters*: The next step is to determine the optimal number of clusters for the data. This can be done using visualization techniques such as the elbow method or using statistical validation measures.

6. *Cluster assignment*: In this step, each object is assigned to a cluster. This step is done by applying the chosen clustering algorithm to the data. In other words, objects are assigned to the appropriate clusters based on their similarity.

7. *Cluster profiling*: Once the objects have been assigned to clusters, the next step is to profile the clusters. Cluster profiling involves analyzing the characteristics of each cluster, such as the mean value of the attributes or the distribution of the objects within the cluster.

8. *Cluster validation*: The final step is to validate the clustering results to ensure that the clustering results are meaningful, reliable, and appropriate for the data.

These are the general steps involved in cluster analysis. The actual implementation of cluster analysis may involve variations and adjustments to these steps depending on the nature of the data and the purpose of the clustering analysis. Many data mining software apps have built-in tools for several steps, which reduce our efforts in the analysis process. We will perform cluster analysis with the airline recommendation dataset using features provided by SAS Enterprise Miner. I won't present all of the above steps explicitly because some of them have been covered in other chapters or incorporated into the software.

Cluster Distance Measure

Distance measures play a crucial role in the cluster analysis process, in general, and in clustering algorithms, in particular, as they determine the similarity or dissimilarity between data points. We cover some common distance measures in this section. Figure 13.2 illustrates these measures and how they differ.

Euclidean Distance

It is the most common distance measure and is defined as the straight-line distance between two data points in Euclidean space. It is measured as the square root of the sum of the squared differences between the corresponding coordinates of the two points.

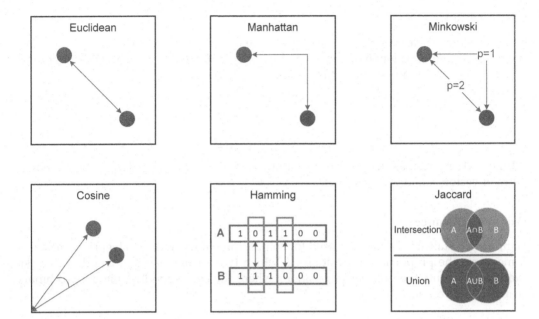

FIGURE 13.2
Different measures of cluster distance.

The formula for the distance is as follows

$$d(x,y) = \sqrt{(x_1 - y_1)^2 + (x_2 - y_2)^2 + \cdots + (x_n - y_n)^2}$$

where
$d(x, y)$ is the distance between two data points, x and y
$(x_1, x_2, ..., x_n)$ and $(y_1, y_2, ..., y_n)$ are the coordinates of the two data points.

Manhattan Distance

Manhattan distance is also known as city block distance or L_1 distance. It measures the distance between two data points by summing the absolute differences between their coordinates. It is named after the city block grid layout, where the shortest path between two points follows a grid-like pattern.

$$d(x,y) = |x_1 - y_1| + |x_2 - y_2| + \cdots |x_n - y_n|$$

Minkowski Distance

Minkowski distance is a generalization of both Euclidean and Manhattan distances. It is defined as the nth root of the sum of the nth powers of the absolute differences between corresponding coordinates of two points.

$$d(x,y) = \left(|x_1 - y_1|^p + |x_2 - y_2|^p + \cdots |x_n - y_n|^p \right)^{1/p}$$

Where p is a parameter. When $p = 1$, it reduces to Manhattan distance, and when $p = 2$, it becomes Euclidean distance.

Cosine Distance

Cosine distance measures the cosine of the angle between two vectors, representing data points. It is often used when dealing with high-dimensional data or when the magnitude of the vectors is not important, but the orientation is crucial.

$$d(x,y) = \frac{1-(x*y)}{\|x\|*\|y\|}$$

Where x*y represents the product of x and y, and ||x|| and ||y|| denote the Euclidean norm of vectors x and y, respectively.

Hamming Distance

Hamming distance is commonly used for comparing binary data or categorical variables. It measures the proportion of positions at which two strings of equal length differ. For example, it counts the number of positions where the corresponding bits in two binary strings are different.

$$d(x,y) = |x_1 - y_1| + |x_2 - y_2| + \cdots |x_n - y_n|$$

$$\textit{If } x_i = y_i \textit{ then } x_i - y_i = 0$$

$$\textit{If } x_i \neq y_i \textit{ then } x_i - y_i = 1$$

Jaccard Distance

Jaccard distance is a measure of dissimilarity between two sets. It is defined as the ratio of the difference between the sizes of the union and the intersection of the sets to the size of the union. It is commonly used in data mining, text analysis, and recommendation systems.

$$d(A,B) = 1 - \frac{|A \cap B|}{|A \cup B|}$$

Where A = set 1 and B = set 2

These are some common distance measures used in cluster analysis. The choice of distance measure depends on the type of data and the specific requirements of the analysis. Each distance measure may be more appropriate for a specific scenario, so it is essential to understand the characteristics of the data and the goals of the analysis when selecting a distance measure.

> In this chapter, we use the Euclidean distance in our examples since it is the most common distance measure in cluster analysis and is measured by a straight-line distance between two data points.

Types of Clustering Algorithms

Two common types of clustering algorithms are hierarchical clustering and partitioning clustering. We discuss these algorithms at a high level and try to avoid mathematical expressions in the algorithms. Most data mining software applications incorporate these algorithms in their interface or menu, which allows us to perform the analysis without having to set up complex configurations.

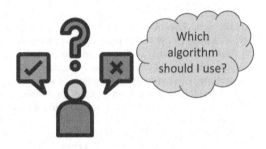

Hierarchical Clustering

Hierarchical clustering is a type of clustering algorithm that groups data points into a tree-like structure called a dendrogram. It starts with assigning each data point into a separate cluster and then merges the closest clusters together based on their similarity. The process continues until all data points are in a single cluster or until a specified number of clusters is reached. Hierarchical clustering can be either agglomerative or divisive.

Partitioning Clustering

Partitioning clustering is a type of clustering algorithm that divides the data points into a predefined number of clusters. The goal is to minimize the distance between data points within each cluster and maximize the distance between clusters. The most commonly used partitioning clustering algorithm is k-means.

Figure 13.3 presents an illustration of hierarchical and partitioning clustering. Table 13.3 summarizes the key differences between them.

HIERARCHICAL CLUSTERING

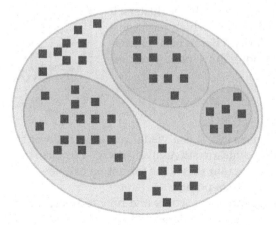

PARTITIONING CLUSTERING

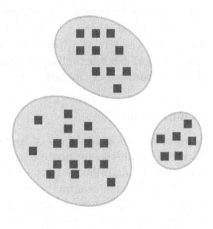

FIGURE 13.3
Hierarchical clustering and partitioning clustering.

TABLE 13.3

Differences between Hierarchical Clustering and Partitioning Clustering

Hierarchical Clustering	Partitioning Clustering
1. *Hierarchy*: Hierarchical clustering creates a hierarchy of clusters by iteratively merging or splitting clusters based on similarity or distance measures.	1. *Fixed number of clusters*: Partitioning clustering methods, such as k-means or k-medoids, require specifying the number of clusters in advance.
2. *Agglomerative and divisive*: It can be agglomerative, starting with individual data points as separate clusters and merging them together, or divisive, starting with a single cluster and splitting it into smaller clusters.	2. *Non-hierarchical*: Partitioning clustering does not create a hierarchy of clusters. It assigns each data point to one and only one cluster based on a predefined criterion.
3. *Number of clusters*: Hierarchical clustering does not require specifying the number of clusters in advance. It produces a hierarchical structure with different levels of granularity, which allows users to choose the number of clusters based on their requirements.	3. *Objective function optimization*: Partitioning methods aim to optimize an objective function, such as minimizing the within-cluster variance or maximizing inter-cluster dissimilarity.
4. *Cluster representation*: The results of hierarchical clustering can be visualized using dendrograms, which show the hierarchical structure of clusters and the distance at which they merge.	4. *Speed*: Partitioning algorithms are generally faster than hierarchical clustering, especially for large datasets, as they do not require pairwise distance calculations for all data points.
5. *Computationally expensive*: Hierarchical clustering can be computationally expensive, especially for large datasets, as it requires computing pairwise distances or similarities between all data points.	5. *Initialization sensitivity*: The initial selection of cluster centroids in partitioning methods can significantly affect the final clustering results, making them sensitive to initialization.
6. *Noisy data handling*: This algorithm is robust to noise and outliers in the data because it does not rely on a global optimization criterion but rather on local similarities.	6. *Difficulty with outliers*: Partitioning methods can be sensitive to outliers because they try to optimize a global criterion. Outliers can influence the cluster centers and distort the resulting clusters.

Hierarchical Clustering

Hierarchical clustering groups data points into a hierarchy of clusters. It creates a tree-like structure known as a dendrogram, which represents the nested clusters at different levels of similarity. Hierarchical clustering is a more flexible method because it does not require us to predetermine the number of clusters.

Dendrogram

Dendrogram is a vital part of hierarchical clustering. It is a visual representation of the hierarchical clustering process in which data points are successively merged into clusters based on their similarity. Each step in the dendrogram shows the formation of a new cluster by joining two existing clusters or individual data points.

In order to help you understand how the dendrogram works and how to interpret the diagram, I provide a simple example. Suppose we have a dataset of six data points: A, B, C, D, E, and F. To create a dendrogram using hierarchical clustering, we first start by considering each data point as an individual cluster. Then, we iteratively merge the closest

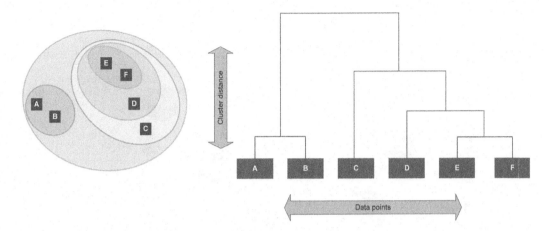

FIGURE 13.4
Example of a dendrogram.

clusters based on a distance metric (e.g., Euclidean distance) until all data points are in one final cluster. Figure 13.4 shows the dendrogram for this example.

- A and B form the cluster [A, B].
- E and F form the cluster [E, F].
- Cluster [E, F] merges with D to form the cluster [D, [E, F]].
- Cluster [D, [E, F]] merges with C to form the cluster [C, [D, [E, F]]].
- All data points now belong to a single cluster.

As you can see, dendrograms allow us to visually examine how data points are successively merged into clusters. It creates a hierarchy of clusters, and the clusters are nested and organized as a tree.

There are two main types of hierarchical clustering, as follows.

Agglomerative clustering (bottom-up): Agglomerative clustering starts with each data point as an individual cluster and iteratively merges the most similar clusters until all data points belong to a single cluster. At each step, the algorithm identifies the closest pair of clusters based on a chosen distance metric and merges them. This process continues until all data points are in a single cluster (Figure 13.5).

Divisive clustering (top-down): Divisive clustering takes the opposite approach. It starts with all data points in a single cluster and recursively splits the clusters into smaller, more distinct clusters until each data point is in its own cluster. At each step, the algorithm identifies the most dissimilar cluster and divides it into two new clusters based on a chosen distance metric. This process continues until each data point forms an individual cluster (Figure 13.6).

The choice of distance measure plays a crucial role in hierarchical clustering. The linkage criterion determines how the distance between clusters is computed during the merging or splitting process. Common linkage methods include single-linkage, complete-linkage, and average-linkage. We will cover different distance measures later.

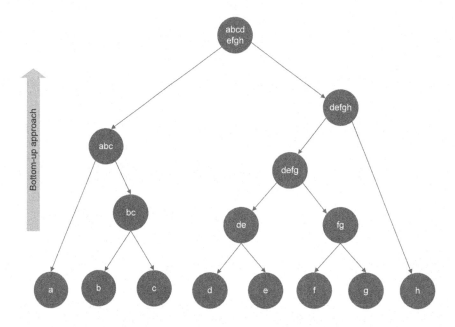

HIERARCHICAL AGGLOMERATIVE CLUSTERING

FIGURE 13.5
Agglomerative clustering (bottom-up).

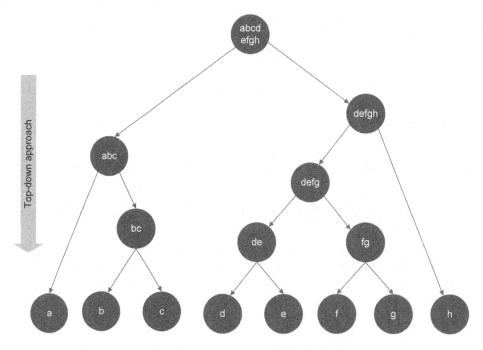

HIERARCHICAL DIVISIVE CLUSTERING

FIGURE 13.6
Divisive clustering (top-down).

Hierarchical clustering has several advantages. It can reveal the inherent structure and relationships in the data by forming a hierarchy of clusters. The dendrogram provides a visual representation of the clustering process, which makes it easy to interpret. Hierarchical clustering is also capable of handling various types of data, including numerical, categorical, and binary data.

However, hierarchical clustering can be computationally expensive, especially with large datasets, as it requires pairwise distance computations. Additionally, the choice of distance metric, linkage criterion, and interpretation of the dendrogram may vary based on the data and application.

Partitioning Clustering

Partitioning clustering, also known as partitional clustering, is a type of clustering algorithm that aims to partition a dataset into non-overlapping clusters. Unlike hierarchical clustering, which creates a hierarchy of clusters, partitioning clustering directly assigns each data point to a specific cluster. The goal is to optimize a predefined objective function, such as minimizing the intra-cluster distance and maximizing the inter-cluster distance.

One of the most well-known partitioning clustering algorithms is k-means. The k-means method partitions the data into K distinct clusters by iteratively updating the cluster centroids and assigning data points to the nearest centroid. The algorithm works iteratively to assign data points to clusters and adjust the cluster centroids until convergence. The objective is to minimize the sum of squared distances between data points and their respective cluster centroids.

The k-means clustering algorithm includes the following steps.

1. *Initialization*: Choose the number of clusters, K, and randomly initialize K centroids within the data range.

2. *Assignment*: Assign each data point to the nearest centroid based on a distance measure, commonly Euclidean distance. This step creates K clusters.

3. *Update*: Recalculate the centroid for each cluster by taking the mean of all data points assigned to that cluster.

4. *Iteration*: Repeat steps 2 and 3 until convergence. Convergence occurs when the centroids no longer change significantly or when a predetermined maximum number of iterations is reached.

5. *Result*: Once the algorithm converges, each data point belongs to a particular cluster, and the cluster centroids represent the center of each cluster.

K-means is a simple and efficient algorithm, but its success depends on the initial choice of centroids and the number of clusters (K). The choice of K, the number of clusters, is typically based on domain knowledge or using techniques such as the elbow method or silhouette analysis to determine the optimal number of clusters. Therefore, multiple runs of the algorithm with different initializations can be performed, and the clustering result with the lowest error is chosen.

K-means clustering is relatively efficient and scalable for large datasets. However, it has a few limitations. First, it assumes that the clusters have a spherical shape and that each data point belongs to only one cluster. It is also sensitive to the initial centroid positions, which can result in different outcomes for different initializations.

Two-Step Cluster Analysis

The two-step cluster analysis algorithm is a common strategy in cluster analysis. It combines elements of hierarchical clustering and k-means clustering to perform the analysis. It is particularly useful when dealing with large datasets or datasets with mixed variable types (both continuous and categorical).

The process involves two main steps as follows.

1. *Pre-clustering*: In the first step, a hierarchical clustering algorithm (such as agglomerative clustering) is used to create a preliminary clustering solution. This pre-clustering step helps to identify potential clusters and reduces the computational complexity for larger datasets.

2. *Two-step clustering*: In this step, the algorithm applies the k-means clustering algorithm to the pre-clustered data. The k-means algorithm iteratively assigns cases to clusters based on their proximity to the cluster centroids. The centroids are recalculated at each iteration until convergence is achieved.

Advantages of Two-Step Cluster Analysis

- *Suitable for large datasets*: Two-step cluster analysis is efficient and scalable for handling large datasets.

- *Automatic determination of the number of clusters*: The technique automatically determines the optimal number of clusters based on statistical criteria, which relieves us from the burden of specifying the number of clusters beforehand.

- *Handles mixed data types*: Two-step cluster analysis can handle both categorical and continuous variables, making it suitable for datasets with different types of variables.

Limitations of Two-Step Cluster Analysis

- *Sensitivity to outliers*: Like other clustering algorithms, two-step cluster analysis can be sensitive to outliers, which may affect the clustering results.

- *Relies on predefined distance measures*: The algorithm assumes that the similarity between data points can be measured using a predefined distance measure which may not always capture the underlying structure of the data accurately.

- *Lack of interpretability*: The resulting clusters may not always have clear and easily interpretable meanings, requiring further analysis and validation.

Overall, two-step cluster analysis is a useful method for data mining projects since it handles well large data with dif-

> In this book, we use the two-step method to perform cluster analysis using SAS Enterprise Miner.

ferent types of variables. In addition, the automatic determination of the number of clusters increases the efficiency of the process.

Cluster Analysis in SAS Enterprise Miner

In SAS Enterprise Miner, cluster analysis is listed under the Explore group instead of the Model group. The reason is that in data mining, cluster analysis is often used to explore the data.

SAS Enterprise Miner provides two different nodes for cluster analysis, the Cluster node in the Model group and the HP Cluster node in the HPDM group. SAS Enterprise Miner preconfigures the cluster analysis steps, so we do not have to perform each step in the cluster analysis process. It is a big advantage compared to traditional statistics software, which requires users to conduct all steps manually. This built-in tool makes the process of running cluster analysis easier, but it also decreases our controllability in the analysis process. Keep in mind that SAS Enterprise Miner uses the two-step clustering algorithm and offers limited changes to configurations. I will show you some key configurations in SAS Enterprise Miner that we could change.

Two-Step Clustering Algorithm

SAS Enterprise Miner has a built-in two-step clustering algorithm, which is described as follows:

- Step 1: Using hierarchical clustering to automatically find the number of clusters. The cubic clustering criterion (CCC) is used to determine the number of clusters.
- Step 2: Using k-mean clustering to assign objects to clusters based on distance measures.

Distance Measures

SAS Enterprise Miner does not provide all distance measures as described before. While some may take it as a disadvantage, others may consider it a plus since we do not have to spend time making decisions in selecting the right measure. The software provides the two most common distance measures, as follows:

- Cluster node: Euclidean distance.
- HP Cluster node: Euclidean distance or Manhattan distance.

Missing Values

SAS Enterprise Miner has a built-in missing value tool to handle missing values. It provides several options, including Default, Ignore, Mean, Midrange, or Omit. This tool makes it easier for us to handle missing values since we do not need to impute the missing values beforehand.

Data Standardization

SAS Enterprise Miner also has a built-in tool to standardize data, which helps address any issues with outliers. It offers several options, including None, Standardization (default), and Range.

SAS ENTERPRISE MINER GUIDELINES

Cluster Node Train Properties

(https://documentation.sas.com)

CLUSTER NODE TRAIN PROPERTIES: NUMBER OF CLUSTERS

Specification Method – Use the Specification Method property to choose the method that SAS Enterprise Miner will use to determine the maximum number of clusters. Choose between Automatic and User-Specified methods.

- The Automatic setting (default) configures SAS Enterprise Miner to automatically determine the optimum number of clusters to create.

  When the Automatic setting is selected, the value in the Maximum Number of Clusters property in the Number of Clusters section is not used to set the maximum number of clusters. Instead, SAS Enterprise Miner first makes a preliminary clustering pass, beginning with the number of clusters that is specified as the Preliminary Maximum value in the Selection Criterion properties.

  After the preliminary pass completes, the multivariate means of the clusters are used as inputs for a second pass that uses agglomerative, hierarchical algorithms to combine and reduce the number of clusters. Then, the smallest number of clusters that meets all four of the following criteria is selected.

  - The number of clusters must be greater than or equal to the number that is specified as the Minimum value in the Selection Criterion properties.

  - The number of clusters must have cubic clustering criterion (CCC) statistic values that are greater than the CCC Cutoff that is specified in the Selection Criterion properties.

  - The number of clusters must be less than or equal to the Final Maximum value.

  - A peak in the number of clusters exists.

- The User-Specified setting enables you to use the Maximum value in the Selection Criterion properties to manually specify an integer value greater than 2 for the maximum number of clusters. Because the Maximum Number of Clusters property is a maximum, it is possible to produce a number of clusters that is smaller than the specified maximum.

  To force the number of clusters to some exact number n, specify n for both the Maximum and Minimum values in the Selection Criterion properties.

Maximum Number of Clusters – Use the Maximum Number of Clusters property to specify the maximum number of clusters that you want to use in your analysis. Permissible values are nonnegative integers. The minimum value for the Maximum Number of Clusters property is 2, and the default value is 10.

SAS ENTERPRISE MINER GUIDELINES

Cluster Node Train Properties

(https://documentation.sas.com)

CLUSTER NODE TRAIN PROPERTIES: SELECTION CRITERION

- **Clustering Method** – If you select Automatic as your Specification Method property, Clustering Method specifies how SAS Enterprise Miner calculates clustering distances.
  - Average – The distance between two clusters is the average distance between pairs of observations, one in each cluster.
  - Centroid – The distance between two clusters is defined as the (squared) Euclidean distance between their centroids or means.
  - Ward – (Default) The distance between two clusters is the ANOVA sum of squares between the two clusters summed over all the variables. At each generation, the within-cluster sum of squares is minimized over all partitions obtainable by merging two clusters from a previous generation.
- Preliminary Maximum – Preliminary Maximum specifies the maximum number of clusters to create during the preliminary training pass. The default setting for the Maximum property is 50. Permissible values are integers greater than 2.
- Minimum – Minimum specifies the minimum number of clusters that is acceptable for a final solution. The default setting for the Minimum property is 2. Permissible values are integers greater than 2.
- Final Maximum – Final Maximum specifies the maximum number of clusters that are acceptable for a final solution. The default setting for the Maximum property is 20. Permissible values are integers greater than 2.
- CCC Cutoff – If you select Automatic as your Specification Method, the CCC Cutoff specifies the minimum cubic clustering cutoff criteria. The default setting for the CCC Cutoff property is 3. Permissible values for the CCC Cutoff property are integers greater than 0.

Example: Cluster Analysis

In this example, we perform a cluster analysis for the *airline recommendation* dataset.

Dataset: AirlineRecommendation.sas7bdat

Target variable: recommendation (binary): 1 – recommend the airline; 0 – do not recommend the airline.

Variables for cluster analysis: Table 13.4 shows variables used for cluster analysis. Note that since cluster analysis is unsupervised learning, only input variables are used for the analysis. The target variable, *recommend*, is omitted in the analysis process. Suppose our purpose is to group similar individuals based on their similarities

TABLE 13.4

Airline Recommendation Data for Cluster Analysis

Variable Name	Label/Description	Scale	Role
recommend	Recommend the airline to others	Binary (Yes/No)	Rejected
airline_st	Airline status	Nominal	Input
age	Age	Interval	Input
gender	Gender	Binary (Male/Female)	Input
price_sensitivity	Price sensitivity	Interval	Rejected
no_years_flying	Number of years flying	Interval	Rejected
no_flt_pa	Average number of flights per year	Interval	Input
pct_ flt_other_airline	Percent of flights with other airlines	Interval	Rejected
type_of_travel	Travel purpose	Nominal	Input
no_other_lty_cards	Number of other loyalty cards	Interval	Rejected
shopping_amt_airpt	Shopping amount at the airport	Interval	Input
eat_drink_airpt	Spending for eating and drinking at the airport	Interval	Rejected
class	Passenger class	Nominal	Rejected
origin_state	Origin state	Nominal	Rejected
destin_state	Destination state	Nominal	Rejected
depart_delay	Departure delay (in minutes)	Interval	Rejected
arrival_delay	Arrival delay (in minutes)	Interval	Rejected
flt_cancel	Flight cancellation	Binary (Yes/No)	Rejected
flt_time	Flight time (in minutes)	Interval	Rejected
flt_distance	Flight distance (miles)	Interval	Input

regarding their demographics and travel experience. In this case, we select seven variables for the cluster analysis purpose as highlighted in Table 13.4: *age, gender, airline status, average number of flights per year, travel purpose, shopping amount at the airport,* and *flight distance.* The clusters derived from those variables allow the airline to identify distinct market segments and establish strategies to target these segments appropriately. Other variables are rejected from this analysis.

Sample-Explore-Modify: Refer to the previous chapters. Since SAS Enterprise Miner has built-in tools to standardize data and handle missing values, we do not need to use the Impute node and Transform Variables node beforehand. Additionally, since we do not use the *price sensitivity* variable in cluster analysis, we do not need the Replacement node, which was used exclusively for this variable.

Cluster Node

Follow the steps below to configure the Cluster node.

1. From the Explore node, drag a Cluster node to the workspace and connect it to the Data Partition node.

2. In the Cluster Training properties
   - Set Internal Standardization to Standardization.
   - Under the Number of Clusters, set Specification Method to Automatic.
   - Under the Selection Criterion, set Clustering Method to Centroid.
   - Under the Missing Values, set Interval Variables to Default and set Nominal Variables to Default.
   - Keep other settings as Default.
3. Run the Cluster node and open the Results window.

Number of Clusters

Figure 13.7 shows the cluster analysis results with the number of clusters and the cluster size. The clustering algorithm indicates there are three main clusters, as follows.

- Cluster 1 with 10,532 cases or 28.21%.
- Cluster 2 with 3,674 cases or 9.84%.
- Cluster 3 with 23,133 cases or 61.95%.

Thus, Cluster 3 is the largest one, followed by Cluster 1 and then Cluster 2. We will look deeper into each cluster soon. (*Note*: SAS Enterprise Miner calls them segments instead of clusters. I will use *clusters* to ensure consistency in the chapter.)

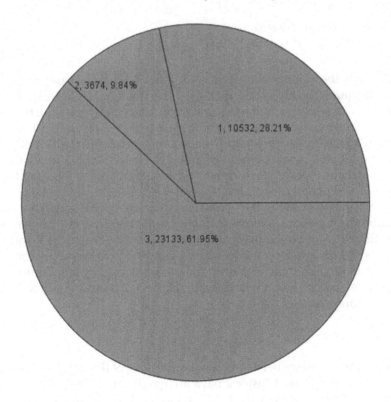

FIGURE 13.7
Cluster size.

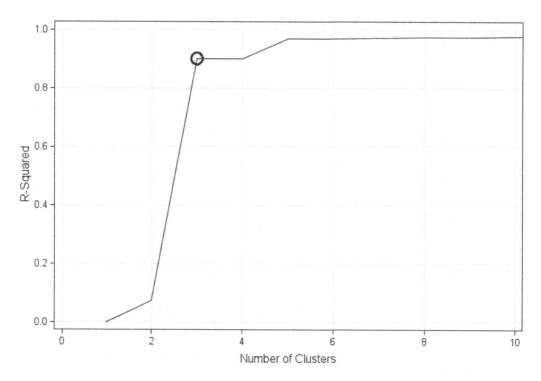

FIGURE 13.8
R-squared value by the number of clusters.

In order to verify the number of clusters, we use the R-squared chart (Figure 13.8), which presents the R-squared value of the model by the number of clusters. Note that, typically, in cluster analysis, we do not use R-squared value strictly as in the linear regression method, since cluster analysis uses a different principle. However, SAS Enterprise Miner produces the R-squared chart as a part of cluster analysis results, which does allow us to interpret the explainable power of the cluster model. Hence, we should use this chart from the general explanatory power perspective and should not try to interpret the R-squared value as a coefficient of determination.

With that in mind, we can see the vertical axis presents the R-squared values, ranging from 0 to 1, and the horizontal axis presents the number of clusters. The chart shows a big hump at the three cluster points, indicating that with three clusters the R-squared is 0.899. In other words, the three-cluster model can explain 89.9% of the variance in the data. We should not use more than three clusters since it does not result in a significant improvement in R-square and can lead to overlapping clusters. Accordingly, this result confirms the selection of three clusters.

Cluster Distance

Table 13.5 shows the distance between each pair of clusters (Euclidean distance measure). It appears that Cluster 1 and Cluster 2 have a large distance (148.26), and Cluster 2 and Cluster 3 also have a large distance (146.50), indicating they are distinct clusters. The distance between Cluster 1 and Cluster 3 is shorter (31.97) but considered acceptable.

TABLE 13.5

Cluster Distance

Clusters	1	2	3
1	0	148.263	31.9703
2	148.263	0	146.501
3	31.9703	146.501	0

Variable Importance

Figure 13.9 shows the variable importance chart, indicating significant variables in cluster formation. The most important variable is the *shopping amount at the airport*, followed by *age, average number of flights per year, travel purpose,* and *flight distance.*

Cluster Profiling

The next step is cluster profiling, which involves reviewing the profile of each cluster (segment), examining the differences between these clusters, and identifying their unique characteristics. In order to do so, we must review the results for all seven variables.

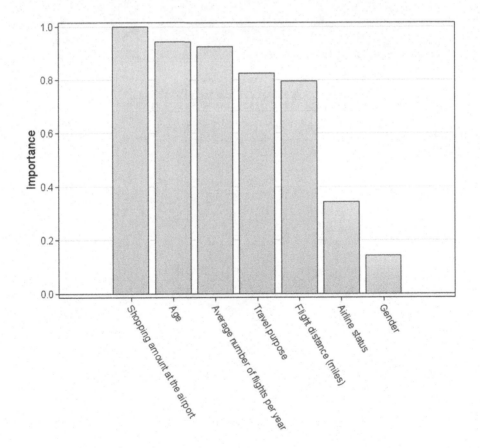

FIGURE 13.9
Variable importance.

Figures 13.10–13.16 present the cluster profiles for those variables. By reviewing each chart, we can summarize the cluster profile for each variable as follows.

- *Age*: Cluster 1 has older passengers; the majority of them have the age range from 59 to 76 years. Clusters 2 and Cluster 3 have younger passengers; the majority have an age range from 34 to 43 years.
- *Gender*: Cluster 1 and Cluster 3 have a more balanced gender split, while Cluster 2 has more females (73%) than males (27%).

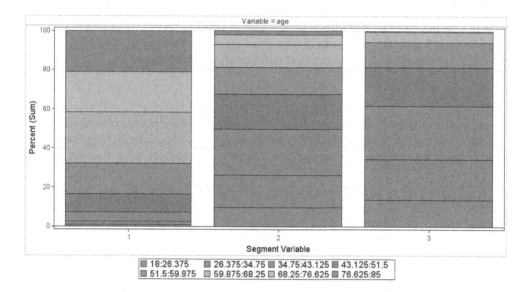

FIGURE 13.10
Cluster profiling – age.

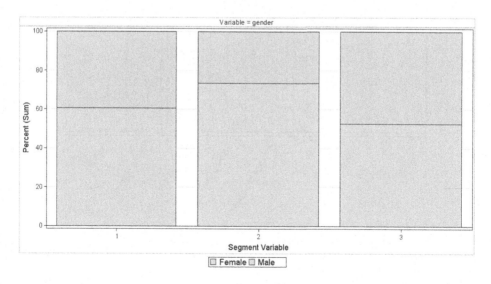

FIGURE 13.11
Cluster profiling – gender.

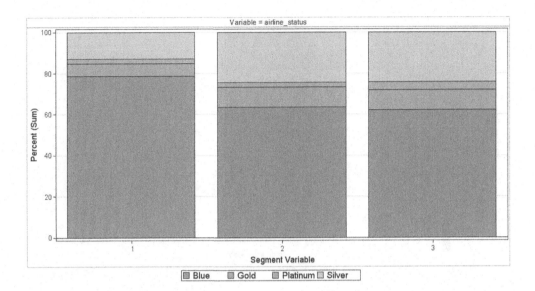

FIGURE 13.12
Cluster profiling – airline status.

- *Airline status*: Cluster 2 and Cluster 3 have similar distribution, with about 60% of passengers having the Blue status, while Cluster 1 has almost 80% of Blue status passengers.
- *Travel purpose*: The three clusters show differences in travel purpose. Cluster 1 includes about 73% of passengers traveling for personal purposes, while Cluster 3 includes more than 80% of passengers traveling for business purposes. Cluster 2 is closer to Cluster 3, with about 63% traveling for business purposes.

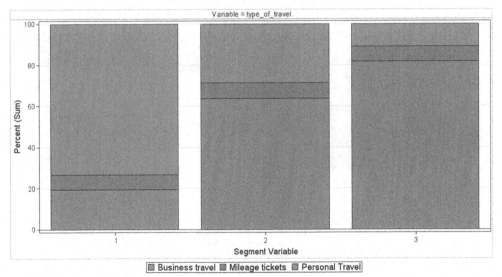

FIGURE 13.13
Cluster profiling – travel purpose.

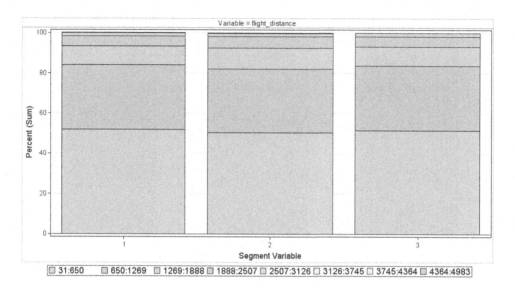

FIGURE 13.14
Cluster profiling – flight distance.

- *Flight distance*: All three clusters have very similar flight distance distributions, in which more than 80% of the passengers have traveled from 34 to 1,269 miles.

- *Number of flights per year*: 57% of passengers in Cluster 1 have 24–48 flights per year. On the other hand, almost 80% of passengers in Cluster 2 and Cluster 3 fly fewer than 24 times per year.

- *Shopping amount at the airport*: Almost all passengers in Cluster 1 and Cluster 3 spend up to 109 shopping units at the airport. On the other hand, 60% of passengers in Cluster 2 spend from 1,098 to 219 shopping units at the airport.

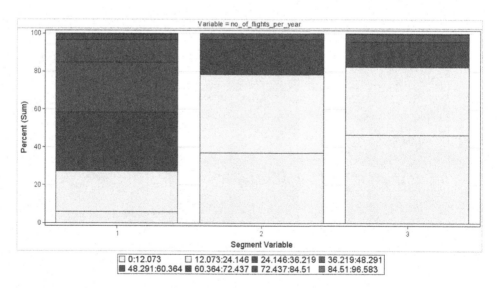

FIGURE 13.15
Cluster profiling – number of flights per year.

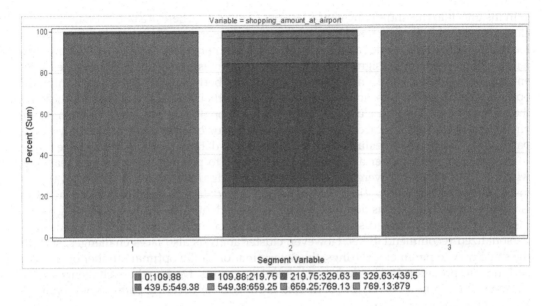

FIGURE 13.16
Cluster profiling – shopping amount at the airport.

Based on that cluster profiling, we describe the unique characteristics of these three clusters as follows (this process could be somewhat subjective since it depends on the researchers' interpretation of the results).

- *Cluster 1*: Older passengers; Blue status; personal travel; very frequent travel; not spending a lot at the airport.
- *Cluster 2*: Younger passengers, more females; business travel; moderate frequent travel; spending more at the airport.
- *Cluster 3*: Younger passengers; mainly business travel; moderate frequent travel; not spending a lot at the airport.

Now that we understand the unique characteristics (profiles) of these three clusters, the next step is to build a predictive model using these clusters as predictors (you can combine them with other predictors in the dataset). The predictive model will show us the relationships between these clusters and the target variable (airline recommendation). Based on these results, airlines can form appropriate marketing strategies for each cluster (segment) to improve their operational efficiency and service quality to attract more passengers.

Summary

Cluster analysis is a data mining method that aims to group data points or objects in a dataset into clusters, or segments, based on their similarities of specific characteristics. It involves partitioning data points into clusters, where objects within the same cluster are more similar to each other than to objects in other clusters. The goal is to uncover hidden structures and gain insights into the underlying characteristics of the data. There are two primary types of clustering algorithms, which are hierarchical clustering and partitioning clustering. While hierarchical clustering creates a hierarchy of clusters by iteratively merging or splitting clusters, partition clustering assigns each data point to one cluster. These algorithms use different approaches to measure similarity or dissimilarity between data points, determine the optimal number of clusters, and assign data points to their respective clusters. K-means is the most popular partition clustering method. Additionally, the two-step clustering combines elements of hierarchical clustering and k-means clustering to perform the analysis. It is particularly useful when dealing with large datasets or datasets with mixed variable types.

The advantages of cluster analysis lie in its ability to provide unsupervised learning, where groupings are discovered without prior knowledge or labeled data. It offers valuable insights for data summarization, data reduction, and data visualization. Cluster analysis is widely applied in various domains, and it helps to identify distinct customer segments, discover meaningful patterns in large datasets, detect outliers or anomalies, and make personalized recommendations. However, cluster analysis also faces challenges, such as the sensitivity to parameter settings, the determination of the optimal number of clusters, and the interpretation and evaluation of clustering results. Despite these challenges, cluster analysis remains a powerful tool in data mining for uncovering patterns and organizing data into meaningful groups.

CHAPTER DISCUSSION QUESTIONS

1. What is cluster analysis? How does cluster analysis work in grouping objects into clusters based on their similarities?

2. What are the key similarities and differences between cluster analysis and PCA?

3. Provide examples and discuss the benefits and challenges of applying cluster analysis in various domains.

4. How does the choice of distance measure impact the results of cluster analysis? Discuss different distance measures and their suitability for different types of data and clustering algorithms.

5. What are the advantages and disadvantages of cluster analysis?

6. Compare hierarchical clustering and partition clustering algorithms. What are their key differences in terms of assumptions, clustering method, strengths, and limitations?

7. What is k-means clustering? Explain how it works and why it is a popular method.

8. What are the challenges of determining the optimal number of clusters in cluster analysis?

9. What is the two-step clustering? Discuss its strengths and weaknesses.

10. Discuss the role of cluster profiling. How can cluster profiles be used to support the decision-making process?

11. What are the different ways to combine cluster analysis results with predictive modeling to produce an effective predictive model?

Exercises

Exercise 1: Cluster analysis for the Bank dataset

1. Open the *bank* dataset in SAS Enterprise Miner.
2. Sample the entire dataset. See the variable names and descriptions in Appendix A.1.
3. Partition the data using a split ratio of 60:40 (train: 60%; validation: 20%; test: 20%).
4. Perform data modification as follows:
   - Impute missing values.
5. Conduct a cluster analysis using the following variables:
   - Age
   - Income
   - Length of residency
   - Teller visit
   - Saving balance
   - CD balance
   - Money market balance
   - Mortgage balance
   - Home value
   - Investment balance
   - Loan balance
6. In the Cluster Training properties:
   - Set Internal Standardization to Standardization.
   - Under the Number of Clusters, set Specification Method to Automatic.
   - Under the Selection Criterion, set Clustering Method to Centroid.
   - Keep other settings as Default.
7. Present the results of the cluster analysis. Explain the number of clusters, cluster size, cluster distance, and variable importance.
8. Perform cluster profiling using the above variables.
9. Describe unique characteristics for each cluster based on the cluster profiling results.
10. Discuss how the cluster analysis results can be used in predicting the individuals' credit scores and what strategies banks and financial organizations can use to target each cluster.

Exercise 2: Neural network models for the Passengers dataset

1. Open the *passengers* dataset in SAS Enterprise Miner.
2. Sample 20% of the full data. Set *return* (decision to return to the airline) as the target variable and change its role to binary. See the variable names and descriptions in Appendix A.2.
3. Partition the data using a split ratio of 60:40 (train: 60%; validation: 20%; test: 20%)
4. Perform data modification as follows:
   - Replace zero values for Likert scale variables with missing values.
   - Impute missing values.
5. Conduct a cluster analysis using the following variables.
   - Gender
   - Age
   - Type of travel
   - Customer type
   - Ticket class
   - Flight distance

6. In the Cluster Training properties
   - Set Internal Standardization to Standardization.
   - Under the Number of Clusters, set Specification Method to Automatic.
   - Under the Selection Criterion, set Clustering Method to Centroid.
   - Keep other settings as Default.
7. Present the results of the cluster analysis. Explain the number of clusters, cluster size, cluster distance, and variable importance.
8. Perform cluster profiling using the above variables.
9. Describe unique characteristics for each cluster based on the cluster profiling results.
10. Discuss how the cluster analysis results can be used in predicting the passengers' decision to return to the same airline and what strategies the airlines can use to target each cluster.

Part III

Advanced Data Mining Methods

14

Random Forest

LEARNING OUTCOMES

Upon the completion of this chapter, you will be able to

1. Describe the principles and concepts of random forest as an ensemble machine learning method.
2. Discuss the advantages and disadvantages of random forest compared to other machine learning methods.
3. Explain how random forest constructs decision trees using random subsets of training data and input variables.
4. Describe how random forest combines predictions from multiple decision trees through voting or averaging.
5. Explore the hyperparameters of random forest and their impact on model performance.
6. Explain the scalability and efficiency of random forest, including its parallelization capabilities.
7. Define Out-of-Bag evaluation and explain how it affects the model performance.
8. Construct random forest modeling using SAS Enterprise Miner.

Introduction

Random forest is one of the most popular and powerful machine learning methods. Random forest is an ensemble learning method that constructs numerous decision trees. We have covered ensemble modeling in Chapter 10, so the concept is basically the same, except here, we ensemble multiple decision trees. Imagine we build many decision tree models (see Chapter 8 for the details) and then combine these trees together into an ensemble

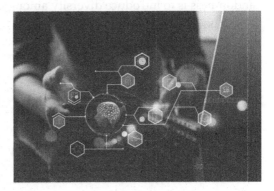

model that can produce a more robust and accurate predictive model. Visually, we have a forest of trees, hence the term *random forest*. Basically, it is a tree-based method. For classification models, the random forest output is the mode of the classes of the individual trees. For association models, the random forest output is the mean prediction of the individual trees.

Random forest is one of the most accurate learning algorithms and can handle a very large number of input variables without variable deletion. It is simple to use, faster to calculate, and more resistant to noise in the data. Additionally, random forests can also prevent overfitting. This chapter introduces and explains the algorithm of random forest and how to perform random forest and interpret the results.

What Is Random Forest?

Random forest is a machine learning algorithm that combines the predictions of multiple decision trees to make more accurate and robust predictions. It falls under the category of ensemble learning, where multiple models are combined to form a more powerful predictive model.

Random forest is actually a bagging algorithm (see Chapter 10 for the details of the bagging algorithm). As a reminder, bagging is an ensemble method that involves training multiple individual models independently on different random subsets of the training data (sampling with replacement). The final prediction is an average or voting over the predictions of all the individual models.

> **DEFINITION**
>
> Random forest is a machine learning algorithm that combines the predictions of multiple decision trees to make more accurate and robust predictions. It falls under the category of ensemble learning, where multiple models are combined to form a more powerful predictive model.

A forest operates under the principle that an ensemble of uncorrelated trees will outperform any of the individual trees. These individual trees are trained like standard trees with separate training data sampled from the dataset. Then, the final prediction of the random forest model is determined based on a majority vote or average of individual trees' prediction outputs. Figure 14.1 illustrates a random forest model. The idea behind this randomness is to introduce diversity among the trees, reducing the risk of overfitting and improving the predictive power.

> Random forest can be used for both association and classification models.
> - For classification, the random forest output is the mode of the classes of the individual trees (majority vote).
> - For regression, the random forest output is the average prediction of the individual trees.

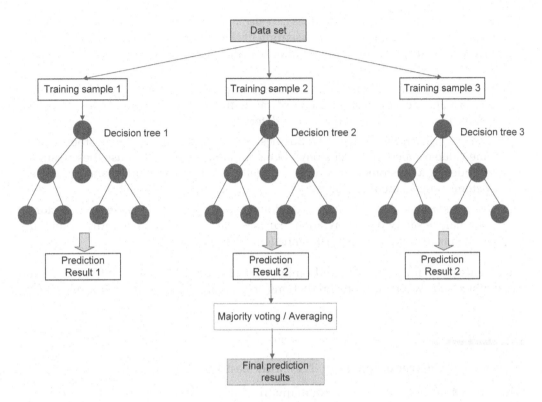

FIGURE 14.1
Illustration of a random forest model.

Practical Applications of Random Forest

Random forest has numerous practical applications in many domains. Below are some of the common applications of random forest.

1. *Anomaly detection*: This method can be applied to identify anomalies or outliers in datasets. It has been used for network intrusion detection, fraud detection in financial transactions, and detecting anomalies in sensor data.

2. *Recommendation systems*: Organizations can use random forest in recommendation systems to provide personalized recommendations. It can analyze user behavior and preferences to suggest movies, products, or content tailored to individual users.

3. *Aircraft maintenance and fault detection*: Random Forest can be applied to predict potential maintenance issues and detect faults in aircraft systems. By analyzing sensor data and historical maintenance records, it can help identify patterns indicative of impending failures or anomalies.

4. *Flight delay prediction*: Airlines can use this method to predict flight delays by analyzing historical data on flight schedules, weather conditions, airport congestion, and other relevant factors. This information can aid airlines in managing their operations and reducing passenger inconvenience.

5. *Passenger sentiment analysis*: Airlines can also use random forest models to analyze passenger feedback, reviews, and sentiments from various sources, such as social media and surveys. This analysis allows airlines to understand customer preferences and improve their services.

6. *Social media analysis*: Sentiment analysis and predicting user behavior in social media data are other applications of random forest. The model helps analyze trends, identify influential users, and detect spam or fake accounts.

7. *Customer relationship management*: Businesses can use this method in customer lifetime value prediction and customer behavior analysis. They can use these results to understand customer preferences, target marketing campaigns, and optimize customer engagement strategies.

8. *Risk assessment and safety analysis*: Random Forest can be used to assess risk factors and analyze safety data in aviation. Airlines use the method to identify potential safety hazards and develop risk management strategies.

Those are just a few examples, and random forest's versatility allows it to be applied in many other fields where accurate predictions or anomaly detection are required.

Differences between Decision Tree and Random Forest

While random forest is a collection of many trees, there are some primary differences between these two algorithms. Understanding these differences allows us to decide when to use which method. Table 14.1 summarizes some major differences between random forests and decision trees.

TABLE 14.1

Differences between Random Forest and Decision Tree

Criteria	Decision Trees	Random Forest
Number of trees	Decision trees consist of a single tree structure.	Random forest is an ensemble method that combines multiple decision trees.
Training process	Decision trees are trained by recursively partitioning the data based on the selected variables and splitting criteria.	Random forest trains each decision tree on a random subset of the training data using bootstrapping.
Variable selection	Decision trees consider all available variables at each split to determine the best predictor and threshold.	Random forest randomly selects a subset of variables at each split, providing randomness and reducing variable correlations.
Prediction	Decision trees make predictions based on the majority class in each leaf node (classification models) or the average of target values (association models).	Random forest combines predictions from multiple trees by voting (classification models) or averaging (association models) to make the final prediction.
Overfitting	Decision trees are prone to overfitting, meaning they can create complex models that fit the training data too closely and generalize poorly to new data.	Random forest mitigates overfitting by aggregating predictions from multiple trees, reducing the variance and improving the model's generalizability.

(Continued)

TABLE 14.1 (*Continued*)

Differences between Random Forest and Decision Tree

Criteria	Decision Trees	Random Forest
Bias-variance tradeoff	Decision trees tend to have low bias but high variance, as they can be sensitive to small changes in the training data.	Random forest strikes a balance between bias and variance by reducing the variance through averaging predictions.
Handling outliers and noisy data	Decision trees can be sensitive to outliers and noisy data, as they can create biased splits.	Random forest is more robust to outliers and noise due to the ensemble of trees, which reduces the impact of individual trees' mistakes.
Interpretability	Decision trees are often more interpretable because they provide a clear decision path.	Since random forest is an ensemble of trees, it can be less interpretable as it combines multiple decision paths. It is hard to visually follow the decision path with the random forest.
Performance	Decision trees are computationally efficient to train and make predictions.	As an ensemble model, random forest can be more computationally expensive during training and prediction due to the combination of multiple trees.
Variable importance	Decision trees can provide variable importance measures based on the variable's contribution to the splits.	Random forest can also provide variable importance measures, which are aggregated across multiple trees and can be more reliable.

Basic Concepts

Random forest is a bagging ensemble method that combines multiple decision trees to make predictions. Table 14.2 presents the key concepts in random forest and their descriptions. It is important to understand these concepts since they form the foundation of random forest and contribute to its effectiveness and versatility as a machine learning method.

TABLE 14.2

Basic Concepts and Descriptions in Random Forest

Terms	Descriptions
Random Forest	Random forest is a machine learning algorithm that combines the predictions of multiple decision trees to make more accurate and robust predictions. It falls under the category of ensemble learning, where multiple models are combined to form a more powerful predictive model.
Ensemble learning	Random forest uses ensemble learning that creates a collection of decision trees and combines their predictions to make a final prediction. The principle of ensemble learning is that the collective decision of multiple models can yield better results than a single model.
Random subset selection	Each decision tree in the random forest is built using a random subset of the training data. This process, known as bootstrap aggregating or "bagging," involves randomly sampling data points with replacement to create diverse subsets for training each tree.
Random variable selection	The random forest algorithm selects a random subset of input variables for each decision tree. This technique, known as variable bagging or variable subsampling, introduces additional randomness and helps to reduce the dominance of any single variable in the ensemble.

(Continued)

TABLE 14.2 (*Continued*)

Basic Concepts and Descriptions in Random Forest

Terms	Descriptions
Sampling with replacement	Sampling with replacement occurs when a randomly chosen unit from the population is put back into the population, and subsequently, another element is chosen at random. In this process, the population consistently retains all its original units, allowing for the possibility of selecting the same unit multiple times.
Voting/averaging	During prediction, each decision tree independently generates a prediction, and the final prediction of the random forest is determined through voting (for classification models) or averaging (for association models) the individual tree predictions. This ensemble approach helps reduce bias and variance in the modeling and improves the overall accuracy and robustness of the model.
Out-of-bag evaluation	Random forest utilizes an out-of-bag (OOB) evaluation technique. Since each decision tree is trained on a different subset of the training data, the samples not included in a tree's training subset can be used for evaluation. This provides an unbiased estimate of the model performance without the need for a separate validation set.
Variable importance	Random forest provides the variable importance plot, which indicates the relative contribution of each predictor in making predictions. This information can be used to assess the relevance of variables and assist in variable selection.
Robustness	The algorithm is known for its robustness against overfitting, noisy data, and outliers. By aggregating multiple decision trees, it can capture complex relationships and handle noisy datasets more effectively.
Scalability	Random forest can be parallelized, as each decision tree in the ensemble can be built independently. This allows for efficient computation and scalability to large datasets.

Advantages and Disadvantages

Random forest is a machine learning algorithm that can be used for both classification and association models. It is a powerful and widely used algorithm, but like all algorithms, it has both strengths and limitations. In this section, we discuss the main advantages and disadvantages of the random forest method so we can decide whether to use it for a particular task.

Advantages of random forest

1. *Robustness*: Random Forest is a highly robust machine learning algorithm that can handle missing data and outliers. It is also less sensitive to noise than other methods.

2. *Accuracy*: This method often performs well in both classification and association models, and it is known to be one of the most accurate machine learning algorithms. It has a low bias and moderate variance, which helps reduce overfitting.

3. *Scalability*: It can handle large datasets with many variables and can handle high-dimensional data without the need for variable selection. It can also be easily parallelized, which makes it a good choice for big data applications.

4. *Interpretability*: Random Forest can provide variable importance rankings, which are useful for understanding the relative importance of different variables in the model.

5. *Preventing overfitting*: Random Forest can be used to prevent overfitting by randomly selecting subsets of the data and variables to build multiple decision trees, which can then be averaged to obtain a final prediction. This process of bootstrapping helps reduce the variance of the model and can improve the predictive power.

Disadvantages of random forest

1. *Complexity*: The algorithm can be complex, and it can be difficult to interpret the results of the model.

2. *Computationally expensive*: When dealing with large datasets, random forest can be computationally expensive. This can make it impractical for real-time or online applications.

3. *Memory consumption*: This method requires a large amount of memory, especially when dealing with large datasets with many variables.

4. *Non-deterministic*: It is a non-deterministic algorithm, which means results obtained from a random forest model may vary when the algorithm is trained on the same dataset multiple times. This can make it difficult to reproduce results and can lead to the model's unreliability.

5. *Biased toward categorical variables*: Random Forest can be biased toward categorical variables that have many levels, which can lead to the overfitting of these variables.

Random Forest Process

Random Forest is one of the most accurate learning algorithms and can handle a very large number of input variables without variable deletion. It is simple to use, faster to calculate, and more resistant to noise in the data. Additionally, random forest can also prevent overfitting.

The implementation of the random forest consists of the following steps:

1. *Data preprocessing*: The first step is to prepare the data for modeling. This includes data cleaning, handling missing values, and transforming data into a suitable format for random forest modeling.

2. *Splitting the data*: The next step is to split the data into training and validation samples. The training sample is used to train the model, while the validation sample is used to evaluate the model's performance.

3. *Random Forest configuration*: This step involves configuring the hyperparameters of the random forest model, such as the number of trees, the maximum depth of the trees, and other parameters like minimum samples per leaf or the number of variables considered for splitting.

4. *Aggregating the trees*: Once the decision trees have been built, they are combined using a technique called ensemble learning. This involves aggregating the predictions of the individual trees to make a final prediction.

5. *Model training*: In this step, the random forest model is trained with the training sample using the chosen hyperparameters.

6. *Model evaluation*: The final step is to evaluate the performance of the random forest model using the validation sample. This involves evaluating model metrics. If the performance is not satisfactory, the model can be further optimized by adjusting hyperparameters such as the number of trees, maximum depth of the trees, and minimum samples per leaf.

Remember that random forest is an ensemble method, and its strength lies in building multiple decision trees and combining their predictions. The process of conducting random forest modeling may require experimentation with hyperparameters and data preprocessing to achieve the best possible results.

Out-of-Bag

In random forest, the out-of-bag (OOB) error estimation is a technique used to estimate the model performance without the need for a separate validation set. The OOB samples are the data points that were not included in the bootstrap sample used to train each individual decision tree in the random forest.

The OOB error estimation works as follows.

- *Bootstrap sampling*: Random Forest creates multiple bootstrap samples by randomly selecting data points with replacement from the original training dataset. Each bootstrap sample is used to train an individual decision tree in the random forest.

- *OOB samples*: Since the bootstrap sampling involves selecting data points with replacement, some data points are left out in each bootstrap sample. These omitted data points are called OOB samples.

> **DEFINITION**
>
> What is sampling with replacement?
>
> Sampling is called with replacement when a unit selected at random from the population is returned to the population and then a second element is selected at random. Whenever a unit is selected, the population contains all the same units, so a unit may be selected more than once.

- *OOB predictions*: Each decision tree in the random forest is trained on a different bootstrap sample and can be evaluated using the OOB samples that were not included in its training. These OOB samples are passed through the decision tree, and their predictions are recorded.

- *OOB error calculation*: The OOB predictions from all the decision trees in the random forest are aggregated, and the OOB error is calculated by comparing the aggregated predictions to the true target values of the OOB samples. This error estimate provides an approximation of the model performance on unseen data.

The OOB error estimation serves as an internal validation mechanism within the random forest algorithm. It helps assess the model's predictive power without the need for a separate validation sample, saving computational resources and simplifying the training process. The OOB error can be used as a model fit metric to compare different random forest models or to guide hyperparameter tuning decisions, such as determining the optimal number of trees or other parameters. Overall, the OOB estimation is a valuable feature of random forest that provides a reliable estimate of the model performance on unseen data while training the ensemble of decision trees.

Random Forest and Overfitting Prevention

Random forest is known for its ability to mitigate overfitting, which is a common problem in predictive modeling. Below are some ways in which random forest helps prevent overfitting.

1. *Random subsampling*: Random Forest applies bootstrapping to create multiple subsets of the original training data. Each decision tree in the random forest is trained on a different bootstrap sample. This random subsampling introduces variability and reduces the chances of overfitting to specific patterns in the training data.

2. *Variable randomness*: At each split in the decision tree construction, the random forest randomly selects a subset of variables to consider. This random variable selection decorrelates the trees and prevents overfitting by reducing the impact of individual variables or subsets of variables that may dominate the decision-making process.

3. *Ensemble of trees*: The final prediction in the random forest is obtained by aggregating the predictions from all the individual trees. By combining the predictions of multiple trees, the random forest reduces the variance and tends to generalize better to unseen data. The ensemble nature of the random forest smooths out the individual tree's idiosyncrasies and reduces overfitting.

4. *Out-of-bag evaluation*: During the training process of each decision tree in the random forest, some data points are left out due to bootstrapping. These OOB samples can be used for evaluation. OOB evaluation provides an estimate of the model performance on unseen data without the need for a separate validation sample. It serves as an additional measure to assess the model's predictive power and helps detect overfitting.

5. *Hyperparameter tuning*: Random Forest has several hyperparameters that can be tuned to control the model's complexity and prevent overfitting. Parameters such as the number of trees, maximum depth of trees, minimum number of samples required for a split, and maximum number of variables considered at each split can be adjusted to find the right balance between underfitting and overfitting.

6. *Early stopping*: Random Forest training can be stopped early if there is no significant improvement in the model performance. Monitoring the performance on a validation sample or using techniques like cross-validation can help determine the optimal number of trees to include in the random forest and prevent overfitting.

It's important to note that while random forest helps in reducing overfitting, it may still be possible for individual decision trees within the random forest to overfit the data. However, the aggregation of multiple trees in the ensemble typically compensates for this issue and results in a more robust and generalized model.

Random Forest Hyperparameter Tuning

Hyperparameter tuning is an essential step in optimizing the performance of a random forest model. I describe below some key hyperparameters that can be tuned in random forest modeling.

1. *Number of trees*: It determines the number of decision trees in the random forest. Increasing the number of trees can improve performance, but it comes with a tradeoff of increased computational time. It is important to find the right balance to avoid overfitting or unnecessary computational burden.

2. *Maximum depth*: It sets the maximum depth allowed for each decision tree in the random forest. A deeper tree can capture more complex relationships but increases the risk of overfitting. Tuning this parameter can help control the complexity of individual trees and prevent overfitting.

3. *Minimum samples for split*: It defines the minimum number of samples required to perform a split at a node. Increasing this value can prevent overfitting by enforcing a higher threshold for node splitting.

4. *Minimum samples per leaf*: It specifies the minimum number of samples required to be in a leaf node. Similar to the minimum samples for split, increasing this value can control overfitting by ensuring a minimum number of samples in each leaf.

5. *Maximum variables*: It determines the number of variables to consider when looking for the best split at each node. Reducing the number of variables can introduce randomness and decorrelation between trees, preventing overfitting.

6. *Variable subset sampling*: It controls whether random variable selection is performed for each tree. Enabling this option introduces additional randomness and diversity among trees, reducing the risk of overfitting.

7. *OOB evaluation*: It enables the use of OOB samples to estimate the model performance during training. The OOB error can provide a measure of model performance without requiring a separate validation sample. It can be used to compare different hyperparameter settings.

These are just a few examples of hyperparameters that can be tuned in configuring the random forest model. Hyperparameter tuning can be performed using techniques like grid search, random search, or Bayesian optimization. It involves searching through different combinations of hyperparameter values and evaluating their impact on the model performance using appropriate model fit metrics such as accuracy, precision, recall, or mean squared error. The goal is to find the set of hyperparameter values that optimize the model performance on the specific task at hand.

SAS Enterprise Miner, the HP Forest node is in the High Performance Data Mining (HPDM) group. SAS Enterprise Miner provides many auto configurations for the HP Forest node, which makes our modeling job easier. Nonetheless, it still allows us to change certain configurations on the tree size as needed. I will provide some examples of how to reconfigure the HP Forest node to produce better results.

SAS ENTERPRISE MINER GUIDELINES

HP Forest Node Train Properties
(https://documentation.sas.com)

HP FOREST NODE TRAIN PROPERTIES: TREE OPTIONS

- **Maximum number of trees** – Specifies the number of trees in the forest. The number of trees in the resulting forest can be less than the value specified here when the HP Forest node fails to split the training data for a tree. The HP Forest node attempts to create up to twice the number of trees specified. The default value is 100.

- The **Significance Level, Smallest Number of Obs in Node,** and **Minimum Category Size** options constrain the split search to form trees that are more likely to predict well using new data. Setting all of these options to 1 generally frees the search algorithm to find a split and train a tree. However, a tree generated with such constraints might not help the forest predict well.

- **Seed** – Use the Seed property to specify an integer value to use as a random seed for the pseudorandom number generator that chooses observations for sampling. The default value for the Random Seed property is 12345. The HP Data Partition node does not use the system data and time when the seed property is 0. Instead, a positive constant is used.

- **Type of Sample** – Specifies whether the number of observations or the percentage of observations is used to determine the training sample. Specify **Count** to use number of observations and **Proportion** to use percentage of observations.

- **Proportion of Obs in Each Sample** – Specifies what percentage of observations is used for each tree when the **Type of Sample** property is set to **Proportion**.

- **Number of Obs in Each Sample** – Specifies the number of observations that are used for each tree when the **Type of Sample** property is set to **Count**.

HP FOREST NODE TRAIN PROPERTIES: NODE OPTIONS

- **Method for Leaf Size** – Specifies the method used to determine the leaf size value. Specify **Default** to let the HP Forest node determine the method that is used for each leaf. Specify **Count** to use number of observations and **Proportion** to use the percentage of observations.

- **Smallest Percentage of Obs in Node** – Specifies the smallest number of training observations that a new branch can have, expressed as the fraction of the number of available observations. The number of available observations does not include observations with missing target values and observations with a nonpositive value for the frequency variable. The value specified here must be between 0 and 1, exclusive. The default value is 0.00001.

- **Smallest Number of Obs in Node** – Specifies the smallest number of training observations a new branch can have. The default value is 1.

- **Split Size** – Specifies the requisite number of training observations a node must have for the HP Forest node to consider splitting it. The default value is either twice the value specified by the **Smallest Number of Obs in Node** property or twice the number of observations implied by the **Smallest Percentage of Obs in Node** property. The HP Forest node counts the number of observations in a node without adjusting for the frequency variable.

- **Use as Modeling Node** – Specifies whether the HP Forest node should behave as a modeling node and create flow code, create publish score code, and perform assessment. When set to **No**, the analytic store files for scoring, score.sasast, and score.sas, are still created. The default value is **Yes**.

SAS ENTERPRISE MINER GUIDELINES

HP Forest Node Train Properties

(https://documentation.sas.com)

HP FOREST NODE TRAIN PROPERTIES: SPLITTING RULE OPTIONS

- **Maximum Depth** – Specifies the maximum depth of a node in any tree that the HP Forest node creates. The root node has depth 0. The children of the root have depth 1, and so on. The smallest acceptable value is 1. The default value is 50.

- **Missing Values** – Specifies how the training procedure handles an observation with missing values. If you specify **Use in Search** and enough training observations in the node are missing the value of the candidate variable, then the missing value is used as a separate value in the test of association and the split search. If you specify **Distribute**, observations with a missing value of the candidate variable are omitted from the test of association and split search in that node. A splitting rule distributes such an observation to all branches. See Missing Values for a more complete explanation. The default value of policy is **Use in Search**. **Note:** Using the **Distribute** option for the **Missing Values** property invokes a processor-intensive algorithm that can result in significantly longer training times.

- **Minimum Use in Search** – Specifies the minimum number of observations with a missing value in a node to initiate the **Use in Search** option for missing values. See Missing Values for a more complete explanation. The default value is 1.

- **Number of Variables to Consider in Split Search** – Specifies the number of input variables to consider splitting on in a node. Valid values are integers between 1 and the number of variables in the training data, inclusive.
- **Significance Level** – Specifies a threshold p-value for the significance level of a test of association of a candidate variable with the target. If no association meets this threshold, the node is not split. The default value is 0.05.
- **Max Categories in Split Search** – Specifies the maximum number of categories of a nominal candidate variable to use in the association test. This value refers only to the categories that are present in the training data in the node and that satisfy the **Minimum Category Size** option. The categories are counted independently in each node. If more categories are present than the value specified here, then the least frequent categories are removed from the association test. Many infrequent categories can dilute the strong predictive ability of common categories. The search for a splitting rule uses all categories that satisfy the **Minimum Category Size** option. The value specified here must be a positive integer. The default value is 30.
- **Minimum Category Size** – Specifies the minimum number of observations that a given nominal input category must have in order to use the category in a split search. Categorical values that appear in fewer observations than the value specified here are handled as if they were missing. The policy for assigning such observations to a branch is the same as the policy for assigning missing values to a branch. The default value is 5.
- **Exhaustive** – Specifies the maximum number of splits to examine in a complete enumeration of all possible splits when the input variable is nominal and the target has more than two nominal categories. The exhaustive method of searching for a split examines all possible splits. If the number of possible splits is greater than the value specified here, then a heuristic search is done instead of an exhaustive search. The default value is 5,000.

Example: Random Forest

In this example, we build predictive models for the *airline recommendation* dataset using the random forest algorithm with various configurations.

Dataset: AirlineRecommendation.sas7bdat

Target variable: *recommendation* (binary): 1 – recommend the airline; 0 – do not recommend the airline.

Sample-Explore-Modify: Refer to previous chapters.

Random Forest Configurations

In this example, we train four random forest models. From the HPDM tab, drag four HP Forest nodes to the diagram workspace. Connect them to the Replacement node. Name them HP Forest Default, HP Forest 1, HP Forest 2, and HP Forest 4. Then from the Assess tab, drag a Model Comparison node to the diagram workspace and connect it to these four HP Forest nodes. The diagram should look like the one below.

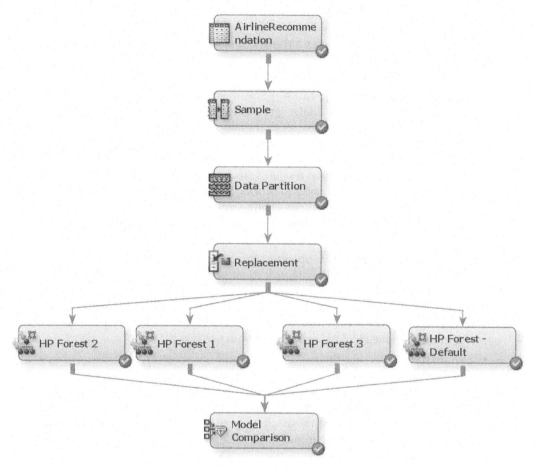

Use the details below to set the configurations for each HP Forest model. We focus on the number of trees, maximum depth, number of variables considered, split size, category size, and maximum number of splits.

Model 1: HP Forest Default (using default properties; the primary ones are included below)

In the HP Forest Train properties

- Under Tree Options:
  - Set Maximum number of trees to 100.
  - Set Type of Sample to Proportion.
  - Set Proportion of Obs in Each Sample to 0.6.
- Under Splitting Rule Options:
  - Set Maximum Depth to 20.
  - Set Number of Variables to Consider to undefined.
  - Set Minimum Category Size to 5.

- Under Node Options
  - Set Method for Leaf Size to Default.
  - Set Split Size to undefined.
- Under Score
  - Set Variable Importance Method to Loss Reduction (Note: If the target is interval, the Absolute Error is used for the importance measure; otherwise, the Margin Reduction is used. The measure based on the validation data is used if present; otherwise, the OOB measure is used.)

Model 2: HP Forest 1

In the HP Forest Train properties

- Under Tree Options:
  - Set Maximum number of trees to 200.
- Under Splitting Rule Options:
  - Set Maximum Depth to 20.
  - Set Number of Variables to Consider to 100.
  - Set Minimum Category Size to 2.
- Under Node Options
  - Set Split Size to 2.
- Keep other properties the same as the HP Forest Default model.

Model 3: HP Forest 2

In the HP Forest Train properties

- Under Tree Options:
  - Set Maximum number of trees to 500.
- Under Splitting Rule Options:
  - Set Maximum Depth to 20.
  - Set Number of Variables to Consider to 200.
  - Set Minimum Category Size to 2.
  - Set Exhaustive to 50,000.
- Under Node Options
  - Set Split Size to 3.
- Keep other properties the same as the HP Forest Default model.

Model 4: HP Forest 3

In the HP Forest Train properties

- Under Tree Options:
  - Set Maximum number of trees to 2,000.

- Under Splitting Rule Options:
  - Set Maximum Depth to 50.
  - Set Number of Variables to Consider to 1,000.
  - Set Minimum Category Size to 2.
  - Set Exhaustive to 50,000.
- Under Node Options
  - Set Split Size to 5.
- Keep other properties the same as the HP Forest Default model.
- Keep other properties the same as the HP Forest Default model.

In the Model Comparison Train properties

- Under the Model Selection:
  - Set Selection Statistic to Misclassification Rate
  - Set Selection Table to Validation

Run the Model Comparison node and open the Results window.

Results

The model comparison results are presented in Table 14.3 using the model fit metrics for the validation samples: misclassification rate, Gini coefficient, ROC index, and Lift value. In addition, Figures 14.2 and 14.3 show the ROC chart and Lift chart, respectively. As you can see, the metrics are very close between these models. Three models, HP Forest 2, HP Forest 1, and HP Forest 3 have almost identical model fit, while HP Forest – Default is the worst model (it is not considered). It is confirmed by the ROC chart and Lift chart, where most curves overlap. Thus, the champion model is not a clear choice. In order to give you a perspective of the HP Forest model performance in comparison with the individual tree model, I added the best individual tree model we found in Chapter 8, Pruned CART tree, to Table 14.3. As you can see, all three random forest models, HP Forest 1, HP Forest 2, and HP Forest 3 outperform the individual tree in all metrics. This evidence shows that the random forest model performs better than individual trees.

We also compare the misclassification rate between three samples: training, validation, and test. The results show very consistent values, indicating the reliability of those models (Table 14.4). These results further confirm that there is no clear winner between HP Forest 1, HP Forest 2, and HP Forest 3. Essentially, any of these models can be selected as the champion model.

TABLE 14.3

Model Comparison Results

Model Description	Valid: Misclassification Rate	Valid: Gini	Valid: ROC	Valid: Lift
HP Forest 2	0.207	0.716	0.858	1.716
HP Forest 1	0.207	0.716	0.858	1.716
HP Forest 3	0.207	0.716	0.858	1.716
HP Forest – Default	0.213	0.709	0.854	1.695
Pruned CART tree	0.209	0.660	0.830	1.610

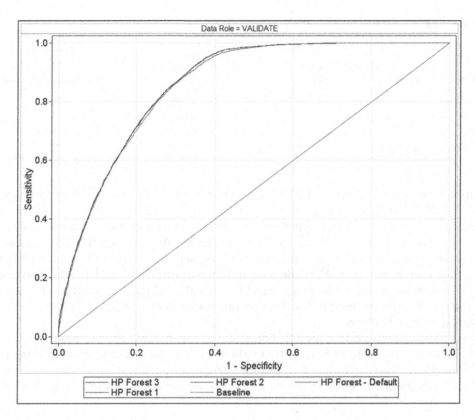

FIGURE 14.2
ROC chart.

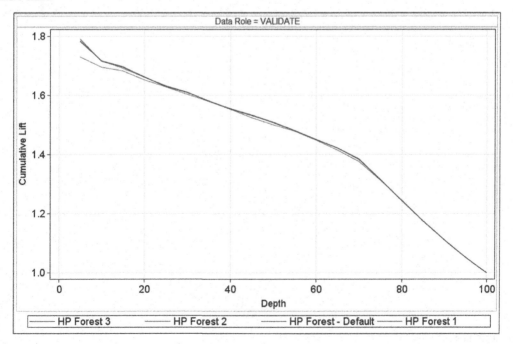

FIGURE 14.3
Lift chart.

TABLE 14.4

Comparison of Misclassification Rates between Three Samples

Model Description	Valid: Misclassification Rate	Train: Misclassification Rate	Test: Misclassification Rate
HP Forest 2	0.20719	0.19027	0.200434
HP Forest 1	0.20719	0.19104	0.200916
HP Forest 3	0.20744	0.19072	0.200193
HP Forest - Default	0.21282	0.20671	0.210958

Suppose we select HP Forest 2 as the champion model. By reviewing the Results window for HP Forest 2, we can get more details of this model, especially the OOB results. Figure 14.4 presents the iteration plots for the misclassification rates with three samples: training, OOB, and validation. Note that the misclassification rate for the OOB is closer to the validation sample and higher than the training sample. With 500 trees, the OOB has a misclassification rate of 0.204, while the validation sample has a misclassification rate of 0.207. The misclassification rate plot seems to flatten after 100 trees, meaning adding more trees may not improve the misclassification rate much. It explains the close call between models we noticed before.

From the Results window for HP Forest 2, we can receive the variable importance table, as shown in Table 14.5, with two values: Gini reduction and margin reduction. SAS Enterprise Miner uses these values for variable importance since we selected Loss Reduction as the method for measuring variable importance. In addition to the values

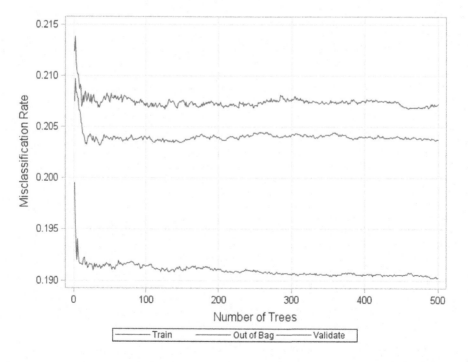

FIGURE 14.4
Iteration plot.

TABLE 14.5

Variable Importance

Variable	OOB: Gini Reduction	Valid: Gini Reduction	OOB: Margin Reduction	Valid: Margin Reduction
Travel purpose	0.151	0.155	0.303	0.306
Airline status	0.029	0.022	0.058	0.051
Arrival delay (in minutes)	0.015	0.015	0.032	0.031
Age	0.009	0.009	0.023	0.024
Gender	0.003	0.003	0.006	0.007
Flight cancellation	0.000	0.001	0.001	0.001
Average number of flights per year	0.000	0.000	0.003	0.003
Number of other loyalty cards	0.000	0.000	0.001	0.001
Replacement: Price sensitivity	0.000	0.000	0.001	0.001
Departure delay (in minutes)	−0.001	0.000	0.001	0.001
Passenger class	−0.001	−0.001	0.000	0.000
Flight time (in minutes)	−0.001	−0.001	0.000	0.000
Number of years flying	−0.001	−0.001	0.001	0.000
Spending for eating and drinking at the airport	−0.001	−0.001	0.000	0.000
Percent of flights with other airlines	−0.001	−0.001	0.000	0.000
Flight distance (miles)	−0.001	−0.001	0.000	0.000
Shopping amount at the airport	−0.001	−0.001	0.000	0.000
Destination state	−0.001	−0.001	0.000	0.000
Origin state	−0.001	−0.001	0.001	0.001

for the validation sample, I also present the values for the OOB sample for comparison since the OOB tends to be less biased. Figures 14.5 and 14.6 present the variable importance plots using Gini reduction with the OOB and validation samples, respectively.

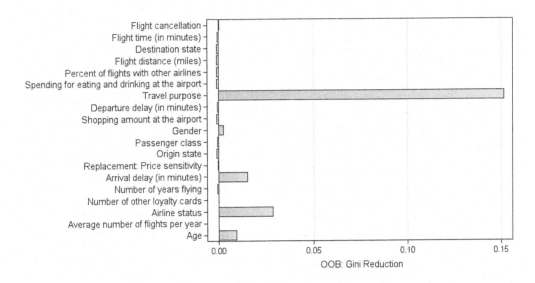

FIGURE 14.5
Variable importance – OOB Gini reduction.

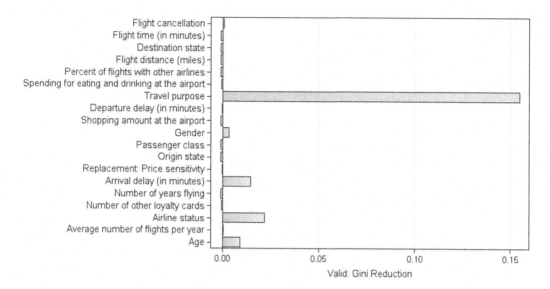

FIGURE 14.6
Variable importance – Validation Gini reduction.

Similarly, Figures 14.7 and 14.8 present the variable importance plots using margin reduction with the OOB and validation samples, respectively. All outputs show consistent results that *travel purpose* is the most important predictor, followed by *airline status, arrival delay time,* and *age.*

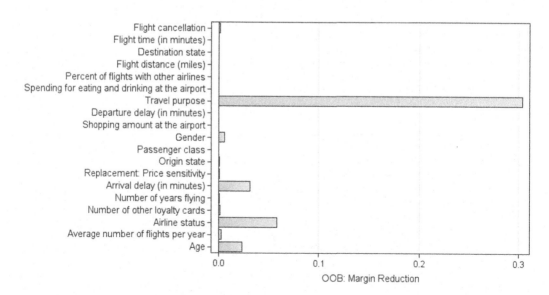

FIGURE 14.7
Variable importance – OOB: Margin reduction

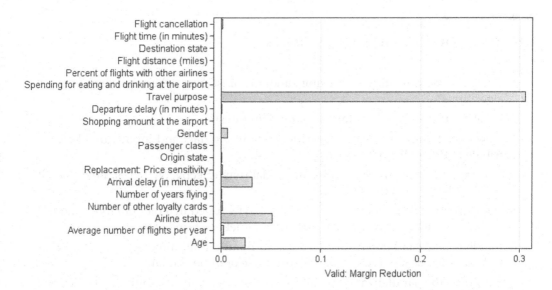

FIGURE 14.8
Variable importance – Valid: Margin reduction.

Summary

Random forest is a popular ensemble machine learning method that combines multiple decision trees to make more robust and accurate predictions. It is a bagging method that constructs each decision tree using a random subset of the training data and a random subset of input variables. This randomness reduces overfitting and enhances the model's ability to generalize to new data. During prediction, the random forest aggregates the predictions of individual trees through either voting (for classification models) or averaging (for association models), resulting in a final prediction that benefits from the collective predictions of the individual trees. It also uses out-of-bag (OOB) evaluation for unbiased performance estimation. The random forest also provides a measure of variable importance, allowing users to understand the relative contribution of different predictors in making predictions. This information can be useful for variable selection and identifying the most relevant factors influencing the output.

The random forest offers several advantages. First, it is known for its robustness against noise and outliers in the data. By combining multiple decision trees, each trained on different subsets of the data, the random forest can effectively handle noisy data. Additionally, random forest is versatile and applicable to various domains and data types, including categorical, numerical, and text data. It is capable of handling high-dimensional datasets and is less sensitive to the curse of dimensionality compared to some other algorithms. Random forest is also parallelizable, which ensures efficient computations and scalability to large datasets. Overall, random forest is a powerful and widely-used machine learning method that combines the strengths of individual decision trees to deliver accurate and robust predictions.

CHAPTER DISCUSSION QUESTIONS

1. What are the advantages of using random forest over other machine learning algorithms?
2. What are the primary limitations of random forest?
3. How does the random subset selection of training data and input variables contribute to the performance of random forest?
4. Can random forest handle imbalanced datasets effectively? If yes, how does it address the issue of class imbalance?
5. What are the main hyperparameters that can be tuned in a random forest model? How do these hyperparameters affect the model performance?
6. Random forest is known for its ability to handle high-dimensional data. What techniques does it employ to handle the curse of dimensionality?
7. How does the parallelization of random forest impact its scalability and efficiency for large datasets?
8. In what scenarios would random forest be a suitable choice for a machine learning task, and when might it be less appropriate?
9. What is OOB evaluation? How does it help address overfitting?

Exercises

Exercise 1: Random forest models for the Bank dataset

1. Open the *bank* dataset in SAS Enterprise Miner.
2. Sample the entire dataset. See the variable names and descriptions in Appendix A.1.
3. Partition the data using a split ratio of 60:40 (train: 60%; validation: 20%; test: 20%).
4. Perform data modification as follows:
   - Impute missing values.
   - Normalize the data.
5. Set *CRSCORE* (credit scores) as the target variable.
6. Configure five random forest models for this dataset as follows.
   - HP Forest Default (using default properties).
   - HP Forest 1
     - Set Maximum number of trees to 200.
     - Set Number of Variables to Consider to 100.
     - Set Split Size to 2.
   - HP Forest 2
     - Set Maximum number of trees to 500.
     - Set Maximum Depth to 20.

  – Set Number of Variables to Consider to 200.
  – Set Exhaustive to 50,000.
  – Set Split Size to 3.
- HP Forest 3
  – Set Maximum number of trees to 1,000.
  – Set Maximum Depth to 50.
  – Set Number of Variables to Consider to 500.
  – Set Exhaustive to 50,000.
  – Set Split Size to 5.
- HP Forest 4
  – Set Maximum number of trees to 2,000.
  – Set Maximum Depth to 50.
  – Set Number of Variables to Consider to 1,000.
  – Set Exhaustive to 100,000.
  – Set Split Size to 5.

7. Compare the model fit metrics between these five models using the validation results.
8. Select the champion model and justify this selection with the necessary evidence.
9. Present the results of the champion model.
10. Evaluate the reliability and validity of the champion model.
11. Present the variable importance information and interpret the results.

Exercise 2: Random forest models for the Passengers dataset

1. Open the *passengers* dataset in SAS Enterprise Miner.
2. Sample 20% of the full data. Set *return* (decision to return to the airline) as the target variable and change its role to binary. See the variable names and descriptions in Appendix A.2.
3. Partition the data using a split ratio of 60:40 (train: 60%; validation: 20%; test: 20%).
4. Perform data modification as follows:
   - Replace zero values for Likert scale variables with missing values.
   - Impute missing values.
5. Configure five random forest models for this dataset as follows.
   - HP Forest Default (using default properties).
   - HP Forest 1
     – Set Maximum number of trees to 200.
     – Set Number of Variables to Consider to 100.
     – Set Split Size to 2.
   - HP Forest 2
     – Set Maximum number of trees to 500.
     – Set Maximum Depth to 20.
     – Set Number of Variables to Consider to 200.
     – Set Exhaustive to 50,000.
     – Set Split Size to 3.
   - HP Forest 3
     – Set Maximum number of trees to 1,000.
     – Set Maximum Depth to 50.
     – Set Number of Variables to Consider to 500.
     – Set Exhaustive to 50,000.
     – Set Split Size to 5.

- HP Forest 4
    - Set Maximum number of trees to 2,000.
    - Set Maximum Depth to 50.
    - Set Number of Variables to Consider to 1,000.
    - Set Exhaustive to 100,000.
    - Set Split Size to 5.
6. Compare the model fit metrics between these five models using the validation results.
7. Select the champion model and justify this selection with the necessary evidence.
8. Present the results of the champion model.
9. Evaluate the reliability and validity of the champion model.
10. Present the variable importance information and interpret the results.

15

Gradient Boosting

LEARNING OUTCOMES

Upon the completion of this chapter, you will be able to

1. Describe the principles and concepts of gradient boosting as a powerful machine learning algorithm.
2. Discuss the advantages and disadvantages of using gradient boosting compared to other machine learning methods.
3. Explain the iterative process of building an ensemble of weak learners in gradient boosting.
4. Categorize different loss functions in gradient boosting.
5. Define gradient descent and explain its important role in gradient boosting.
6. Compare traditional gradient boosting, Gradient Boosting Additive Models (GBAM), and Stochastic Gradient Boosting (SGB).
7. Describe the importance of hyperparameter tuning in gradient boosting and its impact on model performance.
8. Build and train gradient boosting models using SAS Enterprise Miner.

Introduction

This chapter introduces gradient boosting, another method that is an ensemble of decision trees. Gradient boosting is an ensemble learning technique that constructs a sequence of decision trees, collectively forming a unified predictive model. Gradient boosting is a powerful prediction method that is very effective at selecting variables. Does it sound similar to Random Forest? Yes, because both methods involve ensembling multiple individual trees to 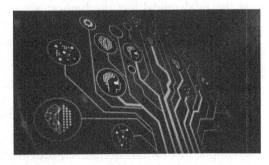 produce more robust and accurate predictions. But they are not the same. We will compare these two methods later in this chapter.

Gradient boosting starts with an initial decision tree model and updates it by using residuals from the model in the previous step as the target. Imagine we have multiple trees

DOI: 10.1201/9781003162872-18

lined up in sequence, with one connected to another. It forms the structure of a gradient boosting model. If the dataset used to create each tree in the sequence of trees is a random sample of the training dataset, then the method is called Stochastic Gradient Boosting (SGB). This chapter explains the principles and concepts of gradient boosting, its differences from the random forest method, the gradient boosting process, and how to perform gradient boosting using SAS Enterprise Miner.

What Is Gradient Boosting?

Gradient boosting is a machine learning method widely used for classification and association models. It is a type of ensemble learning that involves combining multiple weak models to create a strong model. The principle behind gradient boosting is to iteratively add new models to the ensemble, each correcting the previous models' errors.

> **DEFINITION**
>
> Gradient boosting is a machine learning ensemble method that sequentially combines weak base learners (individual decision trees) to create a powerful predictive model by minimizing errors using gradient descent.

Here is how gradient boosting works. Gradient boosting algorithm uses a loss function to measure the difference between predicted and actual values (prediction errors) and then iteratively train new models to reduce the errors. At each iteration, a new model is trained to predict the difference between the current predictions and the actual values. In gradient boosting modeling, this difference is called the *residuals*, and the new model is trained to predict the residuals using the variables in the data. The new model is added to the ensemble, and the predictions of the ensemble are updated by adding the predictions of the new model. This process is repeated iteratively, with each new model correcting the errors of the previous models until the error is minimized or a predefined number of iterations is reached.

The term *gradient* in gradient boosting refers to the fact that the algorithm uses the gradient of the loss function to optimize the model. The gradient provides information about the direction and magnitude of the error, which can be used to update the model parameters.

Unlike random forest, which is a bagging method, gradient boosting is a boosting method. We have covered the boosting ensemble method in Chapter 10. As a reminder, boosting combines weak learners into strong learners by creating sequential models such that the final model has the highest accuracy. Figure 15.1 illustrates how the gradient boosting algorithm works with multiple decision tree models. Keep in mind that gradient boosting is commonly used with decision trees.

Practical Applications of Gradient Boosting

Gradient boosting is a powerful machine learning algorithm that has been applied in various domains. I provide some practical applications of gradient boosting as follows.

- *Ranking and recommendation systems*: Gradient boosting can be used in ranking and recommendation systems. It learns to rank items or recommend personalized content by optimizing ranking metrics such as the pairwise or listwise loss functions.

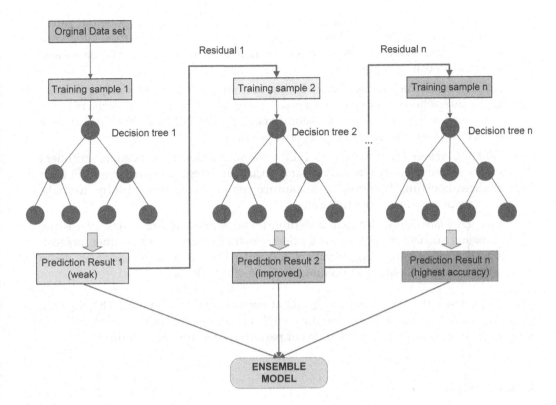

FIGURE 15.1
Gradient boosting algorithm.

This capability makes it useful for applications like search engines, recommender systems, and personalized advertising.

- *Anomaly detection*: Gradient boosting models can be employed for anomaly detection in various domains, including cybersecurity, network intrusion detection, and fraud detection. By learning the normal patterns from labeled data, the algorithm can identify deviations or anomalies in new instances.

- *Medical diagnosis and healthcare*: Healthcare providers can use this algorithm for medical diagnosis and healthcare-related tasks. It helps predict disease outcomes, detect diseases from medical imaging data (e.g., cancer detection in mammograms), and assist in personalized treatment recommendations.

- *Predictive aviation maintenance*: Airlines can utilize gradient boosting to predict maintenance requirements for their aircraft and engines. By analyzing historical maintenance data and sensor readings, the model can identify potential issues and recommend timely maintenance actions, reducing unplanned downtime and improving operational efficiency.

- *Fuel consumption optimization*: Gradient boosting models can be used to optimize fuel consumption by analyzing various factors, including aircraft type, route, weather conditions, and flight altitude. Such optimization can lead to significant cost savings and reduce the environmental impact of air travel.

- *Safety and risk analysis*: Gradient boosting can aid in identifying potential safety risks by analyzing incident data, pilot performance, and other safety-related variables. By proactively addressing risks, airlines can enhance safety standards and maintain a positive reputation.

- *Customer sentiment analysis*: By analyzing customer feedback, reviews, and social media interactions, service providers can use gradient boosting to perform sentiment analysis and understand customer perceptions. This insight helps improve services and address customer concerns promptly.

- *Natural Language Processing (NLP)*: NLP tasks such as text classification, sentiment analysis, named entity recognition, and document categorization can benefit from gradient boosting. It allows us to capture complex language patterns to make accurate predictions on textual data.

- *Time series forecasting*: Gradient boosting can be applied to time series forecasting problems, such as predicting stock prices, electricity demand, or weather forecasting. By incorporating lagged values and other time-dependent variables, it can capture temporal patterns and make accurate predictions.

As you can see, the applications of gradient boosting are tremendous. The algorithm's flexibility, accuracy, and ability to handle complex relationships make it a valuable tool in various fields where accurate predictions or pattern recognition are required.

Differences between Random Forest and Gradient Boosting

Random Forest and gradient boosting are popular machine learning algorithms used for supervised learning tasks. In addition, they both are ensembles of multiple decision trees. While they share some similarities, there are significant differences between the two. Understanding these differences will help us select the right method for our data mining projects. The choice between the two algorithms depends on the specific problem, the characteristics of the data, and the tradeoff between interpretability and performance. Table 15.1 summarizes the key differences between them.

TABLE 15.1

Differences between Random Forest and Gradient Boosting

Items	Random Forest	Gradient Boosting
Ensemble method	Random forest is an ensemble bagging method that combines multiple decision trees parallelly to make predictions.	Gradient boosting is an ensemble boosting method that combines weak decision trees in a sequential manner.
Training process	Random forest builds each decision tree independently, where each tree is trained on a random subset of the training data (bootstrap aggregating or bagging).	Gradient boosting trains the decision trees sequentially. Each new tree is trained to correct the mistakes made by the previous tree.
Bias-variance tradeoff	Random forest reduces variance by averaging predictions from multiple trees. It is less prone to overfitting and performs well with noisy data.	Gradient boosting aims to reduce bias and variance by minimizing the errors made by the previous trees. It tends to achieve lower bias but can be more prone to overfitting.

(Continued)

TABLE 15.1 (*Continued*)

Differences between Random Forest and Gradient Boosting

Items	Random Forest	Gradient Boosting
Variable selection	Random forest randomly selects a subset of variables for each tree, which leads to a relatively lower correlation among trees. It can handle a large number of variables and can provide estimates of variable importance.	In gradient boosting, variable selection is based on the information gain or gradient importance, and variables are typically used in a deterministic order.
Parallelism	Random forest can train trees in parallel since each tree is independent. This makes it computationally efficient and suitable for parallel and distributed computing.	Gradient boosting trains trees sequentially, limiting parallelism. However, there are techniques like parallelized gradient boosting implementations that can be used to overcome this limitation.
Hyperparameters	Random forest has hyperparameters such as the number of trees, the maximum depth of trees, and the number of variables considered for each split.	Gradient boosting has hyperparameters such as the learning rate, number of trees, and maximum depth of trees.
Prediction	Random forest predictions are made by averaging or voting the predictions of all the trees.	In gradient boosting, predictions are made by summing the predictions of all the trees, where the contribution of each tree depends on its learning rate.
Interpretability	Random forest is relatively easier to interpret since it provides variable importance measures and can show how much each variable contributes to the overall prediction.	Gradient boosting, especially with a large number of trees, can be more complex to interpret due to the sequential nature of the training process.

Basic Concepts in Gradient Boosting

Gradient boosting is a powerful ensemble learning method that iteratively combines weak learners to create a strong predictive model. There are some important concepts that we need to understand to be able to perform this method correctly. Table 15.2 presents the key concepts and their descriptions.

TABLE 15.2

Basic Concepts in Gradient Boosting

Terms	Description
Gradient boosting	Gradient boosting is a machine learning ensemble method that sequentially combines weak learners to create a powerful predictive model by minimizing errors using gradient descent.
Ensemble learning	Gradient boosting is an ensemble learning method, which combines multiple weak learners (individual models with limited predictive power) to create a robust and accurate predictive model. The final prediction is obtained by aggregating the predictions of all individual weak learners.
Weak learners	In the context of gradient boosting, weak learners are individual models that perform slightly better than random guessing but are not highly accurate on their own. Decision trees are commonly used as weak learners in gradient boosting, but other models can also be used.

(Continued)

TABLE 15.2 (*Continued*)

Basic Concepts in Gradient Boosting

Terms	Description
Gradient descent	Gradient boosting minimizes a specified loss function by using gradient descent optimization. It computes the gradients of the loss function and adjusts the subsequent weak learner to correct the errors made by previous learners. The learning process aims to iteratively reduce the loss and improve the overall model performance.
Boosting	Gradient boosting employs a boosting algorithm, which builds the ensemble sequentially, with each weak learner focusing on the mistakes of its predecessors. Subsequent learners give more weight to the misclassified examples in the training data to correct the errors made by previous models.
Residuals	In gradient boosting, the subsequent weak learners are trained to predict the residuals or errors made by the previous learners. The goal is to progressively reduce the remaining errors by refining the model's predictions.
Loss function	The loss function measures the model performance and quantifies the difference between predicted and actual values. In gradient boosting, the algorithm minimizes the loss function during the training process to iteratively improve the model's predictive power.
Learning rate	The learning rate is a hyperparameter that controls the step size in gradient descent. It determines how much each weak learner's contribution affects the final ensemble. A lower learning rate makes the algorithm converge slowly but can improve generalizability, while a higher learning rate leads to faster convergence but may increase the risk of overfitting.
Tree depth and number of trees	These are hyperparameters that control the complexity and size of the individual decision trees. The tree depth affects the model's capacity to capture complex relationships in the data, while the number of trees determines the boosting iterations and overall model complexity.
Stochastic Gradient Boosting	Stochastic Gradient Boosting (SGB) is a variant of the traditional gradient boosting algorithm that introduces randomness during the training process. It combines the concepts of gradient boosting and stochastic learning to enhance the model's generalizability and reduce the risk of overfitting.
Gradient Boosting Additive Model	Gradient Boosting Additive Models (GBAM) is a variant of gradient boosting that extends the traditional algorithm to handle additive models. An additive model is a model that consists of a sum of functions of individual input variables, where each function depends only on a single input variable.
Variable importance	Gradient boosting provides a measure of variable importance, indicating the relative contribution of each input variable in making predictions. It allows users to identify the most influential predictors and gain insights into the underlying data patterns.

Advantages and Disadvantages of Gradient Boosting Method

Gradient boosting is a powerful and widely used machine learning algorithm that has several advantages and disadvantages. Understanding those strengths and weaknesses allows us to decide when to use this method and choose the right configurations for the predictive modeling step.

Advantages of gradient boosting

1. *High predictive accuracy*: Gradient boosting is known for its exceptional predictive accuracy. By combining multiple weak learners, it creates a strong ensemble model that can capture complex relationships in the data and produce highly accurate predictions.

2. *Capturing nonlinear relationships*: Nonlinear relationships between predictors and the target variable can be captured effectively by a gradient boosting model, making it suitable for a wide range of real-world applications where the data exhibit intricate patterns.

3. *Variable importance*: The method provides insights into variable importance, which allows us to identify which predictors are most influential in making predictions. This information aids in variable selection and provides a better understanding of the underlying problem.

4. *Flexibility*: Gradient boosting can handle various data types, including numerical, categorical, and textual data. It can be used for both association and classification models, making it a versatile method.

5. *Robustness to outliers*: Due to its ensemble nature gradient boosting is relatively robust to outliers. The impact of outliers is minimized as the model learns from the collective behavior of multiple weak learners.

6. *Handling missing data*: The method can handle missing data without requiring explicit data imputation techniques. Decision trees in the gradient boosting can handle missing values internally during the training process.

7. *No assumptions about data distribution*: Gradient boosting does not assume any specific distribution of the data, making it applicable in situations where the underlying data distribution is unknown.

Disadvantages of gradient boosting

1. *Potential overfitting*: Gradient boosting can be susceptible to overfitting, especially when the model is complex or when the dataset is relatively small. Proper hyperparameter tuning and configurations are essential to mitigate this risk.

2. *Computationally intensive*: Training a gradient boosting model can be computationally intensive and time-consuming, especially when dealing with large datasets or deep trees. Parallelization and optimized implementations can help address this issue.

3. *Hyperparameter tuning*: Finding the optimal hyperparameters for gradient boosting can be a challenging task. The performance of the model is sensitive to hyperparameter settings, and extensive experimentation is often required to find the right configurations.

4. *Black box model*: The ensemble nature of gradient boosting makes it a black box model. In other words, it is challenging to interpret the complete structure of the model and explain its predictions fully.

5. *Data imbalance*: Gradient boosting can struggle with imbalanced datasets, where one class significantly outnumbers the other. Techniques such as class weighting and data resampling may be necessary to address this issue.

Gradient Boosting Steps

Gradient boosting is an iterative algorithm that combines weak learners (individual decision trees) in a sequential manner to create a strong predictive model. So, how does it work? Below are the general steps involved in training a gradient boosting model.

1. *Initialize the model*: Initialize the model by defining the initial prediction, which is often set to the average value of the target variable in association models or the logarithm of the odds ratio in classification models.

2. *Calculate residuals*: Calculate the residuals or errors between the actual target values and the initial predictions. These residuals represent the information that the model needs to learn and improve upon.

3. *Train weak learners*: Train a weak learner (e.g., a decision tree) on the variables and the calculated residuals. The weak learner is typically shallow, meaning it has a small depth and few splits. The goal is to find the best split points that minimize the loss function (e.g., Mean Squared Error (MSE) for association models or log loss for classification models) based on the residuals.

4. *Compute the learning rate*: Decide on a learning rate, which controls the contribution of each weak learner to the final prediction. The learning rate helps to prevent overfitting and control the impact of each weak learner on the ensemble.

5. *Update the model*: Update the model by adding the weak learner's prediction to the previous predictions. The predictions are weighted by the learning rate, which determines how much each weak learner contributes to the overall model.

6. *Update residuals*: Update the residuals by subtracting the predicted values from the actual target values. These updated residuals represent the remaining information that the next weak learner needs to focus on.

7. *Repeat steps 3–6*: Repeat steps 3–6 for a specified number of iterations or until a stopping criterion is met. In each iteration, train a new weak learner on the updated residuals and update the model and residuals accordingly.

8. *Finalize the model*: Once all the iterations are completed, the final model is obtained by combining the predictions of all the weak learners. The learning rate determines the contribution of each weak learner to the final prediction.

9. *Prediction*: To make predictions for new data, pass the data through each weak learner and combine their predictions using the learning rate. The final prediction is the sum of the predictions from all the weak learners.

It's worth noting that there are variations of gradient boosting algorithms, which incorporate additional optimizations and enhancements to improve performance and training speed.

These steps outline the general process of training a gradient boosting model. The actual implementation may involve additional hyperparameter tuning and handling specific nuances based on the chosen gradient boosting algorithm.

Gradient Boosting Loss Function

In gradient boosting, the choice of the loss function is crucial as it determines how the algorithm updates the model at each iteration. The loss function measures the difference between the predicted values and the actual values, and the algorithm aims to minimize this difference by iteratively adding new models to the ensemble.

The most commonly used loss function in gradient boosting is the MSE for association models and the cross-entropy loss (also called log loss) for classification models. The MSE measures the average squared difference between the predicted values and the actual values, while the cross-entropy loss measures the difference between the predicted probability distribution and the actual probability distribution. I will provide the list of common loss functions in this section.

Regardless of the specific loss function used, the algorithm updates the model parameters by calculating the negative gradient of the loss function with respect to the predicted values. This gradient provides information about the direction and magnitude of the prediction error and is used to update the model in the direction that minimizes the loss.

The learning rate is also used to control the size of the updates at each iteration. A lower learning rate results in smaller updates and a slower convergence, while a higher learning rate results in larger updates and a faster convergence. The choice of learning rate is important as it determines the balance between accuracy and convergence speed.

> The loss function is an indicator of both the quality of a model's coefficients and its fit to the underlying fundamental data. The residual is defined in terms of the derivative of a loss function. Loss function must be optimized to minimize prediction errors.

Below are the most common loss functions for association models and classification models and when they can be used.

Loss functions for association models with a continuous target variable

1. *Mean Squared Error (MSE)*: The most widely used loss function for association problems, MSE calculates the average squared difference between predicted and actual values.

2. *Mean Absolute Error (MAE)*: MAE measures the average absolute difference between predicted and actual values, making it less sensitive to outliers than MSE.

3. *Huber loss*: Huber loss is a combination of MSE and MAE, acting like MSE when the error is small and like MAE when the error is large. It provides a balance between the two and is robust to outliers.

4. *Quantile loss*: Quantile loss is useful for quantile regression, where the goal is to predict specific quantiles of the target distribution. It optimizes the difference between predicted quantiles and actual quantiles.

5. *Poisson loss*: This loss function is used when the target variable follows a Poisson distribution, such as in count data regression problems.

Classification loss functions for classification models with a categorical target variable

1. *Log loss (binary cross-entropy)*: The most commonly used function for binary classification models. Log loss measures the performance of a classifier by penalizing false classifications with logarithmic terms.

2. *Multi-class log loss (multi-class cross-entropy)*: For multi-level (multinomial) classification models, this loss function extends binary cross-entropy to handle multiple classes, measuring the dissimilarity between predicted class probabilities and the actual class values.

3. *Exponential loss (AdaBoost)*: Primarily used for binary classification models in the AdaBoost algorithm. This loss function assigns higher weights to misclassified samples to give them more emphasis during boosting.

These loss functions play a critical role in guiding the gradient boosting algorithm to optimize the model performance. Each loss function has its strengths and weaknesses, and the choice of the appropriate loss function depends on the characteristics of the data, the type of target variable, and the specific objectives of the modeling task.

Gradient Boosting Additive Models and Stochastic Gradient Boosting

In addition to the traditional gradient boosting algorithm we have discussed so far, there are two popular variants of gradient boosting that extend the traditional algorithms. They are GBAM and SGB. We discuss key differences among these algorithms which give us a deeper understanding of this popular machine learning method. Table 15.3 summarizes the similarities and differences between the three types of gradient boosting algorithms.

Gradient Boosting Additive Models (GBAM)

Essentially, GBAM is a variant of gradient boosting that extends the traditional algorithm to handle additive models. An additive model is a model that consists of a sum of functions of individual predictors, where each function depends only on a single predictor. Unlike traditional gradient boosting, in which each new model in the ensemble is trained on the residuals of the previous model, in GBAM, the new models are not trained on the residuals, but on the original input variables.

The GBAM algorithm works by constructing a set of basis functions for each predictor and then fitting a linear combination of these functions to the target variable. The basis functions can be any type of function, and they can be chosen based on the specific problem and the complexity of the predictors. At each iteration, the algorithm adds a new basis function to the linear combination by fitting a model to the gradient of the loss function with respect to the current prediction. This allows the algorithm to gradually refine the model and improve its performance on the training data.

GBAM has several advantages over traditional gradient boosting. First, it handles well non-linear relationships between the predictors and the target variable, which is important for many real-world problems. Second, it incorporates domain knowledge into the model by

TABLE 15.3

Differences among Traditional Gradient Boosting, GBAM, and SGB

Items	Traditional Gradient Boosting	Gradient Boosting Additive Models	Stochastic Gradient Boosting
Training approach	Traditional gradient boosting trains weak learners, usually decision trees, sequentially, with each new learner focused on minimizing the errors made by the previous learners.	GBAM extends traditional gradient boosting by allowing the inclusion of different types of weak learners, not limited to decision trees. It allows the combination of diverse models, such as linear models, decision trees, or neural networks.	SGB introduces randomness into the training process by using random subsets of the training data for training each weak learner.
Learning rate	Traditional gradient boosting uses a fixed learning rate that determines the contribution of each weak learner to the overall ensemble. It is typically manually tuned.	GBAM uses a learning rate that controls the contribution of each model component, similar to traditional gradient boosting.	SGB uses a fixed learning rate similar to traditional gradient boosting.
Split selection	**Deterministic split selection:** Traditional gradient boosting selects the best split points deterministically, aiming to minimize the loss function based on the residuals.	**Flexibility in weak learner selection:** GBAM provides flexibility in selecting the weak learners. This allows for the use of different models suitable for different types of variables and data characteristics.	**Random subsampling:** SGB randomly samples a subset of the training data for each iteration, leading to diversity in the weak learners and reducing overfitting.
Model	Traditional gradient boosting tends to create complex models with high variance, especially when the number of iterations is large.	GBAM can offer better model interpretability compared to traditional gradient boosting, especially when linear models or other inherently interpretable models are included.	**SGB** introduces a variance-reduction tradeoff due to the random subsampling. It can reduce overfitting but may increase bias.
Training efficiency	Traditional gradient boosting can be slower compared to other boosting algorithms due to its sequential nature and the need to train each weak learner in order.	Training GBAM can be slower than traditional gradient boosting, especially if it involves computationally intensive models like neural networks.	SGB can be faster compared to traditional gradient boosting since it trains each weak learner on a smaller subset of data. This makes it more scalable for large datasets.

selecting appropriate basis functions for each predictor. Finally, it provides a more interpretable model by decomposing the prediction into a sum of functions of individual predictors.

However, GBAM also has some limitations. First, it requires the choice of appropriate basis functions for each predictor, which can be time-consuming and require expert knowledge. Second, it may not be able to capture complex interactions between the predictors, which may limit its performance on certain problems. Finally, it may be slower and require more memory than traditional gradient boosting due to the need to store the basis functions for each predictor.

Stochastic Gradient Boosting (SGB)

SGB is a variant of gradient boosting that introduces randomness into the training process. In traditional gradient boosting, each new model in the ensemble is trained on the same set of samples and variables, which can lead to overfitting and poor model generalizability. SGB addresses this issue by randomly sampling a subset of the data and variables at each iteration, leading to a more diverse set of models and better predictive power.

The key difference between SGB and traditional gradient boosting is that SGB only uses a subset of the training data at each iteration, which is randomly sampled from the original dataset. This sampling process is typically done with replacement (refer to Chapter 15 regarding sampling with replacement), and the size of the sample is a hyperparameter that can be tuned based on the size of the original dataset and the complexity of the problem.

In addition to sampling the data, SGB also randomly samples a subset of the variables at each iteration. This helps reduce the correlation between the models in the ensemble and makes the algorithm more robust to noisy data. The sampling process introduces randomness into the training process, which can improve the performance of the algorithm and reduce overfitting. However, it also increases the variance of the model, which can lead to a higher training error and slower convergence. To address this issue, SGB introduces a new hyperparameter called the subsample rate, which controls the fraction of the training data that is used at each iteration. A lower subsample rate results in a more diverse set of models but may increase the variance of the model and require more iterations to converge. On the other hand, a higher subsample rate results in a more stable set of models but may increase the risk of overfitting.

In summary, traditional gradient boosting trains weak learners sequentially, uses a fixed learning rate and selects splits deterministically. GBAM extends this approach to include different types of weak learners and offers flexibility and interpretability. Finally, SGB introduces random subsampling to improve training efficiency and reduce overfitting but introduces a variance-bias tradeoff. The choice between these algorithms depends on factors such as the dataset size, interpretability requirements, and tradeoff preferences between accuracy and training efficiency.

Gradient Boosting Hyperparameter Tuning Guide

As mentioned before, gradient boosting involves hyperparameter tuning, which is a crucial step in finding the optimal configurations and addressing overfitting. There are many hyperparameters in gradient boosting given its complexity and numerous variants. When tuning hyperparameters, it's important to consider the computational resources, time constraints, and the size of the dataset. It is recommended to use cross-validation to evaluate the model performance for different hyperparameter settings. By iteratively tuning the hyperparameters and evaluating the model performance, you can find the optimal combination that maximizes the model's accuracy and generalizability.

Below are some important hyperparameters to consider and techniques for tuning them.

1. *Number of trees*: This hyperparameter determines the number of weak learners (trees) in the ensemble. Increasing the number of trees can improve the model performance, but it also increases training time. It is essential to find the right balance to avoid overfitting. You can try different values and use cross-validation to select the optimal number.

2. *Learning rate*: The learning rate controls the contribution of each weak learner to the overall model. A lower learning rate makes the model more robust but increases the number of iterations needed for convergence. A higher learning rate may lead to faster convergence but could result in overfitting. Experiment with different learning rates to find the optimal value.

3. *Maximum depth of trees*: This hyperparameter determines the depth of the individual decision trees. A deeper tree can capture more complex relationships in the data but is prone to overfitting. Shallower trees reduce overfitting but may result in underfitting. It's important to tune the maximum depth based on the complexity of the problem and the available data.

4. *Subsampling*: Subsampling refers to the fraction of training samples to be used for training each weak learner. Using a value less than 1.0 introduces randomness and can reduce overfitting. However, setting it too low may result in underfitting. Cross-validation can help identify the optimal subsampling value.

5. *Variable subsampling*: This hyperparameter determines the fraction of variables to be used for training each weak learner. It introduces randomness and helps reduce overfitting. You can try different values (e.g., 0.5, 0.8) to find the optimal variable subsampling ratio.

6. *Automated hyperparameter optimization*: There are also automated hyperparameter optimization techniques available, such as Bayesian optimization, genetic algorithms, or gradient-based optimization. These methods can efficiently search the hyperparameter space and find optimal values, often using a guided exploratory process.

SAS ENTERPRISE MINER GUIDELINES

Gradient Boosting Node Train Properties
(https://documentation.sas.com)

GRADIENT BOOSTING NODE TRAIN PROPERTIES: SERIES OPTIONS

- **N Iterations** – Use the N Iterations property to specify the number of terms in the boosting series. For interval and binary targets, the number of iterations equals the trees. For a nominal target, a separate tree is created for each target category in each iteration series.

- **Train Proportion** – Use the Train Proportion property to specify the proportion of training observations to train a tree with. A different training sample is taken in each iteration. Trees trained in the same iteration have the same training data.

GRADIENT BOOSTING NODE TRAIN PROPERTIES: NODE

- **Leaf Fraction** – Use the Leaf Fraction property to specify the smallest number of training observations that a new branch can have. This property value is expressed as the proportion of the number N of available training observations in the data. N can be less than the total number of observations in the data set because observations with a missing target value are excluded. The default value is 0.001. If the Leaf Fraction property is set too high for your data, the Gradient boosting node can still run, but complete without finding any splits. A workaround for this no-split scenario is to specify a smaller value for the Leaf Fraction property.

- **Number of Surrogate Rules** – Use the Number of Surrogate Rules property to specify the maximum number of surrogate rules that the Gradient boosting node seeks in each non-leaf node. The first surrogate rule is used when the main splitting rule relies on an input whose value is missing. If the first surrogate rule also relies on an input whose value is missing, the next surrogate rule is invoked. If missing values prevent the main rule and all of the surrogate's rules from applying to an observation, then the main rule assigns the observation to the branch that it has designated as receiving missing values. Permissible values are nonnegative integers. The default value for the Number of Surrogate Rules property is 0.

- **Split Size** – Use the Split Size property to specify the smallest number of training observations that a node must have before it is eligible to be split. Permissible values are integers greater than or equal to 2. The default value is determined based on the data.

SAS ENTERPRISE MINER GUIDELINES

Sample Node Train Properties

(https://documentation.sas.com)

GRADIENT BOOSTING NODE TRAIN PROPERTIES: SPLITTING RULE

- **Huber M-Regression** – Use the Huber M-regression loss function instead of square error loss with an interval target. The Huber loss function is less sensitive to extreme target values. The Huber threshold value must be between 0.6 and 1. A value close to 1, such as 0.9, is reasonable. The default value is No. The HUBER option is ignored unless the target has interval measurement level.

- **Maximum Branch** – Use the Maximum Branch property to specify the maximum number of branches that you want a splitting rule to produce from one node. This property restricts the number of subsets that a splitting rule can produce to the specified number or fewer. Permissible values for the Maximum Branch property are integers between 2 and 100. The minimum value of 2 results in binary trees. The default value for the Maximum Branch property is 2.

- **Maximum Depth** – Use the Maximum Depth property to specify the maximum depth of a node that will be created. The depth of a node equals the number of splitting rules needed to define the node. The root node has depth zero. The children of the root node are the first generation and have depth one.

- **Minimum Categorical Size** – Use the Minimum Categorical Size property to specify the minimum number of training observations that a categorical value must have before the category can be used in a split search. Categorical values that appear in fewer than the number specified (n) are regarded as if they were missing. If the Missing Values property is set to Use in Search, the categories occurring in fewer than n observations are merged into the pseudo category for missing values for the purpose of finding a split. Otherwise, observations with infrequent categories are excluded from the split search. The policy for assigning such observations to a branch is the same as the policy for assigning missing values to a branch. Permissible values are integers greater than or equal to 1. The default value for the Minimum Categorical Size property is 5.

- **Re-use Variable** – Use the Reuse Variable property to specify how many splitting rules in a path can use the same variable.

  When a splitting rule is considered for a node, the worth of the rule is multiplied by n if the splitting variable has already been used in a primary splitting rule in an ancestor node. For $n > 1$, once a variable is used in a primary split, it is more likely to appear in a rule in a descendent node because it gets an advantage in competing for splitting in the descendent node. The tree ends up using fewer variables, especially correlated variables. Reducing the number of variables in a tree can make the tree easier to interpret or deploy. Eliminating correlated variables in the tree results in a more accurate measure of the importance of those that are in the tree.

  An appropriate value for n depends on context. A value of two or three might be reasonable. The default value for n is one, giving no advantage or disadvantage for reusing a variable in a path. Set $n = 0$ to avoid using the same variable more than once in a path.

- **Categorical Bins** – Use the Categorical Bins property to specify the number of preliminary bins to collect categorical input values when preparing to search for a split. If an input variable has more than n categories in the node, then the split search uses the most frequent $n - 1$ categories and regards the remaining categories as a single pseudo category. The count of categories is done separately in each node. The default value is 30.

- **Interval Bins** – Use the Interval Bins property to specify the number of preliminary bins to consolidate interval input values into. The width equals $(\max(x) - \min(x))/n$, where $\max(x)$ and $\min(x)$ are the maximum and minimum of the input variable values in the training data in the tree node being searched. The width is computed separately for each input and each node. The search algorithm ignores the Interval Bins property if the number of distinct input values in the node is smaller than n. The default value of n is 100.

- **Missing Values** – Use the Missing Values property to specify how splitting rules handle observations that contain missing values for a variable. If a surrogate rule can assign an observation to a branch, then it does, and the missing value policy is ignored for the specific observation.

  The default value is Use in search. Select from the following available missing value policies:

  - **Use in search** – Uses missing values during the split search.
  - **Largest branch** – Assigns the observations that contain missing values to the branch with the largest number of training observations.
  - **Most correlated branch** – Assigns an observation with missing values to the most correlated branch.

GRADIENT BOOSTING NODE TRAIN PROPERTIES: SPLIT SEARCH

- **Exhaustive** – Use the Exhaustive property to specify the highest number of candidate splits that you want to find in an exhaustive search. If more candidates should be considered, a heuristic search is used instead. The exhaustive method of searching for a split examines all possible splits. If the number of possible splits is greater than n, then a heuristic search is done instead of an exhaustive search. The exhaustive and heuristic search methods apply only to multi-way splits and binary splits on nominal targets with more than two values. The Exhaustive property applies to multi-way splits and binary splits on nominal targets with more than two values. Permissible values are integers between 0 and 2,000,000,000. The default setting for the Exhaustive property is 5,000.

- **Node Sample** – Use the Node Sample property to specify the maximum within-node sample size n that you want to use to find splits. If the number of training observations in a node is larger than n, then the split search for that node is based on a random sample of size n. Permissible values are integers greater than or equal to 2. The default value for the Node Sample property is 20,000.

SAS ENTERPRISE MINER GUIDELINES

Sample Node Train Properties

(https://documentation.sas.com)

GRADIENT BOOSTING NODE TRAIN PROPERTIES: SUBTREE

- **Assessment Measure** – Use the Assessment Measure property to specify the method that you want to use to select the best tree, based on the validation data. If no validation data is available, training data is used. The available assessment measurements are:

  - **Decision** (default setting) – The Decision method selects the tree that has the largest average profit and smallest average loss if a profit or loss matrix is defined. If no profit or loss matrix is defined, the value of model assessment measure will be reset in the training process, depending on the measurement level of the target. If the target is ordinal, the measure is set to Decision. If the target is interval, the measure is set to Average Square Error. If the target is categorical, the measure is set to Misclassification.

  - **Average Square Error** – The Average Square Error method selects the tree that has the smallest average square error.

  - **Misclassification** – The Misclassification method selects the tree that has the smallest misclassification rate.

Example: Gradient Boosting

In this example, we build predictive models for the *airline recommendation* dataset using the gradient boosting algorithm with various configurations.

Dataset: AirlineRecommendation.sas7bdat

Target variable: Recommendation (binary): 1 – recommend the airline; 0 – do not recommend the airline.

Sample-Explore-Modify: Refer to the previous chapters.

Gradient Boosting Models

In this example, we train five gradient boosting models. From the Model tab, drag four Gradient Boosting nodes to the workspace and connect them to the Replacement node. Name them Gradient Boosting Default, Gradient Boosting 1, Gradient Boosting 2, Gradient Boosting 3, and Gradient Boosting 4. Then from the Assess tab, drag a Model Comparison node to the workspace and connect it to those five Gradient Boosting nodes. The diagram should look like the one below.

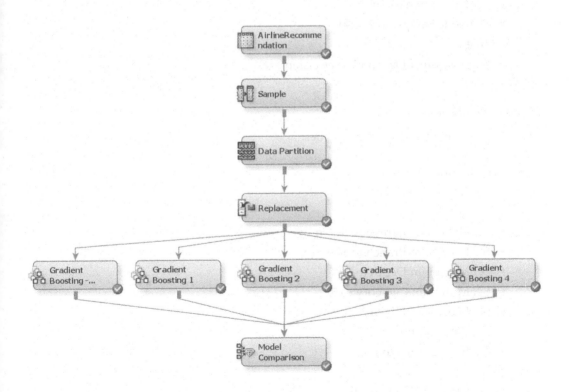

Use the details below to set the configurations for each Gradient boosting model.

Model 1: Gradient Boosting – Default

(Using default properties, the primary settings are included below:
  In the Gradient Boosting Train properties:

- Series Options
  - Set *N* Iteration to 50 (equivalent to 50 trees).
- Splitting Rule
  - Set Huber M-Regression to No.
  - Set Maximum Branch to 2.
  - Set Maximum Depth to 2.
  - Set Minimum Category to 5.
  - Set Reuse Variable to 1.
  - Set Category Bins to 30.
  - Set Interval Bins to 100.
- Node
  - Set Leaf Fraction to 0.001.
  - Set Split Size to undefined.
- Split Search
  - Set Exhaustive to 5,000.
  - Set Node Sample to 20,000.
- Subtree
  - Set Assessment Method to Decision.

Model 2: Gradient Boosting 1

In the Gradient Boosting Train properties:

- Series Options
  - Set *N* Iteration to 100.
- Splitting Rule
  - Set Huber M-Regression to No.
  - Set Maximum Branch to 10.
  - Set Maximum Depth to 50.
  - Set Minimum Category to 5.
  - Set Reuse Variable to 2.
  - Set Category Bins to 50.
  - Set Interval Bins to 200.
- Node
  - Set Leaf Fraction to 0.001.
  - Set Split Size to 5.

- Split Search
  - Set Exhaustive to 10,000.
  - Set Node Sample to 100,000.
- Subtree
  - Set Assessment Method to Misclassification.

Model 3: Gradient Boosting 2

In the Gradient Boosting Train properties:

- Series Options
  - Set N Iteration to 200.
- Splitting Rule
  - Set Huber M-Regression to No.
  - Set Maximum Branch to 20.
  - Set Maximum Depth to 50.
  - Set Minimum Category to 5.
  - Set Reuse Variable to 3.
  - Set Category Bins to 100.
  - Set Interval Bins to 500.
- Node
  - Set Leaf Fraction to 0.001.
  - Set Split Size to 5.
- Split Search
  - Set Exhaustive to 50,000.
  - Set Node Sample to 200,000.
- Subtree
  - Set Assessment Method to Misclassification.

Model 4: Gradient Boosting 3

In the Gradient Boosting Train properties:

- Series Options
  - Set N Iteration to 500.
- Splitting Rule
  - Set Huber M-Regression to No.
  - Set Maximum Branch to 20.
  - Set Maximum Depth to 50.
  - Set Minimum Category to 5.
  - Set Reuse Variable to 3.
  - Set Category Bins to 100.
  - Set Interval Bins to 500.

- Node
  - Set Leaf Fraction to 0.001.
  - Set Split Size to 5.
- Split Search
  - Set Exhaustive to 50,000.
  - Set Node Sample to 200,000.
- Subtree
  - Set Assessment Method to Misclassification.

Model 5: Gradient Boosting 4

In the Gradient Boosting Train properties:

- Series Options
  - Set N Iteration to 500.
- Splitting Rule
  - Set Huber M-Regression to No.
  - Set Maximum Branch to 20.
  - Set Maximum Depth to 50.
  - Set Minimum Category to 5.
  - Set Reuse Variable to 3.
  - Set Category Bins to 100.
  - Set Interval Bins to 1,000.
- Node
  - Set Leaf Fraction to 0.001.
  - Set Split Size to 5.
- Split Search
  - Set Exhaustive to 100,000.
  - Set Node Sample to 200,000.
- Subtree
  - Set Assessment Method to Misclassification.

In the Model Comparison Train Properties:

- Under Model Selection
  - Set Selection Statistic to Misclassification Rate.
  - Set Selection Table to Validation.

Run the Model Comparison node and open the Results window.

Results

As usual, first, we compare the performance of those five models. The model comparison results are presented in Table 15.4 using the validation model fit metrics: misclassification rate, Gini coefficient, ROC index, and Lift value. As we can see, those models are very

TABLE 15.4

Model Comparison Results

Model Description	Valid: Misclassification Rate	Valid: Gini	Valid: ROC	Valid: Lift
Gradient boosting 2	0.20881	0.68	0.84	1.68
Gradient boosting 3	0.20881	0.68	0.84	1.68
Gradient boosting 4	0.20881	0.68	0.84	1.65
Gradient boosting 1	0.20961	0.69	0.85	1.68
Gradient boosting - Default	0.21395	0.69	0.85	1.68
Pruned CART tree	0.209	0.66	0.83	1.61

close, and Gradient boosting 2 and Gradient boosting 3 have identical model fit metrics. Gradient boosting 4 has the same metrics as those two, except for a lower Lift value. This result is confirmed by the ROC chart (Figure 15.2) and Lift chart (Figure 15.3), in which all curves overlap.

In order to compare the gradient boosting model performance with the individual tree model, I included the best individual tree model we found in Chapter 8, Pruned CART tree, at the end of the table. It appears that except for the misclassification rate, Gradient Booting 2, Gradient Boosting 3, and Gradient Boosting 4 outperform the individual tree in all metrics. Gradient Boosting 1 and Gradient Boosting Default have a slightly higher

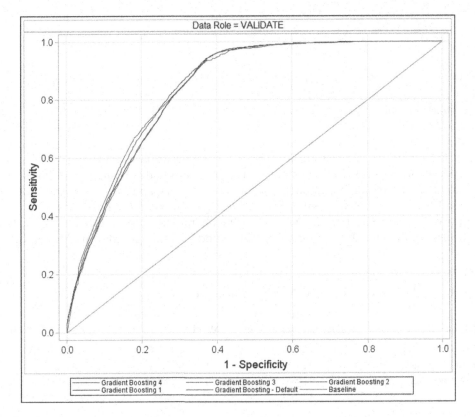

FIGURE 15.2
ROC chart.

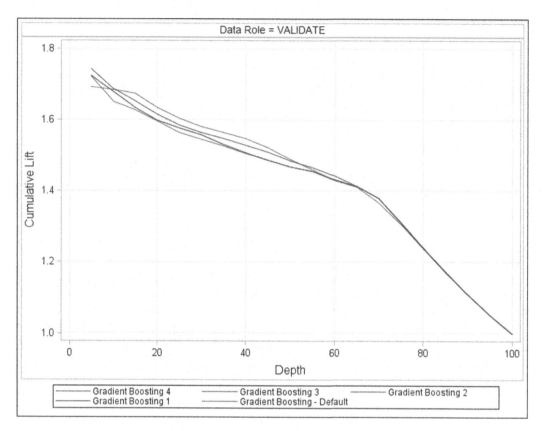

FIGURE 15.3
Lift chart.

misclassification rate but still perform better than the CART tree in the other three metrics. This evidence shows that the gradient boosting model performs better than individual trees due to them being ensemble models.

Table 15.5 shows the misclassification rates for three samples: training, validation, and test. The results show very consistent values, indicating the reliability of these models. Basically, we can conclude that these models are very similar in performance, with Gradient Boosting 2 and Gradient Boosting 3 being slightly superior.

Suppose we select Gradient Boosting 2 as the champion model in this example. Open the Results window for the Gradient Boosting 2 node, we can get the variable importance

TABLE 15.5

Comparison of Misclassification Rates between Three Samples

Model Description	Valid: Misclassification Rate	Train: Misclassification Rate	Test: Misclassification Rate
Gradient boosting 2	0.20881	0.20267	0.2067
Gradient boosting 3	0.20881	0.20267	0.2067
Gradient boosting 4	0.20881	0.20264	0.2065
Gradient boosting 1	0.20961	0.19763	0.2081
Gradient boosting - Default	0.21395	0.21426	0.212

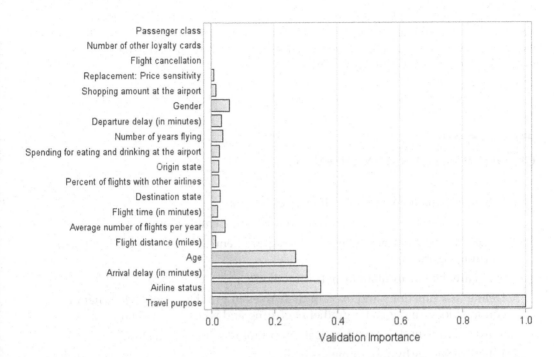

FIGURE 15.4
Variable importance.

results. Figure 15.4 shows the variable importance. The chart shows that the most important predictor is *travel purpose, followed by airline status, arrival delay time,* and *age*. This result is consistent with what we found in Chapter 14, where we used the random forest method.

Summary

Gradient boosting is a powerful ensemble machine learning method that combines weak learners in an iterative fashion to create a strong predictive model. It works by minimizing a specified loss function using gradient descent optimization. Each subsequent weak learner is trained to correct the errors made by the previous learners, emphasizing more the cases that were previously misclassified. This iterative process leads to an ensemble model that can effectively capture complex relationships and make accurate predictions. Gradient boosting has gained popularity due to its ability to handle various types of data and its effectiveness in both classification and association modeling.

One of the key advantages of gradient boosting is its ability to handle heterogeneous data and incorporate different types of weak learners. It can handle categorical variables, numerical variables, and even missing values. Moreover, gradient boosting allows for the use of different loss functions based on the specific problem at hand, providing flexibility and adaptability to different scenarios. Another advantage is the interpretability of the model. By calculating the variable importance, the algorithm allows users to understand the relative importance of each predictor in making predictions, aiding in variable selection and understanding the underlying data patterns. However, it is important to note that gradient boosting is prone to overfitting if not properly configured. Therefore, parameter tuning and configurations are crucial to ensure optimal performance and prevent overfitting in gradient boosting models.

CHAPTER DISCUSSION QUESTIONS

1. What is gradient boosting and how does it work?
2. How does gradient boosting differ from other ensemble methods?
3. What are the main advantages of using gradient boosting over other machine learning algorithms?
4. What are the key limitations of this method?
5. Define loss functions and explain their roles in gradient boosting? What are the common loss functions for gradient boosting and when to use them?
6. What is gradient descent? Why is it important in gradient boosting?
7. What are the key hyperparameters in gradient boosting, and how do they affect the model performance? How would you approach tuning these hyperparameters?
8. Gradient boosting is prone to overfitting, especially when the model becomes too complex. What are some common approaches that can be applied to mitigate overfitting in gradient boosting?
9. Can gradient boosting handle imbalanced datasets effectively? If yes, how does it address the issue of class imbalance?
10. What are the similarities and differences between traditional gradient boosting, GBAM, and SGB?
11. Discuss the computational complexity of gradient boosting. Are there any techniques or optimizations that can be employed to improve its efficiency for large datasets?
12. What are some practical use cases or domains where gradient boosting has shown significant success? Provide examples and discuss the reasons behind its effectiveness in those scenarios.

Exercises

Exercise 1: Gradient boosting models for the Bank dataset

1. Open the *bank* dataset in SAS Enterprise Miner.
2. Sample the entire dataset. See the variable names and descriptions in Appendix A.1.
3. Partition the data using a split ratio of 60:40 (train: 60%; validation: 20%; test: 20%)

4. Perform data modification as follows:
   - Impute missing values.
   - Normalize the data.
5. Set *CRSCORE* (credit scores) as the target variable.
6. Configure five gradient boosting models for this dataset as follows.
   - Gradient Boosting Default (using default properties).
   - Gradient Boosting 1:
     - Set N Iteration to 100.
     - Set Maximum Branch to 10.
     - Set Maximum Depth to 50.
     - Set Split Size to 2.
     - Set Exhaustive to 10,000.
     - Set Node Sample to 100,000.
   - Gradient Boosting 2
     - Set N Iteration to 200.
     - Set Maximum Branch to 20.
     - Set Maximum Depth to 100.
     - Set Split Size to 5.
     - Set Exhaustive to 20,000.
     - Set Node Sample to 200,000.
   - Gradient Boosting 3
     - Set N Iteration to 300.
     - Set Maximum Branch to 50.
     - Set Maximum Depth to 200.
     - Set Split Size to 5.
     - Set Exhaustive to 50,000.
     - Set Node Sample to 200,000.
   - Gradient Boosting 4
     - Set N Iteration to 500.
     - Set Maximum Branch to 50.
     - Set Maximum Depth to 500.
     - Set Split Size to 5.
     - Set Exhaustive to 100,000.
     - Set Node Sample to 300,000.
7. Compare the model fit metrics between these five models using the validation results.
8. Select the champion model and justify this selection with the necessary evidence.
9. Present the results of the champion model.
10. Evaluate the reliability and validity of the champion model.
11. Present the variable importance information and interpret the results.

Exercise 2: Gradient boosting models for the Passengers dataset

1. Open the *passengers* dataset in SAS Enterprise Miner.
2. Sample 20% of the full data. Set *return* (decision to return to the airline) as the target variable and change its role to binary. See the variable names and descriptions in Appendix A.2.
3. Partition the data using a split ratio of 60:40 (train: 60%; validation: 20%; test: 20%)
4. Perform data modification as follows:
   - Replace zero values for Likert scale variables with missing values.
   - Impute missing values.

5. Configure five gradient boosting models for this dataset as follows.
   - Gradient Boosting Default (using default properties).
   - Gradient Boosting 1
     - Set *N* Iteration to 100.
     - Set Maximum Branch to 10.
     - Set Maximum Depth to 50.
     - Set Split Size to 2.
     - Set Exhaustive to 10,000.
     - Set Node Sample to 100,000.
   - Gradient Boosting 2
     - Set *N* Iteration to 200.
     - Set Maximum Branch to 20.
     - Set Maximum Depth to 100.
     - Set Split Size to 5.
     - Set Exhaustive to 20,000.
     - Set Node Sample to 200,000.
   - Gradient Boosting 3
     - Set *N* Iteration to 300.
     - Set Maximum Branch to 50.
     - Set Maximum Depth to 200.
     - Set Split Size to 5.
     - Set Exhaustive to 50,000.
     - Set Node Sample to 200,000.
   - Gradient Boosting 4
     - Set *N* Iteration to 500.
     - Set Maximum Branch to 50.
     - Set Maximum Depth to 500.
     - Set Split Size to 5.
     - Set Exhaustive to 100,000.
     - Set Node Sample to 300,000.
6. Compare the model fit metrics between these five models using the validation results.
7. Select the champion model and justify this selection with the necessary evidence.
8. Present the results of the champion model.
9. Evaluate the reliability and validity of the champion model.
10. Present the variable importance information and interpret the results.

16

Bayesian Networks

LEARNING OUTCOMES

Upon the completion of this chapter, you will be able to

1. Describe the principles and concepts of Bayesian networks.
2. Explain how Bayesian networks capture probabilistic relationships among variables.
3. Discuss the advantages and disadvantages of Bayesian networks compared to other machine learning methods.
4. Describe the structure and components of Bayesian networks, including nodes, directed edges, and conditional probability tables.
5. Evaluate the Bayesian network modeling process.
6. Compare four types of Bayesian networks, Naïve Bayes, Tree Augmented Naïve Bayes (TAN), Bayesian Network Augmented Naïve (BAN), and Markov Blanket.
7. Explore the algorithms for learning the structure of Bayesian networks from data, including constraint-based and score-based algorithms.
8. Interpret a Bayesian network structure, including the identification of causal relationships among variables.
9. Define causal data mining and explain the USELEI process.
10. Construct Bayesian network models using SAS Enterprise Miner.

Introduction

In the final chapter, we cover one of the most advanced and complicated machine learning methods, the Bayesian network. Bayesian networks are probabilistic models that use Bayes' theorem to make predictions based on prior evidence. They create a graphical representation of causal relationships between variables, often in the form of a directed acyclic graph. These networks are valuable for both modeling complex systems and making probabilistic inferences.

DOI: 10.1201/9781003162872-19

This chapter introduces the use of Bayesian network methods in data mining. Specific supervised learning algorithms described in the chapter include Naïve Bayes, Tree Augmented Naïve Bayes, Bayesian Network Augmented Naïve Bayes Classifier, and Markov Blanket. The chapter also describes the causal data mining process using Bayesian network methods and specific examples. Due to the complexity of the mathematical principle of this method, I focus more on the key concepts and how to use this machine learning method. Detailed mathematical formulas are not included to avoid confusion. Since the software automates most steps in Bayesian network modeling, you just need to understand the basic concepts and principles of the method, its strengths and limitations, and how to interpret the results. The probabilistic relationships between predictors and the target variable are explained in a more straightforward way to help you understand the outputs while maintaining the robustness of the analysis.

What Is Bayesian Network?

Correlation vs. Causation

Before we define the Bayesian network, let's discuss the differences between correlation and causation. Data mining has been proven an effective method to detect patterns in large and noisy data sets. In other words, data mining is a great tool to explore large data to find meaningful unknown patterns, which support organizations in the decision-making process. Nonetheless, there have been debates about the limitations of conventional data mining methods such as regression. The most common criticism of conventional data mining methods is the incapability to infer causation among variables (Cox, 2010).

While causation may imply correlation, correlation does not necessarily imply causation. Let's examine an example regarding the level of injury during a car accident (Figure 16.1). We examine the effects of two variables, age and failure to wear seatbelts. Suppose the data analysis indicates a high correlation between age and injury level. Clearly, while age may be highly correlated to the level of injury, it does not cause the injury. The correlation mainly indicates individuals of different ages may experience different levels

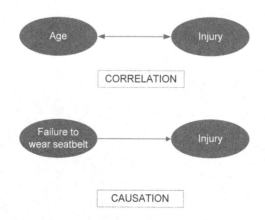

FIGURE 16.1
Correlation vs. causation.

of injury. For risk assessment purposes, it appears that age can be used as one of the predictors for predicting the level of accident injury. However, age is not the cause of the injury, and therefore, it cannot be used to control or mitigate the risk of injury. On the other hand, failure to wear seatbelt is proven to be one of the major factors causing injuries during accidents. Without seatbelt protection, when an accident occurs, the driver will likely suffer severe injuries. Using that result, authorities can reduce the risk of injury by enforcing the seatbelt requirement. This discussion highlights the importance of identifying causal relationships in using data mining for risk prediction.

Now that we understand the differences between correlation and causation, we need to understand how they are tested. There are differences in calculating correlation and causation. The correlation between two variables X and Y can be determined by calculating the correlation coefficient. A positive correlation means if X goes up then Y goes up. On the contrary, a negative correlation means if X goes up then Y goes down. The value of a correlation coefficient indicates the effect size or the extent of the correlation between two variables. It is important to note that while correlation is a common method used in prediction, researchers cannot infer causation from a correlation. In addition, data mining using correlational methods is also subject to overfitting, given the large sample size of the data. The reason is that the larger the sample size, the more likely the relationships between variables are statistically significant.

Causation is much harder to test since it requires isolating variables of interest in a controlled environment. Causation occurs when X actually causes Y to occur. Testing probabilistic relationships is a common method in this case. Using probabilistic analysis, causation can be tested using conditional probabilities.

So, what is a probabilistic relationship? Obviously, it is not a correlational relationship. A probabilistic relationship refers to the existence of a connection or association between two or more variables, where the relationship is characterized by uncertainty and is described using probabilities. More specifically, a probabilistic relationship between two

> **DEFINITION**
>
> A probabilistic relationship refers to the existence of a connection or association between two or more variables, where the relationship is characterized by uncertainty and is described using probabilities.

variables X and Y is determined based on Bayes' theorem. This theorem describes the probability of an event Y given X, based on the probability of each event without regard to each other, and the probability of observing event X given that Y is true. The formula below presents this probabilistic relationship. As you can see the probabilistic relationship between X and Y is represented by the probability of Y, probability or Y, and probability of X given Y.

$$P(Y|X) = \frac{P(X|Y).P(Y)}{P(X)}$$

Where

- $P(Y|X)$ represents the conditional probability of event Y happening, given that event X has already occurred. In other words, it tells us the chance of Y occurring when we know that X has happened.
- $P(X|Y)$ is the conditional probability of event X happening, given that event Y has already occurred. It tells us the chance of X occurring when we know that Y has happened.

- P(Y) is the probability of event Y happening, without considering any other events. It represents the overall chance of Y occurring.

- P(X) is the probability of event X happening, without considering any other events. It represents the overall chance of X occurring.

Definition of Bayesian Network

Bayesian network, also known as a Bayesian belief network or probabilistic graphical model, is a powerful and popular method for representing and reasoning about uncertainty and probabilistic relationships among variables. It is a visual model depicting variables and their conditional dependencies using a directed acyclic graph (DAG). It is named after Thomas Bayes, an 18th-century statistician and philosopher.

> **DEFINITION**
>
> Bayesian network, also known as a Bayesian belief network or probabilistic graphical model, is a powerful and popular method for representing and reasoning about uncertainty and probabilistic relationships between variables. It is a visual model depicting variables and their conditional dependencies using a directed acyclic graph (DAG).

A Bayesian network consists of two main components: nodes and edges. Nodes represent variables of interest, while edges represent probabilistic dependencies between variables. The nodes can be discrete or continuous, and they are connected by directed edges that indicate the cause-and-effect relationships or conditional dependencies between variables.

The structure of a Bayesian network is typically represented by a directed acyclic graph (DAG), where each node corresponds to a variable and the edges (or arcs) capture the probabilistic dependencies. The edges in the graph represent conditional probabilities, indicating the influence of one variable on another. Figure 16.2 shows an illustrated diagram of a Bayesian network structure.

The conditional dependencies are defined using conditional probability tables (CPTs). Each node's CPT describes the probability distribution of that node given its parent nodes in the graph. The CPTs allow for the quantification of uncertain relationships and provide a means to propagate probabilistic inference throughout the network.

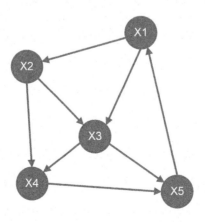

FIGURE 16.2
Annotated direct acyclic graph.

Example of Bayesian Networks

Bayesian network is a rather complex method, so it is understandable that you may get confused. Since its principle lies on the mathematical foundation of probability and Bayes' theorem, it is not easy to understand how it works.

I use a simple example to explain the key concepts and components of a Bayesian network. In this example, we examine the factors that influence the injury level during accidents. We focus on three primary variables: Traffic, Wearing the Seatbelt, Car Accident, and Injury. The goal of this example is to determine the probabilistic relationships between traffic conditions, wearing a seatbelt, the occurrence of a car accident, and the likelihood of sustaining an injury in that accident. The Bayesian network graphical structure for this example would consist of four nodes: Traffic, Wearing Seatbelt, Car Accident, and Injury (Figure 16.3). There would be directed edges from Traffic to Car Accident, from Wearing Seatbelt to Injury, and from Car Accident to Injury. Traffic has two levels, Light or Heavy. Car Accident has two levels, True or False. Wearing Seatbelt has two levels, True or False. Injury has two levels, True or False. We assume that heavy traffic may increase the likelihood of a car accident, and if an accident occurs, not wearing a seatbelt may result in an injury.

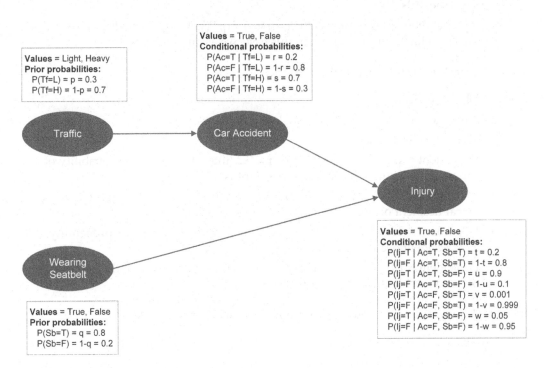

FIGURE 16.3
An example of Bayesian network structure for accident injuries.

In this Bayesian network, the Traffic and Wearing Seatbelt nodes are independent, as they have no direct causal relationship. The Traffic node is the parent of the Car Accident node since heavy traffic increases the risk of accidents. Car Accident node and Wearing Seatbelt are both the parents of the Injury node since an accident occurrence and a failure to wear the seatbelt increases the risk of injury. The probabilities in the CPTs represent the likelihood of different events based on the given conditions. Suppose, after running the analysis, we find the CPT for each node as follows (note that Traffic and Wearing Seatbelt are precursors, so we have prior probabilities for those events; conditional probabilities for the other two variables are determined based on these two precursors).

Node 1 – Traffic:

- Variable: Traffic
- Values: Light, Heavy
- Prior probabilities: P(Traffic = Light) = p; P(Traffic = Heavy) = 1-p (where p is a known probability). In this case, we assume p = 0.3.

Node 2 – Wearing Seatbelt:

- Variable: Wearing Seatbelt
- Values: True, False
- Prior probabilities: P(Wearing Seatbelt = True) = q, P(Wearing Seatbelt = False) = 1-q (where q is a known probability). In this case, we assume p = 0.8.

Node 3 – Car Accident: Influenced by Traffic:

- Variable: Car Accident
- Values: True, False
- Conditional probabilities:
    - P(Accident = True|Traffic = Light) = r = 0.2 (interpretation: the probability of a car accident occurring when traffic is light is 0.2).
    - P(Accident = False|Traffic = Light) = 1-r = 0.8 (interpretation: the probability of no car accident occurring when traffic is light is 0.8).
    - P(Accident = True|Traffic = Heavy) = s = 0.7 (interpretation: the probability of a car accident occurring when traffic is heavy is 0.7).
    - P(Accident = False|Traffic = Heavy) = 1-s = 0.3 (interpretation: the probability of no car accident occurring when traffic is heavy is 0.7).

Node 4 – Injury: Influenced by Car Accident and Wearing Seatbelt:

- Variables: Car Accident, Injury
- Values: True, False
- Conditional probabilities:
    - P(Injury = True|Accident = True, Wearing Seatbelt = True) = t = 0.2 (interpretation: the probability of injury when there is a car accident and the seatbelt is fastened is 0.2).

- P(Injury = False|Accident = True, Wearing Seatbelt = True) = 1-t = 0.8
- *Interpretation*: the probability of no injury when there is a car accident, and the seatbelt is fastened is 0.8.
- P(Injury = True|Accident = True, Wearing Seatbelt = False) = u = 0.9
- *Interpretation*: the probability of injury when there is a car accident, and the seatbelt is not fastened is 0.9.
- P(Injury = False|Accident = True, Wearing Seatbelt = False) = 1-u = 0.1
- *Interpretation*: the probability of no injury when there is a car accident, and the seatbelt is not fastened is 0.1.
- P(Injury = True|Accident = False, Wearing Seatbelt = True) = v = 0.001
- *Interpretation*: the probability of injury when there is no car accident, and the seatbelt is fastened is 0.001.
- P(Injury = False|Accident = False, Wearing Seatbelt = True) = 1-v = 0.999
- *Interpretation*: the probability of no injury when there is no car accident, and the seatbelt is fastened is 0.2.
- P(Injury = True|Accident = False, Wearing Seatbelt = False) = w = 0.05
- *Interpretation*: the probability of injury when there is no car accident, and the seatbelt is not fastened is 0.05.
- P(Injury = False|Accident = False, Wearing Seatbelt = False) = 1-w = 0.95
- *Interpretation*: the probability of no injury when there is no car accident, and the seatbelt is not fastened is 0.95.

Using this Bayesian network, we can perform various types of inference. For example:

- Given the evidence of heavy traffic, we can compute the probability of a car accident. This involves using the conditional probabilities from the CPT of the Car Accident node.
- Given the evidence that a car accident occurred and whether the driver fastened the seatbelt, we can compute the probability of sustaining an injury. This involves using the conditional probabilities from the CPT of the Injury node.

This simple example demonstrates how a Bayesian network can capture dependencies between variables and model probabilistic relationships. In practice, Bayesian networks can become more complex, incorporating additional variables and more intricate causal relationships, which enables more sophisticated inference and decision-making.

Practical Applications of Bayesian Networks

Overall, the versatility of Bayesian networks lies in their ability to model complex dependencies, incorporate domain knowledge, handle uncertainty, and provide probabilistic reasoning and decision support.

They have practical applications in various domains. Some notable applications of Bayesian networks include:

1. *Medical diagnosis*: Bayesian networks can be used for medical diagnosis and decision support systems. They can model the relationships between symptoms, diseases, and test results to provide probabilistic assessments of different diagnoses given observed symptoms and test outcomes.

2. *Risk assessment*: Bayesian networks can model the dependencies between various risk factors and provide probabilistic predictions of the likelihood of specific outcomes or events, such as financial risks, cybersecurity threats, or aviation incidents.

3. *Fraud detection*: This algorithm can be employed for fraud detection in various domains, such as credit card fraud, insurance fraud, or network intrusion detection. They capture the relationships between different variables and can identify patterns and anomalies indicative of fraudulent activities.

4. *Air traffic management*: Bayesian networks help optimize air traffic flow and manage congestion. They can take into account various factors, including weather conditions, aircraft performance, and air traffic control decisions, to make real-time predictions and decisions for efficient traffic management.

5. *Text classification*: This algorithm can model the relationships between words or features in text documents and classify new documents based on their probabilistic dependencies. Hence, it can be applied to text classification tasks, such as sentiment analysis or spam detection.

6. *Image and video processing*: Bayesian networks can capture the relationships between visual features, object appearances, and contextual information to enhance the accuracy of these tasks. Accordingly, they can be used for object recognition, scene understanding, and video analysis.

7. *Incident investigation*: When investigating aviation incidents or accidents, Bayesian networks can be used to analyze data and model the causal relationships between different factors. This can aid in identifying contributing factors and understanding the sequence of events leading to the incident.

8. *Predictive maintenance*: Bayesian networks can support predictive maintenance in industries such as air transportation, manufacturing, and energy. They model the dependencies between sensor data, equipment conditions, and failure events to predict and prevent equipment failures.

Basic Concepts

Bayesian networks are an advanced and complex machine learning algorithm. They are graphical models that represent probabilistic relationships between variables. Hence, it is challenging to use and interpret these models effectively. Table 16.1 presents key concepts in Bayesian networks and their descriptions. By understanding these basic concepts, you can effectively construct, analyze, and perform probabilistic inference in Bayesian networks, making them valuable tools for handling uncertainty and making informed decisions in various domains.

TABLE 16.1

Basic Concepts in Bayesian Networks

Terms	Descriptions
Bayesian network	Bayesian network, also known as a Bayesian belief network or probabilistic graphical model, is a powerful and popular method for representing and reasoning about uncertainty and probabilistic relationships among variables. It is a graphical model that represents a set of variables and their conditional dependencies through a directed acyclic graph.
Bayes' Theorem	Bayes' theorem is a fundamental equation used in Bayesian networks to update probabilities based on new evidence. It calculates the posterior probability of an event given prior knowledge and observed evidence.
Nodes	Nodes represent random variables or events in the domain being modeled. Each node corresponds to a specific quantity or attribute of interest.
Edges	Edges represent probabilistic dependencies between nodes. Directed edges indicate causal or direct influences between variables.
Directed Acyclic Graph (DAG)	The graphical structure of a Bayesian network is represented by a DAG, which is a graph without cycles (no path that starts and ends at the same node). The absence of cycles ensures that the network does not contain feedback loops and allows for efficient probabilistic inference.
Conditional Probability Tables (CPTs)	Each node in a Bayesian network has an associated CPT, which defines the conditional probability distribution of the node given its parents' states. The CPT quantifies the probabilistic relationship between variables.
Parents and children	In a Bayesian network, the parents of a node are the nodes that directly influence it. The children of a node are the nodes that are directly influenced by it.
Probabilistic relationship	A probabilistic relationship refers to the existence of a connection or association between two or more variables, where the relationship is characterized by uncertainty and is described using probabilities.
Probabilistic Inference	Bayesian networks allow for probabilistic inference, which means computing the probability of specific events or variables given evidence (observed data or values) from other variables in the network. Inference is based on Bayes' theorem.
Prior probability	The prior probability represents the initial belief or knowledge about a variable before any evidence or data is observed. It is typically specified as part of the Bayesian network modeling process.
Posterior probability	The posterior probability represents the updated probability of a variable given observed evidence or data. It is calculated by combining the prior probability with the likelihood of the observed data using Bayes' theorem.
Likelihood	The likelihood in Bayesian networks represents the probability of observing specific evidence given the values of the variables in the network. It is derived from the conditional probability tables.
Evidence	Evidence refers to the observed values or states of certain variables in the Bayesian network. It is used to update the probabilities of other variables in the network.
Learning	Learning in Bayesian networks involves estimating the network structure and parameters from data. This can be done using approaches such as constraint-based methods or score-based methods.
Frequentist statistics	Frequentist statistics, also known as frequentist inference, is a statistical framework and approach to data analysis that focuses on the concept of repeated sampling and long-run frequencies of events.
Causal data mining	Causal data mining is a method of using causal machine learning algorithms to detect unknown patterns involving variables and their interrelationships in a causal network from data to predict outcomes.
Score-based algorithm	A score-based algorithm is a Bayesian network structure learning approach that maximizes a scoring metric to identify the most probable network structure given the data. The algorithm aims to find the network structure that best fits the data according to a specific scoring criterion.
Constraint-based algorithm	A constraint-based algorithm is an approach used to learn the network structure from data by discovering the probabilistic dependencies between variables without directly optimizing a scoring metric. It iteratively tests and evaluates conditional independence relationships among variables to determine the network's structure.

Advantages and Disadvantages

Like other methods, Bayesian networks have some important advantages and also disadvantages. It is important to consider these strengths and weaknesses when deciding whether to use Bayesian networks for a particular problem. The suitability of Bayesian networks depends on the specific application, available data, domain expertise, and the trade-off between model complexity and interpretability.

Advantages of Bayesian networks

- *Probabilistic reasoning*: Bayesian networks provide a principled framework for probabilistic reasoning and uncertainty modeling. They can capture complex dependencies between variables and calculate probabilistic inferences, which allow us to gain unique insights from the data.

- *Causal modeling*: Unlike other machine learning methods, Bayesian networks represent causal relationships between variables. By explicitly modeling the causal structure, they enable causal reasoning and help uncover the underlying mechanisms driving the observed data.

- *Efficient inference*: This method provides us with efficient probabilistic inference. Once the network structure and parameters are defined, various inference algorithms can be employed to calculate posterior probabilities, make predictions, or answer queries about the variables in the network.

- *Handling missing data*: Bayesian networks handle missing data more effectively than some other methods. They can perform inference even when some values are missing, making them robust in dealing with incomplete datasets.

- *Modeling complex systems*: This method allows researchers to model complex systems with multiple variables and interactions. We can use Bayesian networks for problems where understanding the relationships between different components is essential.

- *Model transparency*: Bayesian networks offer interpretability and transparency. The graphical representation of dependencies between variables makes it easier to understand and communicate the relationships within the model, aiding in model interpretation and validation.

Disadvantages of Bayesian networks

- *Model complexity*: Constructing Bayesian networks can be challenging, especially when dealing with a large number of variables or complex dependencies. Defining the network structure and estimating the parameters require domain expertise, data availability, and computational resources.

- *Dependency assumptions*: The accuracy of Bayesian networks relies on correctly identifying the dependencies between variables. Incorrect assumptions or limitations in the available data may lead to biased or inaccurate models.

- *Data requirements*: We often need a substantial amount of data to accurately estimate the network structure and parameters. When data is scarce or limited, model performance and generalization may be compromised.
- *Computational complexity*: Inference in Bayesian networks can become computationally intensive, especially when dealing with large or complex networks. Exact inference algorithms may be infeasible, and we need to use approximate methods or sampling techniques.
- *Model uncertainty*: Although Bayesian networks handle uncertainty well, they can also introduce model uncertainty due to the many possible network structures. Determining the best structure and hyperparameters may require expert knowledge or additional model selection techniques.

Bayesian Network Process

Bayesian network modeling requires a complex process. I provide below the important steps in constructing and validating Bayesian networks in data mining projects.

1. Data collection and preprocessing
   - Gather relevant data from various sources, ensuring that it represents the problem domain accurately.
   - Preprocess the data by handling missing values, dealing with outliers, and transforming variables if necessary.
2. Variable selection and domain knowledge
   - Identify the variables of interest for building the Bayesian network. Domain knowledge and expertise play a crucial role in selecting relevant variables.
   - Understand the relationships and dependencies between variables, which can guide the network's structure.
3. Structure learning
   - Determine the network's structure by learning the probabilistic dependencies between variables from the data.
   - Methods such as constraint-based algorithms or score-based algorithms can be used for structure learning.
4. Parameter estimation
   - Estimate the CPTs for each node in the network. This involves calculating the probabilities of each variable given its parent variables.
   - Maximum likelihood estimation (MLE) or Bayesian parameter estimation can be used for parameter estimation.
5. Model evaluation and validation
   - Split the data into training and testing sets for model evaluation.
   - Use appropriate model fit metrics to evaluate the model performance on the test set.

6. Model interpretation and visualization

- Interpret the Bayesian network's structure to understand the relationships and dependencies between variables.
- Visualize the network graphically to aid in model interpretation and communication.

7. Inference and predictions

- Perform probabilistic inference using Bayes' theorem to compute the probabilities of specific events or variables given evidence (observed data).
- Use the Bayesian network to make predictions or decisions based on the inferred probabilities.

8. Model refinement and iteration

- Refine the Bayesian network by making adjustments to the structure or parameters based on feedback, domain knowledge, or additional data.
- Iterate through the process to improve the model performance and accuracy.

It's important to note that constructing a Bayesian network requires a combination of domain knowledge, data analysis, and expert judgment. The iterative nature of the process allows for continuous refinement and improvement of the model's accuracy and performance. I developed a more general process for the so-called causal mining. It is the USELEI process. I will present this process later in this chapter.

Differences between Bayesian Network and Frequentist Statistics

Bayesian network methods and frequentist methods are two different approaches to statistical inference. It is important to understand those differences because you are much more familiar and experienced with frequentist statistics (even though you may not have heard of this term before).

So, what is frequentist statistics? Frequentist statistics, also known as frequentist inference, is a statistical framework and approach to data analysis that focuses on the concept of repeated sampling and long-run frequencies of events. That name comes from the method's emphasis on analyzing the frequency or proportion of events occurring in repeated experiments or observations. In frequentist statistics, the key idea is that probabilities are interpreted as limiting frequencies. It treats the parameters of a statistical model as fixed and unknown quantities that do not have probability distributions. Instead, the focus is on estimating these fixed parameters using observed data and making inferences based on the observed frequencies. Basically, the statistics-based methods we covered before, including linear regression, logistic regression, cluster analysis, principal components, and other statistical methods that you may be familiar with (t-test, ANOVA, MANOVA, discriminant analysis, etc.) are essentially all frequentist statistics.

Since frequentist statistics focuses on frequencies rather than probability distributions, it differs from Bayesian networks. Table 16.2 highlights key differences between these two methods.

TABLE 16.2

Differences between Bayesian Networks and Frequentist Statistics

Items	Bayesian Networks	Frequentist Statistics
Philosophy	Bayesian networks view probability as a measure of subjective belief or degree of uncertainty, incorporating prior knowledge and updating it based on observed data using Bayes' theorem.	Frequentist methods consider probability as the long-run frequency of an event occurring over repeated trials, focusing solely on the properties of the observed data.
Handling uncertainty	Bayesian networks explicitly model and reason uncertainty by assigning prior probabilities to uncertain quantities and updating them based on observed data.	Frequentist methods do not directly incorporate prior beliefs or quantify uncertainty but rely on the concept of sampling variability and estimate parameters based solely on observed data.
Parameter estimation	Bayesian networks estimate parameters by specifying prior probabilities and updating them with observed data to obtain posterior probabilities. The posterior distribution reflects the combined information from the prior knowledge and data.	Frequentist methods estimate parameters using techniques such as maximum likelihood estimation, which aims to find the parameter values that maximize the likelihood of the observed data.
Inference	Bayesian networks provide a framework for probabilistic inference, which enables computation of various probabilities of interest, such as posterior probabilities, conditional probabilities, and predictions.	Frequentist methods focus on point estimation and hypothesis testing. They provide estimates and tests based on the observed data without quantifying probabilities directly.
Sample size	Bayesian networks can handle small sample sizes effectively by incorporating prior knowledge into the analysis. Prior information can act as a regularizer, helping to stabilize estimates and avoid overfitting.	Frequentist methods typically require larger sample sizes for reliable estimation and hypothesis testing due to their reliance on observed data.
Interpretability	Bayesian networks provide a natural framework for interpreting results in terms of probabilities, making it easier to communicate uncertainty and make informed decisions based on the posterior distribution.	Frequentist methods tend to focus more on correlation estimates and p-values, which can sometimes be misinterpreted or lead to binary decisions without explicit consideration of uncertainty.

Bayesian Network and Causal Inference

One common question in implementing the Bayesian network method is whether we can make causal inferences based on the results. As described before, Bayesian networks can provide valuable insights into the dependencies and conditional relationships between variables. Basically, they capture and represent causal relationships between variables through probabilistic relationships. However, it's important to note  that Bayesian networks alone cannot establish causal relationships or infer causation in the strict sense without prior domain knowledge or theoretical foundation. While they do not explicitly determine causation, they can infer causal relationships based on the probabilistic dependencies modeled in the network. Let's get into further details of these points.

Bayesian networks primarily capture statistical dependencies between variables based on observed data and assumptions. They model the conditional probabilities and the directionality of the relationships between variables, which can be helpful for making predictions, performing probabilistic reasoning, and estimating probabilities of events given observed evidence. In a Bayesian network, the directed edges between nodes represent the conditional dependencies or causal relationships. For example, if variable A is a parent of variable B in the network, it implies that A has a direct causal influence on B. The network structure, along with the CPTs associated with each node, encodes the probabilistic relationships between variables.

As stated before, Bayesian networks alone do not prove causation. To prove a true causal relationship, we need to isolate the input variable A and test its effect on the output variable B, while holding all other input variables constant. It is usually conducted in a controlled environment, which allows us to conclude that A indeed causes B. However, this method is not suitable for data mining projects since it requires setting up experiments and can only examine the causal effect of one or two input variables. In data mining, Bayesian network results can suggest causal relationships based on the observed data and the network structure, but further empirical evidence or domain knowledge is often required to establish causation definitively. In our previous example, the probabilistic relationship derived from the Bayesian network suggests that A can have a direct causal relationship with B. Then, researchers use further theoretical foundation, domain knowledge, and even additional empirical evidence to prove whether A in fact causes B.

Nonetheless, Bayesian networks can be used as a tool to help understand and represent causal hypotheses. By incorporating domain knowledge and causal assumptions into the network structure and conditional probabilities, Bayesian networks can provide a framework for reasoning about potential causal relationships and their implications. More specifically, Bayesian networks allow us to make probabilistic inferences based on observed evidence. This inference can be used to analyze the causal relationships within the network.

> Bayesian networks alone cannot establish causal relationships or infer causation in the strict sense without prior domain knowledge or theoretical foundation. Nonetheless, they can infer causal relationships based on the probabilistic dependencies modeled in the network.

Accordingly, in this book, when we use the term "causal inference" or "infer causality," we mainly refer to the causal relationships determined by the Bayesian network structure in terms of probabilistic inference, assuming we have prior domain knowledge and causal assumptions.

Different Types of Bayesian Networks

Bayesian network is an advanced and powerful method that can be used in supervised learning when the target variable is identified along with predictors. The Bayesian network model can capture the dependencies between variables and make predictions or classifications based on the learned probabilities. It is a powerful approach for tasks such as

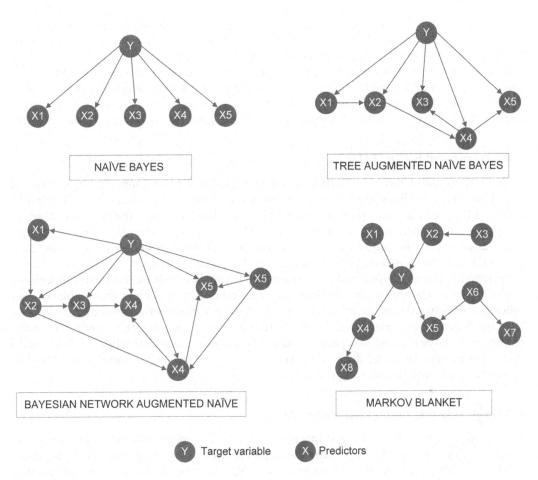

FIGURE 16.4
Four types of Bayesian network learning algorithms.

classification, association, and probabilistic inference in domains where labeled training data is available.

There are four primary types of Bayesian network structures: Naïve Bayes, Tree Augmented Naïve Bayes (TAN), Bayesian Networks Augmented Naïve Bayes (BNAN), and Markov Blanket. Figure 16.4 presents the structures of these network structures in diagram forms.

Naïve Bayes

The Naïve Bayes method is frequently used for constructing Bayesian networks, primarily due to its simplicity. In a Naïve Bayesian network, the target variable serves as the parent node for all other nodes (predictors), resulting in a straightforward structure. There are no other connections between the predictors because the input variables are assumed to be conditionally independent of each other. This assumption allows for fast and efficient training and classification. However, Naive Bayes can be limited when the predictors are dependent on each other, as it ignores any dependencies among the variables.

This method is known for its simplicity and ease of construction, making it an efficient choice that demands a small training sample size. It is a commonly used supervised learning algorithm in data mining projects, allowing direct comparisons with other machine learning techniques. However, its applicability is constrained by the assumption of conditional independence, restricting its use to a simple network with direct relationships between predictors and the target variable. In more complex networks, where predictors are anticipated to exhibit causal dependencies, this assumption is typically violated.

Tree-Augmented Naïve (TAN)

TAN extends Naive Bayes by adding a tree structure to capture dependencies between variables. The TAN Bayesian network connects the target variable to each predictor and connects the predictors in a tree structure. This algorithm constructs the network based on the maximum spanning tree algorithm. In a TAN, each predictor node has no more than two parent nodes, the target node, and at most one another predictor node. Thus, each predictor node can have only one augmenting edge pointing to it.

By relaxing the assumption of conditional independence, this method can outperform Naïve Bayes while preserving its simplicity and efficiency. It retains the simplicity and efficiency of Naïve Bayes but allows for more expressive models by incorporating limited variable dependencies. However, due to the tree structure's constraint, where each predictor node can have at most two parent nodes (the target node and another predictor node as an optional parent node), it doesn't permit a comprehensive exploration of the complete causal network structure among predictors.

Bayesian Network Augmented Naive (BAN)

BAN is an extension of TAN that incorporates a more general Bayesian network structure. It allows for arbitrary inter-variable dependencies by learning a complete Bayesian network structure among the variables. In a BAN, predictor nodes are direct children of the target node, yet a nearly comprehensive Bayesian network is established among the predictor nodes, extending beyond a simple tree structure. Thus, each predictor node can have multiple parents, but one of which must be the target variable. In addition, the target variable must be the parent node and cannot be a child node. The BAN learning algorithm is similar to TAN learning algorithm, with the key difference being the use of an unconstrained Bayesian network (BN) learning algorithm rather than a tree-based learning approach. Unrestricted Bayesian network learning algorithms are commonly employed in practical machine learning applications.

BAN provides a more flexible modeling approach compared to Naive Bayes and TAN. The BAN algorithm is appropriate for learning a causal network structure from big data in a complex system. It can capture more complex relationships among variables but at the cost of increased computational complexity for training and inference.

Markov Blanket

In the context of Bayesian networks, the Markov blanket of a node is a concept that defines a minimal set of nodes that render the node conditionally independent of all other nodes in the network. In other words, given the Markov blanket nodes, the node is probabilistically independent of all other nodes in the network. A Markov blanket network establishes connections between the target variable and its predictors while also allowing connections between specific input variables. Only the children of the target variable are permitted to have an additional parent node, while all other variables remain conditionally independent of the target variable.

The Markov blanket of a target variable includes three types of nodes:

- *Parents*: The parents of the target variable in the Bayesian network. These are the nodes directly connected to the target variable by incoming edges.
- *Children*: The children of the target variable. These are the nodes directly connected to the target variable by outgoing edges.
- *Spouses*: The parents of the children of the target variable. These are the nodes that are directly connected to the children of the target variable, excluding the target variable itself.

The Markov blanket is important because it represents a minimal set of variables that need to be observed or considered when predicting the target variable or performing probabilistic inference. Variables outside the Markov blanket are irrelevant to the target variable once the Markov blanket variables are known. The Markov blanket provides a way to identify and exploit the conditional independence relationships between variables in a Bayesian network. It helps reduce the computational complexity of probabilistic inference by focusing on the minimal set of relevant variables.

Network Structure Learning Algorithms

One important step in the Bayesian network process is learning the network structure from data. In data mining, learning algorithms are employed to complete this task. In the context of Bayesian networks, there are two primary learning algorithms, score-based algorithm and constraint-based algorithm (see Table 16.3). In this section, we gain a fundamental understanding of these algorithms and their differences.

A score-based algorithm is a Bayesian network structure learning approach that maximizes a scoring metric to identify the most probable network structure given the data. The algorithm aims to find the network structure that best fits the data according to a specific scoring criterion. The most commonly used scoring metrics include log-likelihood, Bayesian Information Criterion (BIC), and Akaike Information Criterion (AIC). The higher the score, the better the fit of the model to the data.

A constraint-based algorithm is an approach used to learn the network structure from data by discovering the probabilistic dependencies between variables without directly optimizing a scoring metric. Instead of exhaustively searching the entire space of possible network structures, a constraint-based algorithm iteratively tests and evaluates conditional independence relationships among variables to determine the network's structure.

Each of these approaches has its strengths and weaknesses, and the choice of the method depends on factors such as the size of the dataset, the complexity of the network, the availability of domain knowledge, and the desired interpretability of the resulting model.

TABLE 16.3

Differences between Score-Based Algorithm and Constraint-Based Algorithm

Item	Score-Based Algorithm	Constraint-Based Algorithm
Approach	Optimizes a scoring metric (e.g., log-likelihood, BIC, AIC) to find the network structure that best fits the data.	Identifies conditional independence relationships between variables to infer the network structure without directly optimizing a scoring metric.
Objective	Maximizes a scoring metric to balance model complexity and data fit.	Focuses on capturing direct conditional dependencies between variables to construct a more interpretable network.
Search space	Explores the search space by making local modifications to the network structure, such as adding, deleting, or reversing edges.	Utilizes statistical tests to identify conditional independence relationships and construct a skeleton graph, which is later refined into a partially directed acyclic graph.
Scoring metric	Directly uses a scoring metric to evaluate and compare different network structures.	Does not directly use a scoring metric, but the resulting network structure can be scored using a separate scoring method.
Strengths	• Efficient and scalable for large datasets. • Provides a direct measure of model fit. • Can handle both categorical and continuous variables.	• Robust to overfitting and requires fewer data samples. • Captures direct conditional dependencies, leading to a more interpretable network. • Handles mixed data types.
Limitations	• Sensitive to local optima and may not explore the entire search space thoroughly. • Requires a larger sample size for reliable parameter estimation.	• May not capture some complex relationships due to the focus on direct dependencies. • Can be computationally demanding when testing for conditional independence with many variables.
Interpretability	The resulting network may be complex and harder to interpret.	The network structure often reflects direct causal relationships and is more interpretable.
Common algorithms	Hill Climbing, Tabu Search, Genetic Algorithms, and Max-Min Hill Climbing (MMHC).	Greedy Equivalence Search (GES), Incremental Association Markov Blanket (IAMB), and the PC (Peter & Clark) algorithm.

Causal Data Mining Process

Given the Bayesian networks' capability to capture the probabilistic relationships among variables in a complex network, I want to introduce the concept of causal data mining and how Bayesian networks can be used in causal data mining projects.

In common data mining projects, as described in previous chapters, our goal is to use machine learning algorithms to detect unknown relationships from data, which allows us to predict the target variable. In these projects, the outcome is a predictive model that can predict the target variable accurately based on important predictors.

DEFINITION

Causal data mining can be defined as a method of using causal machine learning algorithms to detect unknown patterns involving variables and their interrelationships in a causal network from data to predict outcomes (Truong, 2021).

The specific relationships among variables, capturing how variables interact and influence one another, are usually not the focus of the study. What the users need is the champion model that can make accurate predictions of the risk or event of interest.

What if, in some cases, the users want to dig deeper into the patterns in the data, pertaining to how variables interact and influence one another, because they need deeper insights into the patterns? Or furthermore, they want to know which variable has a direct causal influence on another variable, which, in its turn, influences another variable, and so on. Understanding the causal relationships in a complex network enables organizations to make sense of the predictions and establish effective business strategies in the long term. In this case, the ordinal data mining may not work. We need a new type of data mining. I call it *causal data mining*.

In my article published in the Journal of Air Transport Management in 2021, I define *causal data mining* as a "method of using causal machine learning algorithms to detect unknown patterns involving variables and their interrelationships in a causal network from data to predict outcomes." For this type of data mining project, the common processes such as SEMMA or CRISP-DM may not be the best fit since they do not reflect the causality nature of the problem. Hence, I developed a six-step process of causal data mining: Understanding, Sampling, Exploring, Learning, Evaluating, and Inferring or USELEI (Truong, 2021b). In this section, I describe this process and how it can be used in causal data mining.

Figure 16.5 presents six steps of the USELEI process, and Table 16.4 describes the detailed purpose and details of each step (Truong, 2021b).

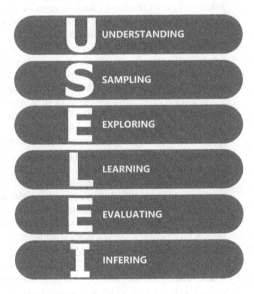

FIGURE 16.5
USELEI process (Truong, 2021b).

TABLE 16.4

USELEI Causal Data Mining Process

Steps	Descriptions
STEP 1: UNDERSTANDING Purpose: Understanding the research problem and objectives	This step focuses on understanding the research problem and research objectives from a business perspective. Information about the industry, market, stakeholders, systems, or organizations must be gathered and then converted into a problem statement and research questions that require mining large data to predict an outcome. Researchers need to identify what they expect to gain from causal data mining. The complexity and dynamism of the system should be described, along with possible variables in the model.
STEP 2: SAMPLING Purpose: Selecting data set, sampling, and partitioning	Data are collected and sampled from reliable data sources. The sampling method is decided depending on the target population and the scope of the research. The dataset should be large enough to contain sufficient information for knowledge discovery but should not be too large to ensure the efficiency of the modeling process. Then, the data is partitioned into training and validation samples. The training sample is used to train the model, whereas the validation sample is used to validate the model. If the cross-validation method is chosen, the data should be partitioned into more sub-samples.
STEP 3: EXPLORING Purpose: Exploring and preparing the data	The dataset is explored carefully to gain a sufficient understanding of variables, descriptive statistics, missing values, and outliers. Missing data and outliers must be analyzed and handled correctly to avoid losing information and, at the same time, to reduce biases. One crucial step in data preparation for causal data mining is discretization, which uses discretization algorithms such as equal distance, normalized equal distance, equal frequency, K-means, and tree algorithms.
STEP 4: LEARNING Purpose: Learning unsupervised and supervised causal networks and performing cross-validation	First, an unsupervised network structure is constructed to explore preliminary causal relationships among variables without identifying a target variable. While this network allows causal inference between individual variables and identifies the most important variables to the entire network, it does not indicate the importance and effect of each variable to the target variable. This network serves as the starting point for constructing the full network. Then, a supervised network is constructed using causal learning algorithms with an identified target variable. This network allows researchers to predict the target variable and examine the importance and effect of each predictor to the target variable. Since the network structure is learned from data, it is important to validate the created network by comparing training and validation samples. With large data, a more robust validation method, such as k-fold cross-validation, is recommended to minimize the overfitting issue.
STEP 5: EVALUATING Purpose: Evaluating the network performance and predictive precision	The causal network performance is evaluated using model fit metrics to ensure the reliability and validity of the model. A post hoc analysis is needed if the developed model does not meet the evaluation criteria. In this step, the model could be modified to improve the network performance by removing variables with the lowest contribution to the prediction of the target variable, one at a time. It is an iterative process and should continue until a satisfactory network performance is achieved.
STEP 6: INFERRING Purpose: Performing target analysis, sensitivity analysis, and causal inference	Influential predictors are reported along with the magnitude of their effects on the target variables. Total effects and direct effects should both be interpreted. In addition, sensitivity analysis can be performed to find how a change in one predictor will affect the target variable. Finally, causal inference is conducted to examine a causal connection between selected predictors and the target variable based on the conditions of the occurrence of an effect. The inference can be used to develop different what-if scenarios, based on which decision-makers can form necessary strategies to prepare for the incidents or mitigate the risk.

Differences between USELEI and SEMMA and CRISP-DM

You may ask: Why do we need another data mining process? How does USELEI differ from the other two processes (SEMMA and CRISP-DM)?

Table 16.5 provides a summary and comparison of three data mining processes (USELEI, CRISP-DM, and SEMMA). These processes show similarities in various steps like sampling, data exploration and preparation, modeling, and model evaluation. However, regarding causal data mining, the USELEI process offers distinct advantages over the other two. It places a stronger emphasis on constructing a causal network structure, performing causal inference and conducting sensitivity analysis. These capabilities prove valuable for organizations in making informed business decisions. Additionally, USELEI highlights the importance of understanding research problems and identifying research objectives from the business perspective, a dimension not prominently featured in SEMMA.

Overall, SEMMA and CRISP-DM are excellent processes for ordinal data mining projects, in which causal relationships among variables are not needed. USELEI is designed specifically for causal data mining. While it serves a narrower audience, this process provides rigorous and thorough steps for conducting a causal data mining project.

I want to mention that the Bayesian networks play a vital role in causal data mining this method allows us to build a causal network from data, which provides probabilistic relationships among variables. We use the Bayesian network structure not only to make a prediction of the target variable but also to examine causal relationships among the variables in the network via probabilistic inference. We won't use the USELEI process in this book, but I will show you how to make the probabilistic inference from the Bayesian network structure in the example.

TABLE 16.5

Comparison between USELEI, CRISP-DM, and SEMMA

Items	USELEI	CRISP-DM	SEMMA
Steps	Understanding→Sampling → Exploring and preparing→Learning and validation→ Evaluating→Inferring	Business understanding →Data understanding →Data preparation →Modeling→Evaluation →Deployment	Sample→Explore →Modify→Model → Assess
Emphasis on understanding of business problems	Yes	Yes	No
Sampling process	Yes	Marginal	Yes
Data exploration and preparation	Yes	Yes	Yes
Modeling and validation	Yes	Yes	Yes
Full causal network structure	Yes	No	No
Model evaluation	Yes	Yes	Yes
Decision support (causal inference)	Yes	No	No
Decision support (sensitivity analysis)	Yes	No	No

Hyperparameter Tuning for Bayesian Networks

Hyperparameter tuning for Bayesian networks typically involves finding the best structure and parameter settings that optimize the model performance. Unlike other machine learning algorithms that often have hyperparameters related to the optimization process, Bayesian networks have hyperparameters associated with the network structure and the parameter estimation process. Below are some key hyperparameters to consider when tuning Bayesian networks.

- *Network structure configuration*: Arrangement of nodes (variables) and edges (directed connections) in the Bayesian network. Different configurations of the network structure can result in different causal relationships and dependencies between variables.

- *Nodes and edges*: Configurations involving adding or deleting nodes and edges can alter the network structure. Adding new nodes can incorporate additional variables while deleting nodes can simplify the model.

- *Maximum number of parents per node*: Maximum number of parent nodes each node can have in the network. Setting this parameter can control the complexity of the network and prevent overfitting.

- *Prior probabilities for CPTs*: Bayesian networks require estimating CPTs for each node. Configuring prior probabilities can influence the learning process and incorporate prior beliefs or knowledge about the variable relationships.

- *Scoring metric*: The choice of the scoring metric, such as log-likelihood, Bayesian Information Criterion (BIC), or Akaike Information Criterion (AIC), influences the evaluation of different network structures during learning.

- *Search algorithm*: The search algorithm determines how the network structure is explored during learning. Score-based and constraint-based algorithms are common search algorithms to learn the network structure from data.

- *Prior knowledge*: Incorporating prior knowledge or constraints, such as known causal relationships, can be specified as part of the configuration to guide the learning process.

Remember that Bayesian network tuning is a complex task as the number of possible network structures can grow exponentially with the number of nodes. It is essential to strike a balance between model complexity and performance. Additionally, domain knowledge and understanding of the data are critical for making informed decisions during the hyperparameter tuning process.

Fortunately, SAS Enterprise Miner has a built-in automatic search algorithm that makes configuring Bayesian networks easier, especially for non-programmers. In addition, it still provides users with options for changing certain configurations. We will practice with these configurations in the example.

SAS ENTERPRISE MINER GUIDELINES

HP Bayesian Network Classifier Node Train Properties

(https://documentation.sas.com)

- **Network Model** – Specifies the network structure that is created.
- Specify **Bayesian Network** to create a Markov blanket Bayesian network, PC Bayesian network, or naive Bayesian network based on the **Network Structure** and **Automatic Model Selection** properties. When **Automatic Model Selection** is set to **No**, use the **Maximum Parents**, **Network Structure**, and **Parenting Method** to control network creation.
- **Automatic Model Selection** – Specifies whether multiple network structures are created and compared based on the **Network Model** property. For **Bayesian Network**, The HP Bayesian Classifier node creates and compares a Markov blanket, a BAN, a TAN, and a naive Bayesian network. For **BAN**, the HP Bayesian Classifier node creates and compares a BAN, a TAN, and a naive Bayesian network. For **TAN**, the HP Bayesian Classifier node creates and compares a TAN and a naive Bayesian network.
- Specify **No** to access the **Maximum Parents**, **Network Structure**, and **Parent Method** properties for the network model specified by the **Network Model** property.
- **Prescreen Variables** – Specifies whether the input variables are pre-screened based on an independence test with the target variable.
- **Variable Selection** – Specifies whether the input variables are pre-selected based on a conditional independence with the target variable.
- **Independence Test Statistics** – Specifies which independence test statistic is used. You can use either the Chi-Square statistic, G-Square statistic, or both. When using both statistics, a variable must satisfy the **Significance Level** specified for both statistics.
- **Significance Level** – Specifies the significance level for the independence tests. Specify a smaller value to select fewer variables. The default value is 0.2.
- **Missing Interval Variable** – Specifies how missing values are handled for interval variables. Specify **None** to ignore observations with missing values. Specify **Mean** to impute missing values with the mean value for that variable. The default value is **None**.
- **Missing Class Variable** – Specifies how missing values are handled for class input variables. Specify **None** to ignore observations with missing values. Specify **Mode** to impute missing values with the modal value for that variable. Specify **Level** to treat missing values as their own measurement level. The default value is **None**.
- **Number of Bins** – Specifies the number of bins used to categorize interval input variables. The HP Bayesian Classifier node bins each interval variable into equal-width bins. Valid values are integers between 2 and 1024, inclusive. The default value is 10.
- **Maximum Parents** – Specifies the maximum number of parents that are allowed for each node in the network. This property applies only to the **TAN**, **BAN**, and **Bayesian Network** models. Valid values are integers between 1 and 16, inclusive. The default value is 5.
- **Network Structure** – Specifies the network structure created. This property applies only to the **Bayesian Network** model.
- **Parenting Method** – Specifies how parent nodes are assigned. Specify **One Parent** to test each variable individually and select the single best variable as the parent. Specify **Set of Parents** to test every combination of the available variables and select the best set of variables as the parents.

Example: Bayesian Networks

In this example, we will build predictive models for the *airline recommendation* dataset using the Bayesian network algorithm with various configurations.

> *Dataset*: AirlineRecommendation.sas7bdat
>
> *Target variable: Recommendation (binary)*: 1 – recommend the airline; 0 – do not recommend the airline.
>
> *Sample-Explore-Modify*: Refer to previous chapters.

Bayesian Network Models

In this example, we train five different Bayesian network models. From the HPDM tab, drag five HP BN Classifier nodes to the workspace and connect them to the Replacement node. Name them HP Classifier – Default, HP Classifier – NB, HP Classifier – TAN, HP Classifier – BAN, and HP Classifier – MB. Then from the Assess tab, drag a Model Comparison node to the workspace and connect it to these four HP BN Classifier nodes. The diagram should look like the one below.

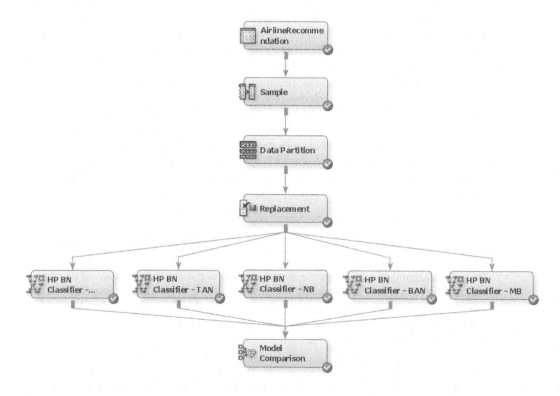

Use the details below to configure those five HP BN Classifier models.

Model 1: HP BN Classifier Default – Automatic Model Selection

Using default properties, primary settings are included below:
  In the HP BN Classifier Training properties

- Set Network Model to Bayesian Network.
- Set Automatic Model Selection to Yes.
- Set Prescreen Variables to Yes.
- Set Variable Selection to No.
- Set Independence Test Statistics to G-Square.
- Set Significance Level to 0.2.
- Set Missing Interval Variable to None.
- Set Missing Class Variable None.
- Set Number of Bins to 10.
- Set Maximum Parents to 5.
- Set Network Structure to Parent-Child.
- Set Parenting Method to Set of Parents.

Model 2: HP BN Classifier NB

Make the changes to property settings as follows:
  In the HP BN Classifier Training properties.

- Set Network Model to Naïve Bayes.
- Set Automatic Model Selection to No.
- Set Variable Selection to Yes.
- Set Missing Interval Variable to Mean.
- Set Missing Class Variable to Mode.
- Set Number of Bins to 20.
- Set Maximum Parents to 5.
- Keep other properties the same as HP BN Classifier Default.

Model 3: HP BN Classifier TAN

Make the changes to property settings as follows
  In the HP BN Classifier Training properties

- Set Network Model to TAN
- Set Independence Test Statistics to Chi-Square and G-Square
- Keep other properties the same as HP BN Classifier NB

Model 4: HP BN Classifier BAN

Make the changes to property settings as follows:
In the HP BN Classifier Training properties

- Set Network Model to BAN
- Set Independence Test Statistics to Chi-Square and G-Square
- Keep other properties the same as HP BN Classifier NB

Model 5: HP BN Classifier MB – Markov Blanket

Make the changes to property settings as follows:
In the HP BN Classifier Training properties

- Set Network Model to Bayesian Network.
- Set Automatic Model Selection to No.
- Set Independence Test Statistics to Chi-Square and G-Square.
- Set Network Structure to Markov Blanket.
- Keep other properties the same as HP BN Classifier NB.

To configure the Model Comparison node:
In the Model Comparison Training properties

- For Model Selection:
  - Set Selection Statistic to Misclassification Rate
  - Set Selection Table to Validation

Run the Model Comparison node and open the Results window.

Results

The model comparison results are presented in Table 16.6 using the validation fit metrics: misclassification rate, Gini coefficient, ROC index, and Lift value. In addition, Figures 16.6 and 16.7 show the ROC chart and Lift chart, respectively. The results indicate that HP BN Classifier – Default is the model with the lowest misclassification rate. In addition, it has the same Gini coefficient, ROC index, and Lift value as HB BN Classifier – MB. On the

TABLE 16.6

Model Comparison Results

Model Description	Valid: Misclassification Rate	Valid: Gini	Valid: ROC	Valid: Lift
HP BN Classifier – Default	0.23098	0.68	0.84	1.7
HP BN Classifier – MB	0.23106	0.68	0.84	1.7
HP BN Classifier – BAN	0.23299	0.68	0.84	1.67
HP BN Classifier – TAN	0.23709	0.67	0.84	1.63
HP BN Classifier – NB	0.23998	0.65	0.83	1.61

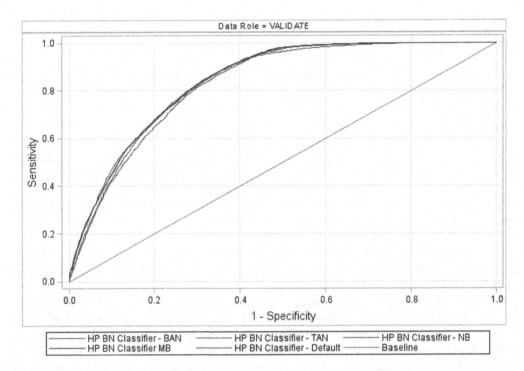

FIGURE 16.6
ROC chart.

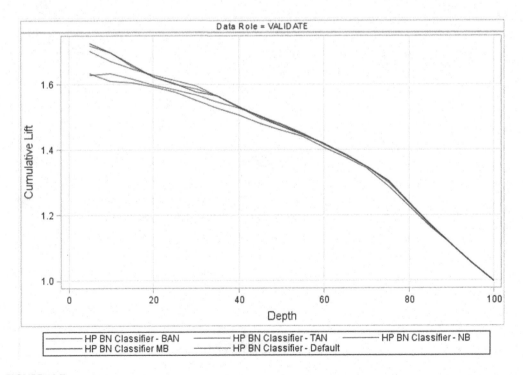

FIGURE 16.7
Lift chart.

TABLE 16.7

Comparison of Misclassification Rates between Three Samples

Model Description	Valid: Misclassification Rate	Train: Misclassification Rate	Test: Misclassification Rate
HP BN Classifier – Default	0.23098	0.23001	0.232969
HP BN Classifier MB	0.23106	0.23012	0.232166
HP BN Classifier – BAN	0.23299	0.22669	0.232085
HP BN Classifier – TAN	0.23709	0.22779	0.236745
HP BN Classifier – NB	0.23998	0.2362	0.239316

other hand, HP BN Classifier – NB has the lowest model fit metrics. This result is confirmed by the ROC chart and Lift chart. However, as you can see those curves overlap, indicating the closeness among those variables.

Table 16.7 compares the misclassification rates between three samples: training, validation, and test. The results show very consistent values, indicating the reliability of those models.

Based on the results, while the models are close enough, we can conclude that HP BN Classifier – Default is the champion model. Since the default settings are used to configure this model with automatic model selection, we review the results to identify the type of Bayesian network structure we have. The Results window of this node shows us more details of this model. Figure 16.8 shows the network structure of this model. As you can

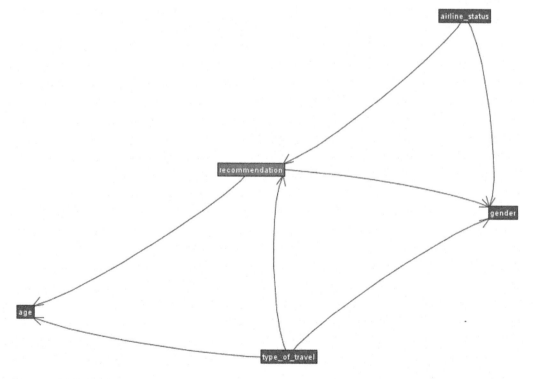

FIGURE 16.8
Bayesian network structure.

see, this network indicates that we have a Market blanket network. The reason is that when we use the default settings and select Yes for Automatic Selection, SAS Enterprise Miner selects the best network structure for training. In this case, it chose the Markov Blanket structure. That explains the closeness of this model and the HP BN Classifier – MB, which also uses the Markov Blanket structure.

The Markov Blanket network in Figure 16.8 indicates three primary predictors used in the model: *travel purpose, airline status, age,* and *gender.* We can also see the directions of relationships among these variables as follows:

- *Recommendation* is the child node of *airline status* and *travel purpose* but is the parent node of *age* and *gender.*
- *Travel purpose* is the parent node of *recommendation, age,* and *gender.*
- *Airline status* is the parent node of *recommendation* and *gender.*
- *Age* is the child node of *recommendation* and *travel purposes.*
- *Gender* is the child node of *recommendation, airline status,* and *travel purpose.*

As stated before, the effects of those predictors on the target variable are not interpreted in the same ways as other machine learning methods. The important output is the CPT for each node. To get the CPTs from SAS Enterprise Miner, in the Results window, go to View, Model, and select CPT. I break them down below so you can see the prior probabilities and posterior probabilities, depending on the node. Note that for *recommendation, age,* and *gender,* since the tables are very long, given the number of variables they associate with and their levels, I only included some conditions for demonstration purposes. These CPTs are shown in Tables 16.8–16.12.

TABLE 16.8

The Conditional Probability Table for *Travel purpose*

Node	Condition	Probability
type_of_travel	BUSINESS TRAVEL	0.6257
type_of_travel	MILEAGE TICKETS	0.0726
type_of_travel	PERSONAL TRAVEL	0.3017

TABLE 16.9

The Conditional Probability Table for *Airline status*

Node	Condition	Probability
airline_status	BLUE	0.6661
airline_status	GOLD	0.0881
airline_status	PLATINUM	0.0321
airline_status	SILVER	0.2138

TABLE 16.10

The Conditional Probability Table for *Recommendation*

Parent Node	Parent Condition	Child Node	Child Condition	Probability
airline_status	BLUE	recommendation	YES	0.6518
type_of_travel	BUSINESS TRAVEL	recommendation	YES	0.6518
airline_status	BLUE	recommendation	NO	0.3482
type_of_travel	BUSINESS TRAVEL	recommendation	NO	0.3482
...				
airline_status	GOLD	recommendation	YES	0.6420
type_of_travel	MILEAGE TICKETS	recommendation	YES	0.6420
airline_status	GOLD	recommendation	NO	0.3580
type_of_travel	MILEAGE TICKETS	recommendation	NO	0.3580
...				
airline_status	PLATINUM	recommendation	YES	0.1218
type_of_travel	PERSONAL TRAVEL	recommendation	YES	0.1218
airline_status	PLATINUM	recommendation	NO	0.8782
type_of_travel	PERSONAL TRAVEL	recommendation	NO	0.8782
...				
airline_status	SILVER	recommendation	YES	0.4636
type_of_travel	PERSONAL TRAVEL	recommendation	YES	0.4636
airline_status	SILVER	recommendation	NO	0.5364
type_of_travel	PERSONAL TRAVEL	recommendation	NO	0.5364

TABLE 16.11

The Conditional Probability Table for *Age*

Parent Node	Parent Condition	Child Node	Child Condition	Probability
recommendation	YES	age	<24.7	0.0524
type_of_travel	BUSINESS TRAVEL	age	<24.7	0.0524
recommendation	YES	age	<31.4	0.1363
type_of_travel	BUSINESS TRAVEL	age	<31.4	0.1363
recommendation	YES	age	<38.1	0.1999
...				
type_of_travel	MILEAGE TICKETS	age	<24.7	0.1003
recommendation	YES	age	<31.4	0.1179
type_of_travel	MILEAGE TICKETS	age	<31.4	0.1179
recommendation	YES	age	<38.1	0.1694
...				
recommendation	NO	age	<24.7	0.1193
type_of_travel	BUSINESS TRAVEL	age	<24.7	0.1193
recommendation	NO	age	<31.4	0.1165
type_of_travel	BUSINESS TRAVEL	age	<31.4	0.1165
recommendation	NO	age	<38.1	0.1448
type_of_travel	BUSINESS TRAVEL	age	<38.1	0.1448
...				
recommendation	NO	age	<24.7	0.1788
type_of_travel	MILEAGE TICKETS	age	<24.7	0.1788
recommendation	NO	age	<31.4	0.1276
type_of_travel	MILEAGE TICKETS	age	<31.4	0.1276
recommendation	NO	age	<38.1	0.1402
type_of_travel	MILEAGE TICKETS	age	<38.1	0.1402

TABLE 16.12

The Conditional Probability Table for *Gender*

Parent Node	Parent Condition	Child Node	Child Condition	Probability
recommendation	YES	gender	FEMALE	0.49216548
airline_status	BLUE	gender	FEMALE	0.49216548
type_of_travel	BUSINESS TRAVEL	gender	FEMALE	0.49216548
recommendation	YES	gender	MALE	0.50783452
airline_status	BLUE	gender	MALE	0.50783452
type_of_travel	BUSINESS TRAVEL	gender	MALE	0.50783452
...				
recommendation	NO	gender	FEMALE	0.56637168
airline_status	BLUE	gender	FEMALE	0.56637168
type_of_travel	MILEAGE TICKETS	gender	FEMALE	0.56637168
recommendation	NO	gender	MALE	0.43362832
airline_status	BLUE	gender	MALE	0.43362832
type_of_travel	MILEAGE TICKETS	gender	MALE	0.43362832

Again, the purpose of the CPT is to encode the conditional dependencies and probabilities between variables in a Bayesian network, enabling probabilistic reasoning, inference, and prediction within the network structure. The table associated with each node specifies the probabilities of the variable taking on different values conditioned on the various states of its parent nodes.

For example, if we want to interpret the target variable, *recommendation*, we need to focus on the influences of its two parent nodes, *airline status*, and *travel purpose*. Based on the CPT, we can state the following.

- If airline status = BLUE, then the probability (recommendation = YES) = 0.6518.
- If airline status = GOLD, then the probability (recommendation = YES) = 0.6420.
- If travel purpose = BUSINESS TRAVEL, then the probability (recommendation = YES) = 0.6518.
- If travel purpose = PERSONAL TRAVEL, then the probability (recommendation = YES) = 0.1218.
- And so on.

We use the same process to interpret the relationships of other variables.

Variable Importance in Bayesian Networks

The variable importance in a Bayesian network is typically determined by examining the conditional probability distributions associated with each node in the network. Nodes with higher conditional probabilities for a given target variable may be considered more important as they have a stronger influence on predicting the target variable. In addition, sensitivity analysis and probabilistic inference techniques can be applied to a Bayesian network to assess how changes in the probabilities of individual predictors propagate and affect the final outcomes, further aiding in understanding variable importance.

The HP BN Classifier node in SAS Enterprise Miner does not produce a variable importance table as with other methods. However, we can use the Score and Reporter nodes to gain the variable importance plot, as described in Chapter 9.

Since the HP BN Classifier node in SAS Enterprise Miner does not produce a variable importance table or plot, we can use the method introduced in Chapter 9 to achieve the variable importance plot. Basically, by using the Score node and Reporter node, the software can generate predictions, simulate the effects of predictors on the target variables, and produce the variable importance plot.

Follow the steps below.

1. From the Assess tab, drag a Score node to the workspace and connect it to the HP BN Classifier – Default node.
2. From the Utility tab, drag a Reporter node to the workspace and connect it to the Score node.
3. Keep all default settings for the Score node.
4. In the Reporter Train properties.
   - Set Nodes to Summary.
   - Set Show All to Yes.
   - Under the Summary Report Options, set Yes to all options.
5. Run the Reporter node and open the Results.

This node creates a report in PDF format. Click View to open the report. The variable importance plot is included in this report. Figure 16.9 shows the variable importance

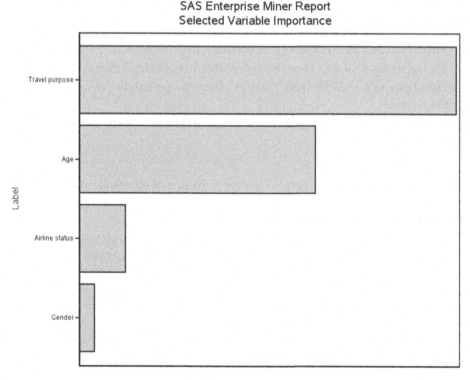

FIGURE 16.9
Variable importance plot.

chart for HP BN Classifier – Default that I extracted from the report. The results indicate that *travel purpose* is the most important predictor, followed by *age, airline status,* and *gender.* As you can see the rank of the top three factors is the same as we get in other models.

Summary

Bayesian network method is a powerful and widely used approach in data mining for modeling and analyzing complex systems with uncertain relationships between variables. It is a probabilistic graphical model that represents the dependencies among variables using directed acyclic graphs (DAGs). In a Bayesian network, each node represents a random variable, and the directed edges between nodes indicate the causal relationships or dependencies between them. The method uses Bayes' theorem to perform probabilistic inference, enabling the calculation of posterior probabilities of variables given observed data. This ability to handle uncertainty and provide interpretable representations of causal relationships makes Bayesian networks valuable in various data mining applications.

In data mining, Bayesian networks are applied in diverse fields, including healthcare, finance, biology, and engineering. They are effective in handling missing data and noisy features, making them robust in real-world scenarios. Moreover, Bayesian networks aid in discovering important features and causal factors in complex systems, assisting researchers in understanding the underlying mechanisms and making informed decisions.

The process of building Bayesian networks involves learning the network structure and estimating the CPTs from data. Structure learning involves exploring the space of possible network structures using score-based or constraint-based algorithms. Score-based algorithms maximize a scoring metric like log-likelihood or BIC, while constraint-based algorithms identify conditional independence relationships between variables. After obtaining the network structure, CPTs are estimated using maximum likelihood or Bayesian parameter estimation. Bayesian networks excel in situations with limited data, making them a valuable tool in data mining when dealing with uncertainty and complex relationships between variables.

CHAPTER DISCUSSION QUESTIONS

1. Differentiate correlation and causation. Give specific real-world examples.
2. What is Bayesian network method? Explain the principle of Bayesian networks.
3. What are the key advantages of the Bayesian network method compared to other machine learning approaches?
4. How does the incorporation of probabilistic reasoning and uncertainty modeling in Bayesian networks benefit decision-making and prediction tasks?

5. Explain the process of learning the structure and parameters of a Bayesian network from data.

6. What are the different algorithms for learning the network structure? Explain their similarities and differences.

7. Discuss the challenges or limitations of the Bayesian network method.

8. What are the four primary types of Bayesian network structures? Explain their similarities and differences.

9. What is frequentist statistics? Compare Bayesian network method with frequentist method.

10. What is causal inference? Can we infer causality using Bayesian networks? Why?

11. Define causal data mining. Provide practical examples of causal data mining projects.

12. Describe the USELEI process. Compare it with SEMMA and CRISP-DM. When should we use the USELEI?

Exercises

Exercise 1: Bayesian network models for the Bank dataset

1. Open the *bank* dataset in SAS Enterprise Miner.
2. Sample the entire dataset. See the variable names and descriptions in Appendix A.1.
3. Partition the data using a split ratio of 60:40 (train: 60%; validation: 20%; test: 20%)
4. Perform data modification as follows:
   - Impute missing values.
   - Normalize the data.
5. Set *CRSCORE* (credit scores) as the target variable.
6. Configure five Bayesian network models for this dataset as follows.
   - HP BN Classifier Default (using default properties).
   - HP BN Classifier NB:
     – Set Network Model to Naïve Bayes.
     – Set Automatic Model Selection to No.
     – Set Variable Selection to Yes.
     – Set Number of Bins to 20.
     – Set Maximum Parents to 5.
   - HP BN Classifier TAN:
     – Set Network Model to TAN.
     – Set Automatic Model Selection to No.
     – Set Variable Selection to Yes.
     – Set Number of Bins to 30.
     – Set Maximum Parents to 5.
   - HP BN Classifier BAN:
     – Set Network Model to BAN.
     – Set Automatic Model Selection to No.

- Set Variable Selection to Yes.
- Set Independence Test Statistics to Chi-Square and G-Square.
- Set Number of Bins to 50.
- Set Maximum Parents to 5.
- HP BN Classifier MB:
  - Set Network Model to Bayesian Network.
  - Set Automatic Model Selection to No.
  - Set Variable Selection to Yes.
  - Set Independence Test Statistics to Chi-Square and G-Square.
  - Set Number of Bins to 50.
  - Set Maximum Parents to 5.
  - Set Network Structure to Markov Blanket.

7. Compare the model fit metrics between those five models using the validation results.
8. Select the champion model and justify this selection with the necessary evidence.
9. Present the results of the champion model.
10. Evaluate the reliability and validity of the champion model.
11. Present the variable importance information and interpret the results.

Exercise 2: Bayesian network models for the Passengers dataset

1. Open the *passengers* dataset in SAS Enterprise Miner.
2. Sample 20% of the full data. Set *return* (decision to return to the airline) as the target variable and change its role to binary. See the variable names and descriptions in Appendix A.2.
3. Partition the data using a split ratio of 60:40 (train: 60%; validation: 20%; test: 20%)
4. Perform data modification as follows:
   - Replace zero values for Likert-scale variables with missing values.
   - Impute missing values.
5. Configure five Bayesian network models for this dataset as follows.
   - HP BN Classifier Default (using default properties).
   - HP BN Classifier NB:
     - Set Network Model to Naïve Bayes.
     - Set Automatic Model Selection to No.
     - Set Variable Selection to Yes.
     - Set Number of Bins to 20.
     - Set Maximum Parents to 5.
   - HP BN Classifier TAN:
     - Set Network Model to TAN.
     - Set Automatic Model Selection to No.
     - Set Variable Selection to Yes.
     - Set Number of Bins to 30.
     - Set Maximum Parents to 5.
   - HP BN Classifier BAN:
     - Set Network Model to BAN.
     - Set Automatic Model Selection to No.
     - Set Variable Selection to Yes.
     - Set Independence Test Statistics to Chi-Square and G-Square.
     - Set Number of Bins to 50.
     - Set Maximum Parents to 5.

- HP BN Classifier MB:
    - Set Network Model to Bayesian Network.
    - Set Automatic Model Selection to No.
    - Set Variable Selection to Yes.
    - Set Independence Test Statistics to Chi-Square and G-Square.
    - Set Number of Bins to 50.
    - Set Maximum Parents to 5.
    - Set Network Structure to Markov Blanket.
6. Compare the model fit metrics between those five models using the validation results.
7. Select the champion model and justify this selection with the necessary evidence.
8. Present the results of the champion model.
9. Evaluate the reliability and validity of the champion model.
10. Present the variable importance information and interpret the results.

Term Definitions

Activation function: An activation function is a function that determines the output of a neuron based on the weighted sum of its inputs. Common activation functions include sigmoid, ReLU (Rectified Linear Unit), and tanh (hyperbolic tangent).

Actual by predicted chart: The actual by predicted chart compares the actual values with the predicted values, showing us how well the trained model fits the data.

Adaptive stepwise: Adaptive stepwise is a forward stepwise method that allows removing a variable currently in the model but no longer significant. It is adaptive.

Aggregation methods: Ensemble models combine the predictions of base learners using aggregation methods. Common aggregation methods include averaging, voting, and weighted voting. The aggregated result is often more accurate and reliable than the predictions of individual models.

Artificial Intelligence (AI): AI is a system that simulates human intelligence for solving problems or making decisions. AI can learn, predict, improve, and solve. Basically, AI could be an application or solution that automatically operates and acts with minimal human interference.

Association model: A predictive model with an interval target variable.

Backward propagation (or backpropagation): Backward propagation is the process of adjusting the weights and biases in the network based on the prediction error. It involves calculating the gradients of the loss function and adjusting the parameters to minimize the error.

Backward stepwise: Backward stepwise is the method in which the model starts with all predictor variables, and at each step, the variable that contributes the least to the model's performance is removed until no further improvement is achieved or a predefined stopping criterion is met.

Bagging: Bagging is an ensemble method that involves training multiple base learners independently on different random subsets of the training data (sampling with replacement). The final prediction is typically an average or voting over the predictions of all the base learners.

Bar chart: A bar chart is a graphical representation of categorical data that uses rectangular bars of varying lengths to visualize the frequency or count of each category.

Base learners (individual models): Base learners are the individual models that constitute the ensemble. Base learners can be any machine learning algorithm, such as decision trees, support vector machines, neural networks, etc.

Bayes' Theorem: Bayes' theorem is a fundamental equation used in Bayesian networks to update probabilities based on new evidence. It calculates the posterior probability of an event given prior knowledge and observed evidence.

Bayesian network: Bayesian network, also known as a Bayesian belief network or probabilistic graphical model, is a powerful and popular method for representing and reasoning about uncertainty and probabilistic relationships between variables. It is a graphical model that represents a set of variables and their conditional dependencies through a directed acyclic graph.

Bias: A bias term is added to the weighted sum of inputs in each neuron. It allows the network to learn a bias toward certain values and improves the accuracy of the model.

Big data: Big data is a term that describes the large volume of data – both structured and unstructured – that inundates a business on a day-to-day basis.

Boosting: Boosting is an iterative ensemble method where base learners are trained sequentially, and each learner focuses on correcting the mistakes made by its predecessors. Boosting assigns higher weights to misclassified instances, effectively giving more attention to challenging samples.

Box plot: A box plot (box-and-whisker plot) is a graphical summary of the distribution of numerical data that displays the median, quartiles, and potential outliers, providing a concise view of the data's central tendency and spread.

Branch or sub-tree: A branch or a sub-tree is a sub-section of a decision tree.

Category: See Class.

Causal data mining: Causal data mining is a method of using causal machine learning algorithms to detect unknown patterns involving variables and their interrelationships in a causal network from data to predict outcomes.

Centroids: Centroids are the mean values of the attributes for the objects in a cluster. They are used to represent the cluster and are often used as the basis for assigning new objects to a cluster.

Champion model: Champion model is the predictive model with the best model performance among the compared models in a data mining project. It is a relative best.

Chi-Squared Automatic Interaction Detection (CHAID): CHAID is a non-parametric method used for creating decision trees by recursively splitting the data into homogeneous subgroups based on the categorical predictor variables, using the Chi-Squared test to assess the independence between variables and find significant splits.

Class: A class refers to a distinct category or label that represents a specific group or type of data instances in a dataset, which is often the target.

Classification and Regression Tree (CART): CART is a binary tree, which uses an algorithm to split a parent node into TWO child nodes repeatedly. CART can be used for both classification and association models.

Classification model: A predictive model with a binary or nominal target variable.

Cluster assignment: Cluster assignment is a process of assigning each object to a specific cluster based on its similarity to the cluster centroids. The assignment is usually done by comparing the distance or similarity of the object to the centroids.

Cluster or segment: A cluster, also known as a segment, refers to a group of data points or objects that are similar to each other based on certain characteristics or attributes.

Cluster profiling: Cluster profiling involves analyzing the characteristics of each cluster, such as the mean value of the attributes or the distribution of the objects within the cluster.

Cluster sampling: Cluster sampling is a sampling method where the population is divided into clusters or groups, and a random selection of entire clusters is chosen, followed by data collection from all the members within the selected clusters.

Cluster validation: Cluster validation is a process of assessing the quality and reliability of the clusters obtained. It involves evaluating the internal cohesion and separation of the clusters, as well as their stability and meaningfulness.

Clustering: A process of grouping objects or observations into clusters (segments) based on their similarity or proximity. The goal is to create clusters that are internally homogeneous (objects within the same cluster are similar) and externally heterogeneous (objects from different clusters are dissimilar).

Clustering algorithms: A clustering algorithm determines the number of clusters and assigns observations to clusters. Cluster algorithms can be categorized into hierarchical clustering and partitioning clustering.

Component rotation: Component rotation is used to transform the principal components to align these components with the original variables, which achieves a more interpretable and meaningful representation of the data.

Conditional Probability Tables (CPTs): Each node in a Bayesian network has an associated CPT, which defines the conditional probability distribution of the node given its parents' states. The CPT quantifies the probabilistic relationship between variables.

Confidence level: The confidence level represents the degree of certainty or confidence we have in the estimates obtained from the sample.

Confusion matrix: Confusion matrix, also called the classification matrix, is the table that summarizes the performance of a classification algorithm.

Connection (edge) (in neural networks): A connection connects neurons. Each connection has an associated weight that determines the level of the influence between connected neurons.

Constraint-based algorithm: A constraint-based algorithm is an approach used to learn the network structure from data by discovering the probabilistic dependencies between variables without directly optimizing a scoring metric. It iteratively tests and evaluates conditional independence relationships among variables to determine the network's structure.

Convenience sampling: Convenience sampling is a non-probabilistic sampling method where researchers select the most readily available individuals to be part of the sample, leading to a lack of randomization and potential bias.

Cost sensitive learning: Cost sensitive learning is a method to evaluate and select a model based on the costs of misclassification.

Covariance: Covariance between two variables measures how much they vary together. If two variables have a high covariance, it means they are positively correlated, while a low covariance indicates no correlation. In PCA, we choose the principal components with the expectation that they are uncorrelated.

CRISP-DM process: Cross-Industry Standard Process for Data Mining.

Data de-identification: Data de-identification is the process of removing or altering identifying information from a dataset to protect the privacy and anonymity of individuals.

Data mining: Data mining is a method of using machine learning algorithms to detect unknown patents involving relationships among variables within large datasets to predict outcomes of interest, which can lead to informed business decisions.

Data mining model: See Predictive model.

Data mining process: Data mining process refers to steps involved in discovering meaningful patterns, relationships, and insights from large datasets using various techniques and algorithms.

Data modification: Data modification involves preparing and transforming the raw data to make it suitable for training our predictive models.

Data science: Data science is a larger and multidisciplinary field, focusing on capturing and extracting knowledge from data and communicating the outcomes. Data science consists of data mining as an essential part of analyzing data and other components such as data collection and management, data treatment, data visualization, computer programming, and artificial intelligence applications.

Data scientist: Data scientist is a professional who does a task or a combination of tasks involving analytics, data collection and treatment, data mining, machine learning, and programming

Data visualization: Data visualization is the graphical representation of data and information through charts, graphs, and other visual elements to help understand patterns, trends, and insights in a more intuitive and accessible way.

Decision matrix: Decision matrix is the table that presents the costs of misclassifications, including costs of false positives and costs of false negatives.

Decision node: When a sub-node is divided into additional sub-nodes, it is referred to as a decision node.

Decision tree: Decision tree is a logical rule-based method that presents a hierarchical structure of variables, including the root node, parent nodes, and child nodes.

Deep learning: Deep learning is a complex neural network with many hidden layers. Deep learning breakthroughs lead to an AI boom.

Dendrograms: A dendrogram is a tree-like diagram that shows the hierarchical relationship between clusters in hierarchical clustering. The height of each branch represents the distance between clusters at that level.

Density plot: A density plot is a graphical representation of the distribution of continuous data, providing an estimate of the underlying probability density function, often using smoothed curves.

Dependent variable: See Target variable.

Descriptive statistics: Descriptive statistics is a branch of statistics that involves the summarization and presentation of data to provide a clear and concise understanding of its main characteristics, such as measures of central tendency, dispersion, and distributions.

Dimensionality reduction: Once the principal components have been identified, PCA can be used to transfer the high-dimensional data into lower-dimensional data, while still retaining as much of the original variation as possible. The number of principal components retained determines the dimensionality of the new data.

Directed Acyclic Graph (DAG): The graphical structure of a Bayesian network is represented by a DAG, which is a graph without cycles (no path that starts and ends at the same node). The absence of cycles ensures that the network does not contain feedback loops and allows for efficient probabilistic inference.

Distance or similarity measures: A distance, also known as a similarity measure, quantifies the similarity or dissimilarity between pairs of objects. These measures are used to determine the proximity between objects and form the basis for clustering algorithms. Common distance measures include Euclidean distance, Manhattan distance, and cosine similarity.

Diversity: The primary strength of ensemble models lies in the diversity of their individual models. By using different learning algorithms or training on different subsets of the data, the ensemble captures various patterns and reduces the risk of overfitting.

Edges (in Bayesian networks): Edges represent probabilistic dependencies between nodes. Directed edges indicate causal or direct influences between variables.

Eigenvectors and eigenvalues: PCA seeks to identify the directions of maximum variability in the data. Eigenvectors are the directions in the data that are not affected by a linear transformation, while eigenvalues indicate how much variance is captured by each eigenvector. In PCA, the principal components are the eigenvectors of the covariance matrix, sorted by their corresponding eigenvalues.

Ensemble: Ensemble is a machine learning method that involves combining the predictions of multiple models to produce a more accurate and robust prediction.

Ensemble size: The number of base learners in an ensemble is an important consideration. Increasing the ensemble size can lead to better performance up to a point, after which the returns diminish, and the model may become computationally expensive.

Error term: Error term (also known as the residual term) represents the discrepancy between the observed values of the target variable and the predicted values obtained from the linear regression model. It captures the part of the target variable that cannot be explained by the linear relationship with the predictors.

Ethical consideration: Ethical consideration refers to the principles, guidelines, and moral values that govern the responsible and respectful use of data throughout the entire data mining process. It is to ensure that we comply with any requirements and restrictions regarding data access to protect human subjects and avoid violating privacy.

Evaluation criteria: See Model fit metrics.

Evaluation metrics: See Model fit metrics.

Evidence: Evidence refers to the observed values or states of certain variables in the Bayesian network. It is used to update the probabilities of other variables in the network.

Explained variance: The proportion of variance explained by each principal component is crucial for understanding the importance of each component in the data. It helps us determine how many principal components to retain for dimensionality reduction while preserving significant information.

Explanatory Power (EP): EP refers to the ability of a predictive model, especially an association model, to explain or predict the variability observed in the data. It measures how well the model captures the underlying relationships between the input variables (predictors) and the target variable.

F-test: F-test is a test of the significance of the overall model. In other words, a significant F-test indicates that our regression model fits the data better than the model without any predictors.

F1 score: F1-score is the harmonic mean of the sensitivity (recall) and precision (positive predicted value); a high F1 score means low false positives (FP) and low false negatives (FN).

Factor analysis: See Principal component analysis.

False Negative (FN): FN is the prediction that wrongly indicates the absence of the event.

False Positive (FP): FP is the prediction that wrongly indicates the presence of the event.

Feature importance: See Variable importance.

Features: See Predictors.

Forward propagation: Forward propagation is the process of transmitting input signals through the network, layer by layer, to produce an output. Each neuron in a layer receives input from the previous layer, performs computations using its activation function, and passes the output to the next layer.

Forward stepwise: Forward stepwise is the method in which the model starts with no predictor variables and iteratively adds one variable at a time, and at each step, the variable that improves the model's performance the most is added to the model until no further improvement is achieved or a predefined stopping criterion is met.

Frequentist statistics: Frequentist statistics, also known as frequentist inference, is a statistical framework and approach to data analysis that focuses on the concept of repeated sampling and long-run frequencies of events.

Gini coefficient: Gini coefficient is a measure of the model's discriminatory power, which is the effectiveness of the model in differentiating between positives and negatives. The Gini coefficient measures how equal the positive rates are across the attributes of a characteristic.

Goodness of fit: See Model fit.

Goodness-of-fit indices: See Model fit metrics.

Gradient boosting: Gradient boosting is a machine learning ensemble method that sequentially combines weak learners to create a powerful predictive model by minimizing errors using gradient descent.

Gradient Boosting Additive Model: Gradient Boosting Additive Models (GBAM) is a variant of gradient boosting that extends the traditional algorithm to handle additive models. An additive model is a model that consists of a sum of functions of individual input variables, where each function depends only on a single input variable.

Gradient descent: Gradient boosting minimizes a specified loss function by using gradient descent optimization. It computes the gradients of the loss function and adjusts the subsequent weak learner to correct the errors made by previous learners. The learning process aims to iteratively reduce the loss and improve the overall model performance.

Hierarchical clustering: Hierarchical clustering builds a hierarchy of clusters, forming a tree-like structure called a dendrogram.

Histogram: A histogram is a graphical representation of continuous data that uses adjacent rectangles to display the distribution and frequency of data within specified intervals (bins).

Imbalanced dataset: An imbalanced dataset refers to a dataset where the number of samples in different classes significantly varies, resulting in an unequal representation of the classes. In an imbalanced dataset, one class (the minority class) typically has significantly fewer instances than the other classes (majority classes).

Imputation: Imputation is a process of estimating or filling in missing values in a dataset with estimated values.

Independent variables: See Predictors.

Input variables: See Predictors.

Institutional Research Board (IRB): Institutional Research Board (IRB) is a type of committee that applies research ethics by reviewing the methods proposed for research to ensure that they are ethical.

Intercept: Intercept is the constant term in the regression equation, representing the predicted value of Y (target variable) when all predictors are zero.

K-means clustering: K-means is a partitioning clustering algorithm that partitions the data into K distinct clusters by iteratively updating the cluster centroids and assigning data points to the nearest centroid. The objective is to minimize the sum of squared distances between data points and their respective cluster centroids.

Label: See Class.

Layers: Neurons are organized into layers in a neural network. The input layer receives the input data, the output layer produces the final output, and there can be one or more hidden layers in between.

Leaf node : Nodes that do not split are called leaf nodes. They represent the output or the predicted value/class for the specific subgroup of data that reaches that node.

Learning (in Bayesian networks): Learning in Bayesian networks involves estimating the network structure and parameters from data. This can be done using approaches such as constraint-based methods or score-based methods.

Learning rate: The learning rate is a hyperparameter that controls the step size in gradient descent. It determines how much each weak learner's contribution affects the final ensemble. A lower learning rate makes the algorithm converge slowly but can improve generalizability, while a higher learning rate leads to faster convergence but may increase the risk of overfitting.

Level: See Class.

Level of measurement: See Variable scale.

Lift chart: Lift is a measure of the effectiveness of a predictive model calculated as the ratio between the results obtained with and without the predictive model. The Lift chart, or Lift curve, presents the graphic representation between the lift values and response rates.

Likelihood: The likelihood in Bayesian networks represents the probability of observing specific evidence given the values of the variables in the network. It is derived from the conditional probability tables.

Line chart: A line chart is a graph that displays data points connected by straight lines, commonly used to visualize trends or changes over time or ordered categories.

Linear regression: Linear regression is a regression method model in which the target variable is interval. Linear regression is an association model.

Logistic regression: Logistic regression is a regression method in which the target variable is categorical (binary or nominal). It is a classification model.

Loss function: A loss function measures the discrepancy between the predicted output of the neural network and the actual target values. It quantifies the error and guides the adjustment of the parameters during training.

Machine learning: Machine learning is a data analytic method that detects unknown patterns from large data to predict the outcomes of interest.

Machine learning model: See Predictive model.

Machine learning process: See Predictive modeling.

Margin of error: The margin of error is a measure of the uncertainty or variability in the estimates obtained from the sample.

Mean Absolute Percentage Error (MAPE): MAPE is a common metric for association models. It measures the percentage difference between the predicted values and the actual values in a dataset.

Measurement of variable: See Variable scale.

Measurement scale: See Variable scale.

Misclassification Rate (MR): MR is a measure of how often a model misclassifies (makes incorrect predictions) the target variable (including actual positives and actual negatives).

Model fit: Model fit measures how well the model fits the data.

Model fit metrics: Criteria used to evaluate model fit.

Model performance: See Model fit.

Model reliability: Model reliability refers to the internal consistency of a model. It means the model produces consistent results with different runs using different data sets.

Model selection and tuning: Ensemble models require careful selection and tuning of base learners and configurations. Different combinations of models and configurations can significantly impact the model's performance.

Model validity: Model validity refers to the accuracy of the model. It means the model consistently produces an accurate prediction of the target variable.

Neuron (node) (in neural networks): A neuron, also called a node or unit, is a basic building block of a neural network. It receives inputs, processes them using an activation function, and produces outputs.

Nodes (in Bayesian networks): Nodes represent random variables or events in the domain being modeled. Each node corresponds to a specific quantity or attribute of interest.

Non-probability sampling: Non-probability sampling is the method of selecting individuals based on non-random criteria, and not every individual in the sampling frame has a chance of being included.

Normalization: Data normalization, also known as variable scaling, is a preprocessing step in machine learning that converts the variables of a dataset to a similar range.

Oblimin: Oblimin is an oblique rotation method that allows for correlation or obliqueness between the rotated components. The main objective of Oblimin rotation is to achieve a simpler structure by minimizing the number of variables with high loadings on a component.

Oblique rotation: Oblique rotation is the rotation method, in which the rotated components are allowed to be correlated with each other.

Odds ratio: Odds ratio represents the ratio of the odds of the event occurring for one group compared to another group. In the context of logistic regression, it measures how the odds of the binary outcome change with respect to a one-unit change in the predictor, while holding all other predictors constant.

Optimization algorithm: The optimization algorithm is used during training to adjust the network's parameters based on the computed gradients. Gradient descent is a common optimization algorithm used for this purpose.

Orthogonal rotation: Orthogonal rotation is the rotation method, in which the rotated components are constrained to be orthogonal to each other, meaning they are independent and uncorrelated.

Out-of-bag evaluation: Random forest utilizes an out-of-bag (OOB) evaluation technique. Since each decision tree is trained on a different subset of the training data, the samples not included in a tree's training subset can be used for evaluation. This provides an unbiased estimate of the model's performance without the need for a separate validation set.

Output: See Target variable.

Overfitting: Overfitting is the situation in which the model is overtrained to the training sample and not generalized to other datasets. Hence, the model is invalid and unusable.

Oversampling: Oversampling is a technique that balances the data by incrementing the size of the minority (rare events) to the same size as the majority.

Parent node and child node (in decision trees): These terms are relative in nature. Any node situated below another node is typically referred to as a child node or sub-node, while the node preceding these child nodes is commonly known as the parent node.

Parents and children (in Bayesian networks): In a Bayesian network, the parents of a node are the nodes that directly influence it. The children of a node are the nodes that are directly influenced by it.

Partitioning clustering: Partitioning clustering divides the data into non-overlapping partitions or clusters. It directly assigns each data point to a specific cluster.

Pie chart: A pie chart is a circular chart that represents the proportions of different categories in a whole, with each category represented by a slice of the pie.

Population: Population is the primary target audience of which we want to examine the patterns of the data and make conclusions.

Posterior probability: The posterior probability represents the updated probability of a variable given observed evidence or data. It is calculated by combining the prior probability with the likelihood of the observed data using Bayes' theorem.

Prediction: A general term for a predicting act

Prediction accuracy: Prediction accuracy is a measure of how accurate a model predicts the target variables (including actual positives and actual negatives).

Prediction errors: Errors measure the extent to which the trained model misfits the data. The lower the error, the more accurate the model.

Prediction model: See Predictive model.

Predictive model: A model predicting either a continuous or categorical target variable.

Predictive modeling: A process of using machine learning algorithms to develop a model that predicts future or unseen events or outcomes based on data.

Predictive power: Predictive power is the ability of a model to accurately capture and represent the underlying patterns, relationships, or trends present in the data and generalize the results to other datasets.

Predictive research: Predictive strategy looks into the future. In other words, organizations analyze a large amount of data to predict new potential safety problems in the future. By mining big data, they can develop a predictive model that predicts an incident or accident before it happens.

Predictors: Inputs being used in predicting the output.

Principal components: Principal components are the eigenvectors that correspond to the highest eigenvalues of the covariance matrix. They are ordered in terms of their importance, where the first principal component explains the maximum variance in the dataset, followed by the second principal component, and so on.

Prior probability: The prior probability represents the initial belief or knowledge about a variable before any evidence or data is observed. It is typically specified as part of the Bayesian network modeling process.

Proactive research: Proactive research studies the present. In other words, organizations examine contributing factors to an incident/accident from various aspects of hazardous conditions and organizational processes and see how they are related to the incident or accident.

Probabilistic inference: Bayesian networks allow for probabilistic inference, which means computing the probability of specific events or variables given evidence (observed data or values) from other variables in the network. Inference is based on Bayes' theorem.

Probabilistic relationship: A probabilistic relationship refers to the existence of a connection or association between two or more variables, where the relationship is characterized by uncertainty and is described using probabilities.

Probability sampling: Probability sampling is the method of selecting individuals randomly in such as way each individual in the sampling frame has an equal probability of being chosen.

Promax: Promax is an oblique rotation method that extends the advantages of Varimax rotation while also accounting for possible correlations between the rotated components. It is considered a compromise between the simplicity of orthogonal rotation and the flexibility of oblique rotation.

Pruning: Removing the sub-nodes of a parent node is called pruning. It is a technique used to simplify the decision tree by removing nodes that do not significantly improve its performance on the validation set. A tree is grown through splitting and shrunk through pruning.

Pseudo R-squared: Pseudo R-squared is a metric used in logistic regression to assess the model fit. Unlike the traditional R-squared used in linear regression, which measures the proportion of variance explained by the model, pseudo R-squared measures the proportion of the deviance explained by the model.

Purposive Sampling: Purposive sampling is a non-probabilistic sampling method where researchers deliberately select specific individuals or units based on pre-defined criteria to best represent certain characteristics or traits of interest.

R-squared or coefficient of determination: R-squared is a measure of the percentage of the variance in the target variable that is explained by variance in predictors, collectively.

Random forest: Random forest is a machine learning algorithm that combines the predictions of multiple decision trees to make more accurate and robust predictions. It falls under the category of ensemble learning, where multiple models are combined to form a more powerful predictive model.

Random subset selection: Each decision tree in the random forest is built using a random subset of the training data. This process, known as bootstrap aggregating or "bagging," involves randomly sampling data points with replacement to create diverse subsets for training each tree.

Random variable selection: The random forest algorithm selects a random subset of input variables for each decision tree. This technique, known as variable bagging or variable subsampling, introduces additional randomness and helps to reduce the dominance of any single variable in the ensemble.

Reactive research: Reactive research focuses on examining events that have already happened and identifying the root causes of a specific incident or accident. Based on the identified root causes, the organizations can form appropriate strategies to mitigate the risk.

Receiver Operating Characteristic (ROC) chart: The ROC chart shows the values of the true positive fraction on the vertical axis and the false positive fraction on the horizontal axis. it reflects the tradeoff between sensitivity and specificity.

Reconstruction: PCA allows the inverse transformation of the lower-dimensional data back into the original high-dimensional space. Although some information is lost during dimensionality reduction, the reconstruction can still be useful for interpretation or other downstream tasks.

Recursive partitioning: Recursive partitioning denotes an iterative procedure involving the division of data into partitions, followed by further splitting along each branch.

Regression coefficients: Regression coefficients are the coefficients assigned to each predictor (Xi), indicating the magnitude and direction of their influence on the target variable. A positive coefficient means an increase in the predictor leads to an increase in the target variable, and vice versa for a negative coefficient.

Regression method: Regression is a popular method that estimates the relationship between one dependent variable (target variable) and multiple independent variables (predictors).

Regression model: See Association model.

Relative Squared Error (RSE): RSE is a common metric for association models. It measures the relative improvement of the model's predictions compared to a simple baseline model that always predicts the mean of the actual values.

Replacement: Replacement is a data modification technique to correct errors, reassign values, or remove incorrect information in the data.

Representative sample: Representative sample is a sample that accurately reflects the characteristics and diversity of the population.

Residual by predicted chart: The residual by predicted chart presents not only how close the actual values are to the predicted values but also indicates any patterns in the residuals.

Residuals: Residuals measure the difference between actual values and predicted values in a dataset.

Robustness: The algorithm is known for its robustness against overfitting, noisy data, and outliers. By aggregating multiple decision trees, it can capture complex relationships and handle noisy datasets more effectively.

Root Mean Squared Error (RMSE): RMSE is a common metric for association models. It measures the average difference between the predicted values and the actual values in a dataset, expressed in the same units as the predicted variable.

Root node: A root node is at the beginning of a tree. It represents the initial decision based on a specific feature that has the most significant impact on the target variable. Starting from the root node, the dataset is partitioned based on different features, and subsequently, these subgroups are further divided at each decision node located beneath the root node.

Sample: Sample is a subset of the population. We use the sample for data analysis and make inferences about the population.

Sample size: Sample size refers to the number of individuals or subjects included in the sample. It should be determined based on statistical considerations.

Sampling bias: Sampling bias occurs when the selected sample does not accurately represent the population, leading to skewed or inaccurate results.

Sampling frame: Sampling frame is the actual list of units or sources from which a sample is drawn.

Sampling method: Sampling method is the procedure that we use to select participants and collect the data.

Sampling with replacement: Sampling with replacement occurs when a randomly chosen unit from the population is put back into the population, and subsequently, another element is chosen at random. In this process, the population consistently retains all its original units, allowing for the possibility of selecting the same unit multiple times.

Scalability: Random forest can be parallelized, as each decision tree in the ensemble can be built independently. This allows for efficient computation and scalability to large datasets.

Scale of measurement: See Variable scale.

Scatter plot: A scatter plot is a graphical representation of paired data points on a two-dimensional plane, used to visualize the relationship and correlation between two variables.

Score-based algorithm: A score-based algorithm is a Bayesian network structure learning approach that maximizes a scoring metric to identify the most probable network structure given the data. The algorithm aims to find the network structure that best fits the data according to a specific scoring criterion.

Scree plot: A scree plot is a graphical tool used in PCA to visualize the eigenvalues associated with each principal component. It is a simple line segment plot that shows the eigenvalues for each individual principal component. The scree plot helps determine the number of principal components based on the amount of variance they explain.

SEMMA process: Sample-Explore-Modify-Model-Assess.

Sensitivity, Recall, or True positive rate (TPR): Sensitivity is the probability of a positive result (event) or how well a model can predict true positives (events).

Significance level (alpha): Significance level (alpha) refers to the significance level or the threshold used for hypothesis testing when evaluating the statistical significance of the estimated coefficients.

Significance value (p-value): The significance value (p-value) is a statistical measure for assessing the significance of the estimated coefficients (also known as the regression weights or beta values) of the predictors in the regression. It determines whether the relationship between each predictor and the target variable is statistically significant or if it could have occurred by chance.

Simple random sampling: Simple random sampling is a sampling method that allows every member of the population to have an equal chance of being selected.

Snowball sampling: Snowball sampling is a non-probabilistic sampling method where initial participants are chosen based on specific criteria and then asked to refer other participants, creating a chain of referrals, commonly used for hard-to-reach or hidden populations.

Specificity, Selectivity, or True negative rate (TNR): Specificity is the probability of a negative result (non-event) or how well a model can predict true negatives (non-events).

Splitting: Splitting is a process of dividing a node into two or more sub-nodes.

Splitting criterion: Splitting criterion is a measure used to evaluate and select the best predictor to split the data at each node of the tree. It is a measure of impurity or variance reduction.

Stacking: Stacking (stacked generalization) is a more complex ensemble technique that combines the predictions of multiple base learners by training a meta-model on their outputs. The meta-model learns to weigh the predictions of individual models effectively.

Standardized regression coefficient (beta): Standardized regression coefficient is a measure used in linear regression to quantify the relationship between a predictor and the target variable after standardizing both variables to a common scale. Standardized coefficients range between 0 and 1 and are measured using the same scale in all cases via standard deviation.

Stepwise method: Stepwise method is an iterative variable selection method used in data mining to identify the most relevant subset of variables for a predictive model.

Stochastic Gradient Boosting: Stochastic Gradient Boosting (SGB) is a variant of the traditional gradient boosting algorithm that introduces randomness during the training process. It combines the concepts of gradient boosting and stochastic learning to enhance the model's generalizability and reduce the risk of overfitting.

Stratified sampling: Stratified sampling is a sampling method where the population is divided into distinct subgroups or strata, and a random sample is drawn from each stratum to ensure the representation of different characteristics within the overall population.

Sum of Squared Error (SSE): SSE measures unexplained variance, which is how far the data are from the model's predicted values.

Sum of Squared Regression (SSR): SSE measures explained variance, which is how far the mean is from the model's predicted values.

Sum of Squared Total (SST): SST measures total variance, which is how far the data are from the mean.

Supervised learning: A machine learning approach for structured data, in which a model is trained from labeled data to make predictions of a pre-defined target variable.

Systematic random sampling: Systematic sampling is a sampling method where every nth member is selected from the population after randomly choosing a starting point, ensuring equal and consistent spacing between selected samples.

Target: See Target variable.

Target variable: The output being predicted.

Test sample: A sample of data used to perform the final test of the model.

Training: Training a neural network involves iteratively adjusting the weights and biases using a training dataset. The goal is to minimize the error or loss function and improve the network's prediction accuracy.

Training sample: A sample of data used to train the model.

Tree depth and number of trees: These are hyperparameters that control the complexity and size of the individual decision trees. The tree depth affects the model's capacity to capture complex relationships in the data, while the number of trees determines the boosting iterations and overall model complexity.

True Negative (TN): TN is the prediction that correctly indicates the absence of the event.

True Positive (TP): TP is the prediction that correctly indicates the presence of the event.

Undersampling: Undersampling is a technique that balances the data by reducing the size of the majority class to the same size as the minority class.

Unstandardized regression coefficient (B): Unstandardized regression coefficient is a measure used in linear regression to quantify the relationship between a predictor and the target variable in its original units of measurement.

Unsupervised learning: A machine learning approach for unstructured data, in which a model is trained from unlabeled data without a specific target variable.

USELEI process: Understanding-Sampling-Exploring-Learning-Evaluating-Inferring.

Validation sample: A sample of data used to validate the model.

Variable discretization: Variable discretization is a process of converting a variable with continuous scale (interval variable) into discrete categories (a categorical variable).

Variable importance: A measure of variable importance, indicating the relative contribution of each input variable in making predictions. It allows users to identify the most influential predictors and gain insights into the underlying data patterns.

Variable scale: A characteristic that describes the nature and properties of a variable; it indicates the type of values that a variable can take and the operations that can be performed on it.

Variance: Variance of a variable measures how much the values of that variable vary from their mean. In PCA, the goal is to find the directions in the data with the highest variance, as these directions contain the most information about the data.

Varimax: Varimax is an orthogonal rotation method that aims to maximize the variance of the squared loadings on each component, leading to a simple and sparse structure where each variable has a high loading on one component and close to zero loadings on other components.

Voluntary response sampling: Voluntary response sampling is a non-probabilistic sampling method where participants self-select to be part of the sample, often in response to a survey or study invitation, which can lead to biased results due to the voluntary nature of participation.

Voting/averaging: During prediction, each decision tree independently generates a prediction, and the final prediction of the random forest is determined through voting (for classification models) or averaging (for association models) the individual tree predictions. This ensemble approach helps reduce bias and variance in the modeling and improves the overall accuracy and robustness of the model.

Weak learners: In the context of gradient boosting, weak learners are individual models that perform slightly better than random guessing but are not highly accurate on their own. Decision trees are commonly used as weak learners in gradient boosting, but other models can also be used.

Weight: Each connection between neurons is assigned a weight, which represents the strength or importance of that connection. These weights determine how much influence the input of one neuron has on the output of another.

References

Abramowitz, M., & Stegun, I. A. (1965). *Handbook of mathematical functions: With formulas, graphs, and mathematical tables*. Dover Publications.

Afendras, G., & Markatou, M. (2019). Optimality of training/test size and resampling effectiveness in cross-validation. *Journal of Statistical Planning and Inference*, 199, 286–301.

Aggarwal, C. C. (2015). *Data mining: The textbook*. Springer International Publishing.

Akaike, H. (1973). Maximum likelihood identification of Gaussian autoregressive moving average models. *Biometrika*, 60(2), 255–265.

Akaike, H. (1977). *On the entropy maximization principle, applications of statistics*. Amsterdam, Holland.

Alpaydin, E. (2020). *Introduction to machine learning* (4th ed.). MIT Press.

Barry de Ville. (2006). *Decision trees for business intelligence and data mining: Using SAS Enterprise Miner*. Cary, NC: SAS Institute.

Bengio, Y., Courville, A., & Vincent, P. (2013). Representation learning: A review and new perspectives. *IEEE Transactions on Pattern Analysis and Machine Intelligence*, 35(8), 1798–1828.

Bishop, C. M. (1996). *Neural networks and pattern recognition*. Oxford University Press.

Bishop, C. M. (2006). *Pattern recognition and machine learning*. Springer.

Boser, B. E., Guyon, I. M., & Vapnik, V. N. (1992). A training algorithm for optimal margin classifiers. In Proceedings of the fifth annual workshop on Computational learning theory, July. (144–152).

Box, G. E. P., & Cox, D. R. (1964). An analysis of transformation. *Journal of the Royal Statistical Society Ser. B*, 26, 211–252.

Breiman, L. (1984). *Classification and regression trees*. Routledge.

Breiman, L. (1996). Bagging predictors. *Machine learning*, 24(2), 123–140.

Breiman, L. (2001). Random forests. *Machine learning*, 45(1), 5–32.

Breiman, L. (2003). *Manual on setting up, using, and understanding random forests v3*. 1. University of California, Berkeley, CA.

Breiman, L. (1998). Arcing classifiers. *Annals of Statistics*, 26, 801–824.

Cai, T., & Dodd, L. (2006). Regression analysis for the partial area under the ROC curve. Working Paper 36, Harvard University Biostatistics Working Paper Series.

Camastra, F., & Vinciarelli, A. (2015). *Machine learning for audio, image, and video analysis* (2nd ed.). Springer.

Cao, L. (2017). Data science: A comprehensive overview. *ACM Computing Surveys (CSUR)*, 50(3), 1–42.

Cox, L. A., Jr. (2010). Regression versus causation, revisited. *Risk Analysis*, 30(4), 535–540.

Caruana, R., Niculescu-Mizil, A., Crew, G., & Ksikes, A. (2004). Ensemble selection from libraries of models. In Proceedings of the Twenty-first International Conference on Machine Learning (p. 18).

Cattell, R. B. (1966). The scree test for the number of factors. *Multivariate Behavioral Research*, 1, 245–276.

Chen, T., & Guestrin, C. (2016). Xgboost: A scalable tree boosting system. In Proceedings of the 22nd ACM SIGKDD International Conference on Knowledge Discovery and Data Mining (pp. 785–794).

Cheng, J., & Greiner, R. (1999). Comparing Bayesian network classifiers. Proceedings of the Fifteenth Conference on Uncertainty in Artificial Intelligence, July 30–August 01, 101–108. Stockholm, Sweden.

Cohen, J. (1987). *Statistical power analysis for the behavioral sciences* (2nd ed.). Laurence Erlbaum Associates.

Cohen, J., Cohen, P., West, S. G., & Aiken, L. S. (2003). *Applied multiple regression/correlation analysis for the behavioral sciences* (3rd ed.). Mahwah, NJ: Lawrence Erlbaum Associates.

Cover, T. M., & Hart, P. E. (1967). Nearest neighbor pattern classification. *IEEE Transactions on Information Theory, 13*(1), 21–27.

Davenport, T. H., & Patil, D. J. (2012). Data scientist. *Harvard Business Review, 90*(5), 70–76.

DeVille, B., & Neville, P. (2013). *Decision trees for analytics using SAS Enterprise Miner*. SAS Publishing.

Dhar, V. (2013). Data science and prediction. *Communications of the ACM, 56*(12), 64–73.

Dobbin, K. K., & Simon, R. M. (2011). Optimally splitting cases for training and testing high dimensional classifiers. *BMC Medical Genomics, 4*(31), 1–8.

Domingos, P., & Pazzani, M. (1997). On the optimality of the simple Bayesian classifier under zero-one loss. *Machine Learning, 29*(2–3), 103–130.

Dubbs, A. (2021). Test set sizing via random matrix theory. arXiv preprint arXiv:2112.05977. https://doi.org/10.48550/arXiv.2112.05977

Emerson, J. D., & Stoto, M. A. (1982). Exploratory methods for choosing power transformations. *Journal of the American Statistical Association, 77*, 103–108.

Federal Aviation Administration. (n.d.). Safety management system. Retrieved from https://www.faa.gov/about/initiatives/sms/explained/basis/

Freund, Y. (1995). Boosting a weak learning algorithm by majority. *Information and Computation, 121*, 256–285.

Freund, Y., & Schapire, R. E. (1996). Experiments with a new boosting algorithm. In *Machine learning: Proceedings of the Thirteenth International Conference* (Vol. 96, pp. 148–156).

Freund, Y., & Schapire, R. E. (1997). A decision-theoretic generalization of on-line learning and an application to boosting. *Journal of computer and system sciences, 55*(1), 119–139.

Freund, Y., Schapire, R. E., Abe, N., & Bello, P. (1999). A short introduction to boosting. *Journal of Japanese Society for Artificial Intelligence, 14*(5), 771–780.

Friedman, H. J., Hastie, T., & Tibshirani, R. (1998). Additive logistic regression: A statistical view of boosting. Technical report. Retrieved from http://www.jstor.org/stable/2674028.

Friedman, J. H. (2001). Greedy function approximation: A gradient boosting machine. *The Annals of Statistics, 29*, 1189–1232.

Friedman, J. H. (2002). Stochastic gradient boosting. *Computational Statistics & Data Analysis, 38*, 367–378.

Friedman, N., Geiger, D., & Goldszmidt, M. (1997). Bayesian network classifiers. *Machine Learning, 29*, 131–161.

Gelman, A., Carlin, J. B., Stern, H. S., Dunson, D. B., Vehtari, A., & Rubin, D. B. (2013). *Bayesian data analysis*. CRC Press: New York, NY.

Goodall, C. (1983). *M-Estimators of location: An outline of theory. Understanding Robust and Exploratory Data Analysis*. Wiley.

Goodfellow, I., Bengio, Y., & Courville, A. (2016). *Deep learning*. MIT Press.

Hair, J. F., Black, W. C., Babin, B. J., & Anderson, R. E. (2018). *Multivariate data analysis* (8th ed.). Pearson Education.

Han, J., Kamber, M. and Pei, J. (2011) *Data mining: Concepts and techniques*. (3rd ed.), Morgan Kaufmann Publishers: Burlington, MA.

Han, J., Kimber, M., & Pei, J. (2011). *Data mining: Concepts and techniques* (3rd ed.). Morgan Kaufmann.

Hand, D., & Till, R. (2001). A simple generalization of the area under the curve for multiple class classification problems. *Machine Learning, 45*, 171–186.

Hastie, T., Tibshirani, R., & Friedman, J. H. (2009). *The elements of statistical learning: data mining, inference, and prediction* (2nd ed.). New York, Springer.

Hastie, T., Tibshirani, R., Friedman, J. H., & Friedman, J. H. (2009). *The elements of statistical learning: Data mining, inference, and prediction* (Vol. 2). Springer.

Hayashi, C. (1998). What is data science? Fundamental concepts and a heuristic example. In: Hayashi, C., Yajima, K., Bock, HH., Ohsumi, N., Tanaka, Y., Baba, Y. (eds.) *Data science, classification, and related methods. Studies in classification, data analysis, and knowledge organization*. Springer, Tokyo.

Heinrich Heine University Düsseldorf (2022). G*Power. https://www.psychologie.hhu.de/arbeitsgruppen/allgemeine-psychologie-und-arbeitspsychologie/gpower

Hoaglin, D. C., Mosteller, F., & Tukey, J. W. (1983). *Understanding robust and exploratory data analysis*. New York, NY: John Wiley and Sons, Inc.

Jordan, M. I., & Mitchell, T. M. (2015). Machine learning: Trends, perspectives, and prospects. *Science, 349*(6245), 255–260.

Joseph, V. R. (2022). Optimal ratio for data splitting. *Statistical Analysis and Data Mining: The ASA Data Science Journal, 15*(4), 531–538.

Kohavi, R. and Provost, F. (1998) Glossary of terms. Machine learning—Special issue on applications of machine learning and the knowledge discovery process. *Machine Learning*, 30, 271–274.

Langley, P., Simon, H. A., Bradshaw, G. L., & Zytkow, J. M. (1987). *Scientific discovery: Computational explorations of the creative processes*. MIT Press.

Kullback, S., & Leibler, R. (1951). On information and sufficiency. *Annals of Mathematical Statistics*, 22, 79–86.

Larsen, J., & Goutte, C. (1999). On optimal data split for generalization estimation and model selection. In *Neural networks for signal processing IX: Proceedings of the 1999 IEEE signal processing society workshop* (Cat. No. 98TH8468). 225–234.

Mallows, C. (1973). Some comments on Cp. *Technometrics, 42*, 87–94.

Masters, T. (1993). *Practical neural network recipes in C++*. San Diego, CA: Academic Press, Inc.

Michalski, R. S., Carbonell, J. G., & Mitchell, T. M. (1983). *Machine learning: An artificial intelligence approach*. Springer.

Mitchell, T. M. (1980). *The need for biases in learning generalizations*. Carnegie-Mellon Univ Pittsburgh PA Dept of Computer Science.

Mitchell, T. M. (1997). *Machine learning*. McGraw Hill: New York: NY.

Mitchell, T. M., Keller, R. M., & Kedar-Cabelli, S. T. (1986). Explanation-based learning: A unified view. *Machine learning, 1*(1), 47–80.

Mitchell, T. M., Shinkareva, S. V., Carlson, A., Chang, K. M., Malave, V. L., Mason, R. A., & Just, M. A. (2008). Predicting human brain activity associated with the meanings of nouns. *Science, 320*(5880), 1191–1195.

Mohamadi, A., Asghari, F., & Rashidian, A. (2014). Continuing review of ethics in clinical trials: a surveillance study in Iran. *Journal of Medical Ethics and History of Medicine, 7*, 22.

Murphy, K. P. (2012). *Machine learning: A probabilistic perspective*. MIT Press.

National Institute of Health (2019, June 25). Research involving private information or biospecimens. https://grants.nih.gov/grants/policy/hs/private-information-biospecimens-flowchart.pdf

Nguyen, Q. H., Ly, H. B., Ho, L. S., Al-Ansari, N., Le, H. V., Tran, V. Q., Prakash, I., and Pham, B. T. (2021). Influence of data splitting on performance of machine learning models in prediction of shear strength of soil. *Mathematical Problems in Engineering, 2021*, 1–15.

Nisbet, R., Elder IV, J., and Miner, G. (2009). *Handbook of statistical analysis and data mining applications* (1st ed.). Burlington, MA: Academic Press/Elsevier.

Pearl, J., & Russell, S. (2003). Bayesian analysis. In M. A. Arbib (ed.), *Handbook of brain theory and neural networks* (pp. 157–160). MIT Press.

Picard, R. R., & Berk, K. N. (1990). Data splitting. *The American Statistician, 44*(2), 140–147. https://doi.org/10.2307/2684155

Provost, F., & Fawcett, T. (2013). *Data science for business*. O'Reilly Media: Sebastopol, CA.

Qualtrics (2020, May 21). Sample size calculator & complete guide. https://www.qualtrics.com/blog/calculating-sample-size/

Quinlan, J. R. (1986). Induction of decision trees. *Machine learning, 1*(1), 81–106.

Rawlings, J.O 1988. *Applied regression analysis: A research tool.* Pacific Grove, CA: Wadsworth and Brooks/Cole.

Rokach, L., & Maimon, O. (2014). *Data mining with decision trees: Theory and applications* (2nd ed.). World Scientific.

Provost, F., Fawcett, T., & Kohavi, R. (1998). The case against accuracy estimation for comparing induction algorithms. In *proceedings of the 15th international conference on machine learning* (pp. 445–453). Madison, WI.

Sarma, K. S. (2013). *Predictive modeling with SAS Enterprise Miner – Practical solutions for business applications* (2nd ed.). SAS Press.

SAS. (nd). Big data. Retrieved from https://www.sas.com/en_us/insights/big-data/what-is-big-data.html

SAS. (nd). Data mining. Retrieved from https://www.sas.com/en_us/insights/analytics/data-mining.html

Schapire, R. E. (1990). The strength of weak learnability. *Machine learning, 5*(2), 197–227.

Schechtman, E., & Schechtman, G. (2016). The relationship between Gini methodology and the ROC curve (SSRN Scholarly Paper No. ID 2739245). https://dx.doi.org/10.2139/ssrn.2739245

Scott, A. J., & Wild, C. J. (1989). Selection based on the response variable in logistic regression. In C. J. Skinner, D. Holt, & T. M. F. Smith (eds.), *Analysis of complex surveys* (pp. 191–205). New York: John Wiley & Sons.

Scutari, M., Vitolo, C. & Tucker, A. (2019). Learning Bayesian networks from big data with greedy search: computational complexity and efficient implementation. *Statistics Computing, 29,* 1095–1108.

Shearer, C. (2000). The CRISP-DM Model: The new blueprint for data mining. *Journal of Data Warehousing, 5*(4). 13–22.

Shmueli, G., Bruce, P. C., & Patel, N. R. (2016). *Data mining for business analytics: Concepts, techniques, and applications with XLMiner* (3rd ed.). Wiley Publishing.

Somers, R. (1962). A new asymmetric measure of association for ordinal variables. *American Sociological Review, 27*(6), 799–811.

Soper, D. (nd). Sample size calculators. https://www.danielsoper.com/statcalc/

Soper, D. S. (2023). A-priori sample size calculator for multiple regression [Software]. https://www.danielsoper.com/statcalc

Tan, P. N., Steinbach, M., & Kumar, V. (2021). *Introduction to data mining* (2nd ed.). Pearson: New York: NY.

Tao, K. M. (1993). A closer look at the radial basis function (RBF) networks. In conference record of the twenty-seventh Asilomar conference on signals, systems, and computers (Vol. 1, pp. 401–405). Los Alamitos, CA.

The Office of Human Research Protection (n.d.). Institutional review board guidebook: Chapter 3, Section A, risk/benefit analysis. https://biotech.law.lsu.edu/research/fed/ohrp/gb/irb_chapter3.htm

Truong, D. (2021a). Estimating the impact of COVID-19 on air travel in the medium and long term using neural network and Monte Carlo simulation. *Journal of Air Transport Management, 96,* 102126. https://doi.org/10.1016/j.jairtraman.2021.102126

Truong, D. (2021b). Using causal machine learning for predicting the risk of flight delays in air transportation. *Journal of Air Transport Management, 91,* 101993. https://doi.org/10.1016/j.jairtraman.2020.101993

Truong, D. & Truong, M.D. (2022). How do customers change their purchasing behaviors during the COVID-19 pandemic? *Journal of Retailing and Consumer Services, 67,* 102963.

Truong, D., & Choi, W. (2020). Using machine learning algorithms to predict the risk of small Unmanned Aircraft System violations in the National Airspace System. *Journal of Air Transport Management, 86,* 101822.

Truong, D., & Truong, M. D. (2023). Impacts of daily travel by distances on the spread of COVID-19: an artificial neural network model. *Transportation Research Record, 2677*(4), 934–945.

Truong, D., Friend, M, & Chen, H. (2018). Applications of business analytics in predicting flight on-time performance. *Transportation Journal, 57*(1), 24–52.

Tuffery, S., & Ebrary, I. (2011). *Data mining and statistics for decision making*. Chichester; Wiley.

U.S. Department of Health & Human Service (1979, April 18). The Belmont Report - Ethical principles and guidelines for the protection of human subjects of research. U.S. Department of Health & Human Service. https://www.hhs.gov/ohrp/regulations-and-policy/belmont-report/read-the-belmont-report/index.html#xbasic

Vapnik, V. N. (1998). *Statistical learning theory*. Wiley.

Werntges, H. W. (1993). Partitions of unity improve neural function approximation. In proceedings of the IEEE international conference on neural networks (Vol. 2, pp. 914–918). San Francisco, CA.

Witten, I. H., Frank, E., Hall, M. A., Pal, C. J. (2016). *Data mining: Practical machine learning tools and techniques* (4th Ed.). Morgan Kaufmann.

Zhang, Y., & Zhou, Z. H. (2014). A review on multi-label learning algorithms. *IEEE Transactions on Knowledge and Data Engineering, 26*(8), 1819–1837.

Appendices: Data Descriptions

Appendix A.1

Bank Customers Data – Variable Descriptions

Variable Name	Label/Description	Scale	Role
ACCTAGE	Age of Oldest Account	Interval	Input
AGE	Age	Interval	Input
ATM	ATM	Binary	Input
ATMAMT	ATM Withdrawal Amount	Interval	Input
BRANCH	Branch of Bank	Nominal	Input
CASHBK	Number Cash Back	Interval	Input
CC	Credit Card	Binary	Input
CCBAL	Credit Card Balance	Interval	Input
CCPURC	Credit Card Purchases	Interval	Input
CD	Certificate of Deposit	Binary	Input
CDBAL	CD Balance	Interval	Input
CHECKS	Number of Checks	Interval	Input
DDA	Checking Account	Binary	Input
DDABAL	Checking Balance	Interval	Input
DEP	Checking Deposits	Interval	Input
DEPAMT	Amount Deposited	Interval	Input
DIRDEP	Direct Deposit	Binary	Input
HMOWN	Owns Home	Binary	Input
HMVAL	Home Value	Interval	Input
ILS	Installment Loan	Binary	Input
ILSBAL	Loan Balance	Interval	Input
INAREA	Local Address	Binary	Input
INCOME	Income	Interval	Input
INV	Investment	Binary	Input
INVBAL	Investment Balance	Interval	Input
IRA	Retirement Account	Binary	Input
IRABAL	IRA Balance	Interval	Input
LOC	Line of Credit	Binary	Input
LOCBAL	Line of Credit Balance	Interval	Input
LORES	Length of Residence	Interval	Input
MM	Money Market	Binary	Input
MMBAL	Money Market Balance	Interval	Input
MMCRED	Money Market Credits	Interval	Input
MOVED	Recent Address Change	Binary	Input
MTG	Mortgage	Binary	Input

(Continued)

(*Continued*)

Variable Name	Label/Description	Scale	Role
MTGBAL	Mortgage Balance	Interval	Input
NSF	Number Insufficient Fund	Binary	Input
NSFAMT	Amount NSF	Interval	Input
PHONE	Number Telephone Banking	Interval	Input
POS	Number Point of Sale	Interval	Input
POSAMT	Amount Point of Sale	Interval	Input
RES	Area Classification	Nominal	Input
SAV	Saving Account	Binary	Input
SAVBAL	Saving Balance	Interval	Input
SDB	Safety Deposit Box	Binary	Input
TELLER	Teller Visits	Interval	Input
CRSCORE	Credit Score	Interval	Target

Appendix A.2

Airline Passengers Data – Variable Description

Variable Name	Description	Scale	Role
Gender	Gender	Binary	Input
Customer_Type	Customer type	Nominal	Input
Age	Age	Interval	Input
Type_of_Travel	Type of travel	Nominal	Input
Class	Ticket class	Nominal	Input
Flight_Distance	Flight distance	Interval	Input
Inflight_wifi_service*	Passenger evaluation of inflight Wi-Fi service	Interval	Input
Departure_Arrival_time_convenience*	Passenger evaluation of departure/arrival time convenience	Interval	Input
Ease_of_Online_booking*	Passenger evaluation of ease of online booking	Interval	Input
Gate_location*	Passenger evaluation of gate location	Interval	Input
Food_and_drink*	Passenger evaluation of food and drink	Interval	Input
Online_boarding*	Passenger evaluation of online boarding	Interval	Input
Seat_comfort*	Passenger evaluation of seat comfort	Interval	Input
Inflight_entertainment*	Passenger evaluation of inflight entertainment	Interval	Input
On_board_service*	Passenger evaluation of on-board service	Interval	Input
Leg_room_service*	Passenger evaluation of legroom service	Interval	Input
Baggage_handling*	Passenger evaluation of baggage handling	Interval	Input
Checkin_service*	Passenger evaluation of check-in service	Interval	Input
Inflight_service*	Passenger evaluation of inflight service	Interval	Input
Cleanliness*	Passenger evaluation of cleanliness	Interval	Input
Departure_Delay_in_Minutes	Departure delay in minutes	Interval	Input
Arrival_Delay_in_Minutes	Arrival delay in minutes	Interval	Input
Return	Passenger decision in returning to the same airline in the next flight (0 – No; 1 – Yes)	Binary	Target

* Likert scale 1–5.

Appendix A.3

Boston Housing Data – Variable Descriptions

Variable Name	Description	Scale	Role
CrimePC	Crime rate per capita	Interval	Input
ZonePr	Proportion of residential land zoned for lots over 25,000 sq.ft.	Interval	Input
IndustPr	Proportion of non-retail business acres.	Interval	Input
Charles_River	Charles River dummy variable (1 if tract bounds river; 0 otherwise)	Interval	Input
NiOxSQ	Nitric oxides concentration (parts per 10 million)	Interval	Input
RmSQ	Average number of rooms per dwelling	Interval	Input
AgePre40	Proportion of owner-occupied units built prior to 1940	Interval	Input
LogDisstance	Weighted distances to five Boston employment centers	Interval	Input
LogAccess	Index of accessibility to radial highways	Interval	Input
Tax	Full value property tax rate per $10,000	Interval	Input
PtRatio	Pupil-teacher ratio	Interval	Input
B	$1,000(Bk - 0.63)^2$, where Bk is the proportion of blacks by town	Interval	Input
Lstat	% lower status of the population	Interval	Input
Imv	Median value of owner-occupied homes in $1,000's	Interval	Target

Index

Note: Locators in *italics* represent figures and **bold** indicate tables in the text.

A

Abstract, writing, 367–369
ACC, *see* Accuracy rate
Accuracy rate (ACC), 191, 192, 193
Activation functions, 309, 310–314
Actual by predicted chart, **171**, 186, *187*, *190*, *289*
Adaptive stepwise method, 214, 215, *216*
Adjusted R², **213**
Agglomerative clustering, 405, *436*
Aggregation methods, **341**, 343
 averaging, 343–344
 maximum technique, 344
 voting, 344
 weighted voting, 344
AI, *see* Artificial Intelligence
AIC, *see* Akaike Information Criterion
Aircraft maintenance and fault detection, 457
Airline industry, 8
Airline passengers data, 562
Airline recommendation, 154–155
 imputation example for, 157–158
 replacement example for, 156–157
Airline recommendation paper, 373
 briefly stating the methodology, 375
 describing the delimitations and limitations, 375
 describing the organization of the paper, 376
 hooking the reader, 373
 justifying the significance of the study, 375
 providing the context of, 373
 research problem and research questions, 373–374
 reviewing previous studies, 374
 writing purpose statement, 374–375
Airline recommendation paper, 399
Akaike Information Criterion (AIC), 521
Alexa, 18
Algorithm diversity, 339
Amazon, 4, 8
Amazon Prime, 7
American Airlines credit card, 8

ANN, *see* Artificial Neural Network
Anomaly detection, 457
Apple, 4
Area under the ROC curve (AUROC), 196
Artificial Intelligence (AI), 4, 5, 15, 17, *17*, 18
Artificial Neural Network (ANN), 303, *303*
Auto-pruning, 264
Averaging, 343–344

B

Backward stepwise method, 214, *214*, 215
Bagging, 340–341, **341**, **460**
Balanced dataset, 81–82
 vs. imbalanced dataset, *82*
BAN, *see* Bayesian network augmented Naive
Bank customers data, 561–562
Banking and financing, 9
Bar charts, 104, 119
 for age, *108*
 for departure delay in minutes, *108*
 graph formatting, 105
 and histograms, 103, **104**
 2D and 3D bar charts for two variables, *107*, *107*
Base learners, **341**
Bayesian belief network, *see* Bayesian network
Bayesian Information Criterion (BIC), 521
Bayesian network (BN), 505, **517**
 advantages of, 514
 basic concepts, 512, **513**
 causal data mining process, 522–523
 and causal inference, 517–518
 correlation vs. causation, 506–508, *506*
 definition of, 508
 disadvantages of, 514–515
 example, 509–511, 528
 models, 528–530
 results, 530–535
 vs. frequentist statistics, 516
 hyperparameter tuning for, 526–527
 learning algorithm, 520

network structure learning algorithms, 521
practical applications of, 511–512
process, 515–516
types of, 518
  Bayesian network augmented Naive (BAN), 520
  Markov blanket, 520–521
  Naïve Bayes method, 519–520
  tree-augmented Naïve (TAN), 520
USELEI and SEMMA and CRISP-DM, differences between, 525
variable importance in, 535–537
Bayesian network augmented Naive (BAN), 520
Bayes' theorem, 507, **513**
Bestbuy, 8
BIC, *see* Bayesian Information Criterion
Bidirectional stepwise method, *see* Adaptive stepwise method
Big data, 20–22, *20*
Binary target variables, 191–193
Black box model, 16
Block network, 314
BN, *see* Bayesian network
Boosting, 341–342, **341**, **484**
Bootstrap aggregating, **460**
Boston housing, 158
  data, 563
  dataset, 221, 284
  discretization example for, 162–164
  imputation example for, 159
  normalization example for, 160–162
Box plots, 113–114
Branch/sub-tree, **253**
Brick-and-mortar business model, 8

C

CART, *see* Classification and Regression Tree
Cascade network, 315
Causal data mining process, **513**, 522–523
  USELEI and SEMMA and CRISP-DM, differences between, 525
Causal inference, Bayesian network, 517–518
Causation, correlation vs., 506–508, *506*
CCC, *see* Cubic clustering criterion
Centroids, **428**
CHAID tree, *see* Chi-Squared Automatic Interaction Detection tree
Champion model, **171**, 181
Chat GPT, 18

Chi-Square and variable worth plots, 128–130
Chi-Squared Automatic Interaction Detection (CHAID) tree, **253**, 258, 260–261, **266**, 279–282, **282**
  and Classification and Regression Tree (CART), 265–266
  pruned CHAID tree plot, *281*
  subtree assessment plot for, **280**
  variable importance for, **282**
Classification and Regression Tree (CART), **253**, 258, 259, **266**, 267, **282**
  CART tree interpretation, 287–290
  CART tree plot and leaf node interpretation, 290–291
  and Chi-Squared Automatic Interaction Detection (CHAID), 265–266
  full CART tree, *292*
  subtree assessment plot for, *288*
  variable importance for, **278**
Classification tree, 259
Cloud-based servers, 4
Cluster analysis, 424, *425*
  advantages of, 428–429
  basic concepts in, 427, **428**
  definition of, 425
  disadvantages of, 429
  example, 441
    cluster distance, 444
    cluster node, 442–443
    cluster profiling, 445–449
    number of clusters, 443–444
    variable importance, 445
  hierarchical clustering, 434
    dendrogram, *433*, 434–437
  partitioning clustering, 437–438
  practical applications of, 426
  Principal Component Analysis (PCA) and, 426–427, **427**
  in SAS Enterprise Miner, 439
    data standardization, 440
    distance measures, 439
    missing values, 439
    two-step clustering algorithm, 439
  steps of, 429–430
  two-step cluster analysis, 438
    advantages of, 438
    limitations of, 438–439
Cluster assignment, **428**
Cluster distance measure, 430
  cosine distance, 432
  Euclidean distance, 430–431
  Hamming distance, 432

Jaccard distance, 432
    Manhattan distance, 431
    Minkowski distance, 431
Clustering, **428**
Clustering algorithms, **428**
    types of, 433
        hierarchical clustering, 433, *433*, **434**
        partitioning clustering, 433, *433*, **434**
Cluster profiling, **428**
Cluster sampling, 70, 77
Cluster validation, **428**
CNN, *see* Convolutional neural network
Conclusion section, writing, 393–396
Conditional probability tables (CPTs), 508, **513**
Confidence level, **67**
Configuration diversity, 340
Confusion matrix, **171**
Confusion matrix metrics, 191–193
Constraint-based algorithm, **513**, **522**
Convenience sampling, 71
Convolutional neural network (CNN),
        304, **305**
Correlation vs. causation, 506–508, *506*
Cosine distance, 432
Cost-complexity pruning, 263
Cost-Sensitive Learning (CSL), 83–84, **172**,
        196–198
    using SAS Enterprise Miner (example), 293
        with cost minimization objective,
            293–294
        with profit maximization objective,
            295–296
COVID-19 pandemic, 113
CPTs, *see* Conditional probability tables
CRISP-DM process, 35–37
CSL, *see* Cost-Sensitive Learning
Cubic clustering criterion (CCC), 439
Curse of dimensionality, 403–404
Customer relationship management, 458

D

DAG, *see* Directed acyclic graph
Daniel Soper, sample size calculators by, 75
Data cleaning, 135
Data descriptions, 99, **100**, 561
    airline passengers data, 562
    airline recommendation (case study),
        100–101
    bank customers data, 561–562
    Boston housing data, 563
Data discretization, 151–152, *151*
Data diversity, 339

Data exploration, 98
    statistics exploration (example), 126
        Chi-Square and variable worth plots,
            128–130
        descriptive statistics results, 127–128
        statistics exploration, 122–124
Data mining, 3, 4, 30, 31–32, 380–382
    Artificial Intelligence, *17*, 18
    big data, 20–22, *20*
    categorizing, 38–39
    characteristics of, 14–17
    concept, *6*
    CRISP-DM process, 35–37
    and data science, 11–14, *13*
    deep learning, *17*, 18
    definitions of, 6–7
    de-identifying data, 24–26
    ensemble modeling, 52
    ethical principles and data collection, 22–23
    general structure of project paper using,
        362–363
    histograms in, 112–113
    Institutional Research Board (IRB), 24, *25*
    justifying the use of, 379
    machine learning, *17*, 18, 19
    machine learning methods, 45
        descriptions and characteristics of, 47
        guidelines to choose, 49–51
        supervised vs. unsupervised learning, 46
    "Person of Interest" (TV show), 4–6, *5*
    practical examples of, 7
        airline industry, 8
        banking and financing, 9
        healthcare, 9
        media streaming, 7
        online shopping, 8
        social networks, 7–8
        transportation, 9–10
    predictive strategy, *10*, 11
    proactive strategy, *10*, 11
    reactive strategy, 10–11, *10*
    SEMMA process, 32–35, 54–55, 57
    and traditional statistical methods, **14**
    USELEI process, 37
    variable measurement scales, 42
        interval and ratio, 43
        Likert scale, 43–45
        nominal scale, 43
        ordinal scale, 43
Data mining report, structure of, *362*
Data mining reports, writing, 359
    abstract, writing, 367–369
    airline recommendation paper, 373–376

airline recommendation paper, 399
conclusion section, writing, 393–396
discussion section, writing, 393–395
general structure of a project paper, 362–363
hypothetical research project, 363
introduction section, writing, 370–373
literature review section, writing, 376–377
methodology section, example of writing, 379
    data mining process, 380–382
    data source and variable descriptions, 379–380
    evaluation metrics, 383–384
    justifying the use of the data mining method, 379
    machine learning algorithms and configurations, 382
methodology section, writing, 378–379
reports, types of, 360, **361**
results section, example of writing, 385
    data mining results, 389–390
    demographic information, 385–386
    descriptive statistics results, 388–389
results section, writing, 384–385
title, writing, 366–367
writing guidelines, following, 363
Data mining research, sample size for, 76–77
Data mining results, 389–390
Data mining software comparison, 52
challenges, 55–56
machine learning algorithms, 55
pricing, 55
user interface, 54
workspace diagram, 54–55
Data modification, 133
advantages, 137–138
disadvantages, 138
importance of, 134–135
imputation method, **136**, 137, **144–145**
missing values, imputation for, 141–143
normalization, 148
    advantages, 148–149
    disadvantages, 149–151
replacement, 138
    errors, correcting, 139
    incorrect information, removing., 139
    values, reassigning, 139
replacement node, 136–137, **136**
techniques, 135–136
transformation, 147
transformation node, **136**, 137

using SAS Enterprise Miner
    airline recommendation dataset, 154–155
    Boston housing, 158
    Boston housing, discretization example for, 162–164
    Boston housing, imputation example for, 159
    Boston housing, normalization example for, 160–162
    imputation example for airline recommendation, 157–158
    replacement example for airline recommendation, 156–157
    variable discretization, 151–152, *151*, **153**
Data normalization, 148
advantages, 148–149
disadvantages, 149–151
Data partition, 90, *90*
split ratio, 90–91
Data partition and model validation, 83
Data preprocessing, *see* Data modification
Data quality improvement, 134
Data reduction, 135
Data re-identification, 25
Data sampling, 63, 64, 78–81
basic concepts in, 67
imbalanced dataset, 81
    Cost-Sensitive Learning (CSL), 83–84
    data partition and model validation, 83
    using multiple model fit metrics, 83
population, *64*, 65
resampling
    oversampling, 84–85, *84*
    undersampling, *84*, 85, **89**
resampling data (example), 88–89
sample, *65, 66, 67*
sample size, 72
    data mining research, sample size for, 76–77
    importance, 72–74
    traditional statistical research, sample size for, 74–76
sampling frame, 65–66, *65*
sampling methods, 66
sampling methods, 68
    non-probability sampling methods, 70–72
    probability sampling, 68–70, *69*
secondary data and sample representativeness, 72
Data science, 11–12, *13*
Data science expert, 11

Data scientist, 11, 12, 14
Data source and variable descriptions, 379–380
Data transformation, 135
Data understanding, 98–99
Data visualization, 97, 102
  bar charts, 104
    for age, *108*
    for departure delay in minutes, *108*
    graph formatting, 105
    2D and 3D bar charts for two variables, *107, 107*
  bar charts and histograms, 103, **104**
  box plots, 113–114
  density plots and scatter plots, 117–119
  histograms, 107, *109, 111, 112*
    importance in data mining, 112–113
  line charts, 115, *115, 116, 117*
    line chart for flight time against flight distance, 116–117
    line chart for shopping amount by age, 116
  MultiPlots, 119, *121*
    bar charts, 119
    scatter plots, 119–121
  pie charts, 114–115, *114*
  quick chart explorer, 121–122
Decision matrix, **172**
Decision node, **253**
Decision tree method, 250, **253**
  advantages of, 257
  association model using (example), 284
    assess, 286–287
    CART tree interpretation, 287–290
    CART tree plot and leaf node interpretation, 290–291
    model, 285–286
    sample-explore-modify, 285
    variable importance, 291
  basic concepts in, 252, **253**s
  Chi-Squared Automatic Interaction Detection (CHAID), 260–261, 265–266, 279–282, **282**
  Classification and Regression Tree (CART), 259, 265–266, 267, **282**
  classification model using (example), 266
    assess, 268–275
    leaf nodes, interpreting, 277–278
    model, 267
    model comparison, 282–283
    sample-explore-modify, 266–267
    tree plot interpretation, 275–277
    variable importance, 278–279, **278**

Cost Sensitive Learning (CSL) using SAS Enterprise Miner (example), 293
  with cost minimization objective, 293–294
  with profit maximization objective, 295–296
  disadvantages of, 258
  example of, *251*
  missing values, 254
    creating multiple branches, 255
    handling during prediction, 255
    splitting criteria with, 255
    using imputation, 255
  node splitting, working of, 253–254
  pruning, 262, *263*
    manual/auto-pruning, 264
  vs. Random Forest, 458, **459**
  types of, 258
  working, 251–252
Deep learning, 17, *17*, 18
Default method, 77
Demographic information, 385–386
Dendrograms, **428**, *433*, 434–437
Density plots and scatter plots, 117–119
Dependent variable, 205
Descriptive statistics results, 127–128, 388–389
Dhar, Vasant, 12
Directed acyclic graph (DAG), 508, **513**
Discussion section, writing, 393–395
Distance/similarity measures, **428**
Diversity, **341**
  algorithm, 339
  configuration, 340
  data, 339
  domain, 340
  model architecture, 340
  training, 340
  variable, 339
Divisive clustering, 405, *436*
DMNeural node, 319
Domain diversity, 340

E

Early Stopping Rule, *see* Pre-pruning
Edges, **513**
Eigenvalue, 405
Emergency medical technicians (EMTs), 10
EMTs, *see* Emergency medical technicians
End Groups node, 347
Ensemble learning, **460, 484**

Ensemble methods, 340, **341**
    bagging, 340–341
    boosting, 341–342
    stacking, 343
Ensemble modeling, 52, 338, 339
    advantages of, 345
    aggregation methods, 343
        averaging, 343–344
        maximum technique, 344
        voting, 344
        weighted voting, 344
    basic concepts in., 340, **341**
    classification model using ensemble node
        (example), 348–351
    classification model using start groups and
        end groups nodes (example), 352–355
    disadvantages of, 345–346
    diversity, concept of, 339–340
    SAS Enterprise Miner
        ensemble node, 346–347
        start groups and end groups nodes, 347
Ensemble size, **341**
EP, *see* Explanatory Power
ERB, *see* Ethical Review Board
Errors, correcting, 139
Estimate sign, 244
Ethical principles and data collection, 22–23
Ethical Review Board (ERB), 24
Euclidean distance, 430–431
Evaluation metrics, 383–384
Evidence, **513**
Explanatory Power (EP), **171**, 184,
        185–186, **186**
Exponential loss, 488

F

F1-score, **172**, **192**, 242
FAA, *see* Federal Aviation Administration
Facebook, 4, 7
Fahrenheit degrees, 43
False Negatives (FN), **171**, 191, 192, 199, 242
False Positives (FP), **171**, 191, 192, 199, 242
Federal Aviation Administration (FAA), 10
Feedforward neural network (FNN), 304, **305**
Financing, banking and, 9
Finch, Harold, 4–5
First N sampling, 77
5-point scale, 43
Flight delay prediction, 457
FN, *see* False Negatives
FNN, *see* Feedforward neural network
Forward stepwise method, 214, *214*

FP, *see* False Positives
Frequentist inference, *see* Frequentist statistics
Frequentist statistics, **513**, **517**
    Bayesian network vs., 516
F-test, **213**
Funnel network, 314

G

G*Power software, 75
GBAM, *see* Gradient boosting additive models
GBM, *see* Gradient Boosting Machine
Gini coefficient, **172**, 196
Gini score, 259
Goodness-of-fit, 173
Goodness-of-fit indices, 183
Google, 4
Google Assistant, 18
Gradient boosting, 479, 480, *481*, **484**
    advantages of, 485
    basic concepts in, 482, **484**
    disadvantages of, 485
    example, 495
        models, 495–498
        results, 498–501
    loss function, 487–488
    practical applications of, 480–482
    Random Forest vs., 482, **483**
    steps, 486
    stochastic gradient boosting (SGB),
        489, 490
Gradient boosting additive models (GBAM),
        484, 488–489, **489**
Gradient boosting hyperparameter tuning
        guide, 490–491
Gradient Boosting Machine (GBM), 339
Gradient descent, **484**
Graph formatting, 105

H

Hamming distance, 432
Healthcare, 9
Heterogeneous data, handling, 135
Hierarchical clustering, **428**, 433, *433*, 434, **434**
    dendrogram, *433*, 434–437
Histograms, 103, 107
    for age, *109*, *111*, *112*
    bar charts and, 103, **104**
    in data mining, 112–113
HP Neural Model Performance, 323–326
Huber loss, 487

Hulu, 7
Hyperbolic tangent (tanh) function, 310–314
Hyperparameters of Random Forest
model, 464
Hyperparameter tuning for Bayesian networks,
526–527
Hypothetical research project, 363

I

Identity function, 310
IEC, *see* Independent Ethics Committee
Imbalanced dataset, **67**, 81
balanced dataset vs., *82*
Cost-Sensitive Learning (CSL), 83–84
data partition and model validation, 83
oversampling, 84–85, *84*
undersampling, *84*, 85, **89**
using multiple model fit metrics, 83
Imputation method, **136**, 137, **144–145**
Incorrect information, removing., 139
Independent Ethics Committee (IEC), 24
Independent variable, 205
Institutional Research Board (IRB), 24, *25*
Internet, 4
Interval and ratio, 43
Interval variable, 151
Introduction section, writing, 370–373
IRB, *see* Institutional Research Board

J

Jaccard distance, 432
Judgment sampling, *see* Purposive sampling

K

Key performance indicators (KPIs), 102
K-means clustering algorithm, **428**, 437
KPIs, *see* Key performance indicators

L

Large data, 15
Leaf node, **253**
Leaf nodes, interpreting, 277–278
Learning in Bayesian networks, **513**
Learning rate, **484**
Least-squared-deviation (LSD), 259
Lexus vehicles, 7–8
Lift chart, **172**, 195, *195*

Lift curve, *see* Lift chart
Likelihood, **513**
Likert scale, 43–45, 206
Linear regression, 112, 206–207, **208**, **213**
assumption requirements, 210–212
equation, 210
estimation approach, 210
example, **206**, 221
assess, 227–229
data description, 221
explore, 222–225
model, 226
model comparison, 233
modify, 225–226
regression equation interpretation,
230–232
sample, 222
and logistic regression, 206–207
Linear regression model fit evaluation, 212
Line charts, 115, *115*, *116*, *117*
for flight time against flight distance,
116–117
for shopping amount by age, 116
Literature review section, writing, 376–377
Logistic regression, 206–207, **208**
assumption requirements, 234–235
equation, 234
estimation approach, 234
example, 237
assess, 239
explore, 238
logistic regression result interpretation,
244–247
model, 239
model fit evaluation, 240–243
modify, 238–239
sample, 237–238
stepwise process, number of steps
in, 240
variable importance, 247
model fit evaluation, 235
model selection methods, 236
reading and understanding, 236–237
result interpretation, **246**
Log-likelihood, 521
Log loss, 488
Log transformation, **150**
Long short-term memory (LSTM) network,
304, **305**
Loss function, **484**
LSD, *see* Least-squared-deviation
LSTM network, *see* Long short-term memory
network

M

The Machine, 4
Machine learning, 17, *17*, 18, 19, 45, 55, 135, 382
    descriptions and characteristics of, 47
    guidelines to choose, 49–51
    supervised vs. unsupervised learning, 46
Machine learning (ML) algorithms, 5, 7, 8, 15, 16
MAE, *see* Mean Absolute Error
Manhattan distance, 431
Manual/auto-pruning, 264
MAPE, *see* Mean Absolute Percent Error
Margin of error, **67**
Markov blanket of a node, 520–521
Maximum Likelihood (ML) method, 207
Maximum likelihood estimation (MLE), 234, **245**
Maximum technique, 344
Mean Absolute Error (MAE), 183, 185, 487
Mean Absolute Percent Error (MAPE), **171**, 184, 185, **186**, 189
Mean Squared Error (MSE), 183, 185, 188, 264, 286, 487
Media streaming, 7
Methodology section, writing, 378–379
    example of, 379
        data mining method, justifying the use of, 379
        data mining process, 380–382
        data source and variable descriptions, 379–380
        evaluation metrics, 383–384
        machine learning algorithms and configurations, 382
Minimal cost complexity pruning, *see* Cost-complexity pruning
Minkowski distance, 431
Min-Max normalization, **150**
Misclassification rate (MR), **171**, 191, **192**, 193, 264
Missing data, handling, 134
Missing values, 254
    in data mining, 141–143
    handling during prediction, 255
    multiple branches, creating, 255
    splitting criteria with, 255
    using imputation, 255
ML algorithms, *see* Machine learning algorithms
MLE, *see* Maximum likelihood estimation
ML method, *see* Maximum Likelihood method
MLP network architecture, *see* Multilayer perceptron feedforward network architecture

Model architecture diversity, 340
Model comparison, 180
    steps, 181–182
Model Comparison node, 239–240
Model evaluation, 169
    basic concepts, 170
    binary target variables
        confusion matrix metrics, 191–193
        cost-sensitive learning (CSL), 196–198
        model fit, 172–173, *174*
        nominal (multi-class) target variables, 198–200
        overfitting, 174–175, *175*
            addressing, 175
            solutions for overfitting issue, **176**
        predictive power, 173–174, *174*
Model fit, **171**, 172–173, *174*, 183
Model fit metrics, 182, 194
    for association models, 183
        actual by predicted chart, 186
        example, 187–189
        prediction error measures, 183–186
        residuals by predicted chart, 186–187
    for classification models, 189–193
    Gini coefficient, 196
    lift chart, 195
    receiver operating characteristic (ROC) chart, 194–195
Model reliability, **171**
    and validity, 177
        assessment process, 178–179
        reporting, 179
Model selection and tuning, **341**
Model validity, **171**
MR, *see* Misclassification rate
MSE, *see* Mean Squared Error
MS Excel, 56
Multi-class log loss, 488
Multilayer perceptron feedforward (MLP) network architecture, 314–315, *315*
Multiple model fit metrics, 83
Multiple regression, 44
MultiPlot node, 119, *121*
    bar charts, 119
    scatter plots, 119–121

N

Natural language processing (NLP), 55, 304, 482
Naïve Bayes method, 519–520
NDA, *see* Non-Disclosure Agreement
Netflix, 7
Network connections, 309

Network structure learning algorithms, 521
Neural network (NN), 300, 301–303, 339
    activation functions, 310–314
    advantages of, 307
    architecture/model, 303
    and artificial neural network, *303*
    association model using (example), 328
        assess, 329–334
        model, 329
    basic concepts in, 308, **308**
    classification model using (example), 320
        assess, 322–323
        HP Neural 1 Model Performance, 323–326
        model, 321–322
    disadvantages of, 307
    model connections, 309
        network connections, 309, *309*
    multilayer perceptron feedforward (MLP)
            network architecture, 314–315, *315*
    neural networks, classification model using
            (example), 320
        assess, 322–323
        HP Neural 1 Model Performance, 323–326
        model, 321–322
    neural network searching, 315
        local optimum situation, 316
        SAS Enterpriser Miner's network
            searching methods, 317
    normalization, 318–319
    practical applications of, 303–304
    SAS Enterprise Miner, 319
    searching, 315
        local optimum situation, 316
        SAS Enterpriser Miner's network
            searching methods., 317
    simple diagram of, *302*
    training, 305–306
    types of, 304–305, **305**
    variable importance, 326–328
NLP, *see* Natural language processing
NN, *see* Neural network
Nodes, **513**
Node splitting, working of, 253–254
Noise reduction, 134
Nominal (multi-class) target variables, 198–200
Nominal scale, 43
Non-Disclosure Agreement (NDA), 23
Non-multicollinearity, 212
Non-probability sampling methods, **67**, 68, 70–72
    convenience sampling, 71
    purposive sampling, 71
    snowball sampling, 71
    voluntary response sampling, 71

Normalization and standardization, 134
Normalized and un-normalized data, **148**

O

Oblimin rotation (oblique), 412
Oblique rotation, *411*, 412
OLS, *see* Ordinal Least Square
Online shopping, 8
OOB evaluation, *see* Out-of-bag evaluation
Ordinal Least Square (OLS), 161, 207, 210
Ordinal scale, 43
Orthogonal rotation, 411–412, *411*
Out-of-bag (OOB) evaluation, **460**, 462–463
Overfitting, **171**, 174–175, *175*
    addressing, 175
    solutions for overfitting issue, **176**
Overfitting prevention, Random Forest and, 463
Oversampling, **67**, 84–85, *84*

P

Parent node and child node, **253**
Partitional clustering, *see* Partitioning
            clustering
Partitioning clustering, **428**, 433, *433*, **434**,
            437–438
Passenger sentiment analysis, 458
PCA, *see* Principal Component Analysis
"Person of Interest" (TV show), 4–6, *5*, 22
Pie charts, 114–115, *114*
Poisson loss, 487
Population, *64*, 65, **67**
Posterior probability, **513**
Post-pruning, 264
Power transformation, **150**
Prediction Accuracy (ACC), **171**, **192**
Prediction error measures, 183–186
Prediction errors, **171**
Predictive power, **171**, 173–174, *174*
Predictive strategy, *10*, 11
Pre-pruning, 264
Price sensitivity values, 381, 389
Price sensitivity variable, 127
Pricing, 55
Principal Component Analysis (PCA), 403
    advantages of, 408
    applications in data mining, 408
    basic concepts of, 404, **407**
        eigenvalue, 405
        principal components, 405
    and cluster analysis, 426–427, **427**

component rotation methods in, 411
  rotation methods, 412
    Oblimin rotation (oblique), 412
    Promax rotation (oblique), 412–413
    Varimax rotation (orthogonal), 412
  curse of dimensionality, 403–404
  disadvantages of, 408–409
  example, 414
    dimensionality reduction, 420
    principal components, number of,
      415–416
    principal components matrix plot,
      417–420
    principal components node, 415
  practical applications in the industry, 405
  SAS Enterprise Miner, principal component
    analysis in, 413–414
  scree plot and number of components,
    410–411, *410*
  steps of, 409–410
Principal components, 405
Prior probability, **513**
Private organizations, 23
Proactive strategy, *10*, 11
Probabilistic graphical model, *see* Bayesian
  network
Probabilistic Inference, **513**
Probabilistic relationship, 507, **513**
Probability sampling, **67**, 68–70, *69*
  cluster sampling, 70
  simple random sampling, 68–69
  stratified sampling, 69
  systematic sampling, 69
Profit maximization objective, CSL with
  (example), 295–296
Promax rotation (oblique), 412–413
Pruning, **253**
Pruning, *see* Tree pruning
Purposive sampling, 71
P-value, **219**, 220
Python, 52, 54, 55, 56

Q

Quantile loss, 487
Quick chart explorer, 121–122

R

R (programming language), 52, 54, 55, 56
R² or coefficient of determination, **213**
Radial basis function network (RBFN), 304, **305**

Random Forest, 455, 456, *457*
  advantages of, 459–460
  basic concepts, 458
  decision tree vs., 458, **459**
  disadvantages of, 461
  example, 467
    configurations, 467–470
    results, 470–472
  vs. gradient boosting, 482, **483**
  hyperparameters of, 464
  out-of-bag (OOB) error estimation,
    462–463
  and overfitting prevention, 463
  practical applications of, 457–458
  process, 461–462
Random sampling, 78
Random subset selection, **460**
Random variable selection, **460**
Rapid Miner, 52, 54–55, 56
Ratio, 43
RBFN, *see* Radial basis function network
Reactive strategy, 10–11, *10*
REB, *see* Research Ethics Board
Receiver operating characteristic (ROC) chart,
  172, 194–195
Recommendation systems, 457
Recurrent neural network (RNN), 304, **305**
Recursive partitioning, **253**, 254
Reese, John, 5–6
Regression equation and results, 219
  significance value (p-value), **219**, 220
  standardized regression coefficients (beta),
    219, 220–221
  unstandardized regression coefficients,
    219, 220
Regression methods, 204, 205–206
  advantages and disadvantages, 209, **209**
  linear regression (example), 221
    assess, 227–229
    data description, 221
    explore, 222–225
    model, 226
    model comparison, 233
    modify, 225–226
    regression equation interpretation,
      230–232
    sample, 222
  linear regression, **213**
    assumption requirements, 210–212
    equation, 210
    estimation approach, 210
    example, **206**
    and logistic regression, 206–207

linear regression model fit evaluation, 212
logistic regression
    assumption requirements, 234–235
    equation, 234
    estimation approach, 234
    model fit evaluation, 235
    model selection methods, 236
    reading and understanding, 236–237
logistic regression (example), 237
    assess, 239
    explore, 238
    logistic regression result interpretation,
        244–247
    model, 239
    model fit evaluation, 240–243
    modify, 238–239
    sample, 237–238
    stepwise process, number of steps
        in, 240
    variable importance, 247
    model selection process, 213–217
Regression Node Results, 244
Relative Squared Error (RSE), **171**, 184,
        185, **186**
Replacement, 138
    errors, correcting, 139
    incorrect information, removing., 139
    values, reassigning, 139
Replacement node, 136–137, **136**
Representative sample, **67**
Resampling, 84
    oversampling, 84–85, *84*
    undersampling, *84*, 85, **89**
Resampling data (example), 88–89
Research Ethics Board (REB), 24
Residual by predicted chart, **171**, *190, 290*
Residuals, **171**, **484**
    by predicted chart, 186–187
Results section, writing, 384–385
    example of, 385
        data mining results, 389–390
        demographic information, 385–386
        descriptive statistics results, 388–389
Risk assessment and safety analysis, 458
RMSE, *see* Root Mean Squared Error
RNN, *see* Recurrent neural network
Robustness, **460**
Robust scaling, **150**
ROC chart, *see* Receiver operating
        characteristic chart
Root Mean Squared Error (RMSE), **171**, 183, 185,
        186, 188, 286
Root node, **253**

Rotation methods, 412
    Oblimin rotation (oblique), 412
    Promax rotation (oblique), 412–413
    Varimax rotation (orthogonal), 412
RSE, *see* Relative Squared Error
R-squared values, 444

S

Sample, *65, 66, 67,* **67**
Sample-explore-modify, 266–267, 285
Sample size, **67**
Sampling bias, **67**, 68
Sampling frame, 65–66, *65,* **67**
Sampling methods, 66, **67**, 68
    non-probability sampling methods, 70–72
    probability sampling methods, 68–70, *69*
Sampling the data, *see* Data sampling
Sampling with replacement, **460**
SAS Enterprise Miner, 43, 52, 54, 55–56, 57
    cluster analysis in, 439
        data standardization, 440
        distance measures, 439
        missing values, 439
        two-step clustering algorithm, 439
    Cost Sensitive Learning (CSL) using
        (example), 293
        with cost minimization objective,
            293–294
        with profit maximization objective,
            295–296
    ensemble modeling
        ensemble node, 346–347
        start groups and end groups nodes, 347
    neural network, 319
    principal component analysis in, 413–414
    SEMMA steps in, *35*
SAS Enterprise Miner, data modification using
    airline recommendation, 154–155
        imputation example for, 157–158
        replacement example for, 156–157
    Boston housing, 158
        discretization example for, 162–164
        imputation example for, 159
        normalization example for, 160–162
Scalability, **460**
Scatter plots, 117–121
Score-based algorithm, **513**, 521, **522**
Scree plot, 410–411, *410*
Secondary data and sample
        representativeness, 72
Segment, **428**
SEMMA process, 32–35, 54–55, 57, 102, 380

SEM method, *see* Structural equation
  modeling method
Sensitivity, **171**, **192**
Servers, 4–5
  cloud-based, 4
7-point scale, 43
SGB, *see* Stochastic gradient boosting
Sigmoid function, 310
Significance level (alpha), **219**
Significance value (p-value), **219**, 220
Simple random sampling, 68–69
Single hidden layer network, 314
Siri, 18
SMOTE, *see* Synthetic Minority Oversampling
  Technique
Snowball sampling, 71
Social media analysis, 458
Social networks, 7–8
Softmax function, 314
Somers' D Gini, 196
Specificity, **172**, **192**
Splitting, **253**
Splitting criterion, **253**
SPSS Modeler, 52, 54, 55, 56
SSE, *see* Sum of Squared Error
SSR, *see* Sum of Squared Regression
SST, *see* Sum of Squared Total
Stacking, 343
Stacking method, **341**, *343*
Standardized regression coefficients (beta),
  219, 220–221
Start Groups node, 347
StatExplore node, 126–127
Statistics exploration, 122–124
  Chi-Square and variable worth plots
    (example), 128–130
  descriptive statistics results (example),
    127–128
Stepwise method, 214, **217**
Stochastic gradient boosting (SGB), **489**, 490
Stochastic Gradient Boosting, **484**
Stratified sampling, 69, 78
Streaming services, 7
Structural equation modeling (SEM)
  method, 44
Sum of Squared Error (SSE), **171**, 183,
  184, *184*
Sum of Squared Regression (SSR), **171**, 183,
  184, *184*
Sum of Squared Total (SST), **171**, 183, 184, *184*
Supervised vs. unsupervised learning, 46
Support Vector Machine (SVM), 339

SVM, *see* Support Vector Machine
Synthetic Minority Oversampling Technique
  (SMOTE), 85
Systematic sampling, 69, 78

T

TAN, *see* Tree-augmented Naïve
Tanh function, 310–314
Tesla self-driving, 18
Title, writing, 366–367
TN, *see* True Negatives
TNR, *see* True Negative Rate
TP, *see* True Positives
TPR, *see* True Positive Rate
Traditional Gradient Boosting, **489**
Traditional statistical research, sample size
  for, 74–76
Training diversity, 340
Training the model with data process, 19
Transformation, 147
Transformation node, **136**, 137
Transform Variables node, 160, 162, 164
Transportation, 9–10
Tree-augmented Naïve (TAN), 520
Tree depth and number of trees, **484**
Tree plot interpretation, 275–277
Tree pruning, 262, *263*; *see also* Decision tree
  method
  manual/auto-pruning, 264
True Negative Rate (TNR), **172**, **192**
True Negatives (TN), **171**, 191, 199
True Positive Rate (TPR), **171**, **192**
True Positives (TP), **171**, 191, 199
Twitter, 4, 7
2D and 3D bar charts for two variables,
  107, *107*
Two-step cluster analysis, 438
  advantages of, 438
  limitations of, 438–439

U

Undersampling, **67**, *84*, 85, **89**
Un-normalized data, **148**
Unstandardized regression coefficients,
  219, 220
Unsupervised learning, 46
USELEI process, 37, *523*, **524**
  and SEMMA and CRISP-DM, 525, **525**
User interface, 54

V

Values, reassigning, 139
Variability, 20
Variable descriptions
   airline passengers data, 562
   bank customers data, 561–562
   Boston housing data, 563
Variable discretization methods, 151–152,
    151, **153**
Variable diversity, 339
Variable importance, **460**, **484**
   in Bayesian networks, 535–537
   in cluster analysis, 445
   in decision tree method, 278–279, **278**
   in logistic regression, 247
   in neural network, 326–328
   in regression methods, 247
Variable labels/descriptions, 101
Variable names, 101
Variable scaling, *see* Data normalization
Variable selection and dimensionality
    reduction, 134

Variety, 20
Varimax rotation (orthogonal), 412
Velocity, 20
Veracity, 21
Volume, 20
Voluntary response sampling, 71
Voting, 344
Voting/averaging, **460**

W

Walmart, 8
Weak learners, **484**
Weighted voting, 344
Workspace diagram, 54–55
Writing guidelines, 363
   hypothetical research project, 363

Z

Z-score, 75, 318
Z-score normalization, **150**